The Challenge of
Democracy
American Government in Global Politics

Fourteenth Edition

Kenneth Janda
Northwestern University

Jeffrey M. Berry
Tufts University

Jerry Goldman
Northwestern University

Deborah J. Schildkraut
Tufts University

Paul Manna
College of William and Mary

CENGAGE
Learning·

Australia • Brazil • Mexico • Singapore • United Kingdom • United States

CENGAGE Learning

The Challenge of Democracy: American Government in Global Politics, 14th Edition
Kenneth Janda, Jeffrey M. Berry, Jerry Goldman, Deborah J. Schildkraut, Paul Manna

Product Director: Paul Banks

Product Manager: Bradley Potthoff

Content Developer: Sarah Edmonds

Product Assistant: Staci Eckenroth

Marketing Manager: Valerie Hartman

Content Project Manager: Cathy Brooks

Art Director: Sarah Cole

Manufacturing Planner: Fola Orekoya

IP Analyst: Alexandra Ricciardi

IP Project Manager: Betsy Hathaway

Production Service and Compositor: MPS Limited

Text Designer: Studio Montage

Cover Designer: Sarah Cole

For product information and technology assistance, contact us at **Cengage Learning Customer & Sales Support, 1-800-354-9706.** For permission to use material from this text or product, submit all requests online at **www.cengage.com/permissions.** Further permissions questions can be emailed to **permissionrequest@cengage.com.**

Library of Congress Control Number: 2016947226

Student Edition:
ISBN: 978-1-305-95492-2

Loose-leaf Edition:
ISBN: 978-1-305-95530-1

Cengage Learning
20 Channel Center Street
Boston, MA 02210
USA

Cengage Learning is a leading provider of customized learning solutions with employees residing in nearly 40 different countries and sales in more than 125 countries around the world. Find your local representative at **www.cengage.com.**

Cengage Learning products are represented in Canada by Nelson Education, Ltd.

To learn more about Cengage Learning Solutions, visit **www.cengage.com.**

Purchase any of our products at your local college store or at our preferred online store **www.cengagebrain.com.**

Printed at CLDPC, USA, 08-20

Brief Contents

Contents

★Letter to Instructors

Dear American Politics Instructor:

Teaching an introductory American Politics course is both a challenging and rewarding endeavor. The challenge is to engage a large classroom full of students, class after class, week after week. The reward is seeing students connect to particular issues, get animated about difficult political situations, become intellectually curious enough to continue studying American politics in subsequent semesters, and develop a lifelong interest in the challenge of democracy. Our goal in writing this book is to help you achieve those rewards and overcome the challenges that come with teaching a large introductory course.

The Challenge of Democracy is not a book centered on current events. Rather, we use the recent past to illustrate enduring features of American government. Our text centers on three themes that help readers recognize and analyze the difficult choices they face in politics. The first is the clash among the values of **freedom, order, and equality**. These value conflicts are prominent in contemporary American society, and they help explain political controversy and consensus in earlier eras. We demonstrate that many of the nation's most controversial issues represent conflicts among individuals or groups who hold differing views on the values of freedom, order, and equality. Views on issues such as abortion are not just isolated opinions; they also reflect choices about the philosophy citizens want government to follow. Yet choosing among these values is difficult, sometimes excruciatingly so.

The second theme focuses on the tensions between **pluralist and majoritarian visions of democracy**. Majoritarianism involves following the will of a majority while pluralism involves the interaction of decision makers with groups concerned about issues that affect them. We use these models to illustrate the dynamics of the American political system, including rising partisanship in Congress, the role of interest groups in policymaking, the ways in which public opinion does (or does not) shape public policy, and the influence of money on a range of political processes.

Our third theme is **globalization**. More than ever before, Americans are becoming citizens of the world. Each day, trade, travel, immigration, and the Internet make the world a more interdependent place. We cannot escape the deepening interrelationships with the rest of the world. Thus, our book examines some of the ramifications of a smaller world on the large landscape of American politics.

Our book includes several elements aimed at engaging your students with these enduring themes, including the vignettes at the start of each chapter; features that highlight tensions among freedom, order, and equality; features that situate American government in the context of global politics; critical thinking questions; and updated examples across the text. We do not believe it is our role to tell students our own answers to the broad questions we pose. Instead, we want our readers to learn firsthand that a democracy requires thoughtful and difficult choices. That is why we titled our book *The Challenge of Democracy*.

New to This Edition

While the enduring challenges of democracy have not changed, some aspects of *The Challenge of Democracy* have. These changes are all devised to help you make your course a rewarding experience for you and your students.

- Each opening vignette now ends with a critical thinking question and a brief challenge that students can pursue. These **#ChallengeAccepted** tasks ask students to perform some activity that deepens their engagement with the themes developed in the vignette.

- We updated several examples in our **"Freedom, Order, or Equality"** features. These features highlight the conflicts among these values through an intriguing case study. New examples include the occupation of the Malheur National Wildlife Refuge in Oregon, the Black Lives Matter movement, and debates about the tradeoff between freedom and national security. Each feature ends with a critical thinking question to encourage students to reflect further on the clash of values explored in the feature.

- We updated several examples in our "_____ in Global Politics" feature. The goal of this feature is to draw greater attention to the impact of globalization on American politics and to encourage reflection about some aspect of American politics in comparison to politics in other countries. New examples include global attitudes about climate change and a profile of Aung San Suu Kyi. Each feature ends with a critical thinking question.

- We discuss recent political developments and connect them to our enduring themes. These developments include the **2016 elections**, gay marriage, marijuana legalization, government surveillance, the impact of social media on political activity, gun control, immigration politics, education policy, net neutrality, campaign finance, the death of Supreme Court Justice Antonin Scalia, and more. Several of these topics are explored in the opening vignettes of each chapter and in our chapter features. A new icon in the margins will draw your attention to content related to the 2016 election.

- All images are now numbered, which will enhance navigation in the electronic version of the book.

MindTap: Your Course Stimulus Package

As an instructor tool, MindTap is here to simplify your workload, organize and immediately grade your students' assignments, and allow you to customize your course as you see fit. Through deep-seated integration with your Learning Management System, grades are easily exported and analytics are pulled with just the click of a button. MindTap provides you with a platform to easily add in current events videos and RSS feeds from national or local news sources. Looking to include more currency in the course? Add in our KnowNow American Government Blog link for weekly updated news coverage and pedagogy.

We are thrilled that you are using *The Challenge of Democracy* in your course. We are honored to play a role as you help your students develop the skills they need to be effective democratic citizens.

Sincerely,

Kenneth Janda, Jeffrey M. Berry, Jerry Goldman, Deborah J. Schildkraut, and Paul Manna

Letter to Students

Dear Student:

The title of our book says it all: democracy is a challenge. *The Challenge of Democracy*, however, is designed to help you succeed in your study of American politics. Our goal is to provide perspectives and insights that will connect you to the important and provocative political questions of our time. How can states legalize marijuana if using the drug still violates federal law? Why is it constitutional for the federal government to require you to purchase health insurance? Why is it so difficult for Congress to pass laws these days? Does it matter if most members of Congress are white males? Would you feel safer in class if you knew that your classmates were carrying loaded firearms? Our aim is to help you explore contemporary questions like these in a deep and meaningful way.

Americans of all backgrounds have different ideas about how much freedom should be granted and to what degree they are willing to give up some freedom in exchange for greater equality or greater societal order. Finding the right balance among **freedom, order, and equality** is one of the biggest challenges that democracies face, and it is the first theme of our book. In the interest of public order and safety, should we allow police to stop and question people on the street, or is that an infringement on personal freedom? In the interest of political equality, should we restrict spending on election campaigns, or is that an infringement on freedom of speech? Questions such as these constitute the daily struggles of modern democratic life.

When developing answers to these questions, should policymakers follow the will of the majority, or should they pay more attention to the individuals, groups, and organizations that have the most expertise and experience with the topic? In other words, should they follow **majoritarian or pluralist principles**? Most Americans support universal background checks for the sale of firearms, but certain organized groups in American society do not. Which one should prevail? The tradeoff among these models of democracy is the second theme of the book. Both models are on display throughout the American political system. Our goal is to help you identify them and consider the benefits and drawbacks of each.

Many of you are the children of immigrants, are immigrants yourselves, or have spent time living in another country. Nearly every item of clothing on your body and every item in your book bag (and even the bag itself) was probably manufactured outside of the United States. And with a swipe on your phone, you can be connected to news, entertainment, and people from around the globe. The place of **globalization** in American politics is our third and final theme. The aims of this theme are to help you think about how various aspect of globalization affect politics at home and also to consider the similarities and differences between the American political system and politics in other countries.

Several features of our book are designed to help you succeed in your studies:

- **Chapter-Opening Vignettes:** Each chapter starts with a story selected to spark your interest and encourage your exploration of the book's themes as they relate to that chapter. For example, Chapter 13 ("The Bureaucracy") begins with the topic of fantasy sports and considers the regulations of this industry that are starting to take shape across the country.

- **#ChallengeAccepted:** Each vignette is accompanied by a brief challenge that you can undertake to help deepen your engagement with the topic at hand. For example, the challenge in Chapter 18 ("Policymaking and Domestic Policy") has you determine the income eligibility level for receiving Medicaid benefits in two different states and consider the reasons why the states differ.

- **"Freedom, Order, or Equality":** Each chapter has a feature that highlights the tensions among these values, and connects those values to the specific content of that chapter. For example, the feature in Chapter 5 ("Public Opinion and Political Socialization") examines how self-identified tea party supporters weigh freedom against order on the issue of immigration.

- **"_____ in Global Politics":** Each chapter has a feature that puts political issues in their global context. For example, the feature in Chapter 11 ("Congress") compares the percentage of women in Congress with the percentage of women in national legislatures across a range of countries.

- **Learning Outcomes:** Each chapter begins with a set of clearly-defined learning outcomes. These learning outcomes are restated throughout the chapter. They are summarized at the end of the chapter, and each chapter ends with a set of study questions tied to each outcome.

- **Critical Thinking Questions:** Each vignette and feature ends with critical thinking questions to promote consideration of the implications of the topic at hand.

The Benefits of Using MindTap As a Student

For students, the benefits of using MindTap with this book are endless. With automatically graded practice quizzes and activities, an easily navigated learning path, and an interactive eBook, you will be able to test yourself in and outside of the classroom with ease. The accessibility of current events coupled with interactive media makes the content fun and engaging. On your computer, phone, or tablet, MindTap is there when you need it, giving you easy access to flashcards, quizzes, readings, and assignments.

We are thrilled that you will you be using *The Challenge of Democracy* in your course, and we are honored to play a role as you develop the skills you need to be a thoughtful, engaged, and effective democratic citizen.

Sincerely,

Kenneth Janda, Jeffrey M. Berry, Jerry Goldman, Deborah J. Schildkraut, and Paul Manna

★About the Authors

Kenneth Janda

Kenneth Janda is the Payson S. Wild Professor Emeritus of Political Science at Northwestern University. Dr. Janda has published extensively in comparative party politics, research methodology, and early use of computer technology in political science, for which he received awards from EDUCOM and support from Apple Computer. His APSA awards include the Samuel Eldersveld Lifetime Achievement Award (2000) and the Frank J. Goodnow Award for distinguished service to the profession and the association (2009). Dr. Janda and fellow author Jerry Goldman shared APSA technology awards in 1992 for IDEAlog, the computer program, and in 2005 for IDEAlog, the website.

Jeffrey M. Berry

Jeffrey M. Berry is the John Richard Skuse Professor of Political Science at Tufts University. He was an undergraduate at the University of California, Berkeley, and received his doctorate from Johns Hopkins University. Dr. Berry Is a recipient of the APSA's Samuel Eldersveld Lifetime Achievement Award (2009) and numerous "best book" awards—from the APSA for *The Rebirth of Urban Democracy* (1994), from the Policy Studies Organization for *The New Liberalism* (1999), from the APSA for *A Voice for Nonprofits* (2004), and from the APSA for *Lobbying and Political Change* (2009). His most recent book is *The Outrage Industry: Political Opinion Media and the New Incivility* (with Sarah Sobieraj).

Jerry Goldman

Jerry Goldman is Professor Emeritus of Political Science at Northwestern University. Dr. Goldman is the 2010 recipient of the first APSA/CQ Press Award for Teaching Innovation in Political Science. He has received many other awards, including the American Bar Association's Silver Gavel for increasing the public's understanding of the law, the EDUCOM Medal, and the Roman & Littlefield Prize for Teaching Innovation. In 2012, Dr. Goldman made the Fastcase 50: "the fifty most interesting, provocative, and courageous leaders in the world of law, scholarship, and legal technology." Through the Oyez Project at oyez.org, which uses images, and audio to bring the Supreme Court alive, he has brought the U.S. Supreme Court closer to everyone.

Deborah J. Schildkraut

Deborah J. Schildkraut is Professor of Political Science at Tufts University. She is the author of *Americanism in the Twenty-First Century: Public Opinion in the Age of Immigration* (2011), *Press "One" for English: Language Policy, Public Opinion, and American Identity* (2005), and several other research articles. Her research focuses on the implications of the changing ethnic composition of the United States on public opinion in a variety of domains. Professor Schildkraut has received awards from the American Political Science Association for the best book published in the field of political psychology (2012) and for the best paper presented in the field of elections, public opinion, and voting behavior (2009). She has served on the Board of Overseers for the American National Election Study and as a reviewer for the National Science Foundation.

Paul Manna

Paul Manna is the Isabelle and Jerome E. Hyman Distinguished University Professor of Government at the College of William & Mary, where he also serves as a faculty affiliate in the college's Public Policy Program. His research and teaching focus is on American politics, policy implementation, federalism, bureaucracy, and applied research methods. Manna is the author of *School's In: Federalism and the National Education Agenda* (Georgetown University Press, 2006), which examines the evolving relationship between federal and state education policy since the 1960s, and *Collision Course: Federal Education Policy Meets State and Local Realities* (CQ Press, 2011), which assesses No Child Left Behind's implementation from 2002–2009, early Obama administration initiatives, and potential future directions for federal policy. He is also co-editor, with Patrick McGuinn of Drew University, of *Education Governance for the Twenty-First Century: Overcoming the Structural Barriers to School Reform* (Brookings, 2013). Manna's current research is examining several topics including the role of state education advocacy organizations in the process of policy change, the relationship between neighborhood violence and school performance, and voter participation in elections for state education chief. After graduating with his B.A. in political science from Northwestern University, Manna taught social studies in his hometown public high school for three years before earning his M.A. and Ph.D. in political science from the University of Wisconsin.

★ Career Opportunities: Political Science

Introduction

It is no secret that college graduates are facing one of the toughest job markets in the past fifty years. Despite this challenge, those with a college degree have done much better than those without since the 2008 recession. One of the most important decisions a student has to make is the choice of a major; many consider future job possibilities when making that call. A political science degree is incredibly useful for a successful career in many different fields, from lawyer to policy advocate, pollster to humanitarian worker. Employer surveys reveal that the skills that most employers value in successful employees—critical thinking, analytical reasoning, and clarity of verbal and written communication—are precisely the tools that political science courses should be helping you develop. This brief guide is intended to help spark ideas for what kinds of careers you might pursue with a political science degree and the types of activities you can engage in now to help you secure one of those positions after graduation.

Careers in Political Science

Law and Criminal Justice

Do you find that your favorite parts of your political science classes are those that deal with the Constitution, the legal system, and the courts? Then a career in law and criminal justice might be right for you. Traditional jobs in the field range from lawyer or judge to police or parole officer. Since 9/11, there has also been tremendous growth in the area of homeland security, which includes jobs in mission support, immigration, and travel security, as well as prevention and response.

Public Administration

The many offices of the federal government combined represent one of the largest employers in the United States. Flip to the bureaucracy chapter of this textbook and consider that each federal department, agency, and bureau you see looks to political science majors for future employees. A partial list of such agencies would include the Department of Education, the Department of Health and Human Services, and the Federal Trade Commission. There are also thousands of staffers who work for members of Congress or the Congressional Budget Office, many of whom were political science majors in college. This does not even begin to account for the multitude of similar jobs in state and local governments that you might consider as well.

Campaigns, Elections, and Polling

Are campaigns and elections the most exciting part of political science for you? Then you might consider a career in the growing industry based around political campaigns. From volunteering and interning to consulting, marketing, and fundraising, there are many opportunities for those who enjoy the competitive and high-stakes electoral arena. For those looking for careers that combine political knowledge with statistical skills, there are careers in public opinion polling. Pollsters work for independent national organizations such as Gallup and YouGov, or as part of news operations and campaigns. For those who are interested in survey methodology, there are also a wide variety of non-political career opportunities in marketing and survey design.

Interest Groups, International and Nongovernmental Organizations

Is there a cause that you are especially passionate about? If so, there is a good chance that there are interest groups out there that are working hard to see some progress made on similar issues. Many of the positions that one might find in for-profit companies also exist in their non-profit interest group and nongovernmental organization counterparts, including lobbying and high-level strategizing. Do not forget that there are also quite a few major international organizations—such as the United Nations, the World Health Organization, and the International Monetary Fund—where a degree in political science could be put to good use. While competition for those jobs tends to be fierce, your interest and knowledge about politics and policy will give you an advantage.

Foreign Service

Does a career in diplomacy and foreign affairs, complete with the opportunity to live and work abroad, sound exciting to you? Tens of thousands of people work for the State Department, both in Washington D.C. and in consulates throughout the world. They represent the diplomatic interests of the United States abroad. Entrance into the Foreign Service follows a very specific process, starting with the Foreign Service Officers Test—an exam given three times a year that includes sections on American government, history, economics, and world affairs. Being a political science major is a significant help in taking the FSOT.

Graduate School

While not a career, graduate school may be the appropriate next step for you after completing your undergraduate degree. Following the academic route, being awarded a Ph.D. or Master's degree in political science could open additional doors to a career in academia, as well as many of the professions mentioned earlier. If a career as a researcher in political science interests you, you should speak with your advisors about continuing your education.

Preparing While Still on Campus

Internships

One of the most useful steps you can take while still on campus is to visit your college's career center in regards to an internship in your field of interest. Not only does it give you a chance to experience life in the political science realm, it can also lead to job opportunities later down the road and add experience to your resume.

Skills

In addition to your political science classes, the following skills will prove useful as a complement to your degree:

Writing: Like anything else, writing improves with practice. Writing is one of those skills that is applicable regardless of where your career might take you. Virtually every occupation relies on an ability to write cleanly, concisely, and persuasively.

Public Speaking: An oft-quoted 1977 survey showed that public speaking was the most commonly cited fear among respondents. And yet oral communication is a vital tool in the modern economy. You can practice this skill in a formal class setting or through extracurricular activities that get you in front of a group.

Quantitative Analysis: As the Internet aids in the collection of massive amounts of information, the nation is facing a drastic shortage of people with basic statistical skills to interpret and use this data. A political science degree can go hand-in-hand with courses in introductory statistics.

Foreign Language: One skill that often helps a student or future employee stand out in a crowded job market is the ability to communicate in a language other than English. Solidify or set the foundation for your verbal and written foreign language communication skills while in school.

Student Leadership

One attribute that many employers look for is "leadership potential," which can be quite tricky to indicate on a resume or cover letter. What can help is a demonstrated record of involvement in clubs and organizations, preferably in a leadership role. While many people think immediately of student government, most student clubs allow you the opportunity to demonstrate your leadership skills.

Conclusion

Hopefully reading this has sparked some ideas on potential future careers. As a next step, visit your college's career placement office, which is a great place to further explore what you have read here. You might also visit your college's alumni office to connect with graduates who are working in your field of interest. Political science opens the door to a lot of exciting careers—have fun exploring the possibilities!

Freedom, Order, or Equality?

Suppose that you are sitting in your American politics class. Would you feel safer from being shot knowing that several of your classmates carried loaded firearms?

Some people think that allowing students to carry weapons on campus would counter possible armed attacks. In December 2015, Jerry Falwell, Jr., president of Virginia's Liberty University said, "I've always thought if more good people had concealed carry permits, then we could end those Muslims before they walked in."[1] Others, like Virginia Governor Terry McAuliffe, thought President Falwell's "rash and repugnant" comment detracted from "the safety of all of our citizens."[2]

Packing heat on campus has recently become legal in several states. In 2015, eight states—Colorado, Idaho, Kansas, Mississippi, Oregon, Texas, Utah, and Wisconsin—allowed concealed weapons on public postsecondary campuses.[3] Although educational institutions in most of these states have fought to prevent or minimize the spread of weapons on campus, the policy trend is clear. Students on college campuses are increasingly likely to be armed.

This trend clashes with the long-established political principle that government (the state) should have a monopoly on physical force or violence—that citizens should not act individually as policemen. Policing the population is the job of the state.

Historically, this principle matched conservative values. In the United States, as elsewhere, property owners have been conservative in the sense that they opposed social change and sought to preserve their wealth. Thus, conservatives valued strong government to protect their lives and property, and they wanted police to monopolize the tools of violence. Today, however, conservatives like Jerry Falwell favor widespread distribution of firearms and less government in many areas, while liberals favor gun control and stronger government.

What's going on in American politics? Should citizens carry around firearms as they did in the Wild West? Has the meaning of "conservative" and "liberal" flipped in recent decades? This initial chapter in *The Challenge of Democracy* reviews how informed observers have thought about these matters. Ultimately, you will have to answer these questions for yourself.

#ChallengeAccepted

Take the Challenge on MindTap for American Government

Can you cite two prominent historical examples in Europe when people rebelled against their rulers, forming governments that did not serve the interests of the property classes? What happened in those cases, and is the same result likely to occur today?

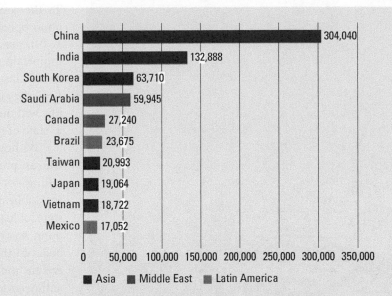

Almost 75 percent of the foreign students were in college or university degree programs. Most came from Asia, about one-third from China alone. Distant Saudi Arabia sent more students here than nearby Canada, a more populous country. The five favorite educational destinations were, in order, the University of Southern California, New York University, Columbia University, University of Illinois, and Purdue University, each receiving between 12,000 and 9,000 students. Nearly 40 percent studied science, technology, engineering, and mathematics, which accounts for the popularity of Illinois and Purdue, both excellent in engineering programs.

Sources: The State Department list is at https://www.csustan.edu/sites/default/files/OIE/documents/YESTERDAYSINTERNATIONALSTUDENTS.pdf; U.S. Immigration and Customs Enforcement, SEVIS by the Numbers, August 2015; and Institute of International Education, Open Doors Data at http://www.iie.org /Research-and-Publications/Open-Doors/Data/International-Students/Enrollment-Trends/1948–2015.

CRITICAL THINKING What good, or harm, do you think might come from having more foreign students study in the United States?

The Purposes of Government

LO2 Identify the purposes that government serves and trace their historical roots.

Governments at any level require citizens to surrender some freedom as part of being governed. Although some governments minimize their infringements on personal freedom, no government has as a goal the maximization of personal freedom. Governments exist to control; to *govern* means "to control." Why do people surrender their freedom to this control? To obtain the benefits of government. Throughout history, government has served two major purposes: maintaining order (preserving life and protecting property) and providing public goods. More recently, some governments have pursued a third purpose, promoting equality, which is more controversial.

Maintaining Order

Maintaining order is the oldest objective of government. **Order** in this context is rich with meaning. Let's start with "law and order." Maintaining order in this sense means

order
Established ways of social behavior. Maintaining order is the oldest purpose of government.

IMAGE 1.1 Leviathan, Hobbes's All-Powerful Sovereign

This engraving is from the 1651 edition of *Leviathan* by Thomas Hobbes. It shows Hobbes's sovereign brandishing a sword in one hand and the scepter of justice in the other. He watches over an orderly town, made peaceful by his absolute authority. But note that the sovereign's body is composed of tiny images of his subjects. He exists only through them. Hobbes explains that such government power can be created only if people "confer all their power and strength upon one man, or upon one assembly of men, that may reduce all their wills, by plurality of voices, unto one will."

Mary Evans Picture Library/Alamy

establishing the rule of law to preserve life and protect property. To the seventeenth-century English philosopher Thomas Hobbes (1588–1679), preserving life was the most important function of government. In his classic philosophical treatise, *Leviathan* (1651), Hobbes described life without government as life in a "state of nature."

Without rules, people would live as predators do, stealing and killing for their personal benefit. In Hobbes's classic phrase, life in a state of nature would be "solitary, poor, nasty, brutish, and short." He believed that a single ruler, or sovereign, must possess unquestioned authority to guarantee the safety of the weak and protect them from the attacks of the strong. Hobbes named his all-powerful government "Leviathan," after a biblical sea monster. He believed that complete obedience to Leviathan's strict laws was a small price to pay for the security of living in a civil society.

Most of us can only imagine what a state of nature would be like. But in some parts of the world, whole nations have experienced lawlessness. After Libya's military strongman Muammar Gaddafi's overthrow in 2011, rival militias fought for power. Armed groups ruled capriciously. Despite the United Nations' efforts to unify Libya, it was still a country without government in 2016. Throughout history, authoritarian rulers have used people's fear of civil disorder to justify taking power. Ironically, the ruling group itself—whether monarchy, aristocracy, or political party—then became known as the *established order*.

Hobbes's conception of life in the cruel state of nature led him to view government primarily as a means of guaranteeing people's survival. Other theorists, taking survival for granted, believed that government protects order by preserving private property (goods and land owned by individuals). Foremost among them was the English philosopher, John Locke (1632–1704). In *Two Treatises on Government* (1690), he wrote that the protection of life, liberty, and property was the basic objective of government. His thinking strongly influenced the Declaration of Independence; it is reflected in the Declaration's famous phrase identifying "Life, Liberty, and the Pursuit of Happiness" as "unalienable Rights" of citizens under government. Locke's defense of property rights became linked with safeguards for individual liberties in the doctrine of **liberalism**, which holds that the state should leave citizens free to further their individual pursuits.[10]

liberalism
The belief that states should leave individuals free to follow their individual pursuits. Note that this differs from the definition of liberal later in this chapter.

Not everyone believes that the protection of private property is a valid objective of government. The German philosopher Karl Marx (1818–1883) rejected the private ownership of property used in the production of goods or services. Marx's ideas form the basis of **communism**, a philosophy that gives ownership of all land and productive facilities to the people—in effect, to the government. In line with communist theory, the 1977 constitution of the former Soviet Union declared that the nation's land, minerals, waters, and forests "are the exclusive property of the state." Years after the Soviet Union collapsed, Russia remains deeply split over abandoning the old communist-era policies to permit the private ownership of land. Even today's market-oriented China still clings to the principle that all land belongs to the state, and not until 2007 did it pass a law that protected private homes and businesses.

communism
A political system in which, in theory, ownership of all land and productive facilities is in the hands of the people, and all goods are equally shared. The production and distribution of goods are controlled by an authoritarian government.

Providing Public Goods

After governments have established basic order, they can pursue other ends. Using their coercive powers, governments can tax citizens to raise money to spend on **public goods**, which are benefits and services available to everyone, such as education, sanitation, and parks. Public goods benefit all citizens but are not likely to be produced by the voluntary acts of individuals. The government of ancient Rome, for example, built aqueducts to carry fresh water from the mountains to the city. Road building was another public good provided by the Roman government, which also used the roads to move its legions and protect the established order.

public goods
Benefits and services, such as parks and sanitation, that benefit all citizens but are not likely to be produced voluntarily by individuals.

Government action to provide public goods can be controversial. During President James Monroe's administration (1817–1825), many people thought that building the Cumberland Road (between Cumberland, Maryland, and Wheeling, West Virginia) was not a proper function of the national government, the Romans notwithstanding. Over time, the scope of government functions in the United States has expanded. During President Dwight Eisenhower's administration in the 1950s, the federal government outdid the Romans' noble road building. Although a Republican opposed to big government, Eisenhower launched the massive interstate highway system at a cost of $27 billion (in 1950s dollars). Yet some government enterprises that have been common in other countries—running railroads, operating coal mines, and generating electric power—are politically controversial or even unacceptable in the United States. People disagree about how far the government ought to go in using its power to tax to provide public goods and services and how much of that realm should be handled by private business for profit.

Promoting Equality

The promotion of equality has not always been a major objective of government. It gained prominence only in the twentieth century, in the

Universal History Archive/UIG via Getty images

IMAGE 1.2   Rosa Parks: She Sat for Equality

Rosa Parks had just finished a day's work as a seamstress and was sitting in the front of a bus in Montgomery, Alabama, going home. A white man claimed her seat, which he could do according to the law in December 1955. When she refused to move and was arrested, outraged blacks, led by Dr. Martin Luther King, Jr., began a boycott of the Montgomery bus company. Rosa Parks died in 2005 at age ninety-two and was accorded the honor of lying in state in the Capitol rotunda, the first woman to receive that tribute.

aftermath of industrialization and urbanization. Confronted by the paradox of poverty amid plenty, some political leaders in European nations pioneered extensive government programs to improve life for the poor. Under the emerging concept of the welfare state, government's role expanded to provide individuals with medical care, education, and a guaranteed income "from cradle to grave." Sweden, Britain, and other nations adopted welfare programs aimed at reducing social inequalities. This relatively new purpose of government has been by far the most controversial. People often oppose taxation for public goods (building roads and schools, for example) because of cost alone. They oppose more strongly taxation for government programs to promote economic and social equality on principle.

Redistributing Income. The key issue here is government's role in redistributing income, that is, taking from the wealthy to give to the poor. Charity (voluntary giving to the poor) has a strong basis in Western religious traditions; using the power of the state to support the poor does not. (In his 1838 novel, *Oliver Twist*, Charles Dickens dramatized how government power was used to imprison the poor, not to support them.) Using the state to redistribute income was originally a radical idea, set forth by Karl Marx as the ultimate principle of developed communism: "from each according to his ability, to each according to his needs."[11] This extreme has never been realized in any government, not even in communist states. But over time, taking from the rich to help the needy has become a legitimate function of most governments.

That function is not without controversy. Especially since the Great Depression of the 1930s, the government's role in redistributing income to promote economic equality has been a major source of policy debate in the United States. Despite inflation, the minimum wage had been frozen at $5.15 per hour from 1997 to 2007, when it was increased to $5.85. In 2009, Congress increased the minimum wage to $7.25 but resisted attempts to raise it further. In his 2014 State of the Union Address, President Obama urged raising the minimum wage to $10.10, but Congress did not comply. Obama then issued an Executive Order, which did not require congressional approval, to raise the wages of workers under federal contracts to $10.10.

Other Policies. Government can also promote social equality through policies that do not redistribute income. For example, in 2015, the U.S. Supreme Court held that state laws banning same-sex marriages were unconstitutional. Laws advancing social equality may clash with different social values held by other citizens. Defying the Court's ruling, a Kentucky county clerk refused to sign marriage licenses for same-sex couples. A district court then ordered them issued without needing her signature.

A Conceptual Framework for Analyzing Government

LO3 Describe how political scientists use concepts to structure events and promote understanding.

Citizens have very different views of how vigorously they want government to maintain order, provide public goods, and promote equality. Of the three objectives, providing for public goods usually is less controversial than maintaining order or promoting equality. After all, government spending for highways, schools, and parks benefits nearly every citizen. Moreover, services merely cost money. The cost of maintaining order and promoting equality is greater than money; it usually means a trade-off in basic values.

To understand government and the political process, you must be able to recognize these trade-offs and identify the basic values they entail. Just as people sit back from a wide-screen motion picture to gain perspective, to understand American government you need to take a broad view—a view much broader than that offered by examining specific political events. You need to use political concepts.

A concept is a generalized idea of a set of items or thoughts. It groups various events, objects, or qualities under a common classification or label. The framework that guides this book consists of five concepts that figure prominently in political analysis. We regard the five concepts as especially important to a broad understanding of American politics, and we use them repeatedly throughout this book. This framework will help you evaluate political events long after you have read this text.

The five concepts that we emphasize deal with the fundamental issues of what government tries to do and how it decides to do it. The concepts that relate to what government tries to do are *order*, *freedom*, and *equality*. All governments by definition value order; maintaining order is part of the meaning of government. Most governments at least claim to preserve individual freedom while they maintain order, although they vary widely in the extent to which they succeed. Few governments even profess to guarantee equality, and governments differ greatly in policies that pit equality against freedom. Our conceptual framework should help you evaluate the extent to which the United States pursues all three values through its government.

How government chooses the proper mix of order, freedom, and equality in its policymaking has to do with the process of choice. We evaluate the American governmental process using two models of democratic government: *majoritarian* and *pluralist*. Many governments profess to be democracies. Whether they are or are not depends on their (and our) meaning of the term. Even countries that Americans agree are democracies—for example, the United States and Britain—differ substantially in the type of democracy they practice. We can use our conceptual models of democratic government both to classify the type of democracy practiced in the United States and to evaluate the government's success in fulfilling that model.

The five concepts can be organized into two groups:

- Concepts that identify the values pursued by government:
    Freedom
    Order
    Equality
- Concepts that describe models of democratic government:
    Majoritarian democracy
    Pluralist democracy

The rest of this chapter examines freedom, order, and equality as conflicting values pursued by government. Chapter 2 discusses majoritarian democracy and pluralist democracy as alternative institutional models for implementing democratic government.

The Concepts of Freedom, Order, and Equality

LO4 Define freedom, order, and equality and discuss the various interpretations of each value.

These three terms—*freedom*, *order*, and *equality*—have a range of connotations in American politics. Both freedom and equality are positive terms that politicians have

Freedom, Order, or Equality and "The Four Freedoms" Posters

Posters by Norman Rockwell

Norman Rockwell became famous in the 1940s for the humorous, homespun covers he painted for the *Saturday Evening Post*, a weekly magazine. Inspired by an address to Congress in which President Roosevelt outlined his goals for world civilization, Rockwell painted The Four Freedoms, which were reproduced in the *Post* during February and March 1943. Their immense popularity led the government to print posters of the illustrations for the Treasury Department's war bond drive.

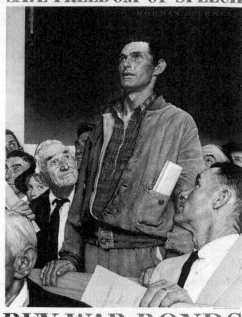

learned to use to their own advantage. Consequently, *freedom* and *equality* mean different things to different people at different times, depending on the political context in which they are used. *Order*, in contrast, usually has negative connotations for people because it symbolizes government intrusion into private lives. It is no coincidence that the film *Star Wars: The Force Awakens* called the dark force "The First Order." Except during periods of social strife or terrorist threat, few politicians in Western democracies openly call for more order. Because all governments infringe on freedom, we examine that concept first.

Freedom

Freedom can be used in two major senses: freedom of and freedom from. President Franklin Delano Roosevelt used the word in both senses in a speech he made shortly before the United States entered World War II. He described four freedoms: freedom of religion, freedom of speech, freedom from fear, and freedom from want. The noted illustrator Norman Rockwell gave Americans a vision of these freedoms in a classic set of paintings published in the *Saturday Evening Post* and subsequently issued as posters to sell war bonds (see "Freedom, Order, or Equality and 'The Four Freedoms' Posters").

The Office of War Information also reproduced The Four Freedoms and circulated the posters in schools, clubhouses, railroad stations, post offices, and other public buildings. Officials even had copies circulated on the European front to remind soldiers of the liberties for which they were fighting. Winning the war would safeguard American culture and preserve order, while equality was implied as an outcome of the other freedoms. It is said that no other paintings in the world have ever been reproduced or circulated in such vast numbers as The Four Freedoms.

OURS...to fight for

FREEDOM FROM WANT

Norman Rockwell/Fine Art/Corbis

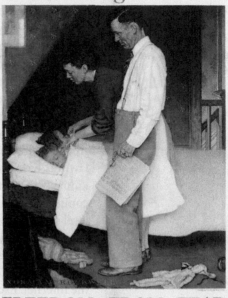

OURS...to fight for

FREEDOM FROM FEAR

Norman Rockwell/Fine Art/CORBIS

CRITICAL THINKING Times have changed since the 1940s. Which of these four freedoms would resonate best today with the American public? Which the least? Why? What has changed over the decades?

Freedom of is the absence of constraints on behavior; it means freedom to do something. In this sense, *freedom* is synonymous with *liberty*.[12] Two of Rockwell's paintings, *Freedom of Worship* and *Freedom of Speech*, exemplify this type of freedom. Freedom of religion, speech, press, and assembly (collectively called "civil liberties") is discussed in Chapter 15.

Freedom from is the message of the other paintings, *Freedom from Fear* and *Freedom from Want*.[13] Here freedom from suggests immunity from fear and want. In the modern political context, freedom from often symbolizes the fight against exploitation and oppression. The cry of the civil rights movement in the 1960s—"Freedom Now!"—conveyed this meaning. This sense of freedom corresponds to the "civil rights" discussed in Chapter 16. If you recognize that freedom in this sense means immunity from discrimination, you can see that it comes close to the concept of equality.[14] In this book, we avoid using freedom to mean "freedom from"; for this sense, we simply use *equality*. When we use *freedom*, we mean "freedom of."

freedom of
An absence of constraints on behavior, as in *freedom of speech* or *freedom of religion*.

freedom from
Immunity, as in *freedom from want*.

Order

When *order* is viewed in the narrow sense of preserving life and protecting property, most citizens concede the importance of maintaining order and thereby grant the need

How far should government go to maintain order, provide public goods, and promote equality? In the United States (as in every other nation), citizens, scholars, and politicians have different answers. We can analyze their positions by referring to philosophies about the proper scope of government—that is, the range of its permissible activities. Imagine a continuum. At one end is the belief that government should do everything; at the other is the belief that government should not exist. These extreme ideologies, from the most government to the least government, and those that fall in between are shown in Figure 1.1.

Totalitarianism

totalitarianism
A political philosophy that advocates unlimited power for the government to enable it to control all sectors of society.

Totalitarianism is the belief that government should have unlimited power. A totalitarian government controls all sectors of society: business, labor, education, religion, sports, and the arts. A true totalitarian favors a network of laws, rules, and regulations that guides every aspect of individual behavior. The object is to produce a perfect society serving some master plan for "the common good." Totalitarianism has reached its terrifying full potential only in literature and films (for example, in George Orwell's *1984*, a novel about "Big Brother" watching everyone), but several societies have come perilously close to "perfection." Think of Germany under Hitler and the Soviet Union under Stalin. Not many people openly profess totalitarianism today, but the concept is useful because it anchors one side of our continuum.

Socialism

socialism
A form of rule in which the central government plays a strong role in regulating existing private industry and directing the economy, although it does allow some private ownership of productive capacity.

Whereas totalitarianism refers to government in general, **socialism** pertains to government's role in the economy. Like communism, socialism is an economic system based on Marxist theory. Under socialism (and communism), the scope of government extends to ownership or control of the basic industries that produce goods and services. These include communications, mining, heavy industry, transportation, and energy.

FIGURE 1.1　Ideology and the Scope of Government

We can classify political ideologies according to the scope of action that people are willing to allow government in dealing with social and economic problems. In this chart, the three rows map out various philosophical positions along an underlying continuum ranging from least to most government. Notice that conventional politics in the United States spans only a narrow portion of the theoretical possibilities for government action. In popular usage, liberals favor a greater scope of government, and conservatives want a narrower scope. But over time, the traditional distinction has eroded and now oversimplifies the differences between liberals and conservatives. Figure 1.2 offers a more discriminating classification of liberals and conservatives.

Although socialism favors a strong role for government in regulating private industry and directing the economy, it allows more room than communism does for private ownership of productive capacity. Many Americans equate socialism with the communism practiced in the old closed societies of the Soviet Union and Eastern Europe, but there is a difference. Although communism in theory was supposed to result in what Marx referred to as a "withering away" of the state, communist governments in practice tended toward totalitarianism, controlling not just economic life but also both political and social life through a dominant party organization. Some socialist governments, however, practice **democratic socialism**. They guarantee civil liberties (such as freedom of speech and freedom of religion) and allow their citizens to determine the extent of the government's activity through free elections and competitive political parties. Outside the United States, socialism is not universally viewed as inherently bad. In fact, the governments of Britain, Sweden, Germany, and France, among other democracies, have at times since World War II been avowedly socialist. More recently, the formerly communist regimes of Eastern Europe have abandoned the controlling role of government in their economies for strong doses of capitalism.

democratic socialism
A socialist form of government that guarantees civil liberties such as freedom of speech and religion. Citizens determine the extent of government activity through free elections and competitive political parties.

Capitalism

Capitalism also relates to the government's role in the economy. In contrast to both socialism and communism, **capitalism** supports free enterprise—private businesses operating without government regulation. Some theorists, most notably the late Nobel Prize-winning economist Milton Friedman, argue that free enterprise is necessary for free politics.[20] This argument, that the economic system of capitalism is essential to democracy, contradicts the tenets of democratic socialism. Whether it is valid depends in part on our understanding of democracy, a subject discussed in Chapter 2. The United States is decidedly a capitalist country, more so than most other Western nations. Despite the U.S. government's enormous budget, it owns or operates relatively few public enterprises. For example, railroads, airlines, and television stations, which are frequently owned by the government in other countries, are privately owned in the United States. But our government does extend its authority into the economic sphere, regulating private businesses and directing the overall economy. Both American liberals and conservatives embrace capitalism, but they differ on the nature and amount of government intervention in the economy they deem necessary or desirable.

capitalism
The system of government that favors free enterprise (privately owned businesses operating without government regulation).

Libertarianism

Libertarianism opposes all government action except what is necessary to protect life and property. **Libertarians** grudgingly recognize the necessity of government but believe that it should be as limited as possible and should not promote either order or equality. For example, libertarians grant the need for traffic laws to ensure safe and efficient automobile travel. But they oppose laws requiring motorcycle riders to wear helmets, and the libertarian ethos in New Hampshire makes it the only state not requiring seat belts. Libertarians believe that social programs that provide food, clothing, and shelter are outside the proper scope of government. Helping the needy, they insist, should be a matter of individual choice. Libertarians also oppose government ownership of basic industries; in fact, they oppose any government intervention in the economy. This kind of economic policy is called **laissez faire**, a French phrase that means "let (people) do (as they please)." Such an extreme policy extends beyond the free enterprise that most capitalists advocate.

Libertarians are vocal advocates of hands-off government in both the social and the economic spheres. Although Kentucky Senator Rand Paul was elected as a Republican, he represented the party's libertarian wing. Other libertarians make no

libertarianism
A political ideology that is opposed to all government action except as necessary to protect life and property.

libertarians
Those who are opposed to using government to promote either order or equality.

laissez faire
An economic doctrine that opposes any form of government intervention in business.

secret of their identity. The Libertarian Party ran candidates in every presidential election from 1972 through 2016, when it won 4 million votes. That was its best showing but was still only 3 percent of all votes cast.

Do not confuse libertarians with liberals—or with liberalism, the John Locke-inspired doctrine mentioned earlier. The words are similar, but their meanings are quite different. *Libertarianism* draws on *liberty* as its root (following Locke) and means "absence of governmental constraint." While both liberalism and libertarianism leave citizens free to pursue their private goals, libertarianism treats freedom as a pure goal; it's liberalism on steroids. In American political usage, *liberalism* evolved from the root word *liberal* in the sense of "freely," like a liberal serving of butter. Liberals see a positive role for government in helping the disadvantaged. Over time, *liberal* has come to mean something closer to generous, in the sense that liberals (but not libertarians) support government spending on social programs. Libertarians find little benefit in any government social program.

Anarchism

anarchism
A political philosophy that opposes government in any form.

Anarchism stands opposite totalitarianism on the political continuum. Anarchists oppose all government in any form. As a political philosophy, anarchism values absolute freedom. Because all government involves some restriction on personal freedom (for example, forcing people to drive on one side of the road), a pure anarchist would object even to traffic laws. Like totalitarianism, anarchism is not a popular philosophy, but it does have adherents on the political fringes. Anarchists also have a website: www.anarchistnews.org.

Liberals and Conservatives: The Narrow Middle

As shown in Figure 1.1, practical politics in the United States ranges over only the central portion of the continuum. The extreme positions—totalitarianism and anarchism—are rarely argued in public debates. And in this era of distrust of "big government," few American politicians openly advocate socialism. When he campaigned for the Democratic presidential nomination in 2016, Vermont Senator Bernie Sanders had trouble explaining his self-description as a democratic socialist. However, more than 120 people ran for Congress in 2014 as candidates of the Libertarian Party without needing to explain libertarianism. Although none won, American libertarians are sufficiently vocal to be heard in the debate over the role of government.

Still, most of that debate is limited to a narrow range of political thought. On one side are people commonly called *liberals*; on the other are *conservatives*. In popular usage, liberals favor more government, conservatives less. This distinction is clear when the issue is government spending to provide public goods. Liberals favor generous government support for education, wildlife protection, public transportation, and a whole range of social programs. Conservatives want smaller government budgets and fewer government programs. They support free enterprise and argue against government job programs, regulation of business, and legislation of working conditions and wage rates.

But on other topics, liberals and conservatives reverse their positions. In theory, liberals favor government activism, yet they oppose government regulation of abortion. In theory, conservatives oppose government activism, yet they support government surveillance of telephone conversations to fight terrorism. What's going on? Are American political attitudes hopelessly contradictory, or is something missing in our analysis of these ideologies today? Actually something is missing. To understand the liberal and conservative stances on political issues, we must look not only at the scope of government action but also at the purpose of government action. That is, to understand a political ideology, it is necessary to understand how it incorporates the values of freedom, order, and equality.

American Political Ideologies and the Purpose of Government

LO7 Explain how liberals, conservatives, libertarians, and communitarians view the role of government.

IMAGE 1.4   A Socialist Candidate?

Although he sought the Democratic Party's presidential nomination in 2016, Vermont Senator Bernie Sanders campaigned as an independent in winning elections for mayor of Burlington, for the U.S. House, and for the Senate. During his campaign, he described himself as a democratic socialist who embraced social policies widely followed in Scandinavian countries.

MICHAEL REYNOLDS/Newscom/European Pressphoto Agency/WASHINGTON/DISTRICT OF COLUMBIA/USA

Much of American politics revolves around the two dilemmas just described: freedom versus order and freedom versus equality. The two dilemmas do not account for all political conflict, but they help us gain insight into the workings of politics and organize the seemingly chaotic world of political events, actors, and issues.

Liberals versus Conservatives: The New Differences

Liberals and conservatives are different, but their differences no longer hinge on the narrow question of the government's role in providing public goods. Liberals do favor more spending for public goods and conservatives less, but this is no longer the critical difference between them. Today that difference stems from their attitudes toward the purpose of government. Conservatives support the original purpose of government: maintaining social order. They are willing to use the coercive power of the state to force citizens to be orderly. They favor firm police action, swift and severe punishment for criminals, and more laws regulating behavior. Conservatives would not stop with defining, preventing, and punishing crime, however. They tend to want to preserve traditional patterns of social relations—the domestic role of women and business owners' authority to hire whom they wish, for example. For this reason, they do not think government should impose equality.

Liberals are less likely than conservatives to want to use government power to maintain order. In general, liberals are more accepting of alternative lifestyles—for example, homosexual behavior. Liberals do not necessarily shy away from using government coercion, but they use it for a different purpose: to promote equality. They support laws that ensure equal treatment of gays in employment, housing, and education; laws that force private businesses to hire and promote women and members of minority groups; laws that require public transportation to provide equal access to people with disabilities; and laws that order cities and states to reapportion election districts so that minority voters can elect

conservatives
Those who are willing to use government to promote order but not equality.

liberals
Those who are willing to use government to promote equality but not order.

minority candidates to public office. Conservatives do not oppose equality, but they do not value it to the extent of using the government's power to enforce equality. For liberals, the use of that power to promote equality is both valid and necessary.

A Two-Dimensional Classification of Ideologies

To classify liberal and conservative ideologies more accurately, we have to incorporate the values of freedom, order, and equality into the classification.[21] We can do this using the model in Figure 1.2. It depicts the conflicting values along two separate dimensions, each anchored in maximum freedom at the lower left. One dimension extends horizontally from maximum freedom on the left to maximum order on the right. The other extends vertically from maximum freedom at the bottom to maximum equality at the top. Each box represents a different ideological type: libertarians, liberals, conservatives, and communitarians.[22]

Libertarians value freedom more than order or equality. (We will use *libertarians* for people who have libertarian tendencies but may not accept the whole philosophy.) In practical terms, libertarians want minimal government intervention in both the economic and the social spheres. For example, they oppose affirmative action and laws that restrict transmission of sexually explicit material.

FIGURE 1.2   Ideologies: A Two-Dimensional Framework

The four ideological types are defined by the values they favor in resolving the two major dilemmas of government: How much freedom should be sacrificed in pursuit of order and equality, respectively? Test yourself by thinking about the values that are most important to you. Which box in the figure best represents your combination of values?

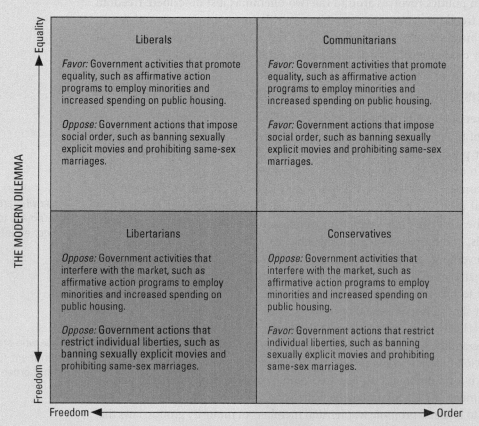

Liberals value freedom more than order but not more than equality. They oppose laws that ban sexually explicit publications but support affirmative action. Conservatives value freedom more than equality but would restrict freedom to preserve social order. Conservatives oppose affirmative action but favor laws that restrict pornography. Finally, we arrive at the ideological type positioned at the upper right in Figure 1.2. This group values both equality and order more than freedom. Its members support both affirmative action and laws that restrict pornography. We will call this new group **communitarians**.[23] The term is used narrowly in contemporary politics to reflect the philosophy of the Communitarian Network, a political movement founded by sociologist Amitai Etzioni.[24] This movement rejects both the liberal-conservative classification and the libertarian argument that "individuals should be left on their own to pursue their choices, rights, and self-interests."[25] Like liberals, Etzioni's communitarians believe that there is a role for government in helping the disadvantaged. Like conservatives, they believe that government should be used to promote moral values—preserving the family through more stringent divorce laws and limiting the dissemination of pornography, for example.[26]

By analyzing political ideologies on two dimensions rather than one, we can explain why people can seem to be liberal on one issue (favoring a broader scope of government action) and conservative on another (favoring less government action). The answer hinges on the purpose of a given government action: Which value does it promote: order or equality?[27] According to our typology, only libertarians and communitarians are consistent in their attitude toward the scope of government activity, whatever its purpose. Libertarians value freedom so highly that they oppose most government efforts to enforce either order or equality. Communitarians (in our usage) are inclined to trade freedom for both order and equality. Liberals and conservatives, on the other hand, favor or oppose government activity depending on its purpose. As you will learn in Chapter 5, large groups of Americans fall into each of the four ideological categories. Because Americans increasingly choose four different resolutions to the original and modern dilemmas of government, the simple labels of *liberal* and *conservative* no longer describe contemporary political ideologies as well as they did in the 1930s, 1940s, and 1950s.

communitarians
Those who are willing to use government to promote both order and equality.

Summary

The challenge of democracy lies in making difficult choices—choices that inevitably bring important values into conflict. This chapter has outlined a normative framework for analyzing the policy choices that arise in the pursuit of the purposes of government in an era of globalization.

LO1 Define globalization and explain how globalization affects American politics and government.

- We live in an era of globalization—a term for the increasing interdependence of citizens and nations across the world. Globalization infringes on national sovereignty, the right of governments to govern their people as they wish. Global forces generate pressures for economic

trade, observance of human rights, and governance by international law. More than ever before, foreign affairs affect American government, and American politics affects government in other nations.

LO2 Identify the purposes that government serves and trace their historical roots.

- Government requires citizens to surrender some freedom as part of being governed. People do so to obtain the benefits of government: maintaining order, providing public goods, and—more controversially—promoting equality.

LO3 **Describe how political scientists use concepts to structure events and promote understanding.**

- Political concepts are generalized ideas about government and politics. They provide broader views than those offered by examining specific political events. Our conceptual framework consists of five concepts organized into two groups: concepts that identify values pursued by government: freedom, order, and equality; and concepts that describe models of democratic government: majoritarian and pluralist democracy.

LO4 **Define freedom, order, and equality and discuss the various interpretations of each value.**

- The terms freedom, order, and equality have varied connotations in American politics. Freedom and equality are positive terms that mean different things to different people at different times. Order has negative connotations for many because it symbolizes government intrusion into private lives. *Freedom* can be used in two major senses: freedom of and freedom from. We use it in the "freedom of" sense. Freedom of speech means freedom to speak. *Order* in politics means more than preserving life and property; it also means established patterns of authority in society and traditional modes of behavior. *Equality* in politics can be viewed narrowly as political equality (each person having one vote) or as social equality (equality in wealth, education, and status). It can also be viewed as equality of opportunity or of outcome.

LO5 **Analyze the inherent conflicts between freedom versus order and freedom versus equality.**

- The conflict between the values of freedom and order represents the original dilemma of government. The modern dilemma of politics is the conflict between the values of freedom and equality.

LO6 **Distinguish among these terms: totalitarianism, socialism, capitalism, libertarianism, and anarchism.**

- Political ideology is defined as a consistent set of values and beliefs about the proper purpose and scope of government. Ideologies differ about the proper range of permissible activities. Totalitarianism is the belief that government should have unlimited power. Socialism extends the scope of government to ownership or control of the basic industries that produce goods and services. Capitalism is committed to free enterprise—private businesses operating without government regulation. Libertarianism opposes all government action except what is necessary to protect life and property. Anarchists oppose all government in any form. In the United States, most political debate is limited to a narrow range of political thought. On one side are liberals; on the other are conservatives.

LO7 **Explain how liberals, conservatives, libertarians, and communitarians view the role of government.**

- In popular usage, liberals favor more government, and conservatives less. That is, liberals support a broader role for government than do conservatives. Liberals and conservatives mainly quarrel over the purpose of government action. Conservatives may want less government, but they are willing to use the government's coercive power to impose social order. Liberals too are willing to use the coercive power of government, but for the purpose of promoting equality. Liberals value freedom more than order and equality more than freedom. Conservatives value order more than freedom and freedom more than equality. Libertarians choose freedom over both order and equality. Communitarians are willing to sacrifice freedom for both order and equality.

Chapter Quiz

LO1 **Define globalization and explain how globalization affects American politics and government.**

1. Define globalization and give an example of globalization's effect on American politics.
2. Give an example of the American government's effects on foreign politics.

LO2 **Identify the purposes that government serves and trace their historical roots.**

1. What are the major purposes of government?
2. Which of these purposes is most controversial?

LO3 **Describe how political scientists use concepts to structure events and promote understanding.**

1. How does the use of political concepts promote understanding?
2. How does the conceptual framework used in this book organize political concepts?

LO4 **Define freedom, order, and equality and discuss the various interpretations of each value.**

1. Which of these concepts is linked most closely to the police power of a state?
2. Which is most closely linked to the concept of rights, and why?

LO5 **Analyze the inherent conflicts between freedom versus order and freedom versus equality.**

1. What are the two dilemmas of government, and which came first?
2. Which dilemma underlies the 1960 law requiring paying men and women the same rate for equal work? Why is it a dilemma?

LO6 **Distinguish among these terms: totalitarianism, socialism, capitalism, libertarianism, and anarchism.**

1. How do the terms libertarianism, liberalism, and liberals differ? In what ways are these terms similar?
2. Give an example of anarchism in contemporary American politics.

LO7 **Explain how liberals, conservatives, libertarians, and communitarians view the role of government.**

1. How can both liberals and conservatives favor greater scope of government?
2. What contemporary politicians exemplify the typological categories of liberal, conservative, libertarian, and communitarian?

2 Majoritarian or Pluralist Democracy?

Smoking marijuana has become fairly commonplace in the United States. Roughly half of all American adults say they have tried smoking pot.[1] Not coincidentally, the percentage of people who believe marijuana should be fully legalized has gone up, and now more than half the public favors this position.

Change in the laws on marijuana has been slow to follow this trend in public opinion. Only four states (Alaska, Colorado, Oregon, and Washington) and the District of Columbia allow the use of recreational marijuana at the time of this publication. In these five places, those of age can legally purchase marijuana without a prescription from a doctor. Twenty-three other states have provisions for legal medical marijuana. Marijuana provides relief to some who suffer from chronic pain and other conditions, and medicinal use generally requires a doctor's prescription.

Clearly, state legislatures have not been eager to enact full legalization of marijuana. One reason may be that opponents feel more strongly about the issue than those who are in favor. Legislators are sensitive to intensity of opinion, not just its overall disposition. Another is that those most supportive of legalization are young, while those most opposed are in the oldest age group and are much more likely to vote in elections. Also, legislators may feel uncomfortable voting for a policy that contradicts federal law.

Due to this opposition in state legislatures, frustrated voters have taken matters into their own hands. In the states that have legalized recreational marijuana, enactment came directly from the voters who acted to pass statewide ballot propositions.[2] As discussed later in this chapter, many states allow for voters to decide on policy questions through initiatives or referenda. In such cases the voters themselves, at election time, pass or reject a proposed law that is listed on their ballots.

In Colorado, for example, after supporters gathered the necessary signatures to get the measure onto the ballot, they then undertook a vigorous campaign aimed at convincing voters that full legalization of marijuana would not create problems in the state. On election day they were successful, winning with 53 percent of the statewide vote. After Colorado voters enacted legalization, a leading campaigner for the initiative noted succinctly, "It's a historic one, man."[3] The marijuana initiatives are historic as these states are fundamentally altering policy from that of the national government. Yet many wonder if allowing voters to make the laws through ballot questions is the best way to formulate public policy. Legislators are likely to spend more time considering a policy issue than is the average citizen.

Most broadly, the question of whether deciding public policy through ballot propositions is a desirable process is about the very nature of democracy. As we'll see in this chapter, there are different models of democracy. These models differ in the degree to which they entrust governing directly to the people or instead rely on the judgment of the people we elect to office.

#ChallengeAccepted

Take the Challenge on MindTap for American Government

Who should decide whether marijuana should be legalized: the public through a statewide vote on a ballot question, or a state's legislature through its normal process?

American Democracy: More Pluralist Than Majoritarian

It is not idle speculation to ask what kind of democracy is practiced in the United States. The answer can help us understand why our government can be called democratic despite a low level of citizen participation in politics and despite government actions that sometimes run contrary to public opinion.

Throughout this book, we probe to determine how well the United States fits the two alternative models of democracy: we judge that across all levels of government, the United States adheres more closely to the pluralist than the majoritarian model. Yet the pluralist model is far from a perfect representation of democracy. Its principal drawback is that it favors the well-organized, and the poor are the least likely to be members of interest groups. Those who are affluent, have professional skills, and are active in the political system have significant advantages in our governmental process.

In recent years, the parties have become more sharply divided along conservative and liberal dimensions, thus making our system a bit more majoritarian than has traditionally been the case. In particular, the two parties in Congress have become more ideologically homogeneous, thus giving voters a clearer opportunity to select a party more cohesive in its programmatic intent.[39] Yet this step toward majoritarianism has led to widespread criticism that our system of government is becoming too bitterly partisan. That is, as the members of Congress have become more ideological, they seem to have become less inclined to work together to achieve moderate, compromise solutions to the nation's problems. Some critics have also charged that ideological activists, who have mobilized more than moderates, have hijacked the parties and pulled them more sharply toward conservative and liberal extremes.[40] For those uncomfortable with more ideological parties, the continuing strong counterbalance of pluralism is welcome.

Given the survey data that show that the people's trust in American government has fallen over the years, it may seem that pluralist democracy is not serving us very well. Indeed, many Americans describe government and politicians in the harshest terms.[41] Radio talk show hosts like Rush Limbaugh and politicians themselves pile invective on top of insult when they talk about what's wrong with Washington.[42] Compared with citizens in other developed nations, Americans fall in the middle concerning their satisfaction with democracy in the United States. But it's not at all clear that Americans would be more satisfied with another type of democracy.

This evaluation of the pluralist nature of American democracy may not mean much to you now. But you will learn that the pluralist model makes the United States look far more democratic than the majoritarian model would. Eventually, you will have to decide the answers to three questions:

1. Is the pluralist model truly an adequate expression of democracy, or is it a perversion of classical ideals, designed to portray America as democratic when it is not?
2. Does the majoritarian model result in a "better" type of democracy?
3. If it does, could new mechanisms of government be devised to produce a desirable mix of majority rule and minority rights?

Let these questions play in the back of your mind as you read more about the workings of American government in meeting the challenge of democracy.

Summary

There are different forms of government around the world, one of which is democracy. But there is no one conception of democracy, and this chapter explores these differing beliefs about how a democracy ought to be constituted.

LO1   Distinguish between the two theories of democratic government used in political science: procedural and substantive.

- The procedural view of democracy emphasizes democratic processes. Four procedural elements seem paramount: universal participation, political equality, majority rule, and government responsiveness to public opinion. Substantive democratic theory focuses on the substance of policies rather than procedures. It holds that there are some rights that are so important that they should not be subject to being overturned by majority decision. Not surprisingly, procedural democracy can come into conflict with substantive democracy. What substantive policies should be beyond the control of popular opinion?

LO2   Consider how indirect democracy diverges from direct democracy.

- Direct democracy allows individuals to participate in making policy themselves, such as through neighborhood government or state-wide referenda. Indirect democracy builds on representation whereby we elect individuals, such as legislators, to act on our behalf. We expect indirect democracy to be responsive to public opinion.

LO3   Compare and contrast the majoritarian and pluralist models of democracy.

- The majoritarian model of democracy is built around majority rule as evidenced by elections. Pluralist democracy conceives of democracy as a competition between opposing groups in society. Elite theorists believe that American government is dominated by a small set of wealthy individuals and large businesses.

LO4   Define the ways in which elite theory differs from pluralist democracy.

- In theory, pluralism holds out the promise of democracy through the competition of interest groups representing various sectors of American society and commerce. Elite theory claims that America is fundamentally undemocratic. Rather, our governmental process is held to be dominated by an oligarchy built on wealth and business connections.

LO5   Evaluate the challenges facing countries trying to move toward a democratic form of government.

- Although the number of democracies in the world increased for a time, this trend has leveled off. The process of democratization is difficult, and many democratizing countries fail and return to some form of authoritarianism. We compare the validity of majoritarian and pluralist models of democracy and conclude that the United States is a mix of both, but closer to pluralism. Majoritarian elements (such as more party-line voting in Congress) are on the rise, though.

Chapter Quiz

LO1 Distinguish between the two theories of democratic government used in political science: procedural and substantive.
1. How do procedural democracy and substantive democracy differ?
2. What is direct democracy? What is indirect democracy?

LO2 Consider how indirect democracy diverges from direct democracy.
1. What are some of the forms of direct democracy?
2. What is the relationship between public opinion and indirect (representative) democracy?

LO3 Compare and contrast the majoritarian and pluralist models of democracy.
1. What are the basic concepts of majoritarian democracy and of pluralist democracy?
2. What criticisms lie at the heart of elite theory?

LO4 Define the ways in which elite theory differs from pluralist democracy.
1. How does pluralist theory compare to the realities of contemporary interest group politics?
2. Neither theory is built around majority public opinion, but the role of a political minority or minorities differs in them. How so?

LO5 Evaluate the challenges facing countries trying to move toward a democratic form of government.
1. How do political and economic instability affect the process of democratization?
2. What trends support the argument that the American system of democracy is becoming more majoritarian?

3 The Constitution

What can a hit Broadway musical tell you about American political history—especially if it is told in hip-hop? *Hamilton*—the wildly successful, unorthodox musical—tells the story of Alexander Hamilton, a central figure in the formation of the United States.[1] Many of you may know that Hamilton's portrait appears on the $10 bill. Some of you may recall that Hamilton's life ended at age forty-nine in a duel with Vice President Aaron Burr. A few of you may recall that Hamilton was the first Secretary of the Treasury under President George Washington, launching the nation's first fiscal and monetary systems. But what did Hamilton and his contemporaries accomplish and why should we care *today*?

Lin-Manuel Miranda—the American composer, lyricist, librettist, rapper, and actor—probably had similar thoughts when he picked up a copy of Ron Chernow's 800-page biography *Alexander Hamilton* while on vacation in 2008.[2] Miranda was mesmerized by Hamilton's life and decided to retell that story in a hip-hop, rap, and pop musical. He began audaciously:

> How does a bastard, orphan, son of a whore and a
> Scotsman, dropped in the middle of a
> Forgotten spot in the Caribbean by providence
> Impoverished, in squalor
> Grow up to be a hero and a scholar?[3]

Miranda faced the challenge of re-telling the story of America's beginning to a new generation: to a society far more racially, ethnically, and religiously diverse than anyone imagined 230 years ago. With enormous success, Miranda used today's musical medium to relate the lives of Hamilton and his contemporaries—Burr, Washington, Thomas Jefferson, James Madison, and others—to illustrate the contentious political issues leading to independence, revolution, federation, and finally, to "a more perfect union." As Miranda explained in an interview:

> [Rap] is uniquely suited to tell Hamilton's story. Because it has more words per measure than any other musical genre. It has rhythm and it has density. And if Hamilton had anything in his writings it was this density.[4]

Hamilton was born on the small Caribbean island of Nevis, then part of the British West Indies. He participated in the Constitutional Convention in 1787 as a delegate from New York, but his proposals never mustered much support. Nevertheless, he signed the final document and became a powerful advocate for its ratification through a series of influential newspaper articles published anonymously (we'd call them op-ed articles today) with assists from Madison and John Jay.

Miranda has brought back the story of America's founding to a new generation. Its retelling—whether in hip-hop or in prose—implicates core values of freedom, order, and equality.

#ChallengeAccepted

Take the Challenge on MindTap for American Government

The Census Bureau predicts that white Americans will be in the minority by 2043. In light of our increasingly multiethnic, multiracial population, how would you tell the story of America's founding to the next generation of students?

Sara Krulwich/The New York Times/Redux

Learning Outcomes

LO1 Explain the reasons for the colonies' declaration of independence from British rule.

LO2 Identify the factors that led to the failure of the Confederation.

LO3 Explain the major points of contention in the writing of the Constitution.

LO4 Explain the contribution of the Constitution to the American political tradition and the principles it establishes.

LO5 Describe the actions taken to ensure the ratification of the Constitution.

LO6 Explain the procedures required to amend the Constitution.

LO7 Evaluate the extent to which the Constitution reflects and embodies the principles of majoritarian or pluralist democracy.

Constitutions Come of Age in Global Politics

Compared with other constitutions across the world, the U.S. Constitution is an antique. Ratified in 1788, it is the world's second oldest constitution. (The tiny landlocked microstate of San Marino boasts the oldest constitution, dating to 1600.) But few 230-year-old antiques still work more or less as their designers intended. Other countries have constitutions, but they tend to come and go.

A national constitution is the fundamental law of a land. It must give voice to a set of inviolable principles that limit the powers of government by setting up governmental institutions and defining their relationships and patterns of authority. Even dictatorships require institutions through which to govern.

Some stable democracies lack a single document as a written constitution. Perhaps the most notable example is Britain, whose fundamental law inheres in other documents, such as the Magna Carta. Other democracies, like Brazil, have gone in the opposite direction by adopting "hyperconstitutions." Brazil tries to pack into its 1988 charter just about every facet of public life, making it one of the longest constitutions ever drafted, nearly six times the length of the U.S. Constitution.

Leaders frequently remake constitutions. They replace their founding documents on average every nineteen years and amend them in smaller ways yearly. These changes may correct unforeseen problems or reflect new conditions or understandings. And occasionally these alterations aim to keep the ruling elite in power.

Three reasons may explain constitutional durability: (1) they tend to derive from an open, participatory process; (2) they tend to be specific; and (3) they tend to be flexible through amendment and interpretation.

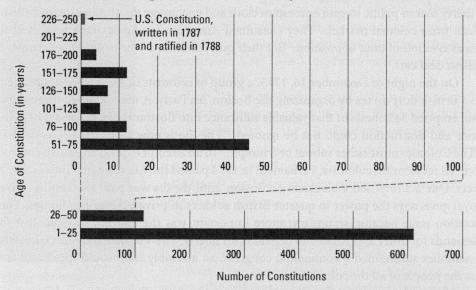

Source: Tom Ginsburg, Zachary Elkins, and James Melton, "The Lifespan of Written Constitutions," *The Record* (Alumni Magazine), Spring 2009, www.law.uchicago.edu/alumni/magazine/lifespan; Zachary Elkins, Tom Ginsburg, James Melton, Robert Shaffer, Juan F. Sequeda, and Daniel P. Miranker, "Constitute: The World's Constitutions to Read, Search, and Compare," *Web Semantics: Science, Services and Agents on the World Wide Web* 27–28 (2014): 10–18.

CRITICAL THINKING What might be some of the advantages and disadvantages of having a durable constitution?

the congress adjourned, planning to reconvene in May 1775.

Revolutionary Action

By early 1775, however, a movement that the colonists themselves were calling a revolution had already begun. Colonists in Massachusetts were fighting the British at Concord and Lexington. Delegates to the Second Continental Congress, meeting in May, faced a dilemma: Should they prepare for war, or should they try to reconcile with Britain? As conditions deteriorated, the Second Continental Congress remained in session to serve as the government of the colony-states while George III assembled a massive force to crush the rebellion once and for all.[10]

On June 7, 1776, owing in large part to the powerful advocacy of John Adams of Massachusetts, a strong supporter of independence, the Virginia delegation called on the Continental Congress to resolve "that these United Colonies are, and of right ought to be, free and Independent States, that they are absolved from all allegiance to the British Crown, and that all political connection between them and the State of Great Britain is, and ought to be, totally dissolved." This was a difficult decision. Independence meant disloyalty to Britain and war, death, and devastation. The congress debated but did not immediately adopt the resolution. A committee of five men was appointed to prepare a proclamation expressing the colonies' reasons for declaring independence.

The Declaration of Independence

Thomas Jefferson, a young farmer and lawyer from Virginia who was a member of the committee, became the "pen" to John Adams's "voice."[11] Because Jefferson was erudite, a Virginian, and an extremely skilled writer, he drafted the proclamation. Jefferson's document, the **Declaration of Independence**, was modestly revised by the committee and then further edited by the congress. It remains a cherished statement of our heritage, expressing simply, clearly, and rationally the many arguments for separation from Great Britain.

The principles underlying the Declaration were rooted in the writings of the English philosopher John Locke and had been expressed many times by speakers in the congress and the colonial assemblies. Locke argued that people have God-given, or natural, rights that are inalienable—that is, they cannot be taken away by any government. According to Locke, all legitimate political authority exists to preserve these natural rights and is based on the consent of those who are governed. The idea of consent is

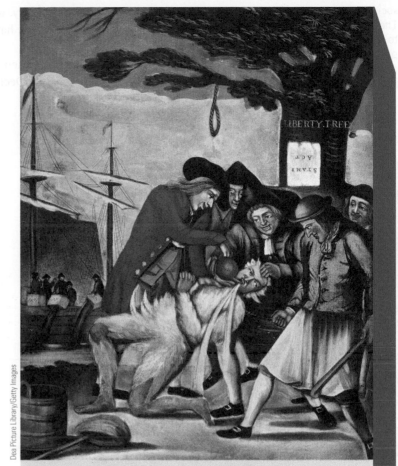

Dea Picture Library/Getty Images

IMAGE 3.2 Uniquely American Protest

Americans protested the Tea Act (1773) by holding the Boston Tea Party (background, left) and by using a unique form of painful punishment, tarring and feathering, on the tax collector (see "STAMP ACT" upside-down on the Liberty Tree). An early treatise on the subject offered the following instructions: "First, strip a person naked, then heat the tar until it is thin, and pour upon the naked flesh, or rub it over with a tar brush. After which, sprinkle decently upon the tar, whilst it is yet warm, as many feathers as will stick to it." Tar is a dark, thick, flammable liquid. When it was smeared on a person's body and covered with feathers the goal was to humiliate the victim. In an act of spite, Loyalists felled the Liberty Tree for firewood during the siege of Boston (1775–1776).

Declaration of Independence Drafted by Thomas Jefferson, the document that proclaimed the right of the colonies to separate from Great Britain.

social contract theory
The belief that the people agree to set up rulers for certain purposes and thus have the right to resist or remove rulers who act against those purposes.

derived from **social contract theory**, which states that the people agree to establish rulers for certain purposes, but they have the right to resist or remove rulers who violate those purposes.[12]

Jefferson used similar arguments in the Declaration of Independence. Taking his cue from a draft of the Virginia Declaration of Rights,[13] Jefferson wrote,

North Wind Picture Archives

AP Images/Sergei Chuzavkov

IMAGES 3.3 AND 3.4   Toppling Tyrants: Then and Now

A gilded equestrian statue of George III once stood at the tip of Manhattan. On July 9, 1776, citizens responded to the news of the Declaration of Independence by toppling the statue. It was melted down and converted into musket balls. The same rage seemed apparent in December 2013, when anti-government protesters in Ukraine used sledgehammers to topple a statue of Soviet state founder Vladimir Lenin. The protesters eventually brought down the government of Russian-leaning Ukrainian President Viktor Yanukovyich. Ukraine remains in turmoil, with its Crimean Peninsula annexed by Russia and the eastern and southern portions of the country occupied by Russian-supported insurgents.

> We hold these truths to be self-evident, that all men are created equal, that they are endowed by their Creator with certain unalienable rights, that among these are life, liberty, and the pursuit of happiness. That to secure these rights, governments are instituted among men, deriving their just powers from the consent of the governed. That whenever any form of government becomes destructive of these ends, it is the right of the people to alter or to abolish it, and to institute new government, laying its foundation on such principles, and organizing its power in such form, as to them shall seem most likely to effect their safety and happiness.

Historian Jack Rakove maintains that Jefferson was not proposing equality for individuals. Rather, he was asserting the equality of peoples to enjoy the same rights of self-government that other peoples enjoyed. "It was the collective right of revolution and self-government that the Declaration was written to justify—not a visionary or even utopian notion of equality within American society itself."[14]

Jefferson went on to list the many deliberate acts of the king that had exceeded the legitimate role of government. The last and lengthiest item on Jefferson's original draft of the Declaration was the king's support of the slave trade. Although Jefferson did not condemn slavery, he denounced the king for enslaving a people, engaging in the slave trade, and proposing that if the slaves were freed, they would attack their masters. When South Carolina and Georgia, two states with an interest in continuing the wretched practice, objected, Jefferson and the committee dropped the offending paragraph. Finally, Jefferson declared that the colonies were "Free and Independent States," with no political connection to Great Britain.

To restate the argument in its simplest terms: (1) the people have a right to revolt if they determine that their government is denying them their legitimate rights; and (2) the long list of the king's actions was evidence of such denial; therefore (3) the people had the right to rebel, to form a new government.

On July 2, 1776, the Second Continental Congress finally voted for independence. The vote was by state, and the motion carried 11–0. (Rhode Island was not present, and the New York delegation, lacking instructions, did not cast its yea vote until July 15.) Two days later, on July 4, the Declaration of Independence was approved, with few changes. Several representatives insisted on removing language they thought would incite the colonists. In the end, even though Jefferson's compelling words were left almost exactly as he had written them, the adjustments tugged at the Virginian's personal insecurities. According to historian Joseph Ellis, while the congress debated various changes to the document, "Jefferson sat silently and sullenly, regarding each proposed revision as another defacement."[15]

By August, fifty-five revolutionaries had signed the Declaration of Independence, pledging "our lives, our fortunes and our sacred honor" in support of their rebellion against the world's most powerful nation. This was no empty pledge: an act of rebellion was treason. Had they lost the Revolutionary War, the signers would have faced a gruesome fate. The punishment for treason was hanging and drawing and quartering—the victim was hanged until half-dead from strangulation, then disemboweled, and finally cut into four pieces while still alive. We celebrate the Fourth of July with fireworks and flag waving, parades, and picnics. We sometimes forget that the Revolution was a matter of life and death. The term revolution belies a fundamental feature of this conflict: it was a civil war "polarizing communities, destroying friendships, [and] dividing families."[16] As one noteworthy example, Benjamin Franklin's only son William was a loyalist.

The war imposed an agonizing choice on colonial Catholics, who were treated with intolerance by the overwhelmingly Protestant population. No other religious group found the choice so difficult. Catholics could either join the revolutionaries, who were opposed to Catholicism, or remain loyal to England and risk new hostility and persecution. But Catholics were few in number, perhaps 25,000 at the time of independence (or 1 percent of the population). Anti-Catholic revolutionaries recognized that if Catholics opposed independence in Maryland and Pennsylvania, where their numbers were greatest, victory might be jeopardized. Furthermore, enlisting the support of Catholic France for the cause of independence would be

H. Armstrong Roberts/ClassicStock/Alamy

IMAGE 3.5   Voting for Independence

The Second Continental Congress voted for independence on July 2, 1776. John Adams of Massachusetts viewed the day "as the most memorable epocha [significant event] in the history of America." In this painting by John Trumbull, the drafting committee presents the Declaration of Independence to the patriots who would later sign it. The committee, grouped in front of the desk, consisted of *(from left to right)* Adams, Roger Sherman (Connecticut), Robert Livingston (New York), Thomas Jefferson (Virginia), and Benjamin Franklin (Pennsylvania).

Trumbull painted the scene years after the event. Relying on Jefferson's faulty memory and his own artistic license, Trumbull created a scene that bears little resemblance to reality. First, there was no ceremonial moment when the committee presented its draft to the congress. Second, the room's elegance belied its actual appearance. Third, the doors are in the wrong place. Fourth, the heavy drapes substitute for actual venetian blinds. And, fifth, the mahogany armchairs replaced the plain Windsor design used by the delegates. Nevertheless, the painting remains an icon of American political history.

against high taxes levied by the state to retire its wartime debt.[22] Later, they attacked an arsenal. Called Shays's Rebellion, the revolt against the established order continued into 1787. Massachusetts appealed to the confederation for help. Horrified by the threat of domestic upheaval, the congress approved a $530,000 requisition for the establishment of a national army. But the plan failed: every state except Virginia rejected the request for money. Finally, the governor of Massachusetts called out the militia and restored order.[23]

The rebellion demonstrated the impotence of the confederation and the urgent need to suppress insurrections and maintain domestic order. Proof to skeptics that Americans could not govern themselves, the rebellion alarmed all American leaders, with the exception of Jefferson. From Paris, where he was serving as American ambassador, he remarked, "A little rebellion now and then is a good thing; the tree of liberty must be refreshed from time to time with the blood of patriots and tyrants."[24]

From Confederation to Constitution

LO3 Explain the major points of contention in the writing of the Constitution.

IMAGE 3.6   "Remember the Ladies"

Abigail Adams, the wife of Continental Congress delegate and future president John Adams, corresponded frequently with her powerful husband. In one such letter on the eve of independence she wrote, "I desire that you would Remember the Ladies, and be more generous and favorable to them.... If particular care and attention is not paid to the Ladies we are determined to foment a Rebellion, and will not hold ourselves bound by any Laws in which we have no Voice, or Representation."

Order, the original purpose of government, was breaking down under the Articles of Confederation. The "league of friendship" envisioned in the Articles was not enough to hold the nation together in peacetime.

Some states had taken halting steps toward encouraging a change in the national government. In 1785, Massachusetts asked the congress to revise the Articles of Confederation, but the congress took no action. In 1786, Virginia invited the states to attend a convention at Annapolis, Maryland, to explore revisions aimed at improving commercial regulation. The meeting was both a failure and a success. Only five states sent delegates, but they seized the opportunity to call for another meeting—with a far broader mission—in Philadelphia the next year. That convention would be charged with devising "such further provisions as shall appear...necessary to render the constitution of the Federal Government adequate to the exigencies of the Union." The congress later agreed to the convention but limited its mission to "the sole and express purpose of revising the Articles of Confederation."[25]

Shays's Rebellion lent a sense of urgency to the task before the Philadelphia convention. The congress's inability to confront the rebellion was evidence that a stronger national government was necessary to preserve order and property—to protect the states from internal as well as external dangers. "While the Declaration was directed against an excess of authority," observed Supreme Court Justice Robert H. Jackson some one hundred fifty years later, "the Constitution [that followed the Articles of Confederation] was directed against anarchy."[26]

Twelve of the thirteen states named seventy-four delegates to convene in Philadelphia, then the most important city in America, in May 1787. (Rhode Island, derisively renamed "Rogue Island" by a Boston newspaper, was the one exception. The state legislature sulkily rejected participating because it feared a strong national government.) Fifty-five delegates eventually showed up at the statehouse in

Philadelphia, but no more than thirty were present at any one time during that swelter-ing spring and summer. The framers were not demigods, but many historians believe that such an assembly will not be seen again. Highly educated, they typically were flu-ent in Latin and Greek. Products of the Enlightenment, they relied on classical liberal-ism for the Constitution's philosophical underpinnings.

They were also veterans of the political intrigues of their states, and so were highly practical politicians who knew how to maneuver. In the words of a leading historian, "The framers built their Constitution with the bricks and mortar of political compro-mise."[27] Although well versed in ideas, they subscribed to the view expressed by one delegate that "experience must be our only guide, reason may mislead us."[28] Fearing for their fragile union, the delegates resolved to keep their proceedings secret. Theirs was a two-fold task: to build a stronger national government and to build a republican gov-ernment, that is, one based on the consent of the people. Each task was daunting; both combined seemed irreconcilable.[29]

The Constitutional Convention, at the time called the Federal Convention, offi-cially opened on May 25. Within the first week, Edmund Randolph of Virginia had presented a long list of changes, suggested by fellow Virginian James Madison, that would replace the weak confederation of states with a powerful national government rather than revise it within its original framework. The delegates unanimously agreed to debate Randolph's proposal, called the **Virginia Plan**. Almost immediately, then, they rejected the idea of amending the Articles of Confederation, working instead to create an entirely new constitution.

The Virginia Plan

The Virginia Plan dominated the convention's deliberations for the rest of the summer, making several important proposals for a strong central government:

- That the powers of the government be divided among three separate branches: a **legislative branch**, for making laws; an **executive branch**, for enforcing laws; and a **judicial branch**, for interpreting laws.
- That the legislature consist of two houses. The first would be chosen by the people, the second by the members of the first house from among candidates nominated by the state legislatures.
- That each state's representation in the legislature be in proportion to the taxes it paid to the national government or in proportion to its free population.
- That an executive, consisting of an unspecified number of people, be selected by the legislature and serve for a single term.
- That the national judiciary include one or more supreme courts and other, lower courts, with judges appointed for life by the legislature.
- That the executive and a number of national judges serve as a council of revision, to approve or veto (disapprove) legislative acts. Their veto could be overridden by a vote of both houses of the legislature.
- That the scope of powers of all three branches be far greater than that assigned the national government by the Articles of Confederation and that the legislature be empowered to override state laws.

By proposing a powerful national legislature that could override state laws, the Virginia Plan clearly advocated a new form of government. It was to have a mixed structure, with more authority over the states and new authority over the people.

Madison was a monumental force in the ensuing debate on the proposals. He kept records of the proceedings that reveal his frequent and brilliant participation and give us insight into his thinking about freedom, order, and equality.

Virginia Plan
A set of proposals for a new government, submitted to the Constitutional Convention of 1787; it included separation of the government into three branch-es, division of the legislature into two houses, and proportional representation in the legislature.

legislative branch
The lawmaking branch of gov-ernment.

executive branch
The law-enforcing branch of government.

judicial branch
The law-interpreting branch of government.

For example, his proposal that senators serve a nine-year term reveals his thinking about equality. Madison foresaw an increase "of those who will labor under all the hardships of life, and secretly sigh for a more equal distribution of its blessings. These may in time outnumber those who are placed above the feelings of indigence."[30] Power, then, could flow into the hands of the numerous poor. The stability of the senate, however, with its nine-year terms and election by the state legislatures, would provide a barrier against the "sighs of the poor" for more equality. Although most delegates shared Madison's apprehension about equality, the nine-year term was voted down.

The Constitution that emerged from the convention bore only a partial resemblance to the document Madison wanted to create. He endorsed seventy-one specific proposals, but he ended up on the losing side on forty of them.[31] And the parts of the Virginia Plan that were ultimately included in the Constitution were not adopted without challenge. Conflicts revolved primarily around the basis for representation in the legislature, the method of choosing legislators, and the structure of the executive branch.

The New Jersey Plan

When in 1787 it appeared that much of the Virginia Plan would be approved by the big states, the small states united in opposition. They feared that if each state's representation in the new legislature was based only on the size of its population, the states with large populations would be able to dominate the new government and the needs and wishes of the small states would be ignored. William Paterson of New Jersey introduced an alternative set of resolutions, written to preserve the spirit of the Articles of Confederation by amending rather than replacing them. The **New Jersey Plan** included the following proposals:

- That a single-chamber legislature have the power to raise revenue and regulate commerce.
- That the states have equal representation in the legislature and choose its members.
- That a multiperson executive be elected by the legislature, with powers similar to those proposed under the Virginia Plan but without the right to veto legislation.
- That a supreme tribunal be created, with a limited jurisdiction. (There was no provision for a system of national courts.)
- That the acts of the legislature be binding on the states—that is, that they be regarded as "the supreme law of the respective states," with the option of force to compel obedience.

After only three days of deliberation, the New Jersey Plan was defeated in the first major convention vote, 7–3. However, the small states had enough support to force a compromise on the issue of representation in the legislature. Table 3.1 compares the New Jersey Plan with the Virginia Plan.

New Jersey Plan
Submitted by the head of the New Jersey delegation to the Constitutional Convention, a set of nine resolutions that would have, in effect, preserved the Articles of Confederation by amending rather than replacing them.

TABLE 3.1 Major Differences Between the Virginia Plan and the New Jersey Plan

Characteristic	Virginia Plan	New Jersey Plan
Legislature	Two chambers	One chamber
Legislative power	Derived from the people	Derived from the states
Executive	Unspecified size	More than one person
Decision rule	Majority	Extraordinary majority
State laws	Legislature can override	National law is supreme
Executive removal	By Congress	By a majority of the states
Courts	National judiciary	No provision for national judiciary
Ratification	By the people	By the states

The Great Compromise

The Virginia Plan provided for a two-chamber legislature, with representation in both chambers based on population. The idea of two chambers was never seriously challenged, but the idea of representation according to population stirred up heated and prolonged debate. The small states demanded equal representation for all states, but another vote rejected that concept for the House of Representatives. The debate continued. Finally, the Connecticut delegation moved that each state have an equal vote in the Senate. Still another poll showed that the delegations were equally divided on this proposal.

A committee was created to resolve the deadlock. It consisted of one delegate from each state, chosen by secret ballot. After working straight through the Independence Day recess, the committee reported reaching the Great Compromise (sometimes called the Connecticut Compromise). Representation in the House of Representatives would be apportioned according to the population of each state. Initially, there would be fifty-six members. Revenue-raising acts would originate in the House. Most important, the states would be represented equally in the Senate, with two senators each. Senators would be selected by their state legislatures, not directly by the people. The deadlock broke when the Massachusetts delegation divided evenly, allowing the equal state vote to pass by the narrowest of margins, five states to four.[32] The small states got their equal representation, the big states their proportional representation. The small states might dominate the Senate and the big states might control the House, but because all legislation had to be approved by both chambers, neither group would be able to dominate the other. To be perpetually assured of state equality, no amendment to the Constitution could violate the equal state representation principle.[33] If the meaning of democracy rests on the "one person, one vote" principle, then the state equality rule must be among the most undemocratic features of the U.S. Constitution.

Great Compromise
Submitted by the Connecticut delegation to the Constitutional Convention, and thus also known as the Connecticut Compromise, a plan calling for a bicameral legislature in which the House of Representatives would be apportioned according to population and the states would be represented equally in the Senate.

Compromise on the Presidency

Conflict replaced compromise when the delegates turned to the executive branch. They did agree on a one-person executive, a president, but they disagreed on how the executive would be selected and what the term of office would be. The delegates distrusted the people's judgment; some feared that popular election of the president would arouse public passions. Consequently, the delegates rejected the idea. At the same time, representatives of the small states feared that election by the legislature would allow the big states to control the executive.

Once again, a committee composed of one member from each participating state was chosen to find a compromise. That committee fashioned the cumbersome presidential election system we still use today, the electoral college. (The Constitution does not use the expression *electoral college*.) Under this system, a group of electors would be chosen for the sole purpose of selecting the president and vice president. Each state legislature would choose a number of electors equal to the number of its representatives in Congress. Each elector would then vote for two people. The candidate with the most votes would become president, provided that the number of votes constituted a majority; the person with the next-greatest number of votes would become vice president. (The procedure was changed in 1804 by the Twelfth Amendment, which mandates separate votes for each office.) If no candidate won a majority, the House of Representatives would choose a president, with each state casting one vote.

The electoral college compromise eliminated the fear of a popular vote for president. At the same time, it satisfied the small states. If the electoral college failed to elect a president, which the delegates expected would happen, election by the House would give every state the same voice in the selection process. Finally, the delegates agreed that the president's term of office should be four years and that presidents should be

electoral college
A body of electors chosen by voters to cast ballots for president and vice president.

eligible for reelection with no limit on the number of terms any individual president could serve. (The Twenty-Second Amendment, ratified in 1951, now limits the presidency to two terms.)

The delegates also realized that removing a president from office would be a serious political matter. For that reason, they involved both of the other two branches of government in the process. The House alone was empowered to charge a president with "Treason, Bribery, or other high Crimes and Misdemeanors" (Article II, Section 4), by a majority vote. The Senate was given the sole power to try the president on the House's charges. It could convict, and thus remove, a president only by a two-thirds vote (an **extraordinary majority**, a majority greater than the minimum of 50 percent plus one). And the chief justice of the Supreme Court was required to preside over the Senate trial. Only two presidents have been impeached by the House: Andrew Johnson in 1868 and Bill Clinton in 1998; neither was convicted.

extraordinary majority
A majority greater than the minimum of 50 percent plus one.

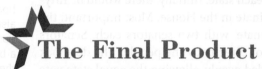

The Final Product

LO4 Explain the contribution of the Constitution to the American political tradition and the principles it establishes.

Once the delegates had resolved their major disagreements, they dispatched the remaining issues relatively quickly. A committee was then appointed to organize and write up the results of the proceedings. Twenty-three resolutions had been debated and approved by the convention; these were reorganized under seven articles in the draft constitution. The preamble, which was the last section to be drafted, begins with a phrase that would have been impossible to write when the convention opened. This single sentence contains four elements that form the foundation of the American political tradition:[34]

- *It creates a people*: "We the people of the United States" was a dramatic departure from a loose confederation of states.
- *It explains the reason for the Constitution*: "in order to form a more perfect Union" was an indirect way of saying that the first effort, the Articles of Confederation, had been inadequate.
- *It articulates goals*: "[to] establish Justice, insure domestic Tranquility, provide for the common defence, promote the general Welfare, and secure the Blessings of Liberty to ourselves and our Posterity"—in other words, the government exists to promote order and freedom.
- *It fashions a government*: "do ordain and establish this Constitution for the United States of America."

The Basic Principles

In creating the Constitution, the founders relied on four political principles—republicanism, federalism, separation of powers, and checks and balances—that together established a revolutionary new political order.

Republicanism is a form of government in which power resides in the people and is exercised by their elected representatives. The idea of republicanism may be traced to the Greek philosopher Aristotle (384–322 B.C.), who advocated a constitution that combined principles of both democratic and oligarchic government. The framers were determined to avoid aristocracy (rule by a hereditary class), monarchy (rule by one person), and direct democracy (rule by the people). A republic was both new and daring: no people had ever been governed by a republic on so vast a scale.

republicanism
A form of government in which power resides in the people and is exercised by their elected representatives.

The framers themselves were far from sure that their government could be sustained. They had no model of republican government to follow; moreover, republican government was thought to be suitable only for small territories, where the interests of the public would be obvious and the government would be within the reach of every citizen. After the convention ended, Benjamin Franklin was asked what sort of government the new nation would have. "A republic," the old man replied, "if you can keep it."

Federalism is the division of power between a central government and regional governments. Citizens are thus subject to two different bodies of law. Federalism can be seen as standing between two competing government schemes. On the one side is unitary government, in which all power is vested in a central authority. On the other side stands confederation, a loose union of powerful states where the states surrender some power to a central government but retain the rest. The Articles of Confederation, as we have seen, divided power between loosely knit states and a weak central government. The Constitution also divides power between the states and a central government, but it confers substantial powers on a national government at the expense of the states.

According to the Constitution, the powers vested in the national and state governments are derived from the people, who remain the ultimate sovereigns. National and state governments can exercise their power over people and property within their spheres of authority. But at the same time, by participating in the electoral process or by amending their governing charters, the people can restrain both the national and the state governments if necessary to preserve liberty.

The Constitution lists the powers of the national government and the powers denied to the states. All other powers remain with the states. Generally, the states are required to give up only the powers necessary to create an effective national government; the national government is limited in turn to the powers specified in the Constitution. Despite the specific lists, the Constitution does not clearly describe the spheres of authority within which the powers can be exercised. As we will discuss in Chapter 4, limits on the exercise of power by the national government and the states have evolved as a result of political and military conflicts; moreover, the limits have proved changeable.

Separation of powers and checks and balances are two distinct principles, but both are necessary to ensure that one branch does not dominate the government. **Separation of powers** is the assignment of the lawmaking, law-enforcing, and law-interpreting functions of government to independent legislative, executive, and judicial branches, respectively. Separation of powers safeguards liberty by ensuring that all government power does not fall into the hands of a single person or group of people. However, the Constitution constrained majority rule by limiting the people's direct influence on the electoral process (see Figure 3.1). In theory, separation of powers means that one branch cannot exercise the powers of the other branches. In practice, however, the separation is far from complete. One scholar has suggested that what we have instead is "separate institutions sharing powers."[35]

Checks and balances is a means of giving each branch of government some scrutiny of and control over the other branches. The aim is to prevent the exclusive exercise of certain powers by any one of the three branches. For example, only Congress can enact laws. But the president (through the veto power) can cancel them, and the courts (by finding that a law violates the Constitution) can strike them down. The process goes on as Congress and the president sometimes begin the legislative process anew, attempting to reformulate laws to address the flaws identified by the Supreme Court in its decisions. In a "check on a check," Congress can override a president's veto by an extraordinary (two-thirds) majority in each chamber. Congress is also empowered to propose amendments to the Constitution, counteracting the courts' power to invalidate. Figure 3.2 depicts the relationship between separation of powers and checks and balances.

federalism
The division of power between a central government and regional governments.

separation of powers
The assignment of lawmaking, law-enforcing, and law-interpreting functions to separate branches of government.

checks and balances
A government structure that gives each branch some scrutiny of and control over the other branches.

FIGURE 3.1   The Constitution and the Electoral Process

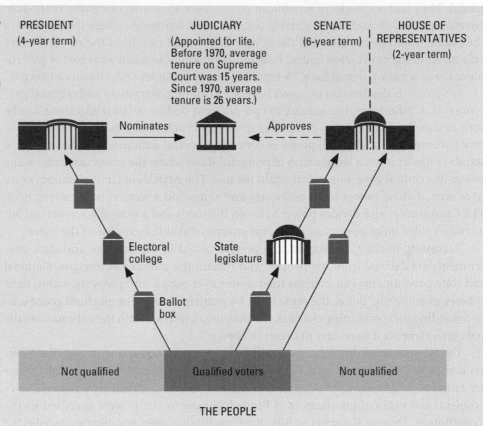

The framers were afraid of majority rule, and that fear is reflected in the electoral process for national office described in the Constitution. The people, speaking through the voters—mostly white men who owned property—participated directly only in the choice of their representatives in the House. The president and senators were elected indirectly, through the electoral college and state legislatures. (Direct election of senators did not become law until 1913, when the Seventeenth Amendment was ratified.) Judicial appointments are, and always have been, far removed from representative links to the people. Judges are nominated by the president and approved by the Senate.

PRESIDENT
(4-year term)

JUDICIARY
(Appointed for life. Before 1970, average tenure on Supreme Court was 15 years. Since 1970, average tenure is 26 years.)

SENATE
(6-year term)

HOUSE OF REPRESENTATIVES
(2-year term)

Nominates   Approves

Electoral college

State legislature

Ballot box

Not qualified   Qualified voters   Not qualified

THE PEOPLE

enumerated powers
The powers explicitly granted to Congress by the Constitution.

necessary and proper clause
The last clause in Section 8 of Article I of the Constitution, which gives Congress the means to execute its enumerated powers. This clause is the basis for Congress's implied powers. Also called the *elastic clause*.

implied powers
Those powers that Congress needs to execute its enumerated powers.

The Articles of the Constitution

In addition to the preamble, the Constitution contains seven articles. The first three establish the separate branches of government and specify their internal operations and powers. The remaining four define the relationships among the states, explain the process of amendment, declare the supremacy of national law, and explain the procedure for ratifying the Constitution.

Article I: The Legislative Article. In structuring their new government, the framers began with the legislative branch because they considered lawmaking the most important function of a republican government. Article I is the most detailed, and therefore the longest, of the articles. It grants substantial but limited legislative power to Congress (Article I begins: "All legislative Power herein granted...."). It defines the bicameral (two-chamber) character of Congress and describes the internal operating procedures of the House of Representatives and the Senate. Section 8 of Article I articulates the principle of **enumerated powers**, which means that Congress can exercise only the powers that the Constitution assigns to it. Eighteen powers are enumerated; the first seventeen are specific powers. For example, the third clause of Section 8 gives Congress the power to regulate interstate commerce. (One of the chief shortcomings of the Articles of Confederation was the lack of a means to cope with trade wars between the states. The solution was to vest control of interstate commerce in the national government.)

The last clause in Section 8, known as the **necessary and proper clause** (or the elastic clause), gives Congress the means to execute the enumerated powers (see the Appendix). This clause is the basis of Congress's **implied powers**—those powers that Congress needs to execute its enumerated powers. For example, the power to levy and

FIGURE 3.2 Separation of Powers and Checks and Balances

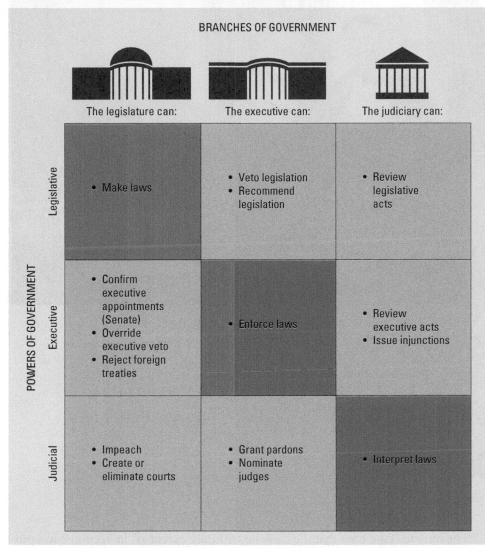

BRANCHES OF GOVERNMENT

The legislature can:

The executive can:

The judiciary can:

POWERS OF GOVERNMENT

Legislative
- Make laws
- Veto legislation
- Recommend legislation
- Review legislative acts

Executive
- Confirm executive appointments (Senate)
- Override executive veto
- Reject foreign treaties
- Enforce laws
- Review executive acts
- Issue injunctions

Judicial
- Impeach
- Create or eliminate courts
- Grant pardons
- Nominate judges
- Interpret laws

Separation of powers is the assignment of lawmaking, law-enforcing, and law-interpreting functions to the legislative, executive, and judicial branches, respectively. The phenomenon is illustrated by the diagonal from upper left to lower right in the figure. Checks and balances give each branch some power over the other branches. For example, the executive branch possesses some legislative power, and the legislative branch possesses some executive power. These checks and balances are listed outside the diagonal.

collect taxes (clause 1) and the power to coin money and regulate its value (clause 5), when joined with the necessary and proper clause (clause 18), imply that Congress has the power to charter a bank. Otherwise, the national government would have no means of managing the money it collects through its power to tax. Implied powers clearly expand the enumerated powers conferred on Congress by the Constitution.

Article II: The Executive Article. Article II grants executive power to a president. The article establishes the president's term of office, the procedure for electing the president by means of electors, the qualifications for becoming president, and the president's duties and powers. The last include acting as commander in chief of the military; making treaties (which must be ratified by a two-thirds vote in the Senate); and appointing government officers, diplomats, and judges (again, with the advice and consent of the Senate).

The president also has legislative powers—part of the constitutional system of checks and balances. For example, the Constitution requires that the president periodically inform Congress of "the State of the Union" and of the policies and programs that the executive branch intends to advocate in the coming year. Today, this is done annually in the president's State of the Union address. Under special circumstances, the president can also convene or adjourn Congress.

IMAGE 3.7   How Many Pens Does It Take to Sign a Bill into Law?

Answer: It depends on the number of people a president wants to thank. The president gives his approval to legislation by signing it into law. Beginning in the 1960s, the bill-signing ceremony became an art form, garnering much press attention. The president would typically employ many pens in small strokes for his signature and then distribute the pens as souvenirs to the people instrumental in the bill's passage. Here, President Barack Obama prepares to use the first of several pens to sign the Child Care Act of 2014 on November 19, 2014. Several congressional sponsors surround him hoping for some of the treasured swag.

The duty to "take Care that the Laws be faithfully executed" in Section 3 has provided presidents with a reservoir of power. President Richard Nixon tried to use this power when he refused to turn over the Watergate tapes despite a judicial subpoena in a criminal trial. He claimed broad executive privilege, an extension of the executive power implied in Article II. But the Supreme Court rejected his claim, arguing that it violated the separation of powers, because the decision to release or withhold information in a criminal trial is a judicial, not an executive, function.

Article III: The Judicial Article. The third article was left purposely vague. The Constitution established the Supreme Court as the highest court in the land. But beyond that, the framers were unable to agree on the need for a national judiciary or on its size, its composition, or the procedures it should follow. They left these issues to Congress, which resolved them by creating a system of federal (that is, national) courts, separate from the state courts.[36]

Unless they are impeached, federal judges serve for life. They are appointed to indefinite terms "during good Behaviour," and their salaries cannot be reduced while they hold office. These stipulations reinforce the separation of powers; they see to it that judges are independent of the other branches and that they do not have to fear retribution for their exercise of judicial power.

Congress exercises a potential check on the judicial branch through its power to create (and eliminate) lower federal courts. Congress can also restrict the power of the federal courts to decide cases. And, as we have noted, the president appoints, with the advice and consent of the Senate, the justices of the Supreme Court and the judges of the lower federal courts. Since the 1980s, especially, the judicial appointment process has become highly politicized, with both Democrats and Republicans accusing each other of obstructionism. Taking obstructionism to new levels in 2016, Senate Republicans vowed neither to hold hearings nor vote on President Obama's nominee Merrick Garland to fill the vacancy created by the death of Supreme Court Justice Antonin Scalia. "Let the people decide [in the 2016 presidential elections]," exhorted Senate Republicans. "Do your job!" shouted Democrats at all levels.

Article III does not explicitly give the courts the power of judicial review, that is, the authority to invalidate congressional or presidential actions because they violate the Constitution. That power has been inferred from the logic, structure, and theory of the Constitution and from important court rulings, some of which we discuss in subsequent chapters.

judicial review
The power to declare congressional (and presidential) acts invalid because they violate the Constitution.

The Remaining Articles. The remaining four articles of the Constitution cover a lot of ground. Article IV requires that the judicial acts and criminal warrants of each state be honored in all other states, and it forbids discrimination against citizens of one state by another state. This provision promotes equality; it keeps the states from treating outsiders differently from their own citizens. For example, suppose Smith and Jones both reside in Illinois, and an Illinois court awards Smith a judgment of $100,000 against Jones. Jones moves to Alaska, hoping to avoid payment. Rather than force Smith to bring a new lawsuit against Jones in Alaska, the Alaska courts give full faith and credit to the Illinois judgment, enforcing it as their own. The origin of Article IV can be traced to the Articles of Confederation.

Article IV also allows the addition of new states and stipulates that the national government will protect the states against foreign invasion and domestic violence.

Article V specifies the methods for amending (changing) the Constitution and guarantees equal state representation in the Senate. We will have more to say about this amendment process shortly.

An important component of Article VI is the supremacy clause, which asserts that when the Constitution, national laws, and treaties conflict with state or local laws, the first three take precedence over the last two. The stipulation is vital to the operation of federalism (and it remains a source of contention within the EU). In keeping with the supremacy clause, Article VI requires that all national and state officials, elected or appointed, take an oath to support the Constitution. The article also mandates that religious affiliation or belief cannot be a prerequisite for holding government office.

supremacy clause
The clause in Article VI of the Constitution that asserts that national laws take precedence over state and local laws when they conflict.

Finally, Article VII describes the ratification process, stipulating that approval by conventions in nine states would be necessary for the Constitution to take effect.

The Framers' Motives

Some argue that the Constitution is essentially a conservative document written by wealthy men to advance their own interests. One distinguished historian who wrote in the early 1900s, Charles A. Beard, maintained that the delegates had much to gain from a strong national government.[37] Many held government securities dating from the Revolutionary War that had become practically worthless under the Articles of Confederation. A strong national government would protect their property and pay off the nation's debts.

Beard's argument, that the Constitution was crafted to protect the economic interests of this small group of creditors, spurred a generation of historians to examine the existing financial records of the convention delegates. Their scholarship has largely discredited his once-popular view.[38] For example, it turns out that seven of the delegates who left the convention or refused to sign the Constitution held public securities worth more than twice the total of the holdings of the thirty-nine delegates who did sign. Moreover, the most influential delegates owned no securities. And only a few delegates appear to have directly benefited economically from the new government.[39] Still, there is little doubt about the general homogeneity of the delegates or about their concern for producing a stable economic order that would preserve and promote the interests of some more than others.

What did motivate the framers? Surely economic considerations were important, but they were not the major issues. The single most important factor leading to the Constitutional Convention was the inability of the national or state governments to maintain order under the loose structure of the Articles of Confederation. Certainly, order involved the protection of property, but the framers had a broader view of property than their portfolios of government securities. They wanted to protect their homes, their families, and their means of livelihood from impending anarchy.

Although they disagreed bitterly on the structure and mechanics of the national government, the framers agreed on the most vital issues. For example, three of the most crucial features of the Constitution—the power to tax, the necessary and proper clause, and the supremacy clause—were approved unanimously without debate; experience had taught the delegates that a strong national government was essential if the United States were to survive. The motivation to create order was so strong, in fact, that the framers were willing to draft clauses that protected the most undemocratic of all institutions: slavery.

The Slavery Issue

The institution of slavery was well ingrained in American life at the time of the Constitutional Convention, and slavery helped shape the Constitution, although it is mentioned nowhere by name in it. (According to the first national census in 1790, nearly 18 percent of the population—697,000 people—lived in slavery.) It is doubtful, in fact, that there would have been a Constitution if the delegates had had to resolve the slavery issue, for the southern states would have opposed a constitution that prohibited slavery. Opponents of slavery were in the minority, and they were willing to tolerate its continuation in the interest of forging a union, perhaps believing that the issue could be resolved another day.

The question of representation in the House of Representatives brought the slavery issue close to the surface of the debate at the Constitutional Convention, and it led to the Great Compromise. Representation in the House was to be based on population. But who counted in the population? States with large slave populations wanted all their inhabitants, slave and free, counted equally; states with few slaves wanted only the free population counted. The delegates agreed unanimously that in apportioning representation in the House and in assessing direct taxes, the population of each state was to be determined by adding "the whole Number of free Persons" and "three fifths of all other Persons" (Article I, Section 2). The phrase "all other Persons" is, of course, a substitute for "slaves."

The three-fifths formula had been used by the 1783 congress under the Articles of Confederation to allocate government costs among the states. The rule reflected the view that slaves were less efficient producers of wealth than free people, not that slaves were three-fifths human and two-fifths personal property.[40]

The three-fifths clause gave states with large slave populations (the South) greater representation in Congress than states with small slave populations (the North). If all slaves had been included in the count, the slave states would have had 50 percent of the seats in the House, an outcome that would have been unacceptable to the North. Had none of the slaves been counted, the slave states would have had 41 percent of House seats, which would have been unacceptable to the South. The three-fifths compromise left the South with 47 percent of the House seats, a sizable minority, but in all likelihood a losing one on slavery issues.[41] The overrepresentation resulting

FIGURE 3.3   Amending the Constitution

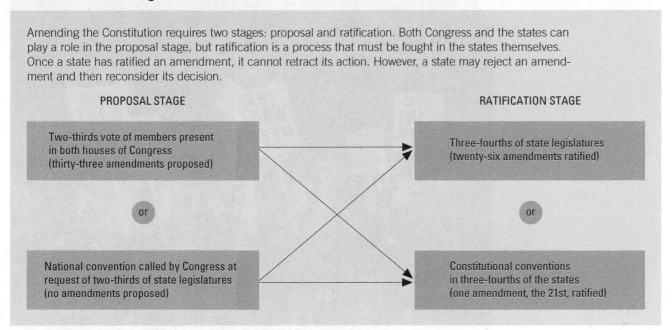

Amending the Constitution requires two stages: proposal and ratification. Both Congress and the states can play a role in the proposal stage, but ratification is a process that must be fought in the states themselves. Once a state has ratified an amendment, it cannot retract its action. However, a state may reject an amendment and then reconsider its decision.

PROPOSAL STAGE   RATIFICATION STAGE

Two-thirds vote of members present in both houses of Congress (thirty-three amendments proposed)

or

National convention called by Congress at request of two-thirds of state legislatures (no amendments proposed)

Three-fourths of state legislatures (twenty-six amendments ratified)

or

Constitutional conventions in three-fourths of the states (one amendment, the 21st, ratified)

by a two-thirds vote in both the House of Representatives and the Senate or by a national convention, summoned by Congress at the request of two-thirds of the state legislatures. All constitutional amendments to date have been proposed by the first method; the second has never been used.

A proposed amendment can be ratified by a vote of the legislatures of three-fourths of the states or by a vote of constitutional conventions held in three-fourths of the states. Congress chooses the method of ratification. It has used the state convention method only once, for the Twenty-first Amendment, which repealed the Eighteenth Amendment (prohibition of intoxicating liquors). Congress may, in proposing an amendment, set a time limit for its ratification. Beginning with the Eighteenth Amendment, but skipping the Nineteenth, Congress has set seven years as the limit for ratification.

Note that the amendment process requires the exercise of extraordinary majorities (two-thirds and three-fourths). The framers purposely made it difficult to propose and ratify amendments (although nowhere near as difficult as under the Articles of Confederation). They wanted only the most significant issues to lead to constitutional change. Note, too, that the president plays no formal role in the process. Presidential approval is not required to amend the Constitution, although the president's political influence affects the success or failure of any amendment effort.

Calling a national convention to propose an amendment has never been tried, and the method raises several thorny questions. For example, the Constitution does not specify the number of delegates who should attend, the method by which they should be chosen, or the rules for debating and voting on a proposed amendment. Confusion surrounding the convention process has precluded its use, leaving the amendment process in congressional hands.[47] The major issue is the limits, if any, on the business of the convention. Remember that the convention in Philadelphia in 1787, charged with revising the Articles of Confederation, drafted an entirely new charter. Would a national convention called to consider a particular amendment be within its bounds to rewrite the Constitution? No one really knows.

AP Images

IMAGE 3.8   "We Want Beer": A Common Refrain

"We want beer" may be a popular refrain at tailgating parties and on certain college campuses today, but it was the basis of political protest in October 1932 when more than 20,000 protesters, many of them women, demanded repeal of the Eighteenth Amendment. The amendment, which was ratified in 1919, banned the manufacture, sale, and transportation of alcoholic beverages. The amendment was spurred by moral and social reform groups, such as the Women's Christian Temperance Union, founded by Evanston, Illinois, resident Frances Willard in 1874. The amendment proved to be an utter failure. People continued to drink, but their alcohol came from illegal sources.

Most of the Constitution's twenty-seven amendments were adopted to reflect changes in political thinking. The first ten amendments (the Bill of Rights) were the price of ratification, but they have been fundamental to our system of government. The last seventeen amendments fall into three main categories: they make public policy, they correct deficiencies in the government's structure, or they promote equality. One attempt to make public policy through a constitutional amendment was disastrous. The Eighteenth Amendment (1919) prohibited the manufacture or sale of intoxicating beverages, extinguishing the fifth largest industry in the nation. This amendment and the Thirteenth, barring the ownership of slaves, were the only provisions to limit the activities of citizens.[48] Prohibition lasted fourteen years and was an utter failure. Gangsters began bootlegging liquor, people died from drinking homemade spirits, and millions regularly broke the law by drinking anyway. Congress had to propose another amendment in 1933 to repeal the Eighteenth. The states ratified this amendment, the Twenty-first, in less than ten months—less time than it took to ratify the Fourteenth Amendment, guaranteeing citizenship, due process, and equal protection of the laws.

Since 1787, about 10,000 constitutional amendments have been introduced; only a fraction has survived the proposal stage. Once Congress has approved an amendment, its chances for ratification are high. The Twenty-seventh Amendment, which prevents members of Congress from voting themselves immediate pay increases, was ratified in 1992. It had been submitted to the states in 1789 without a time limit for ratification, but it languished in a political netherworld until 1982, when a University of Texas student, Gregory D. Watson, stumbled upon the proposed amendment while researching a paper. At that time, only eight states had ratified the amendment. Watson earned a C for the paper; his professor remained unconvinced that the amendment was still pending.[49] (In hindsight, he deserved an A.) Watson took up the cause, prompting renewed interest in the amendment. In May 1992, ratification by the Michigan legislature provided the decisive vote, 203 years after congressional approval of the proposed amendment.[50] Only six amendments submitted to the states have failed to be ratified.

Interpretation by the Courts

In the famous case of *Marbury* v. *Madison* (1803), the Supreme Court declared that the courts have the power to nullify government acts that conflict with the Constitution. This is the power of judicial review. (We will elaborate on judicial review in Chapter 14.) The exercise of judicial review forces the courts to interpret the Constitution. In a way, this makes a lot of sense. The judiciary is the law-interpreting branch of the government; as the supreme law of the land, the Constitution is fair game for judicial interpretation. It is problematic, in theory at least, that the Constitution does not expressly authorize courts to exercise this power. Judicial review is the courts' main check on the other branches of government. But in interpreting the Constitution, the courts cannot help but give new meaning to its provisions. This is why judicial interpretation is a principal form of constitutional change.

What guidelines should judges use in interpreting the Constitution? For one thing, they must realize that the usage and meaning of many words have changed during the past two hundred years. Judges must be careful to think about what the words meant at the time the Constitution was written. Some insist that they must also consider the original intent of the framers—not an easy task. Of course, there are records of the Constitutional Convention and of the debates surrounding ratification. But there are also many questions about the completeness and accuracy of those records, even Madison's detailed notes. And at times, the framers were deliberately vague in writing the document. This may reflect lack of agreement on, or universal understanding of, certain provisions in the Constitution. Some scholars and judges maintain that the search for original meaning is hopeless and that contemporary notions of constitutional provisions must hold sway. Originalists, like Supreme Court Justice Antonin Scalia, claim objectivity in a "dead" constitution and argue that any other approach comes perilously close to amending the Constitution as judges see fit, effectively transforming law interpreters into lawmakers.[51] Still other scholars and judges maintain that judges face the unavoidable challenge of balancing 200-year-old constitutional principles against the demands of modern society. As Judge Richard A. Posner, the most distinguished jurist of our age observed:

> It's difficult enough to figure out what the framers and ratifiers of the Constitution really thought about the problems *they faced*. It is impossible to project their thinking into the twenty-first century and make their words speak to issues they couldn't possibly have had in mind.[52]

Political Practice

The Constitution is silent on many issues. It says nothing about political parties or the president's cabinet, for example, yet both have exercised considerable influence in

American politics. Some constitutional provisions have fallen out of use. The electors in the electoral college, for example, were supposed to exercise their own judgment in voting for the president and vice president. Today, the electors function simply as a rubber stamp, validating the outcome of election contests in their states.

Meanwhile, political practice has altered the distribution of power without changes in the Constitution. The framers intended Congress to be the strongest branch of government. But the president has come to overshadow Congress. Presidents such as Abraham Lincoln and Franklin Roosevelt used their formal and informal powers imaginatively to respond to national crises. And their actions paved the way for future presidents to enlarge further the powers of the office.

The framers could scarcely have imagined an urbanized nation of 323 million people stretching across a landmass some 3,000 miles wide, reaching halfway over the Pacific Ocean, and stretching past the Arctic Circle. Nor could these exceptionally gifted individuals have envisioned an airplane, a man on the moon, a mobile rover on Mars, or a mobile telephone. Never in their wildest nightmares could they have foreseen the destructiveness of nuclear weaponry or envisioned its effect on the power to declare war. The Constitution empowers Congress to consider and debate this momentous step. But with nuclear annihilation perhaps only minutes away and terrorist threats a real if unpredictable prospect since September 11, 2001, the legislative power to declare war is likely to give way to the president's power to wage war as the nation's commander in chief. Strict adherence to the Constitution in such circumstances could destroy the nation's ability to protect itself.

An Evaluation of the Constitution

LO7 Evaluate the extent to which the Constitution reflects and embodies the principles of majoritarian or pluralist democracy.

The U.S. Constitution is one of the world's most praised political documents. It is the oldest written national constitution and one of the most widely copied, sometimes word for word. It is also one of the shortest, consisting of about 4,300 words (not counting the amendments, which add 3,100 words). The brevity of the Constitution may be one of its greatest strengths. As we noted earlier, the framers simply laid out a structural framework for government; they did not describe relationships and powers in detail. For example, the Constitution gives Congress the power to regulate "Commerce... among the several States" but does not define interstate commerce. Such general wording allows interpretation in keeping with contemporary political, social, and technological developments. Air travel, for instance, unknown in 1787, now falls easily within Congress's power to regulate interstate commerce.

The generality of the U.S. Constitution stands in stark contrast to the specificity of most state constitutions and the constitutions of many emerging democracies. The California constitution, for example, provides that "fruit and nut-bearing trees under the age of four years from the time of planting in orchard form and grapevines under the age of three years from the time of planting in vineyard form... shall be exempt from taxation" (Article XIII, Section 12). Because they are so specific, most state constitutions are much longer than the U.S. Constitution. The longest by far is the Alabama constitution, which is more than 300,000 words. That's longer than *Moby-Dick* or the Bible.

For a long period, newly emerging nations viewed the U.S. Constitution and the ideals it embodied as a model worth emulating. But recent evidence reveals that the

Chapter Quiz

LO1 Explain the reasons for the colonies' declaration of independence from British rule.

1. Why did the colonies begin to protest against the British government, and what forms did this protest take?
2. What principles underpin the Declaration of Independence?

LO2 Identify the factors that led to the failure of the Confederation.

1. Why did the delegates to the Second Continental Congress seek to retain power in the states versus creating a strong central government?
2. Provide four reasons that help explain why the Articles of Confederation failed.

LO3 Explain the major points of contention in the writing of the Constitution.

1. What were the primary differences between the Virginia and New Jersey Plans?
2. What major compromises did the drafting of the Constitution entail?

LO4 Explain the contribution of the Constitution to the American political tradition and the principles it establishes.

1. Which powers are provided to Congress through the necessary and proper clause, and why are these important?
2. How did the Constitution originally address the institution of slavery?

LO5 Describe the actions taken to ensure the ratification of the Constitution.

1. Who were the Federalists and Antifederalists, and what were their main points of disagreement?
2. What is the Bill of Rights, and whose rights is it guaranteed to protect?

LO6 Explain the procedures required to amend the Constitution.

1. What are the two methods through which constitutional changes can be proposed, and what are the two methods for ratifying those changes?
2. What are the guidelines used by judges for interpreting the Constitution?

LO7 Evaluate the extent to which the Constitution reflects and embodies the principles of majoritarian or pluralist democracy.

1. What values does the Constitution secure? What values were not priorities at the time the Constitution was drafted?
2. Does the government created by the Constitution reflect the pluralist or majoritarian model of democracy?

4 Federalism

"QUIET: Exam in Progress." If you ever have attended an American public school you've probably seen such warnings posted on classroom doors during the administration of annual state testing. Who do you think should decide the topics that appear on these tests or how the questions are chosen? Your teachers and members of your local school board? State legislators? Leaders in the national government?

Since the 1990s, debates about standards and student testing have intensified in the United States. Examples prompting much discussion include the federal No Child Left Behind Act of 2001 (NCLB), collaborations among state leaders to develop the Common Core State Standards and their accompanying tests, and local efforts, too, that have created teacher and principal evaluation systems that include student test scores.

The education policy landscape shifted again in 2015 when President Obama signed a long-overdue revision of NCLB. The president hailed the new law, known as the Every Student Succeeds Act (ESSA), as "a big step in the right direction."[1] The chair of the National Governors Association, Republican governor Gary Herbert of Utah agreed, calling ESSA "a clear example of cooperative federalism" because it means "states and localities have the freedom to provide students the world-class education they deserve."[2]

Still, others wondered if ESSA struck the proper balance between national, state, and local power. One leading advocate, Kati Haycock of The Education Trust, generally supported ESSA but favored a more assertive national role. "Given the long history of state and local decisions that shortchange vulnerable students, this degree of flexibility is cause for serious trepidation," she said.[3] Others thought the law went too far in extending national authority. The conservative Heritage Foundation urged members of Congress to oppose ESSA because it was a "new federal encroachment on parents' and local communities' abilities to determine how their children are educated."[4]

How to sort out the responsibilities for K–12 schooling? This is not an easy question. The U.S. Constitution never mentions education, but it does declare that the national government was created, among other things, to "promote the general Welfare," which arguably could include helping to educate the population. In contrast, the constitutions of the nation's fifty states address education in detail. Advocates for the states also argue that education is the very sort of topic "reserved to the states" via the Tenth Amendment of the Bill of Rights.

Debates about ESSA reflect different views over **sovereignty**, or the quality of being supreme in power or authority, of national and state governments. In this chapter, we consider American federalism—and its implications for sovereignty—in theory and practice. Is the balance of power between the nation and the states a matter of constitutional principle or practical politics? How does this balance relate to the conflicts between freedom and order and between freedom and equality? How does federalism influence American foreign relations and domestic politics in other countries? Does federalism reflect the pluralist or the majoritarian model of democracy?

#ChallengeAccepted

Take the Challenge on MindTap for American Government

How could the language in the U.S. Constitution be used both to argue for and to argue against a strong national role in K–12 education policy?

Roger Bamber/Alamy

Learning Outcomes

LO1 Compare and contrast two key theories of federalism used to describe the American system of government.

LO2 Identify and explain each of the four forces that stimulate changes in the relationship between the national and state governments.

LO3 Describe the role of ideology in shaping federalism.

LO4 Describe the influence of federalism on elections at the state and national levels.

LO5 Describe the role of local government in a federal system and illustrate how national, state, and local governments sometimes interact.

LO6 Analyze the international dimensions of federalism in the United States and other nations around the world.

LO7 Discuss the changing relationship between federalism, pluralism, and majoritarianism.

The bakery metaphor used to describe this type is *marble-cake federalism*, as Figure 4.1 also illustrates.* The national and state governments do not act in separate spheres; they are intermingled in vertical and diagonal strands and swirls. In short, their functions are mixed in the American federal system. Critical to this theory is an expansive view of the Constitution's supremacy clause (Article VI), which specifically subordinates state law to national law and charges every government official with disregarding state laws that are inconsistent with the Constitution, national laws, or treaties.

Some scholars argue that the layer-cake metaphor has never accurately described the American political structure.[8] In practice, the national and state governments have many common objectives and have often cooperated to achieve them. In the nineteenth century, for example, cooperation, not separation, made it possible to develop transportation systems, such as canals, and to establish state land-grant colleges. Today, the national government and the states share duties for funding and administering numerous programs to protect public health.

A critical difference between the theories of dual and cooperative federalism is the way they interpret two sections of the Constitution that define the relationship between the national and state governments. Article I, Section 8 lists the enumerated powers of Congress and then concludes with the **elastic clause**, which gives Congress the power to "make all Laws which shall be necessary and proper for carrying into Execution the foregoing Powers" (see Chapter 3). The Tenth Amendment reserves for the states or the people powers not assigned to the national government or denied to the states by the Constitution. Dual federalism postulates an inflexible elastic clause and a spacious Tenth Amendment. Cooperative federalism postulates a flexible elastic clause and confines the Tenth Amendment to a self-evident, obvious truth.

Although the Constitution establishes a kind of federalism, the actual and proper balance of power between the nation and states has always been more a matter of debate than of formal theory. Three broad principles help to underscore why. First, rather than operating in a mechanical fashion, American federalism is a flexible and dynamic system. The Constitution's inherent ambiguities about federalism, some of which we have already discussed, generate constraints but also opportunities for politicians, citizens, and interest groups to advance their priorities. Second, because of this flexibility, both elected and appointed officials across levels of government often make policy decisions based on pragmatic considerations without regard to theories of what American federalism should look like. Third, there is a growing recognition among public officials and citizens that public problems (such as questions involving tradeoffs between freedom, order, and equality) cut across governmental boundaries. In sum, politics and policy goals rather than pure theoretical or ideological commitments about federalism tend to dominate decision making.

elastic clause
The last clause in Article I, Section 8, of the Constitution, which gives Congress the means to execute its enumerated powers. This clause is the basis for Congress's implied powers. Also called the necessary and proper clause.

★ Federalism's Dynamics

LO2 Identify and explain each of the four forces that stimulate changes in the relationship between the national and state governments.

In order to grasp how American federalism operates in practice, one must know more than simply the powers that the Constitution assigns the different levels of government. Real understanding stems from recognizing the forces that can prompt changes in relationships between the national government and the states. In this section, we

---

*A marble cake is a rough mixture of yellow and chocolate cake batter resembling marble stone. If you've never seen or eaten a slice of marble cake, imagine mixing a swirl of vanilla and chocolate soft-freeze ice cream.

focus on four specific forces: national crises and demands, judicial interpretations, the expansion of grants-in-aid, and the professionalization of state governments.

National Crises and Demands

The elastic clause of the Constitution gives Congress the power to make all laws that are "necessary and proper" to carry out its responsibilities. By using this power in combination with its enumerated powers, Congress has increased the scope of the national government tremendously during the previous two centuries. The greatest changes have come about in times of crisis and national emergencies, such as the Civil War; the world wars; the aftermath of September 11, 2001; and the economic recession that began in December 2007 and persisted into President Obama's first term. As an example, consider an even more dramatic economic crisis, the Great Depression of the 1930s.

The Great Depression placed dual federalism in repose. The problems of the Great Depression proved too extensive for either state governments or private businesses to handle, so the national government assumed much responsibility for providing relief and pursuing economic recovery. Under the New Deal, President Franklin D. Roosevelt's response to the Great Depression, Congress enacted various emergency programs designed to stimulate economic activity that also required national and state governments to cooperate. For example, the national government offered money to support state relief efforts; however, to receive these funds, states were usually required to provide administrative supervision or contribute some money of their own.[9]

Some call the New Deal era a revolutionary reshaping of American federalism. The national and state governments had cooperated before, but the extent of their interactions during Roosevelt's administration was unprecedented. In addition, the size of the national government and its budget increased tremendously. But perhaps the most significant change was with how Americans thought about their problems and what the national government might do to solve them. Difficulties that people at one time would have considered personal or local were now viewed as national issues requiring national solutions.

In other respects, however, the New Deal was not so revolutionary. For example, Congress did not claim any new powers to address the nation's economic problems. Rather, the national legislature simply used its constitutional powers to suit the circumstances. Arguably those actions were consistent with the overall purpose of the U.S. Constitution, which, as the preamble states, was designed in part to "insure domestic Tranquility . . . [and] promote the general Welfare."

President Obama drew on the logic of the New Deal and the preamble when responding to the economic downturn that afflicted the nation as his first term was beginning. Obama proposed and Congress quickly passed a $787 billion economic stimulus package in February 2009, known as the American Recovery and Reinvestment Act, which included new spending and tax cuts. No Republicans in the House of Representatives and only three Republicans in the Senate voted for the legislation, a clear signal of the charged partisan atmosphere in Washington. The stimulus package offered substantial direct aid to states, which were beleaguered by the recession, in the form of Medicaid payments, extended unemployment benefits, school and infrastructure spending, and other grants. Several Republican governors initially rejected the money, but their bluster receded as furious state legislators in both parties demanded the much needed funds. All governors eventually signed on.[10]

Concerns over terrorist attacks on U.S. soil, a different type of potential crisis, have expanded national power as well. In the month after the events of September 11, 2001, Congress swiftly passed and the president signed into law the USA-PATRIOT Act. Among other provisions, the law expanded significantly the surveillance and investigative powers of the Department of Justice. In a move to further augment domestic

Courtesy of the State Archives of North Carolina

David R. Frazier Photolibrary, Inc./Alamy

IMAGES 4.1A AND 4.1B   Building Roads to Stimulate the Economy: Then and Now

Both Franklin Roosevelt and Barack Obama channeled national funds to states to respond to national economic downturns. Infrastructure spending to improve the nation's roads, shown here during the Great Depression (above) and the Great Recession (below), helped to update the nation's transportation system while putting people back to work.

surveillance activities, President George W. Bush gave approval to wiretaps without warrants of American citizens suspected of terrorist ties. In 2011, President Barack Obama signed a four-year extension of the act's key provisions.[11] These activities continued to blur an already fuzzy line separating the gathering of intelligence to combat the nation's enemies, primarily an activity of the national government, and day-to-day law enforcement, which is an area where state and local police bear large responsibilities.

Judicial Interpretation

How federal courts have interpreted the Constitution and federal law is another factor that has influenced the relationship between the national government and the states. The U.S. Supreme Court, the umpire of the federal system, settles disagreements over the powers that national and state leaders claim by deciding whether the actions of either are unconstitutional (see Chapter 14). As a body, the court's views on federalism have evolved over time, which has had significant impacts on the lives of the nation's people.

Early in the nineteenth century, the nationalist interpretation of federalism prevailed over states' rights. In 1819, under Chief Justice John Marshall (1801–1835), the U.S. Supreme Court expanded the role of the national government in the landmark case of *McCulloch* v. *Maryland*. The Court was asked to decide whether Congress had the power to establish a national bank and, if so, whether states could tax that bank. In a unanimous opinion that Marshall authored, the Court conceded that Congress had only the powers conferred on it by the Constitution, which nowhere mentioned banks. However, Article I granted Congress the authority to enact all laws "necessary and proper" to the execution of Congress's enumerated powers. In other words, Marshall adopted a broad interpretation of the elastic clause. He reasoned that the framers must have meant to give the national government all the powers necessary to carry out its assigned functions, even if those powers were only implied.

The Court clearly agreed that Congress had the power to charter a bank. But did the states (in this case, Maryland) have the power threaten states with the complete loss of federal funding for Medicaid should states refuse to comply with the act's Medicaid expansion.[20] That expansion was a key part of the law, which its proponents assumed all states would accept.[21] As Figure 4.3 shows, however, not all states have agreed, and the Supreme Court's decision allowed them to decline to participate without threatening the Medicaid dollars they previously had been receiving.

Professionalization of State Governments

A final important factor that has produced dynamic changes in the American federal system is that state governments have become more capable policy actors than they were in the past. While political scientists generally agree that the rise of competitive party politics in the South (see Chapter 8), the growth of money in elections (Chapter 9), and the expansion of the interest group system (Chapter 10) have all produced significant changes in American politics, nevertheless many scholars and students rarely consider the expanded capabilities of state governments in the same light.

FIGURE 4.3   Status of State Acceptance of the Affordable Care Act's Medicaid Expansion, February 2016

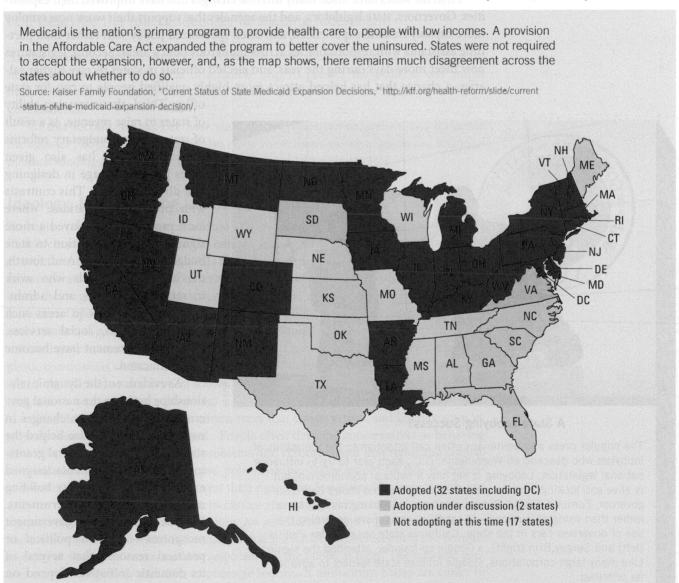

Medicaid is the nation's primary program to provide health care to people with low incomes. A provision in the Affordable Care Act expanded the program to better cover the uninsured. States were not required to accept the expansion, however, and, as the map shows, there remains much disagreement across the states about whether to do so.

Source: Kaiser Family Foundation, "Current Status of State Medicaid Expansion Decisions," http://kff.org/health-reform/slide/current-status-of-the-medicaid-expansion-decision/.

Adopted (32 states including DC)
Adoption under discussion (2 states)
Not adopting at this time (17 states)

Federalism in Global Politics

Serving the Public Across Levels of Government

Each day, nations around the globe attempt to respond to their citizens' needs and meet pressing demands. Educating people, protecting the environment, defending the country; ensuring that roads are paved and that neighborhoods are safe—all of these tasks mobilize into action thousands of government workers on every continent. But although the demands may appear the same, how different nations choose to meet them can vary a lot. As Figure A shows, some nations, such as the United States, Brazil, and Switzerland, rely relatively more on state and local government workers to do the work of government, and relatively less on national government employees. In other countries, including Turkey, Ireland, and New Zealand, the pattern is reversed with national government employees playing a larger role.

FIGURE A   Public Sector Employment in National and Subnational Governments, 2011

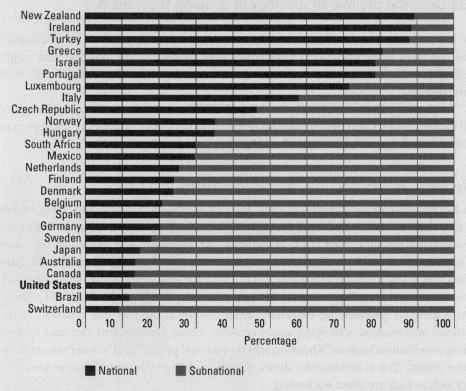

These differences in governmental responsibilities also emerge when one examines which level of government provides the funds for important public services that citizens demand. Figure B shows the percent of government revenues that come from national and subnational (state or local) governments. Here we see additional variation in government responsibilities. In the United States,

In contrast, others often claim that what conservatives hope for, liberals fear. Liberals remember, so the argument goes, that the states' rights model allowed extreme political and social inequalities and that it supported racism. Blacks and city dwellers were often left virtually unrepresented by white state legislators who

Learning Outcomes

LO1 Distinguish the various roles played by public opinion in majoritarian and pluralist democracy.

LO2 Critique polling as a method for measuring public opinion and identify skewed, bimodal, and normal distributions of opinion.

LO3 Explain the influence of the agents of early socialization—family, school, community, and peers—on political learning.

LO4 Compare and contrast the effects of education, income, region, race, ethnicity, religion, and gender on public opinion.

LO5 Define the concept of ideology, describe the liberal-conservative continuum, and assess the influence of ideology on public opinion.

LO6 Assess the impact of knowledge, self-interest, and leadership on political opinions.

public opinion
The collective attitudes of
citizens concerning a given
issue or question.

P ublic opinion is simply the collective attitude of the citizens on a given issue or question. The history of public thinking on issues related to race reveals several characteristics of public opinion:

1. *The public's attitudes toward a given issue or policy can vary over time, often dramatically.* In many areas, opinions about race have moved in the direction of favoring equality over order. Back in 1958, only 4 percent of whites told Gallup that they approve of interracial marriage, compared to 84 percent in 2013.[8]

2. *Public opinion places boundaries on allowable types of policies.* The issue of mass incarceration disproportionately affects racial minorities. It has become a prominent political issue in recent years, with public support for mandatory minimum sentences for drug offenses declining and support for providing treatment for drug users increasing. In the wake of these changes in attitudes, legislation related to sentencing reform advanced in the House and the Senate in 2015.[9]

3. *If asked by pollsters, citizens are willing to register opinions on matters outside their experience.* Although white Americans do not know what it is like to be black, 67 percent of whites report being satisfied with society's treatment of blacks.[10]

4. *Governments tend to respond to public opinion.* This is particularly true regarding civil rights for a nonracial minority group: gays and lesbians. Five years ago, most states prohibited same sex marriage. As the public grew more supportive of gay rights, many policies changed. The federal government eliminated its ban on having openly gay Americans serve in the military in 2011. That same year, the Obama administration said it would no longer defend the Defense of Marriage Act (DOMA), a law that prevented the federal government from recognizing same-sex marriages. In 2015, the Supreme Court ruled that the Constitution guarantees the right to same sex marriage.

5. *The government sometimes does not do what the people want.* Immigration reform is another issue that disproportionately affects racial minorities. A solid majority of Americans, including 80 percent of Democrats and 56 percent of Republicans, favor legislation that would allow immigrants who are in the country illegally to obtain legal status if they meet certain requirements. A majority has felt this way for years. Nonetheless, immigration reform has stalled in Congress for over a decade.[11]

The last two conclusions bear on our understanding of the majoritarian and pluralist models of democracy discussed in Chapter 2. Here, we probe more deeply into the nature, shape, depth, and formation of public opinion in a democratic government. What is the place of public opinion in a democracy? How do people acquire their opinions? What are the major lines of division in public opinion? How do individuals' ideology and knowledge affect their opinions?

Public Opinion and the Models of Democracy

LO1 Distinguish the various roles played by public opinion in majoritarian and pluralist democracy.

Opinion polling, which involves interviewing a sample of citizens to estimate public opinion as a whole, is such a common feature of contemporary life that we often forget it is a modern invention, dating only from the 1930s. In fact, survey methodology did not become a powerful research tool until the advent of computers in the 1950s. Before

Climate Change in Global Politics

Most climate scientists agree that the global climate is changing, that human activity is a major source of such change, and that climate changes will pose very serious problems for people in many ways. Around the world, a majority of people agree that global climate change is a very serious problem. Yet there is also great variation across countries, as the graph below indicates. A recent analysis found that people in countries that are high emitters of CO_2 (an important factor contributing to climate change) are less likely than people elsewhere to express concerns. The United States and China are among the countries with the highest emissions; in both counties, fewer than half of those surveyed agreed that climate change is a very serious problem. Countries in Africa and Latin America tend to produce fewer emissions and have a higher degree of concern.

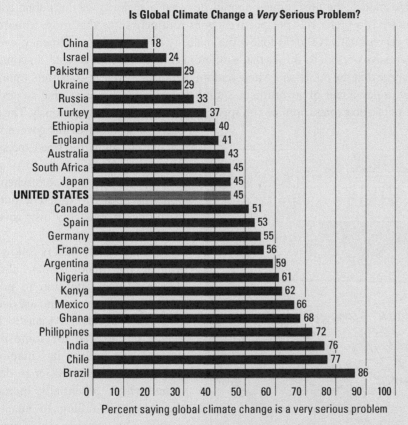

Is Global Climate Change a _Very_ Serious Problem?

Country	Percent
China	18
Israel	24
Pakistan	29
Ukraine	29
Russia	33
Turkey	37
Ethiopia	40
England	41
Australia	43
South Africa	45
Japan	45
UNITED STATES	45
Canada	51
Spain	53
Germany	55
France	56
Argentina	59
Nigeria	61
Kenya	62
Mexico	66
Ghana	68
Philippines	72
India	76
Chile	77
Brazil	86

Percent saying global climate change is a very serious problem

Source: "Global Concern about Climate Change, Broad Support for Limiting Emissions," Pew Research Center, 2015.

CRITICAL THINKING What values might underlie public opinion about global climate change? What factors might influence whether people think that climate change is a serious problem?

polling became a common part of the American scene, politicians, journalists, and everyone else could argue about what the people wanted, but no one really knew. Before the 1930s, observers of America had to guess at national opinion by analyzing newspaper stories, politicians' speeches, voting returns, and travelers' diaries. What if pollsters had been around when the colonists declared their independence from Britain in July 1776? We might have learned (as some historians estimate) that "40 percent of Americans supported the Revolution, 20 percent opposed it, and 40 percent tried to remain neutral."[12]

When no one really knows what the people want, how can the national government be responsive to public opinion? As we discussed in Chapter 3, the founders wanted to build public opinion into our government structure by allowing the direct election of representatives to the House and apportioning representation there according to population. The attitudes and actions of the House of Representatives, the framers thought, would reflect public opinion, especially on the crucial issues of taxes and government spending.

Bills passed by a majority of elected representatives do not necessarily reflect the opinion of a majority of citizens, a fact that would not have bothered the framers because they never intended to create a full democracy, a government completely responsive to majority opinion. Although they wanted to provide for some consideration of public opinion, they had little faith in the ability of the masses to make public policy.

The majoritarian and pluralist models of democracy differ greatly in their assumptions about the role of public opinion in democratic government. According to the classic majoritarian model, the government should do what a majority of the public wants. Americans tend to prefer this perspective—polls routinely show that most Americans think that representatives should follow the majority will of their constituency, even if the representative personally thinks that a different course of action is best.[13] In contrast, pluralists argue that the public as a whole seldom demonstrates clear, consistent opinions on the day-to-day issues of government. Pluralists recognize, however, that subgroups within the public do express opinions on specific matters—often and vigorously. The pluralist model requires that government institutions allow the free expression of opinions by these "minority publics." Democracy is at work when the opinions of many different publics clash openly and fairly over government policy.

Should policymakers follow the will of the majority? Or should they pay most attention to politically engaged groups who are deeply involved in certain issues? This debate has existed for some time, but modern polling has made the will of the majority easier to determine, which potentially increases the stakes of failing to enact its wishes. One expert said, "surveys produce just what democracy is supposed to produce—equal representation of all citizens."[14] Indeed, research shows that public opinion in the polling era has had a strong influence on policy outcomes.[15] At the same time, because government policy sometimes runs against majority opinion, the majoritarian model is considered by some to be an inaccurate description of reality. For example, even though research shows public opinion influences policy outcomes, when opinions of

IMAGE 5.1   How High Will Support for Legalization Go?

Attitudes about marijuana have changed significantly in the past few decades. Pollsters have been asking Americans whether pot should be legal since the 1960s. Data collected in 2013 marked the first time that a majority (52 percent) responded that marijuana should be legal. Americans of all backgrounds have become more supportive over time. Gaps still remain, however, with men, young people, and Democrats more likely than women, older people, and Republicans to favor legalization.

Source: "Majority Now Supports Legalizing Marijuana," Pew Research Center for People and the Press, 4 April 2013.

the richest Americans differ from the opinions of everyone else, policy changes are more likely to reflect the views of the wealthy.[16]

The two models of democracy make different assumptions about public opinion. The majoritarian model assumes that a majority of the people holds clear, consistent opinions on government policy. The pluralist model assumes that the public is often uninformed and ambivalent about specific issues, and opinion polls frequently support that claim. For example, in January 2014, only 54 percent of Americans correctly knew that the Affordable Care Act prohibits companies from denying health insurance to people because of any illnesses they may have.[17] Possessing incorrect information can go on to shape attitudes about the policy itself, which, in turn, can influence the actions of legislators. Would it not be better, some argue, to pay more attention to the preferences of citizens and organizations that are most knowledgeable about, and most involved in, each policy domain?

With this overview of debates about the role of public opinion in the democratic process in place, we now move on to addressing questions about the foundations of public opinion. How do polls measure public opinion? What principles, if any, do people use to organize their beliefs and attitudes about politics? How do individuals form their political opinions? Under what conditions does the public meet the high standards set forth in the majoritarian model of democracy, and when does it fall short?

The Distribution of Public Opinion

LO2 Critique polling as a method for measuring public opinion and identify skewed, bimodal, and normal distributions of opinion.

A government that tries to respond to public opinion soon learns that people seldom think alike. To understand and then act on the public's many attitudes and beliefs, government must pay attention to the way public opinion is distributed among the choices on a given issue. In particular, government must analyze the shape and the stability of that distribution. Understanding how polls work is the first step.

Measuring the Distribution of Public Opinion

How can a pollster tell what the nation thinks by talking to only a few hundred people? The answer lies in the statistical theory of sampling. Briefly, the theory holds that a sample of individuals selected by chance from any population is representative of that population. This means that the traits of the individuals in the sample—their attitudes, beliefs, and sociological characteristics—reflect the traits of the whole population. Sampling theory does not claim that a sample exactly matches the population, only that it reflects the population with some predictable degree of accuracy. Think of a blood test. If your doctor wants to measure your cholesterol level, she does not need to remove all of your blood. She fills one small tube, the contents of which offer a good reflection of the rest of the blood in your body. Sampling works similarly, in theory at least. In reality, ensuring that the test tube of the American public that is included in a survey represents the broader population can be very challenging.

Three important factors determine the accuracy of a sample. The first is how the sample is selected. For maximum accuracy, the individuals in the sample must be chosen randomly. Randomly does not mean "at whim," however; it means that every individual in the population has the same chance of being selected.

Today, many polls conducted by the mass media are done by telephone, with computers randomly dialing numbers within predetermined calling areas. Random dialing ensures that even people with unlisted numbers are called. Most media outlets ensure that they include cell phone numbers in their sampling, since a growing segment of the population (especially younger Americans) only has a cell phone. Surveys are also conducted over the Internet, where it can be even harder to assemble a sample that is representative of the nation as a whole. As one journalist at the *New York Times* wrote, "There's far greater diversity of methods among these polls than among telephone polls. The diversity is a reflection of the still-developing science of Internet polling. *No one is sure of the right way to do it*."[18]

A second factor that affects accuracy is the size of the sample. The larger the sample is, the more accurately it represents the population. For example, a sample of one thousand randomly selected individuals is accurate to within (plus or minus) three percentage points 95 percent of the time.

The third factor that affects the accuracy of sampling is the amount of variation in the population. If there were no variation, every sample would reflect the population's characteristics with perfect accuracy, such as if 100 percent of Americans approved of how the president was handling his job. The greater the variation is within the population, the greater is the chance that one random sample will be different from another, such as if 46 percent of Americans approved of the president. In that case, one poll might find 48 percent approved while another might find that only 45 percent approved.[19]

As shown in Figure 5.1, the predictions of the Gallup Poll for nineteen presidential elections since 1936 have deviated from the voting results by less than 1.0 percentage point. Even this small margin of error can mean an incorrect prediction in a close election. But for the purpose of estimating public opinion on political issues, a sampling error of three percentage points is acceptable.

IMAGE 5.2   Stop the Presses! Oops, Too Late...

As the 1948 election drew near, few people gave President Harry Truman a chance to defeat his Republican opponent, Thomas E. Dewey. Polling was still new, and almost all the early polls showed Dewey far ahead. Most organizations simply stopped polling weeks before the election. The *Chicago Daily Tribune* believed the polls and proclaimed Dewey's victory before the votes were counted. Here, the victorious Truman triumphantly displays the most embarrassing headline in American politics. Later, it was revealed that the few polls taken closer to election day showed Truman catching up to Dewey. Clearly, polls estimate the vote only at the time they are taken.

Poll results can be wrong because of problems that have nothing to do with sampling. Survey questions are prone to random error because interviewers are likely to obtain superficial responses from busy respondents who say anything, quickly, to get rid of them. The way in which survey questions are worded can also change the results. For instance, referring to "Obamacare" as opposed to "the Affordable Care Act" decreases support for the health reform law.[20] But despite the potential for error, modern polling has told us a great deal about public opinion in America.

Shape of the Distribution

The results of public opinion polls are often displayed in graphs such as those in Figure 5.2. The height of the columns indicates the percentage of those polled who gave each response, identified along the baseline. The shape of the opinion distribution depicts the pattern of all the responses when counted and plotted. The figure depicts three patterns of distribution: skewed, bimodal, and normal.

FIGURE 5.1 Gallup Poll Accuracy

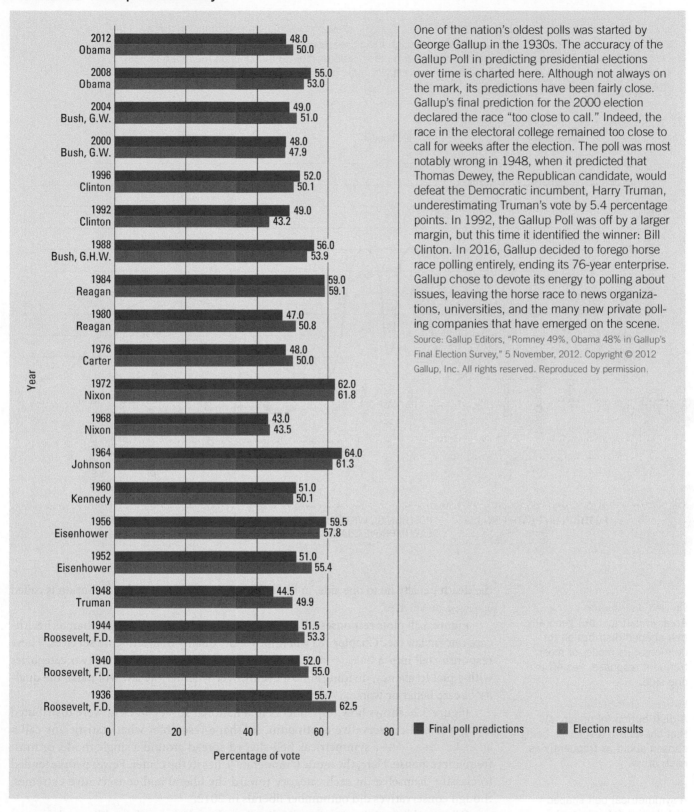

One of the nation's oldest polls was started by George Gallup in the 1930s. The accuracy of the Gallup Poll in predicting presidential elections over time is charted here. Although not always on the mark, its predictions have been fairly close. Gallup's final prediction for the 2000 election declared the race "too close to call." Indeed, the race in the electoral college remained too close to call for weeks after the election. The poll was most notably wrong in 1948, when it predicted that Thomas Dewey, the Republican candidate, would defeat the Democratic incumbent, Harry Truman, underestimating Truman's vote by 5.4 percentage points. In 1992, the Gallup Poll was off by a larger margin, but this time it identified the winner: Bill Clinton. In 2016, Gallup decided to forego horse race polling entirely, ending its 76-year enterprise. Gallup chose to devote its energy to polling about issues, leaving the horse race to news organizations, universities, and the many new private polling companies that have emerged on the scene.

Source: Gallup Editors, "Romney 49%, Obama 48% in Gallup's Final Election Survey," 5 November, 2012. Copyright © 2012 Gallup, Inc. All rights reserved. Reproduced by permission.

Figure 5.2a plots the percentages of respondents surveyed in 2012 who favored or opposed imposing the death penalty for a person convicted of murder. The most frequent response ("favor") is called the *mode*. The mode produces a prominent "hump" in this distribution. The relatively few respondents who didn't know or were opposed to

FIGURE 5.2   Three Distributions of Opinion

Here we superimpose three idealized patterns of distribution—skewed, bimodal, and normal—on three actual distributions of responses to survey questions. Although the actual responses do not match the ideal shapes exactly, the match is close enough that we can describe the distribution of (a) thoughts on the death penalty as skewed, (b) opinions on whether health-care reform will improve care as bimodal, and (c) ideological attitudes as approximately normal.

Source: 2012 American National Election Study, undertaken in collaboration by Stanford University and the University of Michigan, face-to-face sample.

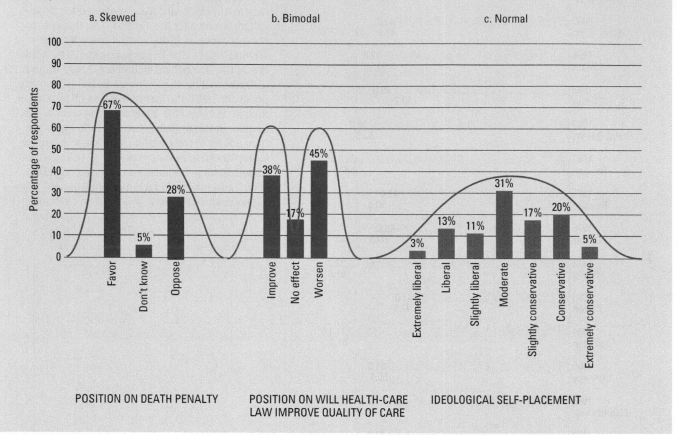

a. Skewed   **b. Bimodal**   **c. Normal**

POSITION ON DEATH PENALTY   POSITION ON WILL HEALTH-CARE LAW IMPROVE QUALITY OF CARE   IDEOLOGICAL SELF-PLACEMENT

skewed distribution
An asymmetrical but generally bell-shaped distribution (of opinions); its mode, or most frequent response, lies off to one side.

bimodal distribution
A distribution (of opinions) that shows two responses being chosen about as frequently as each other.

normal distribution
A symmetrical bell-shaped distribution (of opinions) centered on a single mode, or most frequent response.

the death penalty lie to one side, in its "tail." Such an asymmetrical distribution is called a **skewed distribution**.

Figure 5.2b plots responses when participants were asked whether Obama's health-care reform law (see Chapter 18) will improve the quality of health-care services. These responses fall into a **bimodal distribution**: respondents generally chose two categories with equal frequency, dividing almost evenly over whether the law will make the quality of care better or worse; 17 percent remain in the middle.

Figure 5.2c shows how respondents to a national survey in 2012 were distributed along a liberal-conservative continuum. Its shape resembles what statisticians call a **normal distribution**—a symmetrical, bell-shaped spread around a single mode, or most frequent response. Here, the mode ("moderate") lies in the center. Fewer people tended to classify themselves in each category toward the liberal and conservative extremes, though conservatives did outnumber liberals in 2012.

When public opinion is normally distributed on an issue, the public tends to support a moderate government policy on that issue. It will also tolerate policies that fall slightly to the left or to the right as long as they do not stray too far from the moderate center. In contrast, when opinion is sharply divided in a bimodal distribution, as it is over Obama's health-care reform, there is great potential for political conflict. A skewed

Finally, political education comes simply through exposure and familiarity. One example is voting, which people do with increasing regularity as they grow older.

Social Groups and Political Values

LO4 Compare and contrast the effects of education, income, region, race, ethnicity, religion, and gender on public opinion.

No two people are influenced by precisely the same socialization agents or in precisely the same way. Each individual experiences a unique process of political socialization and forms a unique set of political values. Yet as we noted at the start of this chapter, people with similar backgrounds do share similar experiences, which means they tend to develop similar political opinions. In this section, we examine the ties between people's social background and their political values. In the process, we examine the ties between background and values by looking at responses to two questions posed by the 2012 American National Election Study (ANES).[28] Many questions in the survey tap the freedom-versus-order or freedom-versus-equality dimensions. The two we chose serve to illustrate the analysis of ideological types. These specific questions do not define or exhaust the typology; they merely illustrate it.

The first question dealt with abortion. The interviewer said, "There has been some discussion about abortion during recent years. Which opinion on this page best agrees with your view?":

1. "By law, abortion should never be permitted" [12 percent agreed].
2. "The law should permit abortion only in cases of rape, incest, or when the woman's life is in danger" [28 percent agreed].
3. "The law should permit abortion for reasons other than rape, incest, or danger to the woman's life, but only after the need for the abortion has been clearly established" [18 percent agreed].
4. "By law, a woman should be able to obtain an abortion as a matter of personal choice" [43 percent agreed].[29]

Those who chose the last category most clearly valued individual freedom over order imposed by government. Evidence shows that pro-choice respondents also tend to have concerns about broader issues of social order, such as the role of women and the legitimacy of alternative lifestyles.[30]

The second question posed by the 2012 ANES pertained to the role of government in guaranteeing employment:

> Some people feel the government in Washington should see to it that every person has a job and a good standard of living. Suppose that these people are at one end of the scale. . . . Others think the government should just let each person get ahead on his own. Suppose these people were at the other end. . . . Where would you put yourself on this scale, or haven't you thought much about this?

Excluding respondents who "hadn't thought much" about this question, 28 percent wanted the government to provide every person with a good standard of living, and 23 percent were undecided. That left 49 percent who wanted the government to let people "get ahead" on their own. These respondents valued freedom over government efforts to promote equality.

Together it seems that most people are inclined to value freedom over order or equality. About 61 percent felt that the government should permit abortions in many, if not all, instances while only 39 percent felt government should forbid or severely restrict abortions, and a near-majority thinks people should get ahead on their own efforts without much government aid. However, differences in attitudes emerged for both issues when the respondents were grouped by socioeconomic factors: education, income, region, race, religion, and sex. The differences are shown in Figure 5.4 as positive and negative deviations from the national average for each question. Bars that extend to the right identify groups that are more likely than most other Americans to sacrifice freedom for order (on the left-hand side of the figure) or equality (on the right-hand side). Next, we examine the opinion patterns more closely for each socioeconomic group.

Education

Education increases people's awareness and understanding of political issues. Higher education also promotes tolerance of unpopular opinions and behavior and invites

FIGURE 5.4   How Groups Differ on Two Questions of Order and Equality

Two questions—one posing the dilemma of freedom versus order (regarding government limits on abortion) and the other the dilemma of freedom versus equality (regarding government guarantees of employment)—were asked of a national sample in 2012. Public opinion across the nation as a whole was divided on each question. These two graphs show how respondents in several social groups deviated from the national mean for each question.

Source: Data from the 2012 American National Election Study, undertaken in collaboration by Stanford University and the University of Michigan. Data are from face-to-face interviews and use weights provided by the ANES.

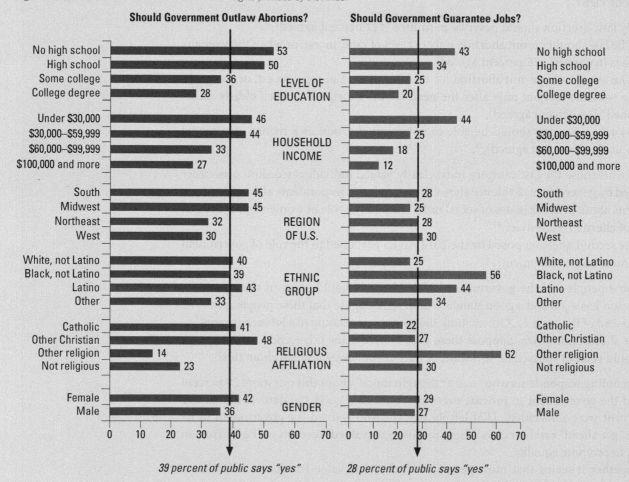

citizens to see issues in terms of civil rights and liberties.[31] This result is clearly shown in the left-hand column of Figure 5.4, which shows that people with less education are more likely to support outlawing abortions, while those with more education view abortion as a matter of a woman's choice.[32] When confronted with a choice between personal freedom and social order, college-educated individuals tend to choose freedom.

With regard to the role of government in reducing income inequality, the right-hand column in Figure 5.4 shows that people with less education favor government action to guarantee jobs and a good standard of living. Those with more education oppose government action, favoring freedom over equality. You might expect better educated people to be humanitarian and to support government programs to help the needy. However, because educated people tend to be wealthier, they would be taxed more heavily for such government programs. Moreover, they may believe that it is unrealistic to expect government to make such economic guarantees.

Income

In many countries, differences in social class, based on social background and occupation, divide people in their politics.[33] In the United States, the majority of citizens regard themselves as "middle class." Yet, as Figure 5.4 shows, wealth is linked to opinions favoring a limited government role in promoting both equality and order. Those with lower incomes are more likely to favor government guarantees of employment and living conditions. Those with incomes under $60,000 also favor outlawing abortions more than those earning over $60,000. For both issues, wealth and education tend to have a similar effect on opinion: the groups with more education and higher income favor freedom.

Region

Early in our country's history, regional differences were politically important-important enough to spark a civil war between the North and South. For nearly a hundred years after the Civil War, regional differences continued to affect American politics. The moneyed Northeast was thought to control the purse strings of capitalism. The Midwest was long regarded as the stronghold of isolationism in foreign affairs. The South was virtually a one-party region, almost completely Democratic. And the individualistic West pioneered its own mixture of progressive politics.

In the past, differences in wealth fed cultural differences between these regions. In recent decades, however, the movement of people and wealth away from the Northeast and Midwest to the Sunbelt states in the South and

John Moore/Getty Images

IMAGE 5.4   In the Eye of the Beholder

In 2015, racial differences in public opinion were on full display when the state of South Carolina decided to remove the Confederate flag from its statehouse. Polls show that in 2015, 66 percent of whites see the flag as a symbol of southern pride, while 72 percent of blacks see it as a symbol of racism.

Source: "Poll: Majority Sees Confederate Flag as Southern Pride Symbol, Not Racist," CNN.com, http://www.cnn.com/2015/07/02/politics/confederate-flag-poll-racism-southern-pride/.

Southwest has equalized the per capita income of the various regions. One result of this equalization is that the formerly "solid South" is no longer solidly Democratic. In fact, the South has tended to vote for Republican presidential candidates since 1968, and the majority of southern congressmen are now Republicans. Political differences between the South and the rest of the country today are often rooted in attitudes about racial politics and social issues in addition to attitudes about the economy.[34]

Figure 5.4 shows public opinion on both an economic and a social issue in the four major regions of the United States. It shows that differences are more pronounced on the social issue: people in the South and Midwest were more likely to favor restricting abortion than people in the Northeast or the West, yet regional differences were minimal regarding government efforts to ensure a decent standard of living.

Ethnicity and Race

Over the course of American history, individuals of diverse ethnic and racial backgrounds have differed with respect to political values and opportunities. In the early twentieth century, the major ethnic minorities in America were composed of immigrants from Ireland, Italy, Germany, Poland, and other European countries who came to the United States in waves during the late 1800s and early 1900s. These immigrants entered a nation that had been founded by British settlers more than a hundred years earlier. They found themselves in a strange land, usually without money and unable to speak the language. Moreover, their religious backgrounds—mainly Catholic and Jewish—differed from that of the predominantly Protestant earlier settlers. These urban ethnics and their descendants became part of the great coalition of Democratic voters that President Franklin Roosevelt forged in the 1930s. And for years after, the European ethnics supported liberal candidates and causes more strongly than the original Anglo-Saxon immigrants did.[35]

From the Civil War through the civil rights movement of the 1950s and 1960s, African Americans fought to secure basic political rights such as the right to vote. Initially mobilized by the Republican Party—the party of Lincoln—following the Civil War, African Americans forged strong ties with the Democratic Party during the New Deal era. Today, African Americans are still more likely to support liberal candidates and identify with the Democratic Party. African Americans constitute 13 percent of the population, with sizable voting blocs in northern cities and in southern states like Mississippi, Georgia, and Louisiana. Over 88 percent of African Americans voted for Democratic candidate Hillary Clinton in 2016.[36]

According to the U.S. Census Bureau, non-Hispanic whites comprised 62 percent of the population in 2014. As we noted earlier, the country is projected to become majority-minority by 2044.[37] Latinos, people of Latin American origin, now make up the largest minority group in the United States: 17.4 percent in 2014. They consist of both whites and nonwhites and are commonly but inaccurately regarded as a racial group. Latinos are projected to be 28.6 percent of the population in 2060.[38] At the national level, Latinos (consisting of groups as different as Cubans, Mexicans, Dominicans, and Puerto Ricans) have lagged behind African Americans in mobilizing and gaining political office. However, they constitute 46 percent of the population in New Mexico and 38 percent in California and Texas—where they have fared better in politics.[39] Like African Americans, Latinos tend to align with the Democratic Party. Over 65 percent of Latino voters voted for Clinton in 2016.[40]

Both Asians and Native Americans account for another 6 percent of the population (5.4 percent Asian; .7 percent Native American). Like other minority groups, their political impact is greatest in cities or regions where they are concentrated and greater in number. For instance, Asian Americans constitute 39 percent of the population in Hawaii and 13 percent in California; Native Americans make up 12 percent of the population of California and 9 percent of Oklahoma.[41] The Asian population in the country overall is expected to increase to 9.1 percent by 2060 while the Native American population is expected to remain the same.[42] Studying the political attitudes of both of these groups is often difficult due to their small number, linguistic diversity, and geographic dispersion. Nonetheless, Asians, like other nonwhites, display a clear preference for Democrats over Republicans, with roughly 65 percent of Asian American voters voting for Clinton in 2016.[43] Information on Native Americans' voting preferences is harder to come by, but estimates suggest that they too vote heavily Democratic.[44]

As we discussed at the outset of this chapter, members of minority groups often differ from whites in their attitudes on issues that pertain to equality.[45] The reasons are twofold.[46] First, racial minorities (excepting second-generation Asians) tend to have lower **socioeconomic status**, a measure of social condition that includes education, occupational status, and income. Second, minorities have been targets of prejudice and discrimination and have benefited from government actions in support of equality. The right-hand column in Figure 5.4 clearly shows the effects of race on the freedom-equality issue. All minority groups, particularly African Americans, are much more likely than whites to favor government action to improve economic opportunity. The abortion issue produces less difference, although Latinos favor government restrictions on abortion more than other groups.[47]

socioeconomic status
Position in society, based on a combination of education, occupational status, and income.

Religion

Religion is another factor that can have a significant impact on public opinion. Today, 49 percent of the population is Protestant or non-Catholic Christian, 21 percent is Catholic, and fewer than 2 percent is Jewish. Almost 23 percent of Americans today claim to be "unaffiliated" with respect to religion, a figure that has grown rapidly in the twenty-first century.[48] Less than 1 percent of the population was Muslim in 2014, a figure that is expected to rise to about 1.7 percent by 2030.[49] For many years, analysts found strong and consistent differences in the political opinions of Protestants, Catholics, and Jews.[50] Protestants were more conservative than Catholics, and Catholics tended to be more conservative than Jews. There have been few surveys of the Muslim population in the United States, though one recent study found that Muslim Americans

Stephen Morton/Stringer/Getty Images

IMAGE 5.5   Word of God?

A person's religiosity may be as important as his or her denominational identification in predicting political opinions. One measure of people's religiosity in a Christian-Judaic society is their opinion about the Bible. When asked about the nature of the Bible in 2012, about 34 percent of respondents said it was the actual word of God and should be taken literally. About 46 percent regarded it as the word of God but believed it should not be taken literally, and 20 percent viewed it as written by men. Among those who believe that the Bible was written by men, 45 percent say that global warming is mainly a product of human activity; among those who believe the Bible is the word of God and should be taken literally, that figure drops to 20 percent. People who think the Bible was written by men were also fifty points more likely than people who say it should be taken literally to believe that abortion should be legal as a matter of personal choice.

Source: 2012 American National Election Study, undertaken in collaboration by Stanford University and the University of Michigan, face-to-face sample.

are more likely to favor "big government" than the rest of the population, and largely consider themselves Democrats.[51]

As Figure 5.4 indicates, such broad religious groupings affect attitudes about economic equality and social order. Protestants ("Other Christian") favor government action to limit abortion even more than Catholics. Non-Christians and people who are not religious overwhelmingly favor a woman's right to choose. Differences among religious subgroups have emerged across many contemporary social and political issues. Evangelical Protestants are more likely than members of other religious groups to oppose gay marriage and support the death penalty while favoring the right to life over abortion. Evangelicals and Jews are more likely to express support for Israel in Middle Eastern politics.

Gender

Men and women differ with respect to their political opinions on a broad array of social and political issues, though their views are similar on the two items depicted in Figure 5.4. Surveys show that women are consistently more supportive than men are of gay marriage, environmental policies, and government spending for social programs. They are consistently less supportive of the death penalty and of going to war.[52] Contemporary politics is marked by a "gender gap": women tend to identify with the Democratic Party more than men do, and they are much more likely than men to vote for Democratic presidential candidates. In the 2016 general election, Clinton won the support of 54 percent of female voters but only 41 percent of male voters.[53]

From Values to Ideology

LO5 Define the concept of ideology, describe the liberal-conservative continuum, and assess the influence of ideology on public opinion.

We have just seen that differences in groups' responses to two survey questions reflect those groups' value choices between freedom and order and between freedom and equality. But to what degree do people's opinions on specific issues reflect their explicit political ideology (the set of values and beliefs they hold about the purpose and scope of government)? Political scientists generally agree that ideology influences public opinion on specific issues; they have much less consensus on the extent to which people think explicitly in ideological terms. They also agree that the public's ideological thinking cannot be categorized adequately in conventional liberal-conservative terms.

The Degree of Ideological Thinking in Public Opinion

Although politicians and the media frequently use the terms *liberal* and *conservative*, many voters tend not to use ideological concepts when discussing politics. For years, surveys have shown that when voters are asked to explain the meaning of the terms "liberal" or "conservative," they often respond with dictionary definitions rather than explicitly political terms. They say that liberals are generous (a *liberal* portion) and conservatives are cautious (a *conservative* estimate). They also say that liberals tend to prefer spending money while conservatives prefer saving money. Very few mention "degree of government involvement" in describing liberals and conservatives.[54]

Ideological labels are technical terms used in analyzing politics, and most citizens don't play that sport. But if you want to play, you need suitable equipment. Scales and typologies, despite their faults, are essential for classification. No analysis, including the study of politics, can occur without classifying the objects being studied. The tendency to use ideological terms in discussing politics grows with increased education, which helps people understand political issues and relate them to one another.

People's personal political socialization experiences can also lead them to think ideologically. For example, children raised in strong union households may be taught to distrust private enterprise and value collective action through government.

True ideologues hold a consistent set of values and beliefs about the purpose and scope of government, and they tend to evaluate candidates in ideological terms. Some people respond to questions in ways that seem ideological but are not because they do not understand the underlying principles. For example, most respondents dutifully comply when asked to place themselves somewhere on a liberal-conservative continuum. The result, as shown earlier in Figure 5.2c, is an approximately normal distribution centering on "moderate," the modal category, which contains 31 percent of all respondents. But many people settle on moderate (a safe choice) when they do not clearly understand the alternatives. When allowed to say, "I haven't thought much about it," 22 percent of respondents in the survey acknowledged that they had not thought much about ideology and were excluded from the distribution.[55] The extent of ideological thinking in America, then, is even less than it might seem from responses to questions asking people to describe themselves as liberals or conservatives.[56] Nonetheless, the majority of Americans do identify themselves as either liberal or conservative.

The Quality of Ideological Thinking in Public Opinion

What people's ideological self-placement means in the twenty-first century is not clear. At one time, the liberal-conservative continuum represented a single dimension: attitudes toward the scope of government activity. Liberals were in favor of more government action to provide public goods, and conservatives were in favor of less. This simple distinction is not as useful today. Many people who call themselves liberal no longer favor government activism in general, and many self-styled conservatives no longer oppose it in principle. As a result, many people have difficulty deciding whether they are liberal or conservative, whereas others confidently choose identical points on the continuum for entirely different reasons. People describe themselves as liberal or conservative because of the symbolic value of the terms as much as for reasons of ideology.[57]

Studies of the public's ideological thinking find that two themes run through people's minds when they are asked to describe liberals and conservatives. One theme associates liberals with change and conservatives with tradition. It corresponds to the distinction between liberals and conservatives on the exercise of freedom and the maintenance of order, a distinction confirmed in research that finds that liberals tend to be more supportive of civil liberties and free speech than conservatives.[58]

The other theme has to do with equality. The conflict between freedom and equality was at the heart of President Roosevelt's New Deal economic policies in the 1930s, which included Social Security (see Chapter 18). The policies expanded the interventionist role of the national government to promote greater economic equality, and attitudes toward government intervention in the economy served to distinguish liberals from conservatives for decades afterward.[59] Attitudes toward government interventionism still underlie opinions about domestic *economic* policies. Liberals support intervention to promote economic equality; conservatives favor less government intervention and more individual freedom in economic activities. Conservatives, however, think differently about government action on *social* policies. (See "Freedom, Order, or Equality: Freedom v. Order: The Tea Party.")

Chapter 1 proposed an alternative system of ideological classification based on people's relative evaluations of freedom, order, and equality. It described liberals as people who believe that government should promote equality, even if some freedom is lost in the process, but who oppose surrendering freedom to government-imposed order. Conservatives do not necessarily oppose equality but put a higher value on freedom than on equality when the two conflict. Yet conservatives are not above restricting freedom when threatened with the loss of order. So both groups value freedom, but one is more willing to trade freedom for equality, and the other is more inclined to trade freedom for order. If you have trouble thinking about these tradeoffs on a single dimension, you are in good company. The liberal-conservative continuum presented to survey respondents takes a two-dimensional concept and squeezes it into a one-dimensional format.[60]

Freedom, Order, or Equality

Freedom v. Order: The Tea Party

"I'll have tea with a generous helping of order." Tea party supporters tout their love of freedom and opposition to government interventions—especially concerning government spending. But tea party supporters favor limits to freedom on some key issues. The figure below compares the attitudes of tea party supporters, opponents, and those who neither support nor oppose the tea party on two questions in which freedom and order conflict: support for the death penalty and support for policies that require local police to determine the immigration status of people they think might be undocumented immigrants. It shows that when freedom and order conflict, tea party supporters are much more likely than other Americans to come down on the side of order.

This preference for order suggests that tea party support is motivated not just by government spending, but also by broad concerns about the social changes occurring in the United States, including ethnic and religious diversity, greater acceptance of gays and lesbians, and an expanded presence of women in leadership roles. Tea partiers, it has been argued, seek to preserve the place of whites, Christians, men, and heterosexuals at the top of the social hierarchy, and are willing to support government intervention in order to do so.

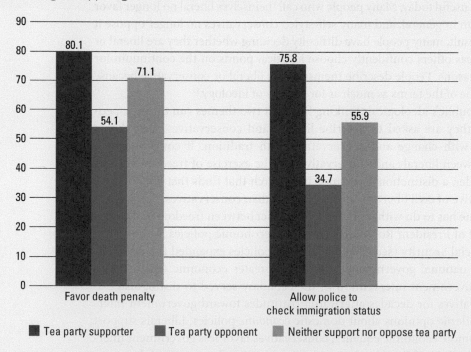

Sources: 2012 American National Election Study; Christopher Parker and Matt Barreto, *Change They Can't Believe In: The Tea Party and Reactionary Politics in America* (Princeton University Press, 2013).

CRITICAL THINKING Which ideological tendency best characterizes tea party supporters: Liberal, Conservative, Libertarian, or Communitarian?

Ideological Types in the United States

Our ideological typology in Chapter 1 (see Figure 1.2) classifies people as Liberals if they favor freedom over order and equality over freedom. Conversely, Conservatives favor freedom over equality and order over freedom. Libertarians favor freedom over both equality and order—the opposite of Communitarians, who favor equality and order over freedom.[61] By cross-tabulating people's answers to the two questions from the 2012 ANES about freedom versus order (abortion) and freedom versus equality (government job guarantees), we can classify respondents according to their ideological tendencies. We can also see that the traditional liberal-to-conservative scale is limited in its ability to capture how people actually feel about the tradeoffs among freedom, order, and equality. As shown in Figure 5.5a, most self-identified liberals favor freedom on abortion and equality on jobs, and self-identified conservatives tend to favor order on abortion and freedom on jobs, just as our ideological typology would expect. But the relationship between self-placement on an ideological scale and issue positions is far from perfect: a majority (51 percent) of self-identified conservatives still prefer to keep abortion legal.

Figure 5.5b illustrates how blunt the liberal-conservative scale is. It shows that among people who are classified as liberal according to their issue positions (i.e. they prefer freedom on abortion and equality on jobs), 59 percent self-identify as liberal, leaving 41 percent who identify as something else (mainly moderate). Among people who are classified as conservative based on their issue positions, 74 percent identify as conservative. What about people whose issue positions are more libertarian or communitarian? The last two bars of Figure 5.5b show that libertarians and communitarians have a harder time locating their ideology on a constrained liberal-conservative scale. These results resemble earlier findings by other researchers who conducted more exhaustive analyses involving more survey questions.[62]

Respondents who readily locate themselves on a single dimension running from liberal to conservative often go on to contradict their self-placement when answering questions that trade freedom for either order or equality. A two-dimensional typology that incorporates freedom and equality on the one hand and freedom and order on the other allows us to analyze responses more meaningfully.[63] A single dimension does not fit many people's preferences for government action concerning both economic and social issues. One reason so many Americans classify themselves as conservative on a one-dimensional scale is that they have no option to classify themselves as libertarian.

The ideological typology also reflects differences between diverse social groups. Blacks and Hispanics are more likely than whites to have liberal policy preferences on the abortion and jobs questions studied here; men are more likely than women to be libertarian; and people with higher degrees tend to be libertarian while people with only a high school diploma are more likely to split between liberal and conservative. Regional differences are small among the types, with libertarians being the most common type everywhere except the Midwest, where conservatives were most common. Liberals were most prominent in the West. People who are not religious were most likely to be classified as libertarian, and Protestants were most likely to be classified as conservative. Finally, the poor were most likely to be classified as liberal, while the affluent were solidly libertarian.

This more refined analysis of political ideology explains why even Americans who pay close attention to politics might find it difficult to locate themselves on the liberal-conservative continuum: they are liberal on some issues and conservative on others. Forced to choose along just one dimension, they opt for the middle category, moderate. However, our analysis indicates that many people who classify themselves as liberal or conservative do fit these two categories in our typology. There is value, then, in the liberal-conservative distinction as long as we understand its limitations.

FIGURE 5.5 **Ideological Self-Placement versus Ideology Based on Issues**

In the 2012 election survey, respondents were asked whether abortion should be outlawed by government or a matter of personal choice, and whether government should guarantee people a job and a good standard of living or people should get ahead on their own. (The questions are given verbatim earlier in the chapter.) These two questions presented choices between freedom and order, and between freedom and equality. Figure 5.5a shows how people who consider themselves liberal, moderate, and conservative answered these questions. In general, self-identified liberals favored freedom regarding abortion and equality regarding guaranteed jobs while conservatives favored order on abortion and freedom on jobs. But the relationship between how people see their ideology and how they feel about specific issues is messy. Figure 5.5b classifies respondents according to four different ideological types based on how they actually answered these two questions: "liberals" favored freedom on abortion and equality on jobs, "conservatives" favored order on abortion and freedom on jobs, "libertarians" favored freedom on both, and "communitarians" favored order on abortion and equality on jobs. The graph shows the proportion within each ideological tendency that considers itself to be liberal, moderate, or conservative.

Source: Data from the 2012 American National Election Study, undertaken in collaboration by Stanford University and the University of Michigan. Data are from face-to-face interviews and use weights provided by the ANES.

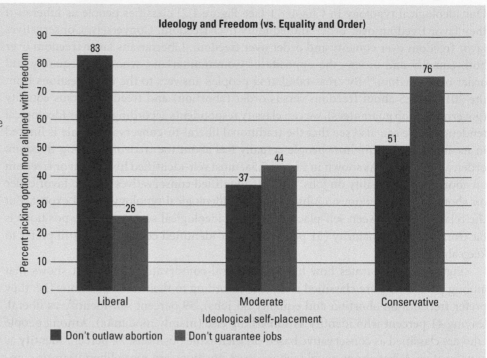

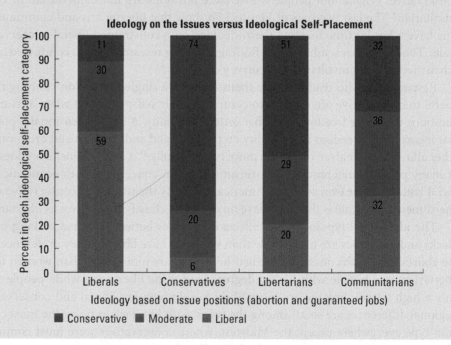

Forming Political Opinions

LO6 Assess the impact of knowledge, self-interest, and leadership on political opinions.

We have seen that people acquire their political values through socialization and that different social groups develop different sets of political values. We have also learned that some people, but only a minority, think about politics ideologically, holding a consistent set of political attitudes and beliefs. But how do those who are not ideologues—in other words, most citizens—form political opinions? Are most people well informed about politics? What can we say about the quality of public opinion in America?

Political Knowledge

In the United States today, education is compulsory (usually to age sixteen), and the literacy rate is relatively high. The country boasts an unparalleled network of colleges and universities. American citizens can obtain information from a variety of news sources. They can keep abreast of national and international affairs through live coverage of world events via satellite from virtually everywhere in the world. But how much do they know about politics?

In a comprehensive study of political knowledge two decades ago, two political scientists collected 3,700 individual survey items that measured some type of factual knowledge about public affairs.[64] They focused on over two thousand items that clearly dealt with political facts, such as knowledge of political institutions and processes, contemporary public figures, political groups, and policy issues. They found that "many of the basic institutions and procedures of government are known to half or more of the public, as are the relative positions of the parties on many major issues."[65] A question that's harder to answer is whether a fact about American politics being known by "more than half" of the public is enough. How much knowledge about public affairs people need to have before they can effectively give their consent to be governed and expect to influence public policy is a profound question that democratic societies face.

Current surveys of political knowledge report mixed findings about public knowledge. Consider Pew Research Center's News IQ Survey, administered two or three times a year. In 2015, Pew researchers found that majorities answered an impressive eleven out of twelve items correctly. Over 80 percent knew that they need to indicate whether they have health insurance when they file their income taxes and 78 percent knew that the U.S. military base at Guantanamo Bay is in Cuba. However, only 33 percent knew that three of the justices on the Supreme Court were women at the time the survey was conducted. But is 33 percent high or low? All else being equal, a higher level of political knowledge is better, but how much people know about particular aspects of the political world rises and falls with media attention. Actual events, and media coverage of those events, signal what is important to the public and can lead to increased information levels.[66]

But perhaps simply calling and asking people if they can recall information like the name of the secretary of state is not the best way to measure political knowledge in the first place. Two researchers conducted an experiment where some people were given a full day to report back their answers to a political knowledge survey. People who were given more time to answer scored somewhat higher than people who had to answer on the spot. The study's authors concluded that in this day and age, people have a range of tools at their disposal, thanks to the Internet, where they can find out what they need to know when they need to know it. Today's wired and interconnected lifestyle means that the public is perhaps more competent regarding political affairs than traditional surveys indicate.[67] It's also the case that people's party affiliations shape how they answer questions about facts. For example, Republicans were less likely than Democrats to answer correctly when asked if the unemployment rate increased during George W. Bush's presidency (it did). It turns out, however, that many Republicans aren't giving a sincere answer when they say that the economy under a Republican president is doing better than it actually is, and likewise for Democrats. How do we know? Recent experiments show that if you offer to pay people for each question they answer correctly, differences in factual knowledge between Democrats and Republicans diminish. The good news is that these findings mean that people often know more about politics than surveys about political knowledge reveal. The bad news is that partisanship can make people care more

IMAGE 5.6   Do As I Say, Not As I Do

A majority of Americans (59 percent) thinks that immigrants do not learn English in a reasonable amount of time. Yet the proportion of immigrants who speak English very well has risen since 1980, and only about 10 percent of the foreign born do not speak English at all. Such misperceptions can affect policy preferences and can also be hard to correct.

Sources: Julia Preston, "Newest Immigrants Assimilating as Fast as Previous Ones, Report Says," *New York Times*, 21 September 2015, http://www.nytimes.com/2015/09/22/us/newest-immigrants-assimilating-as-well-as-past-ones-report-says.html; "Modern Immigration Wave Brings 59 Million to U.S., Driving Population Growth and Change Through 2065," Pew Research Center, 28 September 2015, http://www.pewhispanic.org/2015/09/28/modern-immigration-wave-brings-59-million-to-u-s-driving-population-growth-and-change-through-2065/.

about giving answers that feel good to them than giving answers that are correct.[68]

This is not to say that the public is never uninformed or that incorrect answers to political knowledge questions do not matter. Misperceptions do exist. In 2015, for example, only one-third of Americans knew that about one quarter of immigrants in the United States is undocumented; another third thought it was 45 percent or more. About one-third of Americans also grossly overestimated the percentage of the population that is foreign-born: the correct answer is 13 percent, but many thought it was 39 percent or more.[69] Why are such misperceptions so widespread? Portrayals of Latinos in the media are one culprit. When asked in a 2012 study to recall the kind of roles they have seen Latinos play on television, the most common responses were "criminal," "gardener," and "maid," all of which are associated with an underground economy. That same study included an experiment that found that people who were exposed to negative media portrayals of Latinos were more likely than other people to agree that the term "illegal immigrant" applies well to Latinos.[70]

Although some studies have shown that the *collective* opinion of the public can be interpreted as stable and meaningful—because random ignorance balances off both sides of an issue[71]—the public is simply misinformed on some important issues. Moreover, individuals who strongly believe in certain causes may ignore information that questions their beliefs. Even worse, upon being told that their beliefs are incorrect, some people hold on to their incorrect beliefs even more, a phenomenon called the *backfire effect*. For instance, researchers found that ideological conservatives became more likely to think that Iraq had weapons of mass destruction (WMD) before the 2003 Iraq War *after* they were told that subsequent investigations concluded that Iraq did not have WMD.[72] In their minds, they argued against the evidence presented to them, which strengthened their incorrect beliefs.

The American public, it seems, is not as politically knowledgeable as a pure majoritarian model of democracy would demand. The public's store of information about the structure of American government and about current affairs is far from ideal, and people can be very resistant to new information that might challenge their existing beliefs. But when people are given more time to think about it, and when the news media indicates that new issues are important, levels of political information among the American public do rise.

Costs, Benefits, and Cues

self-interest principle
The implication that people choose what benefits them personally.

Perhaps people do not know a wide variety of political facts, but they can tell whether a policy is likely to directly help or hurt them. The **self-interest principle** states that people choose what benefits them personally.[73] Self-interest affects how people form opinions on policies with clear costs and benefits.[74] Tax payers tend to prefer low taxes to high taxes. Smokers tend to oppose bans on smoking in public places. Gun owners are less likely to support handgun control. People who are well-off financially tend to be less supportive of redistributive social welfare policies than people who are less well-off.

In some cases, individuals are unable to determine personal costs or benefits. This tends to be true of foreign policy, which few people interpret in terms of personal benefits. Here, many people have no opinion, or their opinions are not firmly held and can change quite easily given almost any new information. Attitudes about foreign policy are also powerfully shaped by longstanding predispositions. For example, when it seemed as if the United States might intervene militarily in Syria's civil war in 2013, party and gender were strongly associated with people's preferences: Republicans and men were more likely than Democrats and women to support possible airstrikes.[75]

In other cases, opinions are driven more by what is considered to be in the nation's interest rather than what people think is in their own interest. Such **sociotropic responses** are particularly common with regard to how the economy affects attitudes during elections. Opinions about whether the nation is doing well or not are often more influential over candidate preferences than attitudes about one's own economic standing. It is believed, however, that sociotropic preferences form because people use their ideas about the national condition to help them figure out what to expect in their own lives.[76]

sociotropic responses
Opinions about how the country as a whole is doing affect political preferences more strongly than one's own personal circumstance.

Public opinion that is not based on a complicated ideology may also emerge from the skillful use of cues. Individuals may use heuristics—mental shortcuts that require hardly any information—to make fairly reliable political judgments.[77] For instance, citizens can use political party labels to compensate for low information about the policy positions of candidates. Voters may have well-developed expectations or stereotypes about political parties that structure the way they evaluate candidates and process new information.[78] They assume that Democrats and Republicans differ from each other in predictable ways. Stereotypes about other groups in society, such as women and minorities, can also influence people's political preferences.[79] Similarly, citizens take cues from trusted government officials and interest groups regarding the wisdom of bills pending in Congress or the ideology of Supreme Court nominees.

Political Leadership

Public opinion on specific issues is molded by political leaders, journalists, and policy experts. Politicians serve as cue givers to members of the public. Citizens with favorable views of a politician may be more likely to support his or her values and policy agenda; similarly, unfavorable views of a politician can dampen policy support. In an experiment conducted during the 2008 presidential campaign, 52 percent of Democrats supported a proposal to reform immigration when no party or candidate was mentioned in the policy description, but only 33 percent of Democrats supported the same proposal when it was described as being supported by John McCain, the Republican candidate. Similarly, 66 percent of Republicans opposed the proposal when no candidate was mentioned, and opposition jumped to 90 percent when the policy was attributed to Barack Obama.[80]

Politicians routinely make appeals to the public on the basis of shared political ideology and self-interest. They share information about social trends, policy options, and policy implementation. Competition and controversy among political elites provide the public with a great deal of information. But politicians are well aware that citizen understanding and support for an issue depend on its framing. In **issue framing**, politicians (and interest groups) define the way that issues are presented, selectively invoking values or recalling history in the presentation. For example, opinion leaders might frame a reduction in taxes as "returning money to the people" or, quite differently, as "reducing government services." Politicians and other leaders can frame issues to change or reinforce public opinion.[81]

issue framing
The way that politicians or interest group leaders define an issue when presenting it to others.

The ability of political leaders to influence public opinion has been enhanced enormously by the growth of the broadcast media, especially television.[82] The majoritarian model of democracy assumes that government officials respond to public opinion, and evidence exists to confirm that such responsiveness does occur. But it is also true that political leaders will try to educate or sway the public and convince them to agree that particular courses of action are best.[83] Such attempts to guide public preferences raise important questions about how much potential there is for public opinion to be manipulated by political leaders through the mass media. We examine the relationships among the mass media, political leaders, and the public in the next chapter.

The 2016 Election and Public Opinion about Government

The public holds attitudes not only about policies and particular politicians, but also about elections in general. And their views are complex. Leading up to the 2016 presidential election, an overwhelming majority expressed support for changing campaign finance regulations so as to reduce the role of money in politics. Majorities also felt that politicians are selfish and lose touch with ordinary Americans too quickly. At the same time, however, over 50 percent said that voting gives people some say over how government is run. A majority felt that ordinary Americans could do a better job of solving the nation's problems than elected officials, but only 34 percent said they had a good deal of trust in the "wisdom of the American people when it comes to making political decisions."[84]

This mixed view of the political process and of one's fellow Americans, combined with the many facets of public opinion discussed in this chapter, suggest that it is probably for the best that the American political system allows for both majoritarianism and pluralism to coexist.

Summary

LO1 Distinguish the various roles played by public opinion in majoritarian and pluralist democracy.

- Public opinion is more important to the majoritarian model of democracy than the pluralist model.

LO2 Critique polling as a method for measuring public opinion and identify skewed, bimodal, and normal distributions of opinion.

- At their best, public opinion polls represent the views of the American population as a whole, but there are many challenges to ensuring that polls are generalizable. The shape of the distribution of opinion (skewed, bimodal, or normal) indicates how sharply the public is divided. Bimodal distributions harbor the greatest potential for political conflict. The stability of a distribution over time indicates how settled people are in their opinions.

LO3 Explain the influence of the agents of early socialization—family, school, community, and peers—on political learning.

- People form their values through the process of political socialization. The most important socialization agents in childhood and young adulthood are family, school, community, and peers. Among adults, the workplace is a powerful socialization agent.

LO4 Compare and contrast the effects of education, income, region, race, ethnicity, religion, and gender on public opinion.

- Members of the same social group tend to experience similar socialization processes and thus to adopt similar values, which means people in different social groups tend to have different opinions.

LO5 **Define the concept of ideology, describe the liberal-conservative continuum, and assess the influence of ideology on public opinion.**

- Most people do not think about politics in ideological terms but readily classify themselves along a liberal-conservative continuum, with many choosing the middle category, moderate. Others choose the moderate category because they have liberal views on some issues and conservative views on others. Their political orientation is better captured by a two-dimensional framework that analyzes ideology according to the values of freedom, order, and equality, which classifies people as Liberals, Conservatives, Libertarians, and Communitarians.

LO6 **Assess the impact of knowledge, self-interest, and leadership on political opinions.**

- Surveys show that the public does moderately well on quizzes of political facts, but people sometimes misunderstand critical issues in public policy and can reject evidence that runs counter to their beliefs. Citizens use party labels and cues from elected officials to compensate for their lack of detailed political knowledge. Citizens also respond to the way in which issues are framed when forming their views. The way in which issues are presented to the public through the media can therefore be very important in shaping the relationship between public opinion and political action.

Chapter Quiz

LO1 **Distinguish the various roles played by public opinion in majoritarian and pluralist democracy.**

1. What does the majoritarian model assume about the nature of public opinion?
2. What does the pluralist model assume about public opinion?

LO2 **Critique polling as a method for measuring public opinion and identify skewed, bimodal, and normal distributions of opinion.**

1. Describe three factors that can affect the accuracy of a sample used in a public opinion poll.
2. Explain the differences among a skewed distribution of opinions, a bimodal distribution, and a normal distribution.

LO3 **Explain the influence of the agents of early socialization—family, school, community, and peers—on political learning.**

1. How do the primary principle and the structuring principle affect political learning?
2. What is the transmission model of partisan identification?

LO4 **Compare and contrast the effects of education, income, region, race, ethnicity, religion, and gender on public opinion.**

1. Which social grouping —education, income, region, race, ethnicity, religion, or gender—appears to have the strongest effect on attitudes toward government's role in maintaining order, such as outlawing abortions?
2. Which social grouping appears to have the strongest effect on attitudes toward government's role in promoting equality, such as guaranteeing jobs?

LO5 **Define the concept of ideology, describe the liberal-conservative continuum, and assess the influence of ideology on public opinion.**

1. On which types of issues do liberals tend to support government interventionism? On which types of issues do they oppose it?
2. Why might Americans with a high degree of political engagement have trouble determining whether they are liberal or conservative?

LO6 **Assess the impact of knowledge, self-interest, and leadership on political opinions.**

1. What evidence shows that people know little about politics—or, conversely, that they know a lot about government and political affairs?
2. Using the concept of issue framing, pick a political issue and illustrate how Democratic and Republican candidates present it differently to voters.

6 The Media

Just a few years ago, the term "live tweet" did not exist. But in 2014, it was added to the Oxford Dictionary, and throughout the 2016 presidential election, live tweets of political events were a media phenomenon. As you probably well know, to live tweet is to post comments on Twitter about an event as the event is taking place. During the recent presidential primary season, Democratic candidate Bernie Sanders stole some of the spotlight from his Republican counterparts by live tweeting during their debate. His observations included both substantive policy critiques and sarcastic jabs. He tweeted "Does anybody on the stage believe that our gay brothers and sisters have the same rights as the rest of us? Anybody?" And later, "Does anyone know . . . when will this debate finally end?"[1]

Twitter allows politicians like Sanders to communicate with followers directly, bypassing journalists and traditional media outlets. Sanders was hardly alone in his Twitter presence. Hillary Clinton also live tweeted during Republican debates, while Republicans Donald Trump, Rand Paul, Jeb Bush, and Carly Fiorina sent out tweets to their followers during Democratic debates. You don't have to follow candidates to see their tweets, of course. Many news outlets ran stories throughout the presidential campaign about the candidates' activities on Twitter. And tweets get re-tweeted, leading to further news stories about which live tweets are re-tweeted most.

The use of social media by political leaders during events, or during emergencies such as hurricanes, illustrates how news consumption is no longer a passive, one-way exercise. Journalists, government, and citizens now interact with each other routinely, with each actor producing and receiving information from the other. While most Americans still get most of their news from journalists at traditional outlets, we are in the midst of an era of great change in political communication. Journalists still play a critical role in the media landscape, and news transmitted by social media has its greatest impact when it is also covered by traditional news. But technological change has generated important debates about the role of the media in American democracy.

Some observers say the new media frontier is a threat to democracy. Traditional journalism conducts investigative reporting, follows up on stories once they are no longer on the front page, and sends journalists to report on foreign events and on state and city politics.[2] Journalistic norms of objectivity and accountability provide readers with accurate information that allows them to draw their own conclusions about current affairs. When citizens turn to opinion blogs and social networks, the market for traditional journalism is threatened, and the important services it contributes to the public good could disappear.

On the other side are people who find the new frontier in journalism exciting and democratizing. They argue that the amount of depth and context readers can find about any topic is a huge advance from the limited amount of information that was available when journalists were constrained by the length of a news show or printed article. News sites that exist only on the Web, such as ProPublica, have won Pulitzer Prizes. Champions of new media also say that mobile technology and social networking allow information to reach ever broader audiences.[3]

People on both sides agree on three things. First, the changes—and challenges—facing traditional journalism are here to stay; we cannot put the social networking genie back in the bottle. Second, the media continue to play a critical role in the democratic process. Third, this critical role demands that we carefully and continually study the impact of the rapidly changing media environment.

#ChallengeAccepted

Take the Challenge on MindTap for American Government

What, if anything, is "newsworthy" about tweets from presidential candidates?

140

Magazines

Magazines differ from newspapers not only in the frequency of their publication but also in the nature of their coverage. News-oriented magazines cover the news in a more specialized manner than do daily newspapers and are often forums for opinions, not strictly news. The earliest public affairs magazines were founded in the mid-1800s, and two—*The Nation* and *Harper's*—are still publishing today. Such magazines were often politically influential, especially in framing arguments against slavery and later in publishing exposés of political corruption. Even magazines with limited readerships can wield political power. Magazines may influence **attentive policy elites**—group leaders who follow news in specific areas—and thus influence mass opinion indirectly through a **two-step flow of communication**.

As scholars originally viewed the two-step flow, it conformed to the pluralist model of democracy. Once group leaders (for instance, union or industry leaders) became

IMAGE 6.2   New Ways to Get the News

Printed newspapers have struggled to earn revenue in the digital age. Some try to maintain a subscriber model, requiring people to pay to have full access to a site's content. The very term "news*paper*" is becoming outdated.

informed of political developments, they informed their more numerous followers, mobilizing them to apply pressure on government. Today, according to a revised interpretation of the two-step flow concept, policy elites are more likely to influence public opinion and other leaders by airing their views in the media. In this view, public deliberation on issues is mediated by these professional communicators who frame the issues in the media for popular consumption—that is, they define the way that issues will be viewed, heard, or read.[13]

Only one weekly news magazine—*Time* (founded in 1923)—enjoys big circulation numbers in the United States (3.2 million copies in 2014). Overall, news magazine circulation has declined in recent years much as newspaper circulation has. Once popular as a news weekly, *Newsweek* (founded in 1933) saw a 32 percent decline in circulation from 2009 to 2010. In 2012, *Newsweek* ceased its print publication and is now available only online. Despite these troubles, the magazine publishes in five languages and continues to operate domestic and international bureaus.

attentive policy elites
Leaders who follow news in specific policy areas.

two-step flow of communication
The process in which a few policy elites gather information and then inform their more numerous followers, mobilizing them to apply pressure to government.

Radio

Regularly scheduled, continuous radio broadcasting began in 1920 on stations KDKA in Pittsburgh and WWJ in Detroit. Both stations claim to be the first commercial station, and both broadcast returns of the 1920 election of President Warren G. Harding. The first radio network, the National Broadcasting Company (NBC), was formed in 1926. Soon four networks were on the air, transforming radio into a national medium

FIGURE 6.2   Audiences of Selected Media Sources

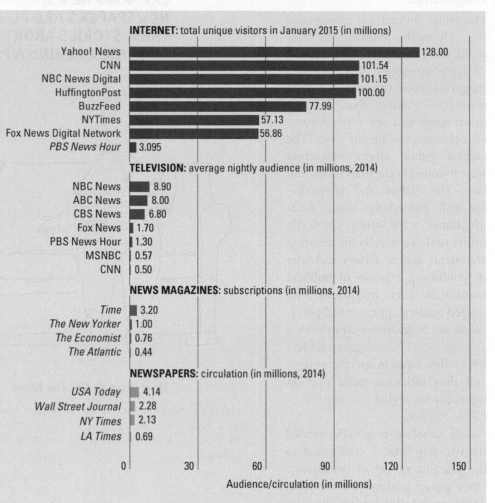

The big story in recent years is the enormous growth in the Internet news audience. The print version of the *New York Times*, for instance, has a circulation of 2.13 million people. Yet over 50 million people visit the paper's website for news every month. Other Internet news sites see more than double that amount of traffic. Some major news magazines (published weekly) have more readers than newspapers do, but newspapers are published daily and there are more of them.

Sources: Pew Research Center, http://www.journalism.org/media-indicators/average-circulation-at-the-top-5-u-s-newspapers-reporting-monday-friday-averages/; Pew Research Center, http://www.journalism.org/files/2015/04/FINAL-STATE-OF-THE-NEWS-MEDIA1.pdf.

INTERNET: total unique visitors in January 2015 (in millions)

Yahoo! News	128.00
CNN	101.54
NBC News Digital	101.15
HuffingtonPost	100.00
BuzzFeed	77.99
NYTimes	57.13
Fox News Digital Network	56.86
PBS News Hour	3.095

TELEVISION: average nightly audience (in millions, 2014)

NBC News	8.90
ABC News	8.00
CBS News	6.80
Fox News	1.70
PBS News Hour	1.30
MSNBC	0.57
CNN	0.50

NEWS MAGAZINES: subscriptions (in millions, 2014)

Time	3.20
The New Yorker	1.00
The Economist	0.76
The Atlantic	0.44

NEWSPAPERS: circulation (in millions, 2014)

USA Today	4.14
Wall Street Journal	2.28
NY Times	2.13
LA Times	0.69

Audience/circulation (in millions)

by linking thousands of local stations. Americans were quick to purchase and use this new technology (see Figure 6.1). Millions of Americans heard President Franklin D. Roosevelt deliver his first "fireside chat" in 1933.

Because the public could sense reporters' personalities over radio in a way they could not in print, broadcast journalists quickly became household names. Edward R. Murrow, one of the most famous radio news personalities, broadcast news of the merger of Germany and Austria by short-wave radio from Vienna in 1938 and during World War II gave stirring reports of German air raids on London.

Today there are over fifteen thousand licensed broadcast radio stations.[14] Despite the advent of iTunes, satellite radio, and podcasts, nine out of ten Americans listen to a traditional AM/FM radio every week.[15] Radio listeners often tune into stations that have news and talk radio formats, and the audience for talk radio continues to grow. The audience of talk radio is more Republican because the majority of talk radio hosts, like Rush Limbaugh, are conservative.[16] Talk radio shows have been criticized for polarizing politics by publicizing extreme views.[17]

Television

Experiments with television began in France in the early 1900s. By 1940, twenty-three television stations were operating in the United States. Two stations broadcast the returns of Roosevelt's 1940 reelection.[18] By 1950, ninety-eight stations covered the major population centers of the country, although only 9 percent of households had televisions (see Figure 6.1).

The first coast-to-coast broadcast came in 1951: President Harry Truman's address to delegates at the Japanese peace treaty conference in San Francisco. That same year, Democratic senator Estes Kefauver of Tennessee called for television coverage of his committee's investigation into organized crime. For weeks, people with televisions invited their neighbors to watch underworld crime figures answering questions before the camera. Kefauver became one of the first politicians to benefit from television coverage. Previously unknown and representing a small state, he won many of the 1952 Democratic presidential primaries and became the Democrats' vice-presidential candidate in 1956.

Many early anchors of television network news programs came

MPI/Stringer/Archive Photos/Getty Images

IMAGE 6.3   Watching the President on Television

Television revolutionized presidential politics by allowing millions of voters to look closely at the candidates' faces and judge their personalities in the process. This close-up of John Kennedy during a debate with Richard Nixon in the 1960 campaign showed Kennedy to good advantage. In contrast, close-ups of Nixon made him look as though he needed a shave. Kennedy won one of the closest elections in history; his good looks on television may have made the difference.

to the medium already famous through their experience on radio. Now that the news audience could see the broadcasters as well as hear them, networks built their evening news around an "anchorman" chosen to inspire trust in viewers.

By 2015, the United States had more than thirteen hundred commercial and three hundred public television stations, and virtually every household had a television (and the vast majority had two or more sets).[19] Today, the three broadcast networks still have large audiences, but millions of viewers have drifted to more opinionated cable networks, especially MSNBC on the left and Fox News on the right. In fact, cable news is becoming a bit of a throwback; more and more it seems analogous to the early newspapers, which were blatantly political organizations. Research suggests that with viewers today having unprecedented choices, people who are more interested in politics increasingly desire partisan shows, while people who are less interested in politics simply avoid news programming altogether. Moreover, some research indicates that people who watch partisan news become more extreme in their political views. Still, some researchers have disputed citizens' "mass migration" from traditional media, concluding instead that these newer venues supplement rather than displace print and broadcast sources. Others contend that viewers of partisan news are already quite partisan themselves, and that the shows they watch do not make them more extreme.[20]

The Internet

What we today call the Internet began in 1969 when, with support from the U.S. Defense Department's Advanced Research Projects Agency, computers at four universities were linked to form ARPANET, which connected thirty-seven universities by 1972. New communications standards developed in 1983 allowed these networks to be

House correspondent, investigative reporting unit, an award-winning congressional reporter, and a growing roster of journalists based in overseas locations including Egypt, Turkey, and Senegal.[27]

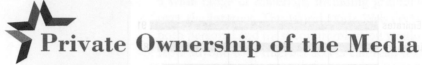

Private Ownership of the Media

LO2 Evaluate the effect of privately owned mass media on the quality of political communication in the United States.

In the United States, people take private ownership of the media for granted. Indeed, most Americans would regard government ownership of the media as an unacceptable threat to freedom that would interfere with the marketplace of ideas and result in one-way communication: from government to citizens. When the government controls the news flow, the people may have little chance to learn what the government is doing or to pressure it to behave differently. Certainly that is true in China. The Chinese government employs thousands of Internet police to prevent "subversive content" from being disseminated to its nearly 650 million Web users. If an Internet user in China searches for "democracy movements," she is met with a screen that reads, "Page cannot be displayed." Every year on June 4, the anniversary of a government crackdown on pro-democracy demonstrators in Tiananmen Square in 1989, activists try to outsmart the censors. They try, for instance, to come up with new ways to highlight the date, including 0.8*8 (which equals 6.4) and May 35 (four days after May 31), and replace censored images with absurd re-creations of the 1989 protests that have included inflatable ducks and Legos.[28]

In other Western democracies, the print media are privately owned, but the broadcast media often are not. In the United States, except for about 350 public television stations (out of about seventeen hundred total) and one thousand public radio stations (out of over fifteen thousand), the broadcast media are privately owned.[29]

The Consequences of Private Ownership

Private ownership of the media gives the news industry in America more political freedom than any other in the world, but it also makes the media more dependent on advertising revenues to cover costs and make a profit. Because advertising rates are tied to audience size, news operations in America must appeal to the audiences they serve.

Much of the content of newspapers is advertising. After fashion reports, sports, comics, and so on, only a relatively small portion of any newspaper is devoted to news of any sort and only a fraction of that

IMAGE 6.5   Ducking the Censors

Pro-democracy activists in China are constantly challenged to find creative ways to evade government censors. This image of ducks in place of tanks in an iconic photo of a pro-democracy protestor was posted on China's version of Twitter in 2013. Soon enough, however, searches for "big yellow duck" were also censored.

Source: Global Internet Phenomena Snapshot: 2H 2013; North America Fixed Access; https://www.sandvine.com/trends/global-internet-phenomena/.

news—excluding stories about fires, murder trials, and the like—can be considered political. In terms of volume, the entertainment content offered by the mass media in the United States can vastly overshadow the news content. In other words, the media function more to entertain than provide news. Entertainment increases the audience, which increases advertising revenues. The profit motive creates constant pressure to increase the ratio of entertainment to news or to make the news itself more entertaining.

You might think that a story's political significance, educational value, or social importance determines whether the media cover it. The truth is that most potential news stories are not judged by such grand criteria. The primary criterion of a story's **newsworthiness** is usually its audience appeal, which is judged according to its potential impact on readers or listeners, its degree of sensationalism (exemplified by violence, conflict, disaster, or scandal), its treatment of familiar people or life situations, its close-to-home character, and its timeliness.[30]

newsworthiness
The degree to which a news story is important enough to be covered in the mass media.

The importance of audience appeal has led the news industry to calculate its audience carefully. Additionally, the media try to increase ratings by tailoring the delivery or content of their news to the desires of their audience. Within the news industry, the process has been termed market-driven journalism—both reporting news and running commercials geared to a target audience.[31] For example, the median age of network evening news viewers is over fifty years old, which is why these shows nearly always feature a health-related story and run one or more commercials related to prescription drugs.[32]

As Figures 6.3a, 6.3b, and 6.3c show, people rely heavily on local news stations to get their news, but few local news stations assign reporters to cover state government. Local news epitomizes market-driven journalism by matching audience demographics to advertising revenue while slighting news about government, policy, and public affairs.[33] Local television newscasts across the nation practice a "hook-and-hold" approach. They hook viewers at the start by airing alarming stories about crime, accidents, fires, and disasters. The middle of the broadcast has informative news about business, science, and politics that are not considered good viewing. To hold viewers to the end, stations tease them by promising soft topics on pop culture, human interest, or health. As a result, local news broadcasts across the country look much the same.[34]

At the national level, the nightly news broadcasts were once the crown jewels of independent broadcasting companies—ABC, CBS, and NBC—and valued for their public service. Now these broadcasts are cogs in huge corporate conglomerates. The Walt Disney Company, for example, owns ABC. NBC was owned by General Electric for years, but merged with the cable company Comcast in 2011, which has created a massive television conglomerate.[35] The merger highlights the fact that television nightly news is no longer a public service, but a profit center.

From 1980 to 2012, ABC, CBS, and NBC suffered severe losses in their prime-time programming audience, though such losses have stabilized in recent years.[36] Many viewers have turned to watching cable stations instead of network programs, or they have turned away from news altogether. Though as Figure 6.3b shows, far more people still turn to the networks for their news than to cable. As parent corporations demand that news programs "pay their way," networks succumb to **infotainment**—a mix of information and diversion oriented to personalities or celebrities, not linked to the day's events, and usually unrelated to public affairs or policy.[37] Over 12 million people tune in for morning shows such as NBC's *Today Show* that have long mixed news and celebrity interviews.

infotainment
A mix of information and diversion oriented to personalities or celebrities, not linked to the day's events, and usually unrelated to public affairs or policy; often called "soft news."

The Concentration of Private Ownership

Media owners can make more money by increasing their audience or by acquiring additional publications or stations. As illustrated by the NBC-Comcast merger discussed earlier, there has been a trend toward concentrated ownership of the media,

FIGURE 6.3   Local TV News Is Most Popular, But Government News Is Not

Although Americans get their news on a variety of platforms, good old television is still the most commonly used source for news, as shown in Figure 6.3a. When watching TV news, Americans are more likely to turn to their local TV news shows over national broadcasts, such as *NBC Nightly News*, and they are far more likely to watch local news over cable news, as can be seen in Figure 6.3b. But when they turn to local news, they are probably more likely to learn about traffic, weather, sports, and crime than about their state government. As Figure 6.3c shows, only 14 percent of local television stations assign reporters to cover state government.

Sources: 6.3a: "How Americans Get Their News," American Press Institute, 17 March 2014, https://www.americanpressinstitute.org/publications/reports/survey-research/how-americans-get-news/; 6.3b: "How Americans Get TV News at Home," Pew Research Center, 11 October 2013, http://www.journalism.org/2013/10/11/how-americans-get-tv-news-at-home/; 6.3c: "Who Covers the Statehouse," Pew Research Center, 10 July 2014, http://www.journalism.org/2014/07/10/who-covers-the-statehouse/.

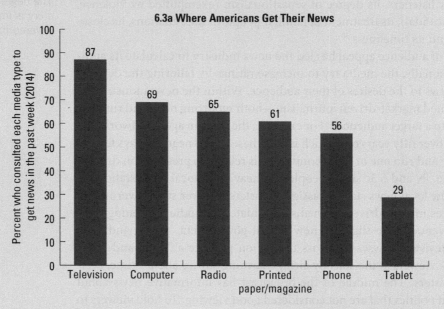

6.3a Where Americans Get Their News

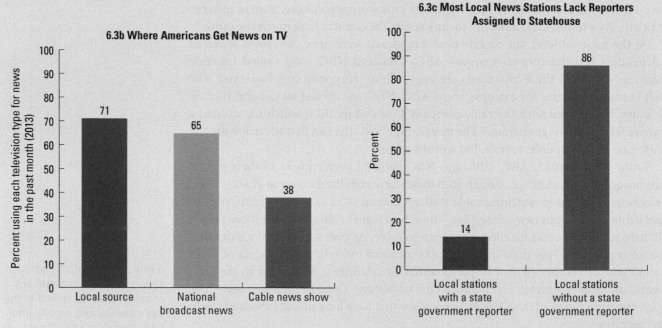

6.3b Where Americans Get News on TV

6.3c Most Local News Stations Lack Reporters Assigned to Statehouse

increasing the risk that a few owners could control the news flow to promote their own interests—much as political parties influenced the content of the earliest American newspapers. Ownership concentration doesn't just affect television news; the number of independent newspapers has declined as newspaper chains (owners of two or more newspapers in different cities) have acquired more newspapers. Research suggests that newspapers owned by publicly traded chains are more likely than other newspapers to resort to negative and positive spins on the news (as opposed to remaining neutral in tone) in order to attract more readers and thus, increase profits. While owners of privately held papers also care about profits, they seem more willing to promote journalistic integrity, even if it might hinder the bottom line.[38]

Some observers argue that since newspapers are under relentless financial stress, they should consider rejecting the for-profit model and instead operate as nonprofits. As nonprofits, newspapers would be financed through endowments, charitable donations, dues-paying members, and even the government, similar to how PBS and NPR operate on television and radio today. To date, a number of nonprofit news organizations have emerged; some focus on local issues, others on national issues, and others track policy-specific issues, such as health care. But no major newspaper has switched to the nonprofit model yet.[39]

At first glance, concentration of ownership does not seem to be a problem in the television industry. Although there are only three major networks, the networks usually do not own their affiliates. Most communities in the United States have a choice of multiple stations. As with newspapers, however, chains sometimes own television stations in different cities, and ownership sometimes extends across different media. Australian media magnate Rupert Murdoch operates two media companies, News Corp and 21st Century Fox, which control newspapers (including the *Wall Street Journal*), cable channels (including Fox News), twenty-seven local Fox stations, several film companies, and more.[40]

Government Regulation of the Media

LO3 Follow the evolution of government regulation of the media and identify the challenges that new media technologies present to existing regulations.

Although most of the mass media in the United States are privately owned, they do not operate free of government regulation. Broadcast media operate under more stringent regulations than print media, initially because of technical aspects of broadcasting. Lately, debates about government regulation of the Internet have become common. In general, government regulation of the mass media addresses three aspects of their operation: technical considerations, ownership, and content.

Technical and Ownership Regulations

In the early days of radio, stations that operated on similar frequencies in the same area often jammed each other's signals, and no one could broadcast clearly. At the broadcasters' insistence, Congress passed the Federal Radio Act (1927), which declared that the public owned the airwaves and private broadcasters could use them only by obtaining a license from the Federal Radio Commission. Thus, government regulation of broadcasting was not forced on the industry by socialist politicians; capitalist owners sought it to impose order on the use of the airwaves (thereby restricting others' freedom to enter broadcasting).

Seven years later, Congress passed the Federal Communications Act of 1934, a more sweeping law that created the **Federal Communications Commission (FCC)**, which has five members (no more than three from the same political party) nominated by the president for terms of five years. The commissioners can be removed from office only

Federal Communications Commission (FCC)
An independent federal agency that regulates interstate and international communication by radio, television, telephone, telegraph, cable, and satellite.

Freedom, Order, or Equality and Net Neutrality

Should Comcast or Verizon be allowed to charge consumers who stream movies on Netflix more for their Internet service than consumers who just use e-mail and surf the Web? Should these Internet service providers (ISPs) be able to block consumers from even accessing sites like YouTube since streaming video eats up so much bandwidth and clogs Internet traffic? These questions are at the heart of debates about *net neutrality*.

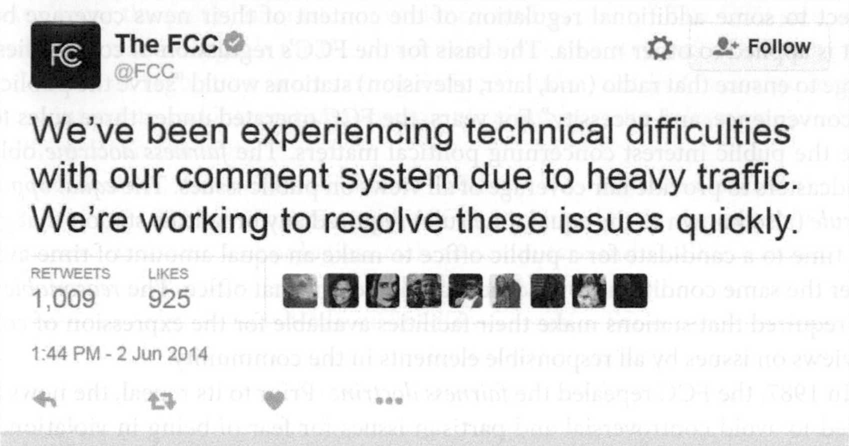

ISPs argue that as private companies, they should be free to set up their businesses as they see fit. They say they want to provide relief from Internet congestion and that establishing the equivalent of first-class mail delivery should be their prerogative. As the graph indicates, Netflix and YouTube alone accounted for over 50 percent of Internet traffic during peak hours in 2015.

In 2014, a federal appeals court ruled that because the Federal Communications Commission (FCC) originally classified broadband as *an information service*, ISPs could not be prohibited from charging for more bandwidth or blocking access to otherwise legal sites.* Supporters of net neutrality say data-intensive information should not be available only to the affluent and that ISPs should not be allowed to determine which sites consumers can access.

When private companies operate within the basic infrastructure that is considered essential to modern democratic life, the government may restrict their freedom to operate as they wish, thus promoting equality of access and order to how the infrastructure is managed. Accordingly, Congress gave the FCC authority to regulate telecommunications. But should ISPs be regulated as one of these so-called *common carriers* that provide "basic telecommunications infrastructure"? Many ordinary Internet users think so, and feel quite strongly about it. As shown in

> **The FCC** ✓
> @FCC   ⚙ ＋ Follow
>
> We've been experiencing technical difficulties with our comment system due to heavy traffic. We're working to resolve these issues quickly.
>
> RETWEETS   LIKES
> 1,009   925
>
> 1:44 PM - 2 Jun 2014

IMAGE 6.6   Traffic Jam

Shortly after John Oliver, host of HBO's "Last Week Tonight," encouraged viewers to call for net neutrality during the FCC's open comment period, the FCC's website crashed under the weight of all of the new activity.

Source: Twitter, Inc

Reporting the News

All major news media seek to cover political events with firsthand reports from journalists on the scene. Because so many significant political events occur in the nation's capital, Washington has an immense press presence, with over 5,000 journalists in the congressional press corps alone.[52] Roughly fifty additional reporters are admitted to the White House press briefing room.[53] Since 1902, when President Theodore Roosevelt first provided space in the White House for reporters, the press has had special access to the president (though as Figure 6.4 shows, the number of presidential news conferences with reporters has declined in recent administrations). The media's relationship with the president is mediated primarily through the Office of the Press Secretary.

To meet daily deadlines, White House correspondents rely heavily on information they receive from the president's staff, each piece carefully crafted in an attempt to control the story. The most frequent form is the news release—a prepared text distributed the FCC's Tweet, the FCC was unable to handle the increased traffic following a call to action on John Oliver's "Last Week Tonight." In 2015, the FCC reclassified the Internet as a telecommunication service, paving the way for more extensive government regulation of how ISPs operate.**

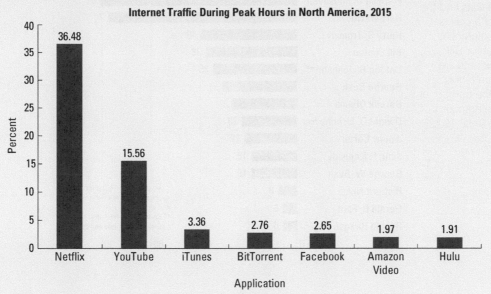

Internet Traffic During Peak Hours in North America, 2015

Source: Global Internet Phenomena Snapshot: 2015; North America Fixed Access; https://www.sandvine.com /downloads/general/global-internet-phenomena/2015/global-internet-phenomena-report-latin-america-and-north -america.pdf.

The net neutrality debate involves clashes between the freedom of ISPs to develop their own business plans and their desire for order in the face of Internet congestion, and equality of access to information among the public. Now that the Internet is an essential medium for news transmission, it is arguably in the public interest to ensure that citizens can find information about politics in the most efficient and equitable way possible. Whether that requires more—or less—government regulation is an ongoing debate.

* Edward Wyatt Lee, "Court Rejects Equal Access Rule for Internet Providers," *New York Times*, 14 January 2014.
** Timothy Lee, "Net Neutrality Is on Trial in Washington: Here's What You Need to Know," *Washington Post*, 10 September 2013. Rebecca Ruiz and Steve Lohr, "In Net Neutrality Victory, F.C.C. Classifies Broadband Internet Service as Public Utility," *New York Times*, 2 February 2015.

CRITICAL THINKING Which types of companies, organizations, and groups do you think are most likely to favor having the FCC promote net neutrality? Which ones are most likely to oppose it?

to reporters in the hope that they will use it verbatim. A daily news briefing enables reporters to question the press secretary about news releases and allows television correspondents time to prepare their stories and film for the evening newscast. A news conference involves questioning high-level officials in the executive branch— including the president.[54] Occasionally, information is given "on background," meaning the information can be quoted, but reporters cannot identify the source. A vague reference—"a senior official says"—is all right. Information disclosed "off the record" cannot even be printed. Journalists who violate these well-known rules risk losing their welcome.

Most news about Congress comes from press releases issued by its 535 members, from congressional reports, and, increasingly, from the members' own social networking accounts. Coverage of policy debates typically mirrors the intensity with which congressional actors seek to promote them.[55] A journalist can therefore report on Congress

FIGURE 6.4   More News = Less Talk?

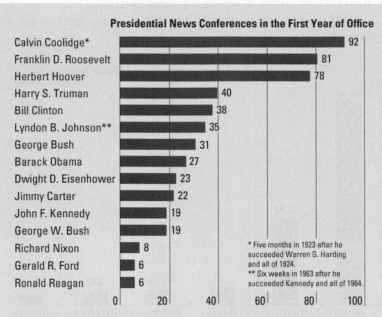

As press conferences have become more formal and scripted, they have also become less frequent. When journalists and the president had more of a collegial relationship, press conferences were common. Except for Bill Clinton, modern presidents are clustered at the bottom of this graph, which shows the number of presidential press conferences in the first year in office since 1922.

Source: "The Frequency of the Message Is Medium," *CQ Weekly Online* 27 (July 2009): 1755. Copyright © 2009 by CQ-ROLL CALL GROUP. Reproduced with permission of CQ-ROLL CALL GROUP via Copyright Clearance Center.

Presidential News Conferences in the First Year of Office

Calvin Coolidge* — 92
Franklin D. Roosevelt — 81
Herbert Hoover — 78
Harry S. Truman — 40
Bill Clinton — 38
Lyndon B. Johnson** — 35
George Bush — 31
Barack Obama — 27
Dwight D. Eisenhower — 23
Jimmy Carter — 22
John F. Kennedy — 19
George W. Bush — 19
Richard Nixon — 8
Gerald R. Ford — 6
Ronald Reagan — 6

* Five months in 1923 after he succeeded Warren G. Harding and all of 1924.
** Six weeks in 1963 after he succeeded Kennedy and all of 1964.

without inhabiting its press galleries. In an effort to save money, many news outlets have cut the size of their Washington staff or eliminated it entirely. In 2015, *World News Tonight* on ABC stopped having a reporter assigned to cover Congress full time. The broadcast instead now sends its White House reporter to cover Congress as needed.[56]

Congress banned microphones and cameras from its chambers until 1979, when the House permitted live coverage. Televised broadcasts of the House were surprisingly successful, thanks to C-SPAN (the Cable-Satellite Public Affairs Network), which feeds to most cable systems across the country. To share in the exposure, the Senate began television coverage in 1986. Occasionally, an event captured on C-SPAN becomes a major news story. In 2009, for example, Representative Alan Grayson (D-Fla.) argued on the floor of the House that the Republican health-care plan had two options: stay healthy or die quickly. The C-SPAN coverage was picked up on YouTube, which then led to days of commentary by pundits. It also led to a fundraising boon: in the two weeks following the broadcast, Grayson's reelection campaign raised over $150,000 from one website alone.[57] But the national attention helped his opponent too, and Grayson lost his 2010 reelection bid (though he won again in 2012). This phenomenon of having a fiery quote picked up by the media, which then generates a spike in fundraising for the speaker (and often for his or her opponent as well), has been termed a "money blurt."[58]

Interpreting and Presenting the News

gatekeepers
Media executives, news editors, and prominent reporters who direct the flow of news.

Media executives, news editors, and prominent reporters function as **gatekeepers** in directing the news flow: they decide which events to report and how to handle the elements in those stories.[59] They not only select what topics go through the gate but also are expected to uphold standards of careful reporting and principled journalism. The rise of the Internet has made more information and points of view available to the public, but the Internet also can spread factual errors and rumors. The Internet has no gatekeepers, and thus no constraints on its content.[60] Most journalists think the Internet has made journalism better, mostly because it is a powerful research tool, it has the ability to deliver information quickly, and it promotes a high degree of engagement from the audience.[61]

Nonetheless, television still remains the most popular source for news. To make televised news understandable and to hold viewers' attention, editors and producers concentrate on individuals because individuals have personalities (political institutions do not—except for the presidency). A study of network news coverage of the president, Congress, and the Supreme Court in 2008–2009 found that 66 percent of the stories were about the presidency, compared with 28 percent on Congress and just 6 percent on the Supreme Court.[62]

During elections, the focus on personalities encourages **horse race journalism**, in which media coverage becomes primarily a matter of which candidate is leading in the polls and who has raised the most money. Study after study of news coverage of presidential elections find that horse race coverage dominates and that horse race content increases as Election Day approaches. Journalists cover the horse race because it offers new material daily, whereas the candidates' programs remain the same.[63] Voters, however, say they want more attention on issues and less on the horse race. After the 2012 election, Americans rated the performance of the press lower than that of the candidates, parties, pollsters, and campaign consultants.[64]

Aside from the day-to-day flow of information from government institutions and the regularity (and frequency) of elections, journalists are drawn to **media events**—situations that are too "newsworthy" to pass up. The media have been described as having an "alarm mode," in which it seems like every news outlet is drawn to a story to the extent that virtually every other issue gets ignored, and a "patrol mode," in which journalists remain focused on the story even after the initial burst of attention has subsided. Once another alarm goes off, the patrol mode ends and attention shifts elsewhere.[65] In early 2016, the alarm sounded when the national media learned that residents in Flint, Michigan, had been told that their drinking water was safe to drink even when government officials knew for months that unsafe lead levels were present. For weeks, the media were in patrol mode, devoting sustained attention to protests, relief efforts, and government investigations. Television is particularly partial to events that have visual impact. Organized protests and fires, for example, "show well" on television, so television covers them.

Where the Public Gets Its News. Until the early 1960s, most people got more of their news from newspapers than from any other source. Television nudged out newspapers as the public's major source of news in the early 1960s and has since remained dominant, as can be seen in Figure 6.3a. Surveys of news consumption consistently indicate that the public consults multiple sources of news during the day—perhaps reading the paper at breakfast, checking the Internet at work, and ending the day watching television news. Increasingly, people have added social networking sites to their list of news sources. Among those Americans who use Twitter or Facebook, over 60 percent say they use these platforms to access the news. Additionally, roughly 25 percent of Facebook and Twitter users tweet or post about the news. Only 4 percent, however, consider these social networking sites to be their most important source for news.[66] A 2015 study showed that about 72 percent of adult Internet users in the United States use Facebook, and 23 percent use Twitter. Facebook users are more likely than non-users to be women, white or Latino, and young. Twitter users are more likely to be nonwhite, have a college degree, live in urban areas, and like Facebook users, are young.[67]

Media Influence on Knowledge and Opinions. If, as surveys indicate, most Americans read or hear the news each day, how much political information do they absorb? Some, but not a lot. A national survey in 2015 asked respondents twelve questions about current events, including the number of women on the Supreme Court and the partisan makeup of the U.S. Senate. The public did well in identifying the current unemployment rate (72 percent got it right), but only one-third knew that three of the

horse race journalism
Election coverage by the mass media that focuses on which candidate is ahead rather than on national issues.

media event
A situation that is so "newsworthy" that the mass media are compelled to cover it. Candidates in elections often create such situations to garner media attention.

(see Chapter 12 for more on going public). The goal is twofold: first, to generate media coverage of the speaking event; and, second, to motivate citizens to pressure their representatives to support the president's agenda. The strategy of going public has become more common over time. Barack Obama attempted this strategy in 2015, when he became the first sitting president to travel to Arctic Alaska to give a speech about climate change. He acknowledged his strategy of visiting places visibly affected by climate change in the hopes of raising awareness and generating public support for his policy agenda, saying, "What's happening here is America's wake-up call. It should be the world's wake-up call."

Socializing the Citizenry

The mass media act as important agents of political socialization, in addition to those described in Chapter 5.[81] Young people who rarely follow the news by choice nevertheless acquire political values through the entertainment function of the media. From the 1930s to the early 1950s, children learned from dramas and comedies on the radio; now they learn from television and other electronic media. The average American teenager consumes close to nine hours of media per day (not including time at school or doing homework)—and sees a lot of sex and hears countless swear words in prime time.[82] In the golden days of radio, youngsters listening to the popular radio drama *The Shadow* heard repeatedly that "crime does not pay . . . the *Shadow* knows!" In program after program—*Dragnet, Junior G-Men, Gangbusters*—the message never varied: criminals are bad; the police are good; criminals get caught and are severely punished for their crimes.

Television today does not portray the criminal justice system in the same way, even in police dramas. Consider programs such as *Blue Bloods, Justified*, and *Hawaii Five-O*, which are among the recent crop of shows that portray law enforcement officers and government agents as lawbreakers. Certainly, one cannot easily argue that years of television messages conveying distrust of law enforcement, disrespect for the criminal justice system, and violence help prepare law-abiding citizens.

Some scholars argue that the most important effect of the mass media, particularly television, is to reinforce the hegemony, or dominance, of the existing culture and order. According to this argument, social control functions not through institutions of force (police, military, and prisons) but through social institutions, such as the media, that cause people to accept "the way things are."[83] By displaying the lifestyles of the rich and famous, for example, the media induce the public to accept the unlimited accumulation of private wealth. Similarly, the media socialize citizens to value "the American way," to be patriotic, to back their country, "right or wrong."

So the media play contradictory roles in the process of political socialization. On the one hand, they promote popular support for government by joining in the celebration of national holidays, heroes' birthdays, political anniversaries, and civic accomplishments. On the other hand, the media erode public confidence by detailing politicians' extramarital affairs, airing investigative reports of possible malfeasance in office, and even showing television dramas about crooked cops.[84]

Evaluating the Media in Government

LO5 Assess the impact of the media on democratic values and politics in the United States.

Are the media fair or biased in reporting the news? What contributions do the media make to democratic government? What effects do they have on the pursuit of freedom, order, and equality?

Is Reporting Biased?

News reports are presented as objective reality, yet critics of modern journalism contend that the news is filtered through the ideological biases of the media owners and editors (the gatekeepers) and the reporters themselves. Even citizens tend to be skeptical of the news and have become even more so over time (see Figure 6.5). Research suggests that as the parties have become more polarized (see Chapter 11) and as the presence of opinionated journalism has proliferated, political leaders increasingly go to ideologically friendly media outlets in order to criticize the rest of the media as an institution (former vice presidential candidate Sarah Palin took to calling the mainstream media the "lame stream" media). This elite criticism of the media in turn leads to greater skepticism of the press among the public. Their skepticism is consequential because people who distrust the media have been shown to be more resistant to learning new information about objective national events, such as changing economic conditions.[85]

The argument that news reports are politically biased has two sides. On the one hand, news reporters are often criticized for tilting their stories in a liberal direction, promoting social equality and undercutting social order.[86] On the other hand, wealthy and conservative media owners are suspected of preserving inequalities and reinforcing the existing order by serving a relentless round of entertainment that numbs the public's capacity for critical analysis.[87] Let's evaluate these arguments, looking first at reporters.

FIGURE 6.5   Rising Distrust in Accuracy and Objectivity of the Press

Over time, people have been asked whether news organizations generally get the facts straight or whether their stories and reports are often inaccurate. They have also been asked if they think that news organizations deal fairly with all sides or whether they tend to favor one side. The graph here shows that the public increasingly sees the news media as inaccurate and biased, especially in the past few years.

Sources: "Press Widely Criticized but Trusted More than Other Information Sources: Views of the News Media: 1985–2011," Report by Pew Research Center for People and the Press, 22 September, 2011. Copyright © 2011 by Pew Research Center. Reproduced by permission. Source for 2013: Pew Research Center, p. 15, http://www.people-press.org/2013/08/08/amid-criticism-support-for-medias-watchdog-role-stands-out/.

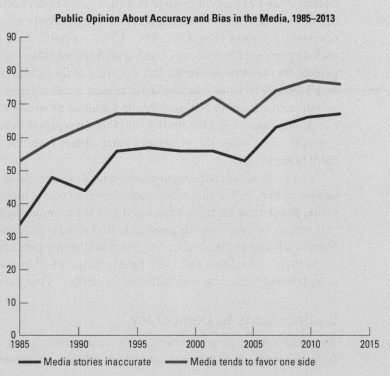

Public Opinion About Accuracy and Bias in the Media, 1985–2013

Although the picture is far from clear, available evidence seems to confirm the charge of liberal leanings among reporters in the major news media. In a 2013 survey of journalists, 28 percent considered themselves to be Democrats compared with only seven percent who said they were Republicans (the rest said they are independent or "other").[88] Content analysis of the tone of ABC, CBS, and NBC network coverage of the 2012 presidential campaign concluded that Barack Obama received more "good press" than Mitt Romney, his Republican challenger.[89] Newspaper coverage of the candidates was more even and for both candidates, the overwhelming majority of newspaper stories were considered neutral in tone.[90]

The counterargument is that working journalists in the national and local media often conflict with their own editors, who tend to be more conservative.[91] Editors, in their function as gatekeepers, tend to tone down reporters' liberal leanings by editing their stories or not placing them well in the medium. Newspaper publishers are also free to endorse candidates. In twelve of seventeen elections from 1948 to 2012, newspaper editorials favored the Republican candidate. In the 2012 election, 45 percent of newspapers endorsed Mitt Romney, 41 percent endorsed Barack Obama, and 14 percent did not issue an endorsement.[92]

In congressional elections, incumbents—as opposed to challengers—enjoy much more news coverage simply from holding office and issuing official statements. Noncampaign news coverage leads to greater incumbent name recognition at election time, particularly for members of Congress (see Chapter 11). This coverage effect is independent of any bias in reporting on campaigns.

Of course, bias in reporting is not limited to election campaigns, and different media may reflect different understandings of political issues. An important series of surveys about perceptions of the Iraq war were taken over the summer of 2003, after Bush had announced the end of combat. Substantial portions of the public held erroneous understandings of the war. For example, 27 percent in the September survey thought that world opinion supported the U.S. war against Iraq (when world opinion opposed the war), 21 percent thought that Iraq had been directly involved in the 9/11 attack (which our government never claimed and President Bush denied at a news conference),[93] and 24 percent thought that the United States had already found Iraqi weapons of mass destruction (when it had not). Respondents who relied on the commercial television networks (Fox, CBS, ABC, CNN, or NBC) held the most misperceptions, with 45 percent of Fox viewers making all three mistakes compared with only about 15 percent for the other networks. Just 9 percent of those who relied on print media erred on all three facts. Broadcast media per se were not to blame, for a scant 4 percent of PBS viewers or listeners to National Public Radio were wrong on all items.[94] Newspapers can display biases too. One study found that newspapers devote more attention to high unemployment when the president's party differs from the papers' partisan endorsement history.[95]

The mere act of choosing to cover some stories while not covering others can also be seen as bias, and in that sense, some degree of bias is inevitable. Those with an optimistic perspective on today's fractured and voluminous media environment maintain that now more than ever, it is possible to find some type of coverage on nearly any topic from nearly any political viewpoint. Such availability puts more pressure on citizens to act as their own editors and learn how to judge whether the information they find is complete and backed up with sufficient evidence.[96] That, however, is a tall order.

Contributions to Democracy

As noted earlier, in a democracy, communication must move in two directions: from government to citizens and from citizens to government. In fact, political communication in the United States mostly goes from government to citizens by passing through the media. The point is important because news reporters tend to be highly critical of politicians; they consider it their job to search for inaccuracies in fact and weaknesses in argument—practicing **watchdog journalism**.[97] Some observers have characterized the news media and the government as adversaries—each mistrusting the other, locked in competition for popular favor while trying to get the record straight. Despite public concerns about the media (see Figure 6.5), recent polling finds that 68 percent of Americans say that the media perform the watchdog function well by preventing public officials from doing things that should not be done.[98]

The mass media transmit information in the opposite direction by reporting citizens' reactions to political events and government actions. The press has traditionally reflected public opinion (and often created it) in the process of defining the news and suggesting courses of government action. But the media's role in reflecting public opinion has become more refined in the information age. Since the 1820s, newspapers conducted straw polls of dubious quality that matched their own partisan inclinations.[99] After commercial polls (such as the Gallup Poll) were established in the 1930s, newspapers began to report more reliable readings of public opinion. By the 1960s, the media began to conduct their own surveys. *The New York Times*, for example, has conducted its own polls at a rate of roughly one poll per month since 2003.[100] Regularly reporting about public opinion is one of the most obvious ways in which the media can tell a story to their consumers—elites and ordinary Americans alike—about what the public believes at any point in time.

Citizens and journalists both complain that heavy reliance on polls during election campaigns causes the media to emphasize the horse race and slights the discussion of issues. But the media also use their polling expertise for other purposes, such as gauging support for going to war and for criminal justice reform. Their net effect has been to generate more accurate knowledge of public opinion and to report that knowledge to public officials as well as to the public. Decades of public opinion research confirm that public opinion often influences policy, a clear indication of government functioning according to the majoritarian model of democracy.[101]

Effects on Freedom, Order, and Equality

The media in the United States have played an important role in advancing equality. Throughout the civil rights movement of the 1950s and 1960s, the media gave national coverage to conflict in the South as black children tried to attend white schools or civil rights workers were beaten and even killed in the effort to register black voters. Partly because of this media coverage, civil rights moved up on the political agenda, and coalitions formed in Congress to pass new laws promoting racial equality. More recently, dramatic video of police using excessive, sometimes deadly, force against African Americans (often coming from witnesses via smartphones) has generated nationwide debates about race relations, criminal justice reform, and police brutality.

Although the media are willing to encourage government action to promote equality at the cost of some personal freedom, journalists resist government attempts to infringe on freedom of the press to promote order.[102] While the public tends to support a free press in theory, public support is not universal and wavers in practice. For example, when asked in 2015 whether the media should be allowed to publish information about "sensitive issues related to national security" or whether the government should be able to prevent publishing such information, a solid majority (59 percent) favored government censorship.[103]

The media's ability to report whatever they wish and whenever they wish certainly erodes efforts to maintain order. For example, sensational media coverage of terrorist

watchdog journalism
Journalism that scrutinizes public and business institutions and publicizes perceived misconduct.

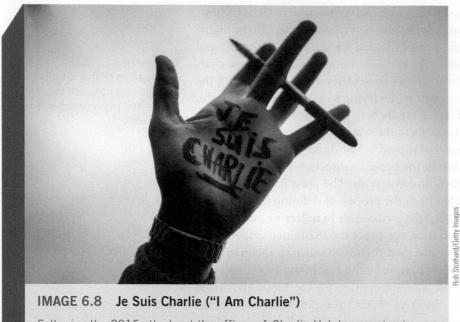

Rob Stothard/Getty Images

IMAGE 6.8   Je Suis Charlie ("I Am Charlie")

Following the 2015 attacks at the offices of *Charlie Hebdo* magazine in Paris, vigils were held around the world in support of a free press, even (or especially) when such freedom threatens order.

acts gives terrorists the publicity they seek, and portrayals of violence on television can encourage copycat crimes. Government officials often criticize media reports about government surveillance programs, charging that coverage of their complex monitoring programs could weaken public and international trust and threaten national security.[104] Freedom of the press is a noble value and one that has been important to democratic government. But we should not ignore the fact that democracies sometimes sacrifice order when they preserve this freedom. In 2015, terrorists attacked the offices of the French satirical newspaper *Charlie Hebdo*. The attackers were allegedly motivated by the magazine's controversial publication of cartoons depicting the prophet Mohammed. Seventeen people were killed as a result of the attack and the subsequent police manhunt.[105] The attack sparked concerns that journalists would be intimidated and led to worldwide debates about the importance of a free press and about whether or when limitations are needed.

Summary

LO1   Trace the evolution of the mass media in the United States and evaluate the impact of new technologies on journalism.

- The mass media transmit information to large, heterogeneous, and widely dispersed audiences through print, broadcasts, and the Internet. The mass media have traditionally been divided into print and broadcast formats, but the rise of digital communications has created a more complicated landscape, rendering this traditional distinction problematic.

LO2   Evaluate the effect of privately owned mass media on the quality of political communication in the United States.

- The mass media in the United States are privately owned and in business to make money, which they do mainly by selling space

or airtime to advertisers. The concern with profit leads both print and electronic media to determine which events are newsworthy on the basis of audience appeal.

LO3   Follow the evolution of government regulation of the media and identify the challenges that new media technologies present to existing regulations.

- The broadcast media operate under technical, ownership, and content regulations imposed by the government. The regulation of media content is minimal and has largely been confined to broadcast media. Comprehensive policy regarding regulation of Internet news has yet to be developed, resulting in clashes between the FCC, Congress, and media corporations.

LO4 Analyze the role of the media in political socialization and the acquisition of political knowledge.

- The main function of the mass media is entertainment, but the media also perform the political functions of reporting news, interpreting news, setting the political agenda, and socializing citizens about politics. Today, gatekeepers (publishers and editors) have less control over what counts as news. Americans get more news from television than from newspapers, and an increasing number of citizens turn to the Internet.
- Despite heavy exposure to news, the ability of most people to retain much political information is low. The media's most important effect on public opinion is in setting the country's political agenda. The media play more subtle, contradictory roles in political socialization, both promoting and undermining certain political and cultural values.

LO5 Assess the impact of the media on democratic values and politics in the United States.

- Reporters from the national media tend to be more liberal than the public while editors and publishers tend to be more conservative.
- From the standpoint of majoritarian democracy, one of the most important roles of the media is to facilitate communication from the people to the government through the reporting of public opinion polls. The media can promote equality, drawing national attention to disadvantaged groups that lack other political resources. They can also disrupt order, spreading information about events that challenge the status quo or that provoke violent reactions.

Chapter Quiz

LO1 Trace the evolution of the mass media in the United States and evaluate the impact of new technologies on journalism.

1. How has the development of the Internet challenged the traditional division between print and broadcast media?
2. Discuss ways in which the mainstream media still matters despite the rise of the Internet, blogs, and social networking as means of transmitting news.

LO2 Evaluate the effect of privately owned mass media on the quality of political communication in the United States.

1. How does the concept of newsworthiness affect the content of the news?
2. List concerns associated with the concentration of media ownership.

LO3 Follow the evolution of government regulation of the media and identify the challenges that new media technologies present to existing regulations.

1. Define the FCC and explain the role it plays in regulating the mass media.
2. What has been the effect of the elimination of the fairness doctrine?

LO4 Analyze the role of the media in political socialization and the acquisition of political knowledge.

1. Which media format is associated with higher levels of political knowledge?
2. What do most scholars believe is the media's greatest influence on politics?

LO5 Assess the impact of the media on democratic values and politics in the United States.

1. Identify the charges behind the claims that the media are liberal and/or that the media are conservative.
2. Discuss whether the media tend to advance order versus equality. What about order versus freedom?

Participation and Voting

Nonvoters have less say in politics than voters, and most young people are nonvoters. U.S. citizens are eligible to vote in elections when they reach eighteen years of age, but only 16 percent between eighteen and twenty-four voted in the 2014 congressional elections.[1] True, 38 percent voted in 2012 when Democrat Barack Obama ran against Republican Mitt Romney, but presidential elections traditionally draw more voters. In 2016, turnout was only 58 percent overall.

Over the twelve previous national elections from 1992 to 2014, the youngest group of citizens averaged only 18 percent voting turnout in six congressional elections. They did double their voting rate to 39 percent in six presidential elections. However, those rates fell far below the comparable averages of 46 percent and 62 percent respectively for all citizens.

The numbers are worse when voting turnout rates for vigorous young citizens from eighteen to twenty-four are compared with creaky old folks over sixty-five. Based on data from just the six elections from 2004 to 2014, citizens over sixty-five voted at a rate of 61 percent in three congressional elections and 71 percent in three presidential elections. In 2016, the youngest group of voters turned out at a rate of 50 percent, substantially below the average of 58 percent.

Simply put, older citizens are more likely to vote than younger citizens. This well-documented trend in political behavior is easily explained. People tend to do things when they understand what they are doing. As people age, their life experiences inform them about politics, and they become more motivated to express their views as citizens.

Let's get personal. The authors of this text—Janda, Berry, Goldman, Schildkraut, and Manna—were in high school during the presidency of George Herbert Walker Bush or even earlier (some of us, much earlier). The sequence of presidential administrations—G.H.W. Bush, Bill Clinton, George W. Bush, and Barack Obama—are fused in our life experiences. We need not memorize their order to keep them straight.

Many readers of our text did not even reach voting age until the Obama administration. To them, earlier presidents are historical figures they only hear about. Young people must learn which parties and politicians proposed and opposed policies on student loans, immigration, economic growth and inequality, Social Security, and other issues in which they are interested. Then too, rules for voting registration tend to frustrate students away at college. Although put off from voting at first, young people inevitably will become informed about politics, register, and increase their turnout rates as they age. Indeed, citizens over sixty-five also had low turnout rates when they were eighteen to twenty-four. Young people, however, are more likely to participate in politics in more unconventional ways.

#ChallengeAccepted

Take the Challenge on MindTap for American Government

Paradoxically, young persons are *more* likely than older people to engage in political protests. How might you explain that?

www.doglikehorse.com/Frotre

Learning Outcomes

LO1 Define political participation and distinguish among types of participation.

LO2 Identify examples of unconventional participation in American history and evaluate their effectiveness.

LO3 Distinguish between supportive acts and influencing acts of political participation.

LO4 Trace the expansion of suffrage in the United States and assess the impact of expanded suffrage on voting turnout.

LO5 Identify the factors that affect political participation, especially voting.

LO6 Evaluate the relationship between the values of freedom, equality, and order and political participation in American democracy.

LO7 Identify the purposes elections serve and explain the relationship between elections and majoritarian and pluralist models of democracy.

In this chapter, we consider various forms of popular participation in politics. We begin by distinguishing between conventional forms of political participation and unconventional forms that still comply with democratic government. Then we evaluate the nature and extent of both types of participation in American politics. Next, we study the expansion of voting rights and voting as the major mechanism for mass participation in politics. Finally, we examine the extent to which the various forms of political participation serve the values of freedom, equality, and order and the majoritarian and pluralist models of democracy.

Democracy and Political Participation

LO1 Define political participation and distinguish among types of participation.

Government ought to be run by the people. That is the democratic ideal in a nutshell. But how much and what kind of citizen participation are necessary for democratic government? Neither political theorists nor politicians, neither idealists nor realists, can agree on an answer. Champions of direct democracy believe that if citizens do not participate directly in government affairs, making government decisions themselves, they should give up all pretense of living in a democracy. More practical observers contend that people can govern indirectly, through their elected representatives. And they maintain that choosing leaders through elections—formal procedures for voting—is the only workable approach to democracy in a large, complex nation.

Elections are a necessary condition of democracy, but they do not guarantee democratic government. Before the collapse of communism, the former Soviet Union regularly held elections in which more than 90 percent of the electorate turned out to vote, but the Soviet Union did not function as a democracy because there was only one political party. Both the majoritarian and pluralist models of democracy rely on voting to varying degrees, but both models expect citizens to participate in politics in other ways. For example, they expect citizens to discuss politics, form interest groups, contact public officials, campaign for political parties, run for office, and even protest government decisions.

We define **political participation** as "those activities of citizens that attempt to influence the structure of government, the selection of government officials, or the policies of government."[2] This definition embraces both conventional and unconventional forms of political participation. In plain language, conventional behavior is behavior that is acceptable to the dominant culture in a given situation. Wearing a swimsuit at the beach in the United States is conventional; wearing one at a formal dance is not. Displaying campaign posters in front yards is conventional; spray-painting political slogans on buildings is not.

Figuring out whether a particular political act is conventional or unconventional can be difficult. We find the following distinction useful:

- **Conventional participation** is a relatively routine behavior that uses the established institutions of representative government, especially campaigning for candidates and voting in elections.
- **Unconventional participation** is a relatively uncommon behavior that challenges or defies established institutions or the dominant culture (and thus is personally stressful to participants and their opponents).

Voting and writing letters to public officials illustrate conventional political participation; staging sit-down strikes in public buildings and chanting slogans outside officials' windows are examples of unconventional participation. Other democratic forms of participation, such as political demonstrations, can be conventional (carrying

political participation
Actions of private citizens by which they seek to influence or support government and politics.

conventional participation
Relatively routine political behavior that uses institutional channels and is acceptable to the dominant culture.

unconventional participation
Relatively uncommon political behavior that challenges or defies established institutions and dominant norms.

signs outside an abortion clinic) or unconventional (linking arms to prevent entrance). Various forms of unconventional participation are often used by powerless groups to gain political benefits while working within the system.[3]

Terrorism is an extreme and problematic case of unconventional political behavior. The U.S. legal code defines **terrorism** as "premeditated, politically motivated violence perpetrated against noncombatant targets by sub-national groups or clandestine agents, usually intended to influence an audience."[4] In 2001, the militant Islamic organization al Qaeda carried out the infamous 9/11 attack on New York and Washington, D.C., killing almost 3,000 Americans and foreign nationals. Since then, terrorist acts of varying severity have occurred across the country. In 2016, a U.S. citizen who pledged loyalty to the Islamic State fired thirteen shots at a policeman driving his car in Philadelphia, hitting him three times but not killing him. Although political goals motivate all acts of terrorism, they do not qualify as political participation because terrorists do not seek to influence government but to destroy it.

Methods of unconventional political behavior, in contrast, are used by disadvantaged groups that resort to them in lieu of more conventional forms of participation used by most citizens. These groups accept government while seeking to influence it. Let us look at both unconventional and conventional political participation in the United States.

terrorism
Premeditated, politically motivated violence perpetrated against noncombatant targets by subnational groups or clandestine agents.

Unconventional Participation

LO2 Identify examples of unconventional participation in American history and evaluate their effectiveness.

On Sunday, March 7, 1965, a group of about six hundred people attempted to march fifty miles from Selma, Alabama, to the state capitol at Montgomery to show their support for voting rights for blacks. (At the time, Selma had fewer than five hundred registered black

IMAGE 7.1   March for Freedom, Fifty Years Later

On Sunday, March 7, 2015, President Barack Obama led marchers, some who had marched fifty years earlier, across the Edmund Pettus Bridge outside Selma, Alabama, to commemorate that "Bloody Sunday" in 1965 when police beat people during a voting rights protest.

voters, out of fifteen thousand eligible.)[5] Alabama governor George Wallace declared the march illegal and sent state troopers to stop it. The two groups met at the Edmund Pettus Bridge over the Alabama River at the edge of Selma. The peaceful marchers were disrupted and beaten by state troopers and deputy sheriffs—some on horseback—using clubs, bullwhips, and tear gas. The day became known as Bloody Sunday.

The march from Selma was a form of unconventional political participation. Marching fifty miles in a political protest is certainly not common; moreover, the march challenged the existing institutions that prevented blacks from voting. But they had been prevented from participating conventionally—voting in elections—for many decades, and they chose this unconventional method to dramatize their cause.

The march ended in violence because Governor Wallace would not allow even this peaceful mode of unconventional expression. The brutal response to the marchers helped the rest of the nation understand the seriousness of the civil rights problem in the South. Unconventional participation is stressful and occasionally violent, but sometimes it is worth the risk. In 2015, hundreds of blacks and whites solemnly but triumphantly reenacted the march on its fiftieth anniversary.

Support for Unconventional Participation

Unconventional political participation has a long history in the United States.[6] The Boston Tea Party of 1773, in which American colonists dumped three cargoes of British tea into Boston Harbor, was only the first in a long line of violent protests against British rule that eventually led to revolution. Yet we know less about unconventional than conventional participation. The reasons are twofold. First, since it is easier to collect data on conventional practices, they are studied more frequently. Second, political scientists are simply biased toward institutionalized, or conventional, politics. In fact, some basic works on political participation explicitly exclude any behavior that is "outside the system."[7] The multinational World Values Survey asked people whether they had engaged in or approved of four types of political participation other than voting: signing petitions, joining boycotts, attending demonstrations, and joining strikes.[8] As shown in Figure 7.1, American respondents regarded only signing petitions as clearly conventional, in the sense that the behavior was widely practiced.

The marchers in Selma, although peaceful, were demonstrating against the established order. If we measure conventional participation according to the proportion of people who disapprove of the act, most demonstrations border on the unconventional, involving relatively few people—often very young people. The same goes for boycotting products—for example, refusing to buy lettuce or grapes picked by nonunion farm workers. Demonstrations and boycotts are problem cases in deciding what is and is not conventional political participation.

The Effectiveness of Unconventional Participation

Vociferous antiabortion protests have discouraged many doctors from performing abortions, but they have not led to outlawing abortions. Does unconventional participation ever work (even when it provokes violence)? Yes. The unconventional activities of civil rights workers produced notable successes. Dr. Martin Luther King, Jr., led the 1955 Montgomery bus boycott (prompted by Rosa Parks's refusal to surrender her seat to a white man), which sparked the civil rights movement. He used **direct action** to challenge specific cases of discrimination, assembling crowds to confront businesses and local governments and demanding equal treatment in public accommodations and government. The civil rights movement organized more than 1,000 such newsworthy demonstrations nationwide—387 in 1965 alone.[9]

direct action
Unconventional participation that involves assembling crowds to confront businesses and local governments to demand a hearing.

FIGURE 7.1 **What Americans Think Is Conventional Political Behavior**

The World Values Survey presented respondents in scores of countries with four forms of political participation outside the electoral process and asked whether they "have done," "might do," or "would never do" any of them. American respondents approved overwhelmingly of signing petitions, which was widely done and rarely ruled out. Even attending demonstrations (a right guaranteed in the Constitution) would "never" be done by 30 percent of Americans. Boycotting products drew similar responses. Joining strikes was more widely rejected.

Source: 2010–2014 World Values Survey. The World Values Survey Association conducts representative surveys in nations across the world. See http://www.worldvaluessurvey.org.

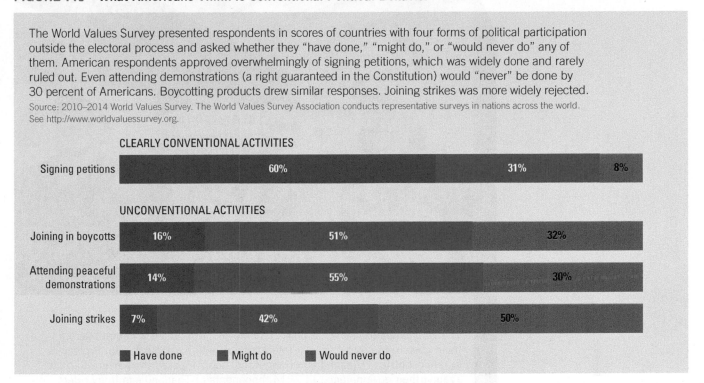

And like the march in Selma, many of these protests provoked violent confrontations between whites and blacks.

Denied the usual opportunities for conventional political participation, minorities used unconventional politics to pressure Congress to pass a series of civil rights laws in 1957, 1960, 1964, and 1968—each one in some way extending national protection against discrimination by reason of race, color, religion, or national origin. (The 1964 act also prohibited discrimination in employment on the basis of sex.)

In addition, the Voting Rights Act of 1965 placed some state electoral procedures under federal supervision, protecting the registration of black voters and increasing their voting rate, especially in the South, where much of the violence occurred. Black protest activity—both violent and nonviolent—has also been credited with increased welfare support for blacks in the South. The civil rights movement showed that social change can occur even when it faces violent opposition at first. In 1970, fewer than fifteen hundred blacks served as elected officials in the United States. In 2006, the number was more than nine thousand, and over five thousand Hispanics held elected office.[10] In 2008, Barack Obama became the first African American to be elected president of the United States.

Although direct political action and the politics of confrontation can work, using them requires a special kind of commitment. Studies show that direct action appeals most to those who both distrust the political system and have a strong sense of political efficacy—the feeling that they can do something to affect political decisions. Whether this combination of attitudes produces behavior that challenges the system depends on the extent of organized group activity. The civil rights movement of the 1960s was backed by numerous organizations across the nation.

The decision to use unconventional behavior also depends on the extent to which individuals develop a group consciousness—identification with their group and awareness of its position in society, its objectives, and its intended course of action. These characteristics were present among blacks and young people in the

IMAGE 7.2 *Hunger Games*-Style Protest in Thailand

The *Hunger Games* series of books and movies introduced a three-fingered hand gesture to protest against totalitarian rule in a mythical land. Protesters in real countries (Thailand and Hong Kong) soon adopted the gesture to protest against their governments. In 2014, opponents of Thailand's military rulers risked arrest by raising three fingers in front of an airport terminal in Bangkok. The salute might look like a conventional act, but it was unconventional in the political context.

mid-1960s and are strongly present today among blacks and, to a lesser degree, among Latinos. Indeed, some researchers contend that black consciousness has heightened both African Americans' distrust of the political system and their sense of individual efficacy, generating more political participation by poor blacks than by poor whites.

Thanks to the Internet, political protests today can pop up spontaneously in the absence of a leader, like Dr. Martin Luther King, Jr.[11] On September 17, 2011, thousands of people swarmed into New York's financial district in response to a tweet from a left-wing Canadian magazine with the hashtag #occupywallstreet to protest corporate greed and wealth inequality. Protesters, mostly under age thirty-four, occupied and reoccupied a park in the district during 2011 and into 2012.[12] Some then created a website, www.occupywallst.org, to "kick the ass of the ruling class" across the world.

Unconventional Participation Around the World

Although most Americans disapprove of using certain forms of participation to protest government policies, the World Values Survey found that U.S. citizens were as inclined to sign petitions, join boycotts, and attend demonstrations as those in Australia, Germany, Japan, the Netherlands, New Zealand, and Spain. Compared with citizens in other democracies, Americans are not noticeably apathetic.

Is something wrong with a political system if citizens resort to unconventional, and often disapproved-of, methods of political participation? To answer this question, we must first learn how much citizens use conventional methods of participation.

Conventional Participation

LO3 Distinguish between supportive acts and influencing acts of political participation.

A practical test of the democratic nature of any government is whether citizens can affect its policies by acting through its institutions—meeting with public officials, supporting candidates, and voting in elections. If people must operate outside government institutions to influence policymaking, as civil rights workers had to do in the South, the system is not democratic. Citizens should not have to risk their life and property to participate in politics, and they should not have to take direct action to force the government to hear their views. The objective of democratic institutions is to make political participation conventional—to allow ordinary citizens to engage in relatively routine, nonthreatening behavior to get the government to heed their opinions, interests, and needs.

It is not unusual in a democracy for a group to gather at a statehouse or city hall to dramatize its position on an issue—say, a tax increase. Such a demonstration is a form of conventional participation. The group is not powerless, and its members are not risking their personal safety by demonstrating. But violence can erupt between opposing groups demonstrating in a political setting, such as between pro-life and pro-choice groups. Circumstances, then, often determine whether organized protest is or is not conventional. In general, the less that the participants anticipate a threat, the more likely it is that the protest will be conventional.

Conventional political behaviors fall into two major categories: actions that show support for government policies and those that try to change or influence policies.

Supportive Behavior

Supportive behavior is action that expresses allegiance to country and government. Reciting the Pledge of Allegiance and flying the American flag on holidays show support for both the country and, by implication, its political system. Such ceremonial activities usually require little effort, knowledge, or personal courage; that is, they demand little initiative on the part of the citizen. The simple act of turning out to vote is in itself a show of support for the political system. Other supportive behaviors, such as serving as an election judge in a nonpartisan election or organizing a holiday parade, demand greater initiative.

> **supportive behavior**
> Action that expresses allegiance to government and country.

At times, people's perception of patriotism moves them to cross the line between conventional and unconventional behavior. In their eagerness to support the American system, they break up a meeting or disrupt a rally of a group they believe is radical or somehow "un-American." Radical groups may threaten the political system with wrenching change, but superpatriots pose their own threat by denying to others the nonviolent means of dissent.

Influencing Behavior

Citizens use **influencing behavior** to modify or even reverse government policy to serve political interests. Some forms of influencing behavior seek particular benefits from government; other forms have broad policy objectives.

> **influencing behavior**
> Behavior that seeks to modify or reverse government policy to serve political interests.

Particular Benefits. Some citizens try to influence government to obtain benefits for themselves, their immediate families, or close friends. For example, citizens might pressure their alderman to rebuild the curbs on their street or to vote against an increase in school taxes, especially if they have no children. Serving one's self-interest through the voting process is certainly acceptable to democratic theory. Each individual has only one vote, and no single voter can wrest particular benefits from government through voting unless a majority of the voters agrees.

Political actions that require considerable knowledge and initiative are another story. Individuals or small groups who influence government officials to advance their self-interest—for instance, to obtain a lucrative government contract—may secretly benefit without others knowing. Those who quietly obtain particular benefits from government pose a serious challenge to a democracy. Pluralist theory holds that groups ought to be able to make government respond to their special problems and needs. In contrast, majoritarian theory holds that government should not do what a majority does not want it to do—if the majority knew what was happening. A majority of citizens might very well not want the government to do what any particular person or group seeks if it is costly to other citizens.

Citizens often ask for special services from local government. Such requests may range from contacting the city forestry department to remove a dead tree in front of a house to calling the county animal control center to deal with a vicious dog in the neighborhood. Studies of such "contacting behavior" find that it tends not to be empirically related to other forms of political activity. In other words, people who complain to city hall do not necessarily vote. Contacting behavior is related to socio-economic status: people of higher socioeconomic status are more likely to contact public officials.

Americans demand much more of their local government than of the national government. Although many people value self-reliance and individualism in national politics, most people expect local government to solve a wide range of social problems. A study of residents of Kansas City, Missouri, found that more than 90 percent thought the city had a responsibility to provide services in thirteen areas, including maintaining parks, setting standards for new home construction, demolishing vacant and unsafe buildings, ensuring that property owners clean up trash and weeds, and providing bus service. The researcher noted that "it is difficult to imagine a set of federal government activities about which there would [be] more consensus."[13] Citizens can also mobilize against a project. Dubbed the "not in my back yard," or NIMBY, phenomenon, such a mobilization occurs when citizens pressure local officials to stop undesired projects from being located near their homes.

Finally, contributing money to a candidate's campaign is another form of influencing behavior. Here, too, the objective can be particular or broad benefits, although determining which is which can sometimes be difficult. Several points emerge from this review of "particularized" forms of political participation. First, approaching government to serve one's particular interests is consistent with democratic theory because it encourages participation from an active citizenry. Second, particularized contact may be a unique form of participation, not necessarily related to other forms of participation such as voting. Third, such participation tends to be used more by citizens who are advantaged in terms of knowledge and resources. Fourth, particularized participation may serve private interests to the detriment of the majority.

Broad Policy Objectives. We come now to what many scholars have in mind when they talk about political participation: activities that influence the selection of government personnel and policies. Here, too, we find behaviors that require little initiative (such as voting) and others that require high initiative (attending political meetings, persuading others how to vote).

Even voting intended to influence government policies is a low-initiative activity. Such "policy voting" differs from voting to show support or to gain special benefits in its broader influence on the community or society. Obviously, this distinction is not sharp: citizens vote for several reasons—a mix of allegiance, particularized benefits, and policy concerns. In addition to policy voting, many other low-initiative forms of conventional participation—wearing a candidate's T-shirt, visiting a party's website, sending tweets for or against candidates—are also connected with elections. In the next section, we focus on elections as a mechanism for participation. For now, we simply note that voting to influence policy is usually a low-initiative activity. As we discuss later, it actually requires more initiative to register to vote in the United States than to vote on election day. It is much easier to e-mail, text, or tweet members of Congress than to vote. Tweeting is so easy that harassed candidates routinely tweeted thanks to volunteers for working on their campaigns. Hillary Clinton gratefully thanked "Students for Hillary" volunteers for their efforts on her behalf.

Other types of participation designed to affect broad policies require high initiative. Running for office requires the most (see Chapter 9). Some high-initiative activities, such as attending party meetings and working on campaigns, are associated with the electoral process; others, such as attending legislative hearings and sending e-mails to Congress, are not. Although many nonelectoral activities involve making personal contact, their objective is often to obtain government benefits for some group of people—farmers, the unemployed, children, oil producers. In fact, studies of citizen contacts in the

Students for Hillary
@Brown_SFH

Our 21 AMAZING volunteers made 947 calls tonight!!! #ImWithHer #603forHRC #FITN #StudentsForHillary http://pbs.twimg.com/media/CabIH2XUAAAlpFY.jpg

Retweeted By HillaryClinton

11:25 PM - 04 Feb 2016

IMAGE 7.3 Twittering Thanks

The morning after Hillary Clinton's February 2016 New Hampshire debate with Senator Bernie Sanders, her campaign retweeted thanks to her volunteers.

Source: Twitter, Inc

United States show that about two-thirds deal with broad social issues and only one-third are for private gain.[14] Few people realize that using the court system is a form of political participation, a way for citizens to press for their rights in a democratic society. Although most people use the courts to serve their particular interests, some also use them, as we discuss shortly, to meet broad objectives. Going to court demands high personal initiative.[15] It also requires knowledge of the law or the financial resources to afford a lawyer.

People use the courts for both personal benefit and broad policy objectives. A person or group can bring a **class action suit** on behalf of other people in similar circumstances. Lawyers for the National Association for the Advancement of Colored People (NAACP) pioneered this form of litigation in the famous school desegregation case *Brown* v. *Board of Education* (1954).[16] They succeeded in getting the Supreme Court to outlaw segregation in public schools, not just for Linda Brown, who brought the suit in Topeka, Kansas, but also for all others "similarly situated"—that is, for all other black students who wanted to attend desegregated schools. Participation through the courts is usually beyond the means of individual citizens, but it has proved effective for organized groups, especially those that have been unable to gain their objectives through Congress or the executive branch. Sometimes such court challenges help citizens without their knowing it. In 2009, Capital One (whose TV slogan is "What's in your

class action suit
A legal action brought by a person or group on behalf of a number of people in similar circumstances.

wallet?") settled a class action suit over its credit cards, agreeing to drop contract language requiring customer disputes to be handled through binding arbitration instead of the legal system.[17]

Individual citizens can also try to influence policies at the national level by participating directly in the legislative process. One way is to attend congressional hearings, which are open to the public and are occasionally held outside Washington, D.C. Especially after World War II, the national government sought to increase citizen involvement in creating regulations and laws by making information on government activities available to interested parties. For example, government agencies were required to publish all proposed and approved regulations in the daily *Federal Register* and to make government documents available to citizens on request.

More recently, the Internet has allowed electronic access to information, allowing citizens to participate in government from their own homes. A comprehensive survey of national government websites reported 1,489 domains and 1,013 websites from 56 agencies.[18] Today, citizens can search the *Federal Register* at www.federalregister.gov.[19] The government website www.USA.gov helps people find information online and offers video tutorials on standard topics. However, the private site www.GovTrack.us provides easier access to congressional voting records than the government site www.Congress.gov. Private sites also monitor more contentious issues. The Center for Responsible Politics at www.OpenSecrets.org covers campaign finance, lobbyists' spending, and other forms of political influence.[20] The National Institute on Money in State Politics covers similar ground for the states.[21] The Center for Effective Government focuses on government spending and the budget deficit, while the Institute for Truth in Accounting lobbies to reduce the national debt.[22] The website of the Center for Responsible Politics at www.OpenSecrets.org makes it easy to obtain data on campaign finance, lobbyists' spending, and other forms of political influence.

voter turnout
The percentage of eligible citizens who actually vote in a given election.

Conventional Participation in America

You may know someone who has testified at a congressional or administrative hearing or who closely monitors governmental actions on the Internet, but the odds are that you do not. Such participation is high-initiative behavior. Relatively few people—only those with high stakes in the outcome of a decision—are willing to participate in this way. How often do Americans contact government officials and engage in other forms of conventional political participation compared with citizens in other countries?

The most common form of political behavior in most industrial democracies is voting for candidates. The rate of voting is known as **voter turnout**, the percentage of eligible voters who actually vote in a given election. Voting eligibility is hard to determine across American states, and there are different ways to estimate voter turnout.[23] However measured, voting for candidates in the United

IMAGE 7.4 Telling Financial Secrets

The Federal Election Commission collects and publishes data on campaign finance and spending, but it is clumsy to use. The private site, OpenSecrets, analyzes and presents the FEC data in a much more usable way.

Source: Center for Responsive Politics

FIGURE 7.2 **Voter Turnout in European and American Elections**

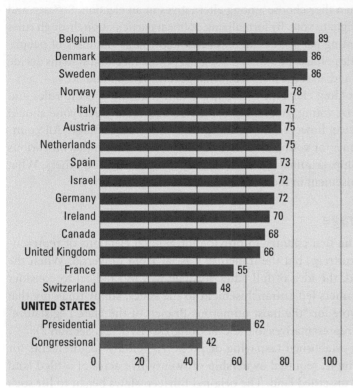

Compared with turnout rates in fifteen established European nations, voter turnout for American presidential elections ranks below all but two countries, and turnout for American congressional elections ranks below all of them. The European data show the percentage of the voting-age population voting in the most recent parliamentary election prior to 2016. The American data show voters as percentages of the eligible voting-age population that voted in the 2012 presidential election and the 2014 congressional election. Turnout in U.S. elections tends to average about twenty points higher in presidential years than in congressional years.

Sources: International IDEA, "Voter Turnout," http://www.idea.int/vt/viewdata .cfm#; and United States Elections Project, http://www.electproject.org/home /voter-turnout/voter-turnout-data.

States is less common than it is in other countries, as demonstrated in Figure 7.2. When voter turnout in the United States is compared with voting in fifteen other countries, the United States ranks at the bottom of the pack. This is a political paradox. On one hand, Americans are as likely as citizens in other democracies to engage in various forms of political participation. But when it comes to voting, the hand that casts the ballot, Americans rank near or at the bottom.

Other researchers noted this paradox and wrote, "If, for example, we concentrate our attention on national elections we will find that the United States is the least participatory of almost all other nations." But looking at the other indicators, they found that "political apathy, by a wide margin, is lowest in the United States. Interestingly, the high levels of overall involvement reflect a rather balanced contribution of both . . . conventional and unconventional politics."[24] Clearly, low voter turnout in the United States constitutes a puzzle, to which we will return.

Participating Through Voting

LO4 Trace the expansion of suffrage in the United States and assess the impact of expanded suffrage on voting turnout.

The heart of democratic government lies in the electoral process. Whether a country holds elections—and if so, what kind—constitutes the critical difference between democratic and nondemocratic governments. Elections institutionalize mass participation in democratic government according to the three normative principles of procedural democracy discussed in Chapter 2: electoral rules specify *who* is allowed to vote, *how much* each person's vote counts, and *how many* votes are needed to win.

suffrage
The right to vote. Also called the *franchise*.

franchise
The right to vote. Also called *suffrage*.

Again, elections are formal procedures for making group decisions. Voting is the act individuals engage in when they choose among alternatives in an election. **Suffrage** and **franchise** both mean the right to vote. By formalizing political participation through rules for suffrage and for counting ballots, electoral systems allow large numbers of people, who individually have little political power, to wield great power. Electoral systems decide collectively who governs and, in some instances, what government should do.

The simple act of holding elections is less important than the specific rules and circumstances that govern voting. According to democratic theory, everyone should be able to vote. In practice, however, no nation grants universal suffrage. All countries have age requirements for voting, and all disqualify some inhabitants on various grounds: lack of citizenship, criminal record, mental incompetence, and others. What is the record of enfranchisement in the United States?

Expansion of Suffrage

The United States was the first country to provide for general elections of representatives through "mass" suffrage, but the franchise was far from universal. When the Constitution was framed, the idea of full adult suffrage was too radical to consider seriously. Instead, the framers left enfranchisement to the states, stipulating only that individuals who could vote for "the most numerous Branch of the State Legislature" could also vote for their representatives to the U.S. Congress (Article I, Section 2).

Initially, most states established taxpaying or property-holding requirements for voting. Virginia, for example, required ownership of twenty-five acres of settled land or five hundred acres of unsettled land. The original thirteen states began to lift such requirements after 1800. Expansion of the franchise accelerated after 1815, with the admission of new "western" states (Indiana, Illinois, Alabama), where land was more plentiful and widely owned. By the 1850s, the states had eliminated almost all taxpaying and property-holding requirements, thus allowing the working class—at least its white male members—to vote. Extending the vote to blacks and women took longer.

The Enfranchisement of Blacks. The Fifteenth Amendment, adopted shortly after the Civil War, prohibited the states from denying the right to vote "on account of race, color, or previous condition of servitude." However, the states of the old Confederacy worked around the amendment by reestablishing old voting requirements (poll taxes, literacy tests) that worked primarily against blacks. Some southern states also cut blacks out of politics through a cunning circumvention of the amendment. Because the amendment said nothing about voting rights in private organizations, these states denied blacks the right to vote in the "private" Democratic primary elections held to choose the party's candidates for the general election. Because the Democratic Party came to dominate politics in the South, the "white primary" effectively disenfranchised blacks, despite the Fifteenth Amendment. Finally, in many areas of the South, the threat of violence kept blacks from the polls.

The extension of full voting rights to blacks came in two phases, separated by twenty years. In 1944, the Court decided in *Smith* v. *Allwright* that laws preventing blacks from voting in primary elections were unconstitutional, holding that party primaries are part of the continuous process of electing public officials.[25] The Voting Rights Act of 1965, which followed Selma's Bloody Sunday by less than five months, suspended discriminatory voting tests. It also authorized federal registrars to register voters in seven southern states, where less than half of the voting-age population had registered to vote in the 1964 election. For good measure, the Supreme Court ruled in 1966 in *Harper* v. *Virginia State Board of Elections* that state poll taxes are unconstitutional.[26] Although long in coming, these actions by the national government to enforce political equality in the states dramatically increased the registration of southern blacks (see Figure 7.3).

Acknowledging that the Voting Rights Act had dramatically changed voting patterns in the South, the Supreme Court voted 5–4 in 2013 to strike down a key part of

FIGURE 7.3   Voter Registration in the South, 1960, 1980, 2000, and 2008

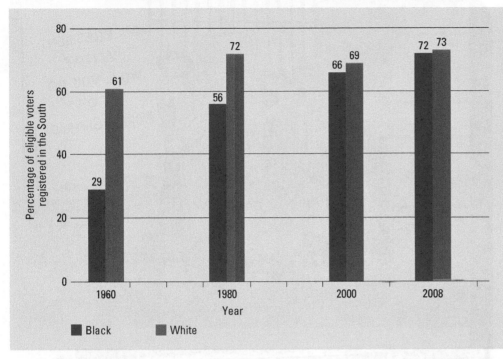

As a result of the Voting Rights Act of 1965 and other national actions, black voter registration in the eleven states of the old Confederacy nearly doubled between 1960 and 1980. By 2008, there was very little difference between the voting registration rates of white and black southern voters.

Sources: Data for 1960 and 1980 are from U.S. Bureau of the Census, *Statistical Abstract of the United States, 1982–1983* (Washington, DC: U.S. Government Printing Office, 1983), p. 488; data for 2000 and 2008 come from the U.S. Census Bureau, *Current Population Reports,* P20, Table 3.

the 1965 Voting Rights Act requiring nine southern states to get national approval to change their election laws. That decision permitted some states to enforce new voter identification laws, which Washington had previously blocked.

The Enfranchisement of Women. The enfranchisement of women in the United States is a less sordid story than enfranchisement of blacks but still nothing to be proud of. Women had to fight long and hard to win the right to vote. Until 1869, women could not vote anywhere in the world.[27] American women began to organize to obtain suffrage in the mid-1800s. Known then as suffragettes, the early feminists initially had a limited effect on politics.* Their first major victory did not come until 1869, when Wyoming, still a territory, granted women the right to vote. No state followed suit until 1893, when Colorado enfranchised women.

In the meantime, the suffragettes became more active. In 1884, they formed the Equal Rights Party and nominated Belva A. Lockwood, a lawyer (who could not herself vote), as the first female candidate for president.[28] Between 1896 and 1918, twelve other states gave women the vote. Most of these states were in the West, where pioneer women often departed from traditional women's roles. Nationally, the women's suffrage movement intensified, often resorting to unconventional political behaviors (marches, demonstrations), which occasionally led to violent attacks from men and even other women. In 1919, Congress finally passed the Nineteenth Amendment, which prohibits states from denying the right to vote "on account of sex." The amendment was ratified in 1920, in time for the November election. A survey of Chicago voters in 1923 found that 75 percent of the men voted in the presidential election but only 46 percent of the women. Among women nonvoters, 11 percent cited "disbelief in woman's voting"; less than 2 percent cited "objection from husband."[29]

Evaluating the Expansion of Suffrage in America. The last major expansion of suffrage in the United States took place in 1971, when the Twenty-sixth Amendment lowered the voting age to eighteen. For most of its history, the United States has been

---

*The term *suffragist* applied to a person of either sex who advocated extending the vote to women, while *suffragette* was reserved for women who did so militantly.

IMAGE 7.5   The Fight for Women's Suffrage . . . and Against It

Militant suffragettes demonstrated outside the White House prior to ratification of the Nineteenth Amendment to the Constitution, which gave women the right to vote. Congress passed the proposed amendment in 1919, and it was ratified by the required number of states in time for the 1920 presidential election. Suffragettes' demonstrations were occasionally disrupted by men—and other women—who opposed extending the right to vote to women.

far from the democratic ideal of universal suffrage. The United States initially restricted voting rights to white male taxpayers or property owners, and wealth requirements lasted until the 1850s. Through demonstrations and a constitutional amendment, women won the franchise only two decades before World War II. Through civil war, constitutional amendments, court actions, massive demonstrations, and congressional action, blacks finally achieved full voting rights only two decades after World War II. Our record has more than a few blemishes.

But compared with other countries, the United States looks pretty democratic.[30] Women did not gain the vote on equal terms with men until 1921 in Norway; 1922 in the Netherlands; 1944 in France; 1946 in Italy, Japan, and Venezuela; 1948 in Belgium; and 1971 in Switzerland. Women are still not universally enfranchised. Among the Arab monarchies, Kuwait granted full voting rights to women in 2005. In 2011, Saudi Arabia finally announced that women could vote in municipal elections—beginning in 2015. Although severely restricted in public speaking and campaigning, Saudi women won 20 seats on local councils—out of over 2,000 contested but still more than expected.

Of course, no one at all can vote in the United Arab Emirates. In South Africa, blacks, who outnumber whites by more than four to one, were not allowed to vote freely in elections until 1994. With regard to voting age, about 85 percent of the world's countries allow eighteen-year-olds to vote. About fifteen countries set the minimum age at twenty or twenty-one. Fewer than ten allow persons under age eighteen to vote—including Austria, which allows voting at sixteen.[31]

When judged against the rest of the world, the United States, which originated mass participation in government through elections, has as good a record of providing for political equality in voting rights as other democracies and a better record than many others.

Voting on Policies

Disenfranchised groups have struggled to gain voting rights because of the political power that comes with suffrage. Belief in the ability of ordinary citizens to make political decisions and to control government through the power of the ballot box was strongest in the United States during the Progressive era, which began around 1900 and lasted until about 1925. **Progressivism** was a philosophy of political reform that trusted the goodness and wisdom of individual citizens and distrusted "special interests" (railroads, corporations) and political institutions (traditional political parties, legislatures).

The leaders of the Progressive movement were prominent politicians (former president Theodore Roosevelt, Senator Robert La Follette of Wisconsin) and eminent scholars (historian Frederick Jackson Turner, philosopher John Dewey). Not content to vote for candidates chosen by party leaders, the Progressives championed the **direct primary**—a preliminary election, run by the state governments, in which the voters choose the party's candidates for the general election. Wanting a mechanism to remove elected candidates from office, the Progressives backed the **recall**, a special election initiated by a petition signed by a specified number of voters. Although about twenty states provide for recall elections, this device is rarely used. Only a few statewide elected officials have actually been unseated through recall. Indeed, only one state governor had ever been unseated until 2003, when California voters threw out Governor Gray Davis in a bizarre recall election that placed movie actor Arnold Schwarzenegger in the governor's mansion. In 2012, Wisconsin voters also sought to recall Republican governor Scott Walker but failed.

The Progressives also championed the power of the masses to propose and pass laws, approximating citizen participation in policymaking that is the hallmark of direct democracy.[32] They developed two voting mechanisms for policymaking that are still in use:

- A **referendum** is a direct vote by the people on either a proposed law or an amendment to a state constitution. The measures subject to popular vote are known as

progressivism
A philosophy of political reform based on the goodness and wisdom of the individual citizen as opposed to special interests and political institutions.

direct primary
A preliminary election, run by the state government, in which the voters choose each party's candidates for the general election.

recall
The process for removing an elected official from office.

referendum
An election on a policy issue.

initiative
A procedure by which voters can propose an issue to be decided by the legislature or by the people in a referendum. It requires gathering a specified number of signatures and submitting a petition to a designated agency.

propositions. Twenty-four states permit popular referenda on laws, and all but Delaware require a referendum for a constitutional amendment. Most referenda are placed on the ballot by legislatures, not voters.

• The initiative is a procedure by which voters can propose a measure to be decided by the legislature or by the people in a referendum. The procedure involves gathering a specified number of signatures from registered voters (usually 5 to 10 percent of the total in the state) and then submitting the petition to a designated state agency. Twenty-four states provide for some form of voter initiative.

Figure 7.4 shows the West's affinity for these democratic mechanisms. In 2014, voters in forty-one states decided on 146 ballot propositions, most placed there by state legislatures, not citizen initiatives.[33] Voters approved most propositions, including ones in Alaska, Oregon, and Washington D.C., on legalizing the recreational use

FIGURE 7.4   Westward Ho!

This map shows quite clearly the western basis of the initiative, referendum, and recall mechanisms intended to place government power directly in the hands of the people. Advocates of "direct legislation" sought to bypass entrenched powers in state legislatures. Established groups and parties in the East dismissed them as radicals and cranks, but they gained the support of farmers and miners in the Midwest and West. The Progressive forces usually aligned with Democrats in western state legislatures to enact their proposals, often against Republican opposition.

Source: Initiative & Referendum Institute at http://iandrinstitute.org/statewide_i%26r.htm.

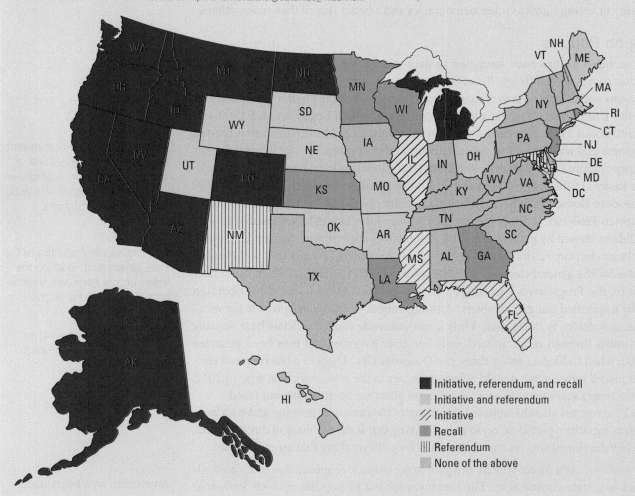

Legend:
- ■ Initiative, referendum, and recall
- ▨ Initiative and referendum
- ⫽ Initiative
- ▦ Recall
- ⦀ Referendum
- ▢ None of the above

of marijuana. In the off-year election of 2015, only nine states voted on twenty-two propositions.[34] Most were approved, but Ohio voters rejected one that permitted recreational use of marijuana.

What conclusion can we draw about the Progressives' legacy of mechanisms for direct participation in government? One seasoned journalist paints an unimpressive picture. He notes that an expensive "industry" developed in the 1980s that makes money circulating petitions and then managing the large sums of money needed to run a campaign to approve (or defeat) a referendum. In 1998, opponents of a measure to allow casino gambling on Native American land in California spent $25.8 million. This huge sum, however, paled in comparison to the $66.2 million spent during the campaign by the tribes that supported the measure. The initiative passed.[35]

Clearly, citizens can exercise great power over government policy through the mechanisms of the initiative and the referendum. What is not clear is whether these forms of direct democracy improve on the policies made by elected representatives.[36] However, recent research has shown that—especially in midterm elections, which are characterized by low turnout—ballot measures tend to increase voting turnout, knowledge of issues, and campaign contributions to interest groups.[37]

If the Internet had been around during their era, Progressives certainly would have endorsed it as a mechanism of direct democracy. At an elementary level, the Internet allows ordinary citizens who seek to initiate legislation to collect on petitions the thousands of signatures needed to place the proposal on the ballot. Pioneering websites, such as www.iSolon.org, aim at "exploring and advancing opportunities for democratic reform brought about by new information technologies," and the Brookings Institution proposes ways that social media can improve citizen engagement in political campaigns and invigorate American democracy.[38] Finally, there have been attempts to implement "deliberative democracy," which involves thorough deliberation of policy options (often involving the Internet) by a random sample of citizens who then propose legislation for adoption in a referendum.[39]

tanuha2001/Shutterstock.com

IMAGE 7.6   So Many Icons, So Little Time

The Internet offers a mind-boggling array of ways to share information on the Internet. The thirty-six icons above are just a sample of the available methods on social media. How many have you used to communicate with your friends? How many have you used to receive or share *political* news?

Voting for Candidates

We have saved for last the most visible form of political participation: voting to choose candidates for public office. Voting for candidates serves democratic government in two ways. First, citizens can choose the candidates they think will best serve their interests. If citizens choose candidates who are "like themselves" in personal traits or party affiliation, elected officials should tend to think as their constituents do on political issues and automatically reflect the majority's views when making public policy.

Second, voting allows the people to reelect the officials they guessed right about and to kick out those they guessed wrong about. This function is very different from the first. It makes public officials accountable for their behavior through the reward-and-punishment mechanism of elections. It assumes that officeholders are motivated to respond to public opinion by the threat of electoral defeat. It also assumes that the voters know what politicians are doing while they are in office and participate actively in the electoral process. We look at the factors that underlie voting choice in Chapter 9. Here, we examine Americans' reliance on the electoral process.

In national politics, voters seem content to elect just two executive officers—the president and vice president—and to trust the president to appoint a cabinet to round out his administration. But at the state and local levels, voters insist on selecting all kinds of officials. Every state elects a governor (and forty-three elect a lieutenant governor). Forty-four elect an attorney general; thirty-seven, a treasurer; and thirty-five, a secretary of state. The list goes on, down through superintendents of schools, secretaries of agriculture, comptrollers, boards of education, and public utilities commissioners. Elected county officials commonly include commissioners, a sheriff, a treasurer, a clerk, a superintendent of schools, and a judge (often several). At the local level, voters elect all but about 600 of 15,300 school boards across the nation.[40] Instead of trusting state and local chief executives to appoint lesser administrators (as we do for more important offices at the national level), we expect voters to choose intelligently among scores of candidates they meet for the first time on a complex ballot in the polling booth.

Around the world, the percentage of countries holding regular, free, and fair elections has risen to 63 percent (see "Electoral Democracy in Global Politics"). However, the criteria for being an electoral democracy are low; witness that Turkey qualified in 2014. In the American version of democracy, our laws recognize no limit to voters' ability to make informed choices among candidates and thus to control government through voting. The reasoning seems to be that elections are good; therefore, more elections are better, and the most elections are best. By this thinking, the United States clearly has the best and most democratic government in the world because it is the undisputed champion at holding elections. The author of a study that compared elections in the United States with elections in twenty-six other democracies concluded:

> No country can approach the United States in the frequency and variety of elections, and thus in the amount of electoral participation to which its citizens have a right. No other country elects its lower house as often as every two years, or its president as frequently as every four years. No other country popularly elects its state governors and town mayors; no other has as wide a variety of nonrepresentative offices (judges, sheriffs, attorneys general, city treasurers, and so on) subject to election. . . . The average American is entitled to do far more electing—probably by a factor of three or four—than the citizen of any other democracy.[41]

However, we learned from Figure 7.2 that the United States ranks at the bottom of fifteen European countries in voter turnout in national elections. How do we square low voter turnout with Americans' devotion to elections as an instrument of democratic government? To complicate matters further, how do we square low voter turnout with the fact that Americans seem to participate in politics in various other ways?

Electoral Democracy in Global Politics

Nations are "electoral democracies" if they have (1) a competitive, multiparty system; (2) universal adult suffrage; (3) regularly contested free elections; and (4) free election campaigns—according to Freedom House. The Washington-based organization has scored nations over the last four decades, during which the spread of electoral democracies can be analyzed in three stages: (1) the period from 1974 to 1989 depicts a "third wave" of democratization caused by social modernization and international influences (the other two waves were in 1828–1926 and 1943–1962); (2) the boom from 1989 to 1994 was sparked by the collapse of communism; and (3) a plateau was reached after 1995.

Growth in Countries and Electoral Democracies, 1973–2014

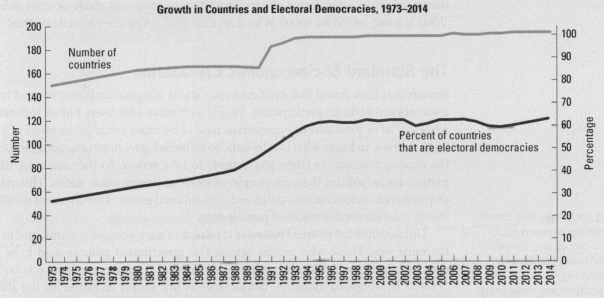

Sources: Larry Diamond, *The Spirit of Democracy* (New York: Times Books, 2008), p. 22 and Appendix, Table 2. Freedom House supplied data after 2007. See https://freedomhouse.org/sites/default/files/ListofElectoralDemocraciesFIW1989-2015.xls.

CRITICAL THINKING The proportion of electoral democracies appears to have "maxed out" below two-thirds of the world's nations. Why?

Explaining Political Participation

LO5 Identify the factors that affect political participation, especially voting.

As explained, political participation can be unconventional or conventional, can require little or much initiative, and can serve to support the government or influence its decisions. Researchers have found that people who take part in some form of political behavior often do not take part in others. For example, citizens who contact public officials to obtain special benefits may not vote regularly, participate in campaigns, or even contact officials about broader social issues. In fact, because particularized contacting serves individual rather than public interests, it is not even considered political behavior by some people.

This section examines some factors that affect the more obvious forms of political participation, with particular emphasis on voting. The first task is to determine how much patterns of participation vary within the United States over time.

FIGURE 7.6   The Decline of Voter Turnout: An Unsolved Puzzle

Education strongly predicts the likelihood of voting in the United States. The percentage of adult citizens with a high school education or more has grown steadily since the end of World War II, but the overall rate of voter turnout trended downward from 1960 to 1996 and is still below the levels two decades after the war. Why turnout decreased as education increased is an unsolved puzzle in American voting behavior.

Sources: U.S. Census Bureau, "Educational Attainment in the United States," at http://www.census.gov/hhes/socdemo/education/data/cps/2014/tables.html; Harold W. Stanley and Richard G. Niemi, *Vital Statistics on American Politics, 2009–2010* (Washington, DC: CQ Press, 2009), Table 1.1; and The United States Election Project at http://www.electproject.org/. Since 2000, the percentage voting in elections is based on the eligible voter population, not the voting-age population.

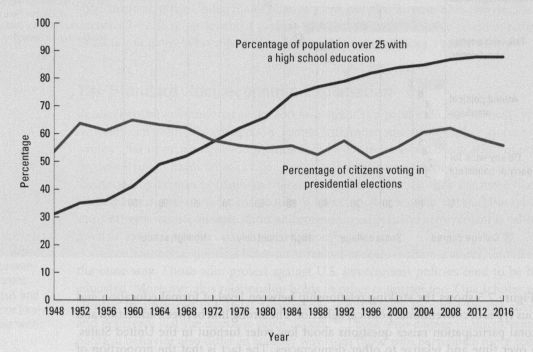

eighteen-year-olds accounts for about one or two percentage points in the total decline in turnout since 1952. Nevertheless, that still leaves more than ten percentage points to be explained in the lower rates since 1972.[54]

Voter turnout has declined in most established democracies since the 1980s, but not as much as in the United States. Given that educational levels are increasing virtually everywhere, the puzzle is why turnout has decreased instead of increased. Many researchers have tried to solve this puzzle. Some attribute most of the decline to changes in voters' attitudes toward politics: beliefs that government is no longer responsive to citizens, that politicians are too packaged, that campaigns are too long.[55] Another is a change in attitude toward political parties, along with a decline in the extent to which citizens identify with a political party (a topic we discuss in Chapter 8).[56] According to these psychological explanations, voter turnout in the United States is not likely to increase until the government does something to restore people's faith in the effectiveness of voting—with or without political parties.

According to the age explanation, turnout in the United States is destined to remain a percentage point or two below its highs of the 1960s because of the lower voting rate of citizens younger than twenty-one. Turnout rates do increase as young people age, which suggests that voting is habit forming.[57] In 2004, almost 49 percent of those eighteen to twenty-nine years old turned out to vote.[58] In 2008, the Obama campaign made a special appeal to young voters, and youth voter turnout increased to 52 percent.[59] Young people actually voted about one point more in 2012 although the overall turnout declined—as it did in 2016.

U.S. Turnout versus Turnout in Other Countries. Scholars cite two factors to explain the low voter turnout in the United States compared with that in other countries. First are the differences in voting laws and administrative machinery. In a few countries, voting is compulsory, and obviously turnout is extremely high. But other methods can encourage voting: declaring election days to be public holidays or providing a two-day voting period. In 1845, Congress set election day for the first Tuesday after the first Monday in November, but a reform group—called Why Tuesday?—wants Congress to change election day to a weekend.[60]

Furthermore, nearly every other democratic country places the burden of registration on the government rather than on the individual voter. This is important. Voting in the United States is a two-stage process, and the first stage (going to the proper officials to register) usually requires more initiative than the second stage (going to the polling booth to cast a ballot). In most American states, the registration process has been separate from the voting process in terms of both time (usually voters had to register weeks in advance of an election) and geography (often voters had to register at the county courthouse, not their polling place). The eleven states that do allow citizens to register and vote on the same day have consistently higher voter participation rates.[61] Turnout is higher in Oregon, where everyone votes by mail.[62] No state votes by Internet, yet. In 2009, the city of Honolulu claimed to hold the first all-digital election—voting online or by phone—but it involved only about 115,000 voters.[63]

Regardless of voting ease, voting registration procedures often are obscure, requiring potential voters to call around to find out what to do. People who move (and younger people move more frequently) have to reregister. In short, although voting requires little initiative, registration usually has required high initiative. If we compute voter turnout on the basis of those who are registered to vote, about 80 percent of Americans vote, a figure that moves the United States to the middle (but not the top) of all democratic nations.

Besides burdensome registration procedures, another factor usually cited to explain low turnout in American elections is the lack of political parties that mobilize the vote of particular social groups, especially lower-income and less educated people. American parties do make an effort to get out the vote, but neither party is as closely linked to specific groups as are parties in many other countries, where certain parties work hand in hand with specific ethnic, occupational, or religious groups. Research shows that strong party–group links can significantly increase turnout.[64] One important study claims that "changing mobilization patterns by parties, campaigns, and social movements accounts for at least half of the decline in electoral participation since the 1960s."[65]

Other research suggests that although well-funded, vigorous campaigns mobilize citizens to vote, the effect depends on the type of citizens, the nature of the election, and (yes) the weather.[66] Highly educated, low-income citizens are more likely to be stimulated to vote than are less educated, high-income citizens, but lower-class citizens can be more easily mobilized to vote in presidential elections than in non-presidential elections.[67] Some thought that the Internet would invite new classes of people to participate in politics, but well-educated and high income people are even more apt to participate online.[68] Citizens are more likely to turn out to vote when the elections are competitive or close.[69] One study observed that college students' decision to register and vote in their home state or in their college state depended in part on which had the more competitive races.[70]

To these explanations for low voter turnout in the United States—the traditional burden of registration and the lack of strong party–group links—we add another. Although the act of voting requires low initiative, the process of learning about the scores of candidates on the ballot in American elections requires a great deal of initiative. Some people undoubtedly fail to vote simply because they feel inadequate to the task of deciding among candidates for the many offices on the ballot in U.S. elections.

Teachers, newspaper columnists, and public affairs groups tend to worry a great deal about low voter turnout in the United States, suggesting that it signifies some sort of political sickness—or at least that it gives us a bad mark for democracy. Some others who study elections closely seem less concerned. One scholar argues:

> Turnout rates do not indicate the amount of electing—the frequency . . . the range of offices and decisions, the "value" of the vote—to which a country's citizens are entitled.... Thus, although the turnout rate in the United States is below that of most other democracies, American citizens do not necessarily do less voting than other citizens; most probably, they do more.[71]

Despite such words of assurance, the nagging thought remains that turnout ought to be higher, so various organizations mount get-out-the-vote campaigns before elections. Civic leaders often back the campaigns because they value voting for its contribution to political order.

Participation and Freedom, Equality, and Order

LO6 Evaluate the relationship between the values of freedom, equality, and order and political participation in American democracy.

As we have seen, Americans do participate in government in various ways and to a reasonable extent, compared with citizens of other countries. What is the relationship of political participation to the values of freedom, equality, and order?

Participation and Freedom

From the standpoint of normative theory, the relationship between participation and freedom is clear. Individuals should be free to participate in government and politics in the way they want and as much as they want. And they should be free not to participate as well. Ideally, all barriers to participation (such as restrictive voting registration and limitations on campaign expenditures) should be abolished, as should any schemes for compulsory voting. According to the normative perspective, we should not worry about low voter turnout because citizens should have the freedom not to vote as well as to vote.

In theory, freedom to participate also means that individuals should be able to use their wealth, connections, knowledge, organizational power (including sheer numbers in organized protests), or any other resource to influence government decisions, provided they do so legally. Of all these resources, the individual vote may be the weakest—and the least important—means of exerting political influence. Obviously, then, freedom as a value in political participation favors those with the resources to advance their own political self-interest.

Participation and Equality

The relationship between participation and equality is also clear. Each citizen's ability to influence government should be equal to that of every other citizen, so that differences in personal resources do not work against the poor or the otherwise disadvantaged.[72]

Elections, then, serve the ideal of equality better than any other means of political participation. Formal rules for counting ballots—in particular, one person, one vote—cancel differences in resources among individuals.

At the same time, groups of people who have few resources individually can combine their votes to wield political power. Various European ethnic groups exercised this type of power in the late nineteenth and early twentieth centuries, when their votes won them entry to the sociopolitical system and allowed them to share in its benefits. More recently, blacks, Hispanics, homosexuals, and those with disabilities have used their voting power to gain political recognition. However, minorities often have had to use unconventional forms of participation to win the right to vote. As two major scholars of political participation put it, "Protest is the great equalizer, the political action that weights intensity as well as sheer numbers."[73]

Participation and Order

The relationship between participation and order is complicated. Some types of participation (pledging allegiance, voting) promote order and so are encouraged by those who value order; other types promote disorder and so are discouraged. Many citizens—men and women alike—even resisted giving women the right to vote for fear of upsetting the social order by altering the traditional roles of men and women.

Both conventional and unconventional participation can lead to the ouster of government officials, but the regime—the political system itself—is threatened more by unconventional participation. To maintain order, the government has a stake in converting unconventional participation to conventional participation whenever possible. We can easily imagine this tactic being used by authoritarian governments, but democratic governments also use it. After September 11, 2001, the FBI not only increased surveillance of groups with suspected ties to foreign terrorists but also began monitoring other groups that protested public policies.[74]

Popular protests can spread beyond original targets. Think about student unrest on college campuses during the Vietnam War. In private and public colleges alike, thousands of students stopped traffic, occupied buildings, destroyed property, boycotted classes, disrupted lectures, staged guerrilla theater, and behaved in other unconventional ways to protest the war, racism, capitalism, the behavior of their college presidents, the president of the United States, the military establishment, and all other institutions. (We are not exaggerating here. Students did such things at our home universities after members of the National Guard shot and killed four students at a demonstration at Kent State University in Ohio on May 4, 1970.)

Confronted by civil strife and disorder in the nation's institutions of higher learning, Congress took action. On March 23, 1971, it enacted and sent to the states the proposed Twenty-sixth Amendment, lowering the voting age to eighteen. Three-quarters of the state legislatures had to ratify the amendment before it became part of the Constitution. Astonishingly, thirty-eight states (the required number) complied by July 1, establishing a new speed record for ratification and cutting the old record nearly in half.[75] (Ironically, voting rights were not high on the list of students' demands.)

Testimony by members of Congress before the Judiciary Committee stated that the eighteen-year-old vote would "harness the energy of young people and direct it into useful and constructive channels," to keep students from becoming "more militant" and engaging "in destructive activities of a dangerous nature."[76] As one observer argued, the right to vote was extended to eighteen-year-olds not because young people demanded it but because "public officials believed suffrage expansion to be a means of institutionalizing youths' participation in politics, which would, in turn, curb disorder."[77]

Freedom, Order, or Equality and Secession

Pro-Russian and Pro-Ukrainian Views on the 2014 Referendum

Do citizens in a region have the right to secede from a nation? Most Americans support President Abraham Lincoln for fighting the Civil War "to save the Union."* By placing the nation's territorial integrity above southern citizens' desire to determine their future, Lincoln valued political order above freedom. Some fifty years later, Woodrow Wilson reversed presidential priorities. By proposing that the 1918 World War I peace treaty provide for self-determination of peoples, Wilson chose freedom over order. The treaty created new nations from subject peoples, and Wilson's principle of self-determination became incorporated into the United Nations Charter.

The freedom versus order conflict was revisited in March 2014, after a popular revolt in Ukraine ousted its corrupt and pro-Russian president. That infuriated Russian President Vladimir Putin and the Russian-speaking majority in Ukraine's Crimean peninsula, home of Russia's Black Sea fleet. Putin sent additional troops to Crimea, which hastily organized a referendum on joining Russia. Ethnic minorities boycotted the vote, but over 90 percent of those who voted chose to join Russia. President Barack Obama opposed the referendum, arguing for Ukrainian territorial integrity (consistent with President Lincoln). President Putin backed the vote, claiming self-determination (consistent with President Wilson).

In 2008, ironically, the American and Russian arguments had been reversed. The majority Albanian population in the Serbian province of Kosovo had revolted against Serbian rule. NATO bombed Serbian forces to stop killings of Albanians. With NATO peace-keeping forces on its ground, Kosovo's parliament voted for independence from Serbia. The United States and most European nations quickly recognized Kosovo as a new nation. Russia and most Slavic nations did not—and still do not. Today, the United States and the European Union do not recognize Crimea as part of Russia.

VIKTOR DRACHEV/Getty Images

*"My paramount object in this struggle *is* to save the Union, and is *not* either to save or to destroy slavery." From Abraham Lincoln's 22 August 1862, letter to Horace Greeley, at http://www.abrahamlincolnonline.org /lincoln/speeches/greeley.htm.

CRITICAL THINKING Two famous American presidents took opposing positions on citizens' rights to self-determination. Were both correct?

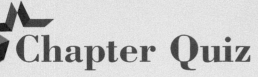

Chapter Quiz

LO1 **Define political participation and distinguish among types of participation.**

1. What distinguishes conventional from unconventional political participation?
2. Is terrorism a form of political participation?

LO2 **Identify examples of unconventional participation in American history and evaluate their effectiveness.**

1. Does unconventional political participation produce results? Give a historical example both ways.
2. Are Americans more or less likely than Europeans to engage in unconventional participation?

LO3 **Distinguish between supportive acts and influencing acts of political participation.**

1. Cite an example of supportive political behavior and an example of influencing political behavior.
2. How can suing in court constitute a form of political behavior?

LO4 **Trace the expansion of suffrage in the United States and assess the impact of expanded suffrage on voting turnout.**

1. Compare the expansion of suffrage in the United States with that in most other democracies.
2. Compare voter turnout in the United States with turnout in other Western democracies.

LO5 **Identify the factors that affect political participation, especially voting.**

1. What is meant by the "standard socioeconomic model" for explaining political participation? Compared with the level of education in the United States, has voting turnout fulfilled the standard socioeconomic model?
2. Which requires more citizen initiative, to register to vote or to vote itself? Why, and why does it matter?

LO6 **Evaluate the relationship between the values of freedom, equality, and order and political participation in American democracy.**

1. Which value—freedom, equality, or order—is best served by voting as a form of participation and why?
2. How can political participation both serve and undermine order?

LO7 **Identify the purposes elections serve and explain the relationship between elections and majoritarian and pluralist models of democracy.**

1. What purposes are served by elections other than selecting candidates or deciding issues?
2. Which model of democracy—majoritarian or pluralist—is better served by elections and why?

8 Political Parties

Do you think that the United States needs another major political party? Most Americans do. In periodic Gallup polls since 2007, a plurality of respondents has agreed that the Republican and Democratic parties "do such a poor job that a third major party is needed."[1]

Beginning in 1796—when John Adams, the Federalist candidate for president, defeated Thomas Jefferson, the Democratic Republican candidate—United States national politics has revolved around two major political parties. The present two-party system began in 1856, when a new Republican Party challenged the governing Democratic Party. Throughout its history, only two major parties have alternated in controlling government. Meanwhile, the United States sustained democracy for 220 years, longer than any other.

Few democracies have two-party systems. Britain's elections were once dominated by the Conservative and Labour parties, but both parties won only two-thirds of the vote in the 2015 parliamentary election. Canada's elections once hinged on votes for the Conservative and Liberal parties, but they accounted for less than 72 percent of the ballots cast for parliament in 2015. Indeed, party voting has fragmented all over Europe in recent decades, as multiple issue-oriented and social protest parties have provoked government instability.[2]

In the United States, however, 95 percent of the voters in 2016 cast their ballots for either the Democratic or Republican presidential candidates, and 95 percent chose either Democratic or Republican congressional candidates. In both elections, voters could have chosen from plenty of other parties and candidates. More than 15 parties backed more than a dozen presidential candidates in 2016, and more than 200 congressional candidates were fielded by a score of parties. The Libertarian Party alone fielded 122 candidates for Congress.

Why does the United States have a two-party system while other democracies have multiparty systems? This chapter points to differences in our government and election rules. Why has the American electorate voted overwhelmingly for the same two parties during much of our history and certainly over the last fifty years? As this chapter shows, it is related to how young citizens are socialized into the political process.

#ChallengeAccepted

Take the Challenge on MindTap for American Government

Suppose that Congress did not consist of only Democrats and Republicans but included members from the Libertarian and Green parties and from new parties formed by blacks, women, Latinos, and Christians. How might that improve or detract from Congress's functioning? Has the United States maintained a democratic form of government in spite of its two-party system—or because of it?

Learning Outcomes

LO1 Define political party and list the functions performed by parties in democratic government.

LO2 Outline the history of the U.S. political party system.

LO3 Explain why two parties dominate the history of American politics.

LO4 Compare and contrast the Democratic and Republican parties on the basis of ideology and organization.

LO5 Identify the principles of responsible party government and evaluate their role in majoritarian democracy.

Why do we have any political parties? What functions do they perform? How did we become a nation of Democrats and Republicans? Do these parties truly differ in their platforms and behavior? Are parties really necessary for democratic government, or do they just get in the way of citizens and their government? In this chapter, we answer these questions by examining political parties, perhaps the most misunderstood element of American politics.

Political Parties and Their Functions

LO1 Define political party and list the functions performed by parties in democratic government.

According to democratic theory, the primary means by which citizens control their government is voting in free elections. Most Americans agree that voting is important. Of those surveyed after the 2012 presidential campaign, 79 percent felt that elections make the government "pay attention to what the people think."[3] Americans are not nearly as supportive of the role played by our major political parties in elections, however. Asked in 2013 whether the "Republican and Democratic parties do an adequate job of representing the American people," only 24 percent thought they performed adequately.[4]

Nevertheless, Americans are quick to condemn as "undemocratic" countries that do not regularly hold elections contested by political parties. In truth, Americans have a love-hate relationship with political parties. They believe that parties are necessary for democratic government; at the same time, they think parties are somehow obstructionist and not to be trusted. This distrust is particularly strong among younger voters. To better appreciate the role of political parties in democratic government, we must understand exactly what parties are and what they do.

What Is a Political Party?

political party
An organization that sponsors candidates for political office under the organization's name.

nomination
Designation as an official candidate of a political party.

A **political party** is an organization that sponsors candidates for political office *under the organization's name.* The italicized part of this definition is important. True political parties select individuals to run for public office through a formal **nomination** process, which designates them as the parties' official candidates. This activity distinguishes the Democratic and Republican parties from interest groups, such as the AFL-CIO and the National Association of Manufacturers. Both of these interest groups support candidates, but they do not nominate them to run as their avowed representatives. If they did, they would be transformed into political parties. Because the so-called tea party does not nominate its own candidates, it is not a political party. True, five congressional candidates in 2010 managed to list themselves on the ballot under the tea party label, but none were endorsed by significant tea party groups and all lost. No one since has run for Congress as a tea party candidate. In short, the sponsoring of candidates, designated as representatives of the organization, is what defines an organization as a party.

Most democratic theorists agree that a modern nation-state cannot practice democracy without at least two political parties that regularly contest elections. In fact, the link between democracy and political parties is so firm that many people define democratic government in terms of competitive party politics.[5] A former president of the American Political Science Association held that even for a small nation, "democracy is impossible save in terms of parties."[6]

Party Functions

Parties contribute to democratic government through the functions they perform for the political system—the set of interrelated institutions that link people with government. Four of the most important party functions are nominating candidates for election to public office, structuring the voting choice in elections, proposing alternative government programs, and coordinating the actions of government officials.

Nominating Candidates. Question: Is *every* American citizen qualified to hold public office? A few scholars have thought so and proposed that government positions be filled "randomly"—that is, through lotteries.[7] Most observers, however, hold that political leadership requires certain abilities (if not special knowledge or public experience) and that not just anyone should be entrusted to hold government office. The question then becomes, who should be chosen among those who offer to lead? Without political parties, voters would confront a bewildering array of self-nominated candidates, each seeking votes on the basis of personal friendships, celebrity status, or family heritage. Parties can provide a form of quality control for their nominees through the process of peer review. Party insiders, the nominees' peers, usually know the strengths and faults of potential candidates much better than average voters do and thus can judge their suitability for representing the party.

In nominating candidates, parties often do more than pass judgment on potential office seekers; sometimes they recruit talented individuals to become candidates. In this way, parties help not only to ensure a minimum level of quality among candidates who run for office but also to raise the quality of those candidates.

Structuring the Voting Choice. Political parties help democratic government by structuring the voting choice—reducing the number of candidates on the ballot to those who have a realistic chance of winning. Established parties—those with experience in contesting elections—acquire a following of loyal voters who guarantee the party's candidates a predictable base of votes. The ability of established parties to mobilize their supporters discourages nonparty candidates from running for office and new parties from forming. Consequently, the realistic choice is between candidates offered by the major parties, reducing the amount of new information that voters need to choose their leaders. Of course, parties seek to structure the voting choice in a way that helps their candidates win.

Contrast the politics of our two-party system with Russian voters' choices among 14 parties in their September 2016 parliamentary election. United Russia, aligned with President Putin, won 54 percent of the vote but 76 percent of the seats. The Communist Party and the Liberal Democratic Party each won 13 percent of the vote but under 10 percent of the seats. A fourth party won 5 percent of the seats, and two seats were won by other parties.

Russia's first parliamentary election in five years had only 48 percent turnout, and some election observers found evidence of voting fraud. Even in honest elections, the presence of multiple parties tends to split opposition to a dominant regime and prevent alternation in power. Two-party systems tend to promote citizens' ability to replace government leaders.

Proposing Alternative Government Programs. Parties help voters choose among candidates by proposing alternative programs of government action—the general policies their candidates will pursue if they gain office. In a stable party system, even if voters know nothing about the qualities of the parties' candidates, they can vote rationally for the candidates of the party that has policies they favor. The specific policies advocated vary from candidate to candidate and from election to election. However, the types of policies advocated by candidates of one party tend to differ from those proposed by candidates of other parties. Although there are exceptions, candidates of the same party

political system
A set of interrelated institutions that link people with government.

tend to favor policies that fit their party's underlying political philosophy, or ideology. Parties in multiparty systems tend to propose more varied and specific programs than parties offer in two-party systems.

In many countries, parties' names, such as Conservative and Socialist, reflect their political stance. The Democrats and Republicans have ideologically neutral names, but many minor parties in the United States have used their names to advertise their policies—for example, the Libertarian Party, the Socialist Party, and the Green Party.[8] The neutrality of the two major parties' names suggests that their policies are similar. This is not true. As we shall see, they regularly adopt very different policies in their platforms.

Coordinating the Actions of Government Officials. Finally, party organizations help coordinate the actions of public officials. A government based on the separation of powers, such as that of the United States, divides responsibilities for making public policy. The president and the leaders of the House and Senate are not required to cooperate with one another. Political party organizations are the major means for bridging the separate powers to produce coordinated policies that can govern the country effectively. Parties do this in two ways. First, candidates' and officeholders' political fortunes are linked to their party organization, which can bestow and withhold favors. Second, and perhaps more important in the United States, members of the same party in the presidency, the House, and the Senate tend to share political principles and thus often voluntarily cooperate in making policy.

Depending on how members view their party, parties differ in how they perform these functions. Two main views prevail. The eighteenth-century thinker Edmund Burke defined a party as "a body of men united for promoting by their joint endeavours the national interest upon some particular principle in which they are all agreed."[9] To Burke, people unite in a party in order to enact agreed policies. In contrast, the mid-twentieth-century economist Anthony Downs defined a party as "a team of men seeking to control the governing apparatus by gaining office in a duly constituted election."[10] To Downs, people unite in a party to get elected. In recent years Republicans have tended to act like Burkeans. For example, they nominated candidates who catered to their conservative base but who often lost in general elections. Democrats have more consistently acted like Downsians, backing policies more popular with ideologically moderate voters.

Leading up to the 2016 presidential election, most Republican candidates who sought the party's nomination certainly acted as Burkeans. They advocated policies that fired up their hard-core conservative Republican primary voters in the spring but did not appeal to others who voted in November. Republican party leaders in Washington (the "establishment") feared losing the election as a consequence. Their fears were unfounded.

So why do we have parties? One expert notes that successful politicians in the United States need electoral and governing majorities and that "no collection of ambitious politicians has long been able to think of a way to achieve their goals in this democracy save in terms of political parties."[11]

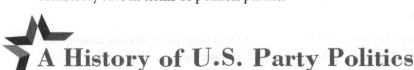

A History of U.S. Party Politics

LO2 Outline the history of the U.S. political party system.

The two major U.S. parties are among the oldest in the world. In fact, the Democratic Party, founded in 1828 but with roots reaching back to the late 1700s, has a strong claim to being the oldest party in existence. Its closest rival is the British Conservative Party,

from a third party (which means any minor party) have little chance of winning office. Third-party candidates tend to be more successful at the local or state level. Since the current two-party system was established, relatively few minor-party candidates have won election to the U.S. House, even fewer have won election to the Senate, and none has won the presidency.

The voters in a given state, county, or community are not always equally divided in their loyalties between the Republicans and the Democrats. In some areas, voters typically favor the Republicans, whereas voters in other areas prefer the Democrats. When one party in a two-party system regularly enjoys support from most voters in an area, it is called the *majority party* in that area; the other is called the *minority party*. Since the inception of the current two-party system, four periods (1860–1894, 1896–1930, 1932–1964, and 1968 to the present) have characterized the balance between the two major parties at the national level.

A Rough Balance: 1860–1894. From 1860 through 1894, the Grand Old Party (or GOP, as the Republican Party is sometimes called) won eight of ten presidential elections, which would seem to qualify it as the majority party. However, seats in the House of Representatives are a better guide to the breadth of national support. Republicans and Democrats won an equal number of congressional elections, each controlling the chamber for nine sessions between 1860 and 1894.

A Republican Majority: 1896–1930. A second critical election, in 1896, transformed the Republican Party into a true majority party. Grover Cleveland, a Democrat, occupied the White House, and the country was in a severe depression. The Republicans nominated William McKinley, governor of Ohio and a conservative, who stood for a high tariff against foreign goods and sound money tied to the value of gold.

IMAGE 8.1   William Jennings Bryan: When Candidates Were Orators

Today, televised images of a candidate waving his hands and shouting to an audience would look silly. But candidates once had to resort to such tactics to be effective with large crowds. One of the most commanding orators around the turn of the twentieth century was William Jennings Bryan (1860–1925), whose stirring speeches extolling the virtues of the free coinage of silver were music to the ears of thousands of westerners and southern farmers.

The Democrats, already in trouble because of the depression, nominated the fiery William Jennings Bryan. In stark contrast to McKinley, Bryan advocated the free and unlimited coinage of silver, which would mean cheap money and easy payment of debts through inflation. Conservatives, especially business-people, were aghast at the Democrats' radical turn, and voters in the heavily populated Northeast and Midwest surged toward the Republican Party, many of them permanently. McKinley carried every northern state east of the Mississippi. The Republicans also won the House, and they retained their control of it in the next six elections.

The election of 1896 helped solidify a Republican majority in industrial America and forged a link between the Republican Party and business. In the subsequent electoral realignment, the Republicans emerged as a true majority party. The GOP dominated national politics—controlling the presidency, the Senate, and the House—almost continuously from 1896 until the Wall Street crash of 1929, which burst big business's bubble and launched the Great Depression.*

A Democratic Majority: 1932–1964. The Republicans' majority status ended in the critical election of 1932 between incumbent president Herbert Hoover and the Democratic challenger, Franklin Delano Roosevelt. Roosevelt promised new solutions to unemployment and the economic crisis of the Great Depression. His campaign appealed to labor, middle-class liberals, and new European ethnic voters. Along with Democratic voters in the Solid South, urban workers in the North, Catholics, Jews, and white ethnic minorities formed "the Roosevelt coalition." The relatively few blacks who voted at that time tended to remain loyal to the Republicans—"the party of Lincoln."

Roosevelt was swept into office in a landslide, carrying huge Democratic majorities with him into the House and Senate to enact his liberal activist programs. The electoral realignment reflected by the election of 1932 made the Democrats the majority party. Not only was Roosevelt reelected in 1936, 1940, and 1944, but also Democrats held control of both houses of Congress in most sessions from 1933 through 1964. The Democrats also won the presidency in seven of nine elections.

A Rough Balance: 1968 to the Present. Scholars agree that an electoral realignment occurred after 1964, and some attribute the realignment to the turbulent election of 1968, sometimes called the fourth critical election.[16] Republican Richard Nixon won in a very close race by winning five of the eleven southern states in the old Confederacy, while Democrat Hubert Humphrey won only one. The other five were won by George Wallace, the candidate of the American Independent Party, made up primarily of southerners who defected from the Democratic Party. Wallace won no states outside the South.

Since 1968, Republican candidates for president have run very well in southern states and tended to win election—Nixon (twice), Reagan (twice), G. H. W. Bush, and G. W. Bush (twice). The record of party control of Congress has been more mixed since 1968. Democrats have controlled the House for most of the sessions, while the parties have split control of the Senate almost evenly. Therefore, the period since 1968 rates as a "rough balance" between the parties, much like the period from 1860 to 1894. Today, both parties nationally are fairly close in electoral strength. However, the North-South coalition of Democratic voters forged by Roosevelt in the 1930s has completely crumbled. Two southern scholars wrote:

> It is easy to forget just how thoroughly the Democratic party once dominated southern congressional elections. In 1950 there were no Republican senators

---

* The only break in the GOP domination was in 1912, when Teddy Roosevelt's Progressive Conservative Party split from the Republicans, allowing Democrat Woodrow Wilson to win the presidency and giving the Democrats control of Congress, and again in 1916 when Wilson was reelected.

from the South and only 2 Republican representatives out of 105 in the southern House delegation. . . . A half-century later Republicans constituted *majorities* of the South's congressional delegations—13 of 22 southern senators and 71 of 125 representatives.[17]

Party loyalty within regions has shifted inexorably since 1968. Moreover, the Democrats' national coalition of blue-collar workers and ethnic minorities has collapsed, while rural voters have become decidedly more Republican.[18] Some scholars say that in the 1970s and 1980s, we were in a period of electoral dealignment, in which party loyalties became less important to voters as they cast their ballots. Others counter that partisanship increased in the 1990s in a gradual process of realignment not marked by a single critical election.[19] We examine the influence of party loyalty on voting in the next chapter, after we look at the operation of our two-party system.

electoral dealignment
A lessening of the importance of party loyalties in voting decisions.

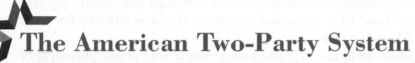

The American Two-Party System

LO3 Explain why two parties dominate the history of American politics.

Our review of party history in the United States has focused on the two dominant parties. But we should not ignore the special contributions of certain minor parties, among them the Anti-Masonic Party, the Populists, and the Progressives of 1912. In this section, we study the fortunes of minor, or third, parties in American politics. We also look at why we have only two major parties, explain how federalism helps the parties survive, and describe voters' loyalty to the two major parties today.

Minor Parties in America

Minor parties have always figured in party politics in America. Most minor parties in our political history have been one of four types:[20]

- *Bolter parties* are formed by factions that have split off from one of the major parties. Seven times in the thirty-eight presidential elections from the Civil War to 2012, disgruntled leaders have "bolted the ticket" and challenged their former parties by forming new parties. Bolter parties have occasionally won significant proportions of the vote. However, with the exception of Teddy Roosevelt's Progressive Party in 1912 and the possible exception of George Wallace's American Independent Party in 1968, bolter parties have not affected the outcome of presidential elections.
- *Farmer-labor parties* represented farmers and urban workers who believed that they, the working class, were not getting their share of society's wealth. The People's Party, founded in 1892 and nicknamed the "Populist Party," was a prime example of a farmer-labor party. The Populists won 8.5 percent of the vote in 1892 and also became the first third party since 1860 to win any electoral votes. Flushed by success, it endorsed William Jennings Bryan, the Democratic candidate, in 1896. When he lost, the party quickly faded. Farm and labor groups revived many Populist ideas in the Progressive Party in 1924, which nominated Robert La Follette for the presidency. Although the party won 16.6 percent of the popular vote, it carried only La Follette's home state of Wisconsin and died in 1925. In 1944, however, the Minnesota Farmer-Labor Party merged with the Democrats to form the Democratic Farmer-Labor (DFL) Party. The DFL is Minnesota's Democratic Party today.

- *Parties of ideological protest* go further than farmer-labor parties in criticizing the established system. These parties reject prevailing doctrines and propose radically different principles, often favoring more government activism. The Socialist Party has been the most successful party of ideological protest. Even at its high point in 1912, however, it garnered only 6 percent of the vote, and Socialist candidates for president have never won a single state. Nevertheless, the Socialist Party persists, fielding a presidential ticket again in 2016. In recent years, protest parties have tended to come from the right, arguing against government action in society. Such is the program of the Libertarian Party, which stresses freedom over order and equality, and reflects its program in the Libertarian's website theme, "Minimum Government, Maximum Freedom." In contrast, the Green Party protests from the left, favoring government action to preserve the environment. Together, the Libertarian and Green parties polled just over 4 percent of the total vote for their presidential candidates in 2016. Although both parties together ran nearly two hundred congressional candidates, they won relatively few votes (see Figure 8.2) and no seats.

- *Single-issue parties* are formed to promote one principle, not a general philosophy of government. The Anti-Masonic parties of the 1820s and 1830s, for example, opposed Masonic lodges and other secret societies. The Free Soil Party of the 1840s and 1850s worked to abolish slavery. The Prohibition Party, the most durable example of a single-issue party, was founded to oppose the consumption of alcoholic beverages, but recently its platform has taken conservative positions: favoring right-to-life, limiting immigration, and urging withdrawal from the World Bank. Prohibition candidates consistently won from 1 to 2 percent of the vote in nine presidential elections between 1884 and 1916, and the party has run candidates in every presidential election since, usually winning only a trickle of votes.

America has a long history of third parties that operate on the periphery of our two-party system. Minor parties form primarily to express some voters' discontent

FIGURE 8.2   Number of 435 House Districts Contested by Parties.

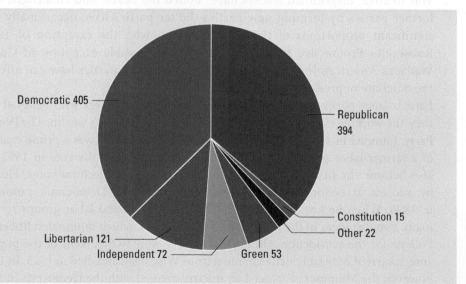

In 2016, as in other recent elections, both the Democratic and Republican parties ran candidates for the House of Representatives in over 90 percent of the 435 congressional districts. Of minor parties, only the Libertarian Party, the best-organized minor party in the nation, ran candidates in more than one hundred districts. None won election, and almost all got less than 10 percent of the votes. All other minor parties ran fewer candidates than the Libertarians, and most got fewer votes. No minor party candidate won election to the House of Representatives.

Source: *Ballot Access News*, 32 (October, 2016), p. 5.

Democratic 405
Republican 394
Constitution 15
Other 22
Green 53
Independent 72
Libertarian 121

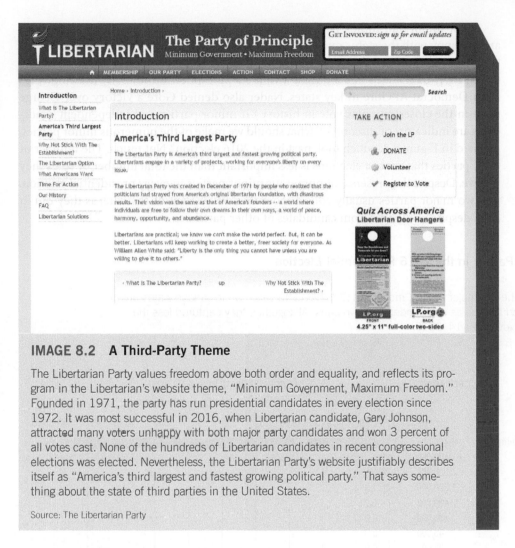

IMAGE 8.2   A Third-Party Theme

The Libertarian Party values freedom above both order and equality, and reflects its program in the Libertarian's website theme, "Minimum Government, Maximum Freedom." Founded in 1971, the party has run presidential candidates in every election since 1972. It was most successful in 2016, when Libertarian candidate, Gary Johnson, attracted many voters unhappy with both major party candidates and won 3 percent of all votes cast. None of the hundreds of Libertarian candidates in recent congressional elections was elected. Nevertheless, the Libertarian Party's website justifiably describes itself as "America's third largest and fastest growing political party." That says something about the state of third parties in the United States.

Source: The Libertarian Party

with choices offered by the major parties and to work for their own objectives within the electoral system.[21]

How have minor parties fared historically? As vote getters, they have not performed well. However, bolter parties have twice won more than 10 percent of the vote. (Although Ross Perot won 19 percent of the vote in 1992, he ran as an independent. When he created the Reform Party and ran as its candidate in 1996, he won only 8 percent.)[22] More significantly, the Republican Party originated in 1854 as a single-issue third party opposed to slavery in the nation's new territories. In its first election, in 1856, the party came in second, displacing the Whigs. (Undoubtedly, the Republican exception to the rule has inspired the formation of other hopeful third parties.) Although surveys repeatedly show over half the public saying they want a third major party, voters tend not to support them at the polls.[23]

As policy advocates, minor parties have a slightly better record. At times, they have had a real effect on the policies adopted by the major parties. Women's suffrage, the graduated income tax, and the direct election of senators all originated with third parties. Of course, third parties may fail to win more votes simply because their policies lack popular support. The Democrats learned this lesson in 1896, when they adopted the Populists' free-silver plank in their own platform. Both their candidate and their platform went down to defeat, hobbling the Democratic Party for decades. Beginning around the 1930s, third-party voting began to decline. Research attributes the decline to the Democratic Party's leftward shift to encompass issues raised by minor parties.[24]

Most important, minor parties function as safety valves. They allow those who are unhappy with the status quo to express their discontent within the system, to contribute to the political dialogue. Surely this was the function of Ralph Nader as the Green Party candidate in 2000, when it won 2.7 percent of the vote. (By drawing votes from Democrat Al Gore in key states, Nader also denied Gore a victory over George Bush in the closest popular vote in history.) If minor parties and independent candidates are indicators of discontent, what should we make of the numerous minor parties, detailed in Figure 8.3, which took part in the 2016 election? Not much. The number of third parties that contest elections is less important than the total number of votes they receive. Despite the presence of numerous minor parties in every presidential election, the two major parties usually collect more than 95 percent of the vote, as they did in 2016 despite challenges from candidates of other parties.

FIGURE 8.3   Candidates and Parties in the 2016 Presidential Election

In addition to the candidates of the two major parties, more than 25 other candidates ran in various states under the banners of more than a dozen parties, as independents, or write-ins. All together, they captured less than 5 percent of the total vote as of November 14, 2016.

Sources: U.S. Election Atlas at http://uselectionatlas.org/RESULTS/ and Politico at http://www.politico.com/2016-election/results/map/president.

CANDIDATE AND PARTY	POPULAR VOTE*	PERCENTAGE OF POPULAR VOTE
Donald Trump, *President* (Republican)	60,700,000	47.0
Hillary Clinton (Democrat)	61,400,000	48.0
Gary Johnson (Libertarian)	4,200,000	3.0
Jill Stein (Green)	1,300,000	1.0
Evan McMullin (Independent)	490,000	0.0
Darrell Castle (Constitution)	180,000	0.0
Gloria La Riva (Socialist)	46,000	0.0
Roque De La Ruenta (Reform)	32,000	0.0
Richard Duncan (Independent)	24,000	0.0
Dan Vacek (Legal Marijuana)	13,500	0.0
Alyson Kennedy (Socialist Workers)	11,000	0.0
Mike Smith (Independent)	9,000	0.0
Chris Keniston (Veterans)	6,600	0.0
Lynn Kahn (New Independent)	5,600	0.0
James Hedges (Prohibition)	5,550	0.0
Monica Moorehead (Workers World)	3,700	0.0
Peter Skewes (American)	3,300	0.0
Emidio Soltisyk (Socialist USA)	2,500	0.0
Arlon Copeland (Constitution)	2,350	0.0
Tom Hoefling (America)	2,220	0.0
Rocky Giordani (Independence)	2,100	0.0
Larry Kotlikoff (It's Our Children)	1,400	0.0
Kyle Kopitke (Ind. American)	1,000	0.0
Joseph Maldonado (Ind. People)	800	0.0
Ryan Scott (Write-in)	690	0.0
Rod Silva (Nutrition)	660	0.0
Bradford Lyttle (Pacifist)	340	0.0
Frank Atwood (Approval Voting)	310	0.0

*Votes are rounded.

Why a Two-Party System?

The history of party politics in the United States is essentially the story of two parties alternating in control of government. With relatively few exceptions, Americans conduct elections at all levels within the two-party system. Nevertheless, surveys show that about half of the population today thinks that the United States needs a third party. Why does the United States have only two major parties? Other democratic countries usually have multiparty systems, but they typically involve more than three parties. In truth, a political system with three relatively equal parties has never existed over a length of time in any country, for it is inherently unstable.[25] Think of an election as a prizefight between two boxers. If a third boxer enters the ring, two gang up on one. A similar dynamic occurs among three parties but not among four or more parties, which pick separate fights with one another.

The two most convincing explanations for the two-party system in the United States lie (1) in its electoral system and (2) in our historical pattern of political socialization. Consider first the electoral system, which sets the "rules of the game" under which the parties play. The two principles of *single winners* chosen by a *simple plurality* of votes produce an electoral system known as **majority representation** (despite its reliance on pluralities rather than majorities). Think about how American states choose representatives to Congress. A state entitled to ten representatives is divided into ten congressional districts, and each district elects one representative. Almost always, the ten representatives are Democrats and Republicans. Majority representation of voters through single-member districts is also a feature of most state legislatures.

Alternatively, a legislature might be chosen through a system of **proportional representation**, which awards legislative seats to each party in proportion to the total number of votes it wins in an election. Under this system, the state might hold a single statewide election for all ten seats, with multiple parties presenting their rank ordered lists of ten candidates. Voters could vote for the party list they preferred, and the party's candidates would be elected from the top of each list, according to the proportion of votes won by the party. Thus, if a party got 30 percent of the vote in this example, its first three candidates would be elected.[26]

Although this form of election may seem strange, more democratic countries use it than use our system of majority representation. Proportional representation tends to produce (or perpetuate) several parties because each can win enough seats nationwide to wield some influence in the legislature. In contrast, our system of elections forces interest groups of all sorts to work within the two major parties, for only one candidate in each race stands a chance of being elected under plurality voting. Therefore, the system tends to produce only two parties. Moreover, the two major parties benefit from state laws that automatically list candidates on the ballot if their party won a sizable percentage of the vote in the previous election. These laws discourage minor parties, which usually have to collect thousands of signatures to get on a state ballot.[27]

The rules of our electoral system may explain why only two parties tend to form in specific election districts, but why do the same two parties (Democratic and Republican) operate within every state? The contest for the presidency is the key to this question. A candidate can win a presidential election only by amassing a majority of electoral votes from across the entire nation. Presidential candidates try to win votes under the same party label in each state in order to pool their electoral votes in the electoral college. The presidency is a big enough political prize to induce parties to harbor uncomfortable coalitions of voters (southern white Protestants allied with northern Jews, Catholic Latinos, and blacks in the Democratic Party, for example) just to win the electoral vote and the presidential election.

The American electoral system may force U.S. politics into a two-party mold, but why must the same two parties reappear from election to election? In fact, they

majority representation
The system by which one office, contested by two or more candidates, is won by the single candidate who collects the most votes.

proportional representation
The system by which legislative seats are awarded to a party in proportion to the vote that party wins in an election.

have not. The earliest two-party system pitted the Federalists against the Democratic Republicans. A later two-party system involved the Democrats and the Whigs. More than 150 years ago, the Republicans replaced the Whigs in what is our two-party system today. But with modern issues so different from the issues then, why do the Democrats and Republicans persist? This is where the second explanation, political socialization, comes into play. The two parties persist simply because they have persisted. After more than one hundred years of political socialization, the two parties today have such a head start in structuring the vote that they discourage challenges from new parties. Third parties still try to crack the two-party system from time to time, but most have had little success. In truth, the two parties in power also write laws that make it hard for minor parties to get on the ballot, such as requiring petitions with thousands of signatures.[28]

The Federal Basis of the Party System

Focusing on contests for the presidency is a convenient and informative way to study the history of American parties, but it also oversimplifies party politics to the point of distortion. By concentrating only on presidential elections, we tend to ignore electoral patterns in the states, where elections often buck national trends. Even during its darkest defeats for the presidency, a party can still claim many victories for state offices. Victories outside the arena of presidential politics give each party a base of support that keeps its machinery oiled and ready for the next contest.[29]

Party Identification in America

party identification
A voter's sense of psychological attachment to a party.

The concept of **party identification** is one of the most important in political science. It signifies a voter's sense of psychological attachment to a party (which is not the same thing as voting for the party in any given election). Scholars measure party identification simply by asking, "Do you usually think of yourself as a Republican, a Democrat, an independent, or what?"[30] Voting is a behavior; identification is a state of mind. For example, millions of southerners voted for Eisenhower for president in 1952 and 1956 but continued to consider themselves Democrats. Again in the 1980s, millions of voters temporarily became "Reagan Democrats." Across the nation, more people identify with one of the two major parties than reject a party attachment. The proportions of self-identified Republicans, Democrats, and independents (no party attachment) in the electorate since 1952 are shown in Figure 8.4. Three significant points stand out:

- The proportion of Republicans and Democrats combined has exceeded that of independents in every year.
- The proportion of Democrats has consistently exceeded that of Republicans but has shrunk over time.
- The proportion of independents has nearly doubled over the period.

Although party identification predisposes citizens to vote for their favorite party, other factors may convince them to choose the opposition candidate. If they vote against their party often enough, they may rethink their party identification and eventually switch. Apparently, this rethinking has gone on in the minds of many southern Democrats over time. In 1952, about 70 percent of white southerners thought of themselves as Democrats, and fewer than 20 percent thought of themselves as Republicans. By 2015, white southerners were only 34 percent Democratic versus 55 percent Republican.[31] Much of the nationwide growth in the proportion of Republicans and independents (and the parallel drop in the number of Democrats) stems from changes in party preferences among white southerners and from migration of northerners, which translated into substantial gains in the proportion of Republicans.

FIGURE 8.4   Distribution of Party Identification, 1952–2016

In every presidential election since 1952, voters across the nation have been asked, "Generally speaking, do you usually think of yourself as a Republican, a Democrat, an independent, or what?" Most voters think of themselves as either Republicans or Democrats, but the proportion of those who think of themselves as independents has increased over time. The size of the Democratic Party's majority has also shrunk. Nevertheless, most Americans today still identify with one of the two major parties, and Democrats still outnumber Republicans.

Source: Data for 1952 to 2012 come from the American National Election Studies Guide to Public Opinion and Electoral Behavior, http://www.electionstudies.org/nesguide/nesguide.htm. Data entering 2016 came from political surveys conducted January–December 2015, N=17,518, by the Pew Research Center. The few respondents (typically under 5 percent) who gave other answers were excluded from the graph.

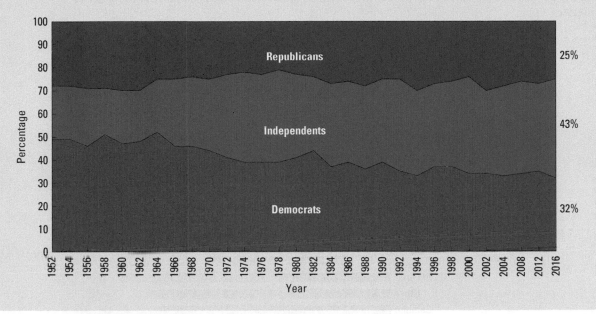

Who are the self-identified Democrats and Republicans in the electorate? Figure 8.5 shows party identification by various social groups entering 2016. The effects of socioeconomic factors are clear. People who have lower incomes and less education are more likely to think of themselves as Democrats rather than as Republicans. However, citizens with advanced degrees (such as college faculty) are more Democratic. The cultural factors of religion and ethnicity produce even sharper differences between the parties. Those who are unaffiliated with a religious group are strongly Democratic compared with those affiliated with religious groups but are mainly independent. Non-Latino whites are markedly more Republican than those in other ethnic groups. Finally, American politics has a gender gap: more women tend to be Democrats than men, and (although not shown here) this gap seems to widen with women's greater education.[32] The youngest citizens are more apt to be Democrats than Republicans, but most are independents. People tend to acquire party identification as they age.

The influence of region on party identification has changed over time, and strong regional differences no longer exist. Because of the high proportion of blacks in the South, it is still predominantly Democratic (in party identity, but not in voting because of lower turnout among low-income blacks). Despite the erosion of Democratic strength in the South, we still see elements of Roosevelt's old Democratic coalition of different socioeconomic groups. Perhaps the major change in that coalition has been the replacement of white European ethnic groups by blacks, attracted by Democrats' backing of civil rights legislation in the 1960s, and by Latinos, attracted by Democrats' supporting more flexible immigration policies.

Nonwhites in general have become more Democratic than Republican today, as the ethnic composition of the United States is inexorably becoming less white. Estimated at

FIGURE 8.5 Party Identification by Social Groups

Respondents to a recent survey were grouped by seven socioeconomic criteria—income, education, religion, gender, ethnicity, region, and age—and analyzed according to their self-descriptions as Democrats, independents, or Republicans. As income increases, people are more likely to vote Republican. The same is true for education, except for those with college degrees. Protestants are far more likely to be Republican than those without religious affiliation, while women, Hispanics, and all nonwhite groups are more likely to be Democrats. Party identification varies relatively little by region. The main effect of age was to reduce the proportion of independents as respondents grew older. Younger citizens who tend to think of themselves as independents are likely to develop an identification with one party or the other as they mature.

Source: Data entering 2016 came from political surveys conducted January–December 2015, N=17,518, by the Pew Research Center. The few respondents (typically under 5 percent) who gave other answers were excluded from the graph. Rounding errors kept all bars from totaling to 100 percent.

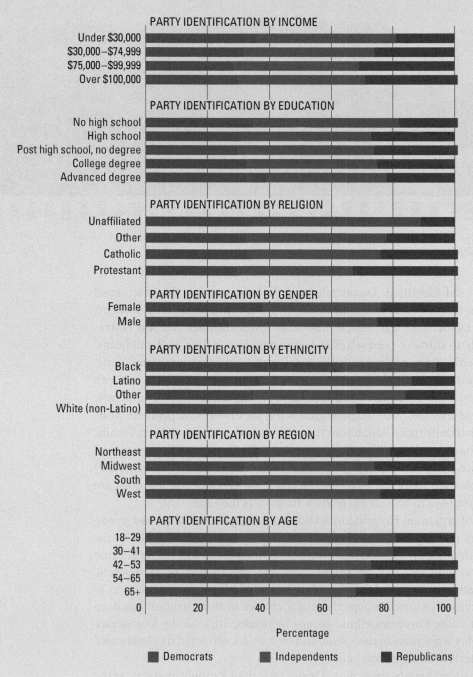

Political Partying in Global Politics

As shown earlier in Figure 8.4, the proportion of Americans who identify with the Republican or Democratic parties has declined over time, while the proportion of independents has increased. This chart shows a similar decline in formal party members for most European countries where citizens formally belong to political parties. Among fifteen European countries with available data over time, only Spain showed an increase in party members as a percentage of the electorate. Citizens everywhere seem less likely to party.

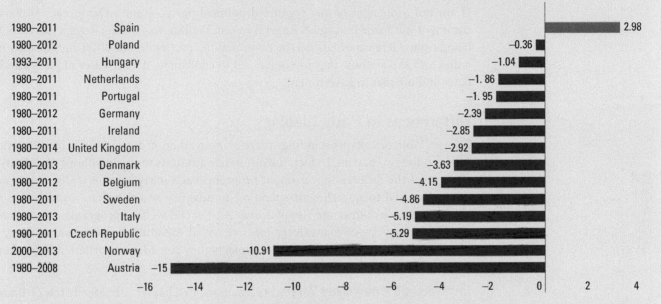

Gain (Green) or Loss (Orange) in Party Members as a Percent of the Electorate over Years Shown

Years	Country	Value
1980–2011	Spain	2.98
1980–2012	Poland	−0.36
1993–2011	Hungary	−1.04
1980–2011	Netherlands	−1.86
1980–2011	Portugal	−1.95
1980–2012	Germany	−2.39
1980–2011	Ireland	−2.85
1980–2014	United Kingdom	−2.92
1980–2013	Denmark	−3.63
1980–2012	Belgium	−4.15
1980–2011	Sweden	−4.86
1980–2013	Italy	−5.19
1990–2011	Czech Republic	−5.29
2000–2013	Norway	−10.91
1980–2008	Austria	−15

Source: Political Party Database Working Group, http://www.politicalpartydb.org. Data were kindly provided by project leaders Susan Scarrow, Paul Webb, and Thomas Pogunke in personal communication.

CRITICAL THINKING Does the decline in party membership suggest an increase or a decrease in political participation? Is that good or bad for democratic government?

62 percent in 2015, the non-Latino white population is projected to be only 55 percent in 2030—resulting in Latinos and non-whites comprising almost half of the electorate.[33] Given that Latinos, blacks, and Asians are strongly Democratic, the Republican Party faces problems in the partisan implications of demographic change.

Studies show that about half of all Americans adopt their parents' party.[34] But it often takes time for party identification to develop. The youngest group of voters is most likely to be independent, but people in their thirties and forties, who were socialized during the Reagan and first Bush presidencies, are more Republican. The oldest group not only is strongly Democratic but also shows the greatest partisan commitment (fewest independents), reflecting the fact that citizens become more interested in politics as they mature.[35] While partisanship has been declining in the United States, that is true elsewhere too.

Americans tend to find their political niche and stay there.[36] The enduring party loyalty of American voters tends to structure the vote even before an election is held, and even before the candidates are chosen. In Chapter 9, we will examine the extent to which party identification determines voting choice. But first we will explore whether the Democratic and Republican parties have any significant differences between them.

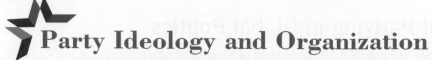

Party Ideology and Organization

LO4 Compare and contrast the Democratic and Republican parties on the basis of ideology and organization.

George Wallace, a disgruntled Democrat who ran for president in 1968 on the American Independent Party ticket, complained that "there isn't a dime's worth of difference" between the Democrats and Republicans. Decades earlier, humorist Will Rogers said, "I am not a member of any organized political party—I am a Democrat." Wallace's comment was made in disgust, Rogers's in jest. Wallace was wrong; Rogers was close to being right. Here we will dispel the myth that the parties do not differ significantly on issues and explain how they are organized to coordinate the activities of party candidates and officials in government.

Differences in Party Ideology

George Wallace notwithstanding, there is more than a dime's worth of difference between the two parties. In fact, the difference amounts to many billions of dollars—the cost of the different government programs each party supports. Democrats are more disposed to government spending to advance social welfare (and hence to promote equality) than are Republicans. And social welfare programs cost money, a lot of money. Republicans decry massive social spending, but they are not averse to spending billions of dollars for the projects they consider important, among them national defense.

Involved and Uninvolved Voters. As discussed in Chapter 5, relatively few ordinary voters think about politics in ideological terms. Party activists often do, however. Figure 8.6 compares all voters with major party identifiers and with party identifiers who voted in their parties' 2016 primaries or caucuses—about 28 percent in each party.

FIGURE 8.6 **Ideologies of Involved and Uninvolved Party Voters in 2016**

The Democratic and Republican parties differed greatly from the public in their ideological centers of gravity. Democratic identifiers were substantially more liberal, while Republican identifiers were far more conservative. Concerning the quarter of each party that voted in their parties' primaries and caucuses, Democratic primary voters were more liberal than party identifiers. Allowing for sampling error, Republican primary voters were no more conservative than party identifiers, but both were at very high levels.

Source: *New York Times*/CBS News poll of 1,753 respondents, September 9–13, 2016. Party identifiers include primary voters. More respondents (28 percent in each party) reported voting in primaries and caucuses than actually did according to voting statistics.

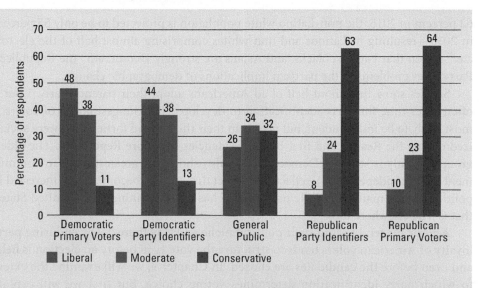

The middle of the graph shows 32 percent of all voters describing themselves as conservative versus 26 percent saying they were liberal. Self-identified Democrats voting in their party's primaries or caucuses were somewhat more liberal than those who did not. Republican identifiers differed little from primary voters. The ideological gap, however, was a yawning chasm between Democratic and Republican primary voters.

Platforms: Freedom, Order, and Equality. Surveys of voters' ideological orientation may merely reflect differences in their personal self-image rather than actual differences in party ideology. For another test of party philosophy, we can look to the platforms adopted at party conventions. Although many people feel that party platforms don't matter very much, several scholars have demonstrated, using different approaches, that winning parties tend to carry out much of their platforms when in office.[37] One study matched the parties' platform statements from 1948 to 1985 against subsequent allocations of program funds in the federal budget. Spending priorities turned out to be quite closely linked to the platform emphases of the party that won control of Congress, especially if the party also controlled the presidency.[38]

Party platforms also matter a great deal to the parties' convention delegates—and to the interest groups that support the parties.[39] The wording of a platform plank often means the difference between victory and defeat for factions within a party. Delegates fight not only over ideas but also over words.

The 2016 Republican platform ran about 35,500 words—about one-third longer than the 26,100 words in the 2016 Democratic platform. The two platforms were also strikingly different in content. The Republicans mentioned "free" or "freedom" nearly five times more often (89 to 18), while the Democrats referred to "equal," "equality," or "inequality" more than three times as much (29 to 9). Republicans also cited public "order" 11 times, while Democrats never mentioned the term. Republicans also talked about "crime," "abortion," and "marriage" more than ten times as often as Democrats.

Different but Similar. The Democrats and the Republicans have very different ideological orientations. Yet many observers claim that the parties are really quite similar in ideology compared to the different parties of other countries. Although both Republicans and Democrats favor a market economy over a planned economy more than parties elsewhere, Republicans do so more strongly than Democrats. A major cross-national study of party positions in Western countries since 1945 concludes that the United States experiences "a form of party competition that is as ideologically (or non-ideologically) driven as the other countries we have studied."[40]

National Party Organization

Most casual observers would agree with Will Rogers's description of the Democrats as an unorganized political party. It used to apply to the Republicans too, but this has changed since the 1970s, at least at the national level. Bear in mind the distinction between levels of party structure. American parties parallel our federal system: they have separate national and state organizations (and functionally separate local organizations, in many cases).

At the national level, each major party has four main organizational components:

- *National convention.* Every four years, each party assembles thousands of delegates from the states and U.S. territories (such as Puerto Rico and Guam) in a national convention for the purpose of nominating a candidate for president. In 2016, the Democratic convention had almost twice the number of delegates as the Republican: 4,784 to 2,472. This presidential nominating convention is also the supreme governing body of the party. It determines party policy through the

Freedom, Order, or Equality

Freedom, Order, or Equality and Party Platforms

As discussed in the text, the 2016 platforms of the Republican and Democratic parties made strikingly different references to freedom, order, and equality. Republicans were almost five times as likely to mention "free" or "freedom" and more than six times as likely to invoke images of public order by mentioning it specifically while also referring to "crime," "marriage," and "abortion." Democrats, however, were more than three times as likely to use "equal" and "equality."

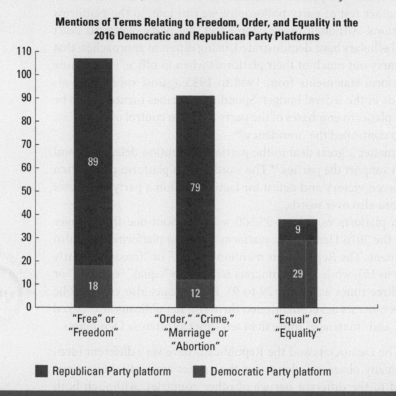

Mentions of Terms Relating to Freedom, Order, and Equality in the 2016 Democratic and Republican Party Platforms

■ Republican Party platform ■ Democratic Party platform

CRITICAL THINKING Do the two parties' usage of these terms in their platforms match or contradict the ideological images that they project?

platform, formulates rules to govern party operations, and designates a national committee, which is empowered to govern the party until the next convention.

national committee
A committee of a political party composed of party chairpersons and party officials from every state.

- *National committee.* The **national committee**, which governs each party between conventions, is composed of party officials representing the states and territories, including the chairpersons of their party organizations. The Republican National Committee (RNC) has about 170 members, consisting of the national committeeman, national committeewoman, and a chairperson from each state and from the District of Columbia, Guam, Puerto Rico, and the Virgin Islands. The Democratic National Committee (DNC) has approximately 450 elected and appointed members, including, in addition to the national committee members and party chairs, members representing auxiliary organizations. The chairperson of each national committee is usually chosen by the party's presidential nominee and then duly elected by the committee. If the nominee loses the election, the national committee usually replaces the nominee's chairperson.

party conferences
A meeting to select party leaders and decide committee assignments, held at the beginning of a session of Congress by Republicans or Democrats in each chamber.

- *Congressional party conferences.* At the beginning of each session of Congress, the Republicans and Democrats in each chamber hold separate **party conferences** (the House Democrats call theirs a caucus) to select their party leaders and decide committee assignments. The party conferences deal only with congressional matters and have no structural relationship to each other and none with their national committees.

- *Congressional campaign committees.* Democrats and Republicans in the House and Senate also maintain separate congressional campaign committees, each of which raises its own funds to support its candidates in congressional elections. The separation of these organizations from the national committee tells us that the national party structure is loose; the national committee seldom gets involved with the election of any individual member of Congress. Moreover, even the congressional campaign organizations merely supplement the funds that senators and representatives raise on their own to win reelection.

It is tempting to think of the national party chairperson as sitting at the top of a hierarchical party organization that not only controls its members in Congress but also issues orders to the state committees and on down to the local level. Few ideas could be more wrong.[41] In fact, the RNC and DNC do not direct or control the crucial presidential campaigns. In 2016, both national committees (the party "establishments") were helpless as outside candidates threatened insiders. Businessman Donald Trump had been a Democrat before seeking the Republican nomination, and Senator Bernie Sanders was an independent who did not become a Democrat until he sought the party's nomination.

In this light, the national committees appear to be relatively useless organizations—as reflected in the 1964 book about them, *Politics Without Power*.[42] For many years, their role was essentially limited to planning for the next party convention. The committee would select the site, invite the state parties to attend, plan the program, and so on. Beginning in the 1970s, however, the roles of the DNC and RNC began to expand—but in different ways.

The Democratic story was dramatic. During the Vietnam War in 1968, an unpopular President Lyndon Johnson was challenged for renomination by prominent Democrats, including Senators Robert F. Kennedy and Eugene McCarthy. On March 31, after primary elections had begun, Johnson chose not to run for reelection. His vice president, Hubert Humphrey, then announced his candidacy. A month later, Senator Kennedy was assassinated. Although Humphrey did not enter a single primary, he won the nomination over McCarthy at a riotous convention angry at the war and the role of party bosses in picking Humphrey. In an attempt to open the party to broader participation, a party commission formulated new guidelines for selecting delegates to the next convention in 1972. These guidelines promised party members a "full, meaningful and timely opportunity" to participate in the process. To comply with the new guidelines, many states used more open procedures, electing convention delegates in party primaries.

While the Democrats were busy in the 1970s with *procedural* reforms, the Republicans were making *organizational* reforms.[43] The RNC did little to open up its delegate selection process; Republicans were not inclined to impose quotas on state parties through their national committee. Instead, the RNC strengthened its fund-raising, research, and service roles. Republicans acquired their own building and their own computer system, and in 1976 they hired the first full-time chairperson in the history of either national party. (Until then, the chairperson had worked part-time.) The new RNC chairman, William Brock, expanded the party's staff, launched new publications, held seminars, conducted election analyses, and advised candidates for state and legislative offices—things that national party committees in other countries had been doing for years. By the 2000 election, campaign finance analysts noted, American parties had become "an important source of funding in the race for the White House."[44]

The vast difference between the Democratic and Republican approaches to reforming the national committees shows in the funds raised by the DNC and RNC during election campaigns. Even though Republicans traditionally raised more campaign money

congressional campaign committee
An organization maintained by a political party to raise funds to support its own candidates in congressional elections.

than Democrats, they no longer relied on a relatively few wealthy contributors. As a matter of fact, the Republicans received more of their funds in small contributions (less than $100), mainly through direct-mail solicitation, than the Democrats. Until the 2008 election, the RNC raised far more money than the DNC, from many more citizens, as part of its long-term commitment to improving its organizational services. Beginning in 2002, however, significant changes occurred in how political parties could collect money to finance their activities. These campaign finance reforms are discussed in Chapter 9.

According to a major study of presidential party building, all Republican presidents, from Eisenhower through G. W. Bush, supported their national committee's organization efforts in order to build a Republican majority in the electorate. In contrast, Democratic presidents from John F. Kennedy through Bill Clinton "were not out to build a new majority but to make use of the one they had."[45] They tended to exploit, not build, the party organization. Obama fell back into the traditional pattern during his first term. By using his party to generate publicity for his administration's policy agenda while neglecting its organizational capacities at the state and local levels, Obama's behavior tended to parallel that of his Democratic predecessors.

State and Local Party Organizations

At one time, both major parties were firmly anchored by powerful state and local party organizations. Big-city party organizations, such as the Democrats' Tammany Hall in New York City and the Cook County Central Committee in Chicago, were called *party machines.*

A **party machine** was a centralized organization that dominated local politics by controlling elections—sometimes by illegal means, often by providing jobs and social services to urban workers in return for their votes. The patronage and social service functions of party machines were undercut when the government expanded unemployment compensation, aid to families with dependent children, and other social services. As a result, most local party organizations lost their ability to deliver votes and thus to determine the outcome of elections. However, machines remained strong in certain areas. In Nassau County, New York, for example, suburban Republicans showed that they could run a machine as well as urban Democrats.[46]

The individual state and local organizations of both parties vary widely in strength, but recent research has found that "neither the Republican nor Democratic party has a distinct advantage with regard to direct campaign activities."[47] Whereas once both the RNC and the DNC were dependent for their funding on "quotas" paid by state parties, now the funds flow the other way. In addition to money, state parties also received candidate training, poll data and research, and campaigning instruction.[48] The national committees have also taken a more active role in congressional campaigns.[49] In the 2014 congressional election cycle, the RNC reported $6 million in "independent expenditures" and the DNC transferred $28 million to state and local parties.[50]

Decentralized but Growing Stronger

Although the national committees have gained strength over the past three decades, American political parties are still among the most decentralized parties in the world.[51] Not even the president can count on loyalty from the legislative members of his party. Consider the 2009 congressional vote on reforming health care, President Obama's most important policy initiative. Although the Democrats held 258 seats in the House, the bill passed only 220–215, as 39 Democrats (15 percent) voted against it. Although all Democrats voted for the bill to reach the sixty votes needed for passage in the Senate (all thirty-nine Republicans opposed it), some Democratic senators demanded and got changes before backing the president's plan.

party machine
A centralized party organization that dominates local politics by controlling elections.

In 2015, the Republican Speaker of the House of Representatives, John Boehner, also had trouble commanding loyalty from his majority in the chamber. The 234 House Republicans were reportedly divided among different party factions: only about forty-four members regularly supported the GOP leadership, but others—including more than sixty aligned with the tea party movement—held to their own demands.[52] A frustrated Boehner abruptly quit as Speaker and retired from Congress, to be replaced by Paul Ryan, thought to be the only person acceptable to the party's warring factions. While competing for the 2016 Republican presidential nomination, most hopefuls openly criticized the party establishment (the RNC and congressional leaders) for not being sufficiently conservative.

Decentralization of power has always been the most distinguishing characteristic of American political parties. Moreover, the rise in the proportion of citizens who style themselves as independents suggests that our already weak parties are in further decline.[53] American political parties are so organizationally diffuse and decentralized that they raise questions about how well they link voters to the government.

The Model of Responsible Party Government

LO5 Identify the principles of responsible party government and evaluate their role in majoritarian democracy.

According to the majoritarian model of democracy, parties are essential to making the government responsive to public opinion. Some scholars view the ideal role of parties in majoritarian democracy in the four principles of **responsible party government:**[54]

1. Parties should present clear and coherent programs to voters.
2. Voters should choose candidates on the basis of party programs.
3. The winning party should carry out its program once in office.
4. Voters should hold the governing party responsible at the next election for executing its program.

responsible party government
A set of principles formalizing the ideal role of parties in a majoritarian democracy.

How well do these principles describe American politics? You've learned that the Democratic and Republican platforms are different and that they are much more ideologically consistent than many people believe. So the first principle is being met fairly well.[55] To a lesser extent, so is the third principle: once parties gain power, they usually try to do what they said they would do.

One can ask whether the model of responsible party government is suited to the American political system. Because governmental power is divided among the House, Senate, and president, a party must control all three components to carry out its program. In national surveys, people only favor one-party control of the presidency and Congress if their party is in control. Otherwise, a majority favors divided government or thinks it makes no difference.[56]

From the standpoint of democratic theory and responsible parties, the real question involves principles 2 and 4: Do voters really pay attention to party platforms and policies when they cast their ballots?[57] And if so, do voters hold the governing party responsible at the next election for delivering, or failing to deliver, on its pledges? To answer these questions, we must consider in greater detail the parties' role in nominating candidates and structuring the voters' choices in elections. At the conclusion of Chapter 9, we will return to evaluating the role of political parties in democratic government.

Summary

LO1   Define political party and list the functions performed by parties in democratic government.

- Political parties perform four important functions: nominating candidates, structuring the voting choice, proposing alternative government programs, and coordinating the activities of government officials. Political parties have been performing these four functions longer in the United States than in any other country.

LO2   Outline the history of the U.S. political party system.

- The Democratic Party, founded in 1828, is the world's oldest political party. The Republican Party emerged as a major party after the 1856 election. Our two-party system has been marked by four critical elections: The election of 1860 established the Republicans as the major party in the North and the Democrats as the dominant party in the South. The election of 1896 strengthened the link between the Republican Party and business interests in the Northeast and Midwest, making it the majority party nationally for more than three decades. The election of 1932 during the Great Depression transformed the Democrats into the majority party for more than three decades. The election of 1968 ended the Democrats' domination of national politics, as Republican presidential candidates ran well in the South.

LO3   Explain why two parties dominate the history of American politics.

- Minor parties have contributed ideas to the Democratic and Republican platforms but have not enjoyed much electoral success in America. Our two-party system is perpetuated by two principles of our electoral system: single-member districts and plurality rule. The political socialization process causes most Americans to identify with either the Democratic or the Republican Party. Over the last sixty years, voters have been leaving the Democratic Party and becoming independents. Still, Democrats nationally outnumber Republicans, and together they outnumber independents.

LO4   Compare and contrast the Democratic and Republican parties on the basis of ideology and organization.

- Democratic identifiers and activists are more likely to describe themselves as liberal; Republican identifiers and activists tend to be conservative. Democratic Party platforms stress equality over freedom; Republican platforms stress freedom but also emphasize the importance of restoring social order. Organizationally, the Republicans have recently become the stronger party at both the national and state levels, and both parties are showing signs of resurgence. Nevertheless, both parties are still very decentralized compared with parties in other countries.

LO5   Identify the principles of responsible party government and evaluate their role in majoritarian democracy.

- According to the four principles of responsible party government, parties should present clear programs to voters and voters should choose candidates on the basis of party programs. The winning party should carry out its program, and voters should hold the party responsible for doing so. However, citizens tend not to pay much attention to platforms when voting.

Chapter Quiz

LO1 **Define political party and list the functions performed by parties in democratic government.**

1. How does a political party differ from an interest group?
2. What are the major functions of political parties?

LO2 **Outline the history of the U.S. political party system.**

1. How did the Twelfth Amendment to the Constitution affect how parties nominated presidential candidates?
2. How did the second party system differ from the first?

LO3 **Explain why two parties dominate the history of American politics.**

1. How does an electoral system based on majority representation favor two parties compared with one based on proportional representation?
2. What does "party identification" mean, how is it measured, and how stable has it been in America since the 1950s?

LO4 **Compare and contrast the Democratic and Republican parties on the basis of ideology and organization.**

1. How do the Democratic and Republican parties' platforms differ in invoking the concepts of freedom, order, and equality?
2. To what extent do the national committees of the Democratic and Republican parties control their parties' presidential campaigns?

LO5 **Identify the principles of responsible party government and evaluate their role in majoritarian democracy.**

1. Describe the ideal role of parties in majoritarian democracy and assess how American politics fits this ideal.
2. Is there any evidence that the two major American political parties fulfill the first principle of responsible party government?

9 Nominations, Elections, and Campaigns

In past presidential campaigns, certain informal rules—"established ways of doing things"—structured candidates' behavior. Politicians followed these rules because they seem to produce desired results. Candidates who broke them usually paid a price. In 2016, candidates in both parties seeking their parties' presidential nomination broke numerous informal rules. Here are nine of the broken rules and the six rule-breakers:

- Businessman and TV star Donald Trump destroyed the rule that candidates without any governmental experience had no chance to gain their party's nomination.
- Former New York Senator and Secretary of State Hillary Clinton demolished the rule that a woman could not win the presidential nomination of a major party.
- Vermont Senator Bernie Sanders refuted the rule that a socialist calling for a political revolution could not seriously challenge the favorite of the Democratic Party's establishment.
- Sanders, by raising small sums from many donors, also invalidated the rule that serious candidates had to get large sums of money from a few donors.
- Trump smashed another rule that candidates should appear "presidential" while campaigning and not insult other candidates, groups, or countries.
- Additionally, Trump shattered the rule that candidates needed to spend large sums of money on advertising to generate attention.
- Trump, by tweeting his thoughts to millions of followers, defied yet another rule: that candidates must coordinate campaign messages with their campaign staffs.
- Texas Senator Ted Cruz and Ohio Governor John Kasich, who plotted to deny the Republican presidential nomination to Donald Trump, ignored the rule that presidential candidates do not collude in campaigning.
- Former Florida governor Jeb Bush disproved the rule that Republican voters would support a well-financed, experienced member of famous Republican family.

Only Ted Cruz, John Kasich, and Jeb Bush (all Republicans) paid any prices. The Cruz–Kasich pact damaged both candidates and failed to stop Trump. Jeb Bush failed to win many votes and withdrew early from the race. However, the serial, four-time rule-breaker, Donald Trump, won each gamble and, against all early expectations, captured his party's nomination.

Others might cite additional rules broken in the 2016 presidential campaign, but these certify the campaign as the most abnormal in American political history. Will the abnormal become the new normal?

#ChallengeAccepted

Take the Challenge on MindTap for American Government

Which of these "broken rules" do you think will have the most impact on the next presidential contest in 2020?

Sources: Donald J. Trump for President, Inc.; Cruz for President; Hillary for America; Bernie 2016

Learning Outcomes

LO1 Describe how election campaigns have changed over time.

LO2 Explain the procedures followed in the nomination of both congressional and presidential candidates.

LO3 Describe the function of the electoral college and formulate arguments for and against the electoral vote system.

LO4 Analyze the American election campaign process in terms of political context, financial resources, and strategies and tactics for reaching the voters.

LO5 Assess the effects of party identification, political issues, and candidate attributes on voter choice.

LO6 Explain the significance of candidate-centered as opposed to party-centered election campaigns for both majoritarian and pluralist democracy.

This chapter examines how candidates are nominated and what factors are important in causing voters to favor one nominee over another. We consider the role of election campaigns and how they have changed over time. We also address these important questions: How well do election campaigns inform voters? How important is money in conducting a winning campaign? What are the roles of party identification, issues, and candidate attributes in influencing voters' choices and thus election outcomes? How do campaigns, elections, and parties fit into the majoritarian and pluralist models of democracy?

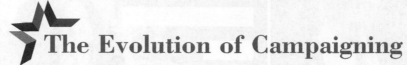

The Evolution of Campaigning

LO1 Describe how election campaigns have changed over time.

Voting in free elections to choose leaders is the main way that citizens control government. As discussed in Chapter 8, political parties help structure the voting choice by reducing the number of candidates on the ballot to those who have a realistic chance of winning or who offer distinctive policies. An **election campaign** is an organized effort to persuade voters to choose one candidate over others competing for the same office. An effective campaign requires sufficient resources to acquire and analyze information about voters' interests, develop a strategy and matching tactics for appealing to these interests, deliver the candidate's message to the voters, and get them to cast their ballots.

In the past, political parties conducted all phases of the election campaign. As recently as the 1950s, state and local party organizations "felt the pulse" of their rank-and-file members to learn what was important to the voters. They helped recruit candidates and then lined up leading officials to support them and to ensure big crowds at campaign rallies. Parties also prepared buttons, banners, and newspaper advertisements that touted their candidates, proudly named under the prominent label of the party. Finally, candidates relied heavily on the local precinct and county party organizations to contact voters before elections, to mention their names, to extol their virtues, and—most importantly—to make sure their supporters voted, and voted correctly.

Today, candidates seldom rely much on political parties to conduct their campaigns. How do candidates learn about voters' interests now? By contracting for public opinion polls, not by asking the party. How do candidates plan their campaign strategy and tactics? By hiring political consultants to devise clever sound bites (brief, catchy phrases) that will capture voters' attention on television, not by consulting party headquarters. How do candidates deliver their messages to voters? By using social media and the mass media, not by counting on party regulars to canvass the neighborhoods. Beginning with the 2004 election, presidential and congressional candidates relied heavily on the Internet to raise campaign funds and mobilize supporters. By the 2016 election, they created Facebook pages, used Twitter to break news and express opinions, hosted chats on Reddit, posted photos on Snapchat and Pinterest, and shared videos on Periscope and Instagram, two social-video services.

Increasingly, election campaigns have evolved from being party centered to being candidate centered.[1] This is not to say that political parties no longer have a role to play in campaigns, for they do. As noted in Chapter 8, the Democratic National Committee now exercises more control over the delegate selection process than it did before 1972. Since 1976, the Republicans have greatly expanded their national organization and fundraising capacity. But whereas the parties virtually ran election campaigns prior to the 1960s, now they exist mainly to support candidate-centered campaigns by providing services or funds to their candidates. National party organizations also lost influence

election campaign
An organized effort to persuade voters to choose one candidate over others competing for the same office.

in conducting campaigns after a 2010 Supreme Court decision (discussed below) that allowed other political organizations to fund candidates. Nevertheless, we will see that the party label is usually a candidate's prime attribute at election time.

Perhaps the most important change in American elections is that candidates don't campaign just to get elected anymore. Due to the Progressive movement in the 1920s that championed use of the direct primary to select party candidates, candidates must campaign for *nomination* as well. As we said in Chapter 8, nominating candidates to run for office under the party label is one of the main functions of political parties. Party organizations once controlled that function. Even Abraham Lincoln served only one term in the House of Representatives before the party transferred the nomination for his House seat to someone else.[2] For most important offices today, however, candidates are no longer nominated by the party organization but *within* the party. Except when recruiting prominent individuals to challenge entrenched incumbents, party leaders seldom choose candidates; they merely organize and supervise the election process by which party voters choose the candidates. Because almost all aspiring candidates must first win a primary election to gain their party's nomination, those who would campaign for election must first campaign for nomination. In the 2016 presidential contest, both national party organizations, but especially the Republicans, stood by helplessly as their favored candidates were battered by newcomers to their parties.

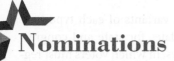

Nominations

LO2 Explain the procedures followed in the nomination of both congressional and presidential candidates.

The distinguishing feature of the nomination process in American party politics is that it usually involves an election by party voters. National party leaders do not choose their party's nominee for president or even its candidates for House and Senate seats. Virtually no other political parties in the world nominate candidates to national legislatures through party elections.[3] In more than half the world's parties, local party leaders choose legislative candidates, and their national party organization usually approve these choices.

Democrats and Republicans nominate their candidates for national and state offices in varying ways across the country, because each state is entitled to make its own laws governing the nomination process. (This is significant in itself, for political parties in most other countries are largely free of laws stating how they must select their candidates.)[4] We can classify nomination practices by the types of party elections held and the level of office sought.

Nomination for Congress and State Offices

In the United States, almost all aspiring candidates for major offices are nominated through a **primary election**, a preliminary election conducted within the party to select its candidates. Some forty states use primary elections alone to nominate candidates for all state and national offices, and primaries figure in the nomination processes of all the other states. The rules governing primary elections vary greatly by state, and they can change between elections. Hence, it is difficult to summarize the types of primaries and their incidence. Every state uses primary elections to nominate candidates for statewide office, but a few also use party conventions to place names on the primary ballots and some allow minor parties to nominate candidates in conventions.[5] The nomination process, then, is highly decentralized, resting on the decisions of thousands, perhaps millions, of the party rank and file who participate in primary elections.

primary election
A preliminary election conducted within a political party to select candidates who will run for public office in a subsequent election.

In both parties, only about half of the regular party voters (about one-quarter of the voting-age population) bother to vote in a given primary, although the proportion varies greatly by state and contest. Moreover, both parties' primary electorate differs from party voters in the general electorate. In 2012, for example, 36 percent of Republican primary voters gave conservative answers to ten questions versus 21 percent who voted only in the general election.[6] (Obama was unchallenged in 2012, preventing a parallel study of Democratic primary voters.)

Some studies support another interpretation: although party activists who turn out for primaries and caucuses are not representative of the average party member, they subordinate their own views to select candidates "who will fare well in the general election."[7] Concerning the 2016 presidential election, leaders in the Republican Party's establishment sought to nominate a candidate whom they thought would actually win the election. Republican primary voters, however, seemed less concerned with nominating someone who appealed to the national electorate than with nominating a candidate who reflected their values and distrust of Washington. In elections at the congressional and state levels, perhaps the most significant trend is the decline in competition for party nominations. In 2014, 327 incumbent members of Congress were renominated by the same party, while only 4 members who sought renomination were defeated.[8] Another study at the state level found that only "about 25 percent of state-wide candidates face serious primary competition."[9]

There are four major types of primary elections, and variants of each type have been used frequently across all states to nominate candidates for state and congressional offices. At one end of the spectrum are **closed primaries**, in which voters must register their party affiliation to vote on that party's potential nominees. At the other end are **open primaries**, in which any voter, regardless of party registration or affiliation, can choose either party's ballot. In between are **modified closed primaries**, in which individual state parties decide whether to allow those not registered with either party to vote with their party registrants, and **modified open primaries**, in which all those not already registered with a party can choose any party ballot and vote with party registrants.

For decades, Louisiana—historically a Democratic state—has used a "blanket primary," which listed all candidates (usually Democrats) on a single ballot. The top two vote-getters ran again in a general election; if one got over 50 percent, that candidate won automatically. Recently voters in two-party states Washington (2004) and California (2010) approved a variant of the blanket primary, called the "top-two." It is open to all candidates, with the top two vote-getters standing for the general election. Brief experience with this "top-two" primary system shows that winning candidates virtually always come from the two major parties.[10] Limited research on its use to date in California shows that the new system has not delivered on its backers' claims. Turnout in top-two primary elections in 2012 and 2014 was less than usual, not more.[11] Moreover, candidates in top-two primaries were not measurably less polarized, perhaps even more polarized.[12] Indeed, researchers have found limited effects of the types of primaries generally on candidates' ideologies—at least at the state level.[13]

Most scholars believe that the type of primary held in a state affects the strength of its party organizations. Open primaries weaken parties more than closed primaries, for they allow voters to float between parties rather than require them to work within one. But the differences among types of primaries are much less important than the fact that our parties have primaries at all—that parties choose candidates through elections. This practice originated in the United States and largely remains peculiar to us. Placing the nomination of party candidates in the hands of voters rather than party leaders is a key factor in the decentralization of power in American parties, which contributes more to pluralist than to majoritarian democracy.

closed primaries
Primary elections in which voters must declare their party affiliation before they are given the primary ballot containing that party's potential nominees.

open primaries
Primary elections in which voters need not declare their party affiliation and can choose one party's primary ballot to take into the voting booth.

modified closed primaries
Primary elections that allow individual state parties to decide whether they permit independents to vote in their primaries and, if so, for which offices.

modified open primaries
Primary elections that entitle independent voters to vote in a party's primary.

dropped out, followed soon by Carson. Rubio left in mid-March, immediately after losing badly in his home state, Florida. Cruz dropped out on May 3, the evening he lost the Indiana primary. Kasich ended his campaign the next day.

Requiring prospective presidential candidates to campaign before many millions of party voters in scores of primaries and hundreds of thousands of party activists in caucus states has several consequences:

- *When no incumbent in the White House is seeking reelection, the presidential nominating process becomes contested in both parties.* This is what occurred in 2016, when seventeen Republicans and six Democrats announced presidential campaigns. In the complex mix of caucus and primary methods that states use to select convention delegates, timing and luck can affect who wins, and even an outside chance of success ordinarily attracts a half-dozen or so plausible contestants in either party lacking an incumbent president.

- *An incumbent president usually encounters little or no opposition for renomination within the party.* Thus, Obama was routinely renominated in 2012, but challenges can occur. In 1992, President George Herbert Walker Bush faced fierce opposition for the Republican nomination from Pat Buchanan. In 1968, President Lyndon Johnson faced such hostility within the Democratic Party that he declined to seek renomination.

- *In the non-incumbent party, numerous hopefuls seek the presidential nomination.* In 2012, twelve notable Republicans sought to run against Barack Obama along with hundreds (yes) of others not so notable who filed candidacy papers.

- *When there is no incumbent president, multiple candidates in both parties will run.* Hence, the twenty-three Republican and Democratic presidential hopefuls in 2016.

- *The Iowa caucuses and New Hampshire primaries do matter.* In 2016, Hillary Clinton placed first (narrowly) in Iowa, and Trump handily won New Hampshire. Since the first Iowa caucus in 1972, each party has nominated twelve presidential candidates. All of the twelve Republican nominees were first (or unopposed) in either Iowa or New Hampshire, as were eleven of the Democrats. Only Bill Clinton in 1992 failed to win either Iowa or New Hampshire.

- *Candidates eventually favored by most party identifiers usually win their party's nomination.* There had been only two exceptions to this rule since 1936, when poll data first became available: Adlai E. Stevenson in 1952 and George McGovern in 1972.[19] Both were Democrats; both lost impressively in the general election. A poll before the 2016 party conventions found only 38 percent of Republicans satisfied with Donald Trump. Democrats slightly favored Hillary Clinton.[20]

- *Candidates who win the nomination do so largely on their own and owe little or nothing to the national party organization, which usually does not promote a candidate.* In fact, Jimmy Carter won the nomination in 1976 against a field of nationally prominent Democrats, although he was a party outsider with few strong connections to the national party leadership. Barack Obama won in 2008 against Hillary Clinton, who had strong ties to Democratic Party leaders. Donald Trump won despite the concerted opposition of Republican Party leaders. The party's 2012 nominee, Mitt Romney, publicly pronounced Trump unfit to be president and led an unsuccessful campaign against his nomination.

Winning the Nomination. Regardless of how parties chose their convention delegates, most must vote on the first convention ballot for the candidates they backed when selected. Over 700 Democratic "super delegates"—seated at the convention because they sat on the Democratic National Committee, formerly held high national office, or were sitting governors or members of Congress—had no voting commitments.

The Republicans had only about 100 such delegates, but the party allowed diverse voting rules for delegates from different states. Trump, whose candidacy was opposed by party leaders, complained that some rules denied him votes at the convention that he had won in state contests. He also claimed that he should be nominated because he had more votes than anyone else—even if not a majority. The convention was, Trump charged, "a rigged system. It's a crooked system."[21] In response, seven former chairs of the Republican National Committee said in the *Wall Street Journal* that historically the majority rules in both parties' conventions. "The majority, no more, no less. Always."[22]

By the Indiana primary on May 3, 2016, party voters in some forty states and territories had chosen over 75 percent of 4,764 Democratic convention delegates and over 80 percent of 2,472 Republican delegates. After losing in Indiana, Ted Cruz and John Kasich—Trump's only remaining opponents—dropped out of the race. Despite polls showing that only 42 percent of all Republican voters viewed him favorably, versus 42 percent unfavorably,[23] Trump became the presumptive nominee of the July 21 Republican convention. While all Democratic voters viewed both Hillary Clinton and Bernie Sanders equally favorably, Clinton soon reached the majority needed for nomination at the July 28 Democratic convention, defeating Bernie Sanders by combining the state delegates she won with the super delegates who favored her. Although Sanders charged that his delegates were denied important roles at the convention, most of his primary voters said that they would support Clinton in the general election. Many Republican primary voters, however, said they sought a third party option, perhaps former New Mexico governor Gary Johnson, running as the presidential candidate of the Libertarian Party.

Elections

LO3 Describe the function of the electoral college and formulate arguments for and against the electoral vote system.

general election
A national election held by law in November of every even-numbered year.

By national law, all seats in the House of Representatives and one-third of the seats in the Senate are filled in a **general election** held in early November in even-numbered years. Every state takes advantage of the national election to fill some of the nearly 500,000 state and local offices across the country, which makes the election even more "general." When the president is chosen every fourth year, the election is identified as a presidential election. The intervening elections are known as *congressional, midterm,* or *off-year elections.*

Presidential Elections and the Electoral College

In contrast to almost all other offices in the United States, the presidency does not go
Unlike almost all other offices in the United States, the presidency does not go automatically to whomever wins the most votes. Donald Trump in 2016 and George W. Bush in 2000 became president despite receiving fewer popular votes than their opponents. Instead, the Constitution specifies a two-stage procedure to decide presidential elections; it requires selection of the president by a group (college) of electors representing the states. Technically, we elect a president not in a national election but in a *federal* election.

The Electoral College: Structure. Surprising as it might seem, the term "electoral college" is not mentioned in the Constitution and is not readily found in books on American politics prior to World War II. One major dictionary defines a college as "a body of persons having a common purpose or shared duties."[24] The electors who choose the president of the United States became known as the electoral college largely during the twentieth century. Eventually, this term became incorporated into statutes relating to presidential elections, so it has assumed a legal basis.[25]

According to the Constitution (Article II, Section 1) each of the fifty states is entitled to one elector for each of its senators (100 total) and one for each of its representatives (435 votes total), totaling 535 electoral votes. In addition, the Twenty-third Amendment to the Constitution awarded three electoral votes (the minimum for any state) to the District of Columbia, although it elects no voting members of Congress. The total number of electoral votes therefore is 538. The Constitution specifies that a candidate needs a majority of electoral votes, or 270 today, to win the presidency. If no candidate receives a majority, the election is thrown into the House of Representatives. The House votes by state, with each state casting one vote. The candidates in the House election are the top three finishers in the general election. A presidential election has gone to the House only twice in American history, in 1800 and 1824, before a stable two-party system had developed.

Electoral votes are apportioned among the states according to their representation in Congress, which depends largely on their population. Because of population changes recorded by the 2010 census, the distribution of electoral votes among the states changed between the 2008 and 2012 presidential elections. Figure 9.2 shows

FIGURE 9.2 Population Shifts and Political Gains and Losses Since 1960

If the states were sized according to their electoral votes for the 2016 presidential election, the nation might resemble this map, on which states are drawn according to their population, based on the 2010 census. Each state has as many electoral votes as its combined representation in the Senate (always two) and the House (which depends on population). Although New Jersey is much smaller in area than Montana, New Jersey has far more people and is thus bigger in terms of "electoral geography." The coloring on this map shows the states that have gained electoral votes since 1960 (in shades of green) and those that have lost electoral votes (in shades of purple). States that have not had the number of their electoral votes changed since 1960 are blue. This map clearly reflects the drain of population (and seats in Congress) from the north-central and eastern states to the western and southern states. California, with two senators and fifty-three representatives in the 2016 election, will have fifty-five electoral votes for presidential elections until 2024, when reapportionment follows the 2020 census.

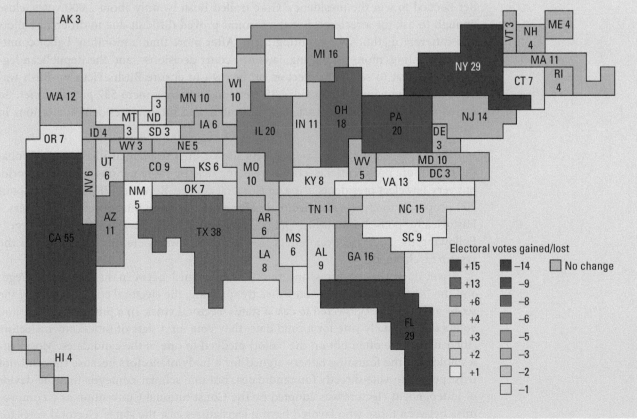

the distribution of electoral votes for the 2016 election, indicating which states have lost and gained electoral votes. The clear pattern is the systemic loss of people and electoral votes in the north-central and eastern states and the gain in the western and southern states.

The Electoral College: Politics. In 1789, the first set of presidential electors was chosen under the new Constitution. Only three states chose their electors by direct popular vote, while state legislatures selected electors in the others. Selection by state legislature remained the norm until 1792. Afterward, direct election by popular vote became more common, and by 1824 voters chose electors in eighteen of twenty-four states. Since 1860, all states have selected their electors through popular vote once they entered the Union.[26] In the disputed 2000 presidential election, the Republican Florida state legislature threatened to resolve the dispute in favor of Bush by selecting its electors itself. There was precedent to do so, but it was a pre–Civil War precedent.

Of course, the situation in Florida was itself unprecedented due to the extremely close election in 2000. Voters nationwide favored the Democratic candidate, Al Gore, by a plurality of approximately 500,000 votes out of 105 million cast. But the presidential election is a *federal* election. A candidate is not chosen president by national popular vote but by a majority of the states' electoral votes. In every state but Maine and Nebraska, the candidate who wins a plurality of its popular vote—whether by 20 votes or 20,000 votes—wins all of the state's electoral votes. Gore and his Republican opponent, George W. Bush, ran close races in many states across the nation. Not counting Florida, Gore had won 267 electoral votes, just three short of the 270 he needed to claim the presidency.

But in Florida, which had twenty-five electoral votes in 2000, the initial vote count showed an extremely close race, with Bush ahead by the slimmest of margins. If Bush outpolled Gore by just a single vote, Bush could add its 25 electoral votes to the 246 he won in the other states, for a total of 271. That was just one more than the number needed to win the presidency. Gore trailed Bush by only about 2,000 votes, close enough to ask for a recount. But the recount proved difficult due to different ballots and different methods for counting them. After more than a month of ballot counting, recounting, more recounting, lawsuits, court decisions—and the Republican legislature's threat to select the electors on its own to ensure Bush's victory—Bush was certified as the winner of Florida's 25 *electoral votes* by a mere 537 *popular votes*. So ended one of the most protracted, complicated, and intense presidential elections in American history.[27]

The Electoral College: Abolish It? As shown in "Presidential Elections in Global Politics," more presidential elections are being held by more nations across the world, but very few elect presidents using an electoral college. Between 1789 and 2000, about 700 proposals to change the electoral college scheme were introduced in Congress.[28] Historically, polls have shown public opinion opposed to the electoral college.[29] Following the 2000 election, letters flooded into newspapers, urging anew that the system be changed.[30]

To evaluate the criticisms, one must first distinguish between the electoral "college" and the "system" of electoral votes. Strictly speaking, the electoral college is merely the set of individuals empowered to cast a state's electoral votes. In a presidential election, voters don't actually vote for a candidate; they vote for a slate of little-known electors (their names are often not on the ballot) pledged to one of the candidates. Most critics hold that the founding fathers argued for a body of electors because they did not trust people to vote directly for candidates. But one scholar contends that the device of independent electors was adopted by the Constitutional Convention as a compromise between those who favored having legislatures cast the states' electoral votes for

Presidential Elections in Global Politics

Today, many nations elect their presidents, and do so differently from how presidents had been chosen. This chart shows how nations chose presidents in 405 elections from 1946 to 2010. Only eleven presidential elections were held in the postwar 1940s and most presidents then were elected by simple plurality vote. Argentina and the United States were the only countries to use an electoral college. As more countries became democratic over the decades, more presidential elections occurred—135 in the 2000s. In that recent decade, only thirty-one elections decided the presidency by a simple plurality vote. In eighty-seven elections, the winning candidate had to win a majority of the vote cast, not a simple plurality. Usually, this meant holding a second ballot some days later. In twelve elections, a qualified majority (more than a simple majority) was needed. The three elections that chose a president by an electoral college in the 2000s were all in the United States (2000, 2004, and 2008). Ireland held two elections by alternative vote, in which voters ranked candidates by their preferences.

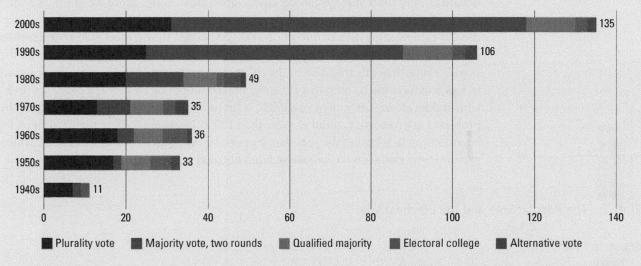

Source: Nils-Christian Bormann and Matt Golder, "Democratic Electoral Systems Around the World, 1946–2011," *Electoral Studies* 32 (2013): 360–369.

CRITICAL THINKING According to the Constitution, candidates must win a majority of the electoral votes (270 out of 538) to claim the presidency. Suppose only a plurality of the vote were needed to become president. How might this simple change affect American politics? Would it advantage or disadvantage minor parties? Would the change be desirable or undesirable?

president and those who favored direct popular election.[31] The electoral college allowed states to choose, and—as described in Chapter 8—all states gravitated to direct election of electors by 1860. Occasionally (but rarely), electors break their pledges when they cast their ballots at their state capitol in December (electors who do so are called "faithless electors"). Indeed, this happened in 2016, when seven electors defected from their states' voting results. Four in Washington and one in Hawaii declined to support Hillary Clinton, while two in Texas voted for John Kasich and Ron Paul, reducing Trump's electoral vote from 306 to 304. Such aberrations make for historical footnotes but do not affect outcomes. Today, voters have good reason to oppose a body of electors to translate their decision, and few observers defend the electoral college itself.

The more legitimate criticism centers on the electoral vote *system*, which makes for a federal rather than a national election. Many reformers favor a majoritarian method for choosing the president by nationwide direct popular vote. They argue that it is simply wrong to have a system that allows a candidate who wins the most popular votes nationally to lose the election. Until 2000, that situation had not occurred since 1888, when

Grover Cleveland won the popular vote but lost the presidency to Benjamin Harrison in the electoral college. During all intervening elections, the candidate winning a plurality of the popular vote also won a majority of the electoral vote. In fact, the electoral vote generally operated to magnify the margin of victory, as Figure 9.3 shows. Some scholars argued that this magnifying effect increased the legitimacy of presidents-elect who failed to win a majority of the popular vote, which happened in the elections of Kennedy, Nixon (first time), Clinton (both times), and certainly George W. Bush (first time).

The 2000 and 2016 elections proved that defenders of the electoral vote system cannot claim that a federal election based on electoral votes yields the same outcome as a national election based on the popular vote. However, three lines of argument support selecting a president by electoral votes rather than by popular vote. First, if one supports a federal form of government as embodied within the Constitution, then one may defend the electoral vote system because it gives small states more weight in the vote: they have two senators, the same as large states. Second, if one favors presidential candidates campaigning on foot and in rural areas (needed to win most states) rather than campaigning via television to the one hundred most populous market areas to win the popular vote, then one might favor the electoral vote system.[33] Third, if you do not want to risk a *nationwide* recount in a close election (multiplying by fifty the counting problems in Florida in 2000), then you might want to keep the current system. Imagine the problems in a national recount of more than 120 million votes cast in the 2016 election. So switching to selecting the president by popular vote has serious implications, which explains why Congress has not moved quickly to amend the Constitution.

FIGURE 9.3   The Popular Vote and the Electoral Vote

Strictly speaking, a presidential election is a federal election, not a national election. A candidate must win a majority (270) of the nation's total electoral vote (538). A candidate can win a plurality of the popular vote and still not win the presidency. That happened in 1888 but not again for over one hundred years—until 2000 and 2016. Unlike 2000, when the popular and electoral votes divided about 50-50, Donald Trump in 2016 won less than 48 percent of the popular vote but 57 percent of the electoral vote. As it has usually worked in the past, the electoral vote system magnified the winner's victory and thus the legitimacy of the president-elect.

Source: Harold W. Stanley and Richard G. Niemi, *Vital Statistics on American Politics, 2011–2012* (Washington, DC: CQ Press, 2014).

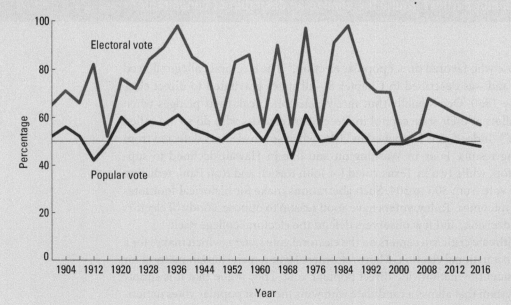

Congressional Elections

In a presidential election, the candidates for the presidency are listed at the top of the ballot, followed by the candidates for other national offices and those for state and local offices. A voter is said to vote a **straight ticket** when she or he chooses the same party's candidates for all the offices. A voter who chooses candidates from different parties is said to vote a **split ticket**. About half of all voters say they split their tickets, and the proportion of voters who chose a presidential candidate from one party and a congressional candidate from the other has varied between 15 and 30 percent since 1952.[34] In the 1970s and 1980s, the common pattern was to elect a Republican as president while electing mostly Democrats to Congress. This produced a divided government, with the executive and legislative branches controlled by different parties (see Chapter 12). In the mid-1990s, the electorate flipped the pattern, electing a Democratic president but a Republican Congress.

Until the 1994 election, Democrats had maintained a lock on congressional elections for decades, winning a majority of House seats since 1954 and controlling the Senate for all but six years during that period. Republicans regularly complained that inequitable districts drawn by Democrat-dominated state legislatures had denied them their fair share of seats. For example, the Republicans won 46 percent of the congressional vote in 1992 but gained only 40 percent of the seats. Despite the Republicans' complaint, election specialists note that sizable discrepancies between votes won and seats won are the inevitable consequence of **first-past-the-post elections**—a British term for elections conducted in single-member districts that award victory to the candidate with the most votes. In all such elections worldwide, the party that wins the most votes tends to win more seats than projected by its percentage of the vote.* In 2014, therefore, the Republicans benefited from the electoral mathematics. They won just 50.5 percent of the congressional vote to the Democrats' 45.5 percent, but Republicans won 57 percent of the seats. These recent election results reveal no evidence of Democratic malapportionment of congressional districts. Both parties have enjoyed, and suffered, the mathematics of first-past-the-post elections.

The Republican Party headed into the 2016 elections worried about the effect of their unorthodox presidential candidate, Donald Trump, on their chances for retaining control of Congress. They anticipated keeping control of the House of Representatives but feared losing control of the Senate. Republicans fared much better from the election results than they expected. They expected to lose perhaps a dozen House seats but lost only half that, easily retaining power, and Democrats fell short of winning enough Senate seats to switch party control.

Campaigns

LO4 Analyze the American election campaign process in terms of political context, financial resources, and strategies and tactics for reaching the voters.

Election campaigns can be analyzed according to their political context, the financial resources available for conducting the campaign, and the strategies and tactics that underlie the dissemination of information about the candidate.

straight ticket
Voting for a single party's candidates for all the offices.

split ticket
Voting for candidates from different parties for different offices.

first-past-the-post elections
A British term for elections conducted in single-member districts that award victory to the candidate with the most votes.

---

*If you have trouble understanding this phenomenon, think of a basketball team that scores, on average, 51 percent of the total points in all the games it plays. That team usually wins more than just 51 percent of the games because it tends to win the close games.

The Political Context

The two most important structural factors that face each candidate planning a campaign are the office the candidate is seeking and whether he or she is the incumbent (the current officeholder running for reelection) or the challenger (who seeks to replace the incumbent). Incumbents usually enjoy great advantages over challengers, especially in elections to Congress. Most congressional elections today are not very competitive. Of 2,175 congressional elections in the 2000s, only 41 (1.9 percent) were decided by two percentage points or fewer.[35] As explained in Chapter 11, incumbents in the House of Representatives are almost impossible to defeat, historically winning more than 95 percent of the time.[36] Incumbent senators are somewhat more vulnerable. An incumbent president is also difficult to defeat—but not impossible. Democrat Jimmy Carter was defeated for reelection in 1980, as was Republican George H. W. Bush in 1992. Of course, a nonincumbent will always triumph in an **open election**, one lacking an incumbent because of a resignation, death, or constitutional requirement.

open election
An election that lacks an incumbent.

Every candidate for Congress must also examine the characteristics of the state or district, including its physical size and the sociological makeup of its electorate. In general, the bigger and more populous the district or state and the more diverse the electorate, the more complicated and costly is the campaign. Obviously, running for president means conducting a huge, complicated, and expensive campaign.

Despite talk about the decreased influence of party affiliation on voting behavior, the party preference of the electorate is an important factor in the context of a campaign. It is easier for a candidate to get elected when her or his party matches the electorate's preference, in part because raising the money needed to conduct a winning campaign is easier. Challengers for congressional seats, for example, get far less money from organized groups than do incumbents and must rely more on their personal funds and raising money from individual donors. So where candidates represent the minority party, they have to overcome not only a voting bias but also a funding bias. Finally, significant political issues—such as economic recession, personal scandals, and war—not only affect a campaign but also can dominate it and even negate such positive factors as incumbency and the advantages of a strong economy.

Financing

Regarding election campaigns, former House Speaker Thomas ("Tip") O'Neill said, "There are four parts to any campaign. The candidate, the issues of the candidate, the campaign organization, and the money to run the campaign with. Without money you can forget the other three."[37] Money pays for office space, staff salaries, cell phones, computers, travel expenses, campaign literature, and, of course, advertising in the mass media. A successful campaign requires a good campaign organization and a good candidate, but enough money will buy the best campaign managers, equipment, transportation, research, and consultants—making the quality of the organization largely a function of money. That may be true, but money alone does not ensure a successful campaign. Entering the 2016 primary election season, Republican Jeb Bush—son of one president and brother of another—led all candidates in funds raised by his campaign and by PACs supporting his candidacy, but he won relatively few primary votes and withdrew early.

Nevertheless, no one can run a successful presidential campaign without raising a great deal of money. Regulations of campaign financing for state elections vary according to the state. Campaign financing for federal elections is regulated by national legislation.

Regulating Campaign Financing. Early campaign financing laws had various flaws, and none provided for adequate enforcement. In 1971, during a period of party reform, Congress passed the Federal Election Campaign Act (FECA), which limited media spending and imposed stringent new rules for full reporting of campaign contributions and expenditures. The need for strict legislation soon became clear. In 1968, before FECA was enacted, House and Senate candidates reported spending $8.5 million on their campaigns. In 1972, with FECA in force, the same number of candidates admitted spending $88.9 million—ten times as much![38]

Financial misdeeds during Nixon's 1972 reelection campaign forced major amendments to the original FECA in 1974. The new legislation created the **Federal Election Commission (FEC)**, an independent agency of six members appointed by the president with approval of the Senate. No more than three members may come from the same party, and their six-year appointments are staggered over time so that no one president appoints the entire commission. The FEC is charged with enforcing limits on financial contributions to national campaigns, requiring full disclosure of campaign spending, and administering the public financing of presidential campaigns, which began with the 1976 election. With its commission divided three-to-three between the two parties, the FEC encountered difficulties in making decision and was ineffective in governing federal elections.

The law also condoned the creation of **political action committees (PACs)** by corporations, labor unions, or "nonconnected" groups that could, under limits, collect money and contribute it to campaigns for federal office—that is, Congress and the presidency. (The role of PACs in congressional elections is discussed at length in Chapter 10.)

Some people opposed any limits on campaign contributions, viewing money as "free speech" and challenging the 1974 limits under the First Amendment. Although the Supreme Court upheld limits on contributions in 1976, it struck down limits on *spending* by individuals or organizations made independently on behalf of a national candidate—holding that such spending constituted free speech, protected under the First Amendment. It also limited the FEC to regulate only advertisements advocating a candidate's election or defeat with such words as "vote for" or "vote against."[39] The 1974 FECA (with minor amendments) governed national elections for almost three decades.

As campaign spending increased, some members of Congress spoke piously about strengthening campaign finance laws but feared altering the process that elected them. In 2002 a bill introduced by Republican senator John McCain (Arizona) and Democratic senator Russell Feingold (Wisconsin) finally passed as the Bipartisan Campaign Reform Act (BCRA; pronounced "bikra"). BCRA was fiercely challenged from several sources, including Republican conservatives who attacked McCain for limiting contributions and weakening the party. Nevertheless, the law was upheld by the Supreme Court in 2003 and took effect for the 2004 election.

In general, BCRA raised the old limits on individual spending and indexed them for inflation in future years. Here are the major BCRA limitations for 2015–2016 contributions by individuals, adjusted for inflation:

- $2,700 to a specific candidate in a separate election during a two-year cycle (primaries, general, and runoff elections count as separate elections);
- $10,000 per year to each state party or political committee;
- $33,400 per year to any national party committee;
- $5,000 per year to any PAC.

Note that the 2002 law did not raise the $5,000 contribution limit for PACs, which many thought already had too much influence in elections, and did not index PAC contributions for inflation.

Within a decade after the 2002 McCain–Feingold BCRA campaign funding limitations went into effect, a more conservative Supreme Court gutted almost all limitations. In 2007, it struck down BCRA's ban of issue ads run before elections, which opened the door to massive independent campaign spending by nonparty groups.

Federal Election Commission (FEC)
A bipartisan federal agency of six members that oversees the financing of national election campaigns.

political action committee (PAC)
An organization that collects campaign contributions from group members and donates them to candidates for political office.

Only 3 percent came from donors who gave the legal maximum of $2,700 under BCRA, while 56 percent came from those who contributed $200 or less.[51] Sanders famously touted that his average donation was only $27, but he had over 4 million individual donors. Sanders demonstrated the power to raise funds over the Internet—as long as the candidate's message appeals broadly to voters.

BCRA did not reduce the amount of money raised (and spent) for presidential campaigns. At least raising money on the Internet has a grassroots basis, in contrast to using money bundlers. But trying to prevent people from spending money to influence elections and politics is like trying to stop water flooding into a basement. Like water, money seeps around barriers. If people could no longer give massively to political parties, they gave to independent groups that campaigned for candidates separate from the parties. Due to the Supreme Court's 5–4 decision in *Citizens United*, citizens—especially wealthy ones—can contribute as much as they want to Super PACs to influence elections. (See "Freedom, Order, or Equality? Freedom v. Equality in Campaign Finance.") The money genie has escaped from the public funding bottle, and future candidates for president are unlikely to accept the public funding limits imposed by the 1974 Federal Election Campaign Act.

Strategies and Tactics

In a military campaign, *strategy* is the overall scheme for winning the war, whereas *tactics* involve the conduct of localized hostilities. In an election campaign, strategy is the broad approach used to persuade citizens to vote for the candidate, and tactics determine the content of the messages and the way they are delivered. Three basic strategies, which campaigns may blend in different mixes, are as follows:

- A *party-centered strategy*, which relies heavily on voters' partisan identification as well as on the party's organization to provide the resources necessary to wage the campaign. Hillary Clinton essentially followed this strategy.
- An *issue-oriented strategy*, which seeks support from groups that feel strongly about various policies. Bernie Sanders clearly followed this strategy, as he campaigned against Wall Street and wealth inequality. So did Ted Cruz, who touted conservative Christian values.
- A *candidate-oriented strategy*, which depends on the candidate's perceived personal qualities, such as experience, leadership ability, integrity, independence, and trustworthiness. Donald Trump employed a candidate-oriented strategy, but one that emphasized his business background, financial independence, and ability to make a deal.

The campaign strategy must be tailored to the political context of the election. Clearly, a party-centered strategy is inappropriate in a primary because all contenders have the same party affiliation. Research suggests that a party-centered strategy is best suited to voters with little political knowledge.[52] How do candidates learn what the electorate knows and thinks about politics, and how can they use this information? Candidates today usually turn to pollsters and political consultants, of whom there are hundreds. Well-funded candidates can purchase a "polling package" that includes:

- A benchmark poll, which provides "campaign information about the voting preferences and issue concerns of various groups in the electorate and a detailed reading of the image voters have of the candidates in the race";
- Focus groups, consisting of ten to twenty people "chosen to represent particular target groups (e.g., Latinos)[53] the campaign wants to reinforce or persuade ... led in their discussion by persons trained in small-group dynamics," giving texture and depth to poll results;

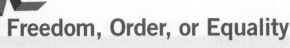

Freedom, Order, or Equality

Freedom v. Equality in Campaign Finance

"Freedom of speech" is guaranteed in the Constitution. Because the Supreme Court regards spending money on political campaigns as a form of speech, it closely scrutinizes limits on campaign spending. The 2002 Bipartisan Campaign Reform Act restricted spending on campaigns. In a series of cases from 2007 to 2014, the Court struck down BCRA's limits. In 2007, the Court ended BCRA's ban on issue ads before elections, allowing outside groups to spend freely on campaigns. The Court's 2010 decision allowed unlimited contributions to Super PACs, and in 2014 it lifted all limits on total donations to candidates, parties, and political committees. Accordingly, wealthy people manage to contribute as much money as they wish to influence elections. This graph identifies the top ten individual contributors to federal election campaigns in the 2015–2016 election cycle as of April 21, 2016. The primary campaigns were not over; the general election campaigns had not begun; and already these ten individuals or families had contributed over $111,000,000—about $32 million to Democrats or liberal groups and $75 million to Republicans or conservative groups. Of course, each member of these families can cast only one vote, the same as any other citizen.

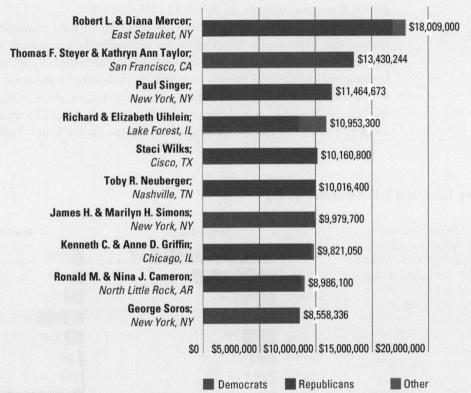

Source: "Top Individual Contributors: All Federal Contributions," The Center for Responsive Politics, 21 April 2016, https://www.opensecrets.org /overview/topindivs.php?view=fc&cycle=2016.

CRITICAL THINKING The First Amendment of the Constitution states, "Congress shall make no laws ... abridging the freedom of speech." Is spending money on election campaigns a legitimate form of speech?

- A trend poll "to determine the success of the campaigns in altering candidate images and voting preferences";
- Tracking polls that begin in early October, "conducting short nightly interviews with a small number of respondents, keyed to the variables that have assumed importance."[54]

Professional campaign managers can use information from such sources to settle on a strategy that mixes party affiliation, issues, and images in its messages.[55] In major campaigns during the past, the mass media disseminated these messages to voters through news coverage, advertising, and Internet services—around which a new industry has grown. In 2016, candidate messages were distributed as well, and often more effectively, through the Internet and the airwaves using social media.

Making the News. Campaigns value news coverage by the media for two reasons: the coverage is free, and it seems objective to the audience. If news stories do nothing more than report the candidate's name, that is important, for name recognition by itself often wins elections. In the past, campaign managers had to cater to reporters' deadlines to get time on television evening news programs and get print in newspapers. Today, cable news programs and social media disseminate information as it is released. Getting free news coverage is yet another advantage that incumbents enjoy over challengers, for incumbents can command attention simply by announcing political decisions—even if they had little to do with them. Members of Congress are so good at this, says one observer, that House members have made news organizations their "unwitting adjuncts."[56] In 2016, however, presidential candidate Donald Trump set a new standard in getting free news coverage, as illustrated in Figure 9.4.

Campaigns vary in the effectiveness with which they transmit their messages through the news media. Effective tactics recognize the limitations of both the audience and the media. The typical voter is not deeply interested in politics and has trouble keeping track of multiple themes supported with details. By the same token, television is not willing to air lengthy statements from candidates. As a result, news coverage is often condensed to sound bites only a few seconds long. The media often use the metaphor of a horse race in covering politics in the United States. Typically, more than

FIGURE 9.4   Money Talks, and Talk Generates Money

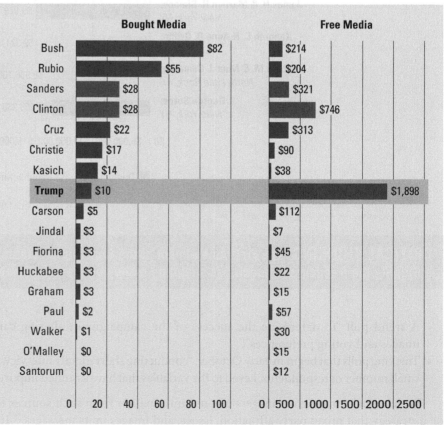

Seeking his party's 2016 presidential nomination, Donald Trump trumped all candidates by drawing free media attention to his unorthodox campaign, during which he became famous for outlandish statements, insulting comments, and otherwise "telling it like it is." The graph lists seventeen candidates in both parties (Republicans in red, Democrats in blue) according to the dollar amount of advertising in millions they purchased through February. In that listing, Trump stood in eighth place. But he stood first—by a wide margin—in the value of free media.

Source: Nicholas Confessore and Karen Yourish, "Measuring Donald Trump's Mammoth Advantage in Free Media," *New York Times*, 15 March 2016, based on mediaQuant, SMG Delta.

half of all election stories on television, in print, and online deal with the horse race.[57] Ironically, evidence suggests that the national media focus more on campaign tactics and positioning than the state or local media do.[58] One longtime student of the media contends that reporters both enliven and simplify campaigns by describing them in terms of four basic scenarios: bandwagons, losing ground, the front-runner, and the likely loser.[59] Once the opinion polls show weakness or strength in a candidate, reporters dust off the appropriate story line.

The more time the press spends on the horse race, the less attention it gives to campaign issues. In fact, recent studies have found that in some campaigns, voters get more information from television ads than they do from television news.[60] Ads are more likely to be effective in low-visibility campaigns below the presidential level because the voters know less about the candidates at the outset and there is little "free" news coverage of the campaigns.[61]

Advertising the Candidate. In all elections, the first objective of paid advertising is name recognition. The next is to promote candidates by extolling their virtues. Finally, campaign advertising can have a negative objective: to attack one's opponent or play on emotions.[62] But name recognition is usually the most important. Studies show that many voters cannot recall the names of their U.S. senators or representatives, but they can recognize their names on a list—as on a ballot. Researchers attribute the high reelection rate for members of Congress mainly to high name recognition (see Chapter 11). Name recognition is the key objective during the primary season even in presidential campaigns, but other objectives become salient in advertising for the general election.

At one time, candidates for national office relied heavily on newspaper advertising; today, they overwhelmingly use the electronic media—primarily television. Political ads convey more substantive information than many people believe, but the amount varies by campaign. In his comprehensive study of campaign advertising in the last seven presidential elections, Darrell West found that political ads tended to mention candidates' policy preferences more in 1984, 1988, 1992, and 2000 and candidates' personal qualities more in 1996, 2004, and 2008.[63] In 1996, Bill Clinton drew fire for lack of "honesty and integrity"; in 2004, John Kerry was attacked for "flip-flopping" on issues and for false "heroism" in Vietnam; and in 2008 Obama was criticized for inexperience and in 2012 for "gutting welfare reform." In turn, Romney was attacked as "catering to the rich at the expense of the middle class."[64] In 2016, Clinton's ads attacked Trump for degrading women, for threatening to expel millions of undocumented immigrants and their families, and as lacking the temperament to be president. Trump's ads characterized her as an untrustworthy liar.

Other scholars have cautioned that the policy positions put forward in campaign ads may be misleading, if not downright deceptive.[65] West found that the 2012 presidential campaign showed "the highest level of campaign negativity in the post–World War II era. Not only were most of the advertisements negative in tone, many of them were highly misleading or characterized by false appeals."[66] Not all negatively toned ads qualify as *attack* ads, which advocate nothing positive.

The term *contrast ads* describes those that both criticize an opponent and advocate policies of the sponsoring candidate.[67] A review of recent studies found that, ironically, both attack and contrast ads "actually carry more policy information than pure advocacy ads."[68] Regardless of whether people learn from political ads, scholars found, advertising does "a great deal to persuade potential voters" who viewed ads compared with those not seeing the ads.[69]

The media often inflate the effect of prominent ads by reporting them as news, which means that citizens are about as likely to see controversial ads during the news as in the ads' paid time slots. Although negative ads do convey information, some studies suggest that negative ads produce low voter turnout.[70] However, recent research shows that the existing level of political mistrust is more important than the negativity of the ads.[71] Moreover, negative ads seem to work differently for challengers (who show a tendency to benefit from them) than for incumbents (who tend to do better with more positive campaigns).[72] If these findings seem confusing, that's essentially the state of research on negative ads.[73] Researchers reviewing studies say that the connection between reality and perceptions is complex. Campaigns seen as negative by scholars are not necessarily viewed that way by voters.[74]

Using the Internet and Social Media. The Internet debuted in presidential campaigns in 1992, when Democratic candidate Jerry Brown, former (and current) governor of California, sent e-mail messages to supporters.[75] Two decades later in 2012, campaigns used the Internet to "microtarget" voters, sending specific messages to computer screens of selected viewers.[76] In 2016, campaigns sent messages to targeted voters' smartphones. As in online marketing, visits to campaign websites generate information for providers who slip digital markers or "cookies" into the users' computers. That information is matched with other user information (e.g., make of car) stored in a huge database. Campaign consultants then match those data with voting records, turnout, and party registration (but not voting choice, which is protected). Then they can frame ads targeted at visitors to conservative (or liberal) websites who shop for Lexus (or Ford) cars, who are registered Republicans (or Democrats), and who are frequent voters. Consultants can produce targeted Internet ads cheaply, transmit them with little expense, and—very importantly—send them quickly in reaction to breaking news.

Candidates like the Internet because it is fast, easy to use, and cheap—saving mailing costs and phone calls. Nevertheless, fewer people get campaign news via the Internet than through television. A national survey in January 2016 asked respondents to name their sources of information about the presidential campaign and which news source was "most helpful."[77] Most people (78 percent) named some form of television (cable news, local TV news, network news, or late night comedy shows), but many (65 percent) also cited digital media (news websites or apps, social networking sites, and other forms). Fewer people identified radio (44 percent) and print newspapers (36 percent), and only 16 percent named candidate or group websites. Only the youngest age group (eighteen to twenty-nine) called social media their "most helpful" news source. Among all adults, more (37 percent) mentioned Facebook as a news source than Twitter (9 percent). Political "insiders," however, burned up the airwaves tweeting about their campaign prowess.

Donald Trump led everyone in campaigning with Twitter, despite its 140 character limit to tweets. Here is a Trump tweet during the May 3 Indiana primary: *Wow, Lyin' Ted Cruz really went wacko today. Made all sorts of crazy charges. Can't function under pressure - not very presidential. Sad!*[78] Trump's 137 characters in that tweet entertained his 7.92 million Twitter followers—almost 2 million more than Clinton's 6.12 million.[79] A specialist in digital media said, "We've never seen this before in politics. . . . This is a continuous Trump rally that happens on Twitter at all hours."[80] Trump also benefitted from the newer Internet service, Reddit, a type of online bulletin board, which posted a video called "The Trump Effect," proposing him as savior of a doomed world.[81] By early April, 90,000 people subscribed to "The Donald" community on Reddit. His campaign also used Instagram, an online mobile service allowing users to share pictures and videos. A social media analytics company reported that through January, "Trump's content has been 'liked' 5.5m times, as opposed to Clinton's 4.3m."[82] Trump, a relatively old candidate at age 69, skillfully exploited the new technology in his presidential campaign.

Explaining Voting Choice

LO5 Assess the effects of party identification, political issues, and candidate attributes on voter choice.

Why do people choose one candidate over another? That is not easy to determine, but there are ways to approach the question. Individual voting choices can be analyzed as products of both long-term and short-term forces. Long-term forces operate throughout a series of elections, predisposing voters to choose certain types of candidates. Short-term forces are associated with particular elections; they arise from a combination of the candidates and issues of the time. Party identification is by far the most important long-term force affecting U.S. elections. The most important short-term forces are candidates' attributes and their policy positions.

Party Identification

Ever since the presidential election of 1952, when the University of Michigan's National Election Studies began, we have known that more than half the electorate decides how to vote before the party conventions end in the summer.[83] And voters who make an early voting decision generally vote according to their party identification. Despite frequent comments in the media about the decline of partisanship in voting behavior, party identification again had a substantial effect on the presidential vote in 2016, as Figure 9.5 shows. Each party's candidates, Hillary Clinton and Donald Trump, won the overwhelming proportions of self-described partisans of their party, with independents splitting their votes in favor of Trump.

This is a common pattern in presidential elections. The winner holds nearly all the voters who identify with the winning party. The loser holds most of his fellow Democrats or Republicans, but some percentage defects to the winner, a consequence of short-term forces—the candidates' attributes and the issues—surrounding the election. Independents usually split disproportionately for the winner, also because of short-term forces. In 2016, the electorate favored the Democratic candidate. But as shown in Figure 8.4, Democrats have consistently outnumbered Republicans over the past fifty years. How, then, have Republican candidates managed to win eight of seventeen presidential elections since 1952? For one thing, Democrats do not turn out to vote as consistently as Republicans do. For another, Democrats tend to defect more readily

FIGURE 9.5 Effect of Party Identification on the Vote, 2016

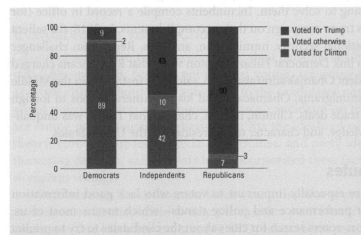

The 2016 election showed that party identification still plays a key role in voting behavior. The chart shows the results of exit polls of thousands of voters as they left hundreds of polling places across the nation on election day. Voters were asked what party they identified with and how they voted for president. Those who identified with one of the two parties voted strongly for their party's candidate.

Source: "Election 2016: Exit Polls," at http://www.nytimes.com/interactive/2016/11/08/us/politics/election-exit-polls.html.

exception arose in 2016. After his competition dropped out in May and handed the Republican presidential nomination to Donald Trump, he was quoted as saying, "This election isn't about the Republican Party, it's about me. . . . I'd rather have a united Republican Party, but I'm not sure that is necessary to the voters. They are voting for me as a person, not a party."[85]

Despite the 2016 Trump vote, the relationship between voters' positions on the issues and their party identification is clearer and more consistent today. For example, Democratic Party identifiers are now more likely than Republican identifiers to describe themselves as liberal and to favor government spending for Social Security and health care. Republicans are more likely to say they are conservative and to oppose federal spending for social programs. The more closely party identification is aligned with ideological orientation, the more sense it makes to vote by party. As shown in Figure 9.6, party identification and ideology became more closely aligned in just over a decade, from 1994 to 2014.

Campaign Effects

If party identification is the most important factor in the voting decision and is also resistant to short-term changes, there are definite limits to the capacity of a campaign to influence the outcome of elections.[86] In a close election, however, changing just a few votes means the difference between victory and defeat, so a campaign can be decisive even if its effects cannot be disentangled.

The Television Campaign. Because of the propensity of television news shows to offer only sound bites, candidates cannot rely on television news to get out their messages. The networks do not give the candidates themselves much time to speak. In the average presidential campaign story, reporters spoke about 74 percent of the time compared with the candidates' 11 percent. No wonder that presidential candidates volunteer to appear on entertainment television shows: they get the chance to talk to the public![87] No wonder that candidates use Twitter and other social media: they can connect directly with voters.

Although candidates seek free coverage on news and entertainment programs, they fight their election campaigns principally through television advertisements and, today, social media. Both parties understand that a presidential election is not truly a national election to be fought across the nation but a *federal* election whose outcome would be decided in certain "battleground" or "swing" states.[88] From 1992 to 2012, eighteen states and Washington D.C.—with 242 electoral votes—voted for Democratic presidential candidates.[89] Only thirteen states with 102 electoral votes voted consistently for Republican candidates. The other nineteen constituted the battleground states, especially those with many electoral votes: Florida (29), Pennsylvania (20), Ohio (18), North Carolina (15), and Virginia (13). The Clinton and Trump television campaigns differed on approach, spending, and effectiveness. Clinton spent over $350 million running more than 300,000 so-called "ad spots," targeted mainly at swing states. Trump spent under $100 million on about 100,000 ad spots, relying more on social media.

The Presidential Debates. In 1960, John F. Kennedy and Richard Nixon held the first televised presidential debate, but debates between the two Democratic and Republican presidential nominees were not used again until 1976. Since then, candidate debates in some form have been a regular feature of presidential elections, especially in primary elections. In 2016, the Republicans held twelve primary debates to the Democrats' ten. Despite the frequency of debates, most were widely viewed. The top three Republican debates, involving more than ten candidates, averaged 20 million viewers, versus 10 million for the top three Democratic debates with never more than five candidates.[90]

FIGURE 9.6   Democrat and Republican Voters: A Decade of Ideological Drift, 1994–2014

Democratic and Republican voters drifted apart ideologically between 1994 and 2014. National surveys in both years asked ten questions concerning government regulation of business, government aid to the poor, immigration policy, environmental regulation, homosexuality, and so on. Answers were scored as liberal or conservative and ranged from –10 (consistently liberal) to +10 (consistently conservative). In 1994, relatively few people had scores of ±10. In 2014, hundreds of Democrats and Republicans did. Those who consistently scored 10s in either direction are bunched up at the graphs' edges.

Source: Pew Research Center, "Political Polarization in the American Public," 14 June 2014, http://www.people-press.org/2014/06/12/section-1-growing-ideological-consistency/#interactive.

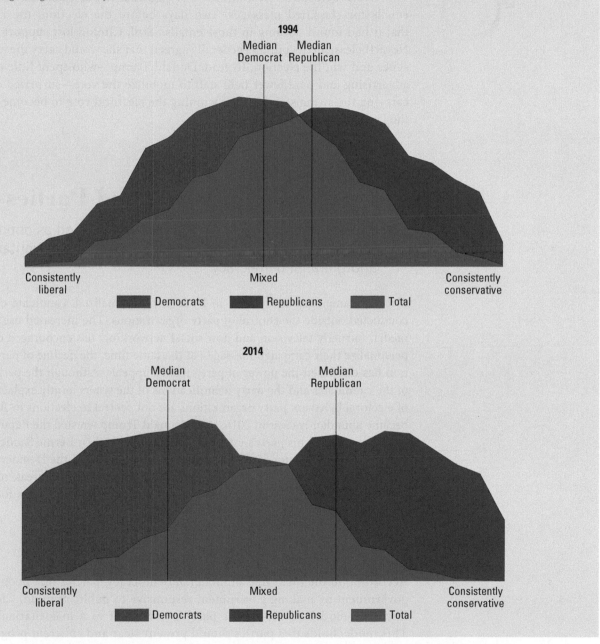

Both campaign staffs agreed to three presidential debates and one vice-presidential debate in October. The first of three debates between Hillary Clinton and Donald Trump occurred on October 26 and was watched by a record 84 million viewers. Judged more poised than Trump, Clinton jumped to a small lead in post-debate polls. Two days before the next presidential debate on October 9, the *Washington Post* released a three minute video, watched by millions, in which Trump spoke vulgarly about women. In the debate, Trump apologized for his "locker room talk" to 66 million viewers. Polls taken afterward showed Clinton surging to a lead of about ten points. Some 70 million people watched the final debate on October 19, which was marked by Trump's refusal to promise to accept the election result.

The Election Strategy and Outcome.

Two weeks before the election, the FBI said that it was examining more Clinton emails for classified messages. Two days before the election, the FBI reported that it had found nothing in those emails. Still, Clinton lost support in the polls. Nevertheless, media pundits generally agreed that she would carry the needed swing states and win the election. Instead, Donald Trump—who spent little on television advertising and paid fewer field staff to mobilize the vote—surprised observers by carrying the swing states and by winning the electoral vote to become President of the United States.

★ Campaigns, Elections, and Parties

LO6 Explain the significance of candidate-centered as opposed to party-centered election campaigns for both majoritarian and pluralist democracy.

Election campaigns today tend to be highly personalized, candidate centered, and conducted outside the control of party organizations. The increased use of electronic media, formerly television and now social networking, has encouraged candidates to personalize their campaign messages; at the same time, the decline of party identification has decreased the power of party-related appeals. Although the party affiliations of the candidates and the party identifications of the voters jointly explain a good deal of electoral behavior, party organizations are not central to elections in America. This became abundantly clear in 2016, when Donald Trump wrested the Republican nomination away from his party's established leaders, and when Bernie Sanders, elected as an Independent Senator from tiny Vermont, almost wrested the Democratic nomination away from Hillary Clinton, the establishment favorite. The weak role played by national parties in choosing presidential candidates has implications for democratic government.

Parties and the Majoritarian Model

According to the majoritarian model of democracy, parties link people with their government by making government responsive to public opinion. Chapter 8 outlined the model of responsible party government in a majoritarian democracy. This model holds that parties should present clear and coherent programs to voters, that voters should choose candidates according to the party programs, that the winning party should carry out its programs once in office, and that voters should hold the governing party responsible at the next election for executing its program. As noted in Chapter 8, the Republican and Democratic parties do follow the model because they formulate different platforms and tend to pursue their announced policies when in office. The weak links in this model of responsible party government are those that connect candidates to voters through campaigns and elections.

You have not read much in this book about the role of the party platform in nominating candidates, conducting campaigns, or explaining voters' choices. In nominating presidential candidates, basic party principles (as captured in the party platform) do interact with the presidential primary process, and the candidate who wins enough convention delegates through the primaries will surely be comfortable with any platform that her or his delegates adopt. But House and Senate nominations are rarely fought over the party platform. And thoughts about party platforms usually are virtually absent from campaigning and from voters' minds when they cast their ballots. Although voters care little about party platforms, platforms reflect party ideology, and Democrats and Republicans in Congress today are divided sharply over ideology.

In theory, the closer the alignment between party voters and their parties' ideologies, the better the operation of responsible party government. However, the theory has not fit the recent operation of Washington politics. Democrats and Republicans in Congress may be behaving "responsibly" when voting cohesively according to their constituents' pronounced liberal and conservative ideological biases, but they are probably not responding to the rest of the voters, who are ideologically more moderate. Moreover, when the presidency and Congress are controlled by different parties—each pushing their constituents' clashing interests—responsible parties produce stalemate in policy making. Such governmental gridlock—Washington's inability to pass legislation and thus govern effectively—concerns all knowledgeable observers. Responsible party government, which fits with the majoritarian model, may simply be incompatible the separation of powers between the president and Congress in American government.

Parties and the Pluralist Model

The way parties in the United States operate is more in keeping with the pluralist model of democracy than the majoritarian model. Our parties are not the basic mechanism through which citizens control their government; instead, they function more as two giant interest groups. The parties' interests lie in electing and reelecting their candidates and in enjoying the benefits of public office. In past elections, the parties cared little about the positions or ideologies favored by their candidates for Congress or state offices. Within today's Republican Party, tea party and evangelical groups work actively to nominate candidates that are suitably conservative. Perhaps to a lesser extent, liberal groups like MoveOn.org and labor unions push to nominate and elect suitably progressive candidates.

Some scholars believe that stronger parties would strengthen democratic government, even if they could not meet all the requirements of the responsible party model.[91] Our parties already perform valuable functions in structuring the vote along partisan lines and in proposing alternative government policies, but stronger parties might also be able to play a more important role in coordinating government policies after elections. Fulfilling that role, however, presumes that the same party controls the House, the Senate, and the presidency. Under the common situation of divided government—when different parties control different branches—strong parties may simply block coordinated policies. At present, the decentralized nature of the nominating process and campaigning for office offer many opportunities for organized groups outside the parties to identify and back candidates who favor their interests. Although this is in keeping with pluralist theory, it is certain to frustrate majority interests on occasion.

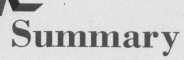

Summary

LO1 Describe how election campaigns have changed over time.

- Campaigning has evolved from a party-centered to a candidate-centered process.

LO2 Explain the procedures followed in the nomination of both congressional and presidential candidates.

- Using primary elections to nominate candidates tends to decentralize power in American political parties. The successful candidate for public office must campaign first to win the party nomination, then to win the general election. Democratic and Republican nominations for president are not decided at the parties' national conventions but determined in advance through the complex process of selecting delegates pledged to particular candidates. Party nominees can legitimately say that they won through their own efforts and owe little to the party organization. However, candidates cannot win the nomination unless they have broad support from party voters.

LO3 Describe the function of the electoral college and formulate arguments for and against the electoral vote system.

- The need to win a majority of votes in the electoral college structures presidential elections. Only twice in more than 100 years has a candidate won a majority of the popular vote and lost in the electoral college; the last time was in 2000. In fact, the electoral college usually magnifies the victory margin of the winning candidate. Since World War II, one party has often won the presidency, while the other party controlled one or more chambers of Congress. Such divided government has interfered with party control of government.

LO4 Analyze the American election campaign process in terms of political context, financial resources, and strategies and tactics for reaching the voters.

- Money is essential in running a modern campaign for major office. Serious attempts to control campaign finance began in 1974 with passage of the Federal Election Campaign Act, which established the Federal Election Commission (FEC). The law restricted campaign contributions by corporations and labor unions and set limits on contributions by individuals. Court decisions in 2010 allowed unlimited contributions by corporations, labor unions, and individuals to influence elections as long as the expenditures were "uncoordinated" with candidates or parties. These decisions gave rise to Super PACs that raised and spent millions of dollars in the 2016 general election. Public funding for presidential elections began with the 1976 election, but by 1996 some candidates learned that they could raise more money privately than provided through public funds. In 2016, no major candidate seeking the presidency sought public funding. The government never provided funding for congressional campaigns, so candidates have raised contributions from individuals, groups, or PACs.

LO5 Assess the effects of party identification, political issues, and candidate attributes on voter choice.

- Voting choice can be analyzed in terms of party identification, candidates' attributes, and policy positions. Party identification is the most important long-term factor in shaping the voting decision, but few candidates rely on it in their campaigns—relying instead on personalized campaigns that stress their attributes and policies. Short-term factors stemming from a combination of the candidates and issues in the election can solidify support from one candidate's partisans nationally, encourage defections from the other's partisans, and capture a majority of the independents. Overall, presidential campaigns are not national but federal elections, and the winning candidate assembles an electoral vote majority by winning traditionally loyal states plus enough swing states.

LO6 **Explain the significance of candidate-centered as opposed to party-centered election campaigns for both majoritarian and pluralist democracy.**

- The way that nominations, campaigns, and elections are conducted in America is out of keeping with the ideals of responsible party government that fit the majoritarian model of

democracy. In particular, campaigns and elections do not function to link parties strongly to voters, as the model posits. American parties are better suited to the pluralist model of democracy, which sees them as major interest groups competing with lesser groups to further their own interests.

Chapter Quiz

LO1 **Describe how election campaigns have changed over time.**

1. Candidates once relied on their parties to run election campaigns; on whom do they rely today?
2. What main role do political parties perform in an election campaign?

LO2 **Explain the procedures followed in the nomination of both congressional and presidential candidates.**

1. What is the difference between an "open" and "closed" party primary? Which weakens political parties?
2. Describe the different methods used to select delegates to a party's national nominating convention.

LO3 **Describe the function of the electoral college and formulate arguments for and against the electoral vote system.**

1. What is the difference between the electoral college and the electoral vote system?
2. Explain why a presidential election is a federal election, not a national election.

LO4 **Analyze the American election campaign process in terms of political context, financial resources, and strategies and tactics for reaching the voters.**

1. By what reasoning has the Supreme Court struck down attempts to regulate campaign finance?
2. Explain how the Court's 2010 decision in the *Citizens United* case has led to increased spending in federal election campaigns.

LO5 **Assess the effects of party identification, political issues, and candidate attributes on voter choice.**

1. Historically, which has the greater effect on voting for president, party identification or the candidates' issue positions?
2. What are "battleground states" in presidential elections, and why are they important?

LO6 **Explain the significance of candidate-centered as opposed to party-centered election campaigns for both majoritarian and pluralist democracy.**

1. How well do political parties fulfill the expectations of the responsible model of party government set forth at the end of the preceding chapter on political parties?
2. Do American political parties operate more in keeping with the majoritarian or pluralist models of democracy?

10 Interest Groups

At age 37, still owing $60,000 in student debt, Kelly Tynan wonders why she borrowed so much to go to college. She could have gone to a less expensive state school rather than the private one she attended. Now, with a small child at home and a job as a special education instructor that is meaningful but not lucrative, her monthly college loan payment of more than $700 a month is a crushing burden. Wistfully, she thinks about how she could live in a larger home or take a vacation once in a while if she didn't have that sizable monthly payment.

Ms. Tynan is not alone. Forty million Americans owe a collective $1.2 trillion in student loan debt. Many who borrow for college do so naively, not fully understanding how the loan payments will impact their lives after they leave school. Those who borrow significant sums may find that they enter a form of debtors' hell. Student loan debt cannot be forgiven by a declaration of bankruptcy. Thus, even if you go broke, you still owe. If you stop making payments because you have no money, more interest builds up and must be paid when payments resume.

The college loan process is a public policy matter since most student loans are either directly funded by government or guaranteed by it for private lenders. Government could, if it desired, eliminate or reduce interest rates, though that would shift costs from student borrowers onto the broader taxpaying public. One argument that could be made for this is that all of society benefits with a better educated workforce and, thus, student loans should be made less expensive.

One might think that college students would organize to try to pressure the government to ease the burden created by loans. In the fall of 2015 there was, in fact, a concerted effort to mobilize students around the country. Among other things, the leadership of the movement used Twitter and the hashtag #MillionStudentMarch to try to build awareness. Protests were held on the same day on campuses, but participation fell far short of a million students. On some campuses only a couple of dozen students showed up to demonstrate.

Despite the difficulties that student loans pose to borrowers, no influential interest group has emerged to champion their cause. Members of Congress and executive branch officials are aware of the depth of the problem, but they have not been able to agree on legislation that would reduce the cost of loans.[1] The failure of borrowers to organize reflects the challenge of trying to build an organization working on behalf of those who have little discretionary income to pay membership dues. Lacking an income stream a new interest group cannot open offices, hire lobbyists and researchers, and publicize their public policy prescriptions.

As we'll see in this chapter, this is a problem that characterizes many groups of people who badly need representation in the policymaking process but yet fail to organize. More broadly here we look at the central dynamic of pluralist democracy: the interaction of interest groups and government. In analyzing the process by which interest groups and lobbyists come to speak on behalf of different groups, we focus on several questions. How do interest groups form? Whom do they represent? What tactics do they use to convince policymakers that their views are best for the nation? Is the interest group system biased in favor of certain types of people? If so, what are the consequences?

#ChallengeAccepted

Take the Challenge on MindTap for American Government

Are you aware of any student-run organization at your school that is working on the college loan issue?

Learning Outcomes

LO1 Identify the different roles that interest groups play in our political system.

LO2 Analyze the role played by entrepreneurs in interest group formation.

LO3 Identify the various resources available to interest groups and evaluate their role in interest group performance.

LO4 Compare and contrast different types of lobbying.

LO5 Evaluate whether the interest group system biases the public policymaking process.

Interest Groups and the American Political Tradition

LO1 Identify the different roles that interest groups play in our political system.

interest group
An organization that tries to influence public policy decisions. Also called a *lobby*.

lobby
See *interest group*.

lobbyist
A representative of an interest group.

An **interest group** is an organization that tries to influence public policy decisions. Among the most prominent interest groups in the United States are the AFL-CIO (representing labor union members), the American Farm Bureau Federation (representing farmers), the Business Roundtable (representing big business), and Common Cause (representing citizens concerned with reforming government). Interest groups are also called **lobbies**, and their representatives are referred to as **lobbyists**.

We use the term interest group because it's convention, but note that it is a bit misleading. Most organizations that lobby are institutions, such as corporations, that are not groups of individuals.[2] Only about 11 percent of interest groups are organizations composed of individuals (see Figure 10.1). It's also important to recognize that most lobbies are primarily focused on some other activity and that their political work is only a small part of what they do. For example, General Motors is in the business of making cars, its principle purpose, but it also has lobbyists in Washington who work to represent the company before government.

Interest Groups: Good or Evil?

A recurring debate in American politics concerns the role of interest groups in a democratic society. Are interest groups a threat to the well-being of the political system, or do they contribute to its proper functioning? A favorable early evaluation of interest groups can be found in the writings of Alexis de Tocqueville, a French visitor to the United States in the early nineteenth century. During his travels, Tocqueville marveled at the array of organizations he found, and he later wrote that "Americans of all ages, all conditions, and

FIGURE 10.1 Not Many Interest Groups Have Individuals as Members

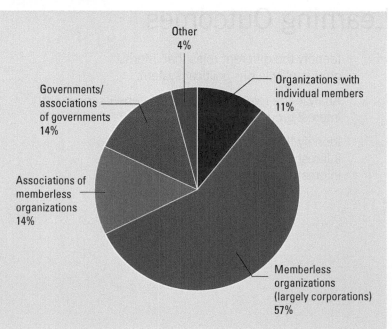

Although we call them interest "groups," most lobbies are not groups of individuals but, rather, are institutions of one type or another. Corporations and associations of corporations dominate the interest group universe.

Source: Kay Lehman Schlozman, Philip Edward Jones, Hye Young You, Traci Burch, Sidney Verba, and Henry E. Brady, "Organizations and the Democratic Representation of Interests," *Perspectives on Politics* 13 (December 2015), p. 1019.

Other
4%

Organizations with individual members
11%

Governments/ associations of governments
14%

Associations of memberless organizations
14%

Memberless organizations (largely corporations)
57%

all dispositions, constantly form associations."[3] Tocqueville was suggesting that the ease with which we form organizations reflects a strong democratic culture.

Yet other early observers were concerned about the consequences of interest group politics. Writing in the *Federalist* papers, James Madison warned of the dangers of "factions," the major divisions in American society. In *Federalist* No. 10, written in 1787, Madison said it was inevitable that substantial differences would develop between factions. It was only natural for farmers to oppose merchants, tenants to oppose landlords, and so on. Madison further reasoned that each faction would do what it could to prevail over other factions; thus, each basic interest in society would try to persuade the government to adopt policies that favored it at the expense of others. He noted that the fundamental causes of faction were "sown in the nature of man."[4]

But Madison argued against trying to suppress factions. He concluded that factions can be eliminated only by removing our freedoms because "Liberty is to faction what air is to fire."[5] Instead, Madison suggested that relief from the self-interested advocacy of factions should come only through controlling the effects of that advocacy. The relief would be provided by a democratic republic in which government would mediate among opposing factions. The size and diversity of the nation as well as the structure of government would ensure that even a majority faction could never come to suppress the rights of others.[6]

How we judge interest groups—as "good" or "evil"—may depend on how strongly we are committed to freedom or equality (see Chapter 1). People dislike interest groups in general because they do not offer equal representation to all; some sectors of society are better represented than others. In a poll asking respondents what they thought of the ethical standards of people working in twenty-two different professions, lobbyists ranked dead last. Only 6 percent of the public thought lobbyists have high ethical standards.[7] Recent filings with Congress listed $3.2 billion in annual spending on lobbying, and as Figure 10.2 shows, individual lobbies spend vast sums as they try to

FIGURE 10.2   Investing in Public Policy

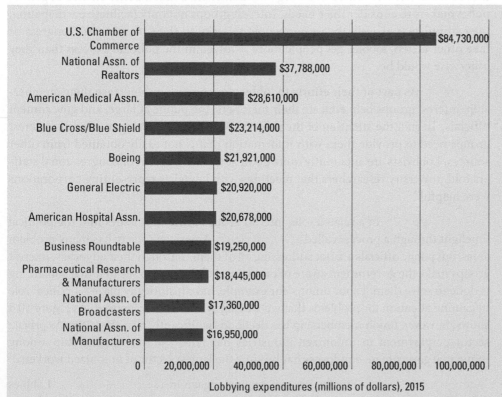

This list of the top ten spenders on lobbying for a single year, 2015, demonstrates the vast sum of money spent to influence public policy. The top spenders are, not surprisingly, business-related lobbies as a change in public policy can result in a business or profession making or losing hundreds of millions of dollars.

Source: Center for Responsive Politics, "Top Spenders," https://www.opensecrets.org/lobby/top.php?showYear=2015&indexType=s.

influence legislation.[8] Interest groups have recently enjoyed unparalleled growth; many new groups have formed, and old ones have expanded. Apparently we distrust interest groups as a whole, but we like those that represent our views. Stated more bluntly, we hate lobbies—except those that speak on our behalf.

The Roles of Interest Groups

The "evil" side of interest group politics is all too apparent. Each group pushes its own selfish interests, which, despite the group's claims to the contrary, are not always in the best interest of other Americans. The "good" side of interest group advocacy may not be so clear. How do the actions of interest groups benefit our political system?[9]

Representation. Interest groups represent people before their government. Just as a member of Congress represents a particular constituency, so does a lobbyist. A lobbyist for the National Association of Broadcasters, for example, speaks for the interests of radio and television broadcasters when Congress or a government agency is considering a relevant policy decision.

Whatever the political interest—the cement industry, Social Security, endangered species—it helps to have an active lobby operating in Washington. Members of Congress represent a multitude of interests, some of them conflicting, from their own districts and states. Government administrators, too, are pulled in different directions and have their own policy preferences. Interest groups articulate their members' concerns, presenting them directly and forcefully in the political process.

Participation. Interest groups are vehicles for political participation. They provide a means by which like-minded citizens can pool their resources and channel their energies into collective political action. People band together because they know it is much easier to get government to listen to a group than to an individual. One farmer fighting against a new pesticide proposal in Congress probably will not get very far, but thousands of farmers united in an organization stand a much better chance of getting policymakers to consider their needs. Interest groups not only facilitate participation; they stimulate it as well. By asking people to write to their member of Congress or take other action, lobbies get people more involved in the political process than they otherwise would be.

Education. As part of their efforts to lobby government and increase their membership, interest groups help educate their members, the public at large, and government officials. To gain the attention of the policymakers they are trying to educate, interest groups need to provide them with information that is not easily obtained from other sources. Lobbyists are apparently quite good at this: 65 percent of congressional staffers told university researchers that meetings with lobbyists representing corporations were helpful.[10]

Agenda Building. In a related role, interest groups bring new issues into the political limelight through a process called agenda building. American society has many problem areas, but public officials are not addressing all of them. Through their advocacy, interest groups make the government aware of problems and then try to see to it that something is done to solve them. Labor unions, for example, have historically played a critical role in gaining attention for problems that were being systematically ignored. As Figure 10.3 shows, however, union membership has declined significantly over the years. As private sector employment in unionized industries has fallen, union membership among municipal government employees has become the largest sector of unionized workers.[11]

Program Monitoring. Finally, interest groups engage in program monitoring. Lobbies follow government programs that are important to their constituents, keeping abreast

agenda building
The process by which new issues are brought into the political limelight.

program monitoring
Keeping track of government programs; usually done by interest groups.

FIGURE 10.3 **Labor Pains**

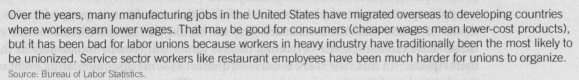

Over the years, many manufacturing jobs in the United States have migrated overseas to developing countries where workers earn lower wages. That may be good for consumers (cheaper wages mean lower-cost products), but it has been bad for labor unions because workers in heavy industry have traditionally been the most likely to be unionized. Service sector workers like restaurant employees have been much harder for unions to organize.
Source: Bureau of Labor Statistics.

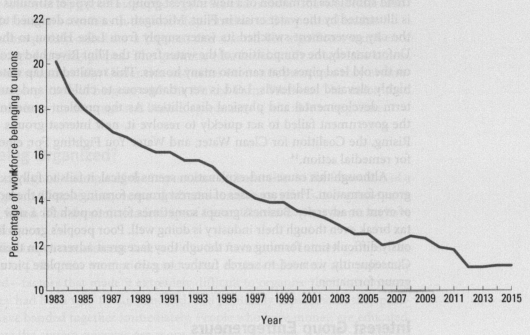

of developments in Washington and the communities where the policies are implemented. When a program is not operating as it should, concerned interest groups push administrators to change it in ways that promote the groups' goals. They also draw attention to proposals that are circulating before governmental bureaucracies. When Trout Unlimited, a lobby representing sport fishermen, learned that a gold mine was proposed near Bristol Bay in Alaska, it immediately went to the Environmental Protection Agency to stop the mining before it began so as to protect a salmon fishery there.[12]

Interest groups do, then, play some positive roles in their pursuit of self-interest. But we should not assume that the positive side of interest groups neatly balances the negative. Questions remain about the overall influence of interest groups on public policymaking. Most important, are the effects of interest group advocacy being controlled, as Madison believed they should be?

How Interest Groups Form

LO2 Analyze the role played by entrepreneurs in interest group formation.

Do some people form interest groups more easily than others? Are some factions represented while others are not? Pluralists assume that when a political issue arises, interest groups with relevant policy concerns begin to lobby. Policy conflicts are ultimately resolved through bargaining and negotiation between the involved organizations and the government. Unlike Madison, who dwelled on the potential for harm by factions,

Brussels Sprouts in Global Politics

The European Union (EU) is now the world's largest economy. The twenty-eight countries that make up the EU are tied together both politically and economically. Most essentially, trade barriers between these countries have been largely eliminated. For example, Italy cannot place a tariff (essentially a tax) on imports of olive oil from Greece even though it might like to do so as a means of protecting its own producers. This elimination of trade barriers has created a dynamic, integrated marketplace for European commerce.

Beyond its borders, the EU is the largest trading partner for the United States. U.S. companies must abide by EU product standards and trade rules if they are to do business in these twenty-eight countries. Moreover, the increasing globalization of the world's economies leads many American companies to focus heavily on international trade. As such, they need representation before EU policymaking bodies as the laws and regulations formulated there affect their businesses. American law and lobbying firms have seen this business opportunity and many branch offices have sprouted up in Brussels, Belgium, in recent years (see the map on the next page). Brussels is home to the European Commission, the regulatory and administrative arm of the EU, and it also serves as one of the two homes of the European Parliament.

Covington & Burling, one of the best known lobbying-focused law firms in Washington, has a significant presence in Brussels. Among its clients are the oil giant Chevron, Microsoft, and the Pharmaceutical Research and Manufacturers of America. Much of what American lobbying firms do in Brussels is to work to harmonize regulations affecting the same industry on both continents. The EU has increasingly moved toward tighter regulations in the areas of consumer and environmental protection. An American chemical manufacturer, for example, might find that the tolerance level for a particular ingredient in a pesticide is lower in the EU than in the United States. This difference could necessitate two separate manufacturing processes.

The Brussels lobbying offices follow a strategy commonly found in the United States: hire former high-ranking government employees and let them use their connections to get their foot in the door of government offices. Covington & Burling employs Jean De Ruyt, a Belgian who previously worked in an important position at the EU.

Just how many lobbyists are working in Brussels is not clear as there is no rule requiring lobbyists or their firms to identify themselves in the Transparency Registry, a voluntary directory of those working to influence EU policymakers. One estimate is that there are 40,000 lobbyists either working in Brussels or sometimes coming there for advocacy purposes. Brussels is starting to look a lot like Washington, where lobbyists like to position their offices near where policymakers are located.

candidates to a much more practical standard and will donate to legislators of various ideological and partisan stripes. The goal of bipartisan contributions is to enhance access, no matter who is in power. Labor unions are an exception to this, donating almost exclusively to Democrats. Nonconnected PACs are highly ideological and tend to give to either conservatives or liberals.

Critics charge that PAC contributions influence public policy, yet political scientists have not been able to document any consistent link between campaign donations and the way members of Congress vote on the floor of the House and Senate.[37] The problem is this: Do PAC contributions influence votes in Congress, or are they just rewards for legislators who would vote for the group's interests anyway because of their long-standing ideology? How do we determine the answer to this question? Simply looking for the influence of PACs in the voting patterns of members of Congress may be shortsighted; influence can also be felt before bills get to the floor of the full House or Senate for a vote. Some sophisticated research shows that PAC donations do seem to influence what goes on in congressional committees.[38] Despite the advantages that organizations with ample resources have through PACs, there are those who defend the current system, emphasizing that interest groups and their members should have the freedom to participate in the political system through campaign donations.

Not surprisingly, lobbyists like to position their offices close to where policymakers are located. The size of the blue dots in the accompanying graphic reflects the density of lobbying firms, American and otherwise, at particular addresses in Brussels. The largest clusters are adjacent to EU buildings.

Source: New York Times, Clustering Near the Seat of Power

Sources: Eric Lipton and Danny Hakim, "Lobbying Bonanza as Firms Try to Influence European Union," *New York Times*, 19 October 2013; David Vogel, *The Politics of Precaution* (Princeton, N.J.: Princeton University Press, 2012); and Justin Greenwood and Joanna Dreger, "The Transparency Register: A European Vanguard of Strong Lobbying Regulation?" *Interest Groups & Advocacy* 2 (2013): 139–162.

CRITICAL THINKING In what ways is lobbying at the EU similar to lobbying in Washington? Why is the EU so important to American firms and industries?

Lobbying Tactics

LO4 Compare and contrast different types of lobbying.

When an interest group decides to try to influence the government on an issue, its staff and officers must develop a strategy, which may include several tactics aimed at various officials or offices. Some tactics are utilized far more frequently than others, but all together, the tactics should use the group's resources as effectively as possible.

We turn here to the different types of lobbying tactics. Keep in mind that lobbying extends beyond the legislative branch. Groups can seek help from the courts and administrative agencies as well as from Congress. Moreover, interest groups may have to shift their focus from one branch of government to another. After a bill becomes a law, for example, a group that lobbied for the legislation will probably try to influence the administrative agency responsible for implementing the new law. Some policy decisions are left unresolved by legislation and are settled through regulations. Interest groups try to influence policy through court suits as well, though litigation can be expensive, and opportunities to go to court may be narrowly structured. Lobbying Congress and agencies is more common.

Direct Lobbying

Direct lobbying relies on personal contact with policymakers. This interaction occurs when a lobbyist meets with a member of Congress, an agency official, or a staff member. In their meetings, lobbyists usually convey their arguments by providing data about a specific issue. If a lobbyist from a chamber of commerce, for example, meets with a member of Congress about a bill the chamber backs, the lobbyist does not say (or even suggest), "Vote for this bill, or our people in the district will vote against you in the next election." Instead, the lobbyist might say, "If this bill is passed, we're going to see hundreds of new jobs created back home." The representative has no trouble at all figuring out that a vote for the bill can help in the next election.

Personal lobbying is a day-in, day-out process. It is not enough simply to meet with policymakers just before a vote or a regulatory decision. Lobbyists must maintain contact with congressional and agency staffers, constantly providing them with pertinent data. In their meetings with policymakers and through other tactics, lobbyists are trying to frame the issue at hand in terms most beneficial to their point of view. Is a gun-control bill before Congress a policy that would make our streets and schools safer from deranged, violent individuals who should not have access to guns—or is it a bill aimed at depriving law-abiding citizens of their constitutional right to bear arms? Research has shown that once an issue emerges, it is very difficult for lobbyists to reframe it—that is, to influence journalists and policymakers alike to view the issue in a new light.[39]

Direct lobbying of legislators was at the heart of a recent victory by a group of corporations, including hotel and restaurant chains, which had been using a tax loophole to escape taxes. One of the companies was Darden Restaurants, which owns the Olive Garden chain among others. Darden sold the land on which its restaurants sit but instead of making conventional real estate sales, the company sold the land to a real estate trust that it created. Darden leased the restaurant land back, pocketed the proceeds of the sales, and avoided paying capital gains taxes. When these companies found that the Congress had had language closing this loophole in some pending legislation, their lobbyists went to legislators they were friendly with (and to whom they contributed campaign funds to) and persuaded them to remove the loophole closing.[40]

Grassroots Lobbying

Grassroots lobbying involves an interest group's rank-and-file members and may include people outside the organization who sympathize with its goals. Grassroots tactics, such as letter-writing campaigns and protests, are often used in conjunction with direct lobbying by Washington representatives. Letters, e-mails, and telephone calls from a group's members to their representatives in Congress or to agency administrators add to a lobbyist's credibility in talks with these officials. Policymakers are more concerned about what a lobbyist says when they know that constituents are really watching their decisions.

Group members—especially influential members (such as corporation presidents or local civic leaders)—occasionally go to Washington to lobby. More ordinary citizens can have an impact too. Research shows that grassroots activity by women's groups is related to passage of legislation aimed at gender equality.[41]

The most common grassroots tactic is letter writing. "Write your member of Congress" is not just a slogan for a civics test. Legislators are highly sensitive to the

Bill Clark/Getty Images

IMAGE 10.2   No Laughing Matter for Jon Stewart

Stewart, the former host of Comedy Central's *The Daily Show*, stands in the Capitol with Senator Kirsten Gillibrand, Democrat of New York. Celebrities can help to call attention to an issue, in this case compensation for first responders whose health was damaged by working inside the rubble of the Twin Towers on 9/11, trying to find survivors.

content of their mail. Interest groups often launch letter-writing campaigns through their regular publications or special alerts. They may even provide sample letters and the names and addresses of specific policymakers. The Internet facilitates mobilization as an interest group office can communicate instantaneously with its members and followers and at virtually no cost through e-mail.

Imaginative grassroots campaigns have been utilized by the car service, Uber. When New York City was resisting Uber's entry into the market there to compete against conventional cabs, the company, which has no membership, offered free rides to people who like Uber to a protest at city hall. The company has mobilized customers in many cities to help it fight local regulators.[42]

As the Uber example illustrates, if people in government seem unresponsive to conventional lobbying tactics, a group might resort to a protest or demonstration, such as picketing or marching, or something else designed to attract media attention to an issue. Protesters hope that television and newspaper coverage will help change public opinion and make policymakers more receptive to their group's demands.

The main drawback to protesting is that policymaking is a long-term, incremental process, and a demonstration is short-lived. It is difficult to sustain anger and activism among group supporters—to keep large numbers of people involved in protest after protest.[43] A notable exception was the civil rights demonstrations of the 1960s, which were sustained over a long period. National attention focused not only on the widespread demonstrations but also on the sometimes violent confrontations between protesters and white law enforcement officers.

Information Campaigns

As the strategy of the civil rights movement shows, interest groups generally feel that public backing adds strength to their lobbying efforts. And because all interest groups

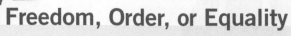

Freedom, Order, or Equality

Does #blacklivesmatter Matter? The Effectiveness of Online Activism

In July of 2013, when a jury acquitted the defendant in the fatal shooting of Trayvon Martin, an unarmed, young black man, an Oakland, California, activist named Alicia Garza took to her computer. She penned an emotional post for her Facebook page. Toward the end of her piece she noted, "I continue to be surprised at how little Black lives matter." In the immediacy of the online world, a close friend 300 miles away quickly tweeted about what Garza had written and created a new hashtag, #blacklivesmatter.

The hashtag evolved into a rallying point, accelerating after a white police officer in Ferguson, Missouri, shot and killed eighteen-year-old Michael Brown, another unarmed African American. The broad anger only increased after more killings by police of unarmed black men.

Black Lives Matter is a different kind of political movement, or, as a writer for the *New Yorker* magazine put it, it is "not your grandfather's civil rights movement." Unlike the 1960s, when activists depended on a combination of protest in the streets and conventional lobbying to effect change, Black Lives Matter has been a combination of protest and online activism. Although this orientation has worked well to gradually solidify the movement's standing with its youthful followers, a focus on raising money and establishing the lobbying offices that could enhance its role in the policymaking process has been absent.

In response to more police shootings of unarmed African Americans in the summer of 2016, #blacklivesmatter helped to rally protests across the country. However, when a single black man shot and killed five white police officers at a rally in Dallas in apparent "payback" for the shootings, the tragedy perversely raised the profile of #blacklivesmatter. The movement was unconnected to the Dallas shooter, the protest there originated from many sources, and the march itself was peaceful. Nevertheless, with more mainstream civil rights groups remaining in the background, Black Lives Matter has become a leading face of black advocacy. What it will do with its growing visibility remains to be seen.

 Black Lives Matter Retweeted

Django Paris @django_paris · Mar 21
Hashtags as movement speech have saved lives, shown us who we are: #Blacklivesmatter #DearNativeYouth #NotYourModelMinority #LoveTwitter

Source: Twitter

 BlackLivesMatterNYC
@BLMNYC   👤+ Follow

No, we're not endorsing any presidential candidate. As a chapter or as the #BlackLivesMatter network.

Source: Twitter

 Black Lives Matter Retweeted

 Jasmyne Cannick @Jasmyne · Apr 16
20 days after she died in a #LAPD jail and 17 days after her family discovered she died, #WakieshaWilson will be laid to rest this morning.

Source: Twitter

CRITICAL THINKING What are the advantages and disadvantages of online activism? How might it be combined with more conventional forms of lobbying to increase a movement's effectiveness in advocacy?

believe they are absolutely right in their policy orientation, they think that they will get that backing if they can only make the public aware of their position and the evidence supporting it. To this end, interest groups launch **information campaigns**, which are organized efforts to gain public backing by bringing their views to the public's attention. The underlying assumption is that public ignorance and apathy are as much a problem as the views of competing interest groups. Various means are used to combat apathy. Some are directed at the larger public; others are directed at smaller audiences with long-standing interest in an issue.

Public relations is one information campaign tactic. A public relations campaign might involve sending speakers to meetings in various parts of the country, generating social media initiatives, taking out newspaper and magazine advertising, or establishing websites. When a group believes that evidence has not been fully developed in a certain area, it may commission research on the subject.

Over time, as public health specialists and government policymakers have emphasized the link between good nutrition and good health, Coca-Cola began to worry that its business would be hurt. Some school districts, for example, limit or forbid altogether the sale of sugary drinks because of health concerns.[44] As a response, Coca-Cola provided money for a nonprofit, Global Energy Balance Network, which began to publicize the value of exercise and claimed that too much emphasis was now being placed on diet.[45] In this particular case the revelation about Coca-Cola's self-interested sponsorship damaged the Global Energy Balance Network's credibility and it disbanded.

information campaign
An organized effort to gain public backing by bringing a group's views to public attention.

Chris McKay/Getty Images

IMAGE 10.3   Coke Gives Advice on Healthy Living

Coca-Cola is skilled at public relations and uses such strategies to try to deflect attention away from health problems relating to sugar intake. This Coke-sponsored tennis clinic reflects a campaign aimed at promoting healthy living through sports.

A central constraint for information campaigns is that they are expensive. In a day and age where we are inundated with advertising, it's a challenge for an interest group to get us to pay attention. Even a deep-pocketed corporation may find that it's prohibitively expensive to repeat its message enough times, in enough places, for it to register with its target audience.

Coalition Building

coalition building
The banding together of several interest groups for the purpose of lobbying.

A final aspect of lobbying strategy is **coalition building**, in which several organizations band together for the purpose of lobbying. Such joint efforts conserve or make more effective use of the resources of groups with similar views. Most coalitions are informal arrangements that exist only for the purpose of lobbying on a single issue. Coalitions most often form among groups that work in the same policy area and have similar constituencies, such as environmental groups or feminist groups. When an issue arises that several such groups agree on, they are likely to develop a coalition.

Yet coalitions often extend beyond organizations with similar constituencies and similar outlooks. Environmental groups and business groups are often thought of as dire enemies. But some businesses support the same goals as environmental lobbies because it is in their self-interest.[46] For example, companies in the business of cleaning up toxic waste sites have worked with environmental groups to strengthen the Superfund program, the government's primary weapon for dealing with dangerous waste dumps. Lobbyists see an advantage in having a diverse coalition. In the words of one lobbyist, "You can't do anything in this town without a coalition. I mean the first question [from policymakers] is, 'Who supports this?'"[47]

Is the System Biased?

LO5 Evaluate whether the interest group system biases the public policymaking process.

As we noted in Chapter 2, our political system is more pluralist than majoritarian. Policymaking is determined more by the interaction of groups with the government than by elections. Indeed, among Western democracies, the United States is one of the most pluralistic governments. The great advantage of majoritarianism is that it is built around the most elemental notion of fairness: what the government does is determined by what most of the people want.

How, then, do we justify the policy decisions made under a pluralist system? How do we determine whether they are fair? There is no precisely agreed-on formula, but most people would agree with the following two simple notions. First, all significant interests in the population should be adequately represented by lobbying groups. That is, if a significant number of people with similar views have a stake in the outcome of policy decisions in a particular area, they should have a lobby to speak for them. If government makes policy that affects farmers who grow wheat, for example, then wheat farmers should have a lobby.

Second, government should listen to the views of all major interests as it develops policy. Lobbies are of little value unless policymakers are willing to listen to them. We should not require policymakers to balance perfectly all competing interests, however, because some interests are diametrically opposed. Moreover, elections inject some of the benefits of majoritarianism into our system because the party that wins an election will have a stronger voice than its opponent in the making of public policy.

Membership Patterns

Public opinion surveys of Americans and surveys of interest groups in Washington can be used to determine who is represented in the interest group system. A clear pattern is evident: some sectors of society are much better represented than others.[48] As noted in the earlier discussions about the United Farm Workers, who is being organized makes a big difference. Those who work in business or in a profession, those with a high level of education, and those with high incomes are the most likely to belong to interest groups. Even middle-income people are much more likely to join interest groups than are those who are poor.

One survey of interest groups is revealing, finding that "the 10 percent of adults who work in an executive, managerial, or administrative capacity are represented by 82 percent" of the organizations that in one way or another engage in advocacy on economic issues. In contrast, "organizations of or for the economically needy are a rarity." Thus, in terms of membership in interest groups, there is a profound bias in favor of those who are well-off financially.[49]

Citizen Groups

Because the bias in interest group membership is unmistakable, should we conclude that the interest group system is biased overall? Before reaching that determination, we should examine another set of data. The actual population of interest groups in Washington surely reflects a class bias in interest group membership, but that bias may be modified in an important way. Some interest groups representing the disadvantaged derive support from sources other than a membership. Thus, although they have no welfare recipients as members, the Center for Budget and Policy Priorities and the Children's Defense Fund have been effective long-term advocates working on behalf of the poor. Poverty groups gain their financial support from philanthropic foundations, government grants, corporations, and wealthy individuals.[50] Given the large numbers of Americans who benefit from welfare and social service programs, poor people's lobbies are not numerous enough. Nevertheless, the poor are represented by these and other organizations (such as labor unions and health lobbies) that regard the poor as part of the constituency they must protect. In short, although the poor are seriously underrepresented in our system, the situation is not as bad as interest group membership patterns suggest.

Another part of the problem of membership bias has to do with free riders. The interests that are most affected by free riders are broad societal problems, such as the environment and consumer protection, in which literally everyone can be considered

IMAGES 10.04a AND 10.04b   Experience Counts

Lobbyists are valued for the connections, and having worked for the president of the United States can lead to a lucrative career in lobbying. Jim Messina, former deputy chief of staff, left the White House to start his own lobbying firm, the Messina Group. Stephanie Cutter, deputy campaign manager for Obama in 2012, also started her own lobbying shop, Precision Strategies.

Douglas Graham/Roll Call/Getty Images

AP Images/Charles Rex Arbogast

citizen group
Lobbying organization built around policy concerns unrelated to members' vocational interests.

as having a stake in the outcome. We are all consumers, and we all care about the environment. But the greater the number of potential members of a group, the more likely it is that individuals will decide to be free riders because they believe that plenty of others can offer financial support to the organization.

Environmental and consumer interests were long underrepresented in the Washington interest group community. In the 1960s, however, a strong citizen group movement emerged. **Citizen groups** are lobbying organizations built around policy concerns unrelated to members' vocational interests. People who join the Natural Resources Defense Council do so because they care about the environment, not because it lobbies on issues related to their profession. If that group fights for stricter pollution control requirements, it doesn't further the financial interests of its members. The benefits to members are largely ideological and aesthetic. In contrast, a corporation fighting the same stringent standards is trying to protect its economic interests. A law that requires a corporation to install expensive antipollution devices can reduce stockholders' dividends, depress salaries, and postpone expansion. Although both the environmental group and the corporation have valid reasons for their stands, their motives are different. Despite the free-rider problem and corporate opposition, citizen groups have had an impressive impact on public policy, with environmental and consumer groups achieving many changes they've lobbied for.[51]

Business Mobilization

Business has always been well represented in Washington.[52] When Congress considers a bill or an agency is formulating a regulation, the stakes for individual corporations and industries can be enormous. Comcast, which owns cable TV systems, NBC, and Universal Pictures, among other enterprises, spends somewhere in the neighborhood of $17 million a year on lobbying. That's a lot of money, but given that the company's 2015 revenues were $69 billion, lobbying expenses are a relatively small expense.[53]

The health-care industry illustrates the level of involvement by business in Washington lobbying. Government regulation is a hugely important factor in determining health-care profits. Through reimbursement formulas for Medicare, Medicaid, and other health-care programs funded by Washington, the national government limits what providers can charge. As regulatory activity has grown, more and more health-care trade associations (like the American Hospital Association) and professional associations (like the American Nurses Association) have come to view Washington lobbying as increasingly significant to the well-being of their members. The number of such lobbies has skyrocketed, and health-care lobbyists cluster around Washington like locusts. Aggregate lobbying expenditures by health-care lobbies in 2015 was around a half a billion dollars.[54]

The advantages of business are enormous.[55] There are more business lobbies, composed of both corporations and trade associations, than any other type (recall Figure 10.1). Professional associations—the American Dental Association, for example—tend to represent business interests as well. Beyond the numbers of groups are the superior resources of business, including lobbyists, researchers, campaign contributions, and well-connected chief executive officers. Whereas citizen groups can try to mobilize their individual members, trade associations can mobilize the corporations that are members of the organization.

Yet the resource advantages of business make it easy to overlook the obstacles that business faces in the political arena. To begin with, business is often divided, with one industry facing another. Apple and Spotify are both gigantic corporations, but they are adversaries on issues relating to music streaming.[56] And even if an industry is unified, it may face strong opposition from labor or citizen groups—sectors that have substantial resources too, even if they don't match up to those of businesses. If both sides have sufficient resources to put up a battle, simply having more money or lobbyists than the other side is unlikely to determine the outcome.[57]

Even though business does not always get its way, or is divided among itself, the affluent and business interests are in the best position to influence policymakers. The aggregate advantages of representation and resources are substantial and give this sector a powerful say in policymaking.[58]

Reform

If the interest group system is biased, should the advantages of some groups somehow be eliminated or reduced? This is hard to do. In an economic system marked by great differences in income, great differences in the degree to which people are organized are inevitable. Moreover, as James Madison foresaw, limiting interest group activity is difficult without limiting fundamental freedoms. The First Amendment guarantees Americans the right to petition their government, and lobbying, at its most basic level, is a form of organized petitioning.

Still, some sectors of the interest group community may enjoy advantages that are unacceptable. If it is felt that the advantages of some groups are so great that they affect the equality of people's opportunity to be heard in the political system, then restrictions on interest group behavior can be justified on the grounds that the disadvantaged must be protected. Pluralist democracy is justified on exactly these grounds: all constituencies must have the opportunity to organize, and competition between groups as they press their case before policymakers must be fair.

Some critics charge that a system of campaign finance that relies so heavily on PACs undermines our democratic system. They claim that access to policymakers is purchased through the wealth of some constituencies. PAC donations come disproportionately from business and professional interests. It is not merely a matter of wealthy interest groups showering incumbents with donations; members of Congress aggressively solicit donations from interest groups. Although observers disagree on whether PAC and Super PAC money actually influences policy outcomes, agreement is widespread that PAC donations give donors better access to members of Congress.

Although some minor reforms have been passed in recent years, the laws surrounding lobbying have altered interest group politics very little. Upon taking office in 2009, President Obama promised to "change the culture of Washington" in terms of the cozy relationship between lobbyists and policymakers. His words were surely sincere but eight years later when he left office, the culture remained unchanged.

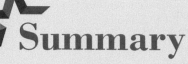
Summary

LO1   Identify the different roles that interest groups play in our political system.

- Interest groups play many important roles in our political process: representation, participation, education, agenda building, and program monitoring. They are a means by which citizens can participate in politics, and they communicate their members' views to those in government. Interest groups make positive contributions, yet the interest group system remains unbalanced, with some segments of society (particularly business, the wealthy, and the educated) considerably better organized than others. Suppressing interest groups, though, runs against our First Amendment freedoms.

LO2   Analyze the role played by entrepreneurs in interest group formation.

- Interest groups are organizations, and they do not form just because a constituency has a need. An organizer or political "entrepreneur" must convince potential members to join. Not all constituencies are created equal in terms of a propensity to join an interest group. Those high in social class are much more likely to join; those in a lower social class are much more challenging to organize. Institutions have an advantage in this process as they do not need to attract a membership—they're already "organized."

LO3   Identify the various resources available to interest groups and evaluate their role in interest group performance.

- The strength and influence of an interest group depends heavily on the organization's resources, which include its membership, lobbyists, and political action committees (PACs). For those interest group that are membership based, there are challenges because of the free-rider problem. Among the most important resources for interest groups are their lobbyists, who have the responsibility for communicating what the organization wants policymakers to know. PACs can facilitate access to policymakers.

LO4   Compare and contrast different types of lobbying.

- Direct lobbying relies on personal contact with policymakers in the legislative and administrative branches. It also includes filing court suits in the legal system. Grassroots lobbying can involve both rank-and-file members communicating with policymakers through letter-writing campaigns and political protests. Common tactics of information campaigns are public relations efforts and sponsoring research.

LO5   Evaluate whether the interest group system biases the public policymaking process.

- Strong growth in the citizen group sector has brought more effective representation on behalf of environmental and consumer interests. Business mobilization has enhanced the advantages already possessed by business in the political system. Little meaningful reform has been enacted to try to change the status quo of interest group politics.

Chapter Quiz

LO1 Identify the different roles that interest groups play in our political system.

1. On balance, are interest groups beneficial to the political system or are they harmful?
2. What roles do interest groups play in American politics?

LO2 Analyze the role played by entrepreneurs in interest group formation.

1. What is an interest group "entrepreneur"?
2. What factors influence the success of an effort to organize a new interest group?

LO3 Identify the various resources available to interest groups and evaluate their role in interest group performance.

1. What is the "free-rider problem"?
2. In our governmental system, what role do lobbyists play?

LO4 Compare and contrast different types of lobbying.

1. How does direct lobbying differ from grassroots lobbying?
2. How do information campaigns work?

LO5 Evaluate whether the interest group system biases the public policymaking process.

1. What advantages does business possess in the lobbying world, and are citizen groups effective counterweights to business groups?
2. Overall, is the interest group system a biased one?

11 Congress

In 2015, Paul Ryan (R-Wisc.) became the fifty-fourth Speaker of the House (the leader of the party with the most seats in the House of Representatives). He was also the fifty-third white male to hold that title. Despite seeming like a traditional choice for the role, he made an unusual demand when he took the reins. He said he would not spend as much time traveling and fundraising as previous speakers. Ryan, a forty-five-year-old father of three, asserted, "I cannot and will not give up my family time."[1] Some observers praised his commitment to his family, noting his stance reflected changing norms about the role of fathers in family life. Others, however, called Ryan a hypocrite for prizing time with his own family while opposing laws that would provide paid family leave and paid sick leave.[2] Others argued that women in Congress would be criticized as unable to balance family and work if they followed his lead.[3]

Ryan's call for family time raises questions about how the demographic makeup of Congress affects the type of representation that Americans get. Is paid family leave a partisan issue, with Republicans generally opposed and Democrats generally in favor? Or does it matter if the people in charge are men or women? If more women were in Congress, would more family leave laws get enacted?

Even though the current Congress is "the most diverse Congress in history," you probably imagine an old white man when you think of what members of Congress look like. That's because Congress is still pretty homogenous: 80 percent male, over 80 percent white, and 92 percent Christian.[4] Why isn't Congress more diverse? Does it matter? Research shows it does matter. Female and nonwhite representatives are more likely to sponsor legislation on issues that disproportionately affect women and minorities.[5]

In doing their jobs, representatives address the interests of many groups. They serve the interests of their constituents in their home districts. They also serve the interests of the nation as a whole. They were also elected to advance their ideology, which means they represent their political party. Representatives readily admit, however, that they also see their job as advancing the interests of people like them, particularly female and nonwhite representatives. As Rep. Louise Slaughter (D-NY) said, "A lot of women are probably represented by some man. I think [women in Congress] have an obligation to make sure that the other women in the country aren't left behind."[6]

So why isn't Congress more diverse? Research points to a pipeline problem, particularly for women. Women are less likely than men in similar occupations, such as lawyers and business leaders, to be encouraged to run for office. Combined with differences in how boys and girls are socialized, women are less likely than similarly-situated men to think of themselves and qualified candidates.[7] Young Americans, the most diverse generation in the nation's history, are especially turned off to electoral politics, a stance attributed to today's partisan warfare.[8]

Members of Congress are continuously pulled in many directions by competing interests. That the institution of Congress as a whole encompasses so many interests contributes to the gridlock that plagues today's Congress and prevents people from a wider array of backgrounds and experiences from throwing their hat into the ring.

#ChallengeAccepted

Take the Challenge on MindTap for American Government

Should it be a representative's job to advance the interests of people like them, even if those people live outside of their district? What might it take for more people of diverse backgrounds to consider running for Congress?

Learning Outcomes

LO1 Explain the structure and powers of Congress as envisioned by the framers and enumerated in the Constitution.

LO2 Analyze the factors that affect the way voters elect members of Congress.

LO3 Describe the ways in which issues get on the congressional agenda.

LO4 Differentiate among the types of congressional committees and evaluate the role of the committee system in the legislative process.

LO5 Identify the leadership structure of the legislative branch and assess the rules and norms that influence congressional operations.

LO6 Appraise the components of the legislative environment that affect decision making in Congress.

LO7 Consider whether members of Congress should vote according to the majority views of their constituents and assess the elements that characterize Congress as a pluralist or majoritarian system.

FIGURE 11.1   Incumbents: Life Is Good

Despite the public's dis-satisfaction with Congress in general, incumbent representatives win reelection at an exceptional rate. Incumbent senators aren't quite as successful, but still do well. Voters seem to believe that their own representatives and senators don't share the same foibles that they attribute to other members of Congress.

Sources: Various sources for 1950–2006. For 2008 and 2010, Harold W. Stanley and Richard G. Niemi (eds.), *Vital Statistics on American Politics, 2011–2012* (Washington, DC: CQ Press, 2011), pp. 43–44. For 2014–2015, Harold W. Stanley and Richard G. Niemi (eds.), *Vital Statistics on American Politics 2014–2015* (Washington, DC: CQ Press), Tables 1–18.

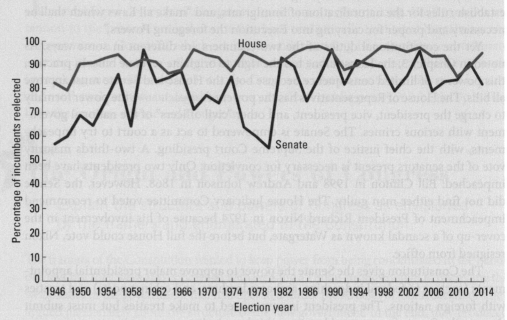

critical of Congress (see Figure 11.2). One reason Americans hold Congress in disdain is that they regard it as overly influenced by interest groups. A struggling economy and persistent partisan disagreements within Congress have also reduced people's confidence in the institution.[11]

Redistricting. One explanation for the incumbency effect centers on redistricting—the way states redraw House districts after a census-based reapportionment.[12] It is

FIGURE 11.2   We Love Our Incumbents, but Congress Itself Stinks

Despite the reelection rate of incumbents reflected in Figure 11.1, public approval of Congress is far less positive. Favorability ratings have never been particularly high, but opinion has turned decidedly negative in recent years. Citizens don't believe that the House and Senate are facing up to the nation's problems.

Sources: "Figure 3–7 Rating of Congress, 1985–2015," in Harold W. Stanley and Richard G. Niemi (eds.), *Vital Statistics on American Politics 2014–2015* (Washington, DC: CQ Press); "Obama in Strong Position at Start of Second Term," Pew Research Center, 17 January 2013, http://www.people-press.org/files/legacy-pdf/01-17-13%20Political%20Release.pdf.

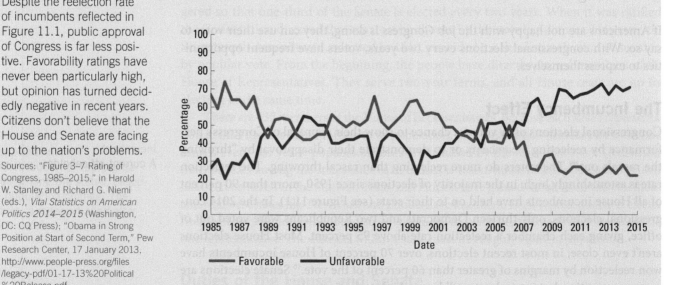

entirely possible for the states to draw the new districts to benefit the incumbents of one or both parties. Altering district lines for partisan advantage is commonly called **gerrymandering**.

Gerrymandering has been practiced since at least the early 1800s, but computer technology makes it incredibly precise today.[13] Precinct voting data can easily be used to manipulate boundary lines and produce districts that enhance or damage a candidate's or party's chances.[14] After the 2010 census, for example, Illinois lost a seat in Congress and had to redraw its districts. The Democratic-controlled state legislature passed a plan that put Republican incumbent Joe Walsh's home in fellow Republican incumbent Randy Hultgren's district, which meant that the two men had to face each other in a primary. Walsh ultimately decided to avoid a bitter and costly primary and run in a neighboring district, which leaned more Democratic. After the 2012 election, he lost the open seat race to Democrat Tammy Duckworth, while Hultgren was reelected. The state's congressional delegation went from eleven Republicans and eight Democrats to six Republicans and twelve Democrats.[15]

Some argue that gerrymandering contributes to increasing polarization between the two parties in the House. Districts that are dominated by one party or another have some tendency to be more ideologically driven. Moreover, representatives elected from new districts after reapportionment tend to exhibit more polarized voting patterns than representatives elected from older districts.[16] Scholars maintain that the polarizing effect of gerrymandering has affected the Senate too. While the Senate doesn't undergo reapportionment, many senators were once members of the House. Their experiences in that polarized body, it is argued, continue to affect their legislative behavior once they move on to the Senate.[17]

Name Recognition. Holding office brings with it some important advantages. First, incumbents develop significant name recognition among voters simply by being members of Congress. Representatives have press secretaries who help with name recognition through their efforts to get publicity for the activities and speeches of their bosses. Another resource available to members of Congress is the *franking privilege*—the right to send mass communications at taxpayer expense. Such communications, which include mailings, e-mails, and messages on social networking sites, work to make constituents aware of their legislators' names, activities, and accomplishments. In 2014, members of Congress sent out $20.9 million worth of mass communications, which critics have derided as "publicly funded campaign literature."[18]

Under current regulations, information about the representative's personal life and political campaign cannot be included in official mailings, websites, or social media messages, and mailings can only target constituents who live in the representatives' districts. Although both chambers have established rules limiting the type of information that members can send out through their official social networking accounts, actual franking regulations do not cover social media.[19] Members of Congress are also free to have their own social networking accounts for personal or campaign use, but they are not allowed to use any resources from their congressional offices, such as staff or technology, when using such accounts. Similarly, they cannot use any of their campaign resources when they use their congressional social networking accounts.[20] By 2015, over 95 percent of members of Congress had Facebook accounts. All senators, and all but fifteen representatives, had Twitter accounts.[21] Twitter even publishes a handbook for politicians, which includes practical information on matters such as how to attack a photo or delete a tweet and advice on using Twitter effectively. In addition to advising representatives to tweet about their media appearances and campaign events, it tells politicians how to be relatable, with suggestions to tweet about favorite TV shows or

gerrymandering
Redrawing a congressional district to intentionally benefit one political party.

The Sweet Potato Taco has a commanding lead right now! Vote on what food you think Al should eat at @MNStateFair

What Should Al Eat At the State Fair?

What Should Al Eat At the State Fair? It's that time again — the Minnesota State Fair is coming up on August 27th. Al will be there. So will a cornucopia of unique foods for him to try. What would...

alfranken.com

IMAGE 11.1   Sweet Potato Taco or Tikka On-a-Stikka?

Today, members of Congress go well beyond the use of franking to keep their constituents informed about their activities and to connect with the folks back home. Many tweet about their personal lives and even ask the public to weigh in, such as when Senator Al Franken (D-Minn.) used Twitter to let people vote on what food he should eat at the Minnesota State Fair. Social media allows members of Congress to connect with people all over the world, not just their constituents. Such technological developments challenge traditional limitations placed on the use of taxpayer funds for congressional outreach. Incidentally, the sweet potato taco won.

Source: Twitter, Inc.

casework
Solving problems for constituents, especially problems involving government agencies.

sports teams.[22] As shown in Image 11.1, members of Congress sometimes ask the public to weigh in on lighthearted topics, such as which food to try at the state fair, in order to boost their relatability.

Casework. Much of the work performed by congressional staff is devoted to casework—services for constituents, such as tracking down a Social Security check or directing the owner of a small business to the appropriate federal agency. Many congressional staffers are employed primarily as caseworkers. Thus, the very structure of congressional offices is built around helping constituents. One caseworker on a staff may be a specialist on immigration, another on veterans' benefits, another on Social Security, and so on. Legislators devote many resources to casework because they assume that when they provide assistance to a constituent, that constituent will be grateful. Not only will that person probably vote for the legislator in the next election, but he or she is also sure to tell family members and friends how helpful the representative or senator was. "Casework is all profit," says one congressional scholar.[23]

Campaign Financing. Anyone who wants to challenge an incumbent needs solid financial backing. Challengers must spend large sums of money to run a strong campaign with an emphasis on advertising—an expensive but effective way to bring their name and record to the voters' attention. But here too the incumbent has the advantage. Challengers have difficulty raising funds because they have to overcome contributors' doubts about whether they can win. In the 2014 elections, incumbents raised 59 percent of all money contributed to campaigns for election to the House and the Senate. Only 20 percent went to challengers (those running for open seats received the rest).[24]

Successful Challengers. Clearly, the deck is stacked against challengers. Yet some challengers do beat incumbents. How? The opposing party and issue-driven donors may target incumbents who seem vulnerable because of age, lack of seniority, a scandal, or unfavorable redistricting. Some incumbents appear vulnerable because they were elected by a narrow margin, or the ideological and partisan composition of their district does not favor their holding the seat. Vulnerable incumbents also bring out higher-quality challengers—individuals who have held elective office previously and are capable of raising adequate funds. Experienced challengers are more likely to defeat incumbents than are amateurs with little background in politics.[25] Senate challengers have a higher success rate than House challengers because they are generally higher-quality candidates. Often they are governors or members of the House who enjoy high name recognition and can attract significant campaign funds because they are regarded as credible candidates.

2016 Election. With some races too close to call as of this writing, it is clear that the Republican Party managed to hang on to its majority in both the House and the Senate following the 2016 Congressional Election. The big story of the election involved the Senate, where the Republican's majority narrowed. Democrats picked up 2 seats, leaving Republicans with 51 (Louisiana is yet to be decided). Despite the fact that Donald Trump's victory at the presidential level signaled a rejection of "politics as usual," incumbents in Congress did very well in 2016. Across both chambers, only 10 incumbents lost (2 Democrats, 8 Republicans). The reelection rate was near 98 percent in the House and 94 percent in the Senate. Although the White House and both houses of Congress will be in Republican hands, enacting policy reforms could still prove elusive in some areas. Democrats in the Senate have the filibuster (discussed later) and Republican members of Congress have state and local constituencies that sometimes put them at odds with their own party and president.

Whom Do We Elect?

As we noted at the start of this chapter, the people we elect to Congress are not a cross-section of American society. Although over half of the American labor force works in blue-collar jobs, someone currently employed as a blue-collar worker rarely wins a congressional nomination. Most members of Congress are upper-class professionals—lawyers and businesspeople—and, at last count, 50.8 percent are millionaires.[26]

Women and minorities have long been underrepresented in elective office, although both groups have increased their representation in Congress over time.

IMAGE 11.2   The Millionaires' Club

In 2015, Representative Darrell Issa (R-Calif.) was the richest lawmaker in Congress, with an estimated net worth of $436 million. While 50.8 percent of lawmakers are millionaires, only about 5 percent of Americans can say the same.

Sources: "Personal Finances, " opensecrets.org/pfds/; Robert J. Samuelson, "The Millionaire's Club Expands," *Washington Post*, 22 October 2014, https://www.washingtonpost.com/opinions/robert-samuelson-the -millionaires-club-expands/2014/10/22/04fcd128-5a01-11e4-8264-deed989ae9a2_story.html.

Women in Legislatures in Global Politics

Compared with other countries, the United States has substantially fewer women serving in the legislature. This figure includes fifteen European countries as well as fifteen countries from the Americas (North America, Central America, and South America) as of November 2015. Ranked by the percentage of women in the lower house of the national legislature, the European countries include, on average, a significantly higher percentage of women than the legislatures of countries in the Western Hemisphere. The United States ranks near the bottom, with women making up only 19.4 percent of the representatives in the House.

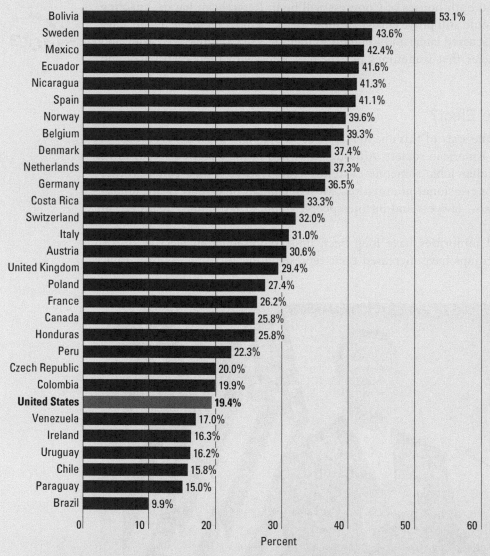

Source: Inter-Parliamentary Union, http://www.ipu.org/wmn-e/classif.htm

CRITICAL THINKING How might the laws passed in countries with more female legislators differ from laws passed in countries with fewer female legislators? How might the percentage of women in office affect how women (and men) feel about government?

Twenty women served in the Senate in the 2013–2014 session, a record number that made it necessary to expand the women's restroom![27] Although the number of women in Congress has grown over time, they comprise only 20 percent of Congress, well below their share of the population. (See "Women in Legislatures in Global Politics" for a comparison of the representation of women in national legislatures.) In recent years, Congress has become more diverse in other ways, including religion and sexual orientation. In addition to having forty-six African Americans, thirty-two Latinos, and eleven Asian Americans, the 114th Congress included five members who were Muslim, Hindu, or Buddhist, as well as seven who were gay or lesbian.[28]

Other members of Congress don't necessarily ignore the concerns of women and minorities.[29] Yet many women and minorities believe that only members of their own group—people who have experienced what they have experienced—can truly represent their interests. This is a belief in descriptive representation—the view that a legislature should resemble the demographic characteristics of the population it represents.[30] The power of descriptive representation was on display in 2014. For years, Rep. Bobby Scott (D-Va.). the first African-American elected to Congress from Virginia since Reconstruction, tried to pass legislation that would require states to report the number of people who died while in police custody, an issue with particular resonance among black Americans. Police brutality toward African Americans became a lead story in 2014, following several incidents that were caught on video and protests nationwide, most notably in Ferguson, Missouri. The national spotlight on this issue gave Scott the opening he needed to finally get enough support in Congress: the Death in Custody Reporting Act became law in December of that year.[31]

It is difficult to promote the descriptive representation of women since women do not live in geographically concentrated areas. But since many racial minorities do live in concentrated areas, the use of racial gerrymandering has helped bring about a more racially diverse legislature (see "Freedom, Order, or Equality: Freedom v. Equality: Redistricting"). In 1993, however, the Supreme Court ruled that racial gerrymandering could violate the rights of whites. In *Shaw* v. *Reno,* the majority ruled in a split decision that a North Carolina district that meandered 160 miles from Durham to Charlotte was an example of "political apartheid." In effect, the Court ruled that racial gerrymandering segregated blacks from whites instead of creating districts built around contiguous communities.[32] In a later decision, the Supreme Court ruled that the "intensive and pervasive use of race" to protect incumbents and promote political gerrymandering violated the Fourteenth Amendment and Voting Rights Act of 1965.[33] In 2001, just before the redistricting from the 2000 census was to begin in the individual states, the Court modified its earlier decisions by declaring that race was not an illegitimate consideration in drawing congressional boundaries as long as it was not the "dominant and controlling" factor.[34]

Racial gerrymandering has been less effective for Hispanics. Hispanic representation lags behind that of blacks, even though there are more Hispanics in the United States than blacks. One reason for this inequity is that Hispanics tend not to live in such geographically concentrated areas as do blacks. Another reason is that an estimated 21.5 percent of adult Hispanics living in the United States are ineligible to vote because they are not American citizens.[35] At only 5.4 percent of the population (with roughly 75 percent foreign born), Asian Americans also face challenges electing a critical mass of representatives who share their racial background.[36] Although this movement over time to draw districts that work to elect minorities has clearly increased the number of black and Hispanic legislators, almost all of whom are Democrats, it has also helped the Republican Party. As more Democratic voting minorities have been packed into some districts, their numbers have diminished in others, leaving the remaining districts not merely "whiter" but also more Republican than they would have otherwise been.[37]

descriptive representation
A belief that constituents are most effectively represented by legislators who are similar to them in such key demographic characteristics as race, ethnicity, religion, or gender.

racial gerrymandering
The drawing of a legislative district to maximize the chance that a minority candidate will win election.

Freedom, Order, or Equality

Freedom v. Equality: Redistricting

Every ten years, state governments use the results of the census to redraw their congressional district lines. They have great freedom in deciding where district boundaries will lie, but in the interest of promoting equality, certain regulations have been imposed on the states by Congress and the courts.

In 1964, the Supreme Court ruled in *Wesberry* v. *Sanders* that all House districts within a state had to have roughly equal population. Prior to this decision, states often drew districts that had over two and three times the number of people than other districts, which the Courts ruled to be a violation of the principle of "one person, one vote."

During the 1980s, both Congress and the Supreme Court affected the freedom of states to draw district lines as they wish by promoting descriptive representation for blacks and Hispanics. When Congress amended the Voting Rights Act in 1982, it encouraged states to draw districts that concentrated minorities together so that black and Hispanic candidates would have a better chance of being elected to office. The Supreme Court decision in *Thornburg* v. *Gingles* in 1986 also pushed states to concentrate minorities in House districts. After the 1990 census was the first time states redrew House boundaries with the intent of creating districts with majority-minority populations. This effort led to a roughly 50 percent increase in the number of black candidates elected to the House. But as the figure below shows, the pace of change for African American representation after the 1990s slowed substantially, and the number of Asian American representatives has been relatively flat since the 1970s. In 2015, there were 117 majority-minority districts in the country (26.9 percent of all districts), seventy of them with minority representatives.

Debates about the extent to which considerations such as race and voting eligibility are necessary when drawing district lines or whether they constitute an undue restriction on both state sovereignty and on the voting rights of other voters continue to emerge with every round of redistricting.

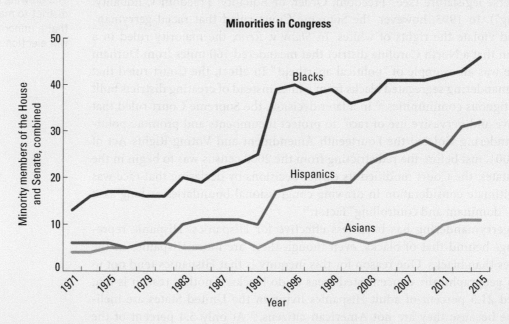

Minorities in Congress

Sources: Harold W. Stanley and Richard G. Niemi (eds.), *Vital Statistics on American Politics 2013–2014* (Washington, DC: CQ Press), Table 5-2, Table 1-17, p. 35, http://www.brookings.edu/~/media/Research/Files/Reports/2013/07/vital-statistics-congress-mann-ornstein/Vital-Statistics-Chapter-1-Demographics-of-Members-of-Congress_UPDATE.pdf?la=en; Harold W. Stanley and Richard G. Niemi (eds.), *Vital Statistics on American Politics 2014–2015* (Washington, DC: CQ Press), Table 5-2, Table 5-3.

CRITICAL THINKING Are there ways to promote racial equality and diversity in Congress that do not conflict with state freedoms in determining how congressional district lines are drawn? What advantages or disadvantages might there be in eliminating state districts altogether and having each voter vote for all of the state's representatives?

How Issues Get on the Congressional Agenda

LO3 Describe the ways in which issues get on the congressional agenda.

The formal legislative process begins when a member of Congress introduces a *bill*, a proposal for a new law. In the House, members drop bills in the "hopper," a mahogany box near the rostrum where the Speaker presides. Senators give their bills to a Senate clerk or introduce them from the floor. But before a bill can be introduced to solve a problem, someone must perceive that a problem exists or that an issue needs to be resolved. In other words, the problem somehow must find its way onto the congressional agenda.

Many issues Congress works on seem to have been around forever. Foreign aid, the national debt, and Social Security have come up in just about every recent session of Congress. Other issues emerge more suddenly, especially those that are the product of technological change.[38] The issue of "geolocation privacy" is one example. Not long ago, the term did not even exist. But today, over 60 percent of Americans own smartphones, which are filled with apps that track the user's location. In 2015, the Senate considered the Location Privacy Protection Act, which included provisions that would require companies to get permission from consumers before collecting location data off of their mobile devices. As of this writing, the bill has yet to become law.

New issues reach the congressional agenda in many ways. Sometimes a highly visible event focuses national attention on a problem. As the number of refugees fleeing civil war in Syria grew throughout 2015 and dominated the news cycle with heartbreaking stories of children dying at sea during their perilous journey, President Obama announced that his administration would increase the number of refugees allowed to resettle in the United States. Motivated by concerns about terrorist attacks that occurred in France that year, the House of Representatives passed a bill that would have set up administrative hurdles aimed at preventing the increase from taking place.[39]

Within Congress, party leaders and committee chairs have the opportunity to move issues onto the agenda, but they rarely act capriciously. They often bide their time, waiting for other members of Congress to learn about an issue as they attempt to gauge the level of support for some kind of action. At times, the efforts of an interest group spark awareness of an issue and support for action.

The Lawmaking Process and the Importance of Committees

LO4 Differentiate among the types of congressional committees and evaluate the role of the committee system in the legislative process.

The process of writing bills and getting them enacted is relatively simple in the sense that it follows a series of specific steps. What complicates the process is the many ways legislation can be treated at each step. Here, we examine the straightforward process by which laws are made. In the next few sections, we discuss some of the complexities of that process.

After a bill is introduced in either house, it is assigned to the committee with jurisdiction over that policy area (see Figure 11.3). A banking bill, for example, would be

FIGURE 11.3   The Legislative Process

The process by which a bill becomes law is subject to much variation. This diagram depicts the typical process a bill might follow. It is important to remember that a bill can fail at any stage because of lack of support.

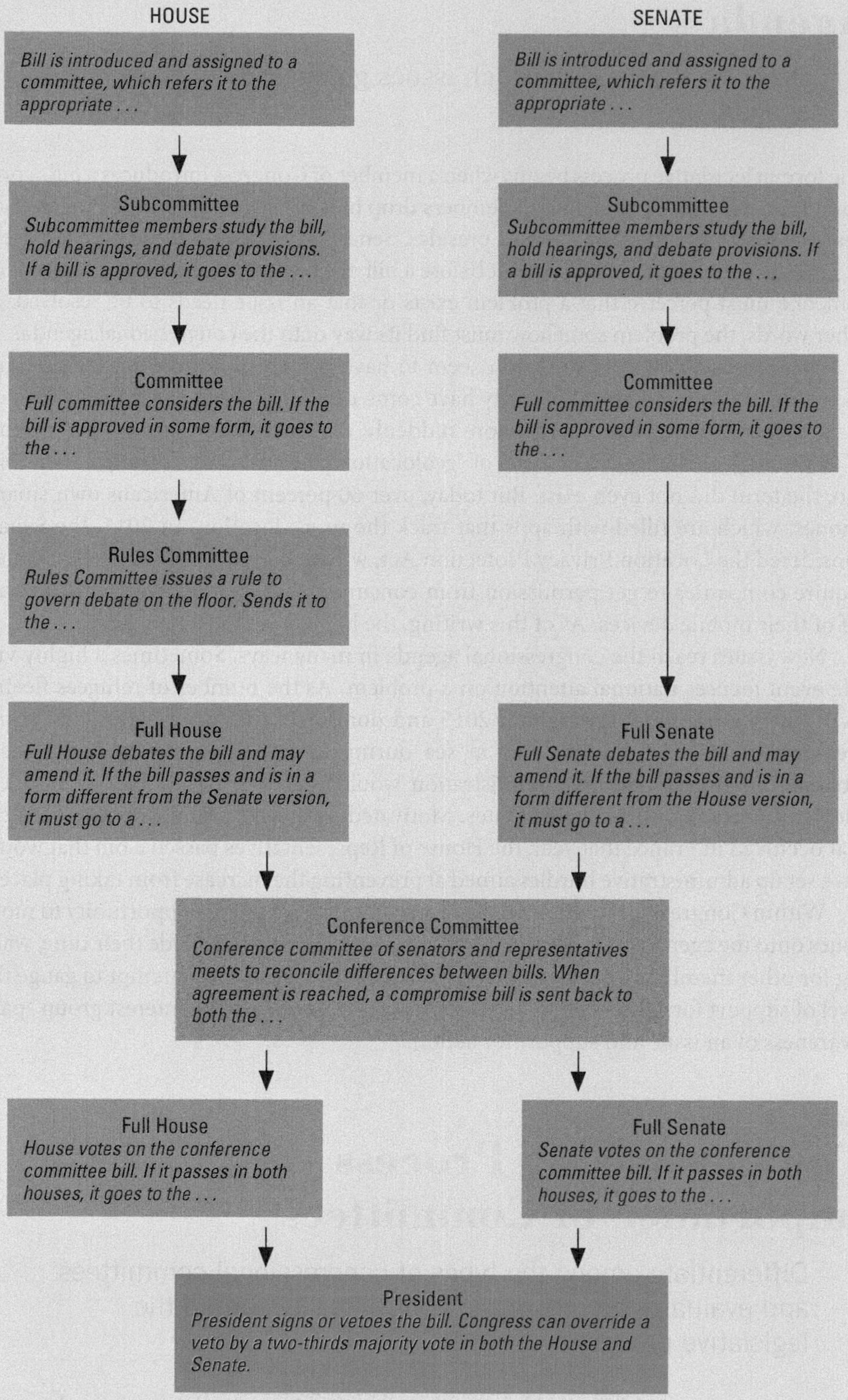

HOUSE

Bill is introduced and assigned to a committee, which refers it to the appropriate . . .

↓

Subcommittee
Subcommittee members study the bill, hold hearings, and debate provisions. If a bill is approved, it goes to the . . .

↓

Committee
Full committee considers the bill. If the bill is approved in some form, it goes to the . . .

↓

Rules Committee
Rules Committee issues a rule to govern debate on the floor. Sends it to the . . .

↓

Full House
Full House debates the bill and may amend it. If the bill passes and is in a form different from the Senate version, it must go to a . . .

SENATE

Bill is introduced and assigned to a committee, which refers it to the appropriate . . .

↓

Subcommittee
Subcommittee members study the bill, hold hearings, and debate provisions. If a bill is approved, it goes to the . . .

↓

Committee
Full committee considers the bill. If the bill is approved in some form, it goes to the . . .

↓

Full Senate
Full Senate debates the bill and may amend it. If the bill passes and is in a form different from the House version, it must go to a . . .

↓ ↓

Conference Committee
Conference committee of senators and representatives meets to reconcile differences between bills. When agreement is reached, a compromise bill is sent back to both the . . .

↓ ↓

Full House
House votes on the conference committee bill. If it passes in both houses, it goes to the . . .

Full Senate
Senate votes on the conference committee bill. If it passes in both houses, it goes to the . . .

↓ ↓

President
President signs or vetoes the bill. Congress can override a veto by a two-thirds majority vote in both the House and Senate.

assigned to the Financial Services Committee in the House or to the Banking, Housing, and Urban Affairs Committee in the Senate. When a committee considers a piece of legislation assigned to it, the bill is usually referred to a subcommittee. The subcommittee may hold hearings, and legislative staffers may do research on the bill. The original bill usually is modified or revised; if passed in some form, it is sent to the full committee. A bill approved by the full committee is sent to the entire membership of the chamber, where it may be debated, amended, and either passed or defeated.

Bills coming out of House committees go to the Rules Committee before going before the full House membership. The Rules Committee attaches a rule to the bill that governs the coming floor debate, typically specifying the length of the debate and types of amendments House members can offer. The Senate does not have a comparable committee, although restrictions on the length of floor debate can be reached through unanimous consent agreements (see the "Rules of Procedure" section later in this chapter).

Even if both houses of Congress pass a bill on the same subject, the Senate and House versions are often different from each other. In that case, a conference committee, composed of legislators from both houses, can work out the differences and develops a compromise version. This version goes back to both houses for another floor vote. If both chambers approve the bill, it goes to the president for his signature or veto.

When the president signs a bill, it becomes law. If the president **vetoes** (disapproves) the bill, he sends it back to Congress with his reasons for rejecting it. The bill then becomes law only if Congress overrides the president's veto by a two-thirds vote in each house. If the president neither signs nor vetoes the bill within ten days (Sundays excepted) of receiving it, the bill becomes law. But if Congress adjourns within the ten days, the president can let the bill die through a *pocket veto*, by not signing it.

The content of a bill can be changed at any stage of the process in either house. Lawmaking in Congress has many access points for those who want to influence legislation. This openness tends to fit within the pluralist model of democracy. As a bill moves through Congress, it is amended again and again, in a search for a consensus that will get it enacted and signed into law. The process can be tortuously slow, and it is often fruitless. Derailing legislation is much easier than enacting it. The process gives groups frequent opportunities to voice their preferences. One foreign ambassador stationed in Washington aptly described the twists and turns of our legislative process this way: "In the Congress of the U.S., it's never over until it's over. And when it's over, it's still not over."[40]

veto
The president's disapproval of a bill that has been passed by both houses of Congress. Congress can override a veto with a two-thirds vote in each house.

Committees: The Workhorses of Congress

President Woodrow Wilson once observed that "Congress in session is Congress on public exhibition, whilst Congress in its committee-rooms is Congress at work."[41] His words are as true today as when he wrote them over 100 years ago. A speech on the Senate floor, for example, may convince the average citizen, but it is less likely to influence other senators. Indeed, few of them may even hear it. The real nuts and bolts of lawmaking go on in the congressional committees.

The House and Senate are divided into committees for the same reason that other large organizations are broken into departments or divisions: to develop and use expertise in specific areas. At Apple, for example, different groups of people design iPhones and iPads, write software, assemble hardware, and sell the company's products. Each task requires an expertise that may have little to do with the others. Likewise, in Congress, decisions on weapons systems require a special knowledge that is of little relevance to decisions on reimbursement formulas for health insurance. It makes sense for some members of Congress to spend more time examining defense issues, becoming increasingly expert on the topic, while others concentrate on health matters. Eventually, all members of Congress vote on each bill that emerges from committees. Those who are not on a particular committee depend on committee members to examine the issues thoroughly, make compromises as necessary, and bring forward a sound piece of legislation that has a good chance of being passed.

standing committee
A permanent congressional committee that specializes in a particular policy area.

Standing Committees. There are several different kinds of congressional committees, but the standing committee is predominant. Standing committees are permanent committees that specialize in a particular area—for example, the House Judiciary Committee or the Senate Foreign Relations Committee. Most of the day-to-day work of drafting legislation takes place in the sixteen standing Senate committees and twenty-one standing House committees. Typically, sixteen to twenty senators serve on each standing Senate committee, and around forty members serve on each standing committee in the House. The proportions of Democrats and Republicans on a standing committee are controlled by the majority party in each house. The majority gives the minority a percentage of seats that, in theory, approximates the minority party's percentage in the entire chamber. However, the majority party usually gives itself enough of a cushion to ensure that it can control each committee.

Standing committees are often broken down further into subcommittees. For instance, the Senate Foreign Relations Committee has seven subcommittees, covering different regions of the world and issues such as human rights. Subcommittees exist for the same reason parent committees exist: members acquire expertise by continually working within the policy area. Typically, members of the subcommittee are the dominant force in shaping the content of a bill.

joint committee
A committee made up of members of both the House and the Senate.

Other Committees. Members of Congress can also serve on joint, select, and conference committees. A joint committee is composed of members of both chambers. Like standing committees, the four joint committees are concerned with particular policy areas. The Joint Economic Committee, for instance, analyzes the country's economic policies. Joint committees are much weaker than standing committees because they typically cannot report bills to the House or Senate. Their role is that of fact finding and publicizing problems and issues that fall within their jurisdiction.

select committee
A temporary congressional committee created for a specific purpose and disbanded after that purpose is fulfilled.

A select committee is a temporary committee created for a specific purpose. Congress establishes select committees to deal with special circumstances or with issues that either overlap or fall outside the areas of expertise of standing committees. In 2011, the Joint Select Committee on Deficit Reduction was created and charged with issuing recommendations by November of that year for reducing the deficit. It was dubbed a "supercommittee" by the media because it included members from both the House and Senate (three members from each party in each chamber).

conference committee
A temporary committee created to work out differences between the House and Senate versions of a specific piece of legislation.

A conference committee is also a temporary committee, created to work out differences between the House and Senate versions of a specific piece of legislation. Its members are appointed from the standing committees or subcommittees from each house that originally crafted and reported the legislation.

Conference committees are not always used, however, to reconcile differing bills. Often, informal negotiations between committee leaders in the House and Senate resolve differences. The increasing partisan conflict between Democrats and Republicans often results in a compromise bill devised solely by the majority party (when a single party controls both chambers).

Congressional Expertise and Seniority

seniority
Years of consecutive service on a particular congressional committee.

Once appointed to a committee, a representative or senator has great incentive to remain there and gain expertise because influence increases with expertise. Influence also grows in a more formal way, with seniority, or years of consecutive service, on a committee. In their quest for expertise and seniority, members tend to stay on the same committees. Within each committee, the senior member of the majority party usually becomes the committee chair. Other senior members of the majority party become subcommittee chairs, whereas their counterparts from the minority party gain influence as ranking minority members.

The way in which committees and subcommittees are led and organized within Congress is significant because much public policy decision making takes place there. The first step in drafting legislation is to collect information on the issue. Committee staffers research the problem, and committees hold hearings to take testimony from witnesses who have some special knowledge of the subject.

At times, committee hearings are more theatrical than informational, designed to draw public attention to them and to offer the majority party a chance to express its views. In 2011, Peter King, the Republican chair of the House Homeland Security Committee who once claimed that there are "too many mosques in the country" and that most are run by extremists, convened highly publicized hearings purportedly aimed at discovering whether American Muslims were becoming increasingly radicalized.[42] Democrats denounced the hearings as inflammatory and as harmful to U.S. relations with the Muslim world. One observer of the contentious hearings wrote, "Mostly, it was the committee itself that appeared to be on trial."[43]

The meetings at which subcommittees and committees actually debate and amend legislation are called *markup sessions*. In some committees, the chair, the ranking minority member, and others work hard, in formal committee sessions and in informal negotiations, to find a middle ground on issues that divide committee members in order to reach consensus. In other committees, members exhibit strong ideological and partisan sentiments. The skill of committee leaders in assembling coalitions that produce legislation that can pass on the floor of their house is critically important. When committees are mired in disagreement, they lose power.

Oversight: Following Through on Legislation

There is general agreement in Washington that knowledge is power. For Congress to retain influence over the programs it creates, it must be aware of how the agencies

Anadolu Agency/Getty Images

IMAGE 11.3   Star Power on the Hill

Famous people often testify before congressional committees in the hopes that their celebrity status will influence legislation. In 2014, actor and comedian Seth Rogen testified before a Senate subcommittee to argue for more government support in combating Alzheimer's disease, a condition that afflicts his mother-in-law.

oversight
The process of reviewing the operations of an agency to determine whether it is carrying out policies as Congress intended.

responsible for them are administering them. To that end, committees engage in oversight, reviewing agencies' operations to determine whether they are carrying out policies as Congress intended.

As the executive branch has grown and policies and programs have become increasingly complex, oversight has become more difficult. On a typical weekday, agencies issue more than a hundred pages of new regulations. Even with the division of labor in the committee system, determining how good a job an agency is doing in implementing a program is no easy task.

Congress performs its oversight function in several different ways. The most visible is the hearing. Hearings may be part of a routine review or can occur when a problem with a program or with an agency's administrative practices emerges. For example, when the new health-care website, healthcare.gov, was unveiled in 2013, it became clear that it was riddled with problems, and people were unable to use it to sign up for health insurance. Committees in both chambers launched investigations, calling government officials and website contractors to testify in order to uncover what went wrong.

Another way Congress keeps track of what departments and agencies are doing is by producing reports on specific agency practices. In 2014, the Senate Intelligence Committee released a 528 page report on CIA interrogation techniques in the so-called War on Terror following the 9/11 terrorist attacks in 2001. The report, which took five years to complete, concluded that the CIA techniques constituted torture, that the techniques were not helpful in the fight against terrorism, and that the CIA misled Congress and administration officials about its tactics.[44]

When the majority party in Congress differs from the party of the president, committees tend to be more aggressive in investigating ethical lapses and policy problems of the executive. President Obama faced a Republican Congress for much of his presidency and had to contend with hearings on a range of issues, including over twenty hearings on the role that Obama's State Department played in anticipating and responding to an attack on the U.S. embassy in Benghazi, Libya, in 2012.

Oversight is often stereotyped as a process in which angry legislators bring some administrators before television cameras at a hearing and proceed to dress them down for some scandal or mistake. Some of this does go on, but the pluralist side of Congress ensures that at least some members of a committee are advocates of the programs they oversee because those programs serve their constituents back home. Members of the House and Senate Agriculture Committees, for example, both Democrats and Republicans, want farm programs to succeed. Thus, most oversight is aimed at trying to find ways to improve programs and is not directed at efforts to discredit them. In short, Congress engages in oversight because it is an extension of their efforts to control public policy.

Majoritarian and Pluralist Views of Committees

Government by committee vests significant power in the committees and subcommittees of Congress—and especially their leaders. This is particularly true in the House, which has more decentralized patterns of influence than the Senate and is more restrictive about letting members amend legislation on the floor. Committee members can bury a bill by not reporting it to the full House or Senate. Many of them also make up the conference committees charged with developing compromise versions of bills.

In some ways, the committee system enhances the force of pluralism in American politics. Representatives and senators are elected by the voters in their particular districts and states, and they tend to seek membership on the committees that make the decisions most important to their constituents. Members from farm areas, for example, want membership on the House and Senate Agriculture Committees, while urban liberals like committees that handle social programs. As a result, committee members tend to represent constituencies with a strong interest in the committee's policy area and are predisposed to write legislation favorable to those constituencies.

Committees have a majoritarian aspect as well, as most committees reflect the general ideological profiles of the two parties' congressional contingents.[45] For example, Republicans on individual House committees tend to vote like all other Republicans in the House. Moreover, even if a committee's views are not in line with those of the full membership, it is constrained in the legislation it writes because bills cannot become law unless they are passed by the parent chamber and the other house. Consequently, in formulating legislation, committees anticipate what other representatives and senators will accept. The parties within each chamber also have means of rewarding members who are loyal to party priorities. Party committees and the party leadership within each chamber make committee assignments and respond to requests for transfers from less prestigious to more prestigious committees. Those who vote in line with the party get better assignments.[46]

Leaders and Followers in Congress

LO5 Identify the leadership structure of the legislative branch and assess the rules and norms that influence congressional operations.

Above the committee chairs is another layer of authority in Congress. The party leaders in each house work to maximize the influence of their own party while keeping their chamber functioning smoothly and efficiently. The operation of the two houses is also influenced by the rules and norms that each chamber has developed over the years.

The Leadership Task

Republicans and Democrats elect party leaders in both chambers who are charged with overseeing institutional procedures, managing legislation, fundraising, and communicating with the press. In the House, the majority party's leader is the **Speaker of the House**. The Speaker is a constitutional officer, but the Constitution does not list the Speaker's duties.[47] The majority party in the House also has a majority leader, who helps the Speaker guide the party's policy program through the legislative process, and a majority whip, who keeps track of the vote count and rallies support for legislation on the floor. The minority party is led by a minority leader who is assisted by the minority whip.

The Constitution makes the vice president of the United States the president of the Senate. But in practice the vice president rarely visits the Senate, unless there is a possibility of a tie vote, in which case he can break the tie. The *president pro tempore* (president "for the time"), elected by the majority party, is supposed to chair the Senate in the vice president's absence, but by custom this constitutional position is entirely honorary. The title is typically assigned to the most senior member of the majority party.

The real power in the Senate resides in the **majority leader**. As in the House, the top position in the opposing party is that of minority leader. Technically, the majority leader does not preside over Senate sessions (members rotate in the president pro tempore's chair), but he or she does schedule legislation, in consultation with the minority leader. More broadly, party leaders play a critical role in getting bills through Congress. The most significant function that leaders play is steering the bargaining and negotiating over the content of legislation. When an issue divides their party, their house, the two houses, or their house and the White House, the leaders try to work out a compromise.

Speaker of the House
The presiding officer of the House of Representatives.

majority leader
The head of the majority party in the Senate; the second-highest ranking member of the majority party in the House.

Much of what leaders do each day is meet with other members of their chamber to try to strike deals that will yield a majority on the floor. It is often a matter of finding out whether one faction is willing to give up a policy preference in exchange for another concession. Beyond trying to engineer trade-offs that will win votes, the party leaders must persuade others (often powerful committee chairs) that theirs is the best deal possible. Former Speaker Dennis Hastert used to say, "They call me the Speaker, but . . . they really ought to call me the Listener."[48]

It is often difficult for party leaders to control rank-and-file members because they have independent electoral bases in their districts and states and receive most of their campaign funds from nonparty sources. Yet party leaders can be aggressive about enforcing party discipline, either by threatening to withdraw support for policy issues near and dear to the defectors or by rewarding those members who toe the party line. When House Republicans had a chance to meet with Obama in the White House in June 2011, the leadership selected freshman Reid Ribble as one of a handful of members who would be able to question the president directly. Ribble was chosen, in part, because "he had never crossed the G.O.P. leadership on anything important."[49] Republican members who had dissented in the past, it was decided, were free to figure out on their own how to have face time with the president.

Rules of Procedure

The operations of Congress are structured by both formal rules and informal norms of behavior. Rules in each chamber are mostly matters of parliamentary procedure. For example, they govern the scheduling of legislation, outlining when and how certain

IMAGES 11.4, 11.5 AND 11.6   The Johnson Treatment

Party leaders in Congress have long played a central role in garnering support for bills and shepherding the party's agenda through the legislative process. When he was Senate majority leader in the 1950s, Lyndon Johnson was well known for his abilities in this regard. In this unusual set of photographs, we see him applying the "Johnson treatment" to Senator Theodore Francis Green (D-R.I.). Washington journalists Rowland Evans and Robert Novak offered the following description of the treatment: "Its tone could be supplication, accusation, cajolery, exuberance, scorn, tears, complaint, the hint of threat. It was all of these together. It ran the gamut of human emotions. Its velocity was breathtaking and it was all in one direction. Interjections from the target were rare. Johnson anticipated them before they could be spoken. He moved in close, his face a scant millimeter from his target, his eyes widening and narrowing, his eyebrows rising and falling. From his pockets poured clippings, memos, statistics. Mimicry, humor, and the genius of analogy made The Treatment an almost hypnotic experience and rendered the target stunned and helpless."

Source: Quote from Rowland Evans and Robert Novak, *Lyndon B. Johnson: The Exercise of Power* (New York: New American Library, 1966), p. 104.

George Tames/The New York Times/Redux

types of legislation can be brought to the floor. Rules also govern the introduction of floor amendments. In the House, amendments must be directly relevant to the bill at hand; in the Senate, except in certain, specified instances, amendments that are not relevant can be proposed.

As noted earlier, an important difference between the two chambers is the House's use of its Rules Committee to govern floor debate. Lacking a similar committee to act as a "traffic cop" for legislation, the Senate relies on unanimous consent agreements to set the starting time and length of debate. If one senator objects, a bill is stalled. Senators do not routinely object to unanimous consent agreements, however, because they will need them when bills of their own await scheduling.

If a senator wants to stop a bill badly enough, she or he may start a **filibuster**. By historical tradition, the Senate gives its members the right of unlimited debate. During a 1947 debate, Idaho Democrat Glen Taylor "spoke for 8½ hours on fishing, baptism, Wall Street, and his children." The record for holding the floor belongs to South Carolina Republican Strom Thurmond for a twenty-four-hour, eighteen-minute marathon in 1957.[50] In the House, no member is allowed to speak for more than an hour without unanimous consent.

After a 1917 filibuster by a small group of senators killed President Wilson's bill to arm merchant ships—a bill favored by a majority of senators—the Senate adopted **cloture**, a means of limiting debate. It takes the votes of sixty senators to invoke cloture. To signal one's intent to filibuster, a senator issues a **hold**, which is a letter requesting that a bill be held from floor debate. In response to a hold, the majority party can take the legislation off the table, try to compromise with the obstructionist lawmaker, or hold a cloture vote.

In today's Congress, the mere threat of a filibuster is common, which means that a bill often needs the support of sixty senators instead of a simple majority in order to pass. It has been argued that filibuster threats have become more common because "the workload of the Senate has increased to the point that wasting time is more costly than accepting the outcome of a cloture vote."[51] In other words, senators are just too busy to wait around while filibustering senators take to the floor. So senators have become more willing to threaten obstruction, knowing that the result will most likely be a cloture vote. Given today's high level of partisan polarization (see Figure 11.4), cloture votes often result in victory for the obstructionist, with few senators willing to cross party lines to end a filibuster. This "60-vote Senate" is often criticized for its ability to thwart the principle of majority rule and to make the legislative process even slower than was originally intended.[52]

In 2013, Senate Democrats became so frustrated with minority filibusters that they enacted a rare change to Senate rules, eliminating the use of filibusters for the confirmation of presidential nominees for the federal courts and executive positions (except in the case of nominees for the Supreme Court). The change has led some observers to believe it is only a matter of time before a majority party decides to eliminate filibusters altogether.

filibuster
A delaying tactic, used in the Senate, that allows any senator to prevent a bill from coming to a vote.

cloture
The mechanism by which a filibuster is cut off in the Senate.

hold
A letter requesting that a bill be held from floor debate.

Edward Steed The New Yorker Collection/The Cartoon Bank

IMAGE 11.7 Help the Bill Find Its Way to Becoming a Law

Political polarization has led elected officials in the House and Senate to try and get their way without having to work with the other side. Their creative use of procedural rules has greatly complicated the process of "how a bill becomes a law."

The most significant reason that parties are important in Congress is that Democrats and Republicans have different ideologies.[56] Both parties have diversity, but as Figure 11.4 illustrates, both parties have become more ideologically cohesive over time. The liberal wing of the Republican Party has practically disappeared, and the party is unified around a conservative agenda. Likewise, the conservative wing of the Democratic Party has declined. The reasons for this increasing ideological homogeneity within the parties are a matter of intense academic debate.[57]

The President

Unlike members of Congress, the president is elected by voters across the entire nation. It can thus be argued that the president has a better claim to representing the nation than does any single member of Congress or even Congress as a whole. As such, presidents try to capitalize on their popular election and usually act as though they are speaking for the majority.

During the twentieth century, the public's expectations of what the president can accomplish in office grew enormously. We now expect the president to be our chief legislator: to introduce legislation on major issues and use his influence to push bills through Congress. This is much different from our early history, when presidents felt constrained by the constitutional doctrine of separation of powers and had to have members of Congress work confidentially for them during legislative sessions.[58]

Today, the White House is openly involved not only in the writing of bills but also in their development as they wind their way through the legislative process. If the White House does not like a bill, it tries to work out a compromise with legislators to have it amended. To monitor Congress and lobby for the administration's policies, many legislative liaison personnel work for the executive branch. On issues of the greatest importance, the president himself may meet with legislators directly. In January 2015, President Obama met personally with Republicans in both the House and the Senate to talk about how he wanted Congress to handle cyber security.[59] As partisan polarization has made it harder for the parties in Congress to work together, meetings between the president and congressional party leadership have become more common.[60] Although members of Congress grant presidents a leadership role in proposing legislation, they jealously guard the power of Congress to debate, shape, and pass or defeat any legislation the president proposes. Congress often clashes sharply with the president.

Constituents

constituents
People who live and vote in a government official's district or state.

Constituents are the people who live and vote in a legislator's district or state. Their opinions are a crucial part of the legislative decision-making process. As much as members of Congress want to please their party's leadership or the president by going along with their preferences, they have to think about what the voters back home want. If they displease enough people by the way they vote, they might lose their seat in the next election.

Constituents' influence contributes to pluralism because the diversity of America is mirrored by the geographical basis of representation in Congress. A representative from Los Angeles needs to be sensitive to issues of particular concern to constituents whose backgrounds are Korean, Vietnamese, Indian, Hispanic, African American, or Jewish. A representative from Montana will have few such constituents but must pay particular attention to issues involving minerals and mining. Such constituencies push and pull Congress in many different directions.

At all stages of the legislative process, the interests of the voters are on the minds of members of Congress. As they decide what to spend time on and how to vote, they

Pool/Getty Images

IMAGE 11.8　We Can Work It Out

As compromise between Republicans and Democrats in Congress has been harder to come by, the president has become more important in helping craft policies that can make it through both chambers. Democratic President Obama and former Republican Speaker of the House John Boehner met many times on matters ranging from immigration to government spending.

weigh how different courses of action will affect their constituents' views of them, and the degree to which they feel they should follow constituency preferences.[61]

Interest Groups

As we pointed out in Chapter 10, interest groups are one way constituents influence Congress. Because they represent a vast array of vocational, regional, and ideological groupings within our population, interest groups exemplify pluralist politics. Interest groups press members of Congress to take a particular course of action, believing sincerely that what they prefer is also best for the country. Legislators are attentive to interest groups not because of an abstract commitment to pluralist politics but because these organizations represent citizens, some of whom live back home in their district or state.

Lobbies are an indispensable source of information for members of Congress. They are also important contributors to and fundraisers for campaigns. Periodic scandals raise concern, however, about potential conflicts of interest and whether legislators do special favors for lobbyists in exchange for campaign contributions or even for personal gain.[62] More common are the entirely legal campaign contributions that individual lobbyists and PACs make to legislators (see Chapter 10). Interest groups don't believe that contributions will necessarily get them what they want, but they certainly expect that significant donations will give them greater access to legislators. And access is the first step toward influencing the process.

With all these strong forces constraining legislators, it's easy to believe that they function solely in response to these external pressures. Legislators, however, bring their own views and life experiences to Congress. The issues they choose to work on and the way they vote reflect these personal values too.[63] But to the degree that the four external sources of influence on Congress—parties, the president, constituents, and interest groups—do influence legislators, they push them in both majoritarian and pluralist directions.

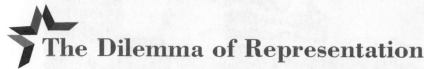

The Dilemma of Representation

LO7 Consider whether members of Congress should vote according to the majority views of their constituents and assess the elements that characterize Congress as a pluralist or majoritarian system.

When candidates for Congress campaign, they routinely promise to work hard for their district's or state's interests. When they get to Washington, though, they all face a troubling dilemma: what their constituents want may not be what the people across the nation want. And as we discussed in the opening section of this chapter, sometimes representatives feel compelled to work on behalf of groups that are not confined to their district, such as women or ethnic minorities.

Every member of Congress lives in two worlds: the world of Washington, D.C., and the world of constituents. A typical week in the life of a representative means working in Washington, then boarding a plane and flying back to the home district. There, the representative spends time meeting with individual constituents and talking to civic groups, church gatherings, business associations, labor unions, and others. A 2013 study found that 78 percent of representatives surveyed said they spent at least forty weekends per year in their districts.[64]

Members of Congress are often criticized for being out of touch with the people they are supposed to represent. This charge does not seem justified. Legislators work extraordinarily hard at keeping in touch with voters and finding out what is on their constituents' minds. The problem is how to act on that knowledge.

Trustees or Delegates?

Are members of Congress bound to vote the way their constituents want them to vote, even if it means voting against their conscience? Some say no. They argue that legislators must be free to vote in line with what they think is best. This view has long been associated with the eighteenth-century English political philosopher Edmund Burke (1729–1797). Burke, who served in Parliament, told his constituents in Bristol that "you choose a member, indeed; but when you have chosen him, he is not a member of Bristol, but he is a member of *Parliament*."[65] Burke reasoned that representatives are sent by their constituents to vote as they think best. As **trustees**, representatives are obligated to consider the views of their constituents, but they are not obligated to vote according to those views if they think they are misguided.

Others hold that legislators should represent the majority view of their constituents—that they are **delegates** with instructions from the people at home on how to vote on critical issues. Delegates, unlike trustees, must be prepared to vote against their own preferences. During the fight over President Obama's health-care reform, Representative Joseph Cao knew he would be in a bind. As a Republican representing a heavily Democratic and black district in Louisiana in which 25 percent of people lacked health insurance, he was torn between his party on the one hand and the desires of his constituents on the other. He ultimately voted for the first reform bill (the only Republican to do so) but against the final version. In the 2010 election, he was one of only two sitting Republicans to be defeated.[66]

trustee
A representative who is obligated to consider the views of constituents but is not obligated to vote according to those views if he or she believes they are misguided.

delegate
A legislator whose primary responsibility is to represent the majority view of his or her constituents, regardless of his or her own view.

and other local projects, but now they have to do more to convince other members of Congress that the projects have merit. Doing so often entails making the case that the projects in question serve the national interest, typically through the job creation or economic development that such projects allegedly produce.

Some members of Congress have been calling for the return of earmarks, claiming that they allow for the exchange of political favors, which enables legislation to move forward. As Representative Tom Cole (R-Okla.) put it, the ban on earmarks removes "all incentive for people to vote on things that are tough."[68] Additionally, members of Congress want to secure projects and programs that will benefit their constituents and help them at election time. To win approval of such projects, members must be willing to vote for other legislators' projects in turn. Such a system promotes pluralism. Survey data suggest that voters like earmarks too, at least in principle if not in name. A 2010 survey asked Americans if certain candidate qualities would make them more or less likely to vote for a particular congressional candidate. Among the eight qualities in the survey, the only one that a majority of Americans said would make them more likely to vote for someone was "has a record of bringing government projects and money to your district." So despite Americans' dislike of so-called wasteful government spending, they still place great pressure on their own representatives to direct federal spending back home.[69]

Proponents of pluralism also argue that the makeup of Congress generally reflects that of the nation—that different members of Congress represent farm areas, low income inner cities, industrial areas, and so on. They point out that America itself is pluralistic, with a rich diversity of economic, social, religious, and racial groups, and even if one's own representatives and senators don't represent one's particular viewpoint, it's likely that someone in Congress does.

Whatever the shortcomings of pluralism, institutional reform aimed at reducing legislators' concern for individual districts and states is difficult. Members of Congress resist any structural changes that might weaken their ability to gain reelection. Nevertheless, the growing partisanship in Congress represents a trend toward greater majoritarianism. As both parties have become more ideologically homogeneous, there is greater unity around policies. To the degree that voters correctly recognize the differences between the parties and are willing to cast their ballots on that basis, increasing majoritarianism constrains pluralism in Congress. Indeed, attachments to partisan identities among voters have become stronger in recent years, and voters are more likely to say that they strongly dislike the other side.[70] In short, the modern Congress is characterized by strong elements of both majoritarianism and pluralism.

Summary

LO1 Explain the structure and powers of Congress as envisioned by the framers and enumerated in the Constitution.

- In designing the legislative branch, the framers wanted a strong union but also wanted to prevent the concentration of power. The Senate consists of two senators from each state elected for six-year terms. The House has 435 members, with each state's representation in proportion to its population. Shared powers include the power to declare war, raise an army and navy, borrow and coin money, regulate interstate commerce, create federal courts, establish rules for the naturalization of immigrants, and make laws. Specific to the Senate are the powers to confirm presidential appointments, ratify treaties, and try cases of impeachment. The House has the power to initiate revenue bills and to impeach.

LO2 Analyze the factors that affect the way voters elect members of Congress.

- Many factors create an electoral advantage for incumbents, including name recognition, casework, campaign fundraising, and weak challengers. The American population is less wealthy and less diverse than members of Congress, though Congress has become more diverse over time.

LO3 Describe the ways in which issues get on the congressional agenda.

- The congressional agenda includes both recurrent issues, such as the national debt and foreign aid, and new issues that may emerge as a result of some highly visible event.

LO4 Differentiate among the types of congressional committees and evaluate the role of the committee system in the legislative process.

- The process by which a bill becomes a law follows a series of specific steps, but the different ways legislation can be treated at each step complicates the process. There are four types of congressional committees: standing, joint, select, and conference; standing committees, which specialize in a particular area of legislation, are predominant. The committee system fosters expertise; representatives and senators who know the most about particular issues have the most influence over them.

LO5 Identify the leadership structure of the legislative branch and assess the rules and norms that influence congressional operations.

- Party leaders in the House and Senate are charged with overseeing institutional procedures, managing legislation, fundraising, and communicating with the press. The majority party leader in the House is the Speaker, who shapes the House agenda and leadership. The vice president of the United States is president of the Senate, but the Senate majority leader exercises the real power in the Senate. Formal rules of procedure structure operations in Congress, while informal norms guide members' behavior. Over time, representatives in both chambers have become more likely to use rules of procedure to avoid compromise.

LO6 Appraise the components of the legislative environment that affect decision making in Congress.

- Political parties, the president, constituents, and interest groups all influence how members of Congress decide issues. Political parties and the president push Congress toward majoritarianism; interest groups exercise a pluralist influence on policymaking; constituents can push representatives in both directions.

LO7 Consider whether members of Congress should vote according to the majority views of their constituents and assess the elements that characterize Congress as a pluralist or majoritarian system.

- Bargaining and compromise play important roles in Congress. Some find this disquieting. They want less deal making and more adherence to principle. This thinking is in line with the desire for a more majoritarian democracy. Others defend the current system, arguing that the United States is a large, complex nation, and

Office are likely to see themselves as being responsible to the president alone. More broadly, presidents use their personal staff and the large Executive Office of the President to centralize control over the entire executive branch. The vast size of the executive branch and the number and complexity of decisions that must be made each day pose a challenge for the White House. Each president must be careful to appoint people to top administration positions who are not merely competent but also passionate about the president's goals and skillful enough to lead others in the executive branch to fight for the president's program instead of their own agendas.

Presidential Leadership

LO4 Defend the argument that "Presidential power is the power to persuade."

A president's influence comes not only from his assigned responsibilities but also from his political skills and from how effectively he uses the resources of his office. His leadership is a function of his own character and skill, as well as the political environment in which he finds himself. Does he work with a congressional majority that favors his policy agenda? Are his goals in line with public opinion? Does he have the interpersonal skills and strength of character to be an effective leader?

Table 12.1 provides two rankings of U.S. presidents. One is based on a Gallup Poll of ordinary Americans; the other is based on a C-SPAN survey of fifty-eight prominent

TABLE 12.1 Presidential Greatness

This table provides two "top twelve" lists of American presidents. The first ranking comes from a Gallup Poll that asked ordinary Americans to name whom they regard as the greatest U.S. president. The second ranking comes from a survey of historians and observers of the presidency, who rated presidents according to their abilities, such as public persuasion, crisis leadership, economic management, moral authority, and relations with Congress. Although the rank order is different, nine presidents appear on both lists. Ordinary Americans are more likely to name recent presidents—Jimmy Carter, Bill Clinton, and George W. Bush—with whom they have had direct experience.

Gallup Poll Ratings		Historians' Ratings	
Rank	President	Rank	President
1	Abraham Lincoln	1	Abraham Lincoln
2	Ronald Reagan	2	Franklin Roosevelt
3	John F. Kennedy	3	George Washington
4	Bill Clinton	4	Theodore Roosevelt
5	Franklin Roosevelt	5	Harry Truman
6	George Washington	6	Woodrow Wilson
7	Harry Truman	7	Thomas Jefferson
8	George W. Bush	8	John F. Kennedy
9	Theodore Roosevelt	9	Dwight Eisenhower
10	Dwight Eisenhower	10	Lyndon Johnson
11	Thomas Jefferson	11	Ronald Reagan
12	Jimmy Carter	12	James K. Polk

historians and professional observers of the presidency. In this section, we look at the factors that affect presidential performance—both those that reside in the person of the individual president and those that are features of the political context that he inherits. Why do some presidents rank higher than others?

Presidential Character

How does the public assess which presidential candidate has the best judgment and whether a candidate's character is suitable to the office? Americans must make a broad evaluation of the candidates' personalities and leadership styles. Although it's difficult to judge, character matters. One of Lyndon Johnson's biographers argues that Johnson had trouble extricating the United States from Vietnam because of insecurities about his masculinity. Johnson wanted to make sure he "was not forced to see himself as a coward, running away from Vietnam."[18] It's hard to know for sure whether this psychological interpretation is valid. Clearer, surely, is the tie between President Nixon's character and the Watergate scandal. Nixon had such an exaggerated fear of what his "enemies" might try to do to him that he created a climate in the White House that nurtured the Watergate break-in and subsequent cover-up.

Presidential character was at the forefront of national politics when it was revealed that President Clinton engaged in a sexual relationship with Monica Lewinsky, a White House intern half his age. Many argued that presidential authority is irreparably damaged when the president is perceived as personally untrustworthy or immoral. Yet despite the disgust and anger that Clinton's actions provoked, most Americans remained unconvinced that his behavior constituted an impeachable offense. The buoyant economy and the public's general satisfaction with Clinton's leadership strongly influenced the country's views on the matter. A majority of the House of Representatives voted to impeach him on the grounds of perjury and obstructing justice, but the Senate did not have the two-thirds majority necessary to convict Clinton, so he remained in office.

Scholars have identified personality traits such as strong self-esteem and emotional intelligence that are best suited to leadership positions like the American presidency.[19] In the media age, it often proves difficult to evaluate a candidate's personality when everyone tries to present himself or herself in a positive light. Even so, voters repeatedly claim that they care about traits such as leadership, integrity, and competence when casting their ballots.[20]

The President's Power to Persuade

In addition to desirable character traits, individual presidents must have the interpersonal and practical political skills to get things done. A classic analysis of the use of presidential resources is offered by Richard Neustadt in his book *Presidential Power*. Neustadt develops a model of how presidents gain, lose, or maintain their influence. His initial premise is simple enough: "Presidential power is the power to persuade."[21] Presidents, for all their resources—a skilled staff, extensive media coverage of presidential actions, the great respect the country holds for the office—must depend on others' cooperation to get things done. Harry Truman echoed Neustadt's premise when he said, "I sit here all day trying to persuade people to do the things they ought to have sense enough to do without my persuading them.... That's all the powers of the President amount to."[22]

Ability in bargaining, dealing with adversaries, and choosing priorities, according to Neustadt, separates above-average presidents from mediocre ones. A president must make wise choices about which policies to push and which to put aside until he can find more support. President Nixon described such decisions as a lot like poker. "I knew when to get out of a pot," said Nixon. "I didn't stick around when I didn't have the cards."[23] The president must decide when to accept compromise and when to stand on principle. He must know when to go public and when to work behind the scenes.

A president's political skills can be important in affecting outcomes in Congress. The president must choose his battles carefully and then try to use the force of his personality and the prestige of his office to forge an agreement among differing factions. When President Lyndon Johnson needed House Appropriations chair George Mahon (D-Tex.) to support him on an issue, he called Mahon on the phone and emphasized the value of Mahon's having a good long-term relationship with him. Speaking slowly to let every point sink in, Johnson told Mahon, "I know one thing ... I know I'm right on this. ... I know I mean more to you, ... and Lubbock [Texas], ... and your district, ... and your State,—and your grandchildren, than Charlie Halleck [the Republican House leader] does."[24]

At the same time, there are real limits to the ability of a president to use his personal resources to persuade recalcitrant legislators, especially those of the opposition party. The opposition party may actually want to do what it can to make the president look bad, rather than helping him accomplish his legislative goals. For presidents, the more important skill may not be bargaining with legislators but forming and timing his legislative agenda.

The President and the Public

A familiar aspect of the modern presidency is the effort presidents devote to mobilizing public support for their programs. A president uses televised addresses (and the media coverage surrounding them), remarks to reporters, and public appearances to speak directly to the American people and convince them of the wisdom of his policies. Scholars have coined the phrase "going public" to describe situations where the president "forces compliance from fellow Washingtonians by going over their heads to

FIGURE 12.1   Race/Ethnicity and Presidential Support

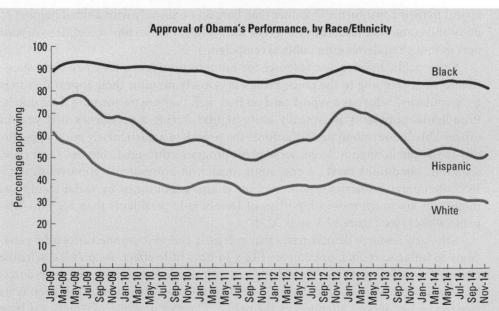

Approval of Obama's Performance, by Race/Ethnicity

As we've noted in previous chapters, party coalitions in America are quite dissimilar in terms of racial and ethnic composition. This, in turn, is reflected in the ways in which Americans of different backgrounds evaluate the president. The gaps between these three demographic sectors were substantial all through President Obama's time in office.

Source: Gary C. Jacobson, "Obama and Nationalized Electoral Politics in the 2014 Midterm," *Political Science Quarterly* 130 (Spring 2015): 6.

Freedom, Order, or Equality

Equality *and* Order and Sexual Assault on Campus

It isn't a typical issue for presidents to take up. But when President Obama created a task force to examine how colleges handle the issue of sexual assault, he indicated that it was time for the White House to become involved because colleges weren't making this issue a priority. Sexual assault is all too common on campuses: one in five women students are assaulted during their time in college. Seven percent of male students admit to having committed or attempted rape.

On the surface, it seemed like this was a case of the president using the bully pulpit to try to galvanize public opinion. Unlike many issues, where there is a tradeoff between the values of freedom, order, and equality, there is no side defending sexual assault. Nor are there advocates of letting colleges have the autonomy to handle cases of violence against its students without any kind of government oversight. Sexual assault is one of those issues on which everyone is aligned in terms of core values, yet generating change is still challenging. And changing the behavior of college students is no easy task.

Rather than trying to mobilize public opinion, Obama used the authority of the federal government to push colleges to do more to create a climate where students understand what constitutes assault and what constitutes consent. Students also need to know that they will be dealt with harshly should they be found guilty of assault. A critical problem is that women often feel that the authorities at their college are not interested in punishing male assailants. Often, women fail to report assaults because they fear the trauma of being questioned skeptically. Although victims can always choose to go to the police instead, many opt for college investigations as they are unsure of what evidence may be necessary to implicate an assailant, may not want to face the possibility of a public trial, or may have more trust in their college than a city's or town's police department.

The Obama plan focused on enforcing civil rights law. Sexual violence and sexual harassment are forms of discrimination and, according to the Department of Education, Obama's initiative "was the first time any administration has called out sexual violence as a civil rights issue." The White House strategy put pressure on colleges to improve the methods by which complaints are handled. It asked colleges to systematically test students' attitudes and awareness of sexual assault; to promote intervention by bystanders to stop misconduct in its tracks; and to better train the college personnel who interact with victims, ensuring that students are treated in a respectful, sensitive, and confidential manner.

The federal government has powerful tools that can be used to punish schools that don't adopt adequate procedures. For example, it can deny federal funds to schools not in compliance with provisions of the law. Thus,

appeal to their constituents."[25] Rather than bargain exclusively with a small number of party and committee leaders in Congress, the president rallies broad coalitions of support as though undertaking a political campaign.

Since public opinion is a resource for modern presidents, they pay close attention to their standing in the polls. Presidents closely monitor their approval ratings or "popularity," which is a report card on how well they are performing their duties. Presidential popularity is typically at its highest during a president's first year in office. This "honeymoon period" affords the president a particularly good opportunity to use public support to get some of his programs through Congress. Over time, economic conditions exert an enormous impact on a president's approval rating.[26] In contemporary America, public support is also conditioned by racial identity as minorities are much more supportive of Democratic presidents than are non-Hispanic whites (see Figure 12.1 on p. 327).

Scholarly research demonstrates that energetic and well-planned efforts by presidents to influence public opinion are likely to have little effect. As political scientist George Edwards concludes, "Presidents cannot reshape the contours of the political landscape to pave the way for change."[27] Perhaps the most difficult obstacle presidents face is a lack of serious attention by the public. The vast majority of Americans have

Presidential leadership is determined in part by whether the president is a member of the dominant political party and whether the public policies and political philosophy associated with his party have widespread support. A president will have a greater opportunity to change public policy when he is in the majority and the opposing political party is perceived to be unable to solve major national problems. Presidents who are affiliated with the dominant political party have larger majorities in Congress and more public support for their party's policy agenda.

Presidents who come to power right after critical elections have the most favorable environment for exerting strong presidential leadership. Franklin Roosevelt, for instance, came to office when the Republican Party was unable to offer solutions to the economic crisis of the Great Depression. He enjoyed a landslide victory and large Democratic majorities in Congress, and he proposed fundamental changes in government and public policy. The weakest presidents are those, like Herbert Hoover, who are constrained by their affiliation with a political party that is perceived to stand for worn-out ideas. Democratic presidents like Truman and Johnson, who followed FDR, were also well positioned to achieve policy success and further their party program since they were affiliated with the dominant New Deal coalition.

The President as National Leader

LO5 Compare and contrast the different roles that the president plays as national leader.

With an election behind him and the resources of his office at hand, a president is ready to lead the nation. Although not every president's leadership is acclaimed, each president enters office with a general vision of how government should approach policy issues. During his term, a president spends much of his time trying to get Congress to enact legislation that reflects his general philosophy and specific policy preferences.

From Political Values . . .

Presidents differ greatly in their views of the role of government. Lyndon Johnson had a strong liberal ideology concerning domestic affairs. He believed that government has a responsibility to help disadvantaged Americans. Johnson described his vision of justice in his inaugural address:

> Justice was the promise that all who made the journey would share in the fruits of the land.
>
> In a land of wealth, families must not live in hopeless poverty. In a land rich in harvest, children just must not go hungry. In a land of healing miracles, neighbors must not suffer and die untended. In a great land of learning and scholars, young people must be taught to read and write.
>
> For [the] more than thirty years that I have served this nation, I have believed that this injustice to our people, this waste of our resources, was our real enemy. For thirty years or more, with the resources I have had, I have vigilantly fought against it.[41]

Johnson used *justice and injustice* as code for *equality and inequality*. He used those words six times in his speech; he used *freedom* only twice. Johnson used his popularity, his skills, and the resources of his office to press for a "just" America—a "Great Society."

To achieve his Great Society, Johnson sent Congress an unprecedented package of liberal legislation. He launched projects such as the Job Corps (which created centers and camps offering vocational training and work experience to youths aged sixteen to twenty-one), Medicare (which provided medical care for the elderly), and the National Teacher Corps (which paid teachers to work in impoverished neighborhoods). Supported by huge Democratic majorities in Congress during 1965 and 1966, he had tremendous success getting his proposals through. Liberalism was in full swing.

In 1985, exactly twenty years after Johnson's inaugural speech, Ronald Reagan took his oath of office for the second time. Addressing the nation, Reagan reasserted his conservative philosophy. He emphasized freedom, using the term fourteen times, and failed to mention justice or equality once. In the following excerpt, we have italicized the term freedom for easy reference:

> By 1980, we knew it was time to renew our faith, to strive with all our strength toward the ultimate in individual *freedom* consistent with an orderly society. . . . We will not rest until every American enjoys the fullness *of freedom*, dignity, and opportunity as our birthright. . . . Americans . . . turned the tide of history away from totalitarian darkness and into the warm sunlight of human *freedom*. . . .
>
>   Let history say of us, these were golden years—when the American Revolution was reborn, when *freedom* gained new life, when America reached for her best. . . . *Freedom* and incentives unleash the drive and entrepreneurial genius that are at the core of human progress. . . . From new *freedom* will spring new opportunities for growth. . . . Yet history has shown that peace does not come, nor will our *freedom* be preserved by goodwill alone. There are those

IMAGES 12.4a AND 12.4b   Different Visions

Lyndon Johnson and Ronald Reagan had strikingly different visions of American democracy and what their goals should be as president. Johnson was committed to equality for all, and major civil rights laws are among the most important legacies of his administration. He is pictured here signing the 1964 Civil Rights Act. Reagan was devoted to reducing the size of government so as to enhance freedom. He worked hard to reduce both taxes and spending.

AP Images; Diana Walker/Time & Life Images/Getty Images

in the world who scorn our vision of human dignity and *freedom.* . . . Human *freedom* is on the march, and nowhere more so than in our own hemisphere. *Freedom* is one of the deepest and noblest aspirations of the human spirit. . . . America must remain *freedom's* staunchest friend, for *freedom* is our best ally. . . . Every victory for human *freedom* will be a victory for world peace. . . . One people under God, dedicated to the dream *of freedom* that He has placed in the human heart.[42]

Reagan turned Johnson's philosophy on its head, declaring that "government is not the solution to our problem. Government is the problem." During his presidency, Reagan worked to undo many welfare and social service programs and cut funding for programs such as the Job Corps and food stamps. By the end of his term, there had been a fundamental shift in federal spending, with sharp increases in defense spending while spending on various social programs went down.

. . . to Policy Agenda

The roots of particular policy proposals, then, can be traced to the more general political ideology of the president. Presidential candidates outline that philosophy of government during their campaign for the White House as they attempt to mobilize voters and interest groups. After the election, presidents and their staffs continue to identify and track support among different kinds of voters as they decide how to translate their general philosophy into concrete legislative proposals.

When the hot rhetoric of the presidential campaign meets the cold reality of what is possible in Washington, the newly elected president must make some hard choices about what to push for during the coming term. There is some urgency early in an administration as the public mood of the nation can turn sharply against the president's ideological orientation. These choices are reflected in the bills the president submits to Congress, as well as in the degree to which he works for their passage. The president's bills, introduced by his allies in the House and Senate, always receive a good deal of initial attention.

The president's role in legislative leadership is largely a twentieth-century phenomenon. A critical change came with Franklin Roosevelt. With the nation in the midst of the Great Depression, Roosevelt began his first term in 1933 with an ambitious array of legislative proposals. During the first one hundred days Congress was in session, it enacted fifteen significant laws, including the Agricultural Adjustment Act, the act creating the Civilian Conservation Corps, and the National Industrial Recovery Act. Never before had a president demanded—and received—so much from Congress. Roosevelt's legacy was that the president would henceforth provide aggressive leadership of Congress through his own legislative program.

Chief Lobbyist

When Franklin D. Roosevelt and Harry Truman first became heavily involved in preparing legislative packages, political scientists typically described the process as one in which "the president proposes and Congress disposes." In other words, once the president sends his legislation to Capitol Hill, Congress decides what to do with it. When the opposition party controls at least one house of Congress, the president can propose all the legislation he wants, but the process has to be collaborative if Congress is to pass some semblance of what was initially proposed.

Over time presidents have become increasingly active in all stages of the legislative process, not just in proposing bills. Most critically, the president is expected

legislative liaison staff
Those people who act as the communications link between the White House and Congress, advising the president or cabinet secretaries on the status of pending legislation.

to do all that he can to push legislation through. The president's efforts to influence Congress are reinforced by the work of his legislative liaison staff. All departments and major agencies have legislative specialists as well. These department and agency people work with the White House liaison staff to coordinate the administration's lobbying on major issues.

The legislative liaison staff is the communications link between the White House and Congress. As a bill slowly makes its way through Congress, liaison staffers advise the president or a cabinet secretary on the problems that emerge. They specify what parts of a bill are in trouble and may have to be modified or dropped. They tell their boss what amendments are likely to be offered, which members of Congress need to be lobbied, and what the bill's chances for passage are with or without certain provisions. Decisions on how the administration will respond to such developments must then be reached.

A certain amount of the president's job consists of stereotypical arm twisting—pushing reluctant legislators to vote a certain way. The president also talks to legislators to seek their advice and takes soundings from committee chairs on what proposals can get through and what must be modified or abandoned. Just in Barack Obama's first four months in office, four hundred representatives and senators were brought to the White House to speak to the president or attend meetings or other events.[43] Yet most day-in, day-out interactions between the White House and Congress tend to be more mundane, with the liaison staff trying to build support by working cooperatively with legislators.

The White House also works directly with interest groups in its efforts to build support for legislation. Presidential aides hope key lobbyists will activate the most effective lobbyists of all: the voters back home. Interest groups can quickly reach the constituents who are most concerned about a bill, using their communications network to mobilize members to write, call, or e-mail their members of Congress. There are so many interest groups in our pluralist political system that they could easily overload the White House with their demands. Consequently, except for those groups most important to the president, lobbies tend to be granted access only when the White House needs them to activate public opinion. During the titanic struggle over health-care legislation, the Obama White House knew it needed a great deal of interest group support. It cut a number of deals with the insurance and pharmaceutical industries to make the president's proposal more palatable to them.[44]

Party Leader

Part of the president's job is to lead his party.[45] This is very much an informal duty, with no prescribed tasks. In this respect, American presidents are considerably different from European prime ministers, who are the formal leaders of their party in the national legislature, as well as the head of their government. In the American system, a president and members of his party in Congress can clearly take very different positions on the issues before them.

As Congress has turned more partisan, presidents have focused more on leadership of their own party rather than trying to bridge differences between the two parties.[46] With less of a moderate middle to work with in Congress, a president needs to work hard to unify his party around his priorities. Increasingly, the public regards presidents as partisan leaders rather than unifying national leaders. Polls show that Americans have evaluated recent presidents, notably Ronald Reagan, Bill Clinton, George W. Bush, and Barack Obama, through a largely partisan prism. Republican identifiers love Republican presidents and despise Democratic ones (see Figure 12.3). Likewise, Democratic identifiers like presidents of their own party and are contemptuous of Republican ones.

FIGURE 12.3　**Polarization and Presidential Approval**

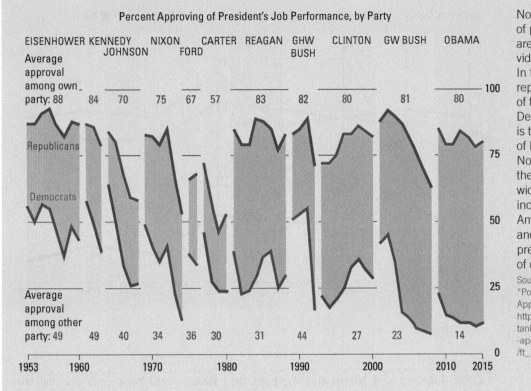

Percent Approving of President's Job Performance, by Party

| EISENHOWER | KENNEDY | NIXON | CARTER | REAGAN | GHW | CLINTON | GW BUSH | OBAMA |

Not surprisingly, evaluations of presidential performance are influenced by individual's partisan leanings. In this figure, the blue line represents the attitude of those who identify as Democrats and the red line is the aggregate opinion of Republican identifiers. Notice how the gap between the blue and red lines has widened over time. The increasing polarization of the American public is evident, and it's become tougher for presidents to gain approval of opposing partisans.

Source: Pew Research Center, "Polarization and Presidential Approval," 12 January 2016, http://www.pewresearch.org/fact-tank/2016/01/12/presidential-job-approval-ratings-from-ike-to-obama/ft_16-01-06_presapproval/.

The president himself has become the "fundraiser in chief" for his party. Since presidents have a vital interest in more members of their party being elected to the House and Senate, they have a strong incentive to spend time raising money for congressional candidates. All incumbent presidents travel frequently to fundraising dinners in different states, where they are the main attraction. Donors pay substantial sums—$1,000 or more a ticket is common—to go to such a dinner. In addition to helping elect more members of his party, a not-so-small by-product for the president is the gratitude of legislators. It's a lot harder to say no to a president's request for help on a bill when he spoke at your fundraiser during the last election.

The President as World Leader

LO6 Analyze the role of the president within the context of the changing nature of global politics.

The president's leadership responsibilities extend beyond Congress and the nation to the international arena. Each administration tries to further what it sees as the country's best interests in its relations with allies, adversaries, and the developing countries of the world. In this role, the president must be ready to act as diplomat and crisis manager. As Figure 12.4 shows, U.S. leadership scores high marks with the rest of the world.

Foreign Relations

From the end of World War II until the late 1980s, presidents were preoccupied with containing communist expansion around the globe. Truman and Korea, Kennedy and

FIGURE 12.4   **U.S. Leadership Scores High Around the World**

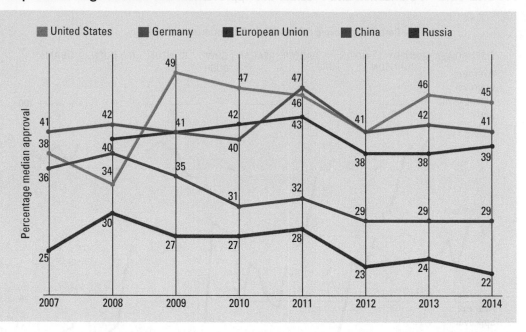

The Gallup Poll periodically surveys people from around the world and asks their opinion of the leadership of some of the most important countries. Across responses from residents of 135 nations, leadership in the United States was rated most highly in comparison to Germany, the European Union, China, and Russia.

Source: Gallup Poll, *Rating World Leaders* (2015), p. 2.

Cuba, Johnson and Nixon and Vietnam, and Reagan and Nicaragua are just some examples of presidents and the communist crosses they had to bear. Presidents not only used overt and covert military means to fight communism but also tried to reduce tensions through negotiations. President Nixon made particularly important strides in this regard, completing an important arms control agreement with the Soviet Union and beginning negotiations with China, with which the United States had had no formal diplomatic relations.

With the collapse of communism in the Soviet Union and Eastern Europe, American presidents entered a new era in international relations, but they are still concerned with three fundamental objectives. First is national security, the direct protection of the United States and its citizens from external threats. National security has been highlighted since the September 11 terrorist attacks. After U.S. intelligence sources pinpointed the hiding place of Osama bin Laden in Pakistan, a special forces operation was carried out during which Navy Seals stormed his compound and shot him to death. President Obama received an immediate boost in the public's estimation of him by appearing to be effective in keeping Americans safe.[47]

Second is fostering a peaceful international environment. Presidents work with international organizations like the United Nations and the North Atlantic Treaty Organization (NATO) to seek an end to regional conflicts throughout the world.

In some cases, like the ongoing dispute between Palestinians and Israelis, the United States has played a central role in mediating conflict and facilitating bargaining between opposing sides. In other cases, presidents send the U.S. military to participate in multinational peace-keeping forces to ensure stability, enforce negotiated peace plans, and monitor democratic elections. The United States may impose trade sanctions to discourage human rights violations.

A third objective is the protection of U.S. economic interests. The new presidential job description places much more emphasis on managing economic relations with the rest of the world. Trade relations are an especially difficult problem because presidents

After the September 11 attacks, there was widespread recognition that our intelligence gathering operations had failed. Although various intelligence agencies had information about al Qaeda, it was never pieced together into an understanding of what was planned. In response, Congress passed the Intelligence Reform and Terrorism Prevention Act of 2004. It amended the 1947 National Security Act, partially restructured the intelligence community, and created an Office of Director of National Intelligence to coordinate all intelligence activities. Since so much of what these agencies do is secret, it's difficult to evaluate whether this administrative reform has actually improved the coordination and performance of the intelligence community.

One part of the intelligence community that has generated a great deal of criticism for its spying activities is the National Security Agency (NSA). Using satellites, supercomputers, and other high-tech equipment, it conducts surveillance around the world. It was created to spy on foreign governments but as noted earlier in this chapter, controversy erupted when it was revealed that the NSA was spying on Americans by gathering phone records.

Crisis Management

Periodically the president faces a grave situation in which conflict is imminent or a small conflict threatens to explode into a larger war. Because handling such episodes is a critical part of the presidency, citizens may vote for candidates who project careful judgment. One reason for Barry Goldwater's crushing defeat in the 1964 election was

IMAGE 12.5 Crisis in Camelot

In October 1962, people gathered in the electronics section of a store to watch President Kennedy address the nation on the Cuban missile crisis. When the United States learned that the Soviet Union was placing missile bases in Cuba, Kennedy demanded that the Soviets remove their missiles, and he ordered a naval blockade. After seven days, Soviet leader Nikita Khrushchev complied with Kennedy's demands, and direct conflict between the two major superpowers was avoided. Cuba's leader at that time, Fidel Castro, had seized power in 1959 and aligned himself with the Soviet Union during the Cold War.

Ralph Crane/Time Life Pictures/Getty Images

his warlike image and rhetoric, which scared many Americans. Fearing that Goldwater would be too quick to resort to nuclear weapons, they voted for Lyndon Johnson instead.

A president must be able to exercise good judgment and remain cool in crisis situations. Henry Kissinger, secretary of state during the Nixon years, notes, "Historians rarely do justice to the psychological stress on a policymaker."[55] John Kennedy's behavior during the Cuban missile crisis of 1962 has become a model of effective crisis management. When the United States learned that the Soviet Union had placed missiles containing nuclear warheads in Cuba, Kennedy saw those missiles as an unacceptable threat to U.S. security. He asked a group of senior aides, including top people from the Pentagon, to advise him on feasible military and diplomatic responses. Kennedy considered an invasion of Cuba and air strikes against the missiles but eventually chose a less dangerous response: a naval blockade. He also privately signaled to Soviet leader Nikita Khrushchev that if the Soviet Union withdrew its missiles from Cuba, the United States would remove American missiles from Turkey. Although the Soviet Union complied, the world held its breath for a short time over the very real possibility of a nuclear war.

What guidelines determine what a president should do in times of crisis? Drawing on a range of advisers and opinions is one. Not acting in unnecessary haste is another. A third is having a well-designed, formal review process with thorough analysis and open debate. A fourth guideline is rigorously examining the reasoning underlying all options to ensure that their assumptions are valid. When President Kennedy backed a CIA plan for a rebel invasion of Cuba by expatriates hostile to Fidel Castro, he did not know that its chances for success were based on unfounded assumptions of immediate uprisings by the Cuban population. Had Kennedy been more aggressive in questioning intelligence officials, he might have chosen to stop the operation. The invasion by a hapless and poorly equipped rebel group went ahead, only to be crushed immediately by the Cuban army. This resulted in an enormous embarrassment for the United States and a stain on Kennedy's reputation.

Summary

LO1 Assess whether the constitutional powers of the president form a strong basis for the modern presidency.

- Presidential leadership is shaped by the president's ability to bargain, persuade, and make wise choices. Over time, presidential power has grown as presidents have interpreted their constitutional authority more broadly. At the same time, there are substantial constraints on presidents, notably Congress, which may have very different goals. The formal powers of the presidency are set forth in Article II of the Constitution.

LO2 Illustrate how claims of inherent powers augment the formal powers of the presidency.

- Informal powers, those not explicitly stated in the Constitution, complement a president's formal powers. A significant source of the growth in presidential power derives from Congress's delegation of authority to the executive branch.

LO3 Assess the role played by the various executive branch institutions as resources for an effective president.

- The president is surrounded by a staff of advisors who provide support and analysis of pending decisions and of broader strategic direction. The primary components of the presidential advisory system are the president's personal staff, the Executive Office of the President, the vice president, and the cabinet.

LO4   Defend the argument that "Presidential power is the power to persuade."

- A part of a president's power is his power to persuade. A president's relationship with the public is highly influenced by Americans' evaluation of his performance in office. A president's ability to get things done is largely contingent on political factors, particularly the relative division of the two parties in Congress.

LO5   Compare and contrast the different roles that the president plays as national leader.

- Leadership is structured by vision, and vision reflects a president's ideological orientation.

Over time, presidents have come to play a critical role in preparing a package of proposals (an agenda) for introduction in Congress. They then lobby for those proposals. Presidents are also leaders of their party, offering direction in terms of policy as well as engaging in more mundane activities, such as raising campaign money for congressional allies.

LO6   Analyze the role of the president within the context of the changing nature of global politics.

- Presidents not only lead the United States but also are important leaders of formal and informal alliances among democracies. The president sits atop a vast set of bureaucracies that aid him in making foreign and defense policy decisions.

Chapter Quiz

LO1   Assess whether the constitutional powers of the president form a strong basis for the modern presidency.

1. What is the underlying philosophy that guided the framers in determining the power of the presidency and, indeed, in structuring the entire Constitution?
2. What are the major formal powers of the presidency as listed in Article II of the Constitution?

LO2   Illustrate how claims of inherent powers augment the formal powers of the presidency.

1. Why have the powers of the presidency grown over time?
2. What are the differences between formal powers and inherent powers?

LO3   Assess the role played by the various executive branch institutions as resources for an effective president.

1. What constitutes the Executive Office of the President?
2. Why does the cabinet not play a major role as a *body* of advisors?

LO4   Defend the argument that "Presidential power is the power to persuade."

1. How might presidential character affect presidential performance?
2. What are the contextual factors that can influence the course of a presidency?

LO5   Compare and contrast the different roles that the president plays as national leader.

1. What fundamental political values distinguish the differences between conservative Republican presidents and liberal Democratic ones?
2. How does a president work to influence Congress?

LO6   Analyze the role of the president within the context of the changing nature of global politics.

1. What are the president's primary responsibilities in terms of leadership in foreign affairs?
2. What guidelines should a president follow in making decisions during crises or urgent situations?

13 The Bureaucracy

Fantasy sports began with groups of friends creating a league of their own. It could be, say, baseball where each participant in the league chooses a team of real-life players from the major leagues. The team "owners" would hold a draft just before the season began and one team might be composed of a first baseman from the St. Louis Cardinals, a catcher from the L.A. Dodgers, a leftfielder from the Chicago Cubs, and so on. The baseball players' real world statistical performance would determine the fantasy winners and, theoretically, the individual who had the sharpest eye for talent and value would win the league at the end of the season. Almost always, there was some gambling involved and the winner would walk away with the entry fee each owner put up.

More recently, fantasy sports became a commercial product. Companies like DraftKings and Fan Duel offer individuals the opportunity to win prizes as big as $1 million. Unlike the amateur leagues, these companies offer betting opportunities not just for a single season, but for any day or week there are games. The TV commercials are as ubiquitous as they are inviting: previous winners talk about how easy it is to enter a contest—just a few keystrokes to select your players—and then experience the fun of seeing how your very temporary team performs. And you might even win some money!

It may all seem like just good, clean fun, but gambling over the Internet is illegal under federal law.[1] However, the law distinguishes between gambling and games of skill. Is choosing players at various prices a matter of skill, or given all that can happen in an individual game, is it just chance as to what works out and what doesn't? Congress has held hearings on this question, but at the time of this writing, seems disinclined to revise existing ambiguous federal law. However, legislators and attorneys general in some states have come to believe that fantasy sports involve a great deal of luck and that these companies exploit people with gambling problems. One rationale for governmental action is that unbeknownst to many who wager, the real winners in fantasy sports are typically people who know how to program their computers to place hundreds or thousands of unique bets on the same day, winning a little more often than not and accruing an advantage through this systematic approach.

As a result, some states have moved forward to regulate fantasy sports—to intervene in a market and to set rules that businesses must abide by. The state of Massachusetts, for example, adopted rules in 2016 aimed at protecting young people, assuming they might not understand the true odds of winning. The state now bans anyone under twenty-one from playing online fantasy sports, and ads targeting minors are forbidden. There can be no betting on college sports. Companies cannot allow clients to put more than $1,000 in their accounts per month unless they've investigated their finances to make sure those individuals can afford to lose more than that.[2]

The decision of Massachusetts and other states to regulate fantasy sports reflects many larger questions about the role of the bureaucracy in American government. With all the problems facing society, why add this one to the responsibilities of government? Is it better to let each state decide how to regulate a market—or not regulate it all—or is it better to have one national set of rules administered by Washington? Should government respect freedom—let people do what they want with their own money—or should it instill order by protecting people from certain business practices?

#ChallengeAccepted

Take the Challenge on MindTap for American Government

Do you know other students who play online fantasy sports? Do they say that overall, they've made money or they've lost money? Should government restrict their right to bet as much they'd like?

Learning Outcomes

LO1 Define the concept of bureaucracy, explain the role of organizations in the administration of the nation's laws, examine the reasons for the growth of the bureaucratic state, and assess arguments for and against its continued expansion.

LO2 Describe the organization of the executive branch, the role of the civil service, and the bureaucracy's responsiveness to presidential control.

LO3 Describe the roles of administrative discretion and rule-making authority in the execution of administrative policymaking.

LO4 Analyze how incrementalism and bureaucratic culture affect policymaking.

LO5 Identify obstacles to effective policy implementation.

LO6 Compare the strengths and weaknesses of reform efforts aimed at increasing the effectiveness of the bureaucracy's performance.

However, government at all levels (national, state, and local) has grown enormously over time, for several major reasons. A principal cause of government expansion is the increasing complexity of society. George Washington did not have an assistant administrator for water and hazardous materials because he had no need for one. The National Aeronautics and Space Administration (NASA) was not necessary until rockets were invented.

Another reason government has grown is that the public's attitude toward business has changed. Throughout most of the nineteenth century, there was little or no government regulation of business. Business was generally autonomous, and any government intervention in the economy that might limit that autonomy was considered inappropriate. This attitude began to change toward the end of the nineteenth century as more Americans became aware that the end product of a laissez-faire approach was not always highly competitive markets that benefited consumers. Instead, businesses sometimes formed oligopolies, such as the infamous "sugar trust," a small group of companies that controlled virtually the entire sugar market.

Gradually government intervention came to be accepted as necessary to protect the integrity of markets. And if government was to police unfair business practices effectively, it needed administrative agencies. During the twentieth century, new bureaucracies were organized to regulate specific industries. Among them are the Securities and Exchange Commission (SEC), which oversees securities trading, and the Food and Drug Administration (FDA), which tries to protect consumers from unsafe food, drugs, and cosmetics. Through bureaucracies such as these, government has become a referee in the marketplace, developing standards of fair trade, setting rates, and licensing individual businesses for operation. As new problem areas have emerged, government has added new agencies, further expanding the scope of its activities.

General attitudes about government's responsibilities in the area of social welfare have changed too. An enduring part of American culture is the belief in self-reliance. People are expected to overcome adversity on their own, to succeed on the basis of their own skills and efforts. Yet certain segments of our population are believed to deserve government support, because we either particularly value their contribution to society or have come to believe that they cannot realistically be expected to overcome adversity on their own.

This belief goes as far back as the nineteenth century. The government provided pensions to Civil War veterans because they were judged to deserve financial support. Later, programs to help mothers and children were developed. Further steps toward income security came in the wake of the Great Depression, when the Social Security Act became law, creating a fund that workers pay into and then collect income from during old age. In the 1960s, the government created Head Start, Medicare, and Medicaid, programs designed to help minorities, the elderly, and the poor. As the government made these new commitments, it also created new bureaucracies and expanded existing ones.

Even today in these tight budgetary times, the pressure to expand government for particular purposes continues. Opioid addiction (both from prescription drugs like OxyContin and Vicodin and illegal drugs such as heroin) has increased and is considered to be an epidemic in certain parts of the United States. In Massachusetts, a relatively prosperous state with strong social services and a broad health-care net, opioid addiction has become a very serious problem. Deaths from both prescription and illegal opioids more than doubled in three years, with over 1,500 deaths in 2015.[6] The state's new governor has promised action, and opioid addiction was discussed in the 2016 presidential campaign. New bureaucracies seem sure to follow.

Can We Reduce the Size of Government?

For many Americans, government is unpopular: they have little confidence in its capabilities and feel that it wastes money and is out of touch with the people. They want a smaller government that costs less and performs better.

Most of the national government is composed of large bureaucracies, so if government is to become smaller, bureaucracies will have to be eliminated or reduced in size. Everyone wants to believe that we can shrink government by eliminating unnecessary bureaucrats. Although efficiencies can be found, serious budget cuts also require serious reductions in programs. Not surprisingly, presidents and members of Congress face opposition when they try to cut spe-

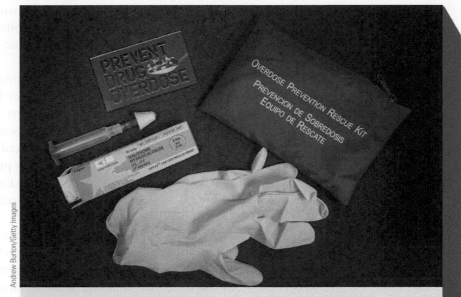

IMAGE 13.1 Lifesaver

Federal, state, and local bureaucracies are struggling to contain a surge in opioid addiction. Unable to stop people from using these dangerous drugs, one recent point of emphasis by policymakers is to arm first responders with Narcan (Naloxone Hydrochloride), which can block overdoses and prevent death if administered quickly enough.

cific programs as those programs may be popular with the public. (See Figure 13.1.) The national government often engages in a bit of a shell game, modestly reducing

FIGURE 13.1 Agency by Agency, Public Attitudes Vary

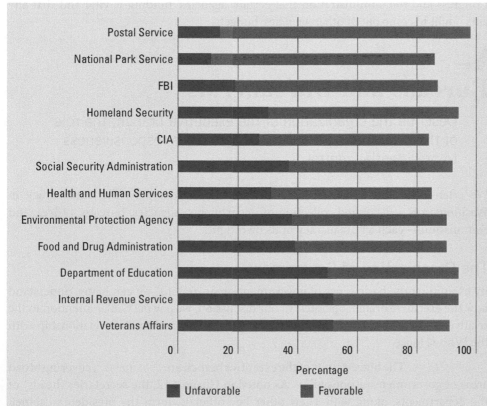

Americans are highly critical of our national government as a whole, but when asked about individual bureaucracies, we tend to be more favorable. Still, attitudes vary considerably by agency. Departments and agencies whose job it is to protect us (FBI, Homeland Security, CIA) are generally held in high esteem. Veterans Affairs, which scores lowest in this 2015 survey, has a reputation for bad service at its medical facilities.

Source: Pew Research Center, "Ratings of Federal Agencies, Congress and the Supreme Court," 23 November 2015, http://www.people-press.org/2015/11/23/4-ratings-of-federal-agencies-congress-and-the-supreme-court/.

the number of bureaucrats (which is popular) without reducing government programs (which is politically risky). The government often turns over the former bureaucrats' jobs to nonprofit or private contractors who do the same job but are not technically government employees.

Beneath the common rhetoric that government needs to be smaller and more efficient, serious efforts to shrink the bureaucracy have varied considerably. Ideological differences between the two parties and the gyrating size of the national budget deficit have shaped the debate. Democrats and liberals generally prefer a more expansive government, one committed to providing social services to those citizens who need them. Republicans and conservatives generally prefer smaller government, one requiring more self-reliance on the part of citizens. Liberals also favor a more active government in regulating the economy, while conservatives want government to play less of a role in supervising the economy.

During the Obama administration, new administrative offices were developed to administer the Dodd-Frank Act, a law designed to prevent the nation's banks from going into free fall after a catastrophic downturn in the economy (as happened in 2008). At the same time, Republican conservatives pushed hard throughout Obama's presidency to cut the nation's budget, thus forcing a reduction in the size of the bureaucracy. The result wasn't so much that agencies were abolished, but that the reduced budgets forced many agencies to make incremental cuts in their size. One of the worst hit has been the Internal Revenue Service (IRS), which no one likes because it collects our taxes, but is especially despised by Republicans. The IRS has lost thousands of staffers in recent years, reducing its ability to do its job, most notably auditing tax returns.[7]

The tendency for big government to endure over the longer term reflects the tension between majoritarianism and pluralism. Even when the public as a whole wants a smaller national government, that sentiment can be undermined by the strong desire of different segments of society for government to continue performing some valuable function for them. Lobbies that represent these segments work strenuously to convince Congress and the administration that certain agencies' funding is vital and that any cuts ought to come out of other agencies' budgets.

Bureaus and Bureaucrats

LO2 Describe the organization of the executive branch, the role of the civil service, and the bureaucracy's responsiveness to presidential control.

We often think of the bureaucracy as a monolith. In reality, the bureaucracy in Washington is a disjointed collection of departments, agencies, bureaus, offices, and commissions—each a bureaucracy in its own right.

The Organization of Government

By examining the basic types of government organizations, we can better understand how the executive branch operates. In our discussion, we pay particular attention to the relative degree of independence of these organizations and to their relationship with the White House.

Departments. The biggest units of the executive branch are **departments**, covering broad areas of government responsibility. As noted in Chapter 12, the secretaries (heads) of the departments, along with a few other key officials, form the president's cabinet.

departments
The biggest units of the executive branch, covering a broad area of government responsibility. The heads of the departments, or secretaries, form the president's cabinet.

various transportation industries. Controversy has swirled for years around a practice of airlines to keep passengers on board an aircraft that has pulled away from the gate but cannot take off (usually due to inclement weather). Horror stories abound. In August 2009, an ExpressJet flight with forty-seven passengers on board stayed overnight on the tarmac at the airport in Rochester, New York. It doesn't take long before a plane runs out of food and water and bathrooms become fouled.

Whenever Congress threatened to enact a "passenger bill of rights" to forbid such unconscionable tarmac delays, the airlines promised to improve their service. At the end of 2009, however, the Department of Transportation announced a new set of rules, limiting tarmac waits to no more than three hours. If that much time elapses, the plane must return to the gate and give passengers the option of deplaning. Airlines claimed there would be unintended consequences and even longer delays as ground crews removed luggage and searched for bags belonging to passengers who deplaned.[17] The new rule, however, has worked well, and according to a 2014 report, "controllable tarmac delays [have] all but vanished."[18]

The regulatory process is controversial because regulations often require individuals and corporations to act against their own self-interest. The airline regulations are a classic case of freedom versus order. The airline companies believed they needed the greater freedom to conduct business in a way that they found most efficient. Consumer groups preferred that the government put more of a premium on maintaining order (preserving the health and well-being of passengers). Administrative rule making gives agencies flexibility as they try to find a balance between conflicting pressures.

Administrative Policymaking: Informal Politics

LO4 Analyze how incrementalism and bureaucratic culture affect policymaking.

When an agency is considering a new regulation and all the evidence and arguments have been presented, how does an administrator reach a decision? Because policy decisions typically address complex problems that lack a single satisfactory solution, these decisions rarely exhibit mathematical precision and efficiency.

The Science of Muddling Through

In his classic analysis of policymaking, "The Science of Muddling Through," Charles Lindblom compared the way policy might be made in the ideal world with the way it is formulated in the real world.[19] The ideal, rational decision-making process, according to Lindblom, begins with an administrator's tackling a problem by ranking values and objectives. After clarifying the objectives, the administrator thoroughly considers all possible solutions to the problem. He or she comprehensively analyzes alternative solutions, taking all relevant factors into account. Finally, the administrator chooses the alternative that appears to be the most effective means of achieving the desired goal and solving the problem.

Lindblom claims that this "rational-comprehensive" model is unrealistic. Policymakers have great difficulty defining precise values and goals. Administrators at the U.S. Department of Energy, for example, want to be sure that supplies of home heating oil are sufficient each winter. At the same time, they want to reduce dependence on foreign oil. Obviously, the two goals are not fully compatible. How should these administrators decide which goal is more important? And how should they relate them to the other goals of the nation's energy policy?

Real-world decision making parts company with the ideal in another way: the policy selected cannot always be the most effective means to the desired end. Even if a tax at the gas pump is the most effective way to reduce gasoline consumption during a shortage, motorists' anger would make this theoretically "right" decision politically difficult. So the "best" policy is often the one on which most people can agree. However, political compromise may mean that the government is able to solve only part of a problem.

Finally, critics of the rational-comprehensive model point out that policymaking can never be based on truly comprehensive analyses. A secretary of energy cannot possibly find the time to read a comprehensive study of all alternative energy sources and relevant policy considerations for the future. A truly thorough investigation of the subject would produce thousands of pages of text. Instead, administrators make choices as to what information to seek out and what to prioritize among all that they are exposed to.[20] Time can also be of the essence, and problems are often too pressing to wait for a complete study. According to Lindblom, policymaking tends to be characterized by **incrementalism**, with policies and programs changing bit by bit, step by step. Decision makers are constrained by competing policy objectives, opposing political forces, incomplete information, and the pressures of time. They choose from a limited number of feasible options that are almost always modifications of existing policies rather than wholesale departures from them.

Because policymaking proceeds by means of small modifications of existing policies, it is easy to assume that incrementalism describes a process that is intrinsically conservative, sticking close to the status quo.[21] Yet even if policymaking moves in small steps, those steps may all be in the same direction. Over time, a series of incremental changes can significantly alter a program. Moreover, although Lindblom offered a more realistic portrayal of the policymaking process, incrementalism is not ubiquitous. There are a minority of cases where decisions are made that move a policy in a significantly new direction. The Obama administration's intervention to resuscitate a collapsing banking industry could not accurately be labeled an incremental change, even though in the past the government has on occasion intervened to shore up an industry in trouble. The staggering sums the government loaned to failed or fragile financial institutions and the level of control the government exerted were without real precedent. It's certainly true that virtually all policy changes have antecedents in current policy, but some changes are considerable in scope.[22]

The Culture of Bureaucracy

How an agency makes decisions and performs its tasks is greatly affected by the people who work there: the bureaucrats. Americans often find their interactions with bureaucrats frustrating because bureaucrats are inflexible (they go by the book) or lack the authority to get things done. Top administrators too can become frustrated with the bureaucrats who work for them.

Why do people act bureaucratically? Individuals who work for large organizations cannot help but be affected by the culture of bureaucracy. Part of that culture is the development of **norms**, an organization's informal, unwritten rules that guide individual behavior. For example, the Individuals with Disabilities Act (IDEA) requires that every child with qualifying disabilities receive an Individualized Education Plan that provides for the necessary, appropriate services. However, school administrators implementing this law frequently offer families fewer services than the law arguably calls for.

incrementalism
Policymaking characterized by a series of decisions, each typically instituting modest change.

norms
An organization's informal, unwritten rules that guide individual behavior.

The reason is not that school administrators don't want to do the maximum for disabled children but that they don't have enough money to provide all services to all qualifying students in their school or district. Norms develop about how to allocate scarce resources even though the law assumes adequate services will be offered.[23]

Bureaucracies are often influenced in their selection of policy options by the prevailing customs, attitudes, and expectations of the people working within them. Departments and agencies commonly develop a sense of mission, where a particular objective or a means for achieving it is emphasized. The Army Corps of Engineers, for example, is dominated by engineers who define the agency's objective as protecting citizens from floods by building dams. There could be other objectives, and there are certainly other methods of achieving this one, but the engineers promote the solutions that fit their conception of what the agency should be doing. More broadly, bureaucracies are influenced by the interest groups that have a vested interest in the policies they develop and administer.[24]

Sometimes we get frustrated with government bureaucrats because we believe that the norms of their agencies have made them timid and too ready to fall back on written rules. We may see formal rules as too cumbersome and requiring too much delay before action can be taken.[25] Bureaucracies can be slow and require a great deal of paperwork before action can be taken but, at the same time, written rules are in place to prevent bureaucrats from acting arbitrarily, impulsively, or without doing the review of evidence necessary to make the most intelligent decision.

Problems in Implementing Policy

LO5 Identify obstacles to effective policy implementation.

The development of policy in Washington is the end of one phase of the policymaking cycle and the beginning of another. After policies have been developed, they must be implemented. **Implementation** is the process of putting specific policies into operation. Ultimately, bureaucrats must convert policies on paper into policies in action. It is important to study implementation because policies do not always do what they were designed to do.

Implementation may be difficult because the policy to be carried out is not clearly stated. Policy directives to bureaucrats sometimes lack clarity and leave them with too much discretion. Implementation can also be problematic because it often involves many different agencies and different layers of government. Take, for example, the case of reducing air pollution in Los Angeles, a city that was afflicted with horrible smog. In 1977 Congress amended the Clean Air Act, which among other things shifted a great deal of responsibility to state, regional, and local institutions. The Environmental Protection Agency (EPA) still retained much authority and continued to issue regulations specifying standards. To implement these regulations in the Los Angeles region, the state of California created the South Coast Air Quality Management District. However, considerable jurisdiction over many sources of pollution lay with another body, the California Air Resources Board. Implementation also involved many city governments in the Los Angeles basin along with a number of transportation agencies.

Despite these challenges of divided responsibilities, considerable progress was made in reducing pollution and smog. But the national government then changed regulatory philosophies, and in 1993 the EPA issued a new set of instructions. The new approach was to move away from "command and control" regulations (basically

implementation
The process of putting specific policies into operation.

Freedom, Order, or Equality

Freedom, Order, and Tanning

A tanned body has long been seen as a sign of health and beauty. If it's not summer or you don't have time to sun yourself at the beach or in the backyard, a convenient option is a tanning salon. Lying under the ultraviolet lamps can turn white skin to brown.

Unfortunately, tanning lamps turn white skin to brown by essentially damaging the skin. (The same is true of tanning from the sun.) The damage is more than skin deep. Among those who use tanning beds or booths, there is a considerably heightened chance of developing melanoma (skin cancer). And skin cancer can metastasize and ultimately turn fatal.

Tanning is especially popular among young, white, non-Hispanic women. Thirty percent of young white high school-age women report going to a tanning parlor at least once a year. Seventeen percent go frequently. Some become addicted.

Due to the dangers of tanning, many states regulate tanning salons in some form or another. California, for example, bans tanning salons for minors under the age of eighteen. Thirty-three states have chosen to regulate these businesses, often by requiring minors to obtain parental consent before using the services of a tanning studio. State governments focus on use by teenagers because they are less likely to understand the health risks associated with tanning and most likely to feel physically invincible. The state's interest is in having a healthy population and not one in which there are unnecessary cancers.

The federal government does not regulate tanning in the same manner as the states do, but under the Affordable Care Act, it now taxes use of tanning studios. Customers have a 10 percent tax added to their bill when they utilize such a facility. This tax is justified as a deterrent to behavior that leads to serious medical problems. All of us who pay for health insurance are adversely affected by those who must be treated for skin cancer. Or more bluntly, we all have to pay more for our health insurance to cover the costs of individuals who must undergo serious and costly treatments for melanoma and related complications.

Despite this new tax, owners of tanning parlors say business has not been affected. The popularity of tanning has not been dimmed.

Sources: National Conference of State Legislatures, "Indoor Tanning Restrictions for Minors," March 2014, http://www.ncsl.org/research/health/indoor-tanning-restrictions.aspx; Karen Kaplan, "Young White Women Still Embrace Indoor Tanning Despite Cancer Risks," *Los Angeles Times*, 19 August 2013, http://articles.latimes.com/2013/aug/19/science/la-sci-sn-indoor-tanning-cancer-white-women-20130819; and Erin Kim, "Obamacare's 'Tanning Tax' Is Here to Stay," CNNMoney, 28 June 2012, http://money.cnn.com/2012/06/28/pf/taxes/tanning-tax/.

CRITICAL THINKING What is the justification for government regulating this business sector through both taxation and restrictions on consumers?

the belief that competition will make government more dynamic and more responsive to changing environments and will weaken the ability of labor unions to raise wages beyond those of nonunion employees.

One widespread adaptation of competitive bidding to administer government programs has come in the area of social services. Over time government welfare programs have increasingly emphasized social services—giving people training and non-cash support—rather than income maintenance (cash support). Social services are labor intensive, and state and local governments have found it efficient to outsource programs to nongovernmental organizations, principally nonprofit organizations like community health centers and day-care centers for elderly persons. For-profit companies compete for the grants and contracts that the government awards through competitive grants or bidding. For example, the for-profit company Maximus is contracted by a number of state agencies responsible for child support to locate noncustodial parents to establish paternity or enforce payments to a custodial parent.[36]

This movement toward **competition and outsourcing** continues to grow. More and more government jobs are open to bidding from nongovernment competitors, and sometimes a government bureau or office competes for the jobs and programs that they used to "own." As the number of federal government employees has declined while the population of Americans increases, some wonder if our country is building a "hollow state." By this, critics mean a government that is distinct from the programs it funds, disengaged from interaction with the people it serves.

competition and outsourcing
Procedures that allow private contractors to bid for jobs previously held exclusively by government employees.

Performance Standards

Another approach to improving the bureaucracy's performance is to focus on performance: To what degree does any individual agency accomplish the objectives that have been set for it? In this view, each agency is held accountable for reaching quantifiable goals each year or budget cycle. Under such a system, congressional and White House overseers examine each agency to see if it meets its objectives, and they reward or punish agencies accordingly. As one scholar noted, this is a philosophy of "making the managers manage."[37]

A major initiative to hold agencies accountable for their performance is the **Government Performance and Results Act.** Passed by Congress, it requires each agency to identify specific goals, adopt a performance plan, and develop quantitative indicators of agency progress in meeting its goals. The law requires that agencies publish reports with performance data on each measure established. This is no small challenge.[38] A case in point is the Healthy Start program funded by the Health Resources and Services Administration (HRSA) and intended to improve infant mortality rates and infant health generally. Among the specific goals are increasing the number of mothers receiving prenatal care during the first trimester and reducing the number of low-weight births. These are measurable, and the hospitals and health centers receiving federal funding for Healthy Start must report the appropriate data to HRSA. More complicated is the degree to which this program makes a difference since infant health can be influenced by many factors.[39]

Government Performance and Results Act
A law requiring each government agency to implement quantifiable standards to measure its performance in meeting stated program goals.

Another problem is that since agencies set their own goals and know they'll be judged on meeting them, they may select indicators where they know they'll do best. One approach to ensure that evaluations are objective is evidence-based policymaking. To achieve objectivity, programs can be assessed through randomized experiments. For example, a reading program for elementary school students can randomly distribute students from the same school to a group using the new (experimental) program while the others are allocated to a group using the approach that has heretofore been in place. Reading scores between the groups are then compared over time. A key is that those programs that work best are rewarded with greater funding—money reserved ahead of time for successful innovations.[40]

Despite the relative appeal of these different approaches to improving the bureaucracy, each has serious shortcomings. There is no magic bullet. The commitment of the government to solve a problem is far more important than management techniques. Still, to return to a theme that we began with, organization does matter. Trying to find ways of improving the bureaucracy is important because bureaucracies affect people's lives, and enhancing their performance, even at the margins, has real consequences.

Summary

LO1 Define the concept of bureaucracy, explain the role of organizations in the administration of the nation's laws, examine the reasons for the growth of the bureaucratic state, and assess arguments for and against its continued expansion.

- As the scope of government activity has grown during the twentieth and early twenty-first centuries, so too has the bureaucracy. The executive branch has evolved into a complex set of departments and independent agencies. The way in which the various bureaucracies are organized matters a great deal because their structure affects their ability to carry out their tasks. Shrinking the government, though popular in the abstract, is difficult to enact because individual programs are popular with individual constituencies.

LO2 Describe the organization of the executive branch, the role of the civil service, and the bureaucracy's responsiveness to presidential control.

- The executive branch is organized around cabinet departments, independent agencies, and a small number of government corporations. Almost all civilian employees of the federal government are protected by civil service employment requirements. Presidents have some control over the bureaucracy, but such authority is constrained by a number of factors.

LO3 Describe the roles of administrative discretion and rule-making authority in the execution of administrative policymaking.

- Administrative discretion is delegated to agencies by the Congress because Congress recognizes that it does not have the staff, time, and expertise to make all the decisions necessary in each policy area. The formulation of regulations follows a formal, legal process termed rule making. Regulations set forth policy and are not mere details of administrative processes.

LO4 Analyze how incrementalism and bureaucratic culture affect policymaking.

- A rational-comprehensive model of administrative policymaking is unrealistic. Instead, agencies make policy through incremental steps. The behavior of bureaucrats is shaped by bureaucratic culture—the norms and informal practices that characterize the internal workings of the organization.

LO5 Identify obstacles to effective policy implementation.

- Implementation is the process by which policies formulated by bureaucracies are put into practice. Lack of clarity in policy directives, involvement of many agencies at different levels of government, time constraints, and the sheer complexity of public policy problems are some of the challenges to effective implementation.

LO6 Compare the strengths and weaknesses of reform efforts aimed at increasing the effectiveness of the bureaucracy's performance.

- Deregulation is a reduction in the level of supervision of a business market or other activity by a government bureaucracy. Recent efforts by government to improve the performance of bureaucracies include competition and outsourcing and setting performance standards.

Chapter Quiz

LO1 **Define the concept of bureaucracy, explain the role of organizations in the administration of the nation's laws, examine the reasons for the growth of the bureaucratic state, and assess arguments for and against its continued expansion.**

1. Why has the bureaucracy grown over the years?
2. What are the obstacles to reducing the size of government?

LO2 **Describe the organization of the executive branch, the role of the civil service, and the bureaucracy's responsiveness to presidential control.**

1. Identify the major structural components of the federal government.
2. How can a change in presidents affect administrative policymaking?

LO3 **Describe the roles of administrative discretion and rule-making authority in the execution of administrative policymaking.**

1. Why does Congress give agencies significant discretion?
2. What is rule making?

LO4 **Analyze how incrementalism and bureaucratic culture affect policymaking.**

1. What is incrementalism?
2. Compare and contrast formal and informal influences on policymaking.

LO5 **Identify obstacles to effective policy implementation.**

1. What is involved in the implementation of policies?
2. What are some of the challenges in implementing policy directives formulated by Washington agencies?

LO6 **Compare the strengths and weaknesses of reform efforts aimed at increasing the effectiveness of the bureaucracy's performance.**

1. What are the potential benefits as well as the negative consequences of deregulation?
2. Why might performance standards be ineffective?

14 The Courts

Suppose someday you would like to serve on the Supreme Court of the United States. How do you realize your ambition? We can break this down to three critical steps: vacancy, nomination, and confirmation.

Step One: there must be a vacancy for you to fill. There are only nine seats on the Court and as the justices have lifetime appointments, they have little incentive to quit (although they can choose to retire at full pay). Justices try to time their departures to give the president of the same party an opportunity to fill the replacement with a sympathetic nominee. Less frequently, justices die in office. Such was the case in February 2016 when Associate Justice Antonin Scalia died in his sleep at a Texas hunting lodge.

Step Two: the president must nominate you. Presidents nominate members of their own party. For example, many a Democratic heart fluttered with the news of Justice Scalia's sudden death because this meant that President Barack Obama would nominate a more moderate replacement for the witty, acerbic, and deeply conservative Scalia. The eight remaining justices were now riven—with four largely conservative justices and four moderate-to-liberal justices—and a new appointment could be a game changer, with pending cases and new cases likely to be decided in a more moderate-to-liberal direction.

With an eye toward Step Three—confirmation—during a term when Republicans controlled the Senate, President Obama sought a "Goldilocks" candidate: not too liberal; not too conservative; but just right—a moderate that even the Republican-dominated Senate would find tough to reject. Obama selected an experienced federal judge, Merrick B. Garland, as his nominee to replace the deceased Scalia. Garland had an enviable résumé: high school valedictorian; Harvard College valedictorian; Harvard Law School; editor of the *Harvard Law Review*; law clerk to renowned federal appellate judge, Henry J. Friendly; law clerk to revered Supreme Court Justice William J. Brennan, Jr.; private law practice; Justice Department prosecutor; federal appellate judge for twenty-one years (appointed by Democratic president Bill Clinton) where he impressed his colleagues and others with his moderation (and these are just the highlights of Garland's amazing career).

Step Three: The Senate must confirm you by a majority vote of the members present. The Senate has the constitutional duty to "advise and consent" to the nomination, and the Republicans held a majority. Given the politics of the moment, would Judge Garland prove "just right"?

This last step remained in limbo because the Senate majority leader, Mitch McConnell (R-KY), decided not to consider Garland's nomination *at all*: no committee hearings, no private meetings, no up-or-down vote on the Senate floor. McConnell claimed that the American people in the 2016 presidential election should decide such a momentous choice—tipping the Supreme Court scale toward more liberal outcomes by electing a Democrat or retaining it in the conservatives' hands by electing a Republican. The Court would be left with an even number of justices and the risk that the Court would be split on many vital decisions. In effect, McConnell broke with long-observed practice to consider a nominee and vote him or her up or down. Instead he chose a decidedly partisan effort to prevent any consideration of President Obama's Goldilocks nominee. But politics in this process is nothing new. Rather than hide politics behind the process, McConnell simply made politics overt.

(By the way, we failed to mention Step Four: luck! Without it, you never even get to Step One.)

#ChallengeAccepted

Take the Challenge on MindTap for American Government
What reasons might explain McConnell's decision?

Learning Outcomes

LO1 Define judicial review, explain the circumstances under which it was established, and assess the significance of the authority it gave the courts.

LO2 Outline the organization of the U.S. court system and identify the principal functions of courts at each tier of the system.

LO3 Describe the process by which cases are both accepted for review and decided by the U.S. Supreme Court and analyze the role played by judicial restraint and judicial activism in judicial decisions.

LO4 Explain how judges at different levels of the federal court system are nominated and confirmed to the federal bench.

LO5 Examine the impact, influence, and acceptance of decisions on issues of national importance by an institution unaccountable to the electorate.

LO6 Evaluate the decision-making authority of the federal judiciary within the context of both majoritarian and pluralist democracy.

The Supreme Court of the United States

IMAGE 14.2 Chief Justice John Marshall

John Marshall (1755–1835) clearly ranks as the Babe Ruth of the Supreme Court. Both Marshall and the Bambino transformed their respective games and became symbols of their institutions. Scholars now recognize both men as originators—Marshall of judicial review and Ruth of the modern age of baseball. (FIAT JUSTITIA is Latin for "Let justice be done.")

judicial review
The power to declare congressional (and presidential) acts invalid because they violate the Constitution.

Marshall's argument vested in the judiciary the power to weigh the validity of congressional acts:

> It is emphatically the province and duty of the judicial department to say what the law is. Those who apply the rule to particular cases, must of necessity expound and interpret that rule. . . . So if a law be in opposition to the constitution; if both the law and the constitution apply to a particular case, so that the court must either decide that case conformably to the law, disregarding the constitution; or conformably to the constitution, disregarding the law; the court must determine which of these conflicting rules governs the case. This is of the very essence of judicial duty.[5]

By invalidating the law that gave Marbury access to the Court for his rightful claim, John Marshall secured the Court's power to strike down acts of Congress and at the same time avoided a confrontation with the Jefferson administration that would leave it ineffectual. Marbury never got his job, but the decision in *Marbury* v. *Madison* firmly established the Supreme Court's power of judicial review—the power to declare congressional acts invalid if they violate the Constitution.** Subsequent cases extended the power to cover presidential acts as well.[6]

Marshall expanded the potential power of the Supreme Court to equal or exceed the power of the other branches of government. Should a congressional act (or, by implication, a presidential act) conflict with the Constitution, the Supreme Court claimed the power to declare the act void. The judiciary would be a check on the legislative and executive branches, consistent with the principle of checks and balances embedded in the Constitution. Although Congress and the president may sometimes wrestle with the constitutionality of their actions, judicial review claimed the final word on the meaning of the Constitution for the courts. The exercise of judicial review—an appointed branch's checking of an elected branch in the name of the Constitution—appears to run counter to democratic theory. But in more than two hundred years of practice, the Supreme Court has invalidated about 180 provisions of national law. Only a small number have had great significance for the political system.[7] The Constitution provides mechanisms to override judicial review (constitutional amendments) and to control excesses of the justices (impeachment), but these steps are more theoretical than practical. In addition, the Court can respond to the continuing struggle among competing interests (a struggle that is consistent with the pluralist model) by reversing itself. It has done so only about 240 times in its entire history.[8]

Although the Constitution did not spell out judicial review of Congress and the president, it did provide such power over state and local government. When such laws conflict with the Constitution or national laws or treaties, the federal courts can invalidate them. That's because the Supremacy Clause obligates state judges to follow the Constitution, national laws, and treaties when state law conflicts with them. Moreover, the Supreme Court ruled that it had final authority to review state court decisions calling for the interpretation of national law.[9] In time, the Supreme Court would use its judicial review power in nearly twelve hundred instances to invalidate state and local laws, on issues as diverse as abortion, the death penalty, the rights of the accused, and gay marriage.[10]

The Exercise of Judicial Review

These early cases, coupled with other historic decisions, established the components of judicial review:

- The power of the courts to declare national, state, and local laws invalid if they violate the Constitution

---

**The Supreme Court had earlier upheld an act of Congress in Hylton v. United States (3 Dallas 171 [1796]). Marbury v. Madison was the first exercise of the power of a court to invalidate an act of Congress.

- The supremacy of national laws or treaties when they conflict with state and local laws
- The role of the Supreme Court as the final authority on the meaning of the Constitution

This political might—the power to undo decisions of the elected branches of the national and state governments—lay in the hands of appointed judges, that is, people who were not accountable to the electorate. Did judicial review square with democratic government?

Alexander Hamilton had foreseen and tackled the problem in *Federalist* No. 78. Writing during the ratification debates surrounding the adoption of the Constitution (see Chapter 3), Hamilton maintained that despite the power of judicial review, the judiciary would be the weakest of the three branches of government because it lacked the strength of the sword or the purse. The judiciary, wrote Hamilton, had "neither FORCE nor WILL, but merely judgment."

Although Hamilton was defending legislative supremacy, he argued that judicial review was an essential barrier to legislative oppression.[11] He recognized that the power to declare government acts void implied the superiority of the courts over the other branches. But this power, he contended, simply reflects the will of the people, declared in the Constitution, as opposed to the will of the legislature, expressed in its statutes. Judicial independence, guaranteed by lifetime tenure and protected salaries, frees judges from executive and legislative control, minimizing the risk of deviation from the law established in the Constitution. If judges make a mistake, the people or their elected representatives have the means to correct the error, through constitutional amendments and impeachment.

Their lifetime tenure does free judges from the direct influence of the president and Congress. And although mechanisms to check judicial power are in place, these mechanisms require extraordinary majorities and remain rarely used. When they exercise the power of judicial review, then, judges can and occasionally do operate counter to majoritarian rule by invalidating the actions of the people's elected representatives.

Courts come under criticism when they uphold or reject the policies of the elected branches as recent high profile rulings on gay marriage, the Affordable Care Act, and the role of money in politics demonstrate. The public and the pundits ask whether the words of the Constitution can be so limited or so expansive—depending on your point of view—to address and answer matters that seem most appropriate for the elected branches. Perhaps the best way to explain such criticism is to understand which ox—liberal or conservative—has been gored.

The Organization of Courts

LO2 Outline the organization of the U.S. court system and identify the principal functions of courts at each tier of the system.

The American court system is complex, partly as a result of our federal system of government. Each state runs its own court system, and no two states' courts are identical. In addition, we have a system of courts for the national government. The national, or federal, courts coexist with the state courts. Individuals and entities fall under the jurisdiction of both court systems. They can sue or be sued in either system, depending mostly on what their case is about. Litigants file nearly all cases (95 percent) in state courts. According to the most recent data, the volume of state court cases has declined from a peak of 106 million cases in 2008—the start of the Great Recession—to about 94 million cases in 2013, dwarfing federal court cases, which amounted to about 411,000 in 2015. Viewed another way, for every case in federal court, state courts handle about 230 cases.[12]

Some Court Fundamentals

Courts are full of mystery to citizens uninitiated in their activities. Lawyers, judges, and seasoned observers understand the language, procedures, and norms associated with legal institutions. Let's start with some fundamentals.

Criminal and Civil Cases. A crime is a violation of a law that forbids or commands an activity. Legislatures create, amend, and repeal criminal laws. Penal codes record these laws and the punishments for violating them. All state penal codes criminalize murder, rape, and arson. A few states decriminalize some activities— marijuana use, for example—that other states still consider criminal. Because crime is a violation of public order, the government prosecutes **criminal cases**. Maintaining public order through the criminal law is largely a state and local function. Criminal cases brought by the national government represent only a small fraction of all criminal cases prosecuted in the United States. In theory, the federalism principle limits the national penal code. The code aims at activities that fall under the delegated and implied powers of the national government, enabling the government, for example, to criminalize tax evasion or the use of computers and laser printers to counterfeit money, bank checks, or even college transcripts.

Fighting crime is popular, and politicians sometimes outbid one another in their efforts to get tough on criminals. National crime-fighting measures have begun to usurp areas long viewed to be under state authority. Since 1975, Congress has added hundreds of new federal criminal provisions covering a wide range of activities once thought to be within the states' domain, including carjacking, willful failure to pay child support, and crossing state lines to engage in gang-related street crime.[13]

Courts decide both criminal and civil cases. **Civil cases** stem from disputed claims to something of value. Disputes arise from accidents, contractual obligations, and divorce, for example. Often the parties disagree over tangible issues (possession of property, custody of children), but civil cases can involve more abstract issues too (the right to equal accommodations, compensation for pain and suffering). The government can be a party to civil disputes, called on to defend its actions or to allege wrongdoing.

Procedures and Policymaking. Most civil and criminal cases never go to trial. In the overwhelming majority of criminal cases, the defendant's lawyer and the prosecutor **plea bargain**, negotiating the severity and number of charges to be brought against the defendant. In a civil case, one side may only be using the threat of a lawsuit to exact a concession from the other. Often the parties settle (or resolve the dispute between themselves) because of the uncertainties in litigation. Though rare, settlement can occur even at the level of the Supreme Court.[14] And sometimes the initiating parties (the plaintiffs in civil cases) may simply abandon their efforts, leaving disputes unresolved.

When cases are neither settled nor abandoned, they end with an *adjudication*, a court judgment resolving the parties' claims and enforced by the government. When trial judges adjudicate cases, they may offer written reasons to support their decisions. When the issues or circumstances of cases are novel, judges may publish *opinions*, explanations justifying their rulings.

Judges make policy in two different ways. The first is through their rulings on matters that no existing legislation addresses. Such rulings set precedents that judges rely on in future, similar cases. We call this body of rules the **common, or judge-made, law**. The roots of the common law lie in the English legal system. Common-law domains include property and torts (injuries or wrongs to the person or property of another). The second area of judicial lawmaking involves the application of statutes enacted by legislatures. The judicial interpretation of legislative acts is called *statutory construction*. The proper application of a statute is not always clear from its wording. To determine how a statute should be applied, judges often look for the legislature's intent, reading reports of committee hearings and debates. If these sources do not clarify the statute's

---

criminal cases
Court cases involving a crime, or violation of public order.

civil cases
Court cases that involve a private dispute arising from such matters as accidents, contractual obligations, and divorce.

plea bargain
A defendant's admission of guilt in exchange for a less severe punishment.

common, or judge-made, law
Legal precedents derived from previous judicial decisions.

meaning, the court does so. With or without legislation to guide them, judges look to the relevant opinions of higher courts for authority to decide the issues before them.

Like the state courts, the federal courts are organized in three tiers, as a pyramid. At the bottom of the pyramid are the **U.S. district courts**, where litigation begins. In the middle are the **U.S. courts of appeals**. At the top is the Supreme Court of the United States. To *appeal* means to take a case to a higher court. The courts of appeals and the Supreme Court are appellate courts; with few exceptions, they review only cases that have already been decided in lower courts. Most federal courts hear and decide a wide array of civil and criminal cases.

The U.S. District Courts

There are ninety-four federal district courts in the United States. Each state has at least one district court, and no district straddles more than one state.[15] In 2015, there were 667 full-time federal district judgeships, and they received over 359,000 new criminal and civil cases.[16]

The district courts are the entry point for the federal court system. When trials occur in the federal system, they take place in the federal district courts. Here is where witnesses testify, lawyers conduct cross-examinations, and judges and juries decide the fate of litigants. More than one judge may sit in each district court, but each case is tried by a single judge, sitting alone. U.S. magistrate judges assist district judges, but they lack independent judicial authority. Magistrate judges have the power to hear and decide minor offenses and conduct preliminary stages of more serious cases. District court judges appoint magistrate judges for eight-year (full-time) or four-year (part-time) terms. As of 2014, there were 534 full-time and 39 part-time and other magistrate judge positions.[17]

Sources of Litigation. Today the authority of U.S. district courts extends to the following:

- Federal criminal cases, as defined by national law (for example, robbery of a nationally insured bank or interstate transportation of stolen securities)
- Civil cases, brought by individuals, groups, or the government, alleging violation of national law (for example, failure of a municipality to implement pollution-control regulations required by a national agency)
- Civil cases brought against the national government (for example, a vehicle manufacturer sues the motor pool of a government agency for its failure to take delivery of a fleet of new cars)
- Civil cases between citizens of different states when the amount in controversy exceeds $75,000 (for example, when a citizen of New York sues a citizen of Alabama in a U.S. district court in Alabama for damages stemming from an auto accident that occurred in Alabama)

The U.S. Courts of Appeals

All cases resolved in a U.S. district court and all decisions of federal administrative agencies can be appealed to one of the twelve regional U.S. courts of appeals. These courts, with 179 full-time judgeships, received nearly 53,000 new cases in 2015.[18] Each appeals court hears cases from a geographical area known as a *circuit*. The U.S. Court of Appeals for the Seventh Circuit, for example, is located in Chicago; it hears appeals from the U.S. district courts in Illinois, Wisconsin, and Indiana. The United States is divided into twelve circuits.*

Appellate Court Proceedings. Appellate court proceedings are public, but they usually lack courtroom drama. There are no jurors, witnesses, or cross-examinations; these

U.S. district courts
Courts within the lowest tier of the three-tiered federal court system; courts where litigation begins.

U.S. courts of appeals
Courts within the second tier of the three-tiered federal court system, to which decisions of the district courts and federal agencies may be appealed for review.

---

*The thirteenth court, the U.S. Court of Appeals for the Federal Circuit, is not a regional court. It specializes in appeals involving patents, contract claims against the national government, and federal employment cases.

are features only of the trial courts. Appeals are based strictly on the rulings made and procedures followed in the trial courts. Suppose, for example, that in the course of a criminal trial, a U.S. district judge allows the introduction of evidence that convicts a defendant but was obtained under questionable circumstances. The defendant can appeal claiming that the evidence was obtained in the absence of a valid search warrant and so was inadmissible. The issue on appeal is the admissibility of the evidence, not the defendant's guilt or innocence. If the appellate court agrees with the trial judge's decision to admit the evidence, the conviction stands. If the appellate court disagrees with the trial judge and rules that the evidence is inadmissible, the defendant must be retried without the incriminating evidence or be released.

The courts of appeals are regional courts. They usually convene in panels of three judges to render judgments. The judges receive written arguments known as *briefs* (which are also sometimes submitted in trial courts). Often the judges hold oral hearings to question the lawyers to probe their arguments.

Precedents and Making Decisions. Following review of the briefs and, in many appeals, oral arguments, the three-judge panel meets to reach a judgment. One judge attempts to summarize the panel's views, although each judge remains free to disagree with the judgment or the reasons for it. When an appellate opinion is published, its influence can reach well beyond the immediate case. For example, a lawsuit turning on the meaning of the Constitution produces a ruling, which then serves as a **precedent** for subsequent cases; that is, the decision becomes a basis for deciding similar cases in the future in the same way. Thus, judges make public policy to the extent that they influence decisions in other courts. Although district judges sometimes publish their opinions, it is the exception rather than the rule. At the appellate level, however, precedent requires that opinions be written.

Making decisions according to precedent is central to the operation of our legal system, providing continuity and predictability. The bias in favor of existing decisions is captured by the Latin expression *stare decisis*, which means "let the decision stand." But the use of precedent and the principle of **stare decisis** do not make lower-court judges cogs in a judicial machine. "If precedent clearly governed," remarked one federal judge, "a case would never get as far as the Court of Appeals: the parties would settle."[19]

Judges on the courts of appeals direct their energies to correcting errors in district court proceedings and interpreting the law (in the course of writing opinions). When judges interpret the law, they often modify existing laws. In effect, they are making policy. Judges are politicians in the sense that they exercise political power, but the black robes that distinguish judges from other politicians signal constraints on their exercise of power.

precedent
A judicial ruling that serves as the basis for the ruling in a subsequent case.

stare decisis
Literally, "let the decision stand"; decision making according to precedent.

★ **The Supreme Court**

LO3 Describe the process by which cases are both accepted for review and decided by the U.S. Supreme Court and analyze the role played by judicial restraint and judicial activism in judicial decisions.

Above the west portico of the Supreme Court building are inscribed the words EQUAL JUSTICE UNDER LAW. At the opposite end of the building, above the east portico, are the words JUSTICE THE GUARDIAN OF LIBERTY. The mottos reflect the Court's difficult task: achieving a just balance among the values of freedom, order, and equality. Consider how these values came into conflict in two controversial issues the Court has faced.

Flag burning as a form of political protest pits the value of order, or the government's interest in maintaining a peaceful society, against the value of freedom, including the individual's right to vigorous and unbounded political expression. In two flag-burning cases, the Supreme Court affirmed constitutional protection for unbridled political expression, including the emotionally charged act of desecrating a national symbol.[20] Because under a pluralist system no decision is ever truly final, the flag-burning decisions hardly quelled the demand for laws to punish flag desecration.

In 2006, Congress inched ever so close to a constitutional amendment banning flag desecration. The proposal passed by more than a two-thirds vote in the House but failed by a single vote in the Senate.

School desegregation pits the value of equality against the value of freedom. In *Brown* v. *Board of Education* (1954), the Supreme Court carried the banner of racial equality by striking down state-mandated segregation in public schools. The decision helped launch a revolution in race relations in the United States. The justices recognized the disorder their decision would create in a society accustomed to racial bias, but in this case, equality clearly outweighed freedom. Twenty-four years later, the Court was still embroiled in controversy over equality when it ruled that race could be a factor in university admissions (to diversify the student body).[21] Having secured equality for blacks, the Court in 2003 faced the charge by white students who sought admission to the University of Michigan that it was denying whites the freedom to compete for admission. A slim Court majority concluded that the equal protection clause of the Fourteenth Amendment did not prohibit the narrowly tailored use of race as a factor in law school admissions but rejected the automatic use of racial categories to award fixed points toward undergraduate admissions.[22] Michigan voters responded by adopting a state constitutional amendment in 2006 banning the use of race or sex considerations in public education. Affirmative action advocates sued the state, arguing that the state amendment violated the Equal Protection Clause of the U.S. Constitution. In 2014, the Roberts Court upheld the amendment by a vote of 6 to 2, declaring that courts possess no authority to set aside state laws that commit such policy determinations to the voters.[23] (See Chapter 16.)

The Supreme Court makes national policy. Because its decisions have far-reaching effects on all of us, it is vital that we understand how it reaches those decisions. With this understanding, we can better evaluate how the Court fits within our model of democracy.

original jurisdiction
The authority of a court to hear a case before any other court does.

Access to the Court

All litigants must follow rules of access to bring a case to the Supreme Court. To succeed, lawyers must be sensitive to the justices' policy and ideological preferences. The notion that anyone can take a case all the way to the Supreme Court is true only in theory, not fact.

The Supreme Court's cases come from two sources. A few arrive under the Court's original jurisdiction, conferred by Article III, Section 2, of the Constitution, which gives the Court the power to hear and decide "all Cases affecting Ambassadors, other public Ministers and Consuls, and those in which a State shall be Party." Cases falling under the Court's original jurisdiction are tried and decided in the Court itself; the cases begin

The Supreme Court of the United States

IMAGE 14.3   The Supreme Court, 2016 Term: The Lineup

The justices of the Supreme Court of the United States. Seated are (left to right) Clarence Thomas, Antonin Scalia (now deceased), Chief Justice John G. Roberts, Jr., Anthony Kennedy, and Ruth Bader Ginsburg. Standing are Sonia Sotomayor, Stephen J. Breyer, Samuel A. Alito, and Elena Kagan.

and end there. For example, the Court is the first and only forum in which legal disputes between states are resolved. It hears few original jurisdiction cases today, however, usually referring them to a special master, often a retired judge, who reviews the parties' contentions and recommends a resolution that the justices are free to accept or reject.

Most cases enter the Supreme Court from the U.S. courts of appeals or the state courts of last resort. This is the Court's **appellate jurisdiction**. These cases have been tried, decided, and reexamined as far as the law permits in other federal or state courts. The Court exercises judicial power under its appellate jurisdiction only because Congress gives it the authority to do so. Congress may change (and, perhaps, eliminate) the Court's appellate jurisdiction. This is a powerful but rarely used weapon in the congressional arsenal of checks and balances.

Litigants in state cases who invoke the Court's appellate jurisdiction must satisfy two conditions. First, the case must have reached the end of the line in the state court system. Litigants cannot jump at will from a state to a federal court. Second, the case must raise a **federal question**, that is, an issue covered by the Constitution, federal laws, or national treaties. But even cases that meet both of these conditions do not guarantee review by the Court.

Since 1925, the Court has exercised substantial (today, nearly complete) control over its **docket**, or agenda (see Figure 14.1). The Court selects a handful of cases (about eighty) for full consideration from the nine thousand requests filed each year. These requests take the form of a *petition for certiorari*, in which a litigant seeking review asks the Court "to become informed" of the lower-court proceeding. For the vast majority of cases, the Court denies the petition for certiorari, leaving the decision of the lower court undisturbed. No explanations accompany these denials, so they have little or no value as Court rulings.

With advance preparation by their law clerks, who screen petitions and prepare summaries, all nine justices make these judgments at secret weekly conferences.[24]

appellate jurisdiction
The authority of a court to hear cases that have been tried, decided, or reexamined in other courts.

federal question
An issue covered by the U.S. Constitution, national laws, or U.S. treaties.

docket
A court's agenda.

FIGURE 14.1 Access to and Decision Making in the U.S. Supreme Court

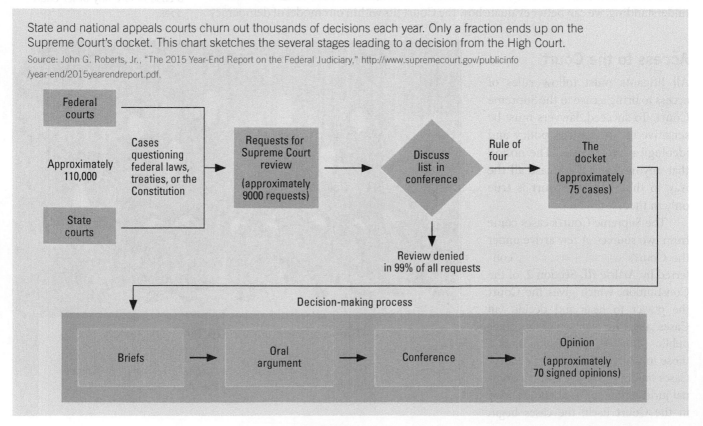

State and national appeals courts churn out thousands of decisions each year. Only a fraction ends up on the Supreme Court's docket. This chart sketches the several stages leading to a decision from the High Court.

Source: John G. Roberts, Jr., "The 2015 Year-End Report on the Federal Judiciary," http://www.supremecourt.gov/publicinfo/year-end/2015yearendreport.pdf.

During the conferences, justices vote on previously argued cases and consider which new cases to add to the docket. The chief justice circulates a "discuss list" of worthy petitions. Cases on the list are then subject to the rule of four, a practice by custom that permits four of the nine justices to grant review of a case. Though it takes only four votes to place a case on the docket, it may ultimately take an enormous leap to garner a fifth, and deciding, vote on the merits of the appeal. This is especially true if the Court is sharply split ideologically. Thus, a minority of justices in favor of an appeal may oppose review if they are not confident the outcome will be to their satisfaction.[25]

It is important to note that business cases represent a substantial portion of the Court's docket, though they receive far less attention than cases addressing social issues such as same-sex marriage, affirmative action, and school prayer. Business disputes are less emotional and the issues more technical. But business cases involve billions of dollars, have enormous consequences for the economy, and affect people's lives more often than the social issues that tend to dominate public debate and discussion. Today's Court has been far friendlier to business since at least World War II.[26]

The Solicitor General

Why does the Court decide to hear certain cases but not others? The best evidence scholars have adduced suggests that agenda setting depends on the individual justices, who vary in their decision-making criteria, and on the issues raised by the cases. Occasionally justices weigh the ultimate outcome of a case when granting or denying review. At other times, they grant or deny review based on disagreement among the lower courts or because delay in resolving the issues would impose alarming economic or social costs.[27] The solicitor general plays a vital role in the Court's agenda setting.

The solicitor general represents the national government before the Supreme Court, serving as the hinge between an administration's legal approach and its policy objectives. Appointed by the president, the solicitor general is the third-ranking official in the U.S. Department of Justice (after the attorney general and the deputy attorney general). Donald B. Verrilli, Jr., served as solicitor general from 2011 to 2016. He succeeded Elena Kagan, the first woman to hold the office. President Obama tapped Kagan to replace Supreme Court Justice John Paul Stevens, who retired in June 2010. Ian Gershengorn assumed the role of acting solicitor general through the end of the Obama administration.

The solicitor general's duties include determining whether the government should appeal lower-court decisions; reviewing and modifying, when necessary, the briefs filed in government appeals; and deciding whether the government should file an amicus curiae brief* in any appellate court.[28] The objective is to create a cohesive program for the executive branch in the federal courts.

Solicitors general play two different, and occasionally conflicting, roles. First, they are advocates for the president's policy preferences; second, as officers of the Court, they traditionally defend the institutional interests of the national government.

Solicitors general usually act with considerable restraint in recommending to the Court that a case be granted or denied review. By recommending only cases of general importance, they increase their credibility and their influence.

By carefully selecting the cases it presses, the solicitor general's office usually maintains a very impressive record of wins in the Supreme Court. Solicitors general are a "formidable force" in the process of setting the Supreme Court's agenda.[29] Their influence in bringing cases to the Court and arguing them there has earned them the informal title of "the tenth justice."

the rule of four
An unwritten rule that requires at least four justices to agree that a case warrants consideration before it is reviewed by the U.S. Supreme Court.

solicitor general
The third highest official of the U.S. Department of Justice, and the one who represents the national government before the Supreme Court.

amicus curiae brief
A brief filed (with the permission of the court) by an individual or group that is not a party to a legal action but has an interest in it.

---

*Amicus curiae is Latin for "friend of the court." Amicus briefs can be filed with the consent of all the parties or with the permission of the court. They allow groups and individuals who are not parties to the litigation but have an interest in it to influence the court's thinking and, perhaps, its decision.

Decision Making

Once the Court grants review, attorneys submit written arguments (briefs). The justices follow an unwritten rule to avoid discussing cases with one another before oral argument. Should the rule be violated, the justices will inform their colleagues in an effort to avoid "little cliques or cabals or little groups that lobby each other before [argument]."[30] Oral argument, typically limited to thirty minutes for each side, is the first time the justices know what their colleagues might be thinking. From October through April, the justices spend two to three hours a day, five or six days a month, hearing arguments. Experience seems to help. Like the solicitor general, seasoned advocates enjoy a greater success rate, regardless of the party they represent.[31] The justices like crisp, concise, conversational presentations; they disapprove of attorneys who read from a prepared text. Some justices are aggressive, relentless questioners who frequently interrupt the lawyers; others are more subdued.

The Court continues to resist video in the courtroom but now releases oral argument transcripts on its website on the day of argument, and it releases argument audio on its website at the end of the week. In 2012, the Court scheduled a whopping 6.5 hours of argument in three cases challenging the constitutionality of the Affordable Care Act (also known as Obamacare) and took the extra step of sharing the audio with the public on each day rather than waiting until the end of the week. But the Court continues to ban tweets and blog posts from the courtroom itself, where computers, mobile phones, and tablets remain off-limits.

Court protocol prohibits the justices from addressing one another directly during oral arguments, but they often debate obliquely through the questions they pose to the attorneys. The justices reach no collective decision at the time of oral arguments. They reach a tentative decision only after they have met in conference.

Our knowledge of the dynamics of decision making on the Supreme Court is all secondhand. Only the justices attend the Court's weekly conferences. By tradition, the justices first shake hands prior to conference and to going on the bench, a gesture of harmony. The handshaking was introduced by Melville Fuller when he was chief justice from 1888 to 1910.[32] The chief justice then begins the presentation of each case with a discussion of it and his vote, which is followed by a discussion and vote from each of the other justices, in order of their seniority on the Court. Justice Antonin Scalia, who joined the Court in 1986, remarked that "not much conferencing goes on." By *conferencing*, Scalia meant efforts to persuade others to change their views by debating points of disagreement. "To call our discussion of a case a conference," he said, "is really something of a misnomer. It's much more a statement of the views of each of the nine Justices, after which the totals are added and the case is assigned" for an opinion.[33]

IMAGE 14.4 The Supreme Court and Information Technology

This cartoon pokes fun at the justices' aversion to technology. Cameras and other electronic devices are banned from the courtroom and the justices firmly resist video of their public sessions. As a concession, the justices release oral argument audio at the end of their weekly sessions. In his 2014 report, Chief Justice John G. Roberts, Jr., announced that the Court will offer all documents from its website as early as 2016—though that step has yet to occur—prompting this cartoon by Ann Telnaes.

Judicial Restraint and Judicial Activism

How do the justices decide to vote on a case? According to some scholars, legal doctrines and previous decisions explain their votes. This explanation, which is consistent with the majoritarian model, anchors the justices closely to the law and minimizes the contribution of their personal values. This view is embodied in the concept of **judicial restraint**, which maintains that the people's elected representatives, not judges, should make the laws. Judges are said to exercise judicial restraint when they defer to decisions of other governmental actors. Other scholars contend that the value preferences and resulting ideologies of the justices provide a more powerful interpretation of their voting.[34] This view is embodied in the concept of **judicial activism**, which maintains that judges should not give deference to the elected branches but should use their judicial power to promote the judges' preferred social and political goals. The concept of judicial activism and its cognate, judicial restraint, has many strands, and scholars sometimes disagree on its many meanings.[35] But at its core, all would agree that judges are activists when their decisions run counter to the will of the other branches of government, in effect substituting their own judgment for the judgment of the people's representatives. By interjecting personal values into court decisions, activist judging is more consistent with the pluralist model.

The terms *judicial restraint* and *judicial activism* describe different relative degrees of judicial assertiveness. Judges acting according to an extreme model of judicial restraint would never question the validity of duly enacted laws but would defer to the superiority of other government institutions in construing the laws. Judges acting according to an extreme model of judicial activism would be an intrusive and ever-present force that would dominate other government institutions. Actual judicial behavior lies somewhere between these two extremes.

How activist is the Supreme Court today? The Court led by Chief Justice John G. Roberts, Jr., has struck down parts of a federal law regulating campaign spending, and parts of the Voting Rights Act and the Defense of Marriage Act. But a look at the overall record across many Courts produces a more nuanced view (see "Freedom, Order, or Equality: Judicial Activism or Judicial Restraint?").

Judgment and Argument. The voting outcome is the **judgment**, the decision on who wins and who loses. The justices often disagree not only on the winner and loser, but also on the reasons for their judgment. This should not be surprising, given nine independent minds and issues that can be approached in several ways. Voting in the conference does not end the justices' work or resolve their disagreements. Votes remain tentative until the Court issues an opinion announcing its judgment.

After voting, the justices in the majority must draft an opinion setting out the reasons for their decision. The **argument** is the kernel of the opinion—its logical content, as distinct from supporting facts, rhetoric, and procedures. If all justices agree with the judgment and the reasons supporting it, the opinion is unanimous. Agreement with a judgment for different reasons from those set forth in the majority opinion is called a **concurrence**. Or a justice can **dissent** if she or he disagrees with a judgment. Both concurring and dissenting opinions may be drafted, in addition to the majority opinion.

The Opinion. After the conference, the chief justice or most senior justice in the majority (in terms of years of service on the Court) decides which justice will write the majority opinion. He or she may consider several factors in assigning the crucial opinion-writing task, including the prospective author's workload, expertise, public opinion, and (above all) ability to hold the majority together. (Remember that the votes are only tentative at this point.) On the one hand, if the drafting justice holds an extreme view on the issues in a case and is not able to incorporate the views of more

judicial restraint
A judicial philosophy by which judges tend to defer to decisions of the elected branches of government.

judicial activism
A judicial philosophy by which judges tend not to defer to decisions of the elected branches of government, resulting in the invalidation or emasculation of those decisions.

judgment
The judicial decision in a court case.

argument
The heart of a judicial opinion; its logical content separated from facts, rhetoric, and procedure.

concurrence
The agreement of a judge with the Supreme Court's majority decision, for a reason other than the majority reason.

dissent
The disagreement of a judge with a majority decision.

Freedom, Order, or Equality: Judicial Activism or Judicial Restraint?

Conservatives like to link judicial activism to liberalism. But that bond is hardly fixed; conservative judges can be activists too. One well-known example tends to upend that association. In *Bush* v. *Gore,* the Supreme Court resolved the contentious 2000 presidential election, which was essentially tied, handing victory to the Republicans. This suggested to many critics that conservative jurists can also be judicial activists, promoting their preferred political goals. Had a majority deferred to the Florida courts on the issue of a recount, the decision would have been hailed as an example of judicial restraint. But overturning the Florida courts and delivering a victory for the Republicans labeled the majority in *Bush* v. *Gore* as conservative judicial activists.

In an effort at greater precision, scholars have used the overturning of legislation as a yardstick for judicial activism; the results are somewhat surprising. Looking solely at the direction of the invalidations in Figure A, the Warren Court is most active and the Roberts Court the most restrained. However, a more refined examination of the evidence looks at individual justice votes in Figure B. The evidence below makes the case. Conservative laws tend to be invalidated by liberal justices, and liberal laws tend to be invalidated by conservative justices. Today, the conservative bent of the Roberts Court makes it a friendly forum to challenge liberal laws. So expect more cases to give today's conservatives a chance to "swing for the fences."

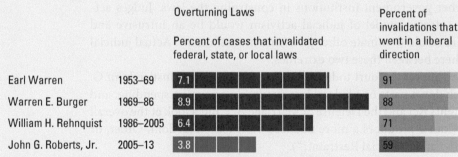

		Overturning Laws Percent of cases that invalidated federal, state, or local laws	Percent of invalidations that went in a liberal direction
Earl Warren	1953–69	7.1	91
Warren E. Burger	1969–86	8.9	88
William H. Rehnquist	1986–2005	6.4	71
John G. Roberts, Jr.	2005–13	3.8	59

Source: Figure A, Adam Liptak, "How Activist Is the Supreme Court?" *New York Times,* 13 October 2013, p. SR4.

moderate colleagues, those justices may withdraw their votes. On the other hand, assigning a more moderate justice to draft an opinion could weaken the argument on which the opinion rests. Opinion-writing assignments can also be punitive. Justice Harry Blackmun once commented, "If one's in the doghouse with the Chief [former Chief Justice Warren Burger], he gets the crud."[36]

Opinion writing is the justices' most critical function. It is not surprising, then, that they spend much of their time drafting opinions. The justices usually call on their law clerks—top graduates of the nation's elite law schools—to help them prepare opinions and carry out other tasks. The commitment can be daunting. All of the justices now rely on their clerks to shoulder substantial responsibilities, including the initial drafts of opinions.[37]

The writing justice distributes a draft opinion to all the justices, who then read it and circulate their criticisms and suggestions. An opinion may have to be rewritten several times to accommodate colleagues who remain unpersuaded by the draft. Justice Felix Frankfurter was a perfectionist; some of his opinions went through thirty or more drafts. Justices can change their votes, and perhaps alter the judgment, until the decision is officially announced. Often, the most controversial cases pile up as coalitions on the

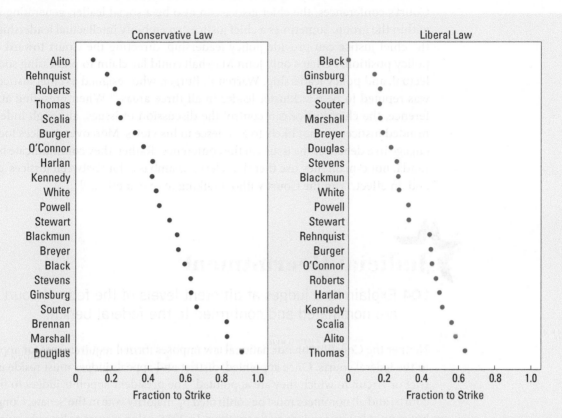

Conservative Law

Liberal Law

Fraction to Strike

Fraction to Strike

Source: Figure B, Lee Epstein and Andrew D. Martin, "Is the Roberts Court Especially Activist?" *Emory Law Journal* 61 (2012): 742.

CRITICAL THINKING Conservative justices tend to vote against liberal policies and liberals tend to vote against conservative policies. But justices are supposed to be above politics. Offer an argument that justifies this apparent contradiction. (*Hint:* What practices come into play when nominating and confirming candidates for the High Court?)

Court vie for support or sharpen their criticisms. When the Court announces a decision, the justices who wrote the opinion read or summarize their views in the courtroom.

Justices in the majority frequently try to muffle or stifle dissent to encourage institutional cohesion. Since the mid-1940s, however, unity has been more difficult to obtain.[38] Gaining agreement from the justices today is akin to negotiating with nine separate law firms. It may be more surprising that the justices ever agree. In 2006, for example, the Court spoke without dissent in more than half of its cases. The conservative shift occasioned by the appointments of Roberts and Alito has infused cohesion among dissenters, who have tended to join a single opinion. And the Court's genteel etiquette appears strained as once collegial justices voice their views publicly and forcefully from the bench.[39]

The justices remain aware of the slender foundation of their authority, which rests largely on public respect. That respect is tested whenever the Court ventures into controversial areas. Banking, slavery, and Reconstruction policies embroiled the Court in the nineteenth century. Freedom of speech and religion, racial equality, the right to privacy, the 2000 election, and gay marriage have led the Court into controversy in the past sixty years.

The Chief Justice

The chief justice is only one of nine justices, but he has several important functions based on his authority. Apart from his role in forming the docket and directing the Court's conferences, the chief justice can also be a social leader, generating solidarity within the group. Sometimes a chief justice can embody intellectual leadership. Finally, the chief justice can provide policy leadership, directing the Court toward a general policy position. Perhaps only John Marshall could lay claim to possessing social, intellectual, and policy leadership. Warren E. Burger, who resigned as chief justice in 1986, was reputed to be a lackluster leader in all three areas.[40] When presiding at the conference, the chief justice can control the discussion of issues, although independent-minded justices are not likely to acquiesce to his views. Moreover, justices today rarely engage in a debate of the issues in the conference. Rather, they communicate by memoranda, not e-mail; they use their law clerks as ambassadors between justices' chambers and, in effect, "run the Court without talking to one another."[41]

Judicial Recruitment

LO4 Explain how judges at different levels of the federal court system are nominated and confirmed to the federal bench.

Neither the Constitution nor national law imposes formal requirements for appointment to the federal courts. Once appointed, district and appeals judges must reside in the district or circuit to which they are appointed. The president appoints judges to the federal courts, and all nominees must be confirmed by majority vote in the Senate. Congress sets, but cannot lower, a judge's compensation. In 2016, salaries were as listed below.

Chief justice of the Supreme Court	$260,700
Associate Supreme Court justices	249,300
Courts of appeals judges	215,400
District judges	203,100
Magistrate judges	185,012

By comparison, in 2015, the average salary of a state supreme court judge was about $166,000. The average for a state trial judge was about $149,000.[42] Although annual compensation for equity partners in major law firms can exceed $10 million, employment prospects for new lawyers remain dim. Jobs have stabilized after a sharp decline with average salaries now around $55,000, though top law firms in big cities offer $180,000 or more for new associates.[43] Supreme Court law clerks entering private practice will earn more than the justices who hired them with signing bonuses upwards of $300,000. This prompted Supreme Court Justice Antonin Scalia to urge bright students to choose other professions, such as engineering and teaching. "Society cannot afford to have such a huge proportion of its best minds going into the law," said Scalia.[44]

In more than half the states, the governor appoints the state judges, often in consultation with judicial nominating commissions. In many of these states, voters decide whether the judges should be retained in office. Other states select their judges by partisan, nonpartisan, or (rarely) legislative election.[45] In some states, nominees must be confirmed by the state legislature. Contested elections for judgeships are on the rise, and at the extreme, such contests may call a judge's impartiality into question. In 2009, the U.S. Supreme Court ruled that the newly elected chief justice of the West Virginia

Supreme Court, Brent Benjamin, had to disqualify himself from deliberations in a case involving a coal company chief executive who had spent $3 million to elect Benjamin.[46] Most other countries appoint their judges, making the United States an outlier nation (see "Judicial Selection in Global Politics").

The Appointment of Federal Judges

One of the great prizes of any presidency is the ability to appoint federal judges. These are lifetime appointments, enabling presidents to extend their legacies well beyond their terms of office. As of July 2016, President Obama had appointed a total of 329 federal judges; fifty-four nominations await Senate action including Judge Merrick Garland to replace Supreme Court Justice Antonin Scalia. An additional sixteen announced vacancies will occur before the end of Obama's presidency.*[47]

Judicial vacancies occur when sitting judges resign, retire, or die. Vacancies also arise when Congress creates new judgeships to handle increasing caseloads. In both cases, the president nominates a candidate, who must be confirmed by the Senate. Under President Obama, the Office of White House Counsel is deeply involved in this screening process. The president also had the help of the Justice Department, primarily through its Office of Legal Policy, which screens candidates before the formal nomination, subjecting serious contenders to FBI investigation. The White House and the Justice Department formed a Judicial Selection Committee as part of this vetting process. The White House and the Senate vie for control in the approval of district and appeals court judges.

The "Advice and Consent" of the Senate. For district and appeals court vacancies, the nomination "must be acceptable to the home state senator from the president's party"[48] (or to the state's House delegation from the president's party if no senator is from the president's party). The Judicial Selection Committee consults extensively with home state senators from which the appointment will be made.[49] Senators' influence is greater for appointments to district court than for appointments to the court of appeals.

This practice, called **senatorial courtesy**, forces presidents to share the nomination power with members of the Senate. The Senate will not confirm a nominee who is opposed by the senior senator from the nominee's state if that senator is a member of the president's party. The Senate does not actually reject the candidate. Instead, the senator of either party whose state is the source of the nomination fails to return a **blue slip** to the Senate Judiciary Committee. In this case, the chairman of the committee, which reviews all judicial nominees, will not schedule a confirmation hearing, effectively killing the nomination.[50]

> **senatorial courtesy**
> A norm under which a nomination must be acceptable to the home state senator from the president's party.
>
> **blue slip**
> The failure of a senator to return a blue slip signals the end of the road for a judicial nomination.

Although the Justice Department is still sensitive to senatorial prerogatives, senators can no longer submit a single name to fill a vacancy. The department searches for acceptable candidates and polls the appropriate senator for her or his reaction to them. President George H. W. Bush asked Republican senators to seek more qualified female and minority candidates. Bush made progress in developing a more diverse bench, and President Clinton accelerated the change.[51] President George W. Bush improved the Republican track record in appointing women and minorities but still lagged behind Clinton. President Obama now ranks at the top in appointing more women during his tenure compared to his predecessors.[52]

The Senate Judiciary Committee conducts a hearing for judicial nominees. The committee chair exercises a measure of control in the appointment process that goes beyond senatorial courtesy. If a nominee is objectionable to the chair, he or she can delay a hearing or hold up other appointments until the president and the Justice Department find an alternative. Such behavior does not win a politician much influence in the long

---

*As of 2016, fifteen federal judges have been impeached. Of these, eight were convicted in the Senate and removed from office. The most recent to be forced to leave office was Judge G. Thomas Porteous, Jr., who was impeached by the House and convicted by the Senate in 2010.

Judicial Selection in Global Politics

The United States is an outlier nation, at least when it comes to the way we select judges. In at least half of the U.S. states, judges run for election. In fact, nearly 90 percent of all state judges face the voters. This practice is in stark contrast to the rest of the world, where governments appoint their judges, either by the executive branch (with or without recommendations from a judicial selection commission), by the judicial selection commission itself, or by the legislative branch. In a few countries, the civil service offers a professional career path leading to a judgeship. In these countries, the route to a judgeship rests on examinations and school programs. In only two nations—Switzerland and Japan—judicial elections hold sway, but only in a very limited way: (1) Some smaller Swiss cantons (subnational units) elect judges, and (2) appointed justices of the Japanese Supreme Court may face retention elections, though scholars regard the practice as a mere formality. Hans A. Linde, a retired justice of the Oregon Supreme Court, captured the essence of the American exception when he observed: "To the rest of the world, American adherence to judicial elections is as incomprehensible as our rejection of the metric system."

The table here shows the judicial selection process used in countries around the world. Some countries use more than one method; the table lists the primary one.

Executive Appointment Without Commission	Executive Appointment with Commission	Appointment by Commission	Legislative Appointment	Career Judiciary
Afghanistan	Albania	Algeria	China	Czech Republic
Argentina	Canada	Andorra	Cuba	France
Australia	Dominican Republic	Angola	Laos	Germany
Bangladesh	England	Bulgaria	Macedonia	Italy
Belarus	Greece	Croatia	Montenegro	Japan
Belgium	Namibia	Cyprus	Poland	
Cambodia	Russia	Israel	Portugal	
Chad	Scotland	Lebanon	Spain	
Egypt	South Africa	Mexico	Turkey	
New Zealand	Ukraine	Rwanda		
Uzbekistan	Zimbabwe	Yemen		

Source: Based on Adam Liptak, "American Exception: Rendering Justice, with One Eye on Re-election," *New York Times*, 25 May 2008, http://www.nytimes.com/2008/05/25/us/25exception.html? pagewanted=1&_r=1.

CRITICAL THINKING What changes, if any, would you implement to the way in which the United States appoints federal judges? Be sure to justify any change as an improvement over the status quo or explain why the status quo is better than the alternatives.

run, however. So committee chairs of the president's party are usually loath to place obstacles in a president's path, especially when they may want presidential support for their own policies and constituencies.

Beginning with the Carter administration, judicial appointments below the Supreme Court have proved a new battleground, with a growing proportion of nominees not confirmed and increasing delays in the process. These appointments were once viewed as presidential and party patronage, but that old-fashioned view has given way to a focus on the president's policy agenda through judicial appointments. This perspective has enlarged the ground on which senators have opposed judicial nominees to include matters of judicial policy (for example, abortion) and theory (for example, delving into a nominee's approach when interpreting the meaning of a statute). Beginning in 2003, Democratic senators used the filibuster to prevent confirmation votes for judicial candidates they deemed "outside the mainstream." This behavior provoked ire from the majority Republicans, who threatened to end the filibuster practice entirely. The parties reached an uneasy compromise in 2005 to invoke a judicial filibuster only for "extraordinary circumstances," but that compromise dissolved in 2011 when the Republicans began employing the judicial filibuster to scuttle Obama nominees. But the turnabout-is-fair-play game ran out of steam in late 2013 when Senate Democrats changed the rules—the so-called nuclear option—to require a simple majority (rather than sixty votes) to end debate for all but Supreme Court nominations. Now for the first time in several years, judges appointed by Democrats outnumber judges appointed by Republicans.[53]

The American Bar Association. The American Bar Association (ABA), the biggest organization of lawyers in the United States, has been involved in screening candidates for the federal bench since 1946.[54] Its role is defined by custom, not law. At the president's behest, the ABA's Standing Committee on the Federal Judiciary routinely rates prospective appointees using a three-value scale: "well qualified," "qualified," and "not qualified." The association no longer has advance notice of possible nominees. The George W. Bush administration considered the ABA too liberal, posing an unnecessary impediment to the confirmation of conservative judges.[55] Nonetheless, the association continued to evaluate the professional qualifications of nominees after they were nominated. President Obama restored the ABA's prenomination review in 2009.[56]

Recent Presidents and the Federal Judiciary

Since the presidency of Jimmy Carter, chief executives have tended—more or less—to make appointments to the federal courts that are more diverse in racial, ethnic, and gender terms than in previous administrations. President Bill Clinton took the lead on diversity, substantially increasing appointments for women or minorities. Clinton pledged to make his appointees "look like America." President Obama has extended that pledge across diverse constituencies (see Figure 14.2).

The racial and ethnic composition of the parties themselves helps explain much of the variation between the appointments of presidents of different parties. It seems clear that political ideology, not demographics, lies at the heart of judicial appointments. Presidents are likely to appoint judges who share similar values.[57]

Appointment to the Supreme Court

The announcement of a vacancy on the High Court usually causes quite a stir. Campaigns for Supreme Court seats are commonplace, although the public rarely sees them. Hopefuls contact friends in the administration and urge influential associates to do the same on their behalf. Some candidates never give up hope. Judge John J. Parker, whose nomination to the Court was defeated in 1930, tried in vain to rekindle interest in his appointment until he was well past the age—usually the early sixties—that appointments are made.[58]

FIGURE 14.2   **The Changing Composition of Federal Judicial Appointments**

As of July 2016, President Obama has appointed 329 federal judges. Their racial, ethnic, and gender makeup stands in contrast to previous presidents with more women, Hispanics, African American, Asian, and openly gay judges than any of his predecessors. Obama's picks come closer to the ethnic and gender composition of the population.

Source: Eliot Slotnick, Sara Schiavoni, and Sheldon Goldman. "Writing the Book of Judges: Part 2," *Journal of Law and Courts* 4, no. 1, (Spring 2016): 227.

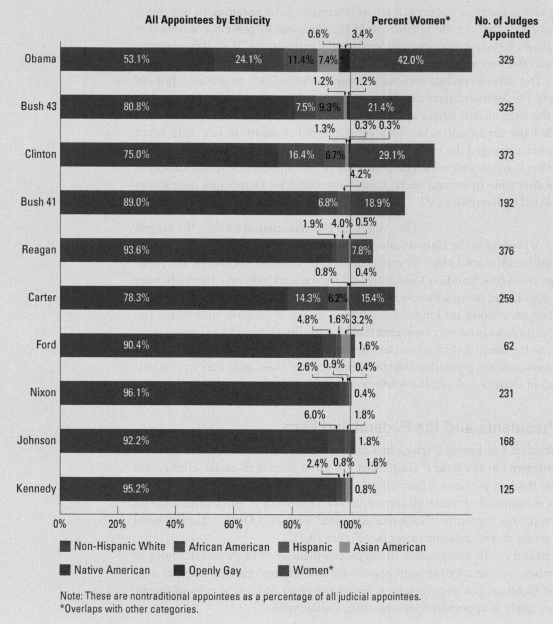

Note: These are nontraditional appointees as a percentage of all judicial appointees.
*Overlaps with other categories.

The president is not shackled by senatorial courtesy when it comes to nominating a Supreme Court justice. However, appointments to the Court attract more intense public scrutiny than do lower-level appointments, effectively narrowing the president's options and focusing attention on the Senate's advice and consent.

Of the 156 men and 5 women nominated to the Court, 11 names have been withdrawn, and 25 have failed to receive Senate confirmation. (Seven confirmed justices declined to serve.)[59] Only six such fumbles have occurred since 1900. The last one was

George W. Bush's nomination of Harriet Miers in 2005 to fill the vacancy created by the retirement of Sandra Day O'Connor. Miers, who was White House counsel, withdrew her candidacy after coming under withering criticism, largely from conservatives, for her lack of clarity on issues likely to come before the Court.

The most important factor in the rejection of a nominee is partisan politics. At least sixteen candidates lost their bids for appointment because the presidents who nominated them were considered likely to become lame ducks: the opposing party in control of the Senate anticipated victory for its candidate in an upcoming presidential race and sought to deny the incumbent president an important political appointment.[60]

Eighteen of the twenty-five successful Supreme Court nominees since 1950 have had prior judicial experience in federal or state courts. This tendency toward "promotion" from within the judiciary may be based on the idea that a judge's previous opinions are good predictors of his or her future opinions on the High Court. After all, a president is handing out a powerful lifetime appointment, so it makes sense to want an individual who is sympathetic to his views. Judges holding lifetime appointments are likely to state their views frankly in their opinions. In contrast, the policy preferences of High Court candidates who have been in legal practice or in political office can only be guessed at, based on the conjecture of professional associates or on speeches they have given to local Rotary Clubs, on the floor of a legislature, and elsewhere.

After a vacancy drought of more than eleven years, President George W. Bush put his stamp on the Supreme Court with two appointments in 2005. He nominated federal judge John G. Roberts, Jr., in July 2005 to replace Associate Justice Sandra Day O'Connor (after the withdrawal of Harriet Miers). But with the death of Chief Justice William H. Rehnquist in September, Bush withdrew Roberts's nomination as associate justice and resubmitted him for the position of chief justice. Roberts was confirmed 78–22. Democrats were evenly split: 22 for and 22 against. Bush then nominated federal judge Samuel A. Alito for the seat vacated by O'Connor. His confirmation hearing was far more contentious, with the Democrats aiming to paint him as "outside the mainstream." The effort failed, as did a last-minute call to filibuster the nomination. Alito was confirmed by the Senate by a narrow margin, 58–42 (nearly all Democrats were opposed), and he took his seat as the 110th justice in January 2006.

The results of the Roberts and Alito appointments were soon apparent. In the 2006 term (October 2006 to June 2007), the first full term with Roberts and Alito on the bench, the Court moved in a decidedly conservative direction. One-third of all the cases were decided by 5–4 votes, almost triple the proportion of close votes from the previous term. In each case, Justice Anthony Kennedy cast the deciding vote.

He joined the majority in all twenty-four 5–4 decisions, siding more often with his conservative colleagues. Subsequently, Kennedy has left his mark by authoring the majority opinion or providing the deciding vote across a range of hot-button issues: declaring the death penalty

Alex Wong/Getty Images

IMAGE 14.5   Can't Spell Truth Without Ruth

President Bill Clinton appointed Justice Ruth Bader Ginsburg to the Supreme Court in 1993. Now 83, Ginsburg has assumed cult status as "Notorious RBG," whose blistering dissents against conservative opinions led to a meme—or Internet-fueled catchphrase—comparing her to the rapper, Notorious B.I.G.

unconstitutional for the rape of a child, supporting a constitutional right for individuals to own a gun for personal use, removing restrictions on corporate spending in election campaigns, and striking down state bans on same-sex marriage.

Justice David H. Souter's decision to retire from the Supreme Court in 2009 gave President Obama the opportunity to appoint a second woman to the Supreme Court, federal judge Sonia Sotomayor of New York. Sotomayor, the first Latina to be nominated to the Court, possessed a sterling résumé with a compelling personal story. Raised by her widowed mother in a Bronx housing project, Sotomayor went on to earn top honors at Princeton and distinction at Yale Law School. She spent years as a federal prosecutor and in private legal practice before she was appointed by Republican president George H. W. Bush to the federal district court in 1992. President Bill Clinton appointed her to the federal appellate court in 1998.

Republicans on the Senate Judiciary Committee tried to derail Sotomayor's nomination, pouring over everything she had written or said. Some senators focused on a comment she made in 2001, that a wise Latina woman "would more often than not reach a better conclusion than a white male who hasn't lived that life."[61] In opposing Sotomayor, some Republicans risked the ire of Hispanic voters, whose role in American politics is destined to grow. By 2050, the percentage of Hispanics in the population is expected to increase from 15 to 30 percent.

Sotomayor deflected the attacks and stuck to her well-rehearsed script, declaring that her core guiding principle was "fidelity to the law." That bromide kept her opponents at bay. In the end, she was confirmed by a vote of 68 to 31, largely along party lines. Given her record as a moderate, Sotomayor's appointment has not been a game changer since she replaced a moderate justice.

President Obama filled a second seat when moderate justice John Paul Stevens announced in April 2010 that he would retire at the end of the current term in June 2010. President Obama nominated Elena Kagan, his solicitor general, to fill the spot. In a departure from recent practice, Obama did not find his choice in the minor leagues of the federal judiciary. Rather, Kagan made her mark as a law professor and law school administrator (and a coveted clerkship with Supreme Court Justice Thurgood Marshall). In a 1995 book review, Kagan wrote that confirmation hearings were "a vapid and hollow charade."[62] But when it was her turn to be interrogated by the Senate Judiciary Committee, she chose the well-worn path of avoiding answers to serious questions. Her bromide: the Court's role "must . . . be a modest one—properly deferential to the decisions of the American people and their elected representatives."[63] The Senate confirmed Kagan by a vote of 63 to 37. On August 7, 2010, she became the 112th justice—and the fourth woman—to serve on the Court.

SCOTUS Nomination @SCOTUSnom   Follow

Meet Chief Judge Merrick Garland, the President's nominee to the Supreme Court. #SCOTUSnominee

The White House

Meet the President's Supreme Court Nominee
Follow @WhiteHouse for the latest from President Obama and his administration.

Source: Twitter, Inc.

IMAGE 14.6   The Goldilocks Candidate?

The Obama administration turned to Twitter in 2016 to mobilize public opinion in support of Judge Merrick Garland's nomination to the Supreme Court. Garland's moderate views would make him a strong candidate if the Senate Republicans would give him a hearing and a vote.

Judge Merrick Garland is Obama's third pick for the Court, filling the vacancy created by Justice Antonin Scalia's death. But the Republican-led Senate has vowed to take no committee or floor action on Garland's candidacy until the outcome of the 2016 presidential election. In the new age of social media, the administration created a Twitter account to push the Garland nomination (see @SCOTUSnom).

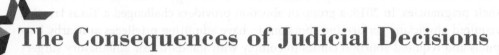

The Consequences of Judicial Decisions

LO5 Examine the impact, influence, and acceptance of decisions on issues of national importance by an institution unaccountable to the electorate.

Judicial rulings represent the tip of the iceberg in terms of all the legal conflicts and disputes that arise in this country. Most cases never surface in court. The overwhelming majority of lawsuits end without a court judgment. Many civil cases are settled, or the parties give up, or the courts dismiss the suits because they are beyond the legitimate bounds of judicial resolution. Most criminal cases end in a plea bargain, with the defendant admitting his or her guilt in exchange for a less severe punishment. Only about 10 percent of criminal cases in the federal district courts are tried; an equally small percentage of civil cases are adjudicated.

Furthermore, the fact that a judge sentences a criminal defendant to ten years in prison or a court holds a company liable for billions in damages does not guarantee that the defendant will lose his or her freedom or the company will give up any assets. In the case of the criminal defendant, the road of seeking an appeal following trial and conviction is well traveled and, if nothing else, serves to delay the day when he or she must go to prison. In civil cases as well, an appeal may be filed to delay the day of reckoning.

Supreme Court Rulings: Implementation and Impact

When the Supreme Court makes a decision, it relies on others to implement it—to translate policy into action. How a judgment is implemented depends in good measure on how it was crafted. Remember that the justices, in preparing their opinions, must work to hold their majorities together, to gain greater, if not unanimous, support for their arguments. This forces them to compromise in their opinions, to moderate their arguments, which introduces ambiguity into many of the policies they articulate. Ambiguous opinions affect the implementation of policy. For example, when the Supreme Court issued its unanimous order in 1955 to desegregate public school facilities "with all deliberate speed,"[64] judges who opposed the Court's policy dragged their feet in implementing it. In the early 1960s, the Supreme Court prohibited prayers and Bible reading in public schools. Yet state court judges and attorneys general reinterpreted the High Court's decision to mean that only compulsory prayer or Bible reading was unconstitutional and that state-sponsored voluntary prayer or Bible reading was acceptable.[65]

Because the Supreme Court confronts issues freighted with deeply felt social values or fundamental political beliefs, its decisions have influence beyond the immediate parties in a dispute. The Court's decision in *Roe* v. *Wade*, legalizing abortion, generated heated public reaction. The justices were barraged with thousands of angry letters. Groups opposing abortion vowed to overturn the decision; groups favoring the freedom to obtain an abortion moved to protect the right they had won. Within eight months of the decision, more than two dozen constitutional amendments had been introduced in Congress, although none managed to carry the extraordinary majority required for passage. Still, the antiabortion faction achieved a modest victory with the passage of a provision forbidding the use of national government funds for abortions except when the woman's life is in jeopardy. (Since 1993, the exception has also included victims of rape or incest.)

Abortion opponents have focused their efforts at state legislatures, hoping to load abortion laws with enough conditions to discourage women from terminating their pregnancies. In 2016, a group of abortion providers challenged a Texas law that required physicians performing abortions to have admitting privileges at nearby hospitals and required abortion clinics comply with standards for ambulatory surgery centers. Both provisions were viewed as unduly restrictive placing a "substantial burden" on the exercise of a woman's right to choose. In a 5–3 decision in June 2016, the Court struck down the Texas law because it imposed an "undue burden" on a woman's liberty protected by the Fourteenth Amendment.[66]

Public Opinion and the Supreme Court

Democratic theorists have a difficult time reconciling a commitment to representative democracy with a judiciary that is not accountable to the electorate yet has the power to undo legislative and executive acts. The difficulty may simply be a problem for theorists, however. The policies coming from the Supreme Court, although lagging years behind public opinion, rarely seem out of line with the public's ideological choices.[67] Surveys in several controversial areas reveal that an ideologically balanced Court seldom departs from majority sentiment or trends.[68] "What history shows," wrote Professor Barry Friedman in the most recent and thorough study in this area, "is assuredly not that Supreme Court decisions always are in line with popular opinion, but rather that they come into line with one another over time."[69] That alignment has yet to materialize nearly five decades later on the issue of school prayer, since the Court struck down the recitation of a nondenominational public school prayer in 1961.[70] A majority of Americans then and now do not agree with the Court's position. And so long as much of the public continues to want prayer in schools, the controversy will continue.

New research has shed valuable light on public knowledge and understanding of the judiciary. It turns out that Americans know more about the Supreme Court than pundits had previously acknowledged. As citizens gain knowledge about the judiciary, they are at the same time confronted with important symbols of judicial power such as the wearing of judicial robes, the use of a privileged form of address (e.g., "Your Honor"), and the requirement to rise when judges enter a court room. These symbols tend to emphasize a special role for the courts. "To know more about courts may not be to love them," wrote James L. Gibson and Gregory A. Caldeira, "but to know them is to learn and think that they are different from other political institutions (and often therefore more worthy of trust, respect, and legitimacy)."[71]

Perhaps it should come as no surprise that the public's negative opinion of the Supreme Court is at a thirty-year high given contentious decisions involving Obamacare, campaign finance, voting rights, and gay marriage. Public opinion of the Court and its ideology "have never been more politically divided." In 2015, 48 percent of the public held a favorable impression of the Court while 43 percent held an unfavorable impression, the most negative in three decades of polling.[72]

The judicial process is imperfect, so it is not surprising that the Court will continue to step into minefields of public criticism. In 2005 the Court ruled that the Constitution did not forbid a city from taking private property for private development.[73] The outrage across the ideological spectrum was enormous and immediate. State legislatures and courts acted swiftly to give greater protection to private property. This was strong evidence that the Court's measured opinion was out of step with conventional wisdom. And while the Court sidestepped a direct challenge to California's Proposition 8 (defining marriage in the state constitution in strictly monogamous, heterosexual terms), the outcome in the lower courts made gay marriage a fact in California. At the national level in 2015, a sharply divided Court struck down state bans on same-sex marriages and refusals to recognize legal same-sex marriage performed in other states. The four moderate-to-liberal justices joined by Justice Anthony Kennedy planted their judgment in the concept of liberty protected by the Due Process Clause and in the Equal Protection Clause of the Fourteenth Amendment, much to the bitter dismay of the conservative minority.[74]

The Courts and Models of Democracy

LO6 Evaluate the decision-making authority of the federal judiciary within the context of both majoritarian and pluralist democracy.

How far should judges stray from existing statutes and precedents? Supporters of the majoritarian model would argue that the courts should adhere to the letter of the law, that judges must refrain from injecting their own values into their decisions. If the law places too much (or not enough) emphasis on equality or order, the elected legislature, not the courts, can change the law. In contrast, those who support the pluralist model maintain that the courts are a policymaking branch of government. It is thus legitimate for the individual values and interests of judges to mirror group interests and preferences and for judges to attempt consciously to advance group interests as they see fit. However, judges at all levels find it difficult to determine when, where, and how to proceed.

The argument that our judicial system fits the pluralist model gains support from a legal procedure called the **class action**. A class action is a device for assembling the claims or defenses of similarly situated individuals so that they can be heard in a single lawsuit. A class action makes it possible for people with small individual claims and limited financial resources to aggregate their claims and resources and thus make a lawsuit viable. The class action also permits the case to be tried by representative parties, with the judgment binding on all. Decisions in class action suits can have broader impact than decisions in other types of cases. Since the 1940s, class action suits have been the vehicles through which groups have asserted claims involving civil rights, legislative apportionment, and environmental problems. For example, schoolchildren have sued (through their parents) under the banner of class action to rectify claimed racial discrimination on the part of school authorities, as in *Brown* v. *Board of Education.*

class action
A procedure by which similarly situated litigants may be heard in a single lawsuit.

Abetting the class action is the resurgence of state supreme courts' fashioning policies consistent with group preferences. Informed Americans often look to the U.S. Supreme Court for protection of their rights and liberties. In many circumstances, that expectation is correct. But state courts may serve as the staging areas for legal campaigns to change the law in the nation's highest court. They also exercise substantial influence over the policies that affect citizens daily, including the rights and liberties enshrined in state constitutions, statutes, and common law.[75]

Furthermore, state judges need not look to the U.S. Supreme Court for guidance on the meaning of certain state rights and liberties. If a state court chooses to rely solely on national law in deciding a case, that case is reviewable by the U.S. Supreme Court. But a state court can avoid review by the U.S. Supreme Court by basing its decision solely on state law or by plainly stating that its decision rests on both state and federal law. If the U.S. Supreme Court is likely to render a restrictive view of a constitutional right and the judges of a state court are inclined toward a more expansive view, the state judges can use the state ground to avoid Supreme Court review. In a period when the nation's highest court has moved in a decidedly conservative direction, some state courts have become safe havens for liberal values. And individuals and groups know where to moor their policies. State supreme courts can turn to their own state constitutions to "raise the ceiling of liberty above the floor created by the federal Bill of Rights."[76]

State courts continue to serve as arenas for political conflict, with litigants, individually or in groups, vying for their preferred policies. The multiplicity of the nation's court system, with overlapping state and national responsibilities, provides alternative points of access for individuals and groups to present and argue their claims. This description of the courts fits the pluralist model of government.

Summary

LO1　Define judicial review, explain the circumstances under which it was established, and assess the significance of the authority it gave the courts.

- Section 1 of Article III of the Constitution creates "one supreme Court," although in its early years the federal judiciary was not a particularly powerful branch of government. With the establishment of judicial review, the Supreme Court's power came to equal or potentially exceed the other branches. The principle of checks and balances can restrain judicial power through several means, such as constitutional amendments and impeachment. But restrictions on that power have been infrequent, leaving the federal courts to exercise considerable influence through judicial review and statutory construction.

LO2　Outline the organization of the U.S. court system and identify the principal functions of courts at each tier of the system.

- The federal court system has three tiers. At the bottom are the district courts, where litigation begins and most disputes end. In the middle are the courts of appeals. At the top is the Supreme Court. The ability of judges to make policy increases as they move up the pyramid from trial courts to appellate courts to the Supreme Court. The American legal system functions with a bias that favors existing decisions. This notion of stare decisis ("let the decision stand")

provides continuity and predictability to the legal process.

LO3　Describe the process by which cases are both accepted for review and decided by the U.S. Supreme Court and analyze the role played by judicial restraint and judicial activism in judicial decisions.

- The Supreme Court harmonizes conflicting interpretations of national law and articulates constitutional rights. The Supreme Court is free to draft its agenda through the discretionary control of its docket. It is helped at this crucial stage by the solicitor general, who represents the executive branch of government before the Court. The solicitor general's influence with the justices affects their choice of cases to review. Given their capacity to accept, consider, and render opinions on issues of national import, the justices on the Supreme Court exercise real political power.

LO4　Explain how judges at different levels of the federal court system are nominated and confirmed to the federal bench.

- Political allegiance and complementary values are necessary conditions for appointment by the president to the coveted position of judge. The president and senators from the same party share appointment power in the case of federal district and appellate judges. The president has more leeway in nominating Supreme Court justices, although all nominees must be confirmed by the Senate. Recent presidents have made efforts to make the federal courts more diverse in racial, ethnic, and gender terms. When it comes to Supreme Court appointments, however, partisan politics is the most important factor affecting which nominees are confirmed.

LO5   Examine the impact, influence, and acceptance of decisions on issues of national importance by an institution unaccountable to the electorate.

- Courts inevitably fashion policy, for each of the states and for the nation. Because the Supreme Court deals with issues that often reflect deeply felt values or political beliefs, the impact of its decisions often extends well beyond the parties in dispute. The crafting of a majority decision often means that justices must moderate their arguments and compromise in their opinions, which can reduce their overall impact on policy implementation. The relationship between the Supreme Court and

public opinion is rarely highly contentious. In fact, the Court's decisions tend to come in line with the views of the general public over time.

LO6   Evaluate the decision-making authority of the federal judiciary within the context of both majoritarian and pluralist democracy.

- The courts provide multiple points of access for individuals to pursue their preferences. Furthermore, class action enables people with small individual claims and limited financial resources to pursue their goals in court, reinforcing the pluralist model. As the U.S. Supreme Court marches in a more conservative direction, some state supreme courts have become safe havens for more liberal policies on civil rights and civil liberties and for legal innovation generally. The state court systems have overlapping state and national responsibilities, offering groups and individuals additional access points to present and argue their claims.

Chapter Quiz

LO1   Define judicial review, explain the circumstances under which it was established, and assess the significance of the authority it gave the courts.

1. Why was the decision in *Marbury* v. *Madison* so important for the Supreme Court?
2. What are the components of judicial review?

LO2   Outline the organization of the U.S. court system and identify the principal functions of courts at each tier of the system.

1. List the different areas over which the U.S. district courts have authority.
2. What is precedent, and how is it used in the court system?

LO3   Describe the process by which cases are both accepted for review and decided by the U.S. Supreme Court and analyze the role played by judicial restraint and judicial activism in judicial decisions.

1. What are the two ways that cases arrive at the Supreme Court?
2. Distinguish between judicial restraint and judicial activism as approaches to decision making.

LO4   Explain how judges at different levels of the federal court system are nominated and confirmed to the federal bench.

1. How does the practice of senatorial courtesy affect the judicial appointment process?
2. Using the confirmation of a recent Supreme Court justice, explain why the appointment process to the Supreme Court can be politically contentious.

LO5   Examine the impact, influence, and acceptance of decisions on issues of national importance by an institution unaccountable to the electorate.

1. What factors affect the impact that Supreme Court decisions can have on policy?
2. Why are many Supreme Court decisions considered ambiguous in nature?

LO6   Evaluate the decision-making authority of the federal judiciary within the context of both majoritarian and pluralist democracy.

1. How does a class action make a lawsuit viable?
2. In what way can state courts diverge from the U.S. Supreme Court on specific decisions?

15 Order and Civil Liberties

How many friends have you texted today? Did your messages include any deep personal secrets or your own views on controversial issues in your school, town, or the nation? Or consider this: Have you ever attended a party where your friends have taken embarrassing photos of themselves—or perhaps you!—and posted them to their social networks? How would you feel if your cell phone company were collaborating with law enforcement authorities to create "back door" ways to hack into your phone, overriding security features that your service agreement said would keep data on your phone private? That question made national news in 2016 in the wake of the San Bernardino, California, terrorist attack that left fourteen people dead and injured another twenty-two.[1]

The gruesome scene began on an otherwise typical day. Syed Rizwan Farook and Tashfeen Malik, a married couple, dropped off their six-month-old daughter with Farook's mother and then drove to the Inland Regional Center where they opened fire. Law enforcement authorities eventually pursued, surrounded, and killed both assailants. During the ensuing investigation, authorities found Farook's iPhone but needed the password to access it. Knowing that too many successful attempts to guess the password could erase the phone's entire contents—a source of potential information about the couple's motives and perhaps even other co-conspirators—the FBI requested that Apple, the maker of the iPhone, override the phone's security features.

Apple CEO Timothy Cook refused the FBI's request, stating his intention to remain loyal to Apple's customers. Engineering a hack into the phone, Cook reasoned, could open up all iPhones to potential security vulnerabilities. Further, "The Founding Fathers would be appalled" at the government's request, he argued, because it represented a worrisome encroachment of law enforcement on the privacy of cell phone users everywhere, potentially setting a dangerous precedent. The director of the FBI, James Comey, strongly disagreed, saying the case "was not about trying to send a message or set a precedent; it was and is about fully investigating a terrorist attack."[2]

In the American political system, courts often resolve such controversies. The iPhone case did go to court where the FBI asked a judge to compel Apple's cooperation, yet the company continued to fight. Eventually, the FBI withdrew its request after hiring hackers who helped it successfully access the phone.[3] Despite that outcome, questions about the case and also larger questions lingered. How well do the courts respond to clashes that pit key values against one another? In this chapter, we explore some value conflicts derived from the Bill of Rights that the judiciary has resolved. After reading it, you will be able to judge whether the American government has met the challenge of democracy by finding the appropriate balance between freedom and order.

#ChallengeAccepted

Take the Challenge on MindTap for American Government

With access to information on smartphones, the FBI says it may be able to stop a future terrorist attack from occurring. Should all Americans sacrifice some of their privacy by allowing government "back doors" into their phones to help prevent potential future attacks?

marijuana use have influenced that relationship. As a result, Cole advised the U.S. Attorneys to monitor closely new state plans to regulate the use of marijuana. As long as those states "have also implemented strong and effective regulatory and enforcement systems," Cole believed they would be "less likely to threaten the federal [enforcement] priorities," which include curtailing marijuana's use as a revenue source for criminals, gangs, and cartels.

In short, Cole's memo reveals the complicated challenge of democracy that government attorneys must manage as they attempt to balance the need to maintain order, via enforcement of the CSA, while simultaneously recognizing the desire that some citizens have for the freedom to use marijuana in ways that they believe poses no threat to others.

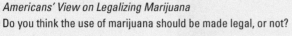

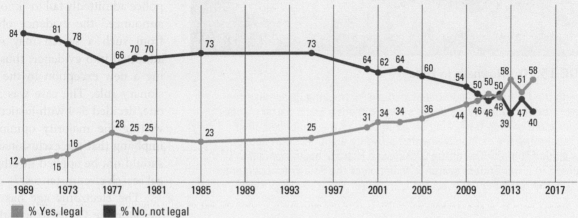

*Note: Blank years represent years when the question was not asked.

Source: Jeffrey M. Jones, Gallup, "In U.S., 58% Back Legal Marijuana Use," 21 October 2015, http://www.gallup.com/poll/186260/back-legal-marijuana.aspx?g_source=legalizing%20marijuana&g_medium=search&g_campaign=tiles.

CRITICAL THINKING Suppose that the federal government were deciding between these two strategies for removing marijuana from Schedule I of the CSA: remove it for all states or only remove it for states that prove they can regulate marijuana effectively. What would be some persuasive arguments for and against each strategy?

struggle with police use of sophisticated electronic eavesdropping devices and searches of movable vehicles. In each case, the justices have confronted a rule that appears to handicap the police and to offer freedom to people whose guilt has been established by the illegal evidence. In the Court's most recent pronouncements, order has triumphed over freedom.

The struggle over the exclusionary rule took a new turn in 1984, when the Court reviewed *United States* v. *Leon.*[77] In this case, the police obtained a search warrant from a judge on the basis of a tip from an informant of unproven reliability. The judge issued a warrant without firmly establishing probable cause to believe the tip. The police, relying on the warrant, found large quantities of illegal drugs. The Court, by a vote of 6–3, established the **good faith exception** to the exclusionary rule. The justices held that the state could introduce at trial evidence seized on the basis of a mistakenly issued search warrant. The exclusionary rule, argued the majority, is not a right but a remedy against illegal police conduct. The rule is costly to society. It excludes pertinent valid evidence, allowing guilty people to go unpunished and generating disrespect for the law.

good faith exception
An exception to the Supreme Court exclusionary rule, holding that evidence seized on the basis of a mistakenly issued search warrant can be introduced at trial if the mistake was made in good faith, that is, if all the parties involved had reason at the time to believe that the warrant was proper.

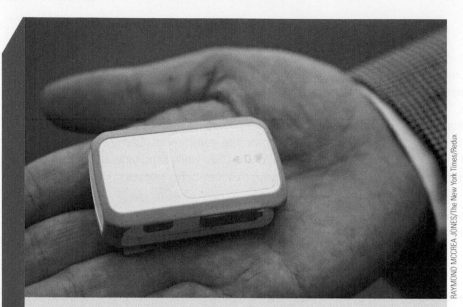

RAYMOND MCCREA JONES/The New York Times/Redux

IMAGE 15.10   Nowhere to Hide

Police in the District of Columbia placed a GPS tracking device like the one pictured here on Antoine Jones's Jeep without a court warrant. Jones was convicted of drug trafficking based in part on the evidence culled from monitoring the car's movements for twenty-eight days. On appeal, Jones argued that the use of the GPS device to track his movement amounted to a warrantless search in violation of the Fourth Amendment. In 2012, the Supreme Court agreed with Jones.

These costs are justifiable only if the exclusionary rule deters police misconduct. Such a deterrent effect was not a factor in *Leon*: the police acted in good faith. Hence, the Court decided, there is a need for an exception to the rule.

The Court recognized another exception in 2006. When police search a home with a warrant, they have been required to "knock and announce" before entering. But the Supreme Court held that when the police admittedly fail to "knock and announce," the evidence obtained from such a search may still be admitted into evidence, thus creating a new exception to the exclusionary rule. The case was a close one, decided 5–4 with Justice Scalia writing the majority opinion and implying that the exclusionary rule should not be applied in other illegal search circumstances.[78]

The electronic age has forced the Supreme Court to wrestle with other types of evidence and searches, as well. Consider the data stored on your smart phone. During or after an arrest, should police officers be able to search through photos, text messages, call history, and other items stored in a phone's memory, much like they would search a suspect's jacket pockets, tote bag, or car? In *Riley* v. *California* (2014) a unanimous Supreme Court said no, unless the law enforcement officials first obtained a warrant to search the phone. Digital data are different than physical personal items, the justices argued, and so merit additional constitutional protections.[79]

The Ninth Amendment and Personal Autonomy

LO6 Explain how the Supreme Court interpreted the Ninth Amendment to broaden the individual's constitutional protection of personal privacy beyond the language in the Bill of Rights.

> The enumeration in the Constitution, of certain rights, shall not be construed to deny or disparage others retained by the people.

The working and history of the Ninth Amendment remain an enigma. The evidence supports two different views: the amendment may protect rights that are not enumerated, or it may simply protect state governments against the assumption of power by the national government.[80] The meaning of the amendment was not an issue until 1965, when the Supreme Court used it to protect privacy, a right that is not enumerated in the Constitution.

From Privacy to Abortion

In *Griswold* v. *Connecticut* (1965), the Court struck down, by a vote of 7–2, a seldom-enforced Connecticut statute that made the use of birth control devices a crime. Justice Douglas, writing for the majority, asserted that the "specific guarantees in the Bill of Rights have penumbras [partially illuminated regions surrounding fully lit areas]" that give "life and substance" to broad, unspecified protections in the Bill of Rights. Several specific guarantees in the First, Third, Fourth, and Fifth Amendments create a zone of privacy, Douglas argued, and the Ninth Amendment protects this zone and applies to the states by the due process clause of the Fourteenth Amendment.[81]

Three justices further emphasized the relevance of the Ninth Amendment, which, they contended, protects fundamental rights derived from those specifically enumerated in the first eight amendments. This view contrasted sharply with the position expressed by the two dissenters, Justices Hugo Black and Potter Stewart. In the absence of some specific prohibition, they argued, the Bill of Rights and the Fourteenth Amendment do not allow judicial annulment of state legislative policies, even if a judge or justice finds those policies abhorrent.

Griswold established the principle that the Bill of Rights as a whole creates a right to make certain intimate, personal choices, including the right of married people to engage in sexual intercourse for reproduction or pleasure. This zone of personal autonomy, protected by the Constitution, was the basis of a 1973 case that sought to invalidate state antiabortion laws. But rights are not absolute, and in weighing the interests of the individual against the interests of the government, the Supreme Court found itself caught up in a flood of controversy that has yet to subside.

In *Roe* v. *Wade* (1973), the Court, in a 7–2 decision, declared unconstitutional a Texas law making it a crime to obtain an abortion except for the purpose of saving the mother's life.[82] Justice Harry Blackmun, who wrote the majority opinion, could not identify a specific constitutional guarantee to justify the Court's ruling. Instead, he based the decision on the right to privacy protected by the due process clause of the Fourteenth Amendment. In effect, state abortion laws were unreasonable and hence unconstitutional. The Court declared that in the first three months of pregnancy, a woman and her physician control the abortion decision. In the interest of protecting the woman's health, states may restrict but not prohibit abortions in the second three months of pregnancy. Finally, in the last three months of pregnancy, states may regulate or even prohibit abortions to protect the life of the fetus, except when medical judgment determines that an abortion is necessary to save the mother's life. In all, the Court's ruling affected the laws of forty-six states. The dissenters—Justices Byron White and William Rehnquist—were quick to assert what critics have frequently repeated since the decision: the Court's judgment was directed by its own dislikes, not by any constitutional compass. In the absence of guiding principles, they asserted, the majority justices simply substituted their views for the views of the state legislatures whose abortion regulations they invalidated.

A perceptible shift away from abortion rights materialized in *Webster* v. *Reproductive Health Services* (1989) after the composition of the Court had shifted in a more conservative direction with new appointments from President Ronald Reagan. In *Webster*, the Supreme Court upheld the constitutionality of a Missouri law that denied the use of public employees or publicly funded facilities to perform an abortion unless the mother's life was in danger.[83] Furthermore, the law required doctors to perform tests to determine whether fetuses twenty weeks and older could survive outside the womb. This was the first time that the Court upheld significant government restrictions on abortion.

The justices issued five opinions, but no single opinion captured a majority. Four justices (Blackmun, William J. Brennan, Jr., Thurgood Marshall, and John Paul Stevens) voted to strike down the Missouri law and hold fast to *Roe*. Four justices (Kennedy, Rehnquist, Scalia, and White) wanted to overturn *Roe* and return to the states the power to regulate abortion. The remaining justice, Sandra Day O'Connor, avoided both camps. Her position was that state abortion restrictions are permissible provided they are not "unduly burdensome." She voted with the conservative plurality to uphold the restrictive Missouri statute on the grounds that it did not place an undue burden on women's rights. But she declined to reconsider (and overturn) *Roe*.

The Court has since moved cautiously down the road toward greater government control of abortion. In 1990, the justices split on two state parental notification laws. The Court struck down a state requirement that compelled unwed minors to notify both parents before having an abortion. In another case, however, the Court upheld a state requirement that a physician notify one parent of a pregnant minor of her intent to have an abortion. In both cases, the justices voiced widely divergent opinions, revealing a continuing division over abortion.[84]

With a clear conservative majority, the Court seemed poised to reverse *Roe* in 1992. But a new coalition—forged by Reagan appointees O'Connor and Kennedy, and George H. W. Bush appointee David Souter—reaffirmed *Roe* yet tolerated additional restrictions on abortions. In *Planned Parenthood* v. *Casey*, a bitterly divided bench opted for the O'Connor "undue burden" test. Eight years later, in 2000, O'Connor sided with a coalition of liberal and moderate justices in a 5–4 decision striking down a Nebraska law that had banned so-called partial-birth abortion. Yet in a different case raising very similar issues in 2007, the Court by a 5–4 vote upheld a federal law banning partial-birth abortion. The narrow margins of these decisions illustrate the Court's continuing and deep division on the abortion issue.[85]

Privacy, Personal Autonomy, and Sexual Orientation

The Court's right-to-privacy cases have involved more than just abortion. For example, does the right to privacy embrace private homosexual acts between consenting adults? Consider the case of Michael Hardwick, who was arrested in 1982 in his Atlanta bedroom while having sex with another man. In a standard approach to prosecuting homosexuals, Georgia charged him with sodomy, which means oral or anal intercourse, under a state criminal statute. The police said that they had gone to his home to arrest him for failing to pay a fine for drinking in public. Although the prosecutor dropped the charges, Hardwick sued to challenge the law's constitutionality. He won in the lower courts, but the state pursued the case.

The conflict between freedom and order lies at the core of the case. "Our legal history and our social traditions have condemned this conduct uniformly for hundreds and hundreds of years," argued Georgia's attorney. Constitutional law, he continued, "must not become an instrument for a change in the social order." Hardwick's attorney, a noted constitutional scholar, said that government must have a more important reason than "majority morality to justify regulation of sexual intimacies in the privacy of the home." He maintained that the case involved two precious freedoms: the right to engage in private sexual relations and the right to be free from government intrusion in one's home.[86]

In a bitterly divided ruling in 1986, the Court held in *Bowers* v. *Hardwick* that the Constitution does not protect homosexual relations between consenting adults, even in the privacy of their own homes. The logic of the findings ran counter to the findings favoring personal autonomy in the contraception and abortion cases discussed earlier. But the 5–4 majority maintained that only heterosexual choices—whether and whom to marry, whether to conceive a child, whether to have an abortion—fall within the zone of privacy the Court had established. "The Judiciary necessarily takes to itself further authority to govern the country without express constitutional authority" when it expands the list of fundamental rights not rooted in the language or design of the Constitution, wrote Justice White, who authored the majority opinion.[87] The arguments on both sides of the privacy issue are compelling. This makes the choice between freedom and order excruciating for ordinary citizens and Supreme Court justices alike.

Justice White's majority opinion was reconsidered in 2003 when the Court heard a "carefully choreographed" challenge to a Texas law that criminalized homosexual but not heterosexual sodomy.[88] This time, in *Lawrence and Garner* v. *Texas*, a new coalition of six justices viewed the issue in a different light. Speaking through Justice Kennedy, the Court observed "an emerging awareness that liberty gives substantial protection to adult persons in deciding how to conduct their private lives in matters pertaining to sex." Since the Texas law furthered no legitimate state interest but intruded into the intimate personal choices of individuals, the law was void. Kennedy along with four other justices then took the unusual step of reaching back in time to declare that the *Bowers* decision was wrong and should be overruled.[89]

Justice Scalia, joined by Chief Justice Rehnquist and Justice Thomas, issued a stinging dissent. Scalia charged the majority with "signing on to the homosexual agenda" aimed at eliminating the moral opprobrium traditionally attached to homosexual conduct. The challenge of democracy calls for the democratic process, not judicial decisions, to sort out value conflicts whenever possible. And, according to Scalia, in overturning *Bowers*, the majority on the Court had moved from its traditional responsibility of umpiring the system to favoring one side over another in the struggle between freedom and order.

For groups dissatisfied with rulings from the nation's courts, the pluralist model provides one avenue for redress. State courts and state legislatures have demonstrated their receptivity to positions that are probably untenable in the federal courts. Pluralist mechanisms such as the initiative and the referendum offer countermeasures to judicial intervention. However, state-by-state decisions offer little comfort to Americans who believe the U.S. Constitution protects them in their most intimate decisions and actions, regardless of where they reside.

Summary

LO1   Explain the role of the Bill of Rights in protecting civil liberties and civil rights.

- When they established the new government of the United States, the states and the people compelled the framers, through the Bill of Rights, to protect their freedoms. The ten original amendments to the Constitution include both civil liberties and civil rights. In interpreting these ten amendments, the courts, especially the Supreme Court, have taken on the task of balancing freedom and order. The adoption of the Fourteenth Amendment in 1868 created a mechanism to extend the guarantees of the Bill of Rights even further. The due process clause of the amendment became the vehicle for applying specific provisions of the Bill of Rights to the states. The Supreme Court has tolerated some variation from state to state in the meaning of certain constitutional rights.

LO2   Identify the mechanisms that guarantee freedom of religion.

- The First Amendment protects several freedoms. The first of these, the freedom of religion, has long been important to American citizens. The establishment clause demands government neutrality toward religions and between the religious and the nonreligious. This clause, instituted to protect all religious beliefs, has nonetheless sparked some controversy in its application. According to judicial interpretations of the free-exercise clause, religious beliefs are inviolable, but the Constitution does *not* protect antisocial actions in the name of religion. Extreme interpretations of the religion clauses could bring the clauses into conflict with each other.

LO3   Identify the free-expression clauses and describe the scope of their protection.

- Freedom of expression encompasses many freedoms, including freedom of speech, freedom of the press, and the right to assemble peaceably and to petition the government. Freedom of speech and freedom of the press are not absolute, but the courts have ruled that the Bill of Rights gives the people far greater protection than other freedoms. Press freedom has enjoyed broad constitutional protection because a free society depends on the ability to collect and report information without government interference. The rights to assemble peaceably and to petition the government stem from the guarantees of freedom of speech and of the press.

LO4   Discuss how the Supreme Court has interpreted the right to bear arms.

- The nature and scope of the Second Amendment have long been a source of contention for gun-control advocates and gun-rights supporters. After nearly seventy years of silence, in 2008 the Supreme Court declared that the right to bear arms protects an individual's right to own a gun for personal use. New legal challenges and court rulings have helped to determine the standards that should apply when judging the appropriateness of gun regulations. For now, however, government may not prohibit individual gun ownership.

LO5   Identify the amendments and development of Supreme Court decisions that protect individuals who have been accused of committing a crime.

- Major advancements of the rights of the accused have occurred as the Supreme Court has interpreted the protections in the Fourth through Eighth amendments and also applied them to the states via the due process clause of the Fourteenth Amendment. The Court's decisions have addressed important procedural matters including the operation of the nation's courtrooms and how the police can conduct work in the field. Although the Supreme Court has declared some such rights fundamental, for others it tolerates variation in state practices.

LO6   Explain how the Supreme Court interpreted the Ninth Amendment to broaden the individual's constitutional protection of personal privacy beyond the language in the Bill of Rights.

- As it has fashioned new fundamental rights from the Constitution, the Supreme Court has become embroiled in controversy. The right to privacy served as the basis for the right of women to terminate a pregnancy, which in turn suggested a right to personal autonomy. The abortion controversy is still evolving, and the justices have heard many cases that have explored under what conditions the right to an abortion can be limited. Beyond the abortion controversy, the justices have advanced freedom over order

by extending protections against state criminal prosecution of private consensual sexual behavior for homosexuals.

Chapter Quiz

LO1   Explain the role of the Bill of Rights in protecting civil liberties and civil rights.

1. Why are civil liberties called "negative rights" and civil rights called "positive rights"?
2. What is the Fourteenth Amendment due process clause, and how does it hold the states to the provisions of the Bill of Rights?

LO2   Identify the mechanisms that guarantee freedom of religion.

1. Which clause in the First Amendment formalizes the separation of church and state?
2. What aspect of religion does the First Amendment not protect?

LO3   Identify the free-expression clauses and describe the scope of their protection.

1. Define the clear and present danger test and explain how it is used in adjudicating cases of freedom of speech.
2. Explain what the right to peaceably assemble entails.

LO4   Discuss how the Supreme Court has interpreted the right to bear arms.

1. What distinguishes the interpretation of the Second Amendment by gun-control advocates from that of gun-rights supporters?

2. Which questions about the Second Amendment has the Supreme Court resolved and which has it left unresolved?

LO5   Identify the amendments and development of Supreme Court decisions that protect individuals who have been accused of committing a crime.

1. Which rights do defendants enjoy in court as a result of the Supreme Court's interpretations of the Bill of Rights and the due process clause of the Fourteenth Amendment?
2. How have Supreme Court decisions influenced how police do their work in the field?

LO6   Explain how the Supreme Court interpreted the Ninth Amendment to broaden the individual's constitutional protection of personal privacy beyond the language in the Bill of Rights.

1. Which principle did the decision in *Griswold v. Connecticut* establish regarding the Bill of Rights as a whole?
2. How have the legal arguments evolved in the Supreme Court's abortion cases and cases involving sexual relations between adults?

KEY CASES

Palko v. *Connecticut* (applying the Bill of Rights to the states, 1937)

Lemon v. *Kurtzman* (religious establishment test, 1971)

Sherbert v. *Verner* (religious free exercise, 1963)

Schenck v. *United States* (free speech, clear and present danger test, 1919)

Brandenburg v. *Ohio* (free speech, 1969)

Tinker v. *Des Moines Independent County School District* (symbolic speech, 1969)

Citizens United v. *Federal Election Commission* (unlimited political campaign spending, 2010)

Cohen v. *California* (free expression, 1971)

Snyder v. *Phelps* (public/private speech; emotional harm, 2011)

New York Times v. *United States* (prior restraint, 1971)

New York Times v. *Sullivan* (free press, 1964)

District of Columbia v. *Heller* (2008) and *McDonald* v. *Chicago* (right to bear arms, 2010)

Gideon v. *Wainwright* (assistance of counsel, 1963)

Miranda v. *Arizona* (self-incrimination, 1966)

Mapp v. *Ohio* (search and seizure, 1961)

Griswold v. *Connecticut* (privacy, 1965)

Roe v. *Wade* (abortion, 1973)

Lawrence and Garner v. *Texas* (gay rights, 2003)

16 Equality and Civil Rights

Every year, high school seniors wait anxiously to learn which college has admitted them. Some, such as Abigail Fisher, receive news that no prospective freshman wants to hear.

Fisher, shown at the Supreme Court in 2012, was a senior at Stephen F. Austin High School in Sugar Land, Texas, when in 2008 she applied but was rejected for admission to the University of Texas–Austin, the state's flagship university. All Texas students who graduate in the top 10 percent of their classes must be admitted to the state university. Students falling short may be admitted nonetheless according to a formula that includes the applicant's race among several other factors. Fisher sued the university in federal court, arguing that using race in university admissions violates the equal protection clause of the Fourteenth Amendment. She lost the first two rounds of her suit in lower federal courts. In 2012, Fisher graduated from Louisiana State University, the same year the Supreme Court finally heard her case.

In a 7–1 decision, the justices decided *Fisher* v. *University of Texas* (2013) and explained that universities could consider race in admissions (consistent with its prior decisions), but only if the court's standard of strict scrutiny, which Chapter 15 described, were met. In this case, however, the lower court had not properly applied strict scrutiny and so the Supreme Court ordered the lower court to review it again. After that review, the U.S. Court of Appeals for the Fifth Circuit still upheld the university's procedures. The case returned to the Supreme Court, and in 2016 the justices agreed with the lower court, this time on a 4–3 vote, that the university's procedures were acceptable. (Seven justices participated because the late Justice Antonin Scalia's seat remained vacant and Justice Sonia Sotomayor recused herself due to prior involvement in the case as U.S. Solicitor General.) The result was a win for supporters of including race in university admissions, but the decision, authored by Justice Anthony Kennedy, was narrowly crafted, suggesting that the Court might rule differently in future cases.[1]

Because people can disagree about what equal treatment involves, cases like Fisher's can be difficult to sort out. Fisher argued that equal treatment means omitting race and letting people compete for spots at UT, or elsewhere, based on their academic records. Asian students have raised these arguments, too. In a recent challenge against Harvard, sixty-four Asian-American organizations complained to the U.S. Department of Education that the university systematically disadvantaged Asians in the admissions process.[2]

Supporters of Texas's and similar policies disagree. To them, equal treatment, means, in part, recognizing important contextual factors. Because Texas previously had prohibited blacks from entering public universities, they argue that contemporary efforts should consider race to help remedy the long-term negative consequences of those policies. Further, universities justify the use of race to assure a critical mass of diverse students in each admitted class. As long as race is considered *a* factor, rather than *the* factor, in admissions, they say, such practices should not run afoul of the Constitution.[3]

In this chapter, we consider different ideals of equality and the quest to realize them through government action. The march forward has been uneven and not without significant challenges. We begin by discussing what makes this march so difficult.

#ChallengeAccepted

Take the Challenge on MindTap for American Government

What do you think would be the consequences for universities and for the nation as a whole if university admissions officers completely ignored race when they made their admissions decisions?

In subsequent years, the Court's decisions narrowed some constitutional protections. In 1876, when a group of Louisiana whites had used violence and fraud to prevent blacks from exercising their basic constitutional rights, including that of peaceable assembly, the justices limited congressional attempts to protect those rights.[8] The Court held that the rights allegedly infringed on were not nationally protected rights and that therefore Congress was powerless to punish those who violated them. On the very same day, the Court ruled that the Fifteenth Amendment did not guarantee all citizens the right to vote; it simply listed grounds that could not be used to deny that right.[9] And in 1883, the Court struck down the public accommodations section of the Civil Rights Act of 1875.[10] The justices declared that the national government could prohibit only *government* action that discriminated against blacks; private acts of discrimination or acts of omission by a state were beyond the national government's reach. For example, a person who refused to serve blacks in a private club was immune from national government control because the discrimination was a private—not a governmental—act. The court chose to protect the freedom to practice invidious discrimination rather than advance equality for blacks.

The Court's decisions gave the states ample room to avoid ensuring civil rights for African Americans. In the matter of voting rights, for example, states could use nonracial means to bar blacks from the polls. One popular tool was the **poll tax**, first imposed by Georgia in 1877. This was a tax of $1 or $2 on every citizen who wanted to vote. The tax did not burden most whites. But many blacks were tenant farmers who lacked extra money for voting because they were deeply in debt to white merchants and landowners. Other bars to black suffrage included literacy tests, minimum education requirements, and a grandfather clause that restricted suffrage to men who could establish that their grandfathers were eligible to vote before 1867 (three years before the Fifteenth Amendment prohibited race from being used to deny individuals the right to vote).[11]

poll tax
A tax of $1 or $2 on every citizen who wished to vote, first instituted in Georgia in 1877. Although it was no burden on most white citizens, it effectively disenfranchised blacks.

From well before the Civil War, racial segregation had been a way of life in the South: blacks lived and worked separately from whites. After the war, southern states began to enact *Jim Crow* laws to reinforce segregation. (Jim Crow was a derogatory term for a black person.) Once the Supreme Court took the teeth out of the Civil Rights Act of 1875, such laws proliferated. They required African Americans to live in separate (usually inferior) areas and restricted them to separate sections of hospitals; separate cemeteries; separate drinking and toilet facilities; separate schools; and separate sections of trains, jails, and parks.

In 1892, Homer Adolph Plessy, who was seven-eighths Caucasian, sat down in a whites-only car of a Louisiana train. He refused to move to the blacks-only car and was arrested. Plessy argued that Louisiana's law mandating racial segregation on its trains was an unconstitutional infringement on both the privileges and immunities guaranteed by the Fourteenth Amendment and its equal protection clause. The Supreme Court disagreed. The majority in **Plessy v. Ferguson*** (1896) upheld state-imposed racial segregation.[12] The decision was based on what came to be known as the **separate-but-equal doctrine**, which held that separate facilities for blacks and whites satisfied the Fourteenth Amendment as long as they were equal. (The Court majority used the phrase "equal but separate" to describe the requirement. Justice John Marshall Harlan's dissenting opinion cast the phrase as "separate but equal," and that wording stuck.) Three years later, the Supreme Court extended the separate-but-equal doctrine to the schools.[13] The justices ignored that black educational facilities (and most other "colored-only" facilities) clearly were far from equal to those reserved for whites.

separate-but-equal doctrine
The concept that providing separate but equivalent facilities for blacks and whites satisfies the equal protection clause of the Fourteenth Amendment.

By the end of the nineteenth century, legal racial segregation was firmly entrenched, affecting life in the South and the North. Although constitutional amendments and

---

*Key cases are highlighted in bold, and a list of key cases appears at the end of the chapter.

national laws to protect equality under the law were in place, the Supreme Court's interpretation of those amendments and laws rendered them ineffective. Several decades would pass before any change was discernible.

Courtroom Efforts to Dismantle Barriers to Full Citizenship

By the 1920s, the separate-but-equal doctrine was so deeply ingrained in American law that no Supreme Court justice would dissent from its continued application to racial segregation. But a few Court decisions offered hope that change would come. In 1935, Lloyd Gaines graduated from Lincoln University, a black college in Missouri, but was rejected when he applied to the state law school. Missouri refused to admit blacks to its all-white law school; instead, the state's policy was to pay the costs of blacks admitted to out-of-state law schools. With the support of the National Association for the Advancement of Colored People (NAACP), Gaines appealed to the courts for admission to the University of Missouri Law School. In 1938, the U.S. Supreme Court ruled that he must be admitted.[14] Under the *Plessy* ruling, Missouri could not shift to other states its responsibility to provide an equal education for blacks.

Later cases helped reinforce the requirement that segregated facilities must be equal in all major respects. One was brought by Heman Sweatt, again with the help of the NAACP. The all-white University of Texas Law School had denied Sweatt entrance because of his race. A federal court ordered the state to provide a black law school for him. The state responded by renting a few rooms in an office building and hiring two black lawyers as teachers. Sweatt refused to attend the school and took his case to the Supreme Court. The Court ruled on *Sweatt* v. *Painter* in 1950. The justices unanimously found that the facilities were inadequate: the separate "law school" provided for Sweatt did not approach the quality of the white state law school. The University of Texas had to give Sweatt full student status. But the Court avoided reexamining the separate-but-equal doctrine.[15]

These decisions suggested to the NAACP that it was time for an attack on segregation itself. In addition to progress in the courtroom, other victories, such as President Harry S Truman's issuing of an executive order in 1948 that ordered the **desegregation** (the dismantling of authorized racial segregation) of the armed forces, convinced NAACP leaders that realizing the full promise of the Civil War amendments—full citizenship and equality for blacks—was within their grasp. Two decades of planning and litigation ultimately led the NAACP to Linda Brown.

Living in Topeka, Kansas, Brown was a black child whose father had tried to enroll her in a white public school because it was close to Linda's home and did not require her to cross a dangerous set of railroad tracks, which she needed to traverse to get to her black-only school. The request was refused because of Linda's race. A federal district court found that the black public school was equal in quality to the white school in all relevant respects; therefore, according to the *Plessy* doctrine, Linda was required to attend the black public school. Brown appealed the decision.

Brown* v. *Board of Education reached the Supreme Court in late 1951. The justices delayed argument on the sensitive case until after the 1952 national election. *Brown* was merged with four similar cases into a class action (see Chapter 14). The NAACP supported the class action, and attorney Thurgood Marshall, who would later become the first black justice on the U.S. Supreme Court, coordinated the effort. The five cases squarely challenged the separate-but-equal doctrine. By several tangible measures (standards for teacher licensing, teacher–pupil ratios, library facilities), the two school systems in each case—one white, the other black—were equal. The issue was legal separation of the races.

On May 17, 1954, Chief Justice Earl Warren, who had only recently joined the Court, delivered a single opinion covering four of the cases. Warren spoke for a unanimous Court when he declared that "in the field of public education the doctrine of 'separate

---

desegregation
The ending of authorized segregation, or separation by race.

but equal' has no place. Separate educational facilities are inherently unequal," depriving the plaintiffs of the equal protection of the laws. Segregated facilities generate in black children "a feeling of inferiority… that may affect their hearts and minds in a way unlikely ever to be undone." In short, the nation's highest court found that state-imposed public school segregation violated the equal protection clause of the Fourteenth Amendment.[16]

A companion case to *Brown* challenged the segregation of public schools in Washington, D.C., where Congress imposed segregation.[17] The equal protection clause of the Fourteenth Amendment did not restrain the national government because the District of Columbia is not a state. The Court unanimously decided that the racial segregation requirement was an arbitrary deprivation of liberty without due process of law, a violation of the Fifth Amendment. In short, the concept of liberty encompassed the idea of equality.

The Court deferred implementation of the school desegregation decisions until 1955. Then, in **Brown v. Board of Education II**, it ruled that school systems must desegregate "with all deliberate

IMAGE 16.1   Anger Erupts in Little Rock

In 1957, the Little Rock, Arkansas, school board attempted to implement court-ordered desegregation: nine black teenagers were to be admitted to Little Rock Central High School. Governor Orval Faubus ordered the National Guard to bar their attendance. A mob blocked a subsequent attempt by the students. Finally, President Dwight Eisenhower ordered federal troops to escort the students to the high school. Among them was fifteen-year-old Elizabeth Eckford (right). Hazel Bryan Massery (left) angrily taunted her from the crowd. This image seared the nation's conscience. The violence and hostility led the school board to seek a postponement of the desegregation plan. The Supreme Court, meeting in special session, affirmed the decision in *Brown* v. *Board of Education* and ordered the plan to proceed. Not to be outdone, Governor Faubus closed all public schools in 1958. They reopened the following year. Fifty years later, a federal judge declared Little Rock's schools desegregated.

speed" and commanded the lower federal courts to supervise the effort.[18]

Some states quietly complied with the *Brown* decree. Others did little to desegregate their schools. And many communities defied the Court, sometimes violently.[19] Gradual desegregation under *Brown* was in some cases no desegregation at all. In 1969, a unanimous Supreme Court ordered that the operation of segregated school systems stop "at once."[20]

Two years later, the Court approved several remedies to achieve integration, including busing, racial quotas, and the pairing or grouping of noncontiguous school zones. In *Swann* v. *Charlotte-Mecklenburg County Schools*, the Supreme Court affirmed the right of lower courts to order the busing of children to ensure school desegregation.[21] But these remedies applied only to **de jure segregation**, government-imposed segregation (for example, government assignment of whites to one school and blacks to another within the same community). Court-imposed remedies did not apply to **de facto segregation**, which is not the result of government action (for example, racial segregation resulting from residential patterns).

The busing of schoolchildren came under heavy attack in both the North and the South. Desegregation advocates saw busing as a potential remedy in many northern cities, where schools had become segregated as white families left the cities for the

de jure segregation
Government-imposed segregation.

de facto segregation
Segregation that is not the result of government influence.

suburbs. This "white flight" had left inner-city schools predominantly black and suburban schools almost all white. Public opinion strongly opposed the busing approach, and Congress sought to limit busing as a remedy to segregation. In 1974, a closely divided Court ruled that lower courts could not order busing across school district boundaries unless each district had practiced racial discrimination or school district lines had been deliberately drawn to achieve racial segregation.[22] This ruling meant an end to large-scale school desegregation in metropolitan areas.

Legislative Efforts to Advance Civil Rights

The legislative branch of government, not just the courts, has been instrumental in advancing civil rights for African Americans. As we saw earlier, even after the Civil War amendments took their place in the Constitution, Congress enacted multiple civil rights acts to help reshape the post-war nation. Nearly a century later, due to the committed efforts of the civil rights movement to advance its cause, and sparked by the assassination of President John F. Kennedy, Congress adopted historic legislation in the 1960s that helped to give teeth to the Court's decisions in *Brown* and other cases. Some research has shown, for example, that it was legislative action, not just iconic battles before the Supreme Court, that marked the turning point for the advancement of civil rights for African Americans.[23]

In June 1963, two months before Martin Luther King, Jr.'s famous "I Have a Dream" speech at the Lincoln Memorial, President Kennedy asked Congress for legislation that would outlaw segregation in public accommodations. Congress had not yet enacted the president's bill when he was assassinated on November 22, 1963. His successor, Lyndon Johnson, considered civil rights his top legislative priority. Johnson masterfully used his previous congressional experience to overcome the considerable opposition to the legislation.[24] Within months, Congress enacted the Civil Rights Act of 1964, which included a vital provision barring segregation in most public accommodations.

Congress had enacted civil rights laws in 1957 and 1960, but they dealt primarily with voting rights. The 1964 act was the most comprehensive legislative attempt ever to erase racial discrimination in the United States. Among its many provisions, the act

- entitled all persons to "the full and equal enjoyment" of goods, services, and privileges in places of public accommodation, without discrimination on the grounds of race, color, religion, or national origin (the inclusion of "national origin" or place of birth would set in motion plans for immigration reform the following year);
- established the right to equality in employment opportunities;
- strengthened voting rights legislation;
- created the Equal Employment Opportunity Commission (EEOC) and charged it with hearing and investigating complaints of job discrimination;*
- and provided that funds could be withheld from federally assisted programs administered in a discriminatory manner.

That last provision had a powerful effect on school desegregation when Congress enacted the Elementary and Secondary Education Act (ESEA) in 1965, which still exists today as the Every Student Succeeds Act. The original ESEA provided billions of federal dollars for the nation's schools; the threat of losing that money spurred local school boards to formulate and implement new plans for desegregation.

The 1964 Civil Rights Act faced an immediate constitutional challenge. Its opponents argued that the Constitution does not forbid acts of private discrimination—the position the Supreme Court had affirmed in the late nineteenth century. But this time,

---

*Since 1972, the EEOC has had the power to institute legal proceedings on behalf of employees who allege that they have been victims of illegal discrimination.

a unanimous Court upheld the law, declaring that acts of discrimination impose substantial burdens on interstate commerce—a topic that the Constitution empowered Congress to regulate—and thus are subject to congressional control.[25]

In a companion case, Ollie McClung, the owner of a small restaurant, had refused to serve blacks. McClung maintained that he had the freedom to serve whomever he wanted in his own restaurant. The justices, however, upheld the government's prohibition of McClung's racial discrimination on the grounds that a substantial portion of the food served in his restaurant had moved in interstate commerce.[26] Thus, the Supreme Court vindicated the Civil Rights Act of 1964 by reason of the congressional power to regulate interstate commerce rather than on the basis of the Fourteenth Amendment.

The Civil Rights Act was one part of President Johnson's strategy to help America become a "great society" for all its people. Soon a constitutional amendment and additional civil rights laws were in place to support that goal:

- The Twenty-fourth Amendment, ratified in 1964, banned poll taxes in primary and general elections for national office.
- The Voting Rights Act of 1965 empowered the attorney general to send voter registration supervisors to areas in which fewer than half the eligible minority voters had been registered.
- The Fair Housing Act of 1968 banned discrimination in the rental and sale of most housing.

In the decades that followed, it became clear that civil rights laws on the books can help, but do not ensure civil rights in action. So legislators in subsequent sessions of Congress, sometimes with and sometimes without presidential support, have enacted additional measures extending and enhancing the laws that emerged from the Great Society era.

In 1988, Congress exercised its lawmaking power to check the law-interpreting power of the judiciary. Congress can revise national laws to counter judicial decisions; in this political chess game, the Court's move is hardly the last one.[27] Legislators protested that in *Grove City College* v. *Bell* (1984) the Court had misinterpreted the intent of antidiscrimination laws, and they forged a bipartisan effort to make legislative intent crystal clear: if any part of an institution gets federal money, no part of it can discriminate.[28] That meant that if a biology department at a university won federal grants, other departments, even if they did not benefit from federal funds, could not discriminate either. This work led to the Civil Rights Restoration Act, which became law in 1988 despite a presidential veto by Ronald Reagan.

Another new civil rights bill emerged a few years later. The Civil Rights Act of 1991 reversed or altered several Court decisions that had narrowed civil rights protections.[29] The new law clarified and expanded earlier legislation and increased the costs to employers for intentional, illegal discrimination.

More contemporary efforts have seen federal officials use these and other laws to defend the civil rights of African Americans. A vivid illustration emerged from the firestorm that erupted in Ferguson, Missouri, after police officer Darren Wilson shot and killed a black teenager, Michael Brown, on August 9, 2014.[30] Wilson ultimately was exonerated of any wrongdoing by a grand jury and a U.S. Department of Justice investigation. Yet Brown's killing sparked protests (some violent) in Ferguson and other cities around the nation. That motivated authorities to scrutinize more closely the conditions in Ferguson, where residents said the city routinely trampled upon the civil rights of African Americans. After a deeper look, the federal government agreed, finding patterns of invidious discrimination against blacks by the Ferguson police department and the city's municipal court that violated federal civil rights

Freedom, Order, or Equality: Enforcement of Order and Unequal Treatment

On October 20, 2014, Chicago police pursued Laquan McDonald, a seventeen-year-old African American youth, after he was reported to have been using a knife to break into vehicles. When the police arrived, McDonald ignored officers' requests to drop his knife and he continued walking down the middle of the street. As recorded in an interview with investigators after the evening, Officer Jason Van Dyke, who came to the scene and shot and killed McDonald, said that he had feared for his life because McDonald had violently attacked him.

Police video footage of the encounter, released thirteen months after the shooting, showed a different story. McDonald had not been violently attacking Van Dyke, but appeared to be in the street, actually veering away from the officer and his car. Van Dyke did, indeed, shoot McDonald, but after landing an initial shot that made McDonald collapse, Van Dyke continued firing. The officer fired fifteen additional shots while McDonald lay on the ground.

The release of the police video prompted protests and calls for the ouster of top city officials, including its police chief and the mayor. The video and further investigation eventually led a grand jury to indict Van Dyke on six counts of first-degree murder and one count of official misconduct. In April 2016, as the proceedings for Van Dyke's trial moved forward, the city released a Police Accountability Task Force Report. While acknowledging the outstanding work done by many dedicated officers on the force, the report nevertheless recognized a history of racism and racist encounters perpetrated by some Chicago police officers, actions that required an aggressive and multifaceted response, the report said.

Laquan McDonald appeared to have broken the law that night, yet even so, the overwhelming response from Van Dyke struck many observers as out of proportion to any potential crime that McDonald might have committed. This case and other examples, such as the longstanding experience of Ferguson, Missouri, residents (see discussion in this chapter) and Officer Michael Slager's actions in North Charleston, North Carolina, in 2015 (Slager also has been indicted for murder after he shot and killed a fleeing Walter Scott—a black man—allegedly planted evidence at the scene, and then lied about what happened) raise doubts about whether equal justice under the law exists for all Americans.

When police use force or other coercive means to uphold the law, their actions can prompt tensions between order and freedom. The experiences of Laquan McDonald, Walter Scott, and residents of Ferguson raise an additional issue. In managing the tensions between freedom and order, the police sometimes impose their powers in an unequal fashion. For example, although blacks report only slightly higher rates of marijuana usage than whites, blacks are arrested three times more frequently than whites for marijuana possession. In short, the evidence shows that some groups, typically racial minorities, receive unequal treatment in the dispute of freedom versus order. Those groups enjoy less freedom before order is imposed—sometimes violently, even—on their actions.

statutes and the First, Fourth, and Fourteenth Amendments. Justice Department officials eventually reached an agreement with Ferguson city officials designed to reform the city's police force and ensure that African Americans in the community receive equal treatment. Only time will tell whether the agreement has its intended effect.[31]

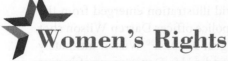

Women's Rights

LO3 Identify how the struggle for civil rights for women has progressed in ways similar to and different from that of African Americans.

The Supreme Court and Congress, once responsible for perpetuating inequality for blacks, have expanded the array of legal tools available to all minorities as they pursue equality. Women, too, have benefited from this change.

Laquan McDonald (middle of street) and Chicago police officers, moments before Officer Jason Van Dyke shot and killed McDonald

Chicago Police Department via AP

Sources: Wayne Drash, "The Killing of Laquan McDonald: The Dashcam Video Vs. Police Accounts," 19 December 2015, http://www.cnn.com/2015/12/17/us/laquan-mcdonald-video-records-comparison/; Steve Schmadeke, "Chicago Cop Indicted on 6 Murder Counts in Laquan McDonald Slaying," *Chicago Tribune*, 16 December 2015, http://www.chicagotribune.com/news/local/breaking/ct-jason-van-dyke-indicted-laquan-mcdonald-met-20151216-story.html; Michael S. Schmidt and Matt Apuzzo, "South Carolina Officer is Charged with Murder of Walter Scott," *New York Times*, 7 April 2015, http://www.nytimes.com/2015/04/08/us/south-carolina-officer-is-charged-with-murder-in-black-mans-death.html; Chicago Police Accountability Task Force, https://chicagopatf.org/; and Dylan Matthews, "The Black/White Marijuana Arrest Gap, in Nine Charts," *Washington Post*, 4 June 2013, https://www.washingtonpost.com/news/wonk/wp/2013/06/04/the-blackwhite-marijuana-arrest-gap-in-nine-charts/.

CRITICAL THINKING Numerous reforms have been proposed to ensure that police do not practice invidious discrimination when they enforce order in the nation's cities and other communities. Identify one of these reforms. Then explain why you believe it would be effective or ineffective.

Protectionism

Until the early 1970s, laws affecting women's civil rights were based on traditional views of the relationship between men and women. At the heart of these laws was protectionism—the notion that women must be sheltered from life's harsh realities. Thomas Jefferson believed, for example, that "were our state a pure democracy there would still be excluded from our deliberations women, who, to prevent deprivation of morals and ambiguity of issues, should not mix promiscuously in gatherings of men."[32] And "protected" they were, through laws that discriminated against them in employment and other areas. With few exceptions, women were also "protected" from voting until early in the twentieth century.

The demand for women's rights arose from the abolition movement and later was based primarily on the Fourteenth Amendment's prohibition of laws that "abridge the privileges or immunities of citizens of the United States." However, the courts consistently rebuffed challenges to protectionist state laws. In 1873, the Supreme Court upheld an Illinois statute that prohibited women from practicing law. The justices

protectionism
The notion that women must be protected from life's cruelties; until the 1970s, the basis for laws affecting women's civil rights.

maintained that the Fourteenth Amendment had no bearing on a state's authority to regulate admission of members to the bar.[33]

In 1908, the Court upheld an Oregon law limiting the number of hours women could work.[34] The decision was rife with assumptions about the nature and role of women, and it supported broad laws that "protected" the "weaker sex." It also prompted protectionist legislation that barred women from working more than forty-eight hours a week and from working at jobs that required them to lift more than thirty-five pounds. (The average work week for men was sixty hours or longer.) In effect, women were locked out of jobs that called for substantial overtime (and overtime pay) and were shunted to jobs that men believed suited their abilities.

Protectionism can take many forms. Some employers hesitate to place women at risk in the workplace. Some have excluded women of child-bearing age from jobs that involve exposure to toxic substances that could harm a developing fetus. Usually such jobs offer more pay to compensate for their higher risk. Although they too face reproductive risks from toxic substances, men have experienced no such exclusions.

In 1991, the Supreme Court struck down a company's fetal protection policy in strong terms. The Court relied on amendments to the 1964 Civil Rights Act providing for only a very few narrow exceptions to the principle that unless some workers differ from others in their ability to work, they must receive equal treatment as other employees. "In other words," declared the majority, "women as capable of doing their jobs as their male counterparts may not be forced to choose between having a child and having a job."[35]

Some versions of protectionism still exist. The abortion controversy, and the Supreme Court's upholding of the practice in *Roe* v. *Wade*, has prompted some states to enact laws that deter women from having abortions even though the procedure is legal. For example, several states require women seeking an abortion first to be shown images of developing fetuses, to hear about potential health risks associated with abortion, and, in some cases, to have a counseling session and then wait up to seventy-two hours before having the procedure. In 2016, waiting periods of some sort existed in twenty-eight states. Rather than having confidence that women will inform themselves about abortion, lawmakers in these states have assumed that women need to be protected from making uninformed choices about whether to terminate their pregnancies.[36]

Victory and Defeat in the Amendment Process

With a few exceptions, women were not allowed to vote in the United States until 1920. In 1869, Francis and Virginia Minor sued a St. Louis, Missouri, registrar for not allowing Virginia to vote. In 1875, the Supreme Court held that the Fourteenth Amendment's privileges and immunities clause did not confer the right to vote on all citizens or require that the states allow women to vote.[37]

The decision clearly slowed but did not stop the women's suffrage movement. In 1878, Susan B. Anthony, a women's rights activist, convinced a U.S. senator from California to introduce a constitutional amendment requiring that "the right of citizens of the United States to vote shall not be denied or abridged by the United States or by any State on account of sex." The amendment was introduced and voted down several times over the next twenty years. Meanwhile, a number of states, primarily in the Midwest and West, did grant limited suffrage to women (see Chapter 7).

The movement for women's suffrage became a political battle to amend the Constitution. In 1917, police arrested 218 women from twenty-six states when they picketed the White House, demanding the right to vote. Nearly one hundred went to jail, some for days and others for months.[38] The movement culminated in the adoption in 1920 of the **Nineteenth Amendment**, which gave women the right to vote. Its wording was that first suggested by Anthony.

Nineteenth Amendment
The amendment to the Constitution, adopted in 1920, that ensures women of the right to vote.

The National Women's Party, one of the few women's groups that remained active after the Nineteenth Amendment was enacted, introduced the proposed **equal rights amendment (ERA)** in 1923. The ERA declared that "equality of rights under the law shall not be denied or abridged by the United States or any State on account of sex." It remained bottled up in committee in every Congress until 1970, when Representative Martha Griffiths filed a discharge petition to bring it to the House floor for a vote, yet the effort still stalled.

A national coalition of women's rights advocates generated enough support to get the ERA through Congress in 1972. Its proponents then had seven years to get the amendment ratified by thirty-eight state legislatures, as the Constitution requires. By 1977, they were three states short of that goal, and three states had rescinded their earlier ratification. Then, in an unprecedented action, Congress extended the ratification deadline. It didn't help. The ERA died in 1982, still three states short of adoption.[39]

Despite its failure, the movement to ratify the ERA produced real benefits. It raised the consciousness of women about their social position, spurred more organizations to form that represented women's interests, contributed to women's participation in politics, and generated important legislation affecting women. As the next section describes, the failure to ratify the ERA stands in stark contrast to the quick enactment of many laws that now protect women's rights. And some scholars argue that for practical purposes, the Supreme Court has implemented the equivalent of the ERA through its decisions.[40] Still, the Supreme Court can reverse course and legislators can repeal statutes. Without an equal rights amendment, argue some advocates, the civil rights of women will lack adequate protection.[41]

equal rights amendment (ERA)
A failed constitutional amendment introduced by the National Women's Party in 1923, declaring that "equality of rights under the law shall not be denied or abridged by the United States or any State on account of sex."

Prohibiting Sex-Based Discrimination in the Workplace

Despite the ERA's repeated defeats, women's rights advocates leveraged the successes of the African American civil rights movement to win additional victories. If years of racial discrimination called for government redress, then so did years of sex discrimination. Furthermore, laws protecting women's rights required only the amending of civil rights bills or the enactment of similar bills.

The movement to provide equal rights to women advanced a step with the passage of the Equal Pay Act of 1963, which required equal pay for men and women doing similar work. Women had entered the workforce in significant numbers during World War I and again during World War II, but they received lower wages than the men they replaced. The justification was the "proper" role of women as mothers and homemakers. Because society expected men to be the principal providers, it followed that women's earnings were less important to the family's support. This thinking perpetuated inequalities in the workplace. Even with the Equal Pay Act, however, state protectionist laws still had the effect of restricting women to jobs that men usually did not want. Where employment was stratified by sex, equal pay was an empty promise. To remove the restrictions of protectionism, women needed equal opportunity for employment. They got it in the Civil Rights Act of 1964 and later legislation.

The objective of the Civil Rights Act of 1964 was to eliminate racial discrimination in America. The original wording of Title VII of the act prohibited employment discrimination based on race, color, religion, and national origin—but not gender. In an effort to scuttle the provision during House debate, Democrat Howard Smith of Virginia proposed an amendment barring job discrimination based on sex. Smith's intention was to make the law unacceptable. His effort to ridicule the law brought gales of laughter to the debate. But Democrat Martha Griffiths of Michigan used Smith's strategy against him. With her support, Smith's amendment carried, as did the act.[42] Congress extended the jurisdiction of the EEOC to cover cases of invidious sex discrimination, or sexism. Another related boost to women came from the Revenue Act of 1972, which provided tax credits for child-care expenses. In effect, the act subsidized parents with young children so that women could enter or remain in the workforce.

Still, progress sometimes stalled, as in 2007, when the Supreme Court tightened the rules over pay discrimination lawsuits under Title VII of the Civil Rights Act.[43] The case involved a woman who did not learn of the pay disparity with sixteen men in her office until years later because salary information was kept secret. But the law required her to file a complaint within 180 days of when her pay was set. The 5–4 decision prompted a bitter oral dissent by Justice Ruth Bader Ginsburg. True to the pluralist character of American democracy, the Obama administration and a Democratic Congress reversed the 2007 decision by passing the Lilly Ledbetter Fair Pay Act, named for the woman whom the Supreme Court had ruled against. It was the first bill that President Obama signed into law upon taking office in 2009. The act allows the filing of complaints beyond the 180-day period.[44] Despite that advance, women's wages still suffer compared to those of men. Data from the U.S. Department of Labor, reported in Figure 16.1, show weekly median earnings in ten professions that employ large numbers of women. The results illustrate that women receive less pay than men for every single profession. The largest disparity shown is in financial management, where women earn 67.4 percent of what men do.

FIGURE 16.1 **Median Weekly Earnings of Women and Men in Occupations with Large Numbers of Women Employees, 2014**

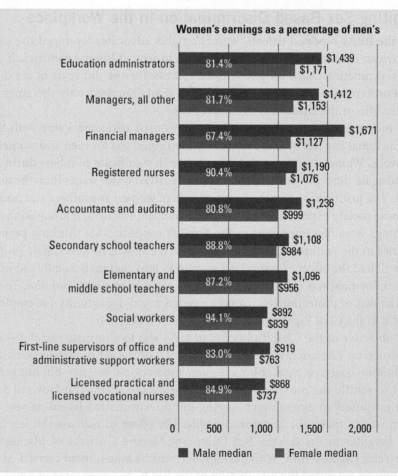

Despite legislative and courtroom victories to secure civil rights in the workplace, women still earn less money than men across different professions.

Source: U.S. Department of Labor, "Most Common Occupations for Women," Chart 2, https://www.dol.gov/wb/stats/most_common_occupations_for_women.htm.

Women's earnings as a percentage of men's

Occupation	Women's %	Male median	Female median
Education administrators	81.4%	$1,439	$1,171
Managers, all other	81.7%	$1,412	$1,153
Financial managers	67.4%	$1,671	$1,127
Registered nurses	90.4%	$1,190	$1,076
Accountants and auditors	80.8%	$1,236	$999
Secondary school teachers	88.8%	$1,108	$984
Elementary and middle school teachers	87.2%	$1,096	$956
Social workers	94.1%	$892	$839
First-line supervisors of office and administrative support workers	83.0%	$919	$763
Licensed practical and licensed vocational nurses	84.9%	$868	$737

■ Male median ■ Female median

Additional Stereotypes Under Scrutiny

The workplace is not the only arena where women have won important civil rights battles. In 1971, for example, the Supreme Court struck down a protectionist state law that gave men preference over women in administering the estate of a person who died without naming an administrator.[45] The state maintained that the law reduced court workloads and avoided family battles; however, the Court dismissed those objections because they were not important enough to justify making gender-based distinctions between individuals. Two years later, the justices declared that paternalism operated to "put women not on a pedestal, but in a cage."[46] They then proceeded to strike down several laws that either prevented or discouraged departures from traditional sex roles. In 1976, the Court finally developed a workable standard for reviewing such laws: gender-based distinctions are justifiable only if they serve some important government purpose.[47] The objective of the standard is to dismantle laws based on sexual stereotypes while fashioning public policies that acknowledge relevant differences between men and women.

AP Images/Elaine Thompson

IMAGE 16.2 Champion on the Field, Loser on Payday

Carli Lloyd, captain of team USA, scored three goals—the third was a blast from mid-field that soared over Japan's stunned goalkeeper—to help the United States win the Women's World Cup final in 2015. Despite the team's frequent success, players still are paid less than players on the men's national team. That prompted Lloyd and other teammates to file a federal wage discrimination complaint against U.S. Soccer, the organization that runs the national teams. Hope Solo, the team's star goalkeeper, noted that the women's squad had won three World Cups and four Olympic gold medals, yet players on the men's team "get paid more to just show up than we get paid to win major championships." Tim Howard, who is Solo's counterpart in goal on the men's team, threw his support behind the effort encourging the women to "fight for their rights."

Sources: Andrew Das, "Top Female Players Accuse U.S. Soccer of Wage Discrimination," *New York Times*, 31 March 2016, http://www.nytimes.com/2016/04/01/sports/soccer/uswnt-us-women-carli-lloyd-alex-morgan-hope-solo-complain.html; and Joe Prince-Wright, "USMNT's Howard: We Support UWSNT's Concerns in Equal Pay Fight," NBC Sports, 31 March 2016, soccer.nbcsports.com/2016/03/31/usmnts-howard-we-support-uswnts-concerns-in-equal-pay-fight.

Further, the courts have extended to women constitutional guarantees won by blacks. In 1994, the Supreme Court extended the Constitution's equal protection guarantee by forbidding the exclusion of potential jurors on the basis of their sex. In a 6–3 decision, the justices held that it is unconstitutional to use gender, and likewise race, as a criterion for determining juror competence and impartiality. "Discrimination in jury selection," wrote Justice Harry Blackmun for the majority, "whether based on race or on gender, causes harm to the litigants, the community, and the individual jurors who are wrongfully excluded."[48] The 1994 decision completed a constitutional revolution in jury selection that began in 1986 with a bar against juror exclusions based on race.

Finally, one of the most important arenas where women have made advances, and by some measures even overtaken men, is in education. A key law that has helped women progress in this area is Title IX of the Education Amendments of 1972, which prohibited sex discrimination in federally aided education programs. People often associate that law with equalizing the athletic opportunities for both sexes, but it actually touches on all aspects of educational life to ensure equality of opportunity.[49]

In 1996, the Court spoke with uncommon clarity when it declared that the men-only admissions policy of the Virginia Military Institute (VMI), a state-supported military college, violated the equal protection clause of the Fourteenth Amendment. Virginia defended the school's policy on the grounds that it was preserving diversity among America's educational institutions. Instead, Virginia established a separate-but-equal institution, the Virginia Women's Institute for Leadership (VWIL). The program was housed at Mary Baldwin College, a private liberal arts college for women, and students enrolled in VWIL received the same financial support as students at VMI. Was the uniqueness of VMI worth preserving at the expense of women who could otherwise meet the academic, physical, and psychological stress imposed by the VMI approach?

In a 7–1 decision, the Supreme Court said no. Writing for the majority in **United States** v. **Virginia,** Justice Ruth Bader Ginsburg applied a demanding test she labeled "skeptical scrutiny" to official acts that deny individuals rights or responsibilities based on their sex. "Parties who seek to defend gender-based government action," she wrote, "must demonstrate an 'exceedingly persuasive justification' for that action." Ginsburg declared that "women seeking and fit for a VMI-quality education cannot be offered anything less, under the State's obligation to afford them genuinely equal protection."[50] The upshot is that distinctions based on sex are almost as suspect as distinctions based on race. Three months after the Court's decision, VMI's board of directors finally voted 9–8 to admit women.[51]

In part due to Title IX and other efforts in the courts and legislatures, women, who used to lag behind their male peers in degree attainment, now have surpassed men. Consider, for example, that in 1980, among people twenty-five to twenty-nine years of age in the United States, 24.0 percent of men had earned bachelor's degrees or higher compared to 21.0 percent of women. By 2015, the trend had reversed with 38.9 percent of women of that same age bracket compared to 32.4 percent of men possessing a bachelor's or more advanced degree.[52] Despite those advances, inequities remain in other aspects of American life for the nation's women on more mundane, but nevertheless important matters. Figure 16.2 shows how state taxation policies treat women's personal health needs differently than others, for example.

Equality for Gay People

LO4 Describe the victories won and challenges remaining for advocates of expanding civil rights protections for gay people.

Numerous advances in civil rights for gay Americans have occurred in recent years. Yet the seeds of this movement were sown many decades ago, emerging out of the same era that saw African Americans and women win victories of their own.

Fringe Movement to Mainstream

June 27, 1969, marked the symbolic beginning of an often overlooked movement for civil rights in the United States. On that Friday evening, plainclothes New York City police officers raided a gay bar in Greenwich Village known as the Stonewall Inn. The police justified the raid because they suspected that Stonewall lacked a proper liquor license. In response, citizens protested in the streets. Violent clashes and a backlash against the police involving hundreds of people ensued for several nights, during which cries of "Gay power!" and "We want freedom!" could be heard. The event became known as the Stonewall Riots and served as the touchstone for the gay liberation movement in the United States.[53]

Native Americans

During the eighteenth and nineteenth centuries, the U.S. government took American Indian lands, isolated Native Americans on reservations, and denied them political and social rights. The government's dealings with them were often marked by violence and broken promises. The agencies responsible for administering Indian reservations kept Native Americans poor and dependent on the national government.

Federal officials switched policies at the beginning of the twentieth century, promoting assimilation instead of separation, yet remaining indifferent to Native Americans' civil rights. The government banned the use of native languages and religious rituals; it sent Indian children to boarding schools and gave them non-Indian names. In 1924, though, American Indians received U.S. citizenship. Until that time, they had been considered members of tribal nations whose relations with the U.S. government were determined by treaties. Today, Native Americans make up less than 1 percent of the population.[64]

Anger bred of poverty, unemployment, and frustration with an uncaring government—all of which produced unequal opportunities and outcomes for Native Americans—exploded in militant action in late 1969, when several American Indians seized Alcatraz Island, an abandoned island in San Francisco Bay. The group cited an 1868 Sioux treaty that entitled them to unused federal lands, and they remained on the island for a year and a half. In 1973, armed members of the American Indian Movement seized eleven hostages at Wounded Knee, South Dakota, the site of an 1890 massacre of two hundred Sioux (Lakota) by U.S. cavalry troops. They remained there, occasionally exchanging gunfire with federal marshals, for seventy-one days, until the government agreed to examine the treaty rights of the Oglala Sioux.[65]

In 1946, Congress had enacted legislation establishing an Indian claims commission to compensate Native Americans for land that had been taken from them. In the 1970s, the Native American Rights Fund and other groups used that legislation to win important victories in the courts. The tribes won the return of lands in the Midwest and in the states of Oklahoma, New Mexico, and Washington. In 1980, the Supreme Court ordered the national government to pay the Sioux $117 million plus interest for the Black Hills of South Dakota, which had been stolen from them a century before.[66]

The special status accorded American Indian tribes in the Constitution has proved attractive to a new group of Indian leaders. Some of the nearly 600 recognized tribes have successfully instituted casino gambling on their reservations, even while facing some state opposition to their plans. The tribes pay no

Congressman Tom Cole

IMAGE 16.4 Not Just Cheap Talk

Although the struggle for Native American civil rights has been an uphill battle, Native Americans have been instrumental in helping to protect the civil rights and civil liberties of all Americans. Congressman Tom Cole (Rep., Oklahoma, pictured at center), a member of the Chicksaw Nation, is one of two Native Americans serving in the U.S. House. Cole appears here in 2013 at a celebration awarding of the Congressional Gold Medal, the highest civilian honor awarded by the national legislature, to commemorate the military service of 33 Native American tribes in World Wars I and II. The tribes provided a valuable service as code talkers who used their Native American languages, which the nation's enemies were unable to translate, to help transmit sensitive messages to American forces and their allies.

taxes on their profits, which has helped them make gambling a powerful engine of economic growth for themselves and has given a once impoverished people undreamed-of riches and responsibilities. Congress has allowed these developments, provided that the tribes spend their profits on Indian assistance programs. In contemporary politics, the evidence shows that despite their continued struggles against poverty and other difficulties, Native Americans have made important strides and have become more potent advocates for their interests and rights.[67]

Immigrant Groups

The Statue of Liberty, a gift from the French to commemorate the American centennial, is a national icon that embodies the belief that the country is a beacon of liberty for countless immigrants far and wide. Although the United States often is called a nation of immigrants, until 1965 the laws that governed immigration were rooted in invidious discrimination.

For most of the first half of the twentieth century, immigration rules established a strict quota system that gave a clear advantage to Northern and Western Europeans and guaranteed that few Southern or Eastern Europeans, Asians, Africans, and Jews would enter the country by legal means. This paralleled the invidious discrimination that had subjugated blacks since the end of the Civil War. In the same spirit that championed civil rights for African Americans, a once-reluctant Congress changed the rules to end discrimination on the basis of national origin. In 1965, President Lyndon Johnson signed a new immigration bill into law at the Statue of Liberty. Henceforth, the invidious quota system was gone; everyone was supposed to have an equal chance of immigrating to the United States. Upon signing the bill, Johnson remarked that there was nothing revolutionary about the law. "It will not reshape the structure of our daily lives or add importantly to either our wealth or our power." Within a few years, Johnson's prediction proved fundamentally wrong.[68]

One purpose of the new law was to reunite families. It gave preference to relatives of immigrants already here, but since the vast majority of these legal immigrants came from Northern or Western Europe, the expectation was that reuniting families would continue the earlier preferences. Another provision gave preference in much smaller numbers to immigrants with coveted skills, such as doctors and engineers. It never occurred to the law's designers that African doctors, Indian engineers, Philippine nurses, or Chinese software programmers would be able to immigrate. Word trickled out to those newly eligible to come. Once here, these immigrants petitioned for their relatives to join them. And those family members petitioned for yet others. As a result of this "chain migration," entire extended families established themselves in the United States.

In addition to legislative changes, historical and more contemporary decisions of the U.S. Supreme Court have helped to shape the immigrant experience in the United States. In the nineteenth century, for example, the Supreme Court considered the case of *Yick Wo* v. *Hopkins* (1886). At that time, the city government in San Francisco had written an ordinance requiring laundries operating in wooden buildings to obtain a permit. The Board of Supervisors was responsible for issuing the permits, which it did in ways that the petitioner argued violated the equal protection clause of the Fourteenth Amendment. The numbers appeared to favor that position: no Chinese owners received a permit even though they operated approximately nine out of ten laundries in the city. The unanimous court was easily persuaded that the city's unequal enforcement of the ordinance violated Yick Wo's rights.[69]

Nearly a century later, in *Lau* v. *Nichols* (1974), another unanimous Supreme Court held that the Civil Rights Act of 1964 required that schools provide linguistic accommodations for students who were still learning English but nevertheless were enrolled in the nation's public schools. The case also arose in San Francisco, where the Court heard arguments showing that approximately 2,800 students of Chinese ancestry who did not speak English attended the public schools, yet 1,800 received no supplemental courses in English to help them learn the language. The Court found that unacceptable.[70] The *Lau* decision has had important implications for the education of children of all backgrounds, especially Hispanics, who comprise more than 75 percent of English-language learners in the nation's public schools.[71]

The civil rights of language minorities, with additionally large implications for Hispanics, also were addressed in a 1975 adjustment to the Civil Rights Act, signed into law by Republican president Gerald Ford. Those revisions, and subsequent changes in other years, required certain jurisdictions to provide voter materials, including registration information, ballot instructions, and ballots themselves, in languages other than English. The requirements applied to jurisdictions with a certain threshold of voters who had limited proficiency in English. As a result of these changes to the Voting Rights Act, for example, jurisdictions within twenty-five states are required to develop these materials, with Hispanics being the main language minority whose needs are addressed by the act's implementation.[72]

As an issue in contemporary American politics, immigration, and especially illegal immigration from Latin America, has frustrated ordinary citizens and elected officials alike. People on all sides of this issue—including advocates for undocumented immigrants and those who favor stricter border security—realize that the nation's policies are broken, and its polarized politics have been unable to find a remedy. As we described in Chapter 4, the Supreme Court weighed in during 2012 on Arizona's attempt to increase immigration enforcement, SB 1070, and civil rights advocates continue to monitor's the state's implementation of the parts of that law, especially its "show me your papers" provision that the Supreme Court let stand.[73]

Given current demographic trends in the United States, Hispanics will continue becoming an increasingly important group in the nation's pluralist political system. Already, they occupy positions of power in national and local arenas, including a seat on the Supreme Court, with President Obama's appointment of Sonia Sotomayor in 2009. The Census Bureau estimates that by 2050, one-third of all residents will be Hispanic. With such growth will come greater political power and, undoubtedly, increased attention to the civil rights afforded to this burgeoning segment of society.[74]

Americans with Disabilities

The status of being a legal or numeric minority is not confined to racial and ethnic groups. After more than two decades of struggle, 43 million Americans with disabilities gained recognition in 1990 as a protected minority with the enactment of the Americans with Disabilities Act (ADA). The law extends the protections embodied in the Civil Rights Act of 1964 to people with physical or mental disabilities, including people with AIDS, alcoholism, and drug addiction. It guarantees them access to employment, transportation, public accommodations, and communication services. Nearly two decades before the ADA became law, schoolchildren with disabilities had earned protections of their own in a different statute. That law, which today is known as the Individuals with Disabilities Education Act, provides federal funds and a mechanism for families of students with disabilities to sue in court to ensure that their civil rights in schools are protected.[75]

The roots of the movement to extend rights to Americans with disabilities stem from the period after World War II. Thousands of disabled veterans returned to a country and a society that were insensitive to their needs. Institutionalization seemed the best way to care for people with disabilities, but this approach came under increasing fire as people with disabilities and their families sought care at home.

Advocates for persons with disabilities found a ready model in the existing civil rights laws. Opponents argued that the changes mandated by the 1990 ADA, such as access for those confined to wheelchairs, could cost billions of dollars. Supporters replied that the costs would be offset by an equal or greater reduction in federal aid to people with disabilities, who would rather be working.[76]

The law's enactment set off an avalanche of job discrimination complaints filed with the national government's discrimination watchdog agency, the EEOC. From 1997 to 2013, the EEOC received about 19,000 ADA-related complaints annually. Curiously, most complaints came from already employed people, both previously and recently disabled. They charged that their employers failed to provide reasonable accommodations as the law required. The disabilities cited most frequently were back problems, mental illness, heart trouble, neurological disorders, and substance abuse.[77]

A deceptively simple question lies at the heart of many ADA suits: What is the meaning of *disability*? According to the EEOC, a disability is "a physical or mental impairment that substantially limits one or more major life activities." This deliberately vague language has thrust the courts into the role of providing needed specificity, and Congress has continued to update the law.[78] In 2008, it revised the ADA and increased protections for people with disabilities by making it easier for workers to prove discrimination. The ADA Amendments Act of 2008 protects people with epilepsy, diabetes, cancer, cerebral palsy, multiple sclerosis, and other ailments. Federal court decisions previously had denied protection under the ADA because the disabling conditions were controlled by medication or were in remission.

Civil rights advocates predict that bias against people with disabilities, like similar biases against other minorities, will wither as they continue to make legal progress and their abilities, rather than their apparent limitations, are more recognized by others. Every October, the United States commemorates their contributions by celebrating National Disability Employment Awareness Month. For 2016, the U.S. Department of Labor estimated that nearly 5.6 million Americans with disabilities were employed in the country's civilian labor force, compelling evidence that the nation benefits when as many of its people as possible are provided with opportunities to excel.[79]

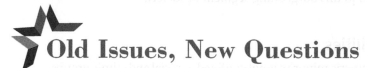

Old Issues, New Questions

LO6 Analyze how contemporary debates about civil rights push new boundaries but have roots in earlier eras.

Just as the overall story of the United States is written each day, so, too, does the nation's pursuit of equality continue to unfold. Sometimes old issues take new forms and raise new questions about the meaning of equality and its tension with other values like freedom.

Racial Equality in Contemporary America

It is undeniable that the United States has made substantial progress in dismantling constitutional and legal barriers that for the majority of American history prevented African Americans from becoming full citizens. Despite overcoming these invidious traditions of America's past, it may be that the easiest battles have been won. Overt racist policies such as the constitutional endorsement of slavery and the black codes were easy for civil rights advocates to identify and target, and with much work, ultimately dismantle. More work remains in numerous areas of American life, as previous discussion in this chapter regarding equality in the nation's criminal justice system illustrates.

The Supreme Court continues to consider such matters. In 2016, for example, an often divided Court nevertheless held 7–1 that Timothy Tyrone Foster, a black man convicted of murder in 1987 and on death row in Georgia, should be allowed to seek a new trial because prosecutors in his case used race as a criterion to strike jurors from the courtroom trial. "Two peremptory strikes on the basis of race are two more than the Constitution allows," argued Chief Justice Roberts in the majority opinion. The case also illustrates the challenge of discovering and then providing remedies in such instances. The fact that prosecutors used race as an unconstitutional criterion to strike potential jurors was only discovered because handwritten notes from prosecutors, which were three decades old, existed and were obtained by Foster's lawyers.[80]

Additionally, college campuses, a hotbed of civil rights activism during the 1960s, provide venues where civil rights advocates have pressed on. The University of Missouri provides a recent example. In 2015, Jonathan Butler was a graduate student at Mizzou (where he also studied as an undergraduate) when he began a hunger strike to protest university leaders whom he and others believed were indifferent to racism. Butler recalled in an interview that he "felt unsafe" upon arriving to campus and that "My first semester here I had someone write the n-word on my wall."[81]

In his letter announcing the hunger strike, Butler called for the university's Board of Curators to fire university president Tim Wolfe. Butler identified examples of racism on campus, beyond his own personal experiences, and reasoned that students could not "achieve their full academic potential because of the inequalities and obstacles they face."[82] Earlier that fall, tensions had been building as protestors had confronted university officials over racist acts on campus. A specific set of demands, issued from a group called Concerned Student 1950—named to commemorate the first year that black students were admitted to the university—called for, among other things, the development of new courses to address racism and inclusion.

Wolfe attempted to respond, admitting that "Racism does exist at our university and it is unacceptable," but his words were not enough to prevent several members of the Missouri football team, black and white, from announcing they would not play until Wolfe was no longer president. Mizzou's coach, Gary Pinkel, supported those players. The next day, Wolfe resigned, and Butler ended his hunger strike.[83]

Voting Rights

Since Florida's recount of the vote in the 2000 presidential election, contemporary elections have become nail-biting affairs, and getting people out to vote matters perhaps more than ever. Today's emphasis on voting has rekindled concerns about the need to protect voting rights, especially for the nation's minority and poor citizens. At issue are recent state policies designed to address voter fraud.[84]

Supporters of these policies, who tend to be Republicans, justify laws requiring people to show official identification—and other related measures—before voting as helping to ensure the integrity of the electoral process. Fraudulent elections are illegitimate, they say, and governments should work hard to ensure that every vote counted is a proper vote. Some evidence does show that gaps exist in the voter registration process that could invite potential fraud. The Pew Center on the States, for example, found that approximately 1.8 million deceased people are listed as voters on state registration rolls, and around 12 million voter registration records list an incorrect address.[85]

IMAGE 16.5   Activism Off the Gridiron

University of Missouri head football coach Gary Pinkel took to social media to express support for students and other protestors who called for the ouster of university president Tim Wolfe. The Mizzou players and coaches pictured here embraced a long tradition of sports figures engaging in civil rights activism. Previous examples include Jackie Robinson, who was signed to the Brooklyn Dodgers by Branch Rickey and subsequently broke baseball's color barrier in 1947, and tennis legend Billie Jean King, winner of thirty-nine grand slam titles on the women's professional tennis tour, who famously defeated Bobby Riggs in the "battle of the sexes" tennis match in 1973.

Critics of these measures, typically Democrats, fire back that concerns about voter fraud mask other motives. They argue there is little evidence that voter fraud exists and what fraud might exist is so minor that it would not change the outcome of elections or threaten the overall voting process. The inaccuracy of state voter rolls does not mean that these errors are altering the results of elections. The real point of these laws, critics say, is to deny potential voters their civil rights, which would have the effect of reducing turnout of black, Hispanic, and poor voters who often tend to support Democrats in state and national elections.

Even though the act of showing a valid ID on election day may be relatively easy, obtaining an ID might be more difficult for some individuals. Elderly people, for example, may lack official copies of required documents like birth certificates. Alternatively, obtaining an ID may require visiting a state department of motor vehicles during regular business hours. This can be difficult for people who lack adequate transportation or work multiple jobs, especially when these offices are located many miles away. Because efforts to minimize these hurdles tend not to accompany new efforts to reduce voter fraud, critics suggest ulterior motives are at work. Supporters answer that these are not unreasonable burdens given the importance of voting to the nation's republican system of government.

Contemporary debates about voter ID laws bear on freedom, order, and equality. States, not the national government, administer elections. And the United States does not require all citizens to carry a common national ID card. Such a policy, as exists in many European countries, could enhance order, but it stokes fears that federal officials could use such a master database to undermine freedom. With the states in charge of voter ID, then, concerns about equity enter the picture for the reasons described above. Elections in which all voters showed a valid picture ID would be more orderly, but that could come at the cost of excluding voters in non-random ways, potentially undermining equity.

Gender Identity

Members of the *transgender* community and their allies have become increasingly active and vocal participants in contemporary debates about civil rights and the lengths to which the nation must go to ensure that all people receive equal treatment. Transgender individuals are people who identify with a gender that does not correspond to their biological sex identified at birth. A transgender man, then, would be a person deemed a female at birth who now identifies as male, and a transgender woman wound be a person deemed a male at birth who now identifies as female. (A related term, *cisgender*, refers to individuals whose gender identity corresponds to their biological sex.)

Although debates about the civil rights of transgender people have been fast moving, in 2015 and 2016 they made national headlines over a somewhat mundane, but fundamentally human issue: the need of all people to use the bathroom. Transgender rights supporters believe that people should be able to use the bathroom that corresponds to the gender with which they identify—they consider bathroom usage as a matter of gender identity and not biological sex. Those who disagree say that people should use the bathroom that corresponds to the sex that appears on their birth certificate. The dispute is a classic case of equality versus order. Transgender people argue that requiring them to use a bathroom at odds with their identities forces them (but not others) to be someone who they are not, a threat to equity, whereas their opponents see potential threats to order if biological men use women's bathrooms and biological women use men's bathrooms.

The stakes in these debates have been high, and the future remains uncertain. For example, in 2016, North Carolina adopted House Bill 2, the Public Facilities Privacy and Security Act, which prohibited people from using bathrooms that do not correspond to their biological sex. The law was in part a response to a local policy adopted by the city of Charlotte that had enabled transgender people to use bathrooms that correspond to their gender identity. The bill prompted swift responses from allies of transgender people, including the company PayPal, which cancelled plans to open a new facility in the state that would have created 400 new jobs. Award-winning musician Bruce Springsteen and his E Street Band cancelled a concert that was slated for the state, issuing ticket refunds to those hoping to attend the show. A statement by Springsteen called transgender advocates "freedom fighters" and supported their battle for "human rights."[86]

Equality of Opportunity or Outcome, or Both?

The vignette about Abigail Fisher that opened this chapter reveals one of the deeper challenges that American democracy faces as we peer into the future. During its history, the country has dismantled many formal barriers to equality, but even with those advances disparities in outcomes between groups, as this chapter has shown, still remain. Addressing these issues is difficult because in many instances they will require more than simply removing a law that produces obvious invidious discrimination. Reducing inequity in outcomes, while still allowing individuals to succeed, is perhaps a harder problem to solve, and it presents an enduring tension between freedom and equality.

Preferential Policies in Global Politics

Americans are not alone in their disagreements over preferential policies. Controversies, even bloodshed, have arisen where the government treats certain groups of citizens preferentially. Of course, countries vary in terms of who benefits from such policies, what types of benefits are bestowed, and even the names of the policies. In India, such policies carry the label "positive discrimination."

Although India is the world's largest democracy, its society is rigidly stratified into groups called castes. The government forbids caste-based discrimination, but members of the lower castes (the lowest being the Dalits, or "untouchables") were historically restricted to the least prestigious and lowest-paying jobs. To improve their status, India has set aside government jobs for the lower castes, which make up half of India's population of 1.2 billion. India now reserves a certain percentage of government jobs for the lower castes and additional ones for untouchables and remote tribe members. Gender equality has also improved since a 1993 constitutional amendment that set aside one-third of all seats in local government councils for women.

Positive discrimination in India has intensified tensions between the lower and upper castes. In 1990, soon after the new quotas were established, scores of young upper-caste men and women set themselves ablaze in protest. And when Indian courts issued a temporary injunction against the positive discrimination policies, lower-caste terrorists bombed a train and killed dozens of people. Adding further strain, a 2010 proposal to create a one-third set-aside for women in the parliament and state legislatures met stiff resistance from the political parties representing the lower castes. The Dalits viewed the proposal as a threat to their monopoly quota. Lower-caste women opposed the idea while feminists from higher-caste parties supported it.

The issue in India is not the use of quotas but which group should benefit from them, as quotas have become a fact of life. In 2016, violent protests over access to quotas in India's Haryana State killed nineteen people and temporarily cut off water supplies. At issue were grievances from members of the Jat caste, who had believed they were to receive status as a "backward" caste group and join more than 2,000 other groups that are so recognized. This would have conferred upon them special status for government hiring and other benefits. Critics charged that the Jat caste is relatively advantaged and so did not merit special treatment.

All governments broker conflict to varying degrees. Under a majoritarian model, group demands could lead quickly to conflict and instability because majority rule leaves little room for compromise. A pluralist model allows different groups to get a piece of the pie. By parceling out benefits, pluralism mitigates disorder in the short term. But in the long term, repeated demands for increased benefits can spark instability. A vigorous pluralist system should provide acceptable mechanisms (legislative, executive, bureaucratic, judicial) to vent such frustrations and yield new allocations of benefits.

affirmative action
Any of a wide range of programs, from special recruitment efforts to numerical quotas, aimed at expanding opportunities for women and minority groups.

In his vision of a Great Society, President Johnson linked economic rights with civil rights and equality of outcome with equality of opportunity. Equal opportunity was not enough, he believed. "We seek not just legal equity but human ability, not just equality as a right and a theory but equality as a fact and equality as a result," Johnson said.[87] This commitment led to **affirmative action** programs, which are efforts by government or another organizations to expand opportunities for women, blacks, Hispanics, and members of other groups, such as veterans.

Affirmative action aims to overcome the effects of present and past discrimination, or disadvantages that certain groups must confront. It embraces a range of public and private programs, policies, and procedures, including special recruitment, preferential treatment, and in some forms even numeric goals in job training and professional education, employment, and the awarding of government contracts. The point of these programs is to move beyond equality of opportunity to equality of outcome.

Advocates on both sides of the affirmative action debate raise good points.[88] Proponents of affirmative action programs tend to argue that certain groups have

REUTERS/Anindito Mukherjee

A tanker truck provides emergency water to residents of New Delhi after Jat protests in early 2016 blocked canals that provided water to millions of the city's people.

Sources: Ramachandra Guha, *India After Gandhi: The History of the World's Largest Democracy* (HarperCollins: New York, 2008); Stuart Corbridge, John Harriss, and Craig Jeffrey, *India Today: Economy, Politics, and Society* (Polity Press: Cambridge, UK, 2013); Press Trust of India, "About a Million Women Elected to Local Bodies in India," 10 February 2004; Somini Sengupta, "Quotas to Aid India's Poor vs. Push for Meritocracy," *New York Times*, 23 May 2006, p. A3; "Caste in Doubt," *The Economist*, 12 June 2010, p. 46; Gardiner Harris, "With Affirmative Action, India's Rich Gain School Slots Meant for Poor," *New York Times*, 8 October 2012, p. A4; and Geeta Anand and Nida Najar, "Haryana State in India Proposes New Caste Status in Bid to Quell Protests," *New York Times*, 22 February 2016, p. A4.

CRITICAL THINKING Preferential policies have at times threatened to disrupt order in rigidly stratified societies. Yet without aggressive reforms, such as preferences, inequities are likely to persist for many years. Are quotas inevitable in these kinds of situations, or might other policies produce better results?

historically suffered invidious discrimination—treatment that sometimes continues today—denying them educational and economic opportunities. To eliminate the effects of such discrimination, the public and private sectors must take action. If the majority once discriminated to hold groups back, discriminating to benefit those groups now is fair. Affirmative action opponents maintain that some of these efforts, especially quotas for designated groups, necessarily create invidious discrimination (in the form of reverse discrimination) against individuals who are themselves blameless. Moreover, they say, such policies lead to the admission, hiring, or promotion of the less qualified at the expense of the well qualified. In the name of equality, such policies thwart individuals' freedom to succeed.

The Supreme Court confronted an affirmative action quota program for the first time in **Regents of the University of California v. Bakke**.[89] Allan Bakke, a thirty-five-year-old white man, had twice applied for admission to the University of California Medical School at Davis and was rejected both times. As part of the university's affirmative action program, the school had reserved sixteen places in each entering class of one hundred for qualified minority applicants. Bakke's academic qualifications exceeded those of all the minority students admitted in the two years his applications were rejected, which he said violated his rights under the Fourteenth Amendment and the Civil Rights Act.

The Court's decision in *Bakke* contained six opinions and spanned 154 pages, but no opinion commanded a majority. Despite the confusing multiple opinions, the Court struck down the school's rigid use of racial quotas, thus admitting Bakke, and it approved of affirmative action programs in education that use race as a plus factor (one of many such factors) but not as the sole factor. Thus, the Court managed to minimize white opposition to the goal of equality (by finding for Bakke) while extending gains for racial minorities through affirmative action.

By 2003—twenty-five years after *Bakke*—the Supreme Court reexamined affirmative action in two cases, both challenging aspects of the University of Michigan's racial preferences policies. In *Gratz v. Bollinger*, the Court considered the university's undergraduate admissions policy, which conferred 20 points automatically to members of favored groups (100 total points guaranteed admission). In a 6–3 opinion, Chief Justice William Rehnquist argued that such a policy violated the equal protection clause because it lacked the narrow tailoring required for permissible racial preferences and it failed to provide for individualized consideration of each candidate.[90]

In the second case, *Grutter v. Bollinger*, the Court considered the University of Michigan's law school admissions policy, which gave preference to minority applicants with lower GPAs and standardized test scores. This time, the Court, in a 5–4 decision authored by Justice Sandra Day O'Connor, held that the equal protection clause did not bar the school's narrowly tailored use of racial preferences to further a compelling interest that flowed from a racially diverse student body. Since each applicant is judged individually on his or her merits, race remains only one among many factors that determine the admissions decision.[91]

The issue of race-based classifications in education arose again in 2007 when parents challenged voluntary school integration plans based on race in *Parents Involved in Community Schools* v. *Seattle School District No. 1*. Chief Justice John G. Roberts, Jr., writing for the 5–4 majority on a bitterly divided bench, invalidated the plans, declaring that the programs were "directed only to racial balance, pure and simple," which the equal protection clause of the Fourteenth Amendment forbids. "The way to stop discrimination on the basis of race is to stop discriminating on the basis of race," he said. Still, Justice Anthony Kennedy, who cast the fifth and deciding vote, wrote separately to say that achieving racial diversity and avoiding racial isolation were "compelling interests" that schools could constitutionally pursue as long as they "narrowly tailored" their programs to avoid racial labeling and sorting of individual children. Justice Stephen Breyer, writing for the minority and speaking from the bench, used pointed language, declaring, "This is a decision that the Court and the nation will come to regret."[92]

Whether Breyer's prediction will come true is difficult to foresee. What the justices' disagreements in the Court's affirmative action decisions illustrate, though, is how the tension between freedom and the many dimensions of equality is unavoidable. Ensuring equal opportunities strikes many people as meaningless if those opportunities are hollow and provide no realistic pathway toward better outcomes. As such, amidst rising inequality, perhaps one of the most important questions facing the country in the twenty-first century is this: How do we balance freedom with real equality of opportunity that gives all Americans a chance to achieve better outcomes for themselves and their families? That is an enduring challenge of democracy, indeed.

Summary

LO1 **Describe how conditions at the founding of the United States have influenced the nation's struggle to expand civil rights.**

- Discrimination simply means making distinctions; by itself discrimination is neither good nor evil. Some forms of discrimination are benign; we want government to engage in such discrimination. Some forms of government discrimination are invidious and violate our understanding of equality. National traditions such as republicanism and a belief in the rule of law have been embraced by civil rights advocates as they have attempted to help the nation overcome other traditions that embraced invidious discrimination. The result has been improvements in equality of opportunities and equality of outcomes.

LO2 **Explain how advocates for African Americans have achieved civil rights victories in the courts and the legislative process, despite sometimes fierce resistance.**

- Congress enacted the Civil War amendments—the Thirteenth, Fourteenth, and Fifteenth amendments—to provide full civil rights to black Americans, yet the Supreme Court and state governments prevented these achievements from fully taking hold in practice. Legal segregation, despite these amendments, persisted because the "separate-but-equal" doctrine ruled the day. Eventually, a series of court cases, culminating in *Brown v. Board of Education*, declared that doctrine unconstitutional. Additional historic legislative victories, such as the Civil Rights Act of 1964 and the Voting Rights Act of 1965, helped advance the cause of African American civil rights. Full equality remains an elusive ideal, yet advocates and their allies continue to press on and fight against injustice.

LO3 **Identify how the struggle for civil rights for women has progressed in ways similar to and different from that of African Americans.**

- Like activists for African Americans' civil rights, women's rights advocates have used the courts and the legislative process to advance their cause. Despite important advances, including the adoption of the Nineteenth Amendment that guaranteed women the right to vote, the states did not ratify the ERA. Still, legislation and judicial rulings have helped to advance progress that the ERA's enthusiasts desired. The Supreme Court now judges sex-based discrimination with "skeptical scrutiny," making distinctions based on sex almost as suspect as distinctions based on race. Although women have made progress, like African Americans, full equality—in particular economic equality—remains elusive.

LO4 **Describe the victories won and challenges remaining for advocates of expanding civil rights protections for gay people.**

- After being confined to the proverbial closet for several generations, gay people have gained greater acceptance in mainstream society and have enjoyed recent victories that protect their civil rights. The Supreme Court has affirmed marriage equality, and gay people can now serve openly in the military. Challenges remain, though, as other court decisions and federal policies, while extending civil rights protections to others, have not yet been extended to gay Americans.

LO5 **Explain how pluralism creates conditions under which numerous groups may advocate for civil rights.**

- Though benefitting African Americans especially, the civil rights movement has worked to the benefit of all minority groups—in fact, it has benefited all Americans. Native Americans obtained some redress for past injustices, winning, for example, the return of lands throughout the country. Immigrant groups press government for a stake in the American experience as many work to gain a better life in jobs that few citizens will do. Hispanics have come to recognize the importance of group action to achieve economic and political equality, and extensions of the Civil Rights Act and Voting Rights Act, for example, have benefited them.

With enactment of laws protecting Americans with disabilities in schools, the workplace, and society more generally, these Americans have won civil rights protections enjoyed by African Americans and others.

LO6 **Analyze how contemporary debates about civil rights push new boundaries but have roots in earlier eras.**

- In a country as vast and dynamic as the United States, it is no wonder that debates about civil rights continue to animate the

country's politics. With new data and revelations come new claims that old promises have yet to be kept. The resurgence of African American civil rights activism around the treatment of blacks in the criminal justice system and in the nation's educational institutions provide one example. New groups, such as the transgender community, have also added their voices to the discussion. Overall, striking the proper balance between the values of equality and freedom remains a persistent challenge of American democracy.

Chapter Quiz

LO1 **Describe how conditions at the founding of the United States have influenced the nation's struggle to expand civil rights.**

1. Provide examples of invidious and benign discrimination across different periods in American history.
2. How have positive and negative American traditions influenced the expansion of civil rights in the nation?

LO2 **Explain how advocates for African Americans have achieved civil rights victories in the courts and the legislative process, despite sometimes fierce resistance.**

1. Define the separate-but-equal doctrine and explain how its supporters said it satisfied the Fourteenth Amendment while upholding racial segregation.
2. How did the Civil Rights Act of 1964 help to give teeth to Supreme Court decisions that dismantled legal segregation?

LO3 **Identify how the struggle for civil rights for women has progressed in ways similar to and different from that of African Americans.**

1. How did protectionism discriminate against women?
2. Describe legislative and judicial efforts that have helped women to fight for equal pay at work.

LO4 **Describe the victories won and challenges remaining for advocates of expanding civil rights protections for gay people.**

1. What evidence exists to suggest that gay people, once shunned from society, have become more part of mainstream America?
2. What were the major lines of debate in the Supreme Court's decision that affirmed marriage equality?

LO5 **Explain how pluralism creates conditions under which numerous groups may advocate for civil rights.**

1. How does the issue of assimilation bear on civil rights concerns of Native Americans, immigrants, and Americans with disabilities?
2. What is the difference between someone who identifies as *transgender* and someone who identifies as *cisgender*, and what implication does that difference have for civil rights?

LO6 **Analyze how contemporary debates about civil rights push new boundaries but have roots in earlier eras.**

1. Why have new state policies regarding election administration prompted recent debates about civil rights?
2. How do affirmative action policies help to illustrate the tension between equality of opportunity and equality of outcome?

KEY CASES

Plessy v. *Ferguson* (racial segregation constitutional, 1896)

Brown v. *Board of Education* (racial segregation unconstitutional, 1954)

Brown v. *Board of Education II* (racial desegregation implementation, 1955)

United States v. *Virginia* (gender equality, 1996)

United States v. *Windsor* (marriage equality under federal law, 2013)

Obergefell v. *Hodges* (marriage equality in the states, 2015)

Regents of the University of California v. *Bakke* (affirmative action, 1978)

Gratz v. *Bollinger* (affirmative action in college admissions, 2003)

Grutter v. *Bollinger* (affirmative action in law school admissions, 2003)

Parents Involved in Community Schools v. *Seattle School District No. 1* (public school racial diversity, 2007)

17 Economic Policy

"Blessed are the young, for they shall inherit the national debt," said former President Herbert Hoover. Hoover was president when the stock market collapsed in 1929 and subsequently lost the 1932 election to Franklin Delano Roosevelt.[1] Hoover was speaking to fellow Republicans in 1936, when the gross debt for the national government (sometimes called the national debt, sometimes the federal debt) was estimated at $39.79 billion.[2] Despite the national debt and the Great Depression, President Roosevelt was overwhelmingly reelected.

Eighty years later, the 1936 national debt of $39.7 billion seems paltry compared with our 2016 debt over $19 *trillion*! (The debt was lower on May 18, 2015, when the photo of National Debt Clock at 110 W 44th St. in New York was taken.) But the teen-trillion number does not take into account eighty years of population increase, economic growth, and inflation. A better way to compare levels of national debt over time is by percentages of gross domestic product (GDP— the total value of all goods and services produced in a given year). In 1936, our GDP was $84.9 billion.[3] As a percentage of GDP, the national debt then was only 39.8 percent. In 2016, the public share of our national debt was 75 percent of GDP.[4] Historically, our national debt as a percent of GDP had been even higher, rising over 100 from 1945 to 1947 and not dropping below 90 percent until 1950. So our nation can tolerate heavy debt without suffering a Great Depression.

How much of this debt do you owe? Let's do the math using round numbers. Dividing the 2016 national debt of $19 trillion by the U.S. population of 323 million was about $59,000 per person. That is indeed bad news, but the good news is that not all the debt needs to be paid off. Nations—like families who borrow to buy homes and cars—are almost never debt-free and pay interest on their loans. About 7 percent of the federal budget in 2016 was just for interest on the national debt.

As with household debt, our national debt should be reduced to avoid large annual interest payments. At present, the U.S. debt payments are relatively low due to historically low interest rates. However, interest rates will rise, and—as President Hoover implied—old people will die before the debt is paid down, leaving the task to the young. Young people may understand better how much money they will have tomorrow if they know more about the economics of government today. How does the national debt relate to the current budget deficit? How did the deficit grow so large and prove so difficult to control against the spending appetites of Congress? More concretely, how is the national budget formulated? How much control of the domestic economy can government really exercise through the judicious use of economic theory? How much is the economy influenced by events that lie outside governmental control? What effects do government taxing and spending policies have on the economy and on economic equality? We address these questions in this chapter. As we shall see, no one person or organization controls the American economy; multiple actors have a voice in economic conditions. And not all of these actors are public—or American.

#ChallengeAccepted

Take the Challenge on MindTap for American Government

What problems follow from spending 7 percent of our annual budget for interest payments on the national debt?

administration in Washington would shoulder responsibility for maintaining a healthy economy. The year Keynes died, Congress passed an employment act establishing "the continuing responsibility of the national government to . . . promote maximum employment, production and purchasing power." The Employment Act of 1946, which reflected Keynesian theory, had a tremendous effect on government economic policy. Many people believe it was the primary source of "big government" in America. Even Richard Nixon, a conservative president, admitted in 1971 that "we are all Keynesians now," by accepting government responsibility for the economy. But not all conservatives buy into that philosophy. In a 2008 editorial, "We're All Keynesians Now," the *Wall Street Journal* deplored George W. Bush's $168 billion fiscal stimulus package of tax rebates to forestall a recession as taking money from one pocket (those with high income) and handing it to another (those with low to moderate income).[11]

IMAGE 17.1   Economists on YouTube

"Fight of the Century: Keynes vs. Hayek, Round Two" is an entertaining ten-minute YouTube video (set to rap music) presenting the clashing views of British economist John Maynard Keynes (left) and Austrian economist Friedrich Hayek (right). Keynes had enormous influence on American economics and government. His *The General Theory of Employment* (1936) advocated deficit spending during economic downturns to maintain employment. Keynesian theory fell out of favor in the 1980s, but Presidents Bush and Obama both embraced it to deal with the 2008 economic collapse. Hayek's *The Road to Serfdom* (1944) argued that government intervention led to socialism and tyranny. Hayek's advocacy of free-market capitalism enjoyed popularity among Republicans who objected to the government bailout of the auto industry.

Source: See https://www.youtube.com/watch?v=GTQnarzmTOc.

Monetary Policy

Although most economists accept Keynesian theory in its broad outlines, they depreciate its political utility. Some especially question the value of fiscal policies in controlling inflation and unemployment. They argue that government spending programs take too long to enact in Congress and to implement through the bureaucracy. As a result, jobs are created not when they are needed but years later, when the crisis may have passed and government spending needs to be reduced.

Also, government spending is easier to start than to stop because the groups that benefit from spending programs tend to defend them even when they are no longer needed. A similar criticism applies to tax policies. Politically, it is much easier to cut taxes than to raise them. In other words, Keynesian theory requires that governments be able to begin and end spending quickly and to cut and raise taxes quickly. But in the real world, these fiscal tools are easier to use in one direction than the other.

Recognizing these limitations of fiscal policies, **monetarists** argue that government can control the economy's performance simply by controlling the nation's money supply.[12] Staunch monetarists, like Nobel Laureate Milton Friedman, favor a long-range policy of small but steady growth in the amount of money in circulation rather than frequent manipulation of monetary policies.

Monetary policies in the United States are under the control of the **Federal Reserve System**, which acts as the country's central bank. Established in 1913, "the Fed" by law has three major goals: controlling inflation, maintaining maximum employment, and

monetarists
Those who argue that government can effectively control the performance of an economy mainly by controlling the supply of money.

Federal Reserve System
The system of banks that acts as the central bank of the United States and controls major monetary policies.

insuring moderate interest rates.[13] The Fed is not a single bank but a system of banks. At the top of the system is the board of governors, seven members appointed by the president for staggered terms of fourteen years. The president designates one member of the board to be its chairperson, who serves a four-year term that extends beyond the president's term of office. This complex arrangement was intended to make the board independent of the president and even of Congress. An independent board, the reasoning went, would be able to make financial decisions for the nation without regard to their political implications.[14] Following the Fed's bold actions taken to combat the financial crisis in 2008, however, members of Congress proposed auditing Fed decisions for the first time. By the summer of 2010, when President Obama signed a financial reform bill, the Fed was granted even greater powers to regulate large complex financial firms.[15]

The Fed controls the money supply, which affects inflation, in three ways. Most important, the Fed can sell and buy government securities (such as U.S. Treasury bills) on the open market. When the Fed sells securities, it takes money out of circulation, thereby making money scarce and raising the interest rate. When the Fed buys securities, the process works in reverse, lowering interest rates. The Fed also sets a target for the *federal funds rate*, which banks charge one another for overnight loans and which is usually cited when newspapers write, "The Fed has decided to lower [or raise] interest rates." Less frequently (for technical reasons), the Fed may change its *discount rate*, the interest rate that member banks pay to borrow money from a Federal Reserve bank. Finally, the Fed can change its *reserve requirement*, which is the amount of cash that member banks must keep on deposit in their regional Federal Reserve bank. An increase in the reserve requirement reduces the amount of money banks have available to lend.

Basic economic theory holds that interest rates should be raised to discourage borrowing and spending when the economy is growing too quickly (this combats inflation) and lowered when the economy is sluggish (thus increasing the money flow to encourage spending and economic growth). Historically, the Fed has adjusted interest rates to combat inflation rather than to stimulate economic growth, which would maximize employment. (A former Fed chairman once said its task was "to remove the punch bowl when the party gets going.")[16] That is, the Fed would dampen economic growth before it leads to serious inflation.

Accordingly, some charge that the Fed acts to further interests of the wealthy (who fear rampant inflation) more than interests of the poor (who fear widespread unemployment). Why so? Although all classes of citizens complain about increasing costs of living, inflation usually harms upper classes (creditors) more than lower classes (debtors). To illustrate, suppose someone borrows $20,000, to be repaid after ten years, during which the inflation rate was 10 percent. When the loan is due, the $20,000 borrowed is "worth" only $18,000. Debtors find the cheaper money easier to raise, and creditors are paid less than the original value of their loan. Hence, wealthy people fear severe inflation, which can erode the value of their saved wealth. As one Federal Reserve bank bluntly stated, "Debtors gain when inflation is unexpectedly high, and creditors gain when it is unexpectedly low."[17]

Formally, the president is responsible for the state of the economy, and voters hold him accountable. As the economy deteriorated in 2008, more people blamed President Bush for its poor performance than blamed Congress, multinational corporations, or financial institutions.[18] However, the president neither determines interest rates (the Fed does) nor controls spending (Congress does). In this respect, all presidents since 1913 have had to work with a Fed made independent of both the president and Congress, and all have had to deal with the fact that Congress ultimately controls spending. These restrictions on presidential authority are consistent with the pluralist model of democracy, but a president held responsible for the economy may not appreciate that theoretical argument.

Although the Fed's economic policies are not perfectly insulated from political concerns, they are sufficiently independent that the president is not able to control monetary policy without the Fed's cooperation. This means that the president cannot be held completely responsible for the state of the economy. Nevertheless, the public blames presidents for poor economic conditions and votes against them in elections. Naturally, a strong economy favors the incumbent party. When people are optimistic about the economic future and feel that they are doing well, they typically see no reason to change the party controlling the White House. But when conditions are bad or worsening, voters often decide to seek a change.

The Fed's activities are essential parts of the government's overall economic policy, but they lie outside the direct control of the president—and directly in the hands of the chair of the Federal Reserve Board. This makes the Fed chair a critical player in economic affairs and can create problems in coordinating economic policy. For example, the president might want the Fed to lower interest rates to stimulate the economy, but the Fed might resist for fear of inflation. Such policy clashes can pit the chair of the Federal Reserve Board directly against the president. So presidents typically court the Fed chair, even one who served a president of the other party.

Alan Greenspan served as Fed chair from 1987 to 2006 under four presidents, both Republican and Democrat. Greenspan was praised for overseeing an economy with low inflation, low unemployment, and strong growth. He believed that markets knew best and should be left unregulated (in keeping with the "efficient market hypothesis"), but Greenspan was later blamed for the financial crisis of 2008. Called before a House committee in October, he admitted that his "whole intellectual edifice collapsed in the summer," when banks held nearly worthless securities that had tumbled from dizzyingly high values.[19] President Bush replaced him in 2006 with Ben Bernanke, who acted boldly in 2008 to rescue the economy, stretching the Fed's authority by arranging bank purchases, emergency loan programs, and the lowest interest rate—zero—in American history. President Obama replaced Bernanke in 2014 with Janet Yellen, the first woman to serve as Fed chair. Under Yellen, the Fed raised the interest rate in 2015 to 0.25 percent, the first increase since 2006.[20]

Historical evidence suggests that government can indeed slow down and smooth out the booms and busts of business cycles through active use of monetary and fiscal policies. From 1855 through World War II—prior to the active employment of Keynesian theory—the nation suffered through economic recessions 42 percent of the time, with each recession averaging twenty-one months. The recession that began in December 2007 lasted for 18 months, officially ending in June 2009. Although unemployment fell under 5 percent in early 2016, Yellen and the Fed still worried about economic growth and temporarily postponed a planned increase in the interest rate.

Alex Wong/Getty Images

IMAGE 17.2   Listening to Yellen

Dr. Janet Yellen, a distinguished professor of economics at the University of California, Berkeley, became the first woman to chair the Federal Reserve System in 2014. Officials at a 2015 meeting of the Financial Stability Oversight Council listen intently to what she has to say.

supply-side economics
Economic policies aimed at increasing the supply of goods (as opposed to decreasing demand); consists mainly of tax cuts for possible investors and less regulation of business.

Supply-Side Economics

When Reagan came to office in 1981, he embraced a school of thought called **supply-side economics** to deal with the stagflation (both unemployment and inflation) that the nation was experiencing. Keynesian theory argues that inflation results when consumers, businesses, and governments have more money to spend than there are goods and services to buy. The standard Keynesian solution is to reduce demand (for example, by increasing taxes). Supply-siders argue that inflation can be lowered more effectively by increasing the supply of goods (that is, they stress the supply side of the economic equation). Specifically, they favor tax cuts to stimulate investment (which leads to the production of more goods) and less government regulation of business (again, to increase productivity—which they hold will yield more, not less, government revenue). Supply-siders also contend that the rich should receive larger tax cuts than the poor because the rich have more money to invest. The benefits of increased investment will then "trickle down" to working people in the form of additional jobs and income.

In a sense, supply-side economics resembles laissez-faire economics because it prefers fewer government programs and regulations and less taxation. Supply-siders believe that government interferes too much with the efforts of individuals to work,

FIGURE 17.1 Budget Deficits and Surpluses over Time

This chart shows the actual deficits and surpluses in constant 2009 dollars incurred under administrations from Johnson to Obama. The deficits were enormous under Reagan, George H. W. Bush, and even during Clinton's early years. Budget deficits were eventually eliminated under Clinton and replaced by surpluses. Larger deficits appeared again under George W. Bush and passed on to Barack Obama, who steadily drew them down.

Source: Executive Office of the President, *Budget of the United States Government, Fiscal Year 217: Historical Tables* (Washington, DC: U.S. Government Printing Office, 2016), Table 1.3.

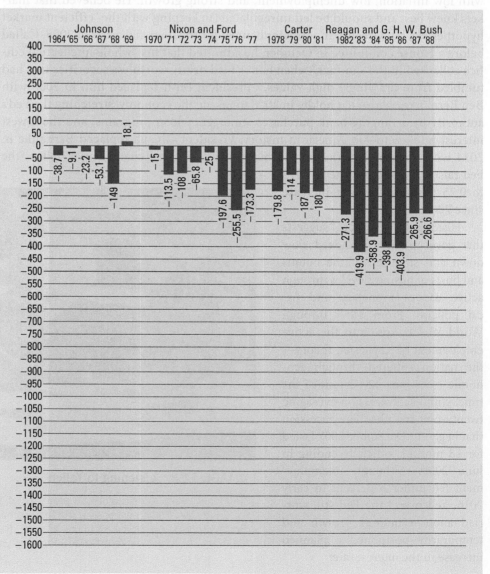

save, and invest. Inspired by supply-side theory, Reagan proposed (and got) massive tax cuts in the Economic Recovery Tax Act of 1981. The act reduced individual tax rates by 23 percent over a three-year period and cut the marginal tax rate for the highest income group from 70 to 50 percent. Reagan also launched a program to deregulate business. According to supply-side theory, these actions would generate extra government revenue, making spending cuts unnecessary to balance the budget. Nevertheless, Reagan also cut funding for some domestic programs, including Aid to Families with Dependent Children. Contrary to supply-side theory, he also proposed hefty increases in military spending. This blend of tax cuts, deregulation, cuts in spending for social programs, and increases in spending for defense became known, somewhat disparagingly, as *Reaganomics*.

How well did Reaganomics work? Although Reaganomics worked largely as expected in the area of industry deregulation, it failed to reduce the budget deficit. Contrary to supply-side theory, the 1981 tax cut was accompanied by a massive drop in tax revenues. Lower tax revenues and higher defense spending produced the largest budget deficits to that time, as shown in Figure 17.1. Economist Gregory Mankiw, advisor to President George W. Bush, said that history failed to confirm the main

FIGURE 17.1   (Continued)

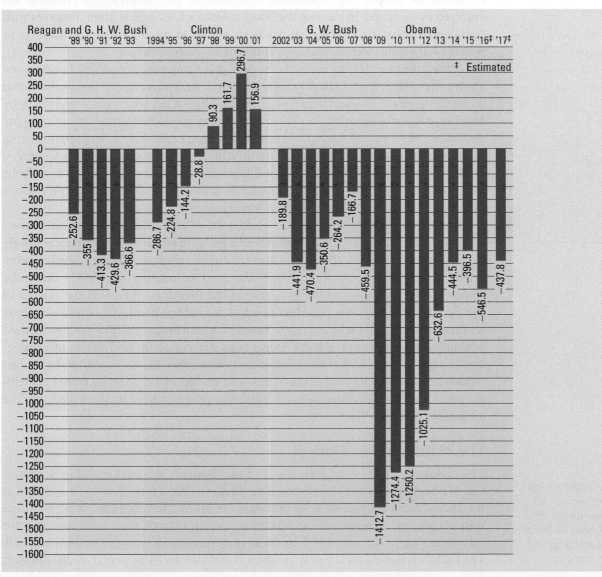

conjecture of supply-side economics: that lower tax revenues would raise tax revenues: "When Reagan cut taxes after he was elected, the result was less tax revenue, not more."[21] Nevertheless, the supply-side idea that cutting taxes raises more revenue is still popular.[22]

Public Policy and the Budget

LO2 Describe the process by which the national budget is prepared and passed into law and the reforms undertaken by Congress to balance the budget.

To most people, the national budget is B-O-R-I-N-G. To national politicians, it is an exciting script for high drama. The numbers, categories, and percentages that numb normal minds cause politicians' nostrils to flare and their hearts to pound. The budget is a battlefield on which politicians wage war over the programs they support.

Control of the budget is important to members of Congress because they are politicians, and politicians want to wield power, not watch someone else wield it. Also, the Constitution established Congress, not the president, as the "first branch" of government and the people's representatives. Unfortunately for Congress, the president has emerged as the leader in shaping the budget. Although Congress often disagrees with presidential spending priorities, it has been unable to mount a serious challenge to presidential authority by presenting a coherent alternative budget.

Today, the president prepares the budget, and Congress approves it. This was not always the case. Before 1921, Congress prepared the budget under its constitutional authority to raise taxes and appropriate funds. The budget was formed piecemeal by enacting a series of laws that originated in the many committees involved in the highly decentralized process of raising revenue, authorizing expenditures, and appropriating funds. Executive agencies even submitted their budgetary requests directly to Congress, not to the president. No one was responsible for the big picture—the budget as a whole. The president's role was essentially limited to approving revenue and appropriations bills, just as he approved other pieces of legislation.

Congressional budgeting (such as it was) worked well enough for a nation of farmers, but not for an industrialized nation with a growing population and an increasingly active government. Soon after World War I, Congress realized that the budget-making process needed to be centralized. The Budget and Accounting Act of 1921 thrust the responsibility for preparing the budget onto the president. It created the Bureau of the Budget to prepare the president's budget for submission to Congress. Congress retained its constitutional authority to raise and spend funds, but now Congress would begin its work with the president's budget as its starting point. And all executive agencies' budget requests had to be funneled for review through the Bureau of the Budget (which became the Office of Management and Budget in 1970); those consistent with the president's overall economic and legislative program were incorporated into the president's budget.

The Nature of the Budget

fiscal year
The twelve-month period from October 1 to September 30 used by the government for accounting purposes. A fiscal year budget is named for the year in which it ends.

The national budget is complex. But its basic elements are not beyond understanding. We begin with some definitions. The Budget of the United States Government is the annual financial plan that the president is required to submit to Congress at the start of each year. It applies to the *next* **fiscal year**, the interval the government uses for accounting purposes. Currently, the fiscal year runs from October 1 to September 30. The budget is named for the year in which it *ends*, so the fiscal year (FY) 2017 budget that Obama submitted in early 2016 applied to the twelve months from October 1, 2016, to September 30, 2017.

Broadly, the budget defines **budget authority** (how much government agencies are authorized to spend on current and future programs); **budget outlays**, or expenditures (how much agencies are expected to spend this year, which includes past authorizations); and **receipts** (how much is expected in taxes and other revenues). President Obama's FY 2017 budget contained *authority* for expenditures of $4,235 billion, but it provided for *outlays* of $4,147 billion (including some previous obligations). His budget also anticipated receipts of $3,644 billion in current dollars, leaving an estimated *deficit* of $503 billion—the difference between receipts and outlays.

When the U.S. government runs a deficit, it borrows funds on a massive scale to finance its operation that fiscal year, thus limiting the supply of loanable funds for business investment. A deficit in the annual budget is different from the **national debt**, which represents the sum of all unpaid government deficits. Various "national debt clocks" calculate real-time estimates of the United States' total national debt.[23] On February 13, 2016, the total was $19 trillion.[24] However, about $5.3 billion of the total debt was "intragovernmental"—money that one part of the government owes to another part. Concerning the $13.7 trillion of "public" debt—money owed to lenders outside the government—almost 50 percent was held by institutions or individuals in other countries. If foreign lenders were to stop financing America's governmental annual deficit and national debt, the economy could suffer a serious blow.

Preparing the President's Budget

The budget that the president submits to Congress each winter is the end product of a process that begins the previous spring under the supervision of the **Office of Management and Budget (OMB)**. The OMB is located within the Executive Office of the President and is headed by a director appointed by the president, with the approval of the Senate. The OMB, with a staff of more than five hundred, is the most powerful domestic agency in the bureaucracy, and its director, who attends meetings of the president's cabinet, is one of the most powerful figures in government. The federal budget, with appendixes, is now available electronically on the OMB website.[25] Thousands of pages long, the budget contains more than numbers. It also explains individual spending programs in terms of national needs and agency objectives, and it analyzes proposed taxes and other receipts. Each year, reporters, lobbyists, and political analysts anxiously await publication of the president's budget, eager to learn his plans for government spending in the coming year.

The OMB initiates the budget process each spring by meeting with the president to discuss the economic situation and his budgetary priorities. It then sends broad budgeting guidelines to every government agency and requests their initial projection of how much money they will need for the next fiscal year. The OMB assembles this information and makes recommendations to the president, who then develops more precise guidelines describing how much each is likely to get. By summer, the agencies are asked to prepare budgets based on the new guidelines. By fall, they submit their formal budgets to the OMB, where budget analysts scrutinize agency requests, considering both their costs and their consistency with the president's legislative program. Much politicking goes on at this stage, as agency heads try to circumvent the OMB by pleading for their pet projects with presidential advisers and perhaps even the president himself.

Political negotiations over the budget may extend into the early winter—and often until it goes to the printer. The voluminous document looks very much like a finished product, but the figures it contains are not final. In giving the president the responsibility for preparing the budget in 1921, Congress simply provided itself with a starting point for its own work. And even with this head start, Congress has a hard time disciplining itself to produce a coherent, balanced budget.

budget authority
The amounts that government agencies are authorized to spend for current and future programs.

budget outlays
The amounts that government agencies are expected to spend in the fiscal year.

receipts
For a government, the amount expected or obtained in taxes and other revenues.

national debt
The accumulated sum of past government borrowing owed to lenders outside the government.

Office of Management and Budget (OMB)
The budgeting arm of the Executive Office; prepares the president's budget.

Passing the Congressional Budget

The president's budget must be approved by Congress. Its process for doing so is a creaky conglomeration of traditional procedures overlaid with structural reforms. The cumbersome process has had difficulty producing a budget according to Congress's own timetable. Traditionally, the tasks of budget making were divided among a number of committees, a process that has been retained. Three types of committees are involved in budgeting:

- **Tax committees** are responsible for raising the revenues to run the government. The Ways and Means Committee in the House and the Finance Committee in the Senate consider all proposals for taxes, tariffs, and other receipts contained in the president's budget.
- **Authorization committees** (such as the House Armed Services Committee and the Senate Banking, Housing, and Urban Affairs Committee) have jurisdiction over particular legislative subjects. The House has about twenty committees that can authorize spending and the Senate about fifteen. Each pores over the portions of the budget that pertain to its area of responsibility. However, in recent years, power has shifted from the authorization committees to the appropriations committees.
- **Appropriations committees** decide which of the programs approved by the authorization committees will actually be funded (that is, given money to spend). For example, the House Armed Services Committee might propose building a new line of tanks for the army, and it might succeed in getting this proposal enacted into law. But the tanks will never be built unless the appropriations committees appropriate funds for that purpose. Twelve distinct appropriations bills are supposed to be enacted each year to fund the nation's spending. Congress had trouble passing those too. It passed none before the end of the year in 2015, but just before Christmas, Congress passed and the president signed an "omnibus" appropriations bill that allowed the government to operate until the end of FY 2016 in September.

Two serious problems are inherent in a budgeting process that involves three distinct kinds of congressional committees. First, the two-step spending process (first authorization, then appropriation) is complex; it offers wonderful opportunities for interest groups to get into the budgeting act in the spirit of pluralist democracy. Second, because one group of legislators in each house plans for revenues and many other groups plan for spending, no one is responsible for the budget as a whole.

In the 1970s, Congress created **budget committees** in each chamber to supervise a comprehensive budget review process. They were directed to pass annual budget resolutions setting spending targets and to work out differences in conferences. They were aided by a new **Congressional Budget Office (CBO)**, with a staff of more than two hundred, to supply budgetary expertise equal to the president's OMB. From 1976 to 2009, Congress usually passed the required budget resolutions but was conflicted to pass *any* for the next five years. In 2015, the Senate approved the House budget resolution, with all forty-six members of the Democratic caucus voting against it.

In 1990, Congress defined two types of spending: **discretionary spending** and **mandatory spending**. Discretionary spending, including annual military expenditures, was authorized annually by each session of Congress and was subject to limits, or caps. Mandatory spending was for programs that have become **entitlements** (such as Social Security and veterans' pensions), which provide benefits to individuals legally entitled to them and cannot be reduced without changing the law.

In 1997, President Clinton and Congress accomplished what most observers thought was beyond political possibility. They not only produced a balanced budget ahead of schedule but actually produced a budget surplus—the first surplus since 1969. In the early 2000s, President Bush and Republicans in Congress advocated using the

tax committees
The two committees of Congress responsible for raising the revenue with which to run the government.

authorization committees
Committees of Congress that can authorize spending in their particular areas of responsibility.

appropriations committees
Committees of Congress that decide which of the programs passed by the authorization committees will actually be funded.

budget committees
One committee in each house of Congress that supervises a comprehensive budget review process.

Congressional Budget Office (CBO)
The budgeting arm of Congress, which prepares alternative budgets to those prepared by the president's OMB.

discretionary spending
In the Budget Enforcement Act of 1990, authorized expenditures from annual appropriations.

mandatory spending
In the Budget Enforcement Act of 1990, expenditures required by previous commitments.

entitlements
Benefits to which every eligible person has a legal right and that the government cannot deny.

budget surplus for large across-the-board tax cuts to return money to taxpayers.[26] Although the caps on discretionary spending helped balance the budget entering 2000, many members of Congress in both parties resented the caps' restrictions on their freedom to make fiscal decisions. Accordingly, Congress allowed the caps on discretionary spending to expire at the end of 2002.[27] Since 2002, the government has run budget deficits, not surpluses.

Repeated failures to eliminate annual budget deficits renewed calls for a constitutional amendment requiring Congress to balance the budget—as required by most state constitutions. Congressional proposals for a balanced budget amendment (BBA) were first introduced in 1936 and often since.[28] Republicans in Congress tend to favor a BBA as a means to limit spending, while Democrats oppose it for reasons similar to those given by most economists: a serious BBA would prevent the government from running a deficit to simulate the economy. Some conservatives feared that a BBA would increase the courts' role in deciding government spending cases certain to arise under it.[29] Others noted that Congress could pass balanced budgets if it wished without a constitutional requirement, which would only encourage Congress to work around the law to increase deficits. In 1985, a desperate Congress set annually decreasing deficit targets that would trigger automatic spending cuts if not met. Each year thereafter, Congress simply raised the targets to meet them. The law was an utter failure, and the deficit targets were eliminated in 1990.

Congress's failure to limit the national debt is similar and instructive. Prior to World War II, Congress limited indebtedness to $45 billion, only 10 percent above the existing debt of $40.4 billion.[30] Every time the debt neared its legal limit—over 100 times since 1940—Congress repeatedly raised the ceiling.[31] Given that the debt ceiling causes so much partisan rancor and that only one other modern democracy (Denmark) legislates a similar debt ceiling, one wonders why it exists at all.[32]

Tax Policies

LO3 Identify the objectives of tax policies and explain why tax reform is difficult.

So far, we have been concerned mainly with the spending side of the budget, for which appropriations must be enacted each year. The revenue side of the budget is governed by overall tax policy, which is designed to provide a continuous flow of income without annual legislation. A major text on government finance says that tax policy is sometimes changed to accomplish one or more of several objectives:

- To adjust overall revenue to meet budget outlays
- To make the tax burden more equitable for taxpayers
- To help control the economy by raising taxes (thus decreasing aggregate demand) or by lowering taxes (thus increasing demand)[33]

If those were the only objectives, the tax code might be simple, but tax policy also reflects two conflicting philosophies for distributing the costs of government: whether citizens should be taxed according to their ability to pay or for benefits they receive. Tax policy is further complicated because it is also used to advance social goals (such as home ownership through the deduction for mortgage interest) or to favor certain industries. To accommodate such deductions and incentives, the tax code (which is available over the Internet) runs over seven thousand pages.[34] Over 90 percent of the government revenue in FY 2017 was expected from three major sources: individual income taxes (49 percent), social insurance taxes (31 percent), and corporate income taxes (12 percent).[35] Because the income tax accounts for most government revenue, discussion of tax policy usually focuses on that source.

Reform

Tax reform proposals are usually so heavily influenced by interest groups looking for special benefits that they end up working against their original purpose.[36] Without question, the tax code is complex. Before 1987, people paid different tax rates depending on where they fit in fourteen income brackets. President Reagan backed a sweeping reform that reduced the number of brackets to two and the rate for the top bracket from 70 to 28 percent. By eliminating many tax brackets, the new tax policy approached the idea of a flat tax—one that requires everyone to pay at the same rate.

A flat tax has the appeal of simplicity, but it violates the principle of **progressive taxation**, under which the rich pay proportionately higher taxes than the poor. The ability to pay has long been a standard of fair taxation, and surveys show that citizens favor this idea in the abstract.[37] In practice, however, they have different opinions, as we will see. Nevertheless, most democratic governments rely on progressive taxation to redistribute wealth and thus promote economic equality. Although wealthy people finance redistributive programs, they also benefit if redistribution alleviates extreme inequalities and prevents poor people from revolting.

In general, the greater the number of tax brackets, the more progressive a tax can be, for higher brackets can be taxed at higher rates. To deal with a budget deficit in 1990, President George H. W. Bush violated his campaign pledge of "no new taxes" by creating a third tax rate, 31 percent, for those with the highest incomes. In 1993, Clinton created a fourth level, 39.6 percent, moving toward a more progressive tax structure, although still less progressive than before 1987. Both presidents acted to increase revenue to reduce a soaring deficit.

Campaigning for president, George W. Bush promised to cut taxes. Soon after his election, he got Congress to pass a complex $1.35 trillion tax cut, with a top personal tax rate of 35 percent. Intended to stimulate the economy, the tax cut also reduced the revenue needed to match government spending.[38] Budget deficits quickly returned under Bush, owing to reduced revenue, a downturn in the stock market, and unanticipated expenses for homeland defense and military action following the September 11 attacks on America. The deficit zoomed to over a trillion dollars (10 percent of GDP) in Bush's last budget (see Figure 17.1), which reflected costs of his $168 billion stimulus package and his $700 billion Troubled Assets

progressive taxation
A system of taxation whereby the rich pay proportionately higher taxes than the poor; used by governments to redistribute wealth and thus promote equality.

IMAGE 17.3   Who Benefits from Tax Policy?

Santa (that is, Congress) often finds that rich constituents don't ask for presents, they demand them.

Tom Toles/Universal Uclick

Relief Program (TARP). The deficit grew further with Obama's $787 billion stimulus package in 2009 but began to decrease in 2010. Obama campaigned to restore the 39.6 percent tax bracket for those with the highest incomes and succeeded in 2013.

Comparing Tax Burdens

No one likes to pay taxes, so politicians find it popular to criticize the agency that collects taxes: the Internal Revenue Service. The income tax itself—and taxes in general—are also popular targets for U.S. politicians who campaign on getting government off the backs of the people. Is the tax burden on U.S. citizens truly too heavy? Compared with what? One way to compare tax burdens is to examine taxes over time in the same country; another is to compare taxes in different countries at the same time. By comparing taxes over time in the United States, we find that the income tax burden on U.S. citizens has actually decreased since the 1950s. The federal income tax rate for a family of four with the median household income was 20 percent in 1955 and 15 percent in 2014.[39] Another way to compare tax burdens is to examine tax rates in different countries. By nearly two to one, more respondents in a post-2000 national survey thought that Americans pay a higher percentage of their income in taxes than citizens in Western Europe.[40] They were flat wrong. Despite Americans' complaints about high taxes, the U.S. tax burden is not large compared with that of other democratic nations. As shown in Figure 17.2, Americans' taxes are quite low

FIGURE 17.2 Tax Burdens in Thirty Countries

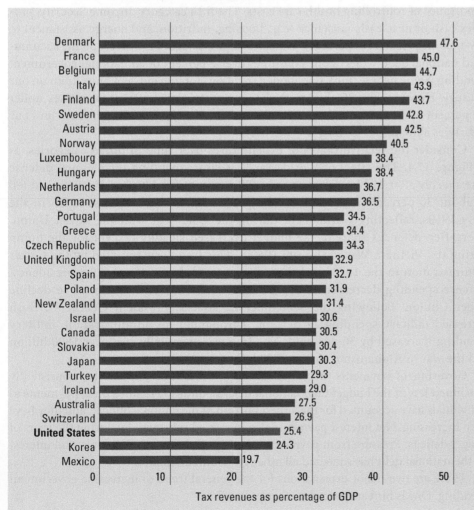

This graph compares tax burdens in 2013 in thirty countries as a percentage of gross domestic product (GDP), which is the market value of goods produced inside the country by workers, businesses, and government. The percentages encompass national, state, and local taxes and Social Security contributions. By this measure, the U.S. government extracts less in taxes from its citizens than do the governments of all Western democratic nations. At the top of the list stands Denmark, well known for providing heavily for social welfare. Despite its low ranking in tax burden, the United States also supports the world's largest military force, to which it allocates about 3 percent of its GDP, or about 15 percent of government expenditures.

Source: OECD, *Revenue Statistics 2015*, OECD Publishing, 3 December 2015.

in general compared with those in twenty-nine other democratic nations. Primarily because they provide their citizens with more generous social benefits (such as health care and unemployment compensation), almost every democratic nation taxes more heavily than the United States does.[41]

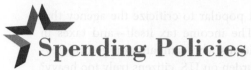

Spending Policies

LO4 Identify the major areas of government outlays and explain the role of incremental budgeting and uncontrollable spending on the growth of government spending.

The FY 2017 budget projects spending over $4,147,000,000,000—that's over $4 trillion (or $4,000 billion, if you prefer). Where does all that money go? Figure 17.3 breaks down the $4.1 trillion in proposed outlays in President Obama's FY 2017 budget by eighteen major governmental functions. The largest amount (23 percent of the total budget) was targeted for Social Security. The next largest amount (15 percent) went for national defense (military spending), which had accounted for most spending from World War II to the collapse of the Soviet Union. The third and fourth largest categories—Medicare and Health (including the National Institutes of Health)—together account for 29 percent of all budgetary outlays, which underscores the importance of controlling health care costs. The fifth category, Income Security, provides cash or near-cash assistance (e.g., housing, nutrition, and energy assistance) to low-income persons (13 percent). The sixth largest category is interest on the accumulated national debt, which alone consumes over 7 percent of all national government spending. Some people think that money spent on "foreign aid" is a huge drain on our treasury. However, the $56 billion outlay for international affairs constitutes under 1.5 percent of the total—and one-quarter of that is for the State Department and our embassies abroad.

Consider the relative shares of expenditures over time in broad categories, as in Figure 17.4. The effect of World War II is clear: spending for national defense rose sharply after 1940, peaked at about 90 percent of the budget in 1945, and fell to about 30 percent in peacetime. The percentage for defense rose again in the early 1950s, reflecting rearmament during the Cold War with the Soviet Union. Thereafter, defense's share of the budget decreased steadily (except for the bump during the Vietnam War in the late 1960s). This trend was reversed by the Carter administration in the 1970s and then shot upward during the Reagan presidency. Defense spending decreased under George H. W. Bush and continued to decline under Clinton. Following the September 11 attacks, President George W. Bush increased military spending 22 percent. Throughout his administration, military spending increased by 30 percent.[42] The Iraq war eventually cost over $800 billion and the war in Afghanistan almost $700 billion.[43]

Government payments to individuals (e.g., Social Security checks) consistently consumed less of the budget than national defense until 1971. Since then, payments to individuals have accounted for the largest portion of the national budget, and they have been increasing. Net interest payments also increased substantially during the years of budget deficits. Pressure from payments for national defense, individuals, and interest on the national debt has squeezed all other government outlays.

There are two major explanations for the general trend of increasing government spending. One is bureaucratic, the other political.

FIGURE 17.3 Federal Spending in FY 2017, by Function

Federal budget authorities and outlays are organized into about twenty categories, some of which are mainly for bookkeeping purposes. This graph shows estimated outlays for each of eighteen substantive functions in President Obama's FY 2017 budget. The final budget differed somewhat from this distribution because Congress amended some of the president's spending proposals. The graph makes clear the huge differences among spending categories. Social Security alone accounts for 23 percent of the budget. Health costs (including Medicare) account for 29 percent more. Military spending costs 15 percent, and income security—housing, nutrition, and energy assistance to low-income persons—takes another 13 percent. Net interest on the national debt alone consumes about 7 percent. This leaves only 15 percent for transportation, agriculture, justice, science, and energy—matters often regarded as important centers of government activity.

Source: Executive Office of the President, *Budget of the United States Government, Fiscal Year 2017: Historical Tables* (Washington, DC: U.S. Government Printing Office, 2016), Table 3.1.

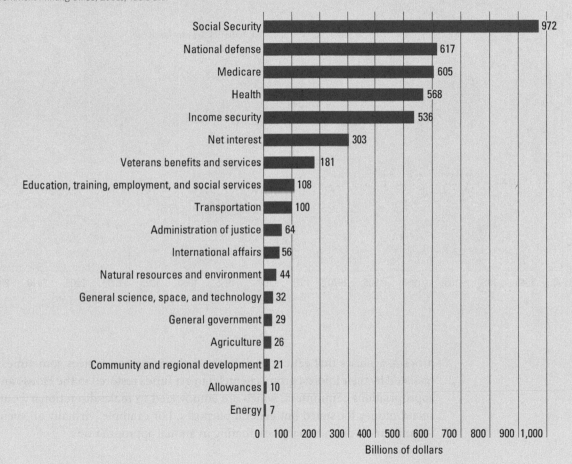

Incremental Budgeting . . .

The bureaucratic explanation for spending increases involves **incremental budgeting**: bureaucrats, in compiling their funding requests for the following year, traditionally ask for the amount they got in the current year plus some incremental increase to fund new projects. Because Congress has already approved the agency's budget for the current year, it pays little attention to the agency's current size (the largest part of its budget) and focuses instead on the extra money (the increment) requested for the next year. As a result, few agencies are ever cut back, and spending continually goes up.

Incremental budgeting generates bureaucratic momentum that continually raises spending. Once an agency is created, it attracts a clientele that defends its existence and supports its requests for extra funds year after year. Because budgeting is a two-step

incremental budgeting
A method of budget making that involves adding new funds (an increment) onto the amount previously budgeted (in last year's budget).

FIGURE 17.4 **National Government Outlays over Time**

This chart plots the percentage of the annual budget devoted to four major expense categories over time. Significant changes have occurred in national spending since 1940. During World War II, defense spending consumed more than 80 percent of the national budget. Defense again accounted for most national expenditures during the Cold War of the 1950s. Following the collapse of communism in the 1990s, the military's share of the budget declined but rose again with the war in Iraq. The major story, however, has been the growth in payments to individuals—for example, in the form of Social Security benefits, Medicare, health care, and various programs that provide a social safety net—including unemployment compensation.

Source: Executive Office of the President, *Budget of the United States Government, Fiscal Year 2017: Historical Tables* (Washington, DC: U.S. Government Printing Office, 2016), Table 6.1.

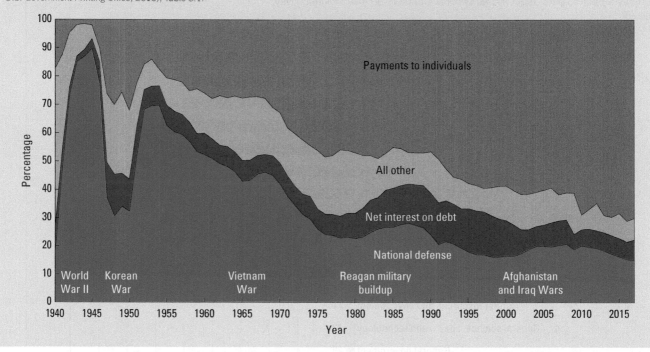

process, agencies that get cut back in the authorizing committees sometimes manage (assisted by their interest group clientele) to get funds restored in the House and Senate appropriations committees, which are empowered to make discretionary outlays—to spend money for stated but general purposes. For example, virtually all spending for the military is discretionary, originating in annual appropriations.

. . . and Uncontrollable Spending

Although each Congress controls discretionary spending, most spending is enshrined in law and uncontrollable unless the law is changed. For example, Social Security legislation guarantees certain benefits to program participants when they retire. Medicare and veterans' benefits also entitle citizens to certain payments. These represent mandatory outlays. In Obama's FY 2017 budget, about 70 percent of all budget outlays were uncontrollable or relatively uncontrollable—mainly for payments to individuals under Social Security, Medicare, and public assistance; for interest on the national debt; and for farm price supports. About half of the rest went for national defense or homeland security, leaving about 15 percent for domestic discretionary spending—excluding homeland security.[44]

To be sure, Congress could change the laws to abolish entitlement payments, and it does modify them through the budgeting process. But politics argues against large-scale reductions. What spending cuts would be acceptable to or even popular with the public? In the abstract, voters favor cutting government spending, but they tend to favor maintaining government programs that help needy people and deal with important national problems. Substantial majorities favor spending the same or even more on Social Security, Medicare, education, job training, programs for poor children, and the military. In fact, when a national poll asked whether respondents thought federal spending should be "increased, decreased, or kept about the same" for eighteen different purposes—education, public schools, veterans' benefits, college financial aid, Medicare, health care, aid to the U.S. needy, Social Security, combating crime, infrastructure, environmental protection, scientific research, energy, agriculture, terrorism, military defense, unemployment aid, and aid to the world's needy—respondents favored increasing or keeping about the same level of spending for *every* purpose except military defense, unemployment aid, and aid to the world's needy.[45]

IMAGE 17.4 **What's In It for Me?**

Citizens demand government benefits (e.g., social security payments, medical care, and a strong military) but resist paying their costs.

In truth, a perplexed Congress, trying to reduce the budget deficit, faces a public that favors funding most programs at even higher levels than those favored by most lawmakers.[46] Moreover, spending for the most expensive of these programs—Social Security and Medicare—is uncontrollable. Americans have grown accustomed to certain government benefits, but they do not like the idea of raising taxes to pay for them. Furthermore, as the deficit shrank under the Obama administration (see Figure 17.1), the public became less concerned about its size. According to a report on national surveys, "The emphasis given to the budget deficit peaked in 2013, the first year of Obama's second term, when 72% called it a top priority," but by 2016, reducing the budget deficit ranked ninth in priority out of eighteen policy areas.[47]

Taxing, Spending, and Economic Equality

LO5 Identify the origins of the income tax, trace the influence of government spending and taxing policies on inequality, and examine these policies from the majoritarian and pluralist perspectives.

As we noted in Chapter 1, the most controversial purpose of government is to promote equality, especially economic equality. Promoting economic equality through government action comes about only at the expense of economic freedom. Wealthy people lose freedom to keep their money when government redistributes wealth from the rich to the poor through a progressive income tax. The goal is not to achieve equality of outcome but to reduce existing levels of inequality.

The national government introduced an income tax in 1862 to help finance the Civil War. That tax was repealed in 1871, and the country relied on revenue from tariffs on imported goods to finance the national government. The tariffs acted as a national sales tax imposed on all citizens, and many manufacturers—themselves taxed at the same rate as a laborer—grew rich from undercutting foreign competition.[48] Followers of a new political movement, the Populists (see Chapter 8), decried the inequities of wealth and called for a more equitable form of taxation, an income tax. An income tax law passed in 1894 was declared unconstitutional by the Supreme Court the next year. The Democratic Party and the Populists accused the Court of defending wealth against equal taxation and called for amending the Constitution to permit an income tax in their 1896 platforms. A bill to do so was introduced in 1909 and ratified in 1913 as the Sixteenth Amendment.

The Sixteenth Amendment gave government the power to levy a tax on individual incomes, and it has done so every year since 1914. From 1964 to 1981, people who reported taxable incomes of $100,000 or more were taxed at least 70 percent on all income above that figure or margin. Individuals with lower incomes paid taxes at progressively lower marginal rates. (Figure 17.5 shows how the top marginal rate has fluctuated over the years.) Let us look at the overall effect of government spending and tax policies on economic equality in America.

Government Effects on Economic Equality

We begin by asking whether government spending policies have any measurable effect on income inequality. Economists call a government payment to individuals through Social Security, unemployment insurance, food stamps, and other programs, such as agricultural subsidies, a transfer payment. Transfer payments need not always go to the poor. In fact, one problem with the farm program is that the wealthiest farmers have often received the largest subsidies. Some—like billionaire Paul Allen (Microsoft co-founder) and Charles Schwab (head of the investment company)—are not usually regarded as farmers.[49] Nevertheless, most researchers have determined that transfer payments have had a definite effect on reducing income inequality. According to the principle of progressive taxation, tax rates are supposed to take more revenue from the rich than from the poor. Although the effective rates have varied during the recent past, the wealthy were always taxed at higher rates than the poor, in line with the principle of progressive taxation. Some oppose progressive taxation as a tool for redistributing income rooted in an "obsession" with inequality.[50] They can point out that the richest 1 percent of taxpayers paid 38 percent of all federal individual income taxes in 2013.[51] Perhaps they paid so much because they made so much. If the richest 1 percent of all taxpayers took in 19 percent of all income in the nation (which they did), some think that they should pay twice that percentage in taxes (which they did).[52]

However, the national income tax is only part of the story. In some cases, poorer citizens pay a larger share of their income in taxes than wealthier citizens. "Stop Coddling the Super-Rich," wrote Warren Buffett. The third richest man in the world reported that he paid only 17.4 percent of his income in income taxes for 2010, while the average tax burden for the other twenty people in his office was 36 percent.[53] How can people in the lowest income group pay a higher percentage of their income in taxes than do those in the very highest group? In part, Buffett wrote, he made most of his money through capital gains on stocks, which were taxed at only 15 percent at the time (the rate is 20 percent today).

The full answer has to do with the combination of national, state, and local tax policies. Only the national income tax is progressive, with rates rising as income rises. The national payroll tax, which funds Social Security and Medicare, has two components—12.4 points go to Social Security and 2.9 to Medicare—for a total tax of 15.3 percent. The tax is regressive: its effective rate decreases as income increases

transfer payment
A payment by government to an individual, mainly through Social Security or unemployment insurance.

FIGURE 17.5 **The Ups and Downs of Top National Tax Rates**

In 1913, the Sixteenth Amendment empowered the national government to collect taxes on income. Since then, the government has levied taxes on individual and corporate income and on capital gains realized by individuals and corporations from the sale of assets, such as stocks or real estate. Incomes above certain levels are taxed at higher rates than incomes below those levels. This chart, which lists only the maximum tax rates, shows that they fluctuated wildly over time, from less than 10 percent to more than 90 percent. (They tend to be highest during periods of war.) During the Reagan administration, the maximum individual income tax rate fell to the lowest level since the Coolidge and Hoover administrations in the late 1920s and 1930s. The top rate increased slightly for 1991, to 31 percent, during George H. W. Bush's administration and jumped to 39.6 percent for 1994 under Clinton. The top rate was reduced in stages to 35 percent by Bush's tax plans in 2001 and 2003, which expired at the end of 2012. Congress and Obama agreed to restore the rate of 39.6 percent in 2013 for individuals making over $400,000.

Sources: *Wall Street Journal*, 18 August 1986, p. 10. Copyright 1986 by Dow Jones & Company, Inc. Reproduced with permission of Dow Jones & Company, Inc., in the format textbook via Copyright Clearance Center. Additional data from the Tax Policy Center, which reports tax brackets for individual years at http://www.taxpolicycenter.org.

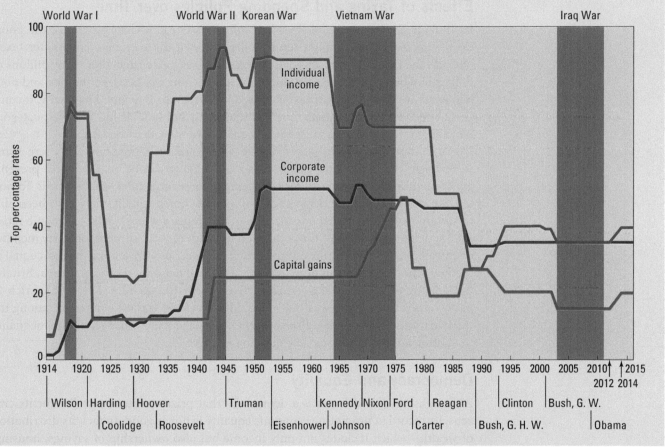

beyond a certain point. Because employers typically pay half, the effective rate for taxpayers is usually 7.65 percent. However, the larger Social Security component is levied on only a set portion of a person's income (the first $115,800 in 2015), and there is no Social Security tax at all on wages over that amount. So the effective rate of the Social Security tax is higher for lower-income groups than for the very top group. In fact, 97 percent of employees in the lowest 20 percent paid more payroll tax than income tax, compared with only 10 percent of employees in the upper 20 percent.[54]

Most state and local sales taxes are equally regressive. Poor and rich usually pay the same flat rate on their purchases. But the poor spend almost everything they earn on purchases, which are taxed, whereas the rich are able to save. A study showed that the effective sales tax rate for the lowest income group was thus about 7 percent, whereas that for the top 1 percent was only 1 percent.[55]

In general, the nation's tax policies at all levels have historically favored not only those with higher incomes, but also the wealthy—those who draw income from capital (wealth) rather than labor—for example:

- There is no national tax at all on investments in certain securities, including municipal bonds (issued by local governments for public projects).
- The tax on earned income (salaries and wages) is withheld from paychecks by employers under national law; the tax on unearned income (interest and dividends) is not.
- The tax on income from the sale of real estate or stocks (called capital gains) has typically been lower than the highest tax on income from salaries. (Income from selling property or from receiving stock dividends is taxed at 20 percent, while income from salaries for highly paid employees is taxed at almost twice that rate.)

Effects of Taxing and Spending Policies over Time

In 1967, at the beginning of President Johnson's Great Society programs, the poorest fifth of American families received 4 percent of the nation's income after taxes, whereas the richest fifth received 43.6 percent. Forty years later, after many billions of dollars had been spent on social programs, the income gap between the rich and poor had actually grown, as illustrated in "Freedom, Order, or Equality: Freedom v. Income Inequality." This is true despite the fact that many households in the lowest category had about one-third more wage-earners, mainly women, decades later.

In a capitalist system, some degree of inequality is inevitable. Is there some mechanism that limits how much economic equality can be achieved and prevents government policies from further equalizing income, no matter what is tried? To find out, we can look to other democracies to see how much equality they have been able to sustain. An international organization of developed nations analyzed income ratios for the richest 10 percent of the population to the poorest 10 percent for thirty member countries in 2013. The northwestern European countries were among the most equal in income ratios, averaging under 7:1.[56] The less equal nations—Portugal, Korea, Britain, Italy, Spain, and Greece—ranged respectively from 10.1 to 12.3. The ratio of rich to poor in the United States was 18.8—only Mexico (30.5) was more unequal among the thirty nations. Other studies also show that our society has more economic inequality than other advanced nations. The question is, why?

Democracy and Equality

Although the United States is a democracy that prizes political equality for its citizens, its record in promoting economic equality is not as good. In fact, its distribution of wealth—which includes not only income but also ownership of savings, housing, automobiles, stocks, and so on—is strikingly unequal. The wealthiest 1 percent of American families control almost 35 percent of the nation's household wealth (property, stock holdings, bank accounts).[57] Moreover, the distribution of wealth among ethnic groups is alarming. The typical white family has an annual income over 1.5 times that of both blacks and Hispanics.[58] If democracy means government "by the people," why aren't the people sharing more equally in the nation's wealth? If one of the supposed purposes of government is to promote equality, why are government policies not working that way?

One scholar theorizes that interest group activity in a pluralist democracy distorts government's efforts to promote equality. His analysis of pluralism sees "corporations and organized groups with an upper-income slant as exerting political power over and above the formal one-man-one-vote standard of democracy."[59] As argued in Chapter 10, the pluralist model of democracy rewards groups that are well organized and well funded.

Freedom, Order, or Equality

Freedom v. Income Inequality

In 2014, the 20 percent of U.S. families with the highest incomes received over 50 percent of all income, and their share has increased since 1967. This distribution of income is one of the most unequal among Western nations. At the bottom of the scale, the poorest 20 percent of families received less than 4 percent of total family income, and their share has decreased since 1967.

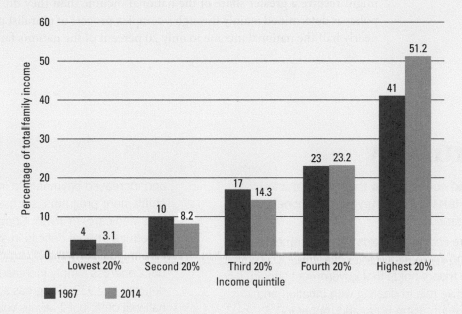

Source: Carmen DeNavas-Walt and Bernadette D. Proctor, U.S. Census Bureau, Current Population Reports, P60-252, *Income and Poverty in the United States: 2014* (Washington, DC: U.S. Government Printing Office, 2015), Table 2.

CRITICAL THINKING Despite nearly fifty years of progressive taxation, high-income people took home a greater share of total income in 2014 than in 1967. What would explain that?

What would happen if national tax policy were determined according to principles of majoritarian rather than pluralist democracy? Perhaps not much, if public opinion is any guide. In a string of Gallup polls from 1985 to 2015, clear majorities consistently said that the distribution of wealth is not fair and favor some redistribution—but the public is roughly evenly split on heavy taxes on the rich.[60] The people of the United States are not eager to redistribute wealth by increasing the only major progressive tax, the income tax. When polls asked over the years about replacing the progressive income tax with a flat tax or a national sales tax, most showed that a plurality of respondents preferred a flat tax, and almost as many favored a sales tax as the current income tax.[61] But a sales tax is a flat tax, paid by rich and poor at the same rate, and it would have a regressive effect on income distribution, promoting inequality. In one poll, the public also preferred a weekly $10 million national lottery to an increase in the income tax.[62] Because the poor are willing to chance more of their income on winning a fortune through lotteries than are rich people, lotteries (run by about forty states) also contribute to wealth inequality.[63]

Majoritarians might argue that most Americans fail to understand the inequities of the national tax system, which hides regressiveness in sales taxes and Social Security taxes. According to a national survey, Americans in the highest income categories (earning over $150,000 a year) understand the tax system much better than those at the lower income levels.[64] In Alabama, for example, income above $4,600 for a family of four went untaxed—meaning that most poor and all rich paid the same income tax, and the state relied mainly on sales and property taxes. In 2003, the conservative Republican governor of Alabama proposed a more progressive system of higher tax rates, mainly on the wealthy, only to have voters reject his reforms 2 to 1.[65] A black preacher and advocate of tax reform said that his parishioners like the (regressive) sales tax because they pay it in small increments.[66]

So majoritarians cannot argue that the public demands "fairer" tax rates that take from richer citizens to help poorer ones. If the public did, the lowest income families might receive a greater share of the national income than they do. Instead, economic policy is determined mainly through a complex process of pluralist politics that returns nearly half the national income to only 20 percent of the nation's families.

★ Summary

LO1 Compare and contrast four theories of market economics: laissez-faire, Keynesian, monetary, and supply-side.

- Laissez-faire economics holds that government should keep its hands off the economy. Keynesian theory holds that government should take an active role in dealing with inflation and unemployment, using fiscal and monetary policies to produce desired levels of aggregate demand. Supply-side economists, popular during the Reagan administration, focus on controlling the supply of goods and services rather than the demand for them.

- Economic growth in the United States during the mid- to late-1990s seemed to support the omniscience of free markets over government regulation. The financial crisis of 2008 and the accompanying recession led to a return to Keynesian principles. The continuing process of globalization has eroded government's ability to manage its own economy completely.

LO2 Describe the process by which the national budget is prepared and passed into law and the reforms undertaken by Congress to balance the budget.

- Congress alone prepared the budget until 1921, when it thrust the responsibility onto the president. In the 1970s, Congress sought to regain control of the process, creating a Congressional Budget Office and new House and Senate budget committees. Congress produced huge budget deficits in the 1980s fueled by tax cuts, increased military spending,

and increased payments to individuals under entitlement programs, such as Social Security and Medicare. In 1985, Congress passed a law to reduce annual deficits in stages, through automatic across-the-board cuts if necessary, but Congress simply increased the allowable deficits. In 1939, Congress set a ceiling for the national debt, but it always voted (over 100 times since) to increase the ceiling to accommodate the debt. Both examples of Congress's failure to control its own spending habits suggest that it would also circumvent any balanced budget amendment to the Constitution.

LO3 Identify the objectives of tax policies and explain why tax reform is difficult.

- Tax policies have several objectives: to adjust revenue to meet budget outlays; to make the tax burden more equitable for taxpayers; and to help control the economy by raising taxes. Tax reform is difficult because tax policies reflect two conflicting philosophies for distributing the costs of government: whether citizens should be taxed according to their ability to pay or for the benefits they receive.

- Despite public complaints about high taxes, current U.S. tax rates are lower than those in most other major countries and lower than they have been since the Great Depression of the 1930s. But even with the heavily progressive tax rates of the past, the national tax system has done little to redistribute income. Government transfer payments to individuals have helped reduce some income inequalities, but the distribution of income is less equal in the United States than in most major Western nations.

LO4 **Identify the major areas of government outlays and explain the role of incremental budgeting and uncontrollable spending on the growth of government spending.**

- Five categories consume about 85 percent of the FY 2017 budget: Social Security payments (the largest portion at 23 percent); Medicare and health, which includes research organizations such as the National Institutes of Health (29 percent); national defense (15 percent); income security (13 percent); and interest on the national debt (7 percent). The remaining 15 percent is distributed among veteran's

affairs, education, transportation, administration of justice, international affairs, natural resources, community development, science and technology, general government, agriculture, and energy.

LO5 **Identify the origins of the income tax, trace the influence of government spending and taxing policies on inequality, and examine these policies from the majoritarian and pluralist perspectives.**

- Pluralist democracy as practiced in the United States has allowed well-organized, well-financed interest groups to manipulate taxing and spending policies to their benefit. Taxing and spending policies in the United States are tipped in the direction of freedom rather than equality.

Chapter Quiz

LO1 **Compare and contrast four theories of market economics: laissez-faire, Keynesian, monetary, and supply-side.**

1. How does the "efficient market hypothesis" relate to laissez-faire economics?
2. How does the concept of "aggregate demand" relate to Keynesian economics?

LO2 **Describe the process by which the national budget is prepared and passed into law and the reforms undertaken by Congress to balance the budget.**

1. What is the difference between a budget authorization and an appropriation?
2. Distinguish between mandatory and discretionary spending.

LO3 **Identify the objectives of tax policies and explain why tax reform is difficult.**

1. What is the difference between a flat tax and a progressive tax? Which do you think is fairer?
2. Compared with other countries, how heavy is the tax burden in the United States?

LO4 **Identify the major areas of government outlays and explain the role of incremental budgeting and uncontrollable spending on the growth of government spending.**

1. Of the twenty or so categories of government functions, which consumes the most federal spending?
2. What percentage of the federal budget is consumed by foreign aid?

LO5 **Identify the origins of the income tax, trace the influence of government spending and taxing policies on inequality, and examine these policies from the majoritarian and pluralist perspectives.**

1. How much effect has national tax policy had on the distribution of family income over time?
2. What might happen if national tax policy were determined according to principles of majoritarian democracy and not pluralist democracy?

18 Policymaking and Domestic Policy

Has your family ever had trouble paying for essential items, like food, heat, and medicine? Have you ever been evicted for not being able to pay the rent? If so, you are not alone. In 2014, the national poverty rate was 14.8 percent, with tremendous variation across groups in society. Among people under age 18, the poverty rate was a whopping 21.1 percent, which means that about one in five children in the United States lives in poverty. Among the elderly, however, the poverty rate is only 10 percent.[1]

What are the elderly doing right? It turns out, the main thing they are doing right is simply being elderly. By virtue of their age, people over sixty-five belong to a group that the government has deemed entitled to important public benefits to help ensure that their basic needs are met. The most notable among these programs are Social Security and Medicare, which we discuss later in this chapter. One recent analysis determined that without Social Security benefits, the poverty rate among the elderly would be an astonishing 41 percent instead of 10 percent.[2]

So why doesn't the government do more to help other groups avoid poverty? Other groups benefit from government antipoverty programs as well, just to a lesser degree. For instance, government programs that provide access to health insurance for children have cut their uninsured rate by half in the past fifteen years.[3] The supplemental nutrition program helped keep nearly 5 million people out of poverty in 2013, including over 2 million children.[4] The fact remains, however, that the elderly have been the group most helped by government antipoverty programs.

Despite the apparent successes of such programs, debates about the government's role in shaping economic and social outcomes remain fierce. First, there are philosophical debates about whether government even has the authority or responsibility to provide a social safety net. Then there are technical debates about the effects of particular policies on areas such as government spending, individual tax burdens, state-level finances, and the quality (or lack thereof) of how laws get implemented. While it is tempting to conclude that policies that reduce poverty should remain in effect, social welfare policies are complicated. The challenge of devising, implementing, and assessing policies that protect the citizenry's standard of living while also satisfying other basic principles, such as federalism, the economic freedom of private employers, and the individual freedom of people to make life choices that endanger their well-being if they want to (such as deciding not to have health insurance), is ongoing.

In modern democracies, many people believe that the government should provide basic services so that no one's quality of life falls below a certain level. Crafting public policies that promote the view that governments have such responsibilities without infringing on personal or economic freedoms is a task that policymakers continually face. If and when a policy is enacted, tracking its progress and determining whether it is achieving its goals without also incurring undesirable, unintended consequences is the next hurdle. Then, deciding what, if any, changes should be made to the policy starts the cycle again.

#ChallengeAccepted

Take the Challenge on MindTap for American Government

Why have the elderly benefited so much from government-run antipoverty programs relative to other groups in society?

Learning Outcomes

LO1 Categorize different types of public policies and outline the process by which policies are formulated and implemented.

LO2 Trace the evolution of social welfare programs as a central element of public policy in the United States.

LO3 Describe the origins and evolution of Social Security as well as the funding and benefit issues facing the program.

LO4 Explain how poverty is defined and trace the evolution of public assistance programs designed to address it.

LO5 Differentiate among Medicare, Medicaid, and the Affordable Care Act of 2010 and explain how each program addresses health-care delivery.

LO6 Describe the role of the federal government in shaping education policy at the state and local government levels.

LO7 Assess alternative policies for addressing illegal immigration into the United States.

LO8 Explain how the issue of fairness shapes perspectives on government benefits.

Previous chapters focused on individual institutions of government. Here we look at government more broadly and ask how policymaking takes place across institutions. We first identify different types of public policies and analyze stages in the policymaking process. We describe policymaking as an ongoing process, often without a clear start or finish. Policies are continually evaluated, altered, and reevaluated. Then we look at specific domestic policies, that is, government plans of action targeting concerns internal to the United States. These are among the most enduring and costly programs that the government has launched on behalf of its citizens. Four questions guide our inquiry: What are the broad contours of the policymaking process? What are the origins and politics of specific domestic policies? What are the effects of these policies once they are implemented? Are disagreements about policy really disagreements about values?

Government Purposes and Public Policies

LO1 Categorize different types of public policies and outline the process by which policies are formulated and implemented.

In Chapter 1, we noted that most citizens accept limitations on their personal freedom in return for various benefits of government. We defined the major purposes of government as maintaining order, providing public benefits, and promoting equality. Different governments place different values on each broad purpose, and those differences are reflected in their public policies. A **public policy** is a general plan of action adopted by a government to solve a social problem, counter a threat, or pursue an objective.

At times, governments choose not to adopt a new policy to deal with a troublesome situation; instead, they muddle through, hoping the problem will diminish in importance. This too is a policy decision because it chooses to maintain the status quo. Whatever their form and effectiveness, all policies are the means by which government pursues certain goals in specific situations. People disagree about public policies because they disagree about one or more of the following elements: the goals government should have, the means it should use to meet them, and how the situation at hand should be perceived.

public policy
A general plan of action adopted by the government to solve a social problem, counter a threat, or pursue an objective.

The Policymaking Process

When people disagree on goals, that disagreement is often rooted in a difference in values. As emphasized throughout this book, such value conflict often involves pitting freedom against order or freedom against equality. Disputes involving values are hard to bridge since they reflect a basic worldview and go to the core of one's sense of right and wrong.

The problem of illegal drugs illustrates how different core values lead us to prefer different policies. Everyone agrees that government should address problems created by drugs. Yet views of what should be done differ sharply. Recall from Chapter 1 that libertarians prioritize individual freedom and want to limit government as much as possible. Many libertarians argue that drugs should be decriminalized; if people want to take drugs, they should be free to do so. If drug use were legal, crimes associated with the drug trade would evaporate. Conservatives emphasize order. In their minds, a safe and civilized society does not allow people to debase themselves through drug abuse, and the government should punish those who violate the law. Liberals promote treatment as a policy option. They regard addiction as a medical problem and believe that government should offer services that help addicts. Government should help people in need, they argue, and many drug offenders cannot pay for treatment because their drug habit has left them impoverished.

Types of Policies

Although values underlie choices, analysis of public policy does not usually focus explicitly on core beliefs. Political scientists often categorize policies by their objectives. One common purpose is to allocate resources so that some segment of society or region of the country can receive a service or benefit. We call these distributive policies. Pork barrel government projects discussed in Chapter 11 are distributive policies. One example of the distribution of resources toward a local project involves the nearly $50,000 that the National Endowment for the Arts recently gave to the Western Folklife Center for its annual Cowboy Poetry Festival in Elko, Nevada. Some argue that the government should not distribute funds for such local projects. Others, such as Senate Majority Leader Harry Reid (D-Nev.), say that the funding preserves and celebrates the culture of the American West while also enhancing the region's economy, since the yearly festival generates millions in economic activity.[5]

distributive policies
Government policies designed to confer a benefit on a particular institution or group.

With distributional policies, all of us, by paying our taxes, support those who receive the benefit, presumably because that benefit works toward the common good, such as stronger security, modernized infrastructure, a cleaner environment, or a richer national culture. In contrast, redistributional policies are explicitly designed to take resources from one sector of society and transfer them to another, reflecting the core value of equality.

redistributional policies
Policies that take government resources, such as tax funds, from one sector of society and transfer them to another.

State-level tax policies offer prime examples of differing ways to think about redistribution. The recession of 2007–2009 led nearly all states to grapple with budget shortfalls and growing numbers of people in hardship. States looked to their tax codes in order to find ways to shore up revenue. Some states, like Connecticut, increased taxes on the wealthiest residents and cut taxes for low-income workers as a way to raise revenue and redistribute income. This approach views taxation as a shared sacrifice that helps people out of poverty (freeing them from government safety net programs) and spurs further economic activity. Other states, like Michigan, reduced tax credits for low-income workers in order to keep more funds for government programs and to finance tax cuts for businesses and corporations. This approach, which minimizes redistribution, views taxes on the wealthy and the business sector as a barrier to economic development. Taking this approach to its extreme, governors in Oklahoma and Kansas have both promoted eliminating their state income tax altogether (an option long practiced in a handful of other states). This plan would essentially require the rich and poor alike to pay the same dollar amount (but vastly different income *percentages*) in taxes through the sales tax.[6] (For public opinion on federal taxes, see Figure 18.1.)

Another policy approach is regulation. In Chapter 13, we noted that regulations are rules that guide the operation of government programs. When regulations apply to businesses, they are an attempt to structure the market in a particular way. Government becomes a referee, establishing rules that set boundaries on how businesses can operate. Prior to the twentieth century, the food industry was unregulated. Since then, both the Food and Drug Administration (FDA) and the U.S. Department of Agriculture have been created to regulate the production and marketing of food. In 2011, the government added to existing regulations by enacting the FDA Food Safety Modernization

regulation
Government intervention in the workings of a business market to promote some socially desired goal.

FIGURE 18.1 **Who Is Paying Their Fair Share?**

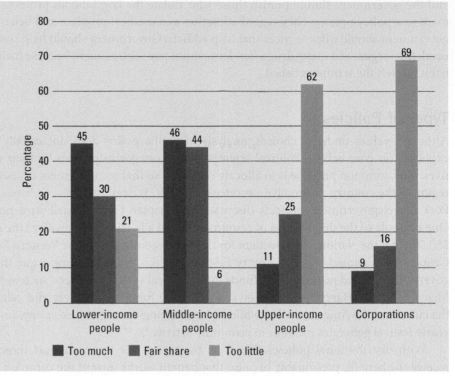

According to a Gallup poll, Americans believe that upper-income Americans and corporations pay too little in the way of taxes. Battles over federal income taxes confront nearly every president and every Congress.

Source: Gallup Poll, 9–12 April 2015.

Act, which was motivated by several high-profile food recalls involving products such as spinach, eggs, and peanut butter. An investigation that followed a *Salmonella* outbreak tied to eggs revealed that the contaminated eggs had been exposed to rodents, flies, maggots, manure, and chicken innards. One provision of the new law empowers the FDA to issue its own recalls instead of relying on voluntary recalls from food producers. It also provides greater inspection authority to the FDA, in the hope of preventing unsafe foods from reaching consumers in the first place, although some people maintain that the FDA does not have enough money to carry out its new prevention authority effectively.[7]

Americans disagree over the extent to which markets should operate freely. Some believe government should be only minimally involved. Others believe markets need close supervision because competitive pressures lead businesses to cut corners on the safety of their products or the integrity of their conduct. On the one hand, the decisions on how to regulate or whether to reduce regulation (to *deregulate*) may involve technical questions and are best left to experts who work for the relevant bureaucratic agencies. What, for example, is a safe level of "rodent filth" to allow in curry powder?[8] On the other hand, regulation and deregulation are subject to the same pulls and pushes of the political process as distributional and redistributional policies. In the case of food safety, the new regulations were supported by major food producers including General Mills and Kraft Foods, while they were opposed by associations representing smaller farms, who feared that the new law would create an insurmountable degree of new regulations and paperwork for them.[9]

This framework of distributional, redistributional, and regulatory policies is rather general, and there are surely policy approaches that don't fit neatly into these categories.[10] Nevertheless, it is a useful prism to examine policymaking. Understanding the broad purposes of public policy allows a better evaluation of the tools necessary to attain these objectives.

Public Policy Tools

There are different ways of achieving public policy objectives. One policy tool is *incentives*. A fundamental element of human behavior is that we can be induced to do certain things if rewards become substantial enough. We should all give to charity simply because it is a generous act. But to promote more giving, the government provides tax deductions for people who donate to nonprofit charities. A taxpayer who makes a $1,000 donation to the Red Cross can subtract that amount from her taxable income when determining how much she owes in taxes. Although giving to charity is a good thing, there's no free lunch. Incentives like these constitute a *tax expenditure*. Since government loses revenue on the charity deduction, it must make up revenue elsewhere. This tax expenditure is quite substantial: over 80 percent of Americans donate to charity each year, totaling over $300 billion annually.[11]

The flip side of incentives are *disincentives*—policies that discourage particular behavior. A tax on pollution, for example, is a disincentive for a factory to continue using high-polluting manufacturing processes. Likewise, taxes on cigarettes are meant to discourage smoking.

Much of what policymakers want to accomplish cannot be done through incentives or disincentives. Rather than coaxing or discouraging behavior, it must take responsibility itself to establish a program. Government's largest expenditures—for health care, education, social services, and defense—come from government's direct payments to its employees or to vendors who implement programs.

Finally, a common policy tool is to set rules. Much of what government does in the form of regulation involves setting rules regarding what businesses or individuals can do in the marketplace, as in the case of food safety discussed earlier. The federal government constantly issues new or revised rules on a variety of policy questions. In 2016, the FDA adopted a new rule that will allow it to regulate electronic cigarettes as a tobacco product. The cigarettes contain nicotine and other chemicals, but are tobacco-free. Before adopting this rule, businesses and state governments could decide for themselves whether e-cigarettes fall under their tobacco-free policies.[12] Now, e-cigarette manufacturers and vendors will have to comply with policies that regulate tobacco products, such as not selling to anyone under 18 and putting health warnings on packaging.

A Policymaking Model

Clearly, different approaches to solving policy problems affect the policymaking process, but common patterns exist. We can separate the policymaking process into four stages: agenda setting, policy formulation, implementation, and policy evaluation. Figure 18.2 shows the four stages in sequence. Note, however, that the process does not end with policy evaluation. Policymaking is a circular process; the end of one phase is the beginning of another.

FIGURE 18.2   The Policymaking Process

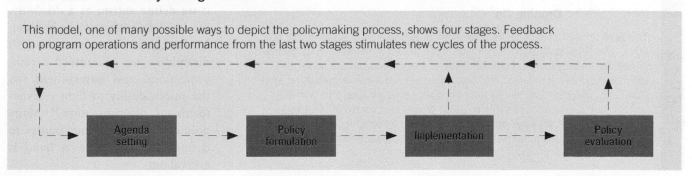

This model, one of many possible ways to depict the policymaking process, shows four stages. Feedback on program operations and performance from the last two stages stimulates new cycles of the process.

Agenda setting → Policy formulation → Implementation → Policy evaluation

Agenda Setting. When we think of the political agenda, we usually think of the broad set of policy areas that are central to American life. This broad agenda changes over time as conditions change, though Americans routinely place the economy and education among the nation's top priorities.

agenda setting
The stage of the policymaking process during which problems get defined as political issues.

Political scientists not only study what's on the agenda at any one time but also **agenda setting**, the part of the process in which problems are defined as political issues. Many problems confront Americans in their daily lives, but government is not actively working to solve them all. Consider Social Security. Today the old-age insurance program seems a hardy perennial of American politics, but it was not created until the New Deal. The problem of poverty among the elderly did not suddenly arise during the 1930s—there had always been poor people of all ages—but that is when inadequate income for the elderly was defined as a political problem. When the government begins to consider acting on an issue it previously ignored, we say that the issue has become part of the political agenda.

Why does a social problem become redefined as a political problem? There is no single reason; many factors stimulate new thinking about a problem. Sometimes highly visible events or developments push issues onto the agenda. Examples are great calamities (such as an oil spill, showing a need for safer offshore drilling rigs), the creation of new technology (such as the invention of mobile location technology, requiring privacy regulations), or irrational human behavior (such as mass shootings, pointing to the need for greater security measures).[13] Whether a certain problem moves onto the agenda is also affected by who controls the government and by broad ideological shifts. Presidential and congressional candidates run for office promising to put neglected issues on the agenda and sometimes succeed.

issue definition
Our conception of the problem at hand.

Part of the politics of agenda building is not just which new issues emerge and which issues decline in visibility, but the way the substantive problem at the heart of an issue is conceived. **Issue definition** is the way we think about a problem. Our conception of an issue is influenced by our own values and the way we see the political world. Interest groups and political parties try to persuade Americans to define issues in ways that are sympathetic to their cause. Ideological conservatives, for example, frame policy problems in terms of market approaches. If we accept that a market approach is better, then we'll shy away from government regulation.[14]

Citizens' views are also colored by what they regard as a government responsibility. Consider autism. If we define autism as a *disease*, then we might see a limited role for government—primarily as a funder of scientific research. But if we define autism as a *disability*, our issue definition will be broader. In the United States, persons with disabilities are guaranteed certain protections, and government has the responsibility to fight relevant forms of discrimination.[15] Many political battles are thus battles to define what the issue at hand is even about.

AMAZON/UPI/Newscom

IMAGE 18.1 Droning On

The development of new technology often puts issues on the agenda. In late 2015, the Federal Aviation Administration unveiled a new system for people to register their unmanned drones, a topic of new importance thanks to technological developments. All "unmanned aircraft systems" weighing more than 0.55 pounds must be registered or the user could face civil or criminal penalties. The potential benefits of using drones in commercial sectors such as agriculture and package delivery—and the individual freedom simply to fly a drone for recreational purposes—need to be balanced against potential risks to safety and privacy.

The most likely form of change in issue definition occurs when an additional *frame* emerges, which happens when a new perspective comes to the fore. For example, for many years the dominant issue frames concerning the death penalty involved punishment and morality. Some argued that the death penalty is a just punishment for a heinous crime. Those on the other side argued that the death penalty was immoral—that the state didn't have the right to take a life. In the late 1990s, stories emerged in the press about people who were wrongly convicted and sentenced to death. DNA testing became an increasing source of exculpatory evidence. This so-called innocence frame became part of the debate over the death penalty, and public support for the death penalty began to drop.[16]

Policy Formulation. Policy formulation is the stage of the process in which formal policy proposals are developed and officials decide whether to adopt them. The most obvious kind of policy formulation is the proposal of a measure by the president or the development of legislation by Congress. Administrative agencies also formulate policy, through the regulatory process. Courts formulate policy too, when their decisions establish new interpretations of the law.

Although policy formulation is depicted in Figure 18.2 as a single stage, it actually takes place over several stages and across different levels of government. In 2013, President Obama signed the Drug Quality and Security Act, which requires stricter oversight of compounding pharmacies (pharmacies that mix their own drugs) after a fatal outbreak of meningitis was linked to unsanitary compounding practices. Bureaucratic agencies then had to develop specific policies for implementing the law. If and when those policies are contested, courts will be called in to settle disputes.[17] Once the policy is in place for some time, it will be periodically evaluated and policymakers will consider further reforms.

As noted in Chapter 13, policy formulation is often *incremental*. As policies are debated, the starting point is the existing policy in that area, and if new policy is adopted, it is usually a modification of what was in place previously. One long-standing policy in the midst of incremental formulation involves fuel efficiency for cars and light trucks, known as Corporate Average Fuel Economy Standards (CAFE Standards). Such standards were first adopted by Congress in 1975, when the average gas mileage for a carmaker's fleet (passenger cars only) could not exceed 18 miles per gallon (mpg). These limits were designed to reduce energy consumption and carbon emissions. By 1990, that average had increased to 27.5 mpg. In 2012, the Environmental Protection Agency changed the standards again. By 2025, the average for a fleet's passenger cars will not be able to exceed 54.5 mpg. This dramatic increase in fuel standards represents a large change from previous limits, but it also represents a continuation and evolution of existing practices.[18]

Keep in mind that policy formulation is only the development of proposals designed to solve a problem. Some issues reach the agenda and stimulate new proposals but then fail to win enactment because political opposition mobilizes.

Implementation. Policies are not self-executing; implementation is the process by which they are carried out. When policies are enacted and when agencies issue regulations, government bodies must put those policies into effect. This process often involves multiple levels of government as well as actors in the private sector. After a major oil spill from the Deepwater Horizon rig in the Gulf of Mexico in 2010, government actors implemented the Oil Pollution Act of 1990, which requires "responsible parties" to establish a way to compensate victims who have suffered personally or professionally as a result of an oil spill. The BP oil company that operated the rig was thus responsible, but the government decided to take the lead in ensuring that the needs of victims were addressed. BP was ordered to establish a $20 billion fund, which was administered by a government-appointed

policy formulation
The stage of the policymaking process during which formal proposals are developed and adopted.

implementation
The process of putting specific policies into operation.

Jake May/The Flint Journal-MLive.com via AP

IMAGE 18.2   A Thirst for Answers

In late 2015, it was discovered that residents of Flint, Michigan, had been drinking water with unsafe lead levels for two years. Amid protests and the emergence of information indicating that government officials knew that the water was contaminated, Congress held hearings to investigate the role of the Environmental Protection Agency in Flint. The Congressional investigation also led the House to pass changes to the Safe Drinking Water Act; if enacted, the changes would require the government to notify the public if unsafe lead levels are detected and would enhance communication and coordination among the different parts of the government responsible for implementing policies related to water safety.

Source: Amanda Emery, "EPA didn't respond to Flint's water crisis as soon as it could have, report says," 18 February 2016, http://www.mlive.com/news/flint/index.ssf/2016/02/epa_didnt_respond _to_flints_wa.html.

"compensation czar." In further response to the spill, the government implemented provisions of the Clean Water Act, which involves charging BP for policy violations, such as negligence. In 2015, BP reached a settlement with the government to the tune of $18.7 billion.[19]

Although it may sound technical, implementation is actually a very political process, involving a great deal of bargaining and negotiation among different groups of people in and out of government. The challenge of implementing complex policies in a federal system, with multiple layers of government, that is also a pluralistic system, with competing interests, seems daunting. Yet there are incentives for cooperation, not the least of which is to avoid blame if a policy fails. (We discuss coordination in more detail in the next section.)

Policy Evaluation. How does the government know whether a policy is working? In some cases, success or failure may be obvious, but at other times, experts in a specific field must tell government officials how well a policy is working.

policy evaluation
Analysis of a public policy so as to determine how well it is working.

feedback
Information received by policymakers about the effectiveness of public policy.

Policy evaluation is the analysis of the results of public policy. Although there is no one method of evaluating policy, evaluation draws heavily on research, including cost-effectiveness analysis and measurement of program outcomes. Such studies influence decisions on whether to continue, expand, alter, reduce, or eliminate programs.

Evaluation is part of the policymaking process because it helps identify problems that arise from current policy. In other words, evaluations provide **feedback** to policymakers on program performance. The dotted line in Figure 18.2 represents a feedback loop. Problems that emerge during implementation also provide feedback to policymakers.

Feedback reflects the dynamic nature of policymaking. By drawing attention to emerging problems, policy evaluation influences the political agenda. The end of the process—evaluating whether the policy is being implemented as it was envisioned—is the beginning of a new cycle of public policymaking.

Fragmentation, Coordination, and Issue Networks

The policymaking process encompasses many stages and includes different participants at each stage. Here we examine some forces that pull the government in different directions and make problem solving less coherent than it might otherwise be. We also look at some structural elements of American government that work to coordinate competing approaches to the same problems.

A single policy problem may be attacked in different ways by government for many reasons. At the heart of this **fragmentation** of policymaking is the fundamental nature of government in America. The separation of powers divides authority among the branches of the national government, and federalism divides authority among the national, state, and local levels of government. These multiple centers of power are a primary component of pluralist democracy. Different groups try to influence different parts of the government; no one entity completely controls policymaking.

Differing policies among the states and between the states and the federal government cause confusion because of the fragmented approach of the different levels of government. Frustrated because the federal government had taken no action regarding the poisoning of children who unknowingly drink out of containers of antifreeze, California and Oregon passed laws requiring manufacturers to add a bitter-tasting ingredient to the mix. But this legislation meant that different states required different things from manufacturers.[20]

Fragmentation often creates a productive pressure to rethink jurisdictions and to create incentives for coordination. In our federal system, for instance, states possess some degree of autonomy. American federalism is often lauded because the states can be "fifty laboratories" for developing policy alternatives. Yet this can be frustrating to the federal government because states may develop policies at odds with federal approaches. Currently, states vary widely in their policies regarding the use of mobile devices while driving. Such distracted driving led to over 3,300 deaths and over 420,000 injuries in the United States in 2013. In response to this problem, some states have banned all handheld phone use by all drivers, some ban handheld phone use only for young drivers, most ban texting while driving, and some have practically no restrictions at all. To encourage coordination, the Distracted Driving Prevention Act has been introduced in Congress many times but has yet to be passed. It would encourage states to adopt laws that ban the use of handheld mobile devices while driving except in emergencies and navigation. States that fail to enact such laws would lose a portion of their federal transportation funds.[21]

The policy fragmentation created by federalism may be solved when an industry asks the national government to develop a single regulatory policy. In the antifreeze case discussed earlier, the state actions convinced the industry trade group that represents antifreeze manufacturers that it should drop its opposition to federal safety regulations.[22] Although an industry may prefer no regulation at all, it generally prefers one instead of fifty.

Another counterweight to fragmentation is the working relationships that develop among the many participants in the pluralist system. Suppose that Congress is considering amendments to the Clean

fragmentation
In policymaking, the phenomenon of attacking a single problem in different and sometimes competing ways.

Philippe TURPIN/Getty Images

IMAGE 18.3   Friends Don't Let Friends Snapchat and Drive

We all know that it's not safe to use our phones while we drive, but most of us are tempted to do it anyway. Some states, like California, have banned all handheld cell phone use while driving. In other states, like Montana, you can text all you want while you drive. Some federal lawmakers want states to have uniform (and strict) policies, but no federal law banning distracted driving has been passed yet.

Air Act. Because Congress does not function in a vacuum, other parts of government affected by the legislation participate in the process too. The Environmental Protection Agency (EPA) has an interest in the outcome because it will have to administer the law. The White House is concerned about legislation that affects such vital sectors of the economy as the steel and coal industries. Thus, officials from the EPA and the White House work with members of Congress and the appropriate committee staffs to try to ensure that their interests are protected. At the same time, lobbyists representing corporations, trade associations, and environmental groups try to influence Congress, agency officials, and White House aides. Experts from think tanks and universities might be asked to testify at hearings or to serve in an informal advisory capacity.

The various individuals and organizations that work in a policy area form a loosely knit community known as an **issue network**, where participants share expertise in a policy domain and interact frequently.[23] Such networks include members of Congress, committee staffers, agency officials, lawyers, lobbyists, consultants, scholars, and public relations specialists. Overall, a network can be quite large. One study identified over twelve hundred interest groups that had some contact with government officials in relation to health care over a five-year period.[24]

The common denominator in a network is not the same political outlook but policy expertise. Consider Medicare. The program is crucial to the health of the elderly, and with millions of baby boomers retiring, it needs to be structured carefully to make sure there will be enough money available to care for them all. But to enter the political debate on Medicare requires specialized knowledge. For instance, what is the difference between "global capitation" and "fee for service"? "Advance directives" and "withholds for never events" may be grating jargon to the uninitiated, but they are meaningful terms to those in this network. In short, members of an issue network speak the same language. They understand the substance of policy, the way Washington works, and one another's viewpoints.

In a number of ways, issue networks promote pluralist democracy. They are open systems, populated by a wide range of interest groups. Decision making is not centralized in the hands of a few key players; policies are formulated in a participatory fashion. But there is still no guarantee that all relevant interests are represented, and those with greater financial resources have an advantage. Nevertheless, issue networks provide access to government for a diverse set of competing interests and thus further the pluralist ideal.

Issue networks are an obstacle to achieving the majoritarian vision of how government should operate. The technical complexity of contemporary issues makes it difficult for the public at large to influence policy outcomes. The more complex an issue, the more elected officials must depend on the technocratic elite that comprise issue networks for policy guidance. Yet majoritarianism still influences policymaking. The broad contours of public opinion can be a dominant force on highly visible issues.[25] Elections, too, send messages to policymakers about the most widely discussed campaign issues. What issue networks have done, however, is facilitate pluralist politics in policy areas in which majoritarian influences are weak.

With this overview of the policymaking process in place, we now turn our attention to some of the largest, most expensive, and politically challenging domestic policy programs in the United States. We discuss how these programs became part of the political agenda and how they have been formulated, implemented, evaluated, and altered over time. We also illustrate how different perspectives on these programs highlight different values placed on freedom, order, and equality.

issue network
A shared-knowledge group consisting of representatives of various interests involved in some particular aspect of public policy.

The Development of the American Welfare State

LO2 Trace the evolution of social welfare programs as a central element of public policy in the United States.

Perhaps the most controversial purpose of government is to promote social and economic equality. To do so may conflict with the freedom of some citizens because it requires government action to redistribute income from rich to poor. This choice between freedom and equality constitutes the modern dilemma of government; it has been at the center of many conflicts in U.S. public policy since World War II. On one hand, most Americans believe that government should help the needy.[26] On the other hand, they do not want to sacrifice their own standard of living in order to do so.

At one time, governments confined their activities to the minimal protection of people and property—to ensuring security and order. Now, almost every modern nation is a **welfare state** serving as the provider and protector of individual well-being through economic and social programs. **Social welfare programs** are government programs designed to provide the minimum living conditions necessary for all citizens. Income for the elderly, health care, public assistance, and education are among the concerns addressed by government social welfare programs.

Social welfare policy is based on the premise that society has an obligation to meet the basic needs of its members. The term *welfare state* describes this protective role of government. To understand American social welfare policies, one must first understand the significance of a major event in U.S. history—the Great Depression— and the two presidential plans that extended the scope of government, the New Deal and the Great Society. Initiatives from these programs dominated national policy and established the idea that it is the role of the federal government to help meet the basic needs of its citizens, though debates about how best to do that remain fierce.

welfare state
A nation in which the government assumes responsibility for the welfare of its citizens by providing a wide array of public services and redistributing income to reduce social inequality.

social welfare programs
Government programs that provide the minimum living standards necessary for all citizens.

The Great Depression and the New Deal

Throughout its history, the U.S. economy has experienced alternating good and bad times, generally referred to as business cycles (see Chapter 17). The **Great Depression** was the longest and deepest setback that the American economy ever experienced. It began with the stock market crash on October 24, 1929, and did not end until the start of World War II. By 1933, one out of every four U.S. workers was unemployed, and millions more were underemployed. To put that in perspective, the annual U.S. unemployment rate since the end of World War II has never topped 10 percent.[27] The effect of the Great Depression on attitudes about the role of government and on the actual operation of governmental institutions is arguably without peer.

In the 1930s, the forces that stemmed earlier business declines were no longer operating. There were no more frontiers, no growth in export markets, no new technologies to boost employment. Unemployment spread, and the crisis fueled itself. Workers who lost their income could not buy the food, goods, and services that kept the economy going. Private industry and commercial farmers produced more than they could sell profitably. Closed factories, surplus crops, and idle workers were the consequences. From 1929 to 1932, more than 44 percent of the nation's banks failed when unpaid loans exceeded the value of bank assets. Farm prices fell by more than half in the same period. Upon accepting the presidential nomination at the 1932 Democratic National Convention, Franklin Delano Roosevelt, then governor of

Great Depression
The longest and deepest setback the American economy has ever experienced. It began with the stock market crash on October 24, 1929, and did not end until the start of World War II.

New Deal
The measures advocated by the Franklin D. Roosevelt administration to alleviate the Depression.

New York, said, "I pledge you, I pledge myself to a new deal for the American people." Roosevelt did not specify the contents of his **New Deal**, but the term was applied to measures Roosevelt's administration undertook to stem the Depression. The most significant New Deal policy created the Social Security program, which is explained in detail later in this chapter. Overall, New Deal policies initiated a long-range trend toward government expansion.

The Great Society

After winning the 1964 presidential election in a landslide, Lyndon Baines Johnson was committed to pushing an aggressive and activist domestic agenda designed to foster equality. In his 1965 State of the Union address, he offered his own version of the New Deal: the **Great Society**, an array of programs designed to redress political, social, and economic inequality. In contrast to the New Deal, which was largely aimed at short-term relief, most of Johnson's programs targeted chronic ills requiring a long-term commitment by the government.

Great Society
President Lyndon Johnson's broad array of programs designed to redress political, social, and economic inequality.

War on Poverty
A part of President Lyndon Johnson's Great Society program, intended to eradicate poverty within ten years.

Central to the Great Society was the **War on Poverty**. The major weapon in this war was the Economic Opportunity Act (1964), which encouraged local programs to educate and train people for employment. Among them were college work-study programs, summer employment for high school and college students, loans to small businesses, a domestic version of the Peace Corps (called VISTA, for Volunteers in Service to America), educational enrichment and nutrition for preschoolers through Head Start, and legal services for the poor. The War on Poverty also saw the passage of the Food Stamp Act, which was a precursor to today's nationwide nutritional assistance program. The year 2014 marked the fiftieth anniversary of the War on Poverty. Some critics say that since the official poverty rate is at roughly the same level as when the War on Poverty began, the policies have not been successful and poverty won. Others contend that without our current antipoverty programs, the poverty rate would be considerably higher.[28]

IMAGES 18.4a AND 18.4b   A Human Tragedy

The Great Depression idled millions of able-bodied Americans. By 1933, when President Herbert Hoover left office, about one-fourth of the labor force was out of work. Private charities were swamped with the burden of feeding the destitute. The hopeless men pictured on the left await a handout from a wealthy San Francisco matron known as the "White Angel," who provided resources for a bread line. Over eighty years later, roughly 14 percent of American families suffer from food insecurity and struggle to find enough to eat, as seen on the right.

Source: "Household Food Security in the United States in 2014," USDA, September 2015, http://www.ers.usda.gov/publications/err-economic-research-report/err194.aspx.

Retrenchment and Reform

In the years following the Great Society era, critics seized on perceived shortcomings of the growing American welfare state. The fact that poverty persisted and had become more concentrated in areas that the Great Society had targeted (inner cities and rural areas) suggested to some observers that the effort was a failure.

Those arguments took hold in the late 1970s and helped Ronald Reagan capture the White House in 1980. Reagan's victory and reelection in 1984 forced a reexamination of social welfare policy. Reagan argued that to the extent that government should guarantee the well-being of less fortunate citizens, state and local governments could do so more efficiently than the national government. Congress, controlled by Democrats, blocked some of Reagan's proposed cutbacks, and many Great Society programs remained in force, although with less funding. The growth of social welfare that began with the New Deal ended with the Reagan administration. Then President Bill Clinton, a Democrat, entered office in 1993 hoping to reform social safety net programs while simultaneously protecting their basic elements. Charting that middle course became essential after 1994 when Republicans took control of Congress. By the end of Clinton's two terms, important reforms emerged in public assistance, which we describe later in this chapter. More recently, President Obama enacted the biggest welfare state reform since the New Deal, with the passage of the Affordable Care Act in 2010, also described later.

Social Security

LO3 Describe the origins and evolution of Social Security as well as the funding and benefit issues facing the program.

Insurance protects against loss. Since the late nineteenth century, there has been a growing tendency for governments to offer social insurance, which is government-backed protection against loss by individuals, regardless of need. Common forms of social insurance offer health protection and guard against losses from sickness, injury and disability, old age, and unemployment. The first social insurance in the United States was workers' compensation. Beginning early in the twentieth century, this insurance compensated workers who lost income because they were injured in the workplace.

Social insurance benefits are distributed to recipients without regard to their economic status. Old-age benefits, for example, are paid to workers—rich or poor—if they have enough covered work experience and have reached the required age. Thus, social insurance programs are examples of entitlements—benefits to which every eligible person has a legal right and that the government cannot deny. The largest entitlement program is Social Security.

Social Security is social insurance that provides economic assistance to people faced with unemployment, disability, or old age. In most social insurance programs, employees and employers contribute to a fund from which employees later receive payments. Contributions to two programs for social insurance in the United States are taken from workers' wages: Social Security and Medicare. The Social Security tax supports disability, survivors' benefits, and retirement benefits. Since 1990, this tax has typically been assessed at a rate of 6.2 percent. In 2016, the tax was only assessed on the first $118,500 earned. The Medicare tax finances much (but not all) of the Medicare program and has been assessed at 1.45 percent of all wages since 1986.[29]

social insurance
A government-backed guarantee against loss by individuals without regard to need.

entitlements
Benefits to which every eligible person has a legal right and that the government cannot deny.

Social Security
Social insurance that provides economic assistance to persons faced with unemployment, disability, or old age. It is financed by taxes on employers and employees.

Juniors Busy
With Variety
Of Activities

Class Officers: Heather Crandall, treasurer; Sue Wendt, secretary; Paul Ryan, president; and Adam Ryan, vice-
president

The Washington Post/Getty Images

IMAGE 18.5   Social Security for Kids?

When Speaker of the House Paul Ryan was 16, his father died from a heart attack. For the next two years, Ryan received government aid in the form of Social Security survivor's benefits, which helped him pay for college. Most people think of the elderly when they think of Social Security, but widows, widowers, children, and dependent parents can also receive benefits when a worker in the family dies.

Source: Bobbie Kyle Sauer, "10 Things You Didn't Know about Paul Ryan," *US News & World Report*, 23 July 2008, http://www.usnews.com/news/campaign-2008/articles/2008/07/23/10-things-you-didnt-know-about-paul-ryan.

Social Security Act
The law that provided for Social Security and is the basis of modern American social welfare.

Origins of Social Security

The idea of Social Security came late to the United States. Most European nations adopted old-age insurance after World War I; many provided income support for the disabled and income protection for families after the death of the principal wage earner. In the United States, however, the needs of the elderly and the unemployed were left largely to private organizations and individuals. Although twenty-eight states had old-age assistance programs by 1934, neither private charities nor state governments could cope with the prolonged unemployment and distress of the Great Depression. It became clear that a national policy was necessary to deal with a national crisis.

In 1935, President Roosevelt signed the **Social Security Act**, which remains the cornerstone of the modern American welfare state. The act developed three approaches to the problem of dependence. The first provided social insurance in the form of old-age and surviving-spouse benefits and cooperative state–national unemployment assistance. To ensure that the elderly did not retire into poverty, it created a program to provide income to retired workers. An unemployment insurance program was also created to provide payments for a limited time to workers who were laid off or dismissed for reasons beyond their control.

The second approach provided aid to the destitute in the form of grants-in-aid to the states. It was the first national commitment to provide financial assistance to the needy aged, needy families with dependent children, the blind, and (since the 1950s) the permanently and totally disabled. The third approach provided health and welfare services through federal aid to the states. Included were health and family services for disabled children and orphans and vocational rehabilitation for the disabled.

How Social Security Works

Although the Social Security Act encompasses many components, when most people think of "Social Security," they have the retirement security element of the law in mind. Revenues for retirement security go into their own *trust fund* (each program contained in the Social Security Act has a separate fund). The fund is administered by the Social Security Administration, an independent government agency. Trust fund revenue can be spent only for the old-age benefits program. Benefits, in the form of monthly payments, begin when an employee reaches retirement age, which is sixty-seven for people born in 1960 or later. People can retire as early as age sixty-two with reduced benefits.

Social Security taxes collected today pay the benefits of today's retirees with any surpluses held over to help finance the retirement of future generations. Thus, Social Security (and social insurance in general) is not a form of savings (your contributions are not set aside for your retirement); it is a pay-as-you-go tax system. Today's workers support today's program beneficiaries. Universal participation is thus essential. Government—the only institution with the authority to coerce—requires all employees and their employers to contribute, thereby imposing restrictions on freedom.

When the Social Security program began, it had many contributors and few beneficiaries. The program could therefore provide relatively large benefits with low taxes. In 1955, Social Security taxes of nearly nine workers supported each beneficiary. Over time, this ratio has decreased, dropping to 2.8 workers for every beneficiary in 2015 (see Figure 18.3).[30] The solvency of the Social Security program will soon be tested. Based on projections from recent analyses, the program's assets will be exhausted by 2029.[31]

People who currently pay into the system receive retirement benefits financed by future participants. If the birthrate remains steady or grows, future wage earners can support today's contributors when they retire. And if the economy expands, there will be more jobs, more income, and a growing wage base to tax for benefits to retirees. But when the birthrate falls or mortality declines or the economy falters, then contributions decline and the financial status of the program suffers. With life expectancy in the United States roughly five years longer than it was when Social Security was created, some argue that it is time to increase the retirement age since retirees today benefit from the program for a longer period of time than was originally envisioned. If the retirement age had been indexed to life expectancy in 1935, the retirement age today would be around seventy-two.[32]

Added to the demographic challenges facing Social Security is the fact that the rising cost of living means that payments to retirees need to increase as well in order for the program to achieve its aim of helping seniors avoid poverty. In 1972, Congress adopted automatic adjustments in benefits and in the dollar amount of contributors' wages subject to tax. The cost of living adjustment (COLA) is now based on changes in the Consumer Price Index. During the recession of 2007–2009, the Consumer Price Index did not rise, which resulted in no COLA in 2010 or 2011, marking the first time that benefits did not rise since adjustments were made automatic. Benefit levels were kept the same in 2016 as well.[33]

FIGURE 18.3   More Seniors, Fewer Workers

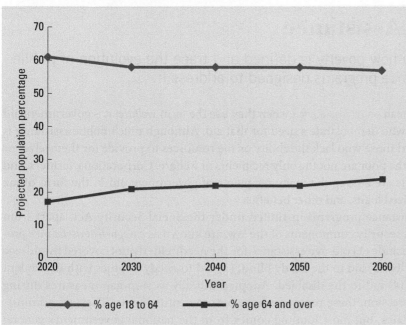

Between now and 2035, the percentage of the population aged sixteen to sixty-four is expected to decrease by 5.1 points while the percentage over sixty-five is expected to grow by 6.1 points. With a smaller percentage contributing to Social Security and a greater percentage receiving benefits, the financing of the program will be challenged. Debate over changes to the program boils down to two questions that politicians politely decline to answer: How soon will the national government change the current system, and how much will the government change it?

Source: Bureau of Census, "Resident Population Projections by Sex and Age: 2015 to 2050 [Quinquennially, as of July 1]," *ProQuest Statistical Abstract of the U.S. 2014 Online Edition*, ed. ProQuest, 2014.

Social Security Reform

Given the fund projections and demographic trends discussed earlier, concern over the future survival of Social Security runs high. For example, in 2014, 50 percent of Americans born after 1980 said that they believed that Social Security would not have money available to pay for their benefits when they retire.[34]

Repeated attempts to reform Social Security have failed to be enacted due to the tough choices involved. President George W. Bush advocated allowing individual workers to invest their own payroll taxes in the stock market in hopes of earning a higher rate of return than currently paid to the Social Security Trust Funds. However, people who wanted to stay in the current Social Security system could choose to do so.[35] But he was unable to generate enough support for the reform, since many Americans and lawmakers alike feared that privatizing the program would expose the elderly to too much risk of lost savings should the stock market decline. Bush left office with the Social Security program unchanged.

When Barack Obama took office in 2009, addressing the economic recession became his first priority; reforming Social Security was on the back burner. In his 2014 budget plan, Obama proposed basing COLAs on *chained CPI* instead of on the traditional CPI. Chained CPI is an alternative measure of inflation, based on the assumption that as the price of goods rises, people look to save money by buying cheaper alternatives. Traditional CPI, on the other hand, does not factor in changes in people's buying habits. The Obama administration and Republicans in Congress supported using chained CPI, which would result in lower COLAs, but Democrats in Congress saw the change as a benefit cut and opposed it.[36]

Despite the difficulty of reforming Social Security in recent years, it is unlikely that Congress or the White House will ever let its fund run dry. Proposals for keeping Social Security solvent include raising the full retirement age, raising the payroll tax rate, eliminating the salary cap and allowing all income to be taxed, reducing benefits for wealthy seniors, and reducing COLAs and benefit levels for all retirees. Of these, allowing all income to be taxed and not just the first $118,500 would help the program the most. It is also the option that most Americans prefer.[37]

Public Assistance

LO4 Explain how poverty is defined and trace the evolution of public assistance programs designed to address it.

public assistance
Government aid to individuals who can demonstrate a need for that aid.

Most people mean **public assistance** when they use the term *welfare*; it is government aid to individuals who demonstrate a need for that aid. Although much public assistance is directed toward those who lack the ability or the resources to provide for themselves or their families, the poor are not the only recipients of welfare. Corporations, farmers, and college students are among the many recipients of government aid in the form of tax breaks, subsidized loans, and other benefits.

Public assistance programs instituted under the Social Security Act, apart from the retirement security components of the law, are known as *categorical assistance programs*. They include (1) old-age assistance for the needy elderly not covered by old-age pension benefits, (2) aid to the needy blind, (3) aid to needy families with dependent children, and (4) aid to the disabled. Adopted initially as stop-gap measures during the Great Depression, these programs have become entitlements. They are administered by the states, but most funding comes from the national government's general tax revenues. Because states also contribute to funding of their public assistance programs, the benefits and some standards that define eligibility can vary widely from state to state.

Poverty in the United States

Until 1996, the government imposed national standards on state welfare programs. It distributed funds to each state based on the proportion of its population living in poverty. That proportion is determined by a federally defined poverty level, or poverty threshold, which is the minimum cash income that will provide for a family's basic needs. The poverty level varies by family size and was originally calculated as three times the cost of a minimally nutritious diet for a given number of people over a given time period. The threshold was computed this way because research suggested that poor families of three or more persons spent approximately one-third of their income on food.[38] Today, the threshold is adjusted using the Consumer Price Index. The poverty threshold is what the Census Bureau uses to determine the number of people who live below the poverty line. In 2015, the poverty threshold for a family of four was a cash income below $24,036.[39] The Department of Health and Human Services uses a slightly different measure, called the poverty guideline, to determine the income level at which families qualify for government assistance.

> **poverty level**
> The minimum cash income that will provide for a family's basic needs; calculated using the Consumer Price Index.

The poverty level is only a rough measure for distinguishing the poor from the nonpoor. For instance, the poverty level has been fairly constant since the early 1970s, even though other indicators of well-being, like the infant mortality rate and the percentage of adults with a high school diploma, show dramatic improvement in that same time period.[40]

The poverty rate in the United States declined after the mid-1960s, rose slightly in the 1980s, then declined again. In 2014, the U.S. Census Bureau estimated that 46.7 million people, or roughly 14.8 percent of the population, were living in poverty (see Figure 18.4).[41]

Poverty was once a condition of old age, but Social Security changed that. As noted in the opening of this chapter, poverty is still related to age, but in the opposite direction: it is largely a predicament of the young. In 2014, 21.1 percent of persons under eighteen years old were in poverty, compared with about 10 percent of people over sixty-five.[42]

Over time, the proportion of income spent on food has declined as the costs of housing, child care, health care, and other expenses have increased. Policymakers have therefore considered different approaches to determine how much a family of four needs to live in the United States, but they have been reluctant to abandon a measure that has been in use since the 1960s. In 2009, officials from several agencies developed a supplemental poverty measure (SPM) that incorporates cost of living changes across a wider range of goods and benefits that people receive from antipoverty programs. According to the SPM, the poverty rate in 2014 was closer to 15.3 percent, half of a point higher than the rate determined by the traditional measure. For young people, the SPM was lower (21.1 percent versus 16.7 percent), while among the elderly, it was higher (10 percent versus 14.4 percent).[43]

Another trend in the United States, which we illustrate in Figure 18.4, is the concentration of poverty in households headed by single women. Over 30 percent of female-headed families are in poverty, compared to only 6.2 percent of families headed by a married couple. Researchers have labeled this trend toward greater poverty among women the feminization of poverty.

> **feminization of poverty**
> The term applied to the fact that a large percentage of all poor Americans are women or the dependents of women.

Welfare Reform

Critics of social welfare spending have long argued that antipoverty policies make poverty more attractive by removing incentives to work. During Reagan's campaign

FIGURE 18.4   The Feminization of Poverty

The twentieth century brought extraordinary changes for women. Women won the right to vote and own property, and they gained some legal and social equality (see Chapter 16). But increases in rates of divorce and adolescent pregnancy have cast more women into the head-of-household role, a condition that tends to push women and children into poverty. In the absence of a national child-care policy, single women with young children face limited employment opportunities and lower wages in comparison to other workers. These factors have contributed to the feminization of poverty—the fact that a high percentage of all poor Americans are women or the dependents of women. In this graph, female-headed households with no husband have the highest poverty rate among the demographic groups depicted.

Sources: Barbara Ehrenreich and Frances Fox Piven, "The Feminization of Poverty," *Dissent* (Spring 1984): 162–170; Harrell R. Rodgers, Jr., *Poor Women, Poor Families: The Economic Plight of America's Female-Headed Households*, 2nd ed. (Armonk, N.Y.: M. E. Sharpe, 1990); U.S. Census Bureau, *Income, Poverty, and Health Insurance Coverage in the United States: 2012* (published 2013), Table 3 People in Poverty by Selected Characteristics: 2011 and 2012, http://www.census.gov/prod/2013pubs/p60-245.pdf; and Carmen DeNavas-Walt and Bernadette D. Proctor, "Income and Poverty in the United States: 2014," (Washington, DC: U.S Census Bureau, 2015).

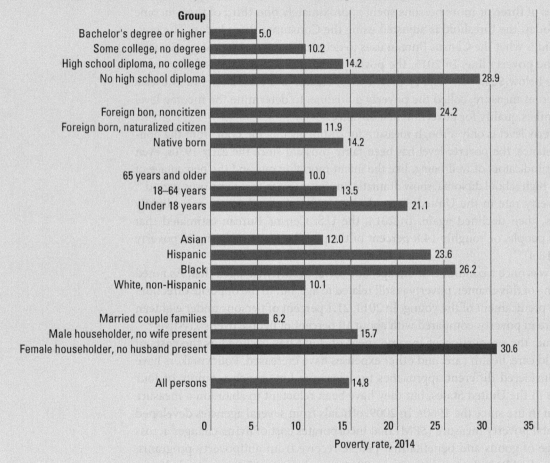

Group

Group	Poverty rate, 2014
Bachelor's degree or higher	5.0
Some college, no degree	10.2
High school diploma, no college	14.2
No high school diploma	28.9
Foreign bon, noncitizen	24.2
Foreign born, naturalized citizen	11.9
Native born	14.2
65 years and older	10.0
18–64 years	13.5
Under 18 years	21.1
Asian	12.0
Hispanic	23.6
Black	26.2
White, non-Hispanic	10.1
Married couple families	6.2
Male householder, no wife present	15.7
Female householder, no husband present	30.6
All persons	14.8

Poverty rate, 2014

Temporary Assistance for Needy Families (TANF)
A 1996 national act that abolished the longtime welfare policy, Aid for Families with Dependent Children (AFDC). TANF gives the states much more control over welfare policy.

for the presidency, he blamed such policies for creating Cadillac-driving "welfare queens."[44] In 1996, the Republican-led Congress sought a fundamental revision of the welfare system and enlisted President Clinton in their cause. When Clinton signed the Personal Responsibility and Opportunity to Work Act into law that year, he abolished the sixty-one-year-old Aid to Families with Dependent Children (AFDC) program, which was created during the New Deal to provide cash assistance to poor families, and replaced it with **Temporary Assistance for Needy Families (TANF)**, a program that is still in place.

Under TANF, which devolves power to the states, adult recipients of welfare payments have to become employed within two years. The law places the burden of job training and creation on the states. Families can receive no more than a total of five years of benefits in a lifetime, and states can set a lower limit.[45] A major feature of the reformed program was to allow states to use the funds for a wide array of programs beyond direct cash assistance as long as those programs were designed to help people get (and keep) jobs and become economically self-sufficient.[46] As Figure 18.5 shows, the amount of welfare funding going directly to cash assistance declined sharply when TANF was implemented.

How has welfare reform affected the states? In terms of funding, federal support for the law has been implemented through block grants, or a lump-sum, to the states totaling $16.5 billion per year. That money helps finance fifty different welfare systems. As in any other complicated piece of legislation, the process of writing regulations and offering guidance to help states implement the law has been an ongoing process. Overall, though, state leaders generally were pleased with the increased flexibility that TANF provided when compared to policy on the books prior to 1996.

What about welfare recipients themselves? How have they fared under the law? Since the implementation of TANF, the number of families on welfare has declined and remained relatively low when compared to the pre-TANF period (5 million families in 1994 versus 1.3 million families in 2015).[47] Large numbers of former welfare recipients were able to find steady work. One of the biggest fears of TANF's critics, that employers would find former welfare recipients undesirable employees and that there would be few jobs available in major urban areas, did not materialize.[48] As a result, Americans' opposition to welfare spending has declined in recent years, and their attitudes about welfare recipients have improved.[49]

Other trends are less promising. Despite former welfare recipients' increased levels of employment, most have not been able to find jobs that pay good wages and offer valuable benefits, such as health care. Thus, many former TANF recipients still live below or close to the poverty level. Moreover, studies have found that these jobs often require workers to have long commutes, which creates added stress as parents need to

FIGURE 18.5   Spending on TANF and Prior Programming, 1994–2014

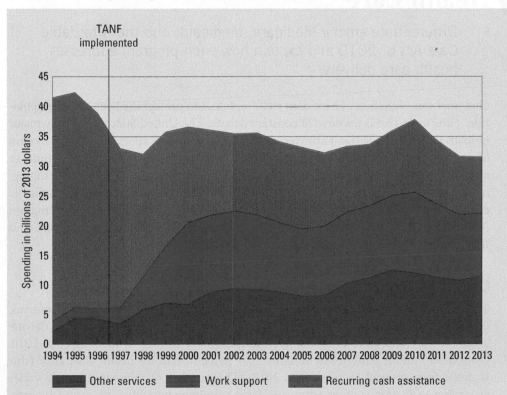

Before TANF was implemented, nearly all welfare spending was in the form of cash assistance to the poor. Now, less than 30 percent of the funds go to cash assistance. The rest goes to related programming, including job training and childcare.

Source: Congressional Budget Office based on data from the Department of Health and Human Services; https://www.cbo.gov/publication/49887#title0.

Supplemental Nutrition Assistance Program (SNAP)
A federal program administered by the states that provides assistance for purchasing food to eligible beneficiaries.

secure child care during their long workday.[50] Other challenges became acute during the recession that started in 2007. Many Americans hit hard by the recession were not helped by TANF. The problem is that the block grant funding is set to a fixed amount and does not change in response to increased need. Moreover, that fixed amount has not changed since TANF was first created. As a result, TANF cases did not increase much during the recession despite widespread job loss and hardship. As a point of comparison, the food stamp program known as **Supplemental Nutrition Assistance Program (SNAP)**, which gets increased funding when the need arises, saw a 45 percent increase in its participation rate from 2007 to 2009, whereas TANF participation only rose by 13 percent. With the dollar amount given to states unchanged and with needs rising, many states actually cut TANF benefits during the recession.[51]

TANF was due to be reauthorized in 2010. During the reauthorization process, Congress debates whether to make changes to both the funding levels and the rules that affect how and under what conditions the funds may be spent. TANF has not yet been formally reauthorized; instead Congress has been passing temporary measures to continue funding the program. When Congress finally turns its attention to TANF, the policy evaluation (recall Figure 18.2) will likely center on how the program fared during the last recession. Although welfare reform was initially hailed as a success, the experiences of the past several years have led many people to conclude otherwise.

SNAP, like TANF, is run through a partnership between the federal government and the states, though the states do not have as much freedom in its administration as they do with TANF. In 2014, the program provided food aid to 46 million Americans, nearly 70 percent of them in families with children. That year, the average benefit was $125 per month (or $4.17 per day; $1.39 per meal). In 2014, President Obama signed into law a farm bill that included cutting $8.6 billion from the $82.5 billion program.[52]

Health Care

LO5 Differentiate among Medicare, Medicaid, and the Affordable Care Act of 2010 and explain how each program addresses health-care delivery.

One important function of a modern welfare state is to protect the health of its population. How to do that is a source of constant debate. The United States is the only major industrialized nation without a universal health-care system. Rather, a patchwork system of care designed to cover different segments of the population has evolved over time. In addition to private insurance, which many Americans receive as a benefit of employment, government programs to provide health care include Medicare, primarily for the elderly; Medicaid, for the qualifying poor; and the Children's Health Insurance Program (CHIP), for children in needy families. This section discusses Medicare, Medicaid, and the Affordable Care Act (ACA) enacted by the Obama administration in 2010.

Cost and Access

To better understand the American system of health care and possibilities for reforms, it is important to consider two issues that animate the nation's health-care debate: access to care and cost. First, many Americans have no health insurance. In 2014, around 33 million Americans, roughly 10.4 percent, had no health insurance (this is down from around 16 percent in 2010). The number of uninsured people varies according to factors such as education level, employment status, race, and income.

People without a high school diploma are less likely to have insurance, as are African Americans, Hispanics, immigrants, people who are unemployed, and families with an income under $50,000. Figure 18.6 lists the states with the highest percentages of uninsured residents. About two-thirds of Americans with health insurance are insured through their employer or have some type of private plan. The practice of employers offering health insurance to their employees became widespread during World War II as employers searched for ways to attract workers in the face of wage controls. The remainder of insured Americans receives coverage through the government, with programs such as Medicaid, Medicare, and the military.[53]

Access to health care depends on more than having insurance. Many Americans with insurance are underinsured, with plans that do not adequately meet their true health-care needs. And even with adequate health insurance, many Americans lack easy access to doctors or hospitals. The supply of physicians in the United States simply does not meet the demand. Increasing the number of insured Americans might only make the problem worse. One study projects that by 2025, the United States will need as many as 90,000 more physicians to meet demand.[54]

The second major issue confronting the nation's health-care system is cost. The health-care sector is a significant portion of the U.S. economy. In 2014, public and private spending on health care reached an all-time high of $3 trillion, which was 17.5 percent of gross domestic product (GDP). Given the aging of the American population, coverage expansions due to the Affordable Care Act (described below), and the development of newer medical technologies, those numbers are projected to increase. By 2024, health care is expected to account for 19.6 percent of GDP.[55] Among advanced industrial nations, the United States spends the largest proportion of its economy on health care. In 2013, it spent more than nations with comprehensive systems of

FIGURE 18.6 Poverty in the States

In 2014, nearly 15 percent of all Americans lived below the poverty line; 10 percent had no health insurance. These national figures mask important differences across states. In New Hampshire, for example, only around 9 percent of the population lives in poverty; in Mississippi, nearly 22 percent of residents live in poverty. In Massachusetts, fewer than 5 percent of state residents are without health insurance, yet 17 percent of Texans don't have health insurance. Variations are due to state laws, social problems, immigration, and local job opportunities. In this figure, we list the top ten states according to the percentage of state residents who live below the poverty line and who are without health insurance (as of 2014).

Source: 2014 Small Area Income and Poverty Estimates, http://www.census.gov/did/www/saipe/data/interactive/saipe.html?s_appName=saipe&map_yearSelector=2014&map_geoSelector=aa_c&menu=grid_proxy&s_inclStTot=y&s_USStOnly=y; and http://kff.org/other/state-indicator/total-population/.

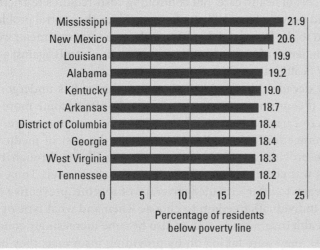
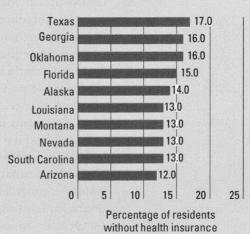

Percentage of residents below poverty line

Percentage of residents without health insurance

Health Spending in Global Politics

Compared to other nations, the United States spends a great deal of money on health care. In 2013, the United States spent more than 17 percent of its gross domestic product on health care. What does spending on health care achieve? Looking just at longevity, life expectancy in developed nations reveals little variation. Babies born in the United States in 2013 can expect to live on average to almost seventy-nine. In contrast, babies born in Switzerland can expect to live past eighty-two, as can those born in Italy and Spain. Despite the fact that Americans outspend other nations on health care, the payoff in life expectancy has not been realized.

Health expenditures in 2013

United States	17.7
Netherlands	11.9
France	11.6
Germany	11.3
Canada	11.2
Switzerland	11.0
Austria	10.8
Belgium	10.5
United Kingdom	9.4
Norway	9.3
Spain	9.3
Italy	9.2

Life expectancy in 2013 (total population)

Italy	82.7
Switzerland	82.6
Spain	82.4
France	82.2
Norway	81.4
Netherlands	81.3
United Kingdom	81.1
Austria	81.1
Canada	81.0
Germany	80.8
Belgium	80.5
United States	78.7

Source: OECD Health Statistics 2013 - Frequently Requested Data, http://www.oecd.org/els/health-systems/oecdhealthdata2013-frequentlyrequesteddata.htm.

CRITICAL THINKING What other factors besides spending might affect a society's life expectancy? Why might the United States rank highest on spending but comparatively low on life expectancy?

coverage, including Switzerland (11 percent of GDP), Germany (11.3 percent), and Canada (11.2 percent) (see "Health Spending in Global Politics").[56]

The two central problems of health care, access and cost, give rise to two goals and a familiar dilemma. First, health care policy should democratize health care by making it available to more people, ideally everyone. But by providing broad access to medical care, we increase the amount we spend on such care and increase the amount of regulations we place on private insurance companies. Second, policies must aim to control the ballooning cost of health care. But controlling costs requires restricting the range of procedures and providers available to patients. Thus, the central problems of the health-care issue go to the heart of the modern dilemma of government: we must weigh greater equality in terms of universal coverage and cost controls against a loss of freedom in markets for health care and in choosing a doctor.

Over the past few decades, the health insurance industry has undergone tremendous change, and it continues to do so as these trade-offs become more acute. Most Americans used to carry what was called catastrophic care insurance, which provided hospital coverage for serious illnesses only. As the cost of medical care ballooned, health-care providers realized that preventing illness through regular physical examinations was cheaper than curing illnesses after onset. Thus, health insurance providers began to offer extended coverage of routine, preventive care in return for limiting an individual's freedom to choose when and what type of medical specialist to see. Health insurance providers also became increasingly concerned with the amount of risk they were taking on by providing insurance; they became more interested in covering healthy people who were likely to consume fewer services and less interested in covering people with existing—and expensive—medical conditions.

Medicare

As early as 1945, public opinion supported some form of national health insurance, and President Harry Truman proposed such a program during his administration. However, that idea became entangled in Cold War politics—the growing crusade against communism in America.[57] The American Medical Association (AMA), representing the nation's physicians, mounted a campaign to link national health insurance (so-called socialized medicine) with socialism; the campaign was so successful that the prospect of a national health-care policy vanished.

Both proponents and opponents of national health insurance tried to cast their positions in terms of deeply rooted American values: advocates emphasized equality and fairness; opponents stressed freedom.

After the 1960 election, however, the terms of the debate changed. It no longer focused on the clash between freedom and equality. Democrats framed the issue of health insurance in terms of providing assistance to the aged, a perspective that brought it back to the national agenda.[58] In 1962, the Senate considered extending Social Security benefits to provide hospitalization and medical care for the elderly. Opponents were concerned that costs would soar without limit. Others, including the AMA, still saw any form of government-provided medical care as a step toward government control of medicine. Such opponents won the battle that day. Three years later, however, the Social Security Act was amended to provide Medicare, a health insurance program for all people aged sixty-five and older.[59]

On July 30, 1965, with Harry Truman at his side, President Johnson signed a bill that provided a number of health benefits to the elderly and the poor. One major provision created a compulsory hospitalization insurance plan for the elderly (known today as Part A of Medicare). In addition, the bill created voluntary government-subsidized insurance to cover physicians' fees (known today as Part B of Medicare). In 2015, 46 million people over age sixty-five received health insurance coverage through Medicare, which costs over $500 billion.[60]

Medicare is compulsory insurance that covers certain hospital services for people aged sixty-five and older. Workers pay a tax, and for certain parts of the program other than Part A, retirees pay premiums deducted from their Social Security payments. Payments for services are made by the government directly to participating hospitals and other qualifying facilities. Citizens with Medicare coverage may also possess private insurance for additional services that the program may not cover or may cover in less generous ways.

The program still contains its original components, Parts A and B, but over the years, Medicare has expanded to cover more services. Today, Part A pays for care in facilities, such as inpatient hospital visits, care in skilled nursing facilities, and hospice. Part B pays for doctors' services and outpatient care. Services under Part A come at no cost to beneficiaries, but Part B services require participants to pay a monthly premium (just over $100 in 2016); the government pays the remaining cost of Part B.

In addition to the original Parts A and B, the program also offers supplemental plans, known as Medigap plans, that are run by private insurance companies and that seniors pay for through a premium, which varies by type of plan.

An important change in Medicare occurred in 2003 with the passage of the Medicare Prescription Drug, Improvement, and Modernization Act. Rather than a single program with simple rules, the drug plan (known as Part D) encouraged private

Medicare
A health insurance program serving primarily persons sixty-five and older.

insurers to offer competing plans. In some locations, seniors may have the option of thirty or more plans from which to choose, each with different costs, deductibles, participating pharmacies, and formularies (covered medications). Like other aspects of Medicare, the costs of the program continue to increase at rates in excess of the cost of living. In 2016, over 15 percent of government spending on Medicare was devoted to the prescription plan (see later section on health-care reform for new provisions related to Medicare).[61]

Medicaid

Medicaid
A need-based comprehensive medical and hospitalization program.

Another important part of the nation's health-care patchwork is **Medicaid**, the main program to provide health care to low-income Americans. Like Medicare, it was the product of the Great Society and was passed as another amendment to the Social Security Act. In 1965, the program was relatively small and enrolled 4 million people at an annual cost of $0.4 billion. It has since become a massive program, enrolling roughly 60 million people.[62] The 2010 Affordable Care Act created additional expansions of the program, which went into effect in 2014.

The program's scope is vast. It insures millions of children and low-income adults and people with disabilities. It also pays for 40 percent of all childbirths.[63] Although Medicaid is designed primarily to cover citizens with low incomes, the pool of eligible people varies significantly across the country. That is because, unlike Medicare, which is solely a federal program, Medicaid is jointly run and financed by the federal government and the states. Federal law defines a certain minimum level of benefits that states must offer through Medicaid, but states vary in the criteria they use to define eligibility and in the types of services the program covers. Because Medicaid expenditures are typically one of the top expenses in state budgets (along with education), benefits are frequently cut when states experience difficult budgetary situations. Such cuts come despite the fact that more and more people rely on Medicaid during economic downturns.

Medicaid participants fall into four main groups: children under age twenty-one, adults (mainly pregnant women, parents, and other caregivers of children), those who are disabled, and those aged sixty-five and over (senior citizens can qualify for Medicare *and* Medicaid if their incomes fall below a certain level). Although their numbers are relatively small compared to other participants in the program, the disabled and elderly account for over half of Medicaid expenditures; the cost of the program is driven by the high cost of medical care for these two groups rather than other factors.[64]

The ACA expanded the pool of eligible beneficiaries in 2014 to include any adult earning up to 138 percent of the federal poverty level ($27,724 for a family of three in 2015). Originally, the health-care law required states to expand eligibility in this manner. Failure to do so would have resulted in the loss of all federal help paying for Medicaid. But in *National Federation of Independent Business* v. *Sebelius* (2012), the Supreme Court ruled that such expansion can only be voluntary; the federal government cannot require it by threatening to remove such a significant portion of states' health-care funding. The threat, it was ruled, was too coercive. Under the ACA, the federal government covers the cost of Medicaid expansion for the first three years. In subsequent years, the federal government will pay 90 percent of the bill. As of this writing, thirty-one states have opted to expand Medicaid eligibility.[65] Even with the refusal of so many states, the expansion thus far has added to the size, scope, and cost of the program. The year 2015 was the first full year of the expanded Medicaid provisions of the ACA, and that year saw an increase in enrollment and spending approaching 14 percent. In states that expanded Medicaid eligibility, the increase in enrollment and spending was around 18 percent; in states that did not expand, the increase was closer to 6 percent.[66]

Health-Care Reform: The Affordable Care Act

In 2010, President Obama signed sweeping health-care reform legislation into law. The law is called the Patient Protection and Affordable Care Act, but has become known as the ACA and as "Obamacare." It has been described as the most wide-ranging policy change in a generation, comparable to the creation of Social Security. Its aim is to provide insurance to as many Americans as possible. To get the law passed, Obama had to scale back some initial ideas (such as offering a health insurance plan administered by the federal government), create new taxes, and ensure that federal funds would not be used to cover the costs of abortions. The legislative battle pitted arguments about equality of access to care against arguments about freedom from government intervention. The arguments about equality won the day, but battles about the scope of this legislation endure.

There are several notable aspects of the law. People aged nineteen to twenty-five immediately became eligible to stay on their parents' insurance plans. By 2014, insurance providers could no longer deny people coverage because of preexisting conditions. To make it possible for insurers to pay for the needs of high-cost treatments, what is perhaps the most controversial aspect of the reform was added, namely that all individuals are now required to have health insurance or pay a fine (some are exempt from this so-called *individual mandate*, including Native Americans and people with religious objections). There are opportunities for people to get government subsidies to help them obtain coverage, and as noted earlier, the bill expands eligibility for Medicaid.

Individuals aren't the only ones subject to mandates under the ACA; employers are as well. As of 2015, all employers with 100 or more employees needed to offer health insurance or pay a fine (employers with fifty to ninety-nine employees had until 2016). Tax credits are available to some small businesses that offer health plans to their workers. Finally, states were encouraged to set up insurance marketplaces, called *exchanges*, by 2014 where people and small businesses can shop for competitively priced health plans.[67] Residents lacking health insurance in the twenty-seven states that did not set up exchanges need to use a federally run marketplace (available at healthcare.gov) if they do not already have health insurance through their employer.

In 2015, the ACA survived another major court challenge. At issue was whether the language of the law allowed people who buy health insurance through healthcare .gov to be eligible for federal subsidies or whether such subsidies are only available to people who use state-run exchanges. Had the court ruled in favor of the plaintiffs (who believed that only people using state-run exchanges were eligible for government aid), nearly 8 million people would have lost their health insurance. The Supreme Court ruled 6–3 in *King* v. *Burwell* that people who use healthcare.gov could also get the subsidies. The ACA lived to see another day.[68]

Expanding Medicaid and providing subsidies for insurance coverage will cost the government hundreds of billions of dollars, but the law also includes provisions that will help pay for it. In fact, the Congressional Budget Office estimated that the bill will reduce deficits in the long run. The ACA places new taxes on high-cost health plans, places new Medicare taxes on wealthy Americans, creates a new tax on indoor tanning, charges fees to employers and private health insurance companies, and reforms some aspects of Medicare spending (including the creation of an advisory board that can alter how Medicare is administered and the introduction of a program in which doctors are paid for the quality of treatment instead of the quantity). The state insurance exchanges are also expected to lower health-care costs; because private insurers will have new competition, insurance premiums are expected to decrease.[69]

That the ACA is not expected to add to the deficit has not silenced critics. For people wary of "big government," any program that results in more bureaucracy, more

Freedom, Order, or Equality

Freedom v. Equality: Health Insurance

Did your mother make you eat broccoli? Could the government? The Affordable Care Act made it illegal for private health insurance companies to deny people health care on the basis of preexisting medical conditions. The law also included a requirement that virtually everyone purchase health insurance by 2014, a provision known as the individual mandate. Several states filed lawsuits in federal court to contest the law. Some courts upheld the individual mandate and others rejected it. In June 2012, the Supreme Court ruled (5–4) that Congress has the authority to levy taxes. The fine for not buying insurance amounts to a tax; therefore, the mandate is constitutional. Despite this ruling, the provision remains controversial and unpopular: 64 percent of Americans surveyed in 2014 viewed the mandate unfavorably.* In his dissent, former Justice Antonin Scalia argued that requiring individuals to purchase insurance means the government essentially has unlimited power and could require citizens to engage in all manner of commercial activity. Could it, he wondered, require Americans to buy broccoli? As his question illustrates, the case of the ACA and the individual mandate creates a dramatic clash between individual freedom and equal access to health care.

*Source: Kaiser Health Policy Tracking Poll: December 2014, http://kff.org/health-reform/poll-finding/kaiser-health -policy-tracking-poll-december-2014/.

CRITICAL THINKING Should the government be able to require that people buy health insurance? What constitutional arguments could be made for or against such a requirement?

regulation, and more taxes is problematic. Additionally, many patients and hospitals harbor fears about how reforms to Medicare will play out despite assurances that benefits will not be affected. Others charge that even with government subsidies, many families will not be able to pay the insurance premiums that the law requires of them.

Still others argue that the federal government is simply not equipped to manage such a massive program successfully, while others have concerns about whether the privacy of their medical and financial records will be protected sufficiently. Finally, other opponents simply charge that it is unconstitutional for the government to require that all individuals purchase health insurance, though the Supreme Court ruled otherwise (see "Freedom, Order, or Equality: Freedom v. Equality: Health Insurance"). Whether the alleged benefits or drawbacks of the ACA will come to pass still remains to be seen. The implementation of the policy is still in its infancy and health-care policy in the United States is in a period of great transformation. Evaluation of the ACA's implementation will be ongoing, and debates about the law will feature prominently in Washington and across the country for decades to come.

 Elementary and Secondary Education

LO6 Describe the role of the federal government in shaping education policy at the state and local government levels.

Although it is no less important, education is unlike the other public policies discussed in this chapter given that responsibility for schooling resides primarily in state and local governments in the United States. Since Horace Mann introduced mandatory public schooling in Massachusetts in the mid-nineteenth century, public schools have been an important part of local government. The federal government covers only around 10 percent of the nation's K–12 education bill.[70]

Concerns Motivating Change

Two main factors, related to freedom, order, and equality, have prompted greater federal involvement in the nation's elementary and secondary schools during the last several decades.

Equity. The overriding and persistent concern has been educational equity. An important part of Lyndon Johnson's Great Society was the American belief that social and economic equality could be attained through equality of educational opportunity. The justices of the Supreme Court argued as much in their landmark decision in *Brown* v. *Board of Education* (1954). Legislatively, the **Elementary and Secondary Education Act of 1965 (ESEA)**, yet another product of the Great Society, was the first major federal effort to address educational equity in a systematic way. The law, which has been reauthorized periodically, provided direct national government aid to local schools in order to improve the educational opportunities of the economically disadvantaged.

> **Elementary and Secondary Education Act of 1965 (ESEA)** The federal government's primary law to assist the nation's elementary and secondary schools. It emerged as part of President Lyndon Johnson's Great Society program.

The original law focused on economic disadvantage; later iterations recognized other groups, such as students for whom English is a second language and Native American students. A separate but related law, the Individuals with Disabilities Education Act (IDEA), is designed to improve educational opportunities for students of all ages (elementary school through college and graduate school) with physical or other disabilities.

Despite the federal policy, improvements in educational, and thus social and economic, equality have been elusive. Differences in student achievement between advantaged and disadvantaged groups have declined since the 1960s. However, gaps remain in test scores and in overall graduation rates.[71] These gaps are important because they tend to correlate with future educational and economic opportunities.[72]

National Security and Prosperity. Concern over educational achievement is not limited to issues of social equality at home. In an increasingly competitive global economy, countries are competing to offer—and attract—highly educated and skilled workers. Thus, a desire to keep the United States competitive with other nations, both economically and militarily, is one reason why education is considered a key public policy area.

The connection between national security and education is not new. It dates back at least to the 1950s when the Eisenhower administration promoted the National Defense Education Act of 1958 (NDEA). The law is considered to be a response to the Soviet Union's launch of a satellite known as *Sputnik*, the first such craft to orbit the earth. This Soviet success, which many interpreted to mean that the United States was losing the "brain race" against its rival, set off calls for improving the nation's stock of scientists and engineers, as well as its cadre of foreign language speakers, to counter the communist threat. Funding from the NDEA supported efforts in all of these areas at the elementary, secondary, and postsecondary levels.

A desire to improve American economic competitiveness has been the most recent force prompting greater efforts to improve the nation's education system. These concerns date back to the 1970s, when state governors realized the link between their own states' economic fortunes and the quality of their schools. These state-level concerns foreshadowed subsequent debates at the national level that forged a similar link between the competitiveness of the entire nation and the educational preparation of the country's young people.

These state- and national-level concerns coalesced in a famous report entitled *A Nation at Risk*, which was released in 1983 by the National Commission on Excellence in Education. The report charged that the nation's schools were inadequate and were getting worse. Its findings, along with improved data comparing American students with their international counterparts, through projects such as the Trends in International Mathematics and Science Study (TIMSS), created momentum for public officials to improve schools.

Values and Reform

At the center of debates over education is the dilemma of freedom versus equality. The American belief in equality is weighted toward equality of opportunity, and equality of opportunity depends on equal access to a good education. At the same time, Americans vehemently support their freedom to choose where to live, what kind of school they want their children to attend, and what their children will be taught while they are there.

As the national and international challenges we face grow in technological and scientific sophistication, the dilemmas of education reform will become more pressing. The questions of who will pay for reform, who will benefit, and how best to improve student learning came to a head in a major reauthorization of the ESEA, known as the **No Child Left Behind Act of 2001 (NCLB)**.

No Child Left Behind Act of 2001 (NCLB)
A reauthorization of the Elementary and Secondary Education Act during the George W. Bush presidency.

The No Child Left Behind Act of 2001. In 2000, Republican candidate George W. Bush made education one of the most important issues in his campaign for the White House, and with much fanfare, he signed the measure into law in January 2002.[73]

Although the law was technically a reauthorization of the ESEA, it also instituted far-reaching changes in education policy. Most significant among them was the law's requirement that states demonstrate that all of their students are performing at proficient levels in reading and math by 2014, leaving states free to determine their own standards of proficiency and means of assessment. Along the way, the law required schools to show the federal government that they were making "Adequate Yearly Progress" among all student groups, be they economically disadvantaged, weak in English language skills, or disabled.

NCLB was initially praised for highlighting educational inequality and asserting that all students deserve qualified teachers. But its implementation was controversial.[74]

Critics charged that the emphasis on testing led teachers to "teach to the test" and ignore subjects that were not tested, like music and social studies. Others charged that the federal government did not spend enough money to help schools live up to the standards that it set and that state and local governments needed to give up too much autonomy to the federal government.

Common Core. In the meantime, the Obama administration granted waivers to forty states in order to free them from the proficiency guidelines of NCLB. In return, those states agreed to adopt a common set of academic standards and develop new systems for evaluating teacher effectiveness (a clear use of incentives as an important public policy tool).[75] During the Obama administration, forty-five states developed and adopted a set of *Common Core Standards*, which lays out a set of skills in math and English language arts that students are encouraged to master in each grade. The goals of the Common Core were to raise standards as well as promote consistency across states. From the start, however, the Common Core had critics. Some said the core still placed too much weight on testing; others said the federal government would be too involved in dictating state standards; others charged that the standards were developed without enough input from educators or the public. Some states then relabeled their initiatives in order to distance themselves from the program. Examples include Iowa's "Iowa Core," and Florida's "Next Generation Sunshine State Standards."[76] Whether such changes are just cosmetic remains to be seen, as the new standards have only been newly implemented.

Every Student Succeeds Act. As states moved forward implementing the Common Core, Congress worked on the next reauthorization of the ESEA. In a rare display of bipartisanship, Congress passed the **Every Student Succeeds Act (ESSA)** in 2015, with the support of 85 Senators and 359 Representatives.[77] The new law, which replaces NCLB, still requires states to test students in reading and math in grades three through eight and again in high school, but the federal government will no longer set performance goals, determine if schools are meeting them, or decide what to do if they are not; those tasks have been returned to the states.

> **Every Student Succeeds Act of 2015 (ESSA)**
> A reauthorization of the Elementary and Secondary Education Act during the Barack Obama presidency.

Not everyone is pleased with the ESSA, of course. Some critics lament the continued reliance on test scores as the primary means of evaluating schools. Others fear that the retreat of the federal government will mean that some states will fail to create assessment methods that reveal the inadequacies of their own schools. Other people worry that the educational needs of traditionally disadvantaged groups will not be addressed adequately.[78] Perhaps nowhere are the challenges of fragmentation and coordination on display more than with education policy. Debates about the 2001 NCLB and the 2015 ESSA illustrate the difficulties of coordinating efforts across the states, devising national objectives that still allow for local flexibility, and evaluating which aspects of a policy work and which ones need reform. As President Obama said when he signed the ESSA, "Now the hard work begins. Laws are only as good as the implementation."[79]

★ Immigration

LO7 Assess alternative policies for addressing illegal immigration into the United States.

Along with health care and education, immigration is also central to the domestic policy agenda. Immigrants today make up around 13 percent of the population. It is estimated that just over 11 million immigrants are here illegally, down from about 12 million in 2007.[80] Americans are divided over whether overall levels of immigration to the United States should be decreased or kept the same, but most agree that addressing the situation of illegal immigration in the United States is important.

Undocumented immigrants are among the poorest and most vulnerable individuals. Whereas roughly 10.4 percent of all Americans are without health insurance, 31.2 percent of foreign-born noncitizens lack health insurance, and 24.2 percent live below the poverty line. The rates for those noncitizens in the country illegally are even higher.[81] Enduring debates about immigration involve whether immigrants should have access to the benefits of the social welfare state such as health care and education and whether they should be eligible to earn citizenship.

The United States didn't regulate immigration until the end of the nineteenth century, and it wasn't until 1924 that the concept of an "illegal immigrant" took hold. It was then that Congress enacted the Johnson-Reed Act, which set strict quotas on the number of immigrants permitted to enter the country and the nations from which they could come. Due to racist concerns about the dilution of American culture, the act favored immigration from western Europe and severely limited immigration from southern and eastern Europe and from Asia. These restrictions were significantly loosened by the Johnson administration in 1965, which is when the rate of legal and illegal immigration began to surge. For several decades, the majority of new immigrants came from Latin America. Today, however, more immigrants come from Asia than from any other region.

Foreigners who wish to work in the United States for an extended period of time need to apply for a permanent resident card, or "green card." Individuals with a green card are known as "legal permanent residents," and they may eventually apply to become U.S. citizens. In 2013, the United States granted permanent admission to nearly 1 million noncitizens.[82] Priority is given to reuniting families, admitting workers in occupations with strong demand for labor, providing a refuge for people who face persecution in their home countries, and providing admission to people from a diverse set of countries.[83] Prior to the 1996 welfare reforms (discussed earlier in this chapter), legal immigrants were eligible for most public benefits on the same terms as citizens. The 1996 reforms, however, prohibited legal immigrants from participating in safety net programs such as SNAP, Medicaid, and TANF until they have been in the country for five years. States are free to enroll legal immigrants sooner, provided that state funds—and not federal funds—are used to supply the benefit.[84]

But it is undocumented immigrants who get the most attention in policy debates. If caught, they may be offered the chance to leave the country voluntarily, or they may be fined, imprisoned, deported, and prohibited from returning to the United States. In 2015, about 235,000 undocumented immigrants were deported, down from a high of 400,000 in 2012.[85] Most undocumented immigrants in the United States come from Mexico and other Latin American countries. They tend to be geographically concentrated in western states and large urban areas, where they provide cheap labor in agriculture and manufacturing industries.

Undocumented immigrants have always been ineligible for the safety net programs discussed in this chapter (their American-born children are eligible), but they enroll in public schools and get treated in hospital emergency rooms, both of which come at a cost to American taxpayers. Most policy debates about illegal immigration focus on how best to increase border security with Mexico, how to get employers to stop hiring undocumented workers, and whether undocumented immigrants currently in the United States should be allowed to become legal residents and/or citizens. Since 2005, Congress and the Bush and Obama administrations sought legislation that would allow undocumented immigrants in the United States to earn citizenship if they paid fines, passed English and civics exams, and remained employed, but every effort has stalled. Conservative groups charge that such legislation would give "amnesty" to people who had broken the law. Pro-immigrant groups have been concerned with proposals that would create a temporary worker program that allows people to work in the United States for a period of time and then force them to return to their home country before reapplying for a temporary permit. Unions fear that legal temporary workers would drive down wages and take jobs away from American workers.

Comprehensive proposals supported by Presidents Bush and Obama would create a lengthy path to citizenship for undocumented immigrants living in the United States, increase the number of temporary visas available for highly skilled and agricultural guest workers, devote more resources to border security, and require employers to use E-Verify (a program that allows employers to check the immigration status of potential employees), but such reform has yet to make it out of Congress. Despite the lack of progress, majorities of the American public consistently support the major elements of this approach, including the path to citizenship for undocumented immigrants.[86]

Another proposal that Americans generally support but that has stalled in Congress is the Development, Relief, and Education for Alien Minors (DREAM) Act. If passed, the act would allow undocumented immigrants who had been brought to the United States as children to become eligible for legalized status. With Congress unable to agree on the DREAM Act, President Obama issued an executive action in 2012, called Deferred Action for Childhood Arrivals (DACA), that directed federal immigration authorities to cease pursuing deportations for most undocumented immigrants who were brought to the United States as children. DACA also allows

Marjorie Kamys Cotera/Bob Daemmrich Photography/Alamy

IMAGE 18.6   An Uncertain Path Ahead

Since the mid-1990s, anywhere from 500,000 to 1 million people become naturalized citizens each year. Today, there are over 19 million naturalized citizens in the United States. If comprehensive immigration reform becomes a reality, over 11 million undocumented immigrants could join their ranks. Their path, however, would take a minimum of thirteen years, according to some proposals.

Source: Jie Zong and Jeanne Batalova, "Frequently Requested Statistics on Immigrants and Immigration in the United States," Migration Information Source, 26 February 2016.

those immigrants to apply for a two-year work authorization. One year later, over 588,000 people applied for the change in status. Over 96 percent of the applications were approved.[87]

In 2014, President Obama issued additional executive actions that expanded DACA eligibility. He also ordered that undocumented immigrants who are parents of U.S. citizens be eligible to apply for deportation relief and work permits under a program called Deferred Action for Parents of Americans (DAPA). Opponents charge that the president overstepped his authority with these measures. Their objections led federal courts to block implementation, and the Supreme Courts agreed to weigh in on the matter in 2016.[88] In June of that year, the court was deadlocked 4–4 over whether Obama had the authority to create DAPA (former Justice Scalia's seat was vacant). The tied ruling meant that the program would remain blocked.

The Constitution grants Congress the authority to "establish a uniform rule of naturalization," which has been interpreted to grant jurisdiction of immigration policy solely to the federal government. Yet in the absence of federal action to address the pressing social needs that illegal immigration produces in social services, states have increasingly enacted their own policies on the issue (see Figure 18.7). Employers in several states must check workers' residency status with E-Verify and could be fined if they knowingly hire undocumented immigrants. Some states, such as California, have enacted immigrant-friendly legislation that allows undocumented immigrants to pay in-state tuition at public universities and get driver's licenses. Others, such as Arizona and Alabama, have enacted policies aimed at creating a climate that drives immigrants away. The Arizona law, for example, directs local law enforcement officials to check the immigration status of people they stop or arrest. In addition to raising fears that the law will promote racial profiling, some believe that only the federal government has the authority to engage in this type of immigration enforcement. In 2012, the Supreme Court ruled that states can direct law enforcement authorities to ask people to demonstrate whether they are in the country legally.[89]

FIGURE 18.7 Absent Federal Action, States Take on Immigration Reform

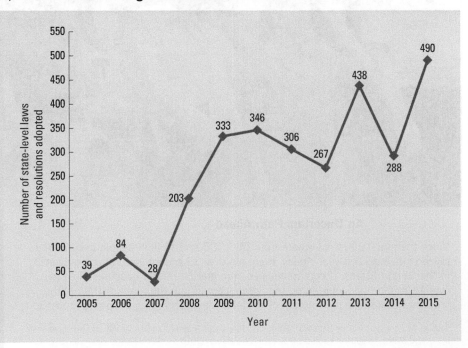

With immigration reform stalled at the federal level, state legislative activity to address issues that arise from immigration has increased dramatically. Some laws are considered immigration-friendly while others are considered hostile. Whether the states even have the jurisdiction to enact these policies is a matter of continuing debate.

Source: National Conference of State Legislatures, "State Laws Related to Immigration and Immigrants," http://www.ncsl.org/research/immigration/state-laws-related-to-immigration-and-immigrants.aspx.

Benefits and Fairness

LO8 Explain how the issue of fairness shapes perspectives on government benefits.

As the policies examined here demonstrate, the national government provides many Americans and noncitizen residents with benefits. Some benefits are conditional. **Means-tested benefits** impose an income test to qualify. For example, Medicaid benefits are available to households with an income that falls below a designated threshold. **Non-means-tested benefits** impose no such income test; benefits such as Medicare and Social Security are available to all.

Some Americans question the fairness of non-means-tested benefits. Benefits are subsidies, and some people need them more than others do. If resources available for such benefits are limited, imposing means tests on more benefits has real allure. For example, historically, all elderly people received the same basic Medicare benefits, regardless of income, and all wage earners paid the same percentage in Medicare taxes. Fairness advocates maintain that the affluent should shoulder a higher share of Medicare costs, shifting more benefits to the low-income elderly. The ACA addresses some of this concern by increasing Medicare taxes for the wealthy. If the idea of shifting benefits gains support in the future, reform debates will focus on the income level below which a program will apply. Thus, the question of fairness is one more problem for policymakers to consider as they try to reform the nation's welfare state programs.

There are many other domestic policy areas that consume significant government resources and that merit attention when analyzing the complex processes by which policies are formulated, implemented, and evaluated. These policy areas include energy policy, the environment, science and technology, transportation, and food policy, just to name a few. As with the policies covered in this chapter, debates in these other areas often come down to differing perspectives on freedom and equality, involve coordination problems across levels of government, and are influenced by complex issue networks that are at the heart of the nation's pluralist system.

means-tested benefits
Conditional benefits provided by government to individuals whose income falls below a designated threshold.

non-means-tested benefits
Benefits provided by government to all citizens, regardless of income; Medicare and Social Security are examples.

The 2016 Election

The 2016 election handed the White House and both houses of Congress to the Republicans. Although Democrats in the Senate have tools they can use to obstruct legislation (see Chapter 11), the Trump administration will have an opportunity to use the first years of the president's term to make significant changes in many of the policy areas discussed in this chapter. The most likely targets for reform include the Affordable Care Act, which Trump and Republicans in Congress want to repeal, and immigration, which was a signature issue of Trump's campaign. Specifically, Trump vowed to build a wall between the United States and Mexico, end DACA and DAPA, and curtail immigration from countries with ties to terrorism. There will be considerable pressure to accomplish some of these goals quickly; Presidents Clinton, Bush, and Obama all experienced unified government, but all three found themselves facing majorities of the opposing party in Congress after only a few years.

Summary

LO1 **Categorize different types of public policies and outline the process by which policies are formulated and implemented.**

- Underlying policy choices are basic values—the core beliefs about how government should work. The basic objectives of government policy tend to be distributional, redistributional, and regulatory.

- The policymaking process consists of four broad stages: agenda setting, formulation, implementation, and evaluation. All three branches of the national government formulate policy, along with policy experts, interest groups, and trade organizations, which together form issue networks. Formulation often involves one of the following tools to achieve objectives: incentives and disincentives, direct provision of services, or rule setting. Implementation and evaluation influence agenda building because program shortcomings become evident during these stages. Thus, the process is circular, with the end often marking the beginning of a new round of policymaking. Policymaking stages are often marked by fragmentation and by efforts intended to achieve coordination.

LO2 **Trace the evolution of social welfare programs as a central element of public policy in the United States.**

- Many domestic policies that provide benefits to individuals and promote economic equality were instituted during the Great Depression and were expanded during President Johnson's Great Society agenda.

LO3 **Describe the origins and evolution of Social Security as well as the funding and benefit issues facing the program.**

- Today, the government plays an active role in providing benefits to the poor, the elderly, and the disabled, which reflects the social welfare function of the modern state.

LO4 **Explain how poverty is defined and trace the evolution of public assistance programs designed to address it.**

- Programs to aid the elderly and the poor have been transformed into entitlements, or rights that accrue to eligible persons. These programs have reduced poverty among some groups, especially the elderly. However, poverty retains a grip on certain segments of the population.

- Temporary Assistance for Needy Families (TANF) was a major overhaul of welfare policy. While initially considered a success for reducing the number of people on welfare and granting more flexibility to the states, recent national economic difficulties have led many to conclude that TANF is inadequate at combating poverty.

LO5 **Differentiate among Medicare, Medicaid, and the Affordable Care Act of 2010 and explain how each program addresses health-care delivery.**

- Recent health-care reform is a reflection of the modern dilemma of democracy: universal coverage and cost controls versus a loss of freedom in health-care choices.

LO6 **Describe the role of the federal government in shaping education policy at the state and local government levels.**

- Education is considered a critical public policy area among Americans, though it remains largely a state and local endeavor. The federal government's education policy centers on providing equal access to a good education for all Americans, often relying on incentives to help achieve these aims.

LO7 **Assess alternative policies for addressing illegal immigration into the United States.**

- While the federal government has long been interested in controlling the number of immigrants who are legal permanent residents, the problem of illegal immigration has only garnered national attention in the past few decades. In the absence of federal legislation addressing illegal immigration, many states have enacted their own policies.

LO8 **Explain how the issue of fairness shapes perspectives on government benefits.**

- Some government subsidy programs provide means-tested benefits, for which eligibility hinges on income. Non-means-tested benefits are available to all, regardless of income. As the demand for such benefits exceeds available resources, their fairness becomes questioned. Departing from non-means-tested benefits in the name of fairness may very well be the next challenge of democracy.

Chapter Quiz

LO1 **Categorize different types of public policies and outline the process by which policies are formulated and implemented.**

1. Identify and explain at least two public policy tools used to achieve objectives.
2. What are the four main stages of the policy-making process?
3. What are issue networks? Do they reflect the pluralist or majoritarian model of democracy?

LO2 **Trace the evolution of social welfare programs as a central element of public policy in the United States.**

1. What are social welfare programs?
2. Summarize the emergence and goals of the New Deal.

LO3 **Describe the origins and evolution of Social Security as well as the funding and benefit issues facing the program.**

1. Why is the success of the Social Security program dependent on such factors as birth rate and life expectancy?
2. Discuss alternative proposed reforms to Social Security recently debated by policymakers.

LO4 **Explain how poverty is defined and trace the evolution of public assistance programs designed to address it.**

1. What is the current poverty rate, and what is the current poverty threshold?
2. What does TANF stand for, and how did this program change welfare policy?

LO5 **Differentiate among Medicare, Medicaid, and the Affordable Care Act of 2010 and explain how each program addresses health-care delivery.**

1. Define Medicare.
2. Explain how federalism shapes the administration and financing of Medicaid.
3. Identify at least three key features of the Affordable Care Act of 2010.

LO6 **Describe the role of the federal government in shaping education policy at the state and local government levels.**

1. Discuss how the dilemma of freedom versus equality shapes debates about education policy.
2. Describe one way in which the Every Student Succeeds Act changes the No Child Left Behind Act.

LO7 **Assess alternative policies for addressing illegal immigration into the United States.**

1. List central features of current policy debates for addressing illegal immigration that have been proposed by the federal government and/or by individual states.

LO8 **Explain how the issue of fairness shapes perspectives on government benefits.**

1. Contrast means-tested and non-means-tested benefits.

Appendix

The Declaration of Independence

In Congress, July 4, 1776

The unanimous Declaration of the thirteen United States of America

When in the course of human events, it becomes necessary for one people to dissolve the political bands which have connected them with another, and to assume, among the powers of the earth the separate and equal station to which the Laws of Nature and of Nature's God entitle them, a decent respect to the opinions of mankind requires that they should declare the causes which impel them to the separation.

We hold these truths to be self-evident, that all men are created equal, that they are endowed by their Creator with certain unalienable rights, that among these are life, liberty, and the pursuit of happiness. That to secure these rights, governments are instituted among men, deriving their just powers from the consent of the governed. That whenever any form of government becomes destructive of these ends, it is the right of the people to alter or to abolish it, and to institute new government, laying its foundation on such principles, and organizing its power in such form, as to them shall seem most likely to effect their safety and happiness. Prudence, indeed, will dictate that governments long established should not be changed for light and transient causes; and accordingly all experience hath shown, that mankind are more disposed to suffer, while evils are sufferable, than to right themselves by abolishing the forms to which they are accustomed. But when a long train of abuses and usurpations, pursuing invariably the same object evinces a design to reduce them under absolute despotism, it is their right, it is their duty, to throw off such government, and to provide new guards for their future security. Such has been the patient sufferance of these Colonies; and such is now the necessity which constrains them to alter their former systems of government. The history of the present King of Great Britain is a history of repeated injuries and usurpations, all having in direct object the establishment of an absolute tyranny over these States. To prove this, let facts be submitted to a candid world.

He has refused his assent to laws, the most wholesome and necessary for the public good.

He has forbidden his governors to pass laws of immediate and pressing importance, unless suspended in their operation till his assent should be obtained; and, when so suspended, he has utterly neglected to attend to them.

He has refused to pass other laws for the accommodation of large districts of people, unless those people would relinquish the right of representation in the legislature, a right inestimable to them, and formidable to tyrants only.

He has called together legislative bodies at places unusual, uncomfortable, and distant from the depository of their public records, for the sole purpose of fatiguing them into compliance with his measures.

He has dissolved representative houses repeatedly, for opposing, with manly firmness, his invasions on the rights of the people.

He has refused for a long time, after such dissolutions, to cause others to be elected; whereby the legislative powers, incapable of annihilation, have returned to the people at large for their exercise; the State remaining, in the meantime exposed to all the dangers of invasions from without and convulsions within.

He has endeavored to prevent the population of these States; for that purpose obstructing the laws for naturalization of foreigners; refusing to pass others to encourage their migration hither, and raising the conditions of new appropriations of lands.

He has obstructed the administration of justice, by refusing his assent to laws for establishing judiciary powers.

He has made judges dependent on his will alone, for the tenure of their offices, and the amount and payment of their salaries.

He has erected a multitude of new offices, and sent hither swarms of officers to harass our people, and eat out their substance.

He has kept among us, in times of peace, standing armies, without the consent of our legislatures.

He has affected to render the military independent of and superior to the civil power.

He has combined with others to subject us to a jurisdiction foreign to our constitution, and unacknowledged by our laws; giving his assent to their acts of pretended legislation: For quartering large bodies of armed troops among us; For protecting them, by a mock trial, from punishment for any murders which they should commit on the inhabitants of these states; For cutting off our trade with all parts of the world; For imposing taxes on us without our consent; For depriving us, in many cases, of the benefits of trial by jury; For transporting us beyond seas, to be tried for pretended offenses; For abolishing the free system of English laws in a neighboring province, establishing therein an arbitrary government, and enlarging its boundaries, so as to render it at once an example and fit instrument for introducing the same absolute rule into these Colonies; For taking away our Charters, abolishing our most valuable laws, and altering fundamentally the forms of our governments; For suspending our own Legislatures, and declaring themselves invested with power to legislate for us in all cases whatsoever.

He has abdicated government here, by declaring us out of his protection and waging war against us.

He has plundered our seas, ravaged our coasts, burned our towns, and destroyed the lives of our people.

He is at this time transporting large armies of foreign mercenaries to complete the works of death, desolation, and tyranny, already begun with circumstances of cruelty and perfidy scarcely paralleled in the most barbarous ages, and totally unworthy the head of a civilized nation.

He has constrained our fellow-citizens taken captive on the high seas to bear arms against their country, to become the executioners of their friends and brethren, or to fall themselves by their hands.

He has excited domestic insurrection among us, and has endeavored to bring on the inhabitants of our frontiers the merciless Indian savages, whose known rule of warfare is an undistinguished destruction of all ages, sexes, and conditions.

In every stage of these oppressions we have petitioned for redress in the most humble terms: our repeated petitions have been answered only by repeated injury. A prince whose character is thus marked by every act which may define a tyrant, is unfit to be the ruler of a free people.

Nor have we been wanting in our attentions to our British brethren. We have warned them, from time to time, of attempts by their Legislature to extend an unwarrantable jurisdiction over us. We have reminded them of the circumstances of our emigration and settlement here. We have appealed to their native justice and magnanimity, and we have conjured them by the ties of our common kindred to disavow these usurpations, which would inevitably interrupt our connections and correspondence. They too have been deaf to the voice of justice and of consanguinity. We must, therefore, acquiesce in the necessity, which denounces our separation, and hold them, as we hold the rest of mankind, enemies in war, in peace friends.

We, therefore, the Representatives of the United States of America, in General Congress assembled, appealing to the Supreme Judge of the world for the rectitude of our intentions, do, in the name, and by the authority of the good people of these Colonies, solemnly publish and declare, That these United Colonies are, and of right ought to be, FREE AND INDEPENDENT STATES; that they are absolved from all allegiance to the British Crown, and that all political connection between them and the State of Great Britain is, and ought to be, totally dissolved; and that, as Free and Independent States they have full power to levy war, conclude peace, contract alliances, establish commerce, and do all other acts and things which independent States may of right do. And for the support of this declaration, with a firm reliance on the protection of Divine Providence, we mutually pledge to each other our lives, our fortunes and our sacred honor.

JOHN HANCOCK
and fifty-five others

The Constitution of the United States of America*

[Preamble: outlines goals and effect]

We the people of the United States, in order to form a more perfect Union, establish Justice, insure domestic Tranquility, provide for the common defence, promote the general Welfare, and secure the Blessings of Liberty to ourselves and our Posterity, do ordain and establish this Constitution for the United States of America.

Article I

[The legislative branch]

[Powers vested]

Section 1 All legislative Powers herein granted shall be vested in a Congress of the United States, which shall consist of a Senate and a House of Representatives.

[House of Representatives: selection, term, qualifications, apportionment of seats, census requirement, exclusive power to impeach]

Section 2 The House of Representatives shall be composed of Members chosen every second Year by the people of the several States, and the Electors in each State shall have the Qualifications requisite for Electors of the most numerous Branch of the State Legislature.

No person shall be a Representative who shall not have attained to the Age of twenty five Years, and been seven Years a Citizen of the United States, and who shall not, when elected, be an Inhabitant of that State in which he shall be chosen.

Representatives and direct Taxes shall be apportioned among the several States which may be included within this Union, according to their respective numbers, which shall be determined by adding to the whole Number of free Persons, including those bound to Service for a Term of Years and excluding Indians not taxed, three-fifths of all other Persons. The actual Enumeration shall be made within three Years after the first Meeting of the Congress of the United States, and within every subsequent Term of ten Years, in such Manner as they shall by Law direct. The number of Representatives shall not exceed one for every thirty Thousand, but each State shall have at Least one Representative; *and until such enumeration shall be made, the State of New Hampshire shall be entitled to choose three, Massachusetts eight, Rhode Island and Providence Plantations one, Connecticut five, New York six, New Jersey four, Pennsylvania eight, Delaware one, Maryland six, Virginia ten, North Carolina five, South Carolina five, and Georgia three.*

When vacancies happen in the Representation from any State, the Executive Authority thereof shall issue Writs of Election to fill such Vacancies.

The House of Representatives shall chuse their Speaker and other Officers; and shall have the sole Power of Impeachment.

[Senate: selection, term, qualifications, exclusive power to try impeachments]

Section 3 The Senate of the United States shall be composed of two Senators from each State, *chosen by the Legislature thereof,* for six years; and each Senator shall have one Vote.

---

*Passages no longer in effect are printed in italic type.

Immediately after they shall be assembled in Consequence of the first Election, they shall be divided as equally as may be into three Classes. The Seats of the Senators of the first Class shall be vacated at the Expiration of the second Year, of the second Class at the expiration of the fourth Year, and of the third Class at the expiration of the sixth Year, so that one-third may be chosen every second Year; and if Vacancies happen by Resignation or otherwise, during the Recess of the Legislature of any State, the Executive thereof may make temporary Appointments until the next meeting of the legislature, which shall then fill such Vacancies.

No person shall be a Senator who shall not have attained to the Age of thirty Years, and been nine Years a Citizen of the United States, and who shall not, when elected, be an Inhabitant of that State for which he shall be chosen.

The Vice-President of the United States shall be President of the Senate, but shall have no Vote, unless they be equally divided.

The Senate shall choose their other officers, and also a President pro tempore, in the absence of the Vice-President, or when he shall exercise the Office of President of the United States.

The Senate shall have the sole Power to try all impeachments. When sitting for that purpose, they shall be on Oath or Affirmation. When the President of the United States is tried, the Chief Justice shall preside: and no Person shall be convicted without the Concurrence of two-thirds of the members Present.

Judgment in Cases of Impeachment shall not extend further than to removal from the Office, and disqualification to hold and enjoy any Office of honor, Trust or Profit under the United States: but the Party convicted shall nevertheless be liable and subject to Indictment, Trial, Judgment and Punishment, according to Law.

[Elections]

Section 4 The Times, Places and Manner of holding Elections for Senators and Representatives shall be prescribed in each State by the Legislature thereof; but the Congress may at any time by Law make or alter such regulations, except as to the Places of chusing Senators.

The Congress shall assemble at least once in every Year, and such meeting *shall be on the first Monday in December, unless they shall by Law appoint a different Day.*

[Powers and duties of the two chambers: rules of procedure, power over members]

Section 5 Each House shall be the Judge of the Elections, Returns and Qualifications of its own Members, and a Majority of each shall constitute a Quorum to do Business; but a smaller Number may adjourn from day to day, and may be authorized to compel the Attendance of absent Members, in such Manner, and under such Penalties as each House may provide.

Each House may determine the Rules of its proceedings, punish its Members for disorderly behaviour, and with the Concurrence of two thirds, expel a Member.

Each House shall keep a Journal of its Proceedings, and from time to time publish the same, excepting such Parts as may in their Judgment require Secrecy; and the Yeas and Nays of the Members of either House on any question shall, at the Desire of one fifth of those Present, be entered on the Journal.

Neither House, during the Session of Congress, shall, without the Consent of the other, adjourn for more than three days, nor to any other Place than that in which the two Houses shall be sitting.

[Compensation, privilege from arrest, privilege of speech, disabilities of members]

Section 6 The Senators and Representatives shall receive a Compensation for their services, to be ascertained by Law, and paid out of the Treasury of the United States. They shall in all Cases, except Treason, Felony and Breach of the Peace, be privileged from Arrest during their Attendance at the Session of their respective Houses, and in going to and returning from the same; and for any Speech or Debate in either House, they shall not be questioned in any other Place.

No Senator or Representative shall, during the Time for which he was elected, be appointed to any civil Office under the Authority of the United States, which shall have been created, or the Emoluments whereof shall have been increased, during such time; and no Person holding any Office under the United States, shall be a Member of either House during his Continuance in Office.

[Legislative process: revenue bills, approval or veto power of president]

Section 7 All bills for raising Revenue shall originate in the House of Representatives; but the Senate may propose or concur with Amendments as on other Bills.

Every Bill which shall have passed the House of Representatives and the Senate, shall, before it become a Law, be presented to the President of the United States; if he approve he shall sign it, but if not he shall return it with Objections to that House in which it originated, who shall enter the Objections at large on their journal, and proceed to reconsider it. If after such Reconsideration two thirds of that House shall agree to pass the Bill, it shall be sent, together with the Objections, to the other House, by which it shall likewise be reconsidered, and, if approved by two thirds of that house, it shall become a Law. But in all such Cases the Votes of both houses shall be determined by yeas and Nays, and the Names of the Persons voting for and against the Bill shall be entered on the journal of each House respectively. If any Bill shall not be returned by the President within ten Days (Sundays excepted) after it shall have been presented to him, the Same shall be a Law, in like Manner as if he had signed it, unless the Congress by their Adjournment prevent its Return, in which Case it shall not be a Law.

Every Order, Resolution, or Vote to which the Concurrence of the Senate and House of Representatives may be necessary (except on a question of Adjournment) shall be presented to the President of the United States; and before the Same shall take Effect, shall be approved by him, or being disapproved by him, shall be repassed by two thirds of the Senate and House of Representatives, according to the Rules and Limitations prescribed in the Case of a Bill.

[Powers of Congress enumerated]

Section 8 The Congress shall have Power

To lay and collect Taxes, Duties, Imposts, and Excises, to pay the Debts and provide for the common Defence and general Welfare of the United States; but all Duties, Imposts and Excises shall be uniform throughout the United States;

To borrow Money on the credit of the United States;

To regulate Commerce with foreign Nations, and among the several States, and with the Indian tribes;

To establish an uniform Rule of Naturalization, and uniform Laws on the subject of Bankruptcies throughout the United States;

To coin Money, regulate the Value thereof, and of foreign Coin, and fix the Standard of Weights and Measures;

To provide for the Punishment of counterfeiting the Securities and current Coin of the United States;

To establish Post Offices and post Roads;

To promote the Progress of Science and useful Arts by securing for limited Times to Authors and Inventors the exclusive Right to their respective Writings and Discoveries;

To constitute Tribunals inferior to the supreme Court;

To define and punish Piracies and Felonies committed on the high Seas, and offenses against the Law of Nations;

To declare War, grant Letters of Marque and Reprisal, and make Rules concerning Captures on Land and Water;

To raise and support Armies, but no Appropriation of Money to that Use shall be for a longer Term than two Years;

To provide and maintain a Navy;

To make rules for the Government and Regulation of the land and naval Forces;

To provide for calling forth the Militia to execute the Laws of the Union, suppress Insurrections, and repel Invasions;

To provide for organizing, arming, and disciplining the Militia, and for governing such Part of them as may be employed in the Service of the United States, reserving to the States respectively the Appointment of the Officers, and the Authority of training the Militia according to the discipline prescribed by Congress;

To exercise exclusive Legislation in all Cases whatsoever, over such District (not exceeding ten Miles square) as may, by cession of particular States, and the Acceptance of Congress, become the Seat of Government of the United States, and to exercise like Authority over all places purchased by the Consent of the Legislature of the State in which the Same shall be, for Erection of Forts, Magazines, Arsenals, dock-Yards, and other needful Buildings;—And

[Elastic clause]

To make all Laws which shall be necessary and proper for carrying into Execution the foregoing Powers, and all other powers vested by this Constitution in the Government of the United States, or in any Department or Officer thereof.

[Powers denied Congress]

Section 9 *The Migration or Importation of such persons as any of the States now existing shall think proper to admit, shall not be prohibited by the Congress prior to the Year 1808; but a Tax or duty may be imposed on such Importation, not exceeding $10 for each Person.*

The Privilege of the Writ of Habeas Corpus shall not be suspended, unless when in Cases of Rebellion or Invasion the public Safety may require it.

No Bill of Attainder or ex post facto Law shall be passed.

No Capitation, or other direct, Tax shall be laid, unless in Proportion to the Census or Enumeration herein before directed to be taken.

No Tax or Duty shall be laid on Articles exported from any State.

No Preference shall be given by any Regulation of Commerce or Revenue to the Ports of one State over those of another; nor shall Vessels bound to, or from, one State, be obliged to enter, clear, or pay Duties in another.

No Money shall be drawn from the Treasury, but in Consequence of Appropriations made by Law; and a regular Statement and Account of the receipts and Expenditures of all public Money shall be published from time to time.

No Title of Nobility shall be granted by the United States: And no Person holding any Office or Profit or trust under them, shall, without the Consent of the Congress, accept of any present, Emolument, Office, or Title, of any kind whatever, from any King, Prince, or foreign State.

[Powers denied the states]

Section 10 No State shall enter into any Treaty, Alliance, or Confederation; grant Letters of Marque and Reprisal; coin Money; emit Bills of Credit; make any Thing but gold and silver Coin a Tender in Payment of Debts; pass any Bill of Attainder, ex post facto law, or Law impairing the obligation of Contracts, or grant any Title of Nobility.

No State shall, without the Consent of Congress, lay any Imposts or Duties on Imports or Exports, except what may be absolutely necessary for executing its inspection Laws: and the net Produce of all duties and imposts, laid by any State on Imports or Exports, shall be for the Use of the Treasury of the United States; and all such Laws shall be subject to the Revision and Controul of the Congress.

No State shall, without the consent of Congress, lay any Duty of Tonnage, keep Troops or Ships of War in time of Peace, enter into any Agreement or Compact with another State, or with a foreign Power, or engage in War, unless actually invaded, or in such imminent Danger as will not admit of delay.

Article II

[The executive branch]

[The president: power vested, term, electoral college, qualifications, presidential succession, compensation, oath of office]

Section 1 The executive Power shall be vested in a President of the United States of America. He shall hold his Office during the Term of four Years, and, together with the Vice President, chosen for the same Term, be elected as follows:

Each State shall appoint, in such Manner as the Legislature thereof may direct, a Number of Electors, equal to the whole Number of Senators and Representatives to which the State may be entitled in the Congress; but no Senator or Representative, or Person holding an Office of Trust or Profit under the United States, shall be appointed an Elector.

The Electors shall meet in their respective States, and vote by Ballot for two Persons, of whom one at least shall not be an inhabitant of the same State with themselves. And they shall make a List of all the Persons voted for, and of the Number of Votes for each; which List they shall sign and certify, and transmit sealed to the Seat of Government of the United States, directed to the President of the Senate. The President of the Senate shall, in the presence of the Senate and House of Representatives, open all the Certificates, and the Votes shall then be counted. The Person having the greatest Number of Votes shall be the President, if such Number be a Majority of the whole number of Electors appointed; and if there be more than one who have such Majority, and have an equal Number of Votes, then the House of Representatives shall immediately chuse by Ballot one of them for President; and if no Person have a Majority, then from the five highest on the List said House shall in like Manner chuse the President. But in chusing the President the Votes shall be taken by States, the Representation from each State having one Vote; a quorum for this purpose shall consist of a Member or Members from two thirds of the States, and a Majority of all the States shall be necessary to a Choice. In every Case, after the Choice of the President, the person having the greatest Number of Votes of the Electors shall be the Vice President. But if there should remain two or more who have equal Votes, the Senate shall chuse from them by Ballot the Vice President.

The Congress may determine the Time of chusing the Electors and the Day on which they shall give their Votes; which Day shall be the same throughout the United States.

No person except a natural born Citizen, or a Citizen of the United States at the time of the Adoption of this Constitution, shall be eligible to the Office of President; neither shall any Person be eligible to that Office who shall not have attained to the age of thirty-five Years, and been fourteen Years a Resident within the United States.

In cases of the Removal of the President from Office or of his Death, Resignation, or Inability to discharge the Powers and Duties of the said Office, the same shall devolve on the Vice President, and the Congress may by law provide for the case of Removal, Death, Resignation, or inability, both of the President and Vice President, declaring what Officer shall then act as President, and such Officer shall act accordingly, until the Disability be removed, or a President shall be elected.

The President shall, at stated Times, receive for his Services, a Compensation, which shall neither be increased nor diminished during the Period for which he shall have been elected, and he shall not receive within that Period any other emolument from the United States, or any of them.

Before he enter on the Execution of his Office, he shall take the following Oath or Affirmation:—"I do solemnly swear (or affirm) that I will faithfully execute the Office of the President of the United States, and will to the best of my Ability preserve, protect and defend the Constitution of the United States."

[Powers and duties: as commander in chief, over advisers, to pardon, to make treaties and appoint officers]

Section 2 The President shall be Commander in Chief of the Army and Navy of the United States, and of the Militia of the several States, when called into the actual service of the United States; he may require the Opinion, in writing, of the principal Officer in each of the executive Departments, upon any Subject relating to the Duties of their respective Offices, and he shall have Power to grant Reprieves and Pardons for Offences against the United States, except in Cases of Impeachment.

He shall have Power, by and with the Advice and Consent of the Senate, to make Treaties, provided two-thirds of the Senators present concur; and he shall nominate, and by and with the Advice and Consent of the Senate, shall appoint Ambassadors, other public Ministers and Consuls, Judges of the supreme Court, and all other Officers of the United States, whose Appointments are not herein otherwise provided for, and which shall be established by Law: but Congress may by Law vest the Appointment of such inferior Officers, as they think proper, in the President alone, in the courts of Law, or in the Heads of Departments.

The President shall have Power to fill up all Vacancies that may happen during the Recess of the Senate, by granting Commissions which shall expire at the end of their next Session.

[Legislative, diplomatic, and law-enforcement duties]

Section 3 He shall from time to time give to the Congress Information of the State of the Union, and recommend to their Consideration such Measures as he shall judge necessary and expedient; he may, on extraordinary Occasions, convene both Houses, or either of them, and in Case of Disagreement between them, with Respect to the Time of Adjournment, he may adjourn them to such Time as he shall think proper; he shall receive Ambassadors and other public Ministers; he shall take Care that the Laws be faithfully executed, and shall Commission all the Officers of the United States.

[Impeachment]

Section 4 The President, Vice President and all civil Officers of the United States shall be removed from Office on Impeachment for, and on Conviction of, Treason, Bribery, or other high Crimes and Misdemeanors.

Article III

[The judicial branch]

[Power vested; Supreme Court; lower courts; judges]

Section 1 The judicial Power of the United States shall be vested in one supreme Court, and in such inferior Courts as the Congress may from time to time ordain and establish. The Judges, both of the supreme and inferior Courts, shall hold their Offices during good Behaviour, and shall, at stated Times, receive for their Services a Compensation which shall not be diminished during their Continuance in Office.

[Jurisdiction; trial by jury]

Section 2 The judicial Power shall extend to all Cases, in Law and Equity, arising under this Constitution, the Laws of the United States, and Treaties made, or which shall be made, under their Authority;—to all Cases affecting Ambassadors, other public Ministers and Consuls;—to all Cases of admiralty and maritime Jurisdiction;—to Controversies to which the United States shall be a Party;—to controversies between two or more States;—*between a State and Citizens of another State*;—between Citizens of different States—between Citizens of the same State claiming Lands under grants of different States, and between a State, or the Citizens thereof, and foreign States, Citizens or Subjects.

In all cases affecting Ambassadors, other public Ministers and Consuls, and those in which a State shall be Party, the supreme Court shall have original Jurisdiction. In all the other Cases before mentioned, the supreme Court shall have appellate Jurisdiction, both as to Law and Fact, with such Exceptions, and under such Regulations, as the Congress shall make.

The Trial of all Crimes, except in cases of Impeachment, shall be by Jury; and such Trial shall be held in the State where said Crimes shall have been committed; but when not committed within any State, the Trial shall be at such Place or Places as the Congress may by Law have directed.

[Treason: definition, punishment]

Section 3 Treason against the United States shall consist only in levying War against them, or in adhering to their Enemies, giving them Aid and Comfort. No Person shall be convicted of Treason unless on the Testimony of two Witnesses to the same overt Act, or on confession in open Court.

The Congress shall have power to declare the Punishment of Treason, but no Attainder of Treason shall work Corruption of Blood, or Forfeiture except during the Life of the Person attainted.

Article IV

[States' relations]

[Full faith and credit]

Section 1 Full Faith and Credit shall be given in each State to the public Acts, Records, and judicial Proceedings of every other State. And the Congress may by general laws prescribe the Manner in which such Acts, Records, and Proceedings shall be proved, and the Effect thereof.

[Interstate comity, rendition]

Section 2 The Citizens of each State shall be entitled to all Privileges and Immunities of Citizens in the several States.

A Person charged in any State with Treason, Felony, or other Crime, who shall flee from Justice, and be found in another State, shall on Demand of the executive Authority of the State from which he fled, be delivered up, to be removed to the State having Jurisdiction of the Crime.

No person held to Service or Labor in one State, under the Laws thereof, escaping into another, shall, in consequence of any Law or Regulation therein, be discharged from such Service or Labor, but shall be delivered up on Claim of the Party to whom such Service or Labor may be due.

[New states]

Section 3 New States may be admitted by the Congress into this Union; but no new State shall be formed or erected within the Jurisdiction of any other State; nor any State be formed by the Junction of two or more States, or parts of States, without the Consent of the Legislatures of the States concerned as well as of the Congress.

The Congress shall have Power to dispose of and make all needful Rules and Regulations respecting the Territory or other Property belonging to the United States; and nothing in this Constitution shall be so construed as to Prejudice any Claims of the United States, or of any particular State.

[Obligations of the United States to the states]

Section 4 The United States shall guarantee to every State in this Union a Republican Form of Government, and shall protect each of them against Invasion; and on Application of the Legislature, or of the Executive (when the Legislature cannot be convened), against domestic Violence.

Article V

[Mode of amendment]

The Congress, whenever two-thirds of both Houses shall deem it necessary, shall propose Amendments to this Constitution, or, on the Application of the Legislatures of two-thirds of the several States, shall call a Convention for proposing Amendments, which, in either Case, shall be valid to all Intents and Purposes, as part of this Constitution, when ratified by the legislatures of three-fourths of the several States, or by Conventions in three-fourths thereof, as the one or the other Mode of Ratification may be proposed by the Congress; Provided *that no Amendment which may be made prior to the Year One thousand eight hundred and eight shall in any Manner affect the first and fourth clauses in the Ninth Section of the first Article;* and that no State, without its Consent, shall be deprived of its equal suffrage in the Senate.

Article VI

[Prior debts, supremacy of Constitution, oaths of office]

All Debts contracted and Engagements entered into, before the Adoption of this Constitution, shall be as valid against the United States under this Constitution, as under the Confederation.

This Constitution, and the Laws of the United States which shall be made in Pursuance thereof; and all Treaties made, or which shall be made, under the Authority of the United States, shall be the supreme Law of the Land; and the judges in every State shall be bound thereby, anything in the Constitution or Laws of any State to the Contrary notwithstanding.

The Senators and Representatives before mentioned, and the Members of the several State Legislatures, and all executive and judicial Officers, both of the United States and of the several States, shall be bound by Oath or Affirmation to support this Constitution; but no religious test shall ever be required as a Qualification to any Office or public Trust under the United States.

Article VII

[Ratification]

The ratification of the Conventions of nine States shall be sufficient for the Establishment of this Constitution between the States so ratifying the Same.

Done in Convention by the Unanimous Consent of the States present, the seventeenth day of September in the Year of our Lord one thousand seven hundred and eighty-seven and of the Independence of the United States of America the twelfth. In WITNESS whereof We have hereunto subscribed our Names.

GEORGE WASHINGTON
and thirty-seven others

Amendments to the Constitution

[The first ten amendments—the Bill of Rights—were adopted in 1791.]

Amendment I

[Freedom of religion, speech, press, assembly]

Congress shall make no law respecting an establishment of religion, or prohibiting the free exercise thereof; or abridging the freedom of speech, or of the press; or the right of the people peaceably to assemble, and to petition the Government for a redress of grievances.

Amendment II

[Right to bear arms]

A well-regulated militia being necessary to the security of a free State, the right of the people to keep and bear arms shall not be infringed.

Amendment III

[Quartering of soldiers]

No Soldier shall, in time of peace, be quartered in any house without the consent of the Owner, nor in time of war, but in a manner to be prescribed by law.

Amendment IV

[Searches and seizures]

The right of the people to be secure in their persons, houses, papers, and effects, against unreasonable searches and seizures, shall not be violated, and no Warrants shall issue but upon probable cause, supported by Oath or Affirmation, and particularly describing the place to be searched, and the persons or things to be seized.

Amendment V

[Rights of persons: grand juries, double jeopardy, self-incrimination, due process, eminent domain]

No person shall be held to answer for a capital, or otherwise infamous crime, unless on a presentment or indictment of a Grand Jury, except in cases arising in the land or naval forces, or in the Militia, when in actual service in time of War or public danger; nor shall any person be subject for the same offense to be twice put in jeopardy of life or limb; nor shall be compelled in any criminal case to be a witness against himself, nor be deprived of life, liberty, or property, without due process of law; nor shall private property be taken for public use without just compensation.

Amendment VI

[Rights of accused in criminal prosecutions]

In all criminal prosecutions, the accused shall enjoy the right to a speedy and public trial, by an impartial jury of the State and district wherein the crime shall have been committed, which district shall have been previously ascertained by law, and to be informed of the nature and cause of the accusation; to be confronted with the witnesses against him; to have compulsory process for obtaining Witnesses in his favor, and to have the assistance of counsel for his defence.

Amendment VII

[Civil trials]

In Suits at common law, where the value in controversy shall exceed twenty dollars, the right of trial by jury shall be preserved, and no fact tried by a jury shall be otherwise reexamined in any Court of the United States, than according to the rules of the common law.

Amendment VIII

[Punishment for crime]

Excessive bail shall not be required, nor excessive fines imposed, nor cruel and unusual punishments inflicted.

Amendment IX

[Rights retained by the people]

The enumeration in the Constitution, of certain rights, shall not be construed to deny or disparage others retained by the people.

Amendment X

[Rights reserved to the states]

The powers not delegated to the United States by the Constitution, nor prohibited by it to the States, are reserved to the States respectively, or to the people.

Amendment XI

[Suits against the states; adopted 1798]

The Judicial power of the United States shall not be construed to extend to any suit in law or equity, commenced or prosecuted against one of the United States by Citizens of another state, or by Citizens or Subjects of any Foreign State.

Amendment XII

[Election of the president; adopted 1804]

The electors shall meet in their respective States, and vote by ballot for President and Vice-President, one of whom, at least, shall not be an inhabitant of the same state with themselves; they shall name in their ballots the person voted for as President, and in distinct ballots the person voted for as

Vice-President, and they shall make distinct lists of all persons voted for as President, and of all persons voted for as Vice-President, and of the number of votes for each, which lists they shall sign and certify, and transmit sealed to the seat of government of the United States, directed to the President of the Senate;—the President of the Senate shall, in the presence of the Senate and House of Representatives, open all the certificates and the votes shall then be counted;—the person having the greatest number of votes for President shall be the President, if such number be a majority of the whole number of electors appointed; and if no person have such majority, then from the persons having the highest numbers not exceeding three on the list of those voted for as President, the House of Representatives shall choose immediately, by ballot, the President. But in choosing the President, the votes shall be taken by States, the representation from each State having one vote; a quorum for this purpose shall consist of a member or members from two-thirds of the States, and a majority of all the States shall be necessary to a choice. And if the House of Representatives shall not choose a President whenever the right of choice shall devolve upon them, before *the fourth day of March* next following, then the Vice-President shall act as President, as in the case of the death or other constitutional disability of the President.—The person having the greatest number of votes as Vice-President shall be the Vice-President, if such number be a majority of the whole number of electors appointed; and if no person have a majority, then from the two highest numbers on the list the Senate shall choose the Vice-President; a quorum for the purpose shall consist of two-thirds of the whole number of Senators, and a majority of the whole number shall be necessary to a choice. But no person constitutionally ineligible to the Office of President shall be eligible to that of Vice-President of the United States.

Amendment XIII

[Abolition of slavery; adopted 1865]

Section 1 Neither slavery nor involuntary servitude, except as a punishment for crime whereof the party shall have been duly convicted, shall exist within the United States, or any place subject to their jurisdiction.

Section 2 Congress shall have power to enforce this article by appropriate legislation.

Amendment XIV

[Adopted 1868]

[Citizenship rights; privileges and immunities; due process; equal protection]

Section 1 All persons born or naturalized in the United States, and subject to the jurisdiction thereof, are citizens of the United States and of the State wherein they reside. No State shall make or enforce any law which shall abridge the privileges or immunities of citizens of the United States; nor shall any State deprive any person of life, liberty, or property, without due process of law; nor deny to any person within its jurisdiction the equal protection of the laws.

[Apportionment of representation]

Section 2 Representatives shall be apportioned among the several States according to their respective numbers, counting the whole number of persons in each State, excluding Indians not taxed. But when the right to vote at any election for the choice of Electors for President and Vice-President of the United States, Representatives in Congress, the Executive and Judicial officers of a State, or the members of the Legislature thereof, is denied to any of the male inhabitants of such State, being twenty-one years of age and citizens of the United States, or in any way abridged, except for participation in rebellion, or other crime, the basis of representation therein shall be reduced in the proportion which the number of such male citizens shall bear to the whole number of male citizens twenty-one years of age in such State.

[Disqualification of Confederate officials]

Section 3 No person shall be a Senator or Representative in Congress, or Elector of President and Vice-President, or hold any Office, civil or military, under the United States, or under any State, who, having previously taken an oath, as a member of Congress, or as an officer of the United States, or as a member of any State legislature, or as an executive or judicial officer of any State, to support the Constitution of the United States, shall have engaged in insurrection or rebellion against the same, or given aid or comfort to the enemies thereof. Congress may, by a vote of two-thirds of each house, remove such disability.

[Public debts]

Section 4 The validity of the public debt of the United States, authorized by law, including debts incurred for payment of pensions and bounties for services in suppressing insurrection or rebellion, shall not be questioned. But neither the United States nor any State shall assume or pay any debt or obligation incurred in aid of insurrection or rebellion against the United States, or any claim for the loss of emancipation of any slave; but all such debts, obligations, and claims shall be held illegal and void.

[Enforcement]

Section 5 The Congress shall have power to enforce, by appropriate legislation, the provisions of this article.

Amendment XV

[Extension of right to vote; adopted 1870]

Section 1 The right of citizens of the United States to vote shall not be denied or abridged by the United States or by any State on account of race, color, or previous condition of servitude.

Section 2 The Congress shall have power to enforce this article by appropriate legislation.

Amendment XVI

[Income tax; adopted 1913]

The Congress shall have power to lay and collect taxes on incomes, from whatever source derived, without apportionment among the several States, and without regard to any census or enumeration.

Amendment XVII

[Popular election of senators; adopted 1913]

Section 1 The Senate of the United States shall be composed of two Senators from each State, elected by the people thereof, for six years; and each Senator shall have one vote. The electors in each State shall have the Qualifications requisite for electors of the most numerous branch of the State legislatures.

Section 2 When vacancies happen in the representation of any State in the Senate, the executive authority of such State shall issue writs of election to fill such vacancies: Provided, that the Legislature of any State may empower the executive thereof to make temporary appointments until the people fill the vacancies by election as the Legislature may direct.

Section 3 This amendment shall not be so construed as to affect the election or term of any Senator chosen before it becomes valid as part of the Constitution.

Amendment XVIII

[Prohibition of intoxicating liquors; adopted 1919, repealed 1933]

Section 1 After one year from the ratification of this article the manufacture, sale or transportation of intoxicating liquors within, the importation thereof into, or the exportation thereof from the United States and all territory subject to the jurisdiction thereof, for beverage purposes, is hereby prohibited.

Section 2 The Congress and the several States shall have concurrent power to enforce this article by appropriate legislation.

Section 3 This article shall be inoperative unless it shall have been ratified as an amendment to the Constitution by the legislatures of the several States, as provided by the Constitution, within seven years from the date of the submission thereof to the States by the Congress.

Amendment XIX
[Right of women to vote; adopted 1920]

Section 1 The right of citizens of the United States to vote shall not be denied or abridged by the United States or by any State on account of sex.

Section 2 The Congress shall have power to enforce this article by appropriate legislation.

Amendment XX
[Commencement of terms of office; adopted 1933]

Section 1 The terms of the President and Vice-President shall end at noon on the 20th day of January, and the terms of Senators and Representatives at noon on the 3d day of January, of the years in which such terms would have ended if this article had not been ratified; and the terms of their successors shall then begin.

Section 2 The Congress shall assemble at least once in every year, and such meetings shall begin at noon on the 3d day of January, unless they shall by law appoint a different day.

[Extension of presidential succession]

Section 3 If, at the time fixed for the beginning of the term of the President, the President-elect shall have died, the Vice-President-elect shall become President. If a President shall not have been chosen before the time fixed for the beginning of his term, or if the President-elect shall have failed to qualify, then the Vice-President-elect shall act as President until a President shall have qualified; and the Congress may by law provide for the case wherein neither a President-elect nor a Vice-President-elect shall have qualified, declaring who shall then act as President, or the manner in which one who is to act shall be selected, and such persons shall act accordingly until a President or Vice-President shall have qualified.

Section 4 The Congress may by law provide for the case of the death of any of the persons from whom the House of Representatives may choose a President whenever the right of choice shall have devolved upon them, and for the case of the death of any of the persons from whom the Senate may choose a Vice-President whenever the right of choice shall have devolved upon them.

Section 5 Sections 1 and 2 shall take effect on the 15th day of October following the ratification of this article.

Section 6 This article shall be inoperative unless it shall have been ratified as an amendment to the Constitution by the Legislatures of three-fourths of the several States within seven years from the date of its submission.

Amendment XXI
[Repeal of Eighteenth Amendment; adopted 1933]

Section 1 The eighteenth article of amendment to the Constitution of the United States is hereby repealed.

Section 2 The transportation or importation into any State, Territory, or Possession of the United States for delivery or use therein of intoxicating liquors, in violation of the laws thereof, is hereby prohibited.

Section 3 This article shall be inoperative unless it shall have been ratified as an amendment to the Constitution by conventions in the several States, as provided in the Constitution, within seven years from the date of submission thereof to the States by the Congress.

Amendment XXII

[Limit on presidential tenure; adopted 1951]

Section 1 No person shall be elected to the Office of President more than twice, and no person who has held the Office of President, or acted as President, for more than two years of a term to which some other person was elected President shall be elected to the Office of President more than once. But this article shall not apply to any person holding the Office of President when this article was proposed by the Congress, and shall not prevent any person who may be holding the Office of President, or acting as President, during the term within which this article becomes operative from holding the Office of President or acting as President during the remainder of such term.

Section 2 This article shall be inoperative unless it shall have been ratified as an amendment to the Constitution by the legislatures of three-fourths of the several States within seven years from the date of its submission to the States by the Congress.

Amendment XXIII

[Presidential electors for the District of Columbia; adopted 1961]

Section 1 The District constituting the seat of Government of the United States shall appoint in such manner as the Congress may direct: A number of electors of President and Vice President equal to the whole number of Senators and Representatives in Congress to which the District would be entitled if it were a State, but in no event more than the least populous State; they shall be in addition to those appointed by the States, but they shall be considered for the purposes of the election of President and Vice President, to be electors appointed by a State; and they shall meet in the District and perform such duties as provided by the twelfth article of amendment.

Section 2 The Congress shall have the power to enforce this article by appropriate legislation.

Amendment XXIV

[Poll tax outlawed in national elections; adopted 1964]

Section 1 The right of citizens of the United States to vote in any primary or other election for President or Vice President, for electors for President or Vice President, or for Senator or Representative in Congress, shall not be denied or abridged by the United States or any State by reason of failure to pay any poll tax or other tax.

Section 2 The Congress shall have the power to enforce this article by appropriate legislation.

Amendment XXV

[Presidential succession; adopted 1967]

Section 1 In case of the removal of the President from Office or of his death or resignation, the Vice President shall become President.

[Vice-presidential vacancy]

Section 2 Whenever there is a vacancy in the Office of the Vice President, the President shall nominate a Vice President who shall take Office upon confirmation by a majority vote of both Houses of Congress.

Section 3 Whenever the President transmits to the President pro tempore of the Senate and the Speaker of the House of Representatives his written declaration that he is unable to discharge the powers and duties of his Office, and until he transmits to them a written declaration to the contrary, such powers and duties shall be discharged by the Vice President as Acting President.

[**Presidential disability**]

Section 4 Whenever the Vice President and a majority of either the principal officers of the executive departments or of such other body as Congress may by law provide, transmit to the President pro tempore of the Senate and the Speaker of the House of Representatives their written declaration that the President is unable to discharge the powers and duties of his Office, the Vice President shall immediately assume the powers and duties of the Office as Acting President.

Thereafter, when the President transmits to the President pro tempore of the Senate and the Speaker of the House of Representatives his written declaration that no inability exists, he shall resume the powers and duties of his Office unless the Vice President and a majority of either the principal officers of the executive department(s) or of such other body as Congress may by law provide, transmit within four days to the President pro tempore of the Senate and the Speaker of the House of Representatives their written declaration that the President is unable to discharge the powers and duties of his Office. Thereupon Congress shall decide the issue, assembling within forty-eight hours for that purpose if not in session. If the Congress, within twenty-one days after receipt of the latter written declaration, or, if Congress is not in session, within twenty-one days after Congress is required to assemble, determines by two-thirds vote of both Houses that the President is unable to discharge the powers and duties of his Office, the Vice President shall continue to discharge the same as Acting President; otherwise, the President shall resume the powers and duties of his Office.

Amendment XXVI

[Right of eighteen-year-olds to vote; adopted 1971]

Section 1 The right of citizens of the United States, who are eighteen years of age or older, to vote shall not be denied or abridged by the United States or by any State on account of age.

Section 2 The Congress shall have power to enforce this article by appropriate legislation.

Amendment XXVII

[Congressional pay raises; adopted 1992]

No law, varying the compensation for the services of the Senators and Representatives shall take effect, until an election of Representatives shall have intervened.

Glossary

A

administrative discretion The latitude that Congress gives agencies to make policy in the spirit of their legislative mandate.

affirmative action Any of a wide range of programs, from special recruitment efforts to numerical quotas, aimed at expanding opportunities for women and minority groups.

agenda building The process by which new issues are brought into the political limelight.

agenda setting The stage of the policymaking process during which problems get defined as political issues.

aggregate demand The total income that consumers, businesses, and government wish to spend for goods and services.

amicus curiae brief A brief filed (with the permission of the court) by an individual or group that is not a party to a legal action but has an interest in it.

anarchism A political philosophy that opposes government in any form.

appellate jurisdiction The authority of a court to hear cases that have been tried, decided, or reexamined in other courts.

appropriations committees Committees of Congress that decide which of the programs passed by the authorization committees will actually be funded.

argument The heart of a judicial opinion; its logical content separated from facts, rhetoric, and procedure.

Articles of Confederation The compact among the thirteen original states that established the first government of the United States.

attentive policy elites Leaders who follow news in specific policy areas.

authorization committees Committees of Congress that can authorize spending in their particular areas of responsibility.

autocracy A system of government in which the power to govern is concentrated in the hands of one individual.

B

benign discrimination Discrimination that causes no harm because it is grounded in reason.

bill of attainder A law that pronounces an individual guilty of a crime without a trial.

Bill of Rights The first ten amendments to the Constitution. They prevent the national government from tampering with fundamental rights and civil liberties, and emphasize the limited character of national power.

bimodal distribution A distribution (of opinions) that shows two responses being chosen about as frequently as each other.

black codes Legislation enacted by former slave states to restrict the freedom of blacks.

block grants Grants-in-aid awarded for general purposes, allowing the recipient great discretion in spending the grant money.

blue slip The failure of a senator to return a blue slip signals the end of the road for a judicial nomination.

budget authority The amounts that government agencies are authorized to spend for current and future programs.

budget committees One committee in each house of Congress that supervises a comprehensive budget review process.

budget outlays The amounts that government agencies are expected to spend in the fiscal year.

bureaucracy A large, complex organization in which employees have specific job responsibilities and work within a hierarchy of authority.

bureaucrats Employees of a bureaucracy, usually meaning a government bureaucracy.

business cycles Expansions and contractions of business activity, the first accompanied by inflation and the second by unemployment.

C

cabinet A group of presidential advisers; the heads of the executive departments and other key officials.

capitalism The system of government that favors free enterprise (privately owned businesses operating without government regulation).

casework Solving problems for constituents, especially problems involving government agencies.

categorical grants Grants-in-aid targeted for a specific purpose by either formula or project.

caucus A closed meeting of the members of a political party to decide questions of policy and the selection of candidates for office.

caucus/convention A method used to select delegates to attend a party's national convention. Generally, a local meeting selects delegates for a county-level meeting, which in turn selects delegates for a higher-level meeting; the process culminates in a state convention that actually selects the national convention delegates.

checks and balances A government structure that gives each branch some scrutiny of and control over the other branches.

citizen group Lobbying organization built around policy concerns unrelated to members' vocational interests.

civil cases Court cases that involve a private dispute arising from such matters as accidents, contractual obligations, and divorce.

civil liberties Freedoms guaranteed to individuals taking the form of restraint on government.

civil rights Powers or privileges guaranteed to individuals and protected from arbitrary removal at the hands of government or individuals.

civil service The system by which most appointments to the federal bureaucracy are made, to ensure that government jobs are filled on the basis of merit and that employees are not fired for political reasons.

Civil War amendments The Thirteenth, Fourteenth, and Fifteenth Amendments to the U.S. Constitution.

class action suit A legal action brought by a person or group on behalf of a number of people in similar circumstances.

clear and present danger test A means by which the Supreme Court has distinguished between speech as the advocacy of ideas, which is protected by the First Amendment, and speech as incitement, which is not protected.

closed primaries Primary elections in which voters must declare their party affiliation before they are given the primary ballot containing that party's potential nominees.

cloture The mechanism by which a filibuster is cut off in the Senate.

coalition building The banding together of several interest groups for the purpose of lobbying.

coercive federalism A view holding that the national government may impose its policy preferences on the states through regulations in the form of mandates and restraints.

commerce clause The third clause of Article I, Section 8, of the Constitution, which gives Congress the power to regulate commerce among the states.

common, or judge-made, law Legal precedents derived from previous judicial decisions.

communism A political system in which, in theory, ownership of all land and productive facilities is in the hands of the people, and all goods are equally shared. The production and distribution of goods are controlled by an authoritarian government.

communitarians Those who are willing to use government to promote both order and equality.

competition and outsourcing Procedures that allow private contractors to bid for jobs previously held exclusively by government employees.

competitive grants Grants-in-aid awarded on the basis of applications submitted by prospective recipients who are eligible to compete for the grant.

concurrence The agreement of a judge with the Supreme Court's majority decision, for a reason other than the majority reason.

confederation A loose association of independent states that agree to cooperate on specified matters.

conference committee A temporary committee created to work out differences between the House and Senate versions of a specific piece of legislation.

Congressional Budget Office (CBO) The budgeting arm of Congress, which prepares alternative budgets to those prepared by the president's OMB.

congressional campaign committee An organization maintained by a political party to raise funds to support its own candidates in congressional elections.

conservatives Those who are willing to use government to promote order but not equality.

constituents People who live and vote in a government official's district or state.

conventional participation Relatively routine political behavior that uses institutional channels and is acceptable to the dominant culture.

cooperative federalism A view holding that the Constitution is an agreement among people who are citizens of both state and nation, so there is much overlap between state powers and national powers.

county governments The government units that administer a county.

criminal cases Court cases involving a crime, or violation of public order.

critical election An election that produces a sharp change in the existing pattern of party loyalties among groups of voters.

D

de facto segregation Segregation that is not the result of government influence.

de jure segregation Government-imposed segregation.

Declaration of Independence Drafted by Thomas Jefferson, the document that proclaimed the right of the colonies to separate from Great Britain.

deficit financing The Keynesian technique of spending beyond government income to combat an economic slump. Its purpose is to inject extra money into the economy to stimulate aggregate demand.

delegate A legislator whose primary responsibility is to represent the majority view of his or her constituents, regardless of his or her own view.

delegation of powers The process by which Congress gives the executive branch the additional authority needed to address new problems.

democracy A system of government in which, in theory, the people rule, either directly or indirectly.

democratic socialism A socialist form of government that guarantees civil liberties such as freedom of speech and religion. Citizens determine the extent of government activity through free elections and competitive political parties.

democratization A process of transition as a country attempts to move from an authoritarian form of government to a democratic one.

departments The biggest units of the executive branch, covering a broad area of government responsibility. The heads of the departments, or secretaries, form the president's cabinet.

deregulation A bureaucratic reform by which the government reduces its role as a regulator of business.

descriptive representation A belief that constituents are most effectively represented by legislators who are similar to them in such key demographic characteristics as race, ethnicity, religion, or gender.

desegregation The ending of authorized segregation, or separation by race.

direct action Unconventional participation that involves assembling crowds to confront businesses and local governments to demand a hearing.

direct lobbying Attempts to influence a legislator's vote through personal contact with the policymaker.

direct primary A preliminary election, run by the state government, in which the voters choose each party's candidates for the general election.

discretionary spending In the Budget Enforcement Act of 1990, authorized expenditures from annual appropriations.

dissent The disagreement of a judge with a majority decision.

distributive policies Government policies designed to confer a benefit on a particular institution or group.

divided government The situation in which one party controls the White House and the other controls at least one house of Congress.

docket A court's agenda.

dual federalism A view holding that the Constitution is a compact among sovereign states, so that the powers of the national government and the states are clearly differentiated.

E

earmark Federal funds appropriated by Congress for use on local projects.

economic depression A period of high unemployment and business failures; a severe, long-lasting downturn in a business cycle.

efficient market hypothesis Financial markets are informationally efficient—they quickly absorb all relevant information about securities into their prices.

e-government Online communication channels that enable citizens to easily obtain information from government and facilitate the expression of opinions to government officials.

elastic clause The last clause in Article I, Section 8, of the Constitution, which gives Congress the means to execute its enumerated powers. This clause is the basis for Congress's implied powers. Also called the *necessary and proper clause*.

election campaign An organized effort to persuade voters to choose one candidate over others competing for the same office.

electoral college A body of electors chosen by voters to cast ballots for president and vice president.

electoral dealignment A lessening of the importance of party loyalties in voting decisions.

electoral realignment The change in voting patterns that occurs after a critical election.

Elementary and Secondary Education Act of 1965 (ESEA) The federal government's primary law to assist the nation's elementary and secondary schools. It emerged as part of President Lyndon Johnson's Great Society program.

elite theory The view that a small group of people actually makes most of the important government decisions.

entitlements Benefits to which every eligible person has a legal right and that the government cannot deny.

enumerated powers The powers explicitly granted to Congress by the Constitution.

equal rights amendment (ERA) A failed constitutional amendment introduced by the National Women's Party in 1923, declaring that "equality of rights under the law shall not be denied or abridged by the United States or any State on account of sex."

equality of opportunity The idea that each person is guaranteed the same chance to succeed in life.

equality of outcome The concept that society must ensure that people are equal, and governments must design policies to redistribute wealth and status so that economic and social equality is actually achieved.

establishment clause The first clause in the First Amendment, which forbids government establishment of religion.

Every Student Succeeds Act of 2015 (ESSA) A reauthorization of the Elementary and Secondary Education Act during the Barack Obama presidency.

ex post facto law A law that declares an action to be criminal after it has been performed.

exclusionary rule The judicial rule that states that evidence obtained in an illegal search and seizure cannot be used in trial.

executive agreement A pact between the heads of two countries.

executive branch The law-enforcing branch of government.

Executive Office of the President The president's executive aides and their staffs; the extended White House executive establishment.

executive orders Presidential directives that create or modify laws and public policies, without the direct approval of Congress.

extraordinary majority A majority greater than the minimum of 50 percent plus one.

F

Federal Communications Commission (FCC) An independent federal agency that regulates interstate and international communication by radio, television, telephone, telegraph, cable, and satellite.

Federal Election Commission (FEC) A bipartisan federal agency of six members that oversees the financing of national election campaigns.

federal question An issue covered by the U.S. Constitution, national laws, or U.S. treaties.

Federal Reserve System The system of banks that acts as the central bank of the United States and controls major monetary policies.

federalism The division of power between a central government and regional governments.

feedback Information received by policymakers about the effectiveness of public policy.

feminization of poverty The term applied to the fact that a large percentage of all poor Americans are women or the dependents of women.

fighting words Speech that is not protected by the First Amendment because it inflicts injury or tends to incite an immediate disturbance of the peace.

filibuster A delaying tactic, used in the Senate, that allows any senator to prevent a bill from coming to a vote.

first-past-the-post elections A British term for elections conducted in single-member districts that award victory to the candidate with the most votes.

fiscal policies Economic policies that involve government spending and taxing.

fiscal year The twelve-month period from October 1 to September 30 used by the government for accounting purposes. A fiscal year budget is named for the year in which it ends.

formula grants Categorical grants distributed according to a particular set of rules, called a *formula*, that specifies who is eligible for the grants and how much each eligible applicant will receive.

fragmentation In policymaking, the phenomenon of attacking a single problem in different and sometimes competing ways.

franchise The right to vote. Also called *suffrage*.

freedom from Immunity, as in *freedom from want*.

freedom of An absence of constraints on behavior, as in *freedom of speech* or *freedom of religion*.

free-exercise clause The second clause in the First Amendment, which prevents the government from interfering with the exercise of religion.

free-expression clauses The press and speech clauses of the First Amendment.

free-rider problem The situation in which people benefit from the activities of an organization (such as an interest group) but do not contribute to those activities.

front-loading States' practice of moving delegate selection primaries and caucuses earlier in the calendar year to gain media and candidate attention.

G

gatekeepers Media executives, news editors, and prominent reporters who direct the flow of news.

general election A national election held by law in November of every even-numbered year.

gerrymandering Redrawing a congressional district to intentionally benefit one political party.

globalization The increasing interdependence of citizens and nations across the world.

going public A strategy whereby a president seeks to influence policy elites and media coverage by appealing directly to the American people.

good faith exception An exception to the Supreme Court exclusionary rule, holding that evidence seized on the basis of a mistakenly issued search warrant can be introduced at trial if the mistake was made in good faith, that is, if all the parties involved had reason at the time to believe that the warrant was proper.

government The legitimate use of force to control human behavior; also, the organization or agency authorized to exercise that force.

government corporations Government agencies that perform services that might be provided by the private sector but that either involve insufficient financial incentive or are better provided when they are somehow linked with government.

Government Performance and Results Act A law requiring each government agency to implement quantifiable standards to measure its performance in meeting stated program goals.

grant-in-aid Money provided by one level of government to another level of government, or sometimes to a nongovernmental organization, to be spent for a given purpose.

grassroots lobbying Lobbying activities performed by rank-and-file interest group members and other supporters.

Great Compromise Submitted by the Connecticut delegation to the Constitutional Convention, and thus also known as the Connecticut Compromise, a plan calling for a bicameral legislature in which the House of Representatives would be apportioned according to population and the states would be represented equally in the Senate.

Great Depression The longest and deepest setback the American economy has ever experienced. It began with the stock market crash on October 24, 1929, and did not end until the start of World War II.

Great Society President Lyndon Johnson's broad array of programs designed to redress political, social, and economic inequality.

gridlock A situation in which government is incapable of acting on important issues.

gross domestic product (GDP) The total value of the goods and services produced by a country during a year.

H

hold A letter requesting that a bill be held from floor debate.

home rule The right to enact and enforce legislation locally.

horse race journalism Election coverage by the mass media that focuses on which candidate is ahead rather than on national issues.

I

impeachment The formal charging of a government official with "treason, bribery, or other high crimes and misdemeanors."

implementation The process of putting specific policies into operation.

implied powers Those powers that Congress needs to execute its enumerated powers.

incremental budgeting A method of budget making that involves adding new funds (an increment) onto the amount previously budgeted (in last year's budget).

incrementalism Policymaking characterized by a series of decisions, each instituting modest change.

incumbent A current officeholder.

independent agencies Executive agencies that are not part of a cabinet department.

inflation An economic condition characterized by price increases linked to a decrease in the value of the currency.

influencing behavior Behavior that seeks to modify or reverse government policy to serve political interests.

information campaign An organized effort to gain public backing by bringing a group's views to public attention.

infotainment A mix of information and diversion oriented to personalities or celebrities, not linked to the day's events, and usually unrelated to public affairs or policy; often called "soft news."

inherent powers Authority claimed by the president that is not clearly specified in the Constitution. Typically, these powers are inferred from the Constitution.

initiative A procedure by which voters can propose an issue to be decided by the legislature or by the people in a referendum. It requires gathering a specified number of signatures and submitting a petition to a designated agency.

interest group An organized group of individuals that seeks to influence public policy; also called a *lobby*.

interest group entrepreneur An interest group organizer or leader.

intergovernmental system The collection of governments made up of national, state, and local units of government.

invidious discrimination Discrimination against persons or groups that works to their harm and is based on animosity.

issue definition Our conception of the problem at hand.

issue framing The way that politicians or interest group leaders define an issue when presenting it to others.

issue network A shared-knowledge group consisting of representatives of various interests involved in some particular aspect of public policy.

J

joint committee A committee made up of members of both the House and the Senate.

judgment The judicial decision in a court case.

judicial activism A judicial philosophy by which judges tend not to defer to decisions of the elected branches of government, resulting in the invalidation or emasculation of those decisions.

judicial branch The law-interpreting branch of government.

judicial restraint A judicial philosophy by which judges tend to defer to decisions of the elected branches of government.

judicial review The power to declare congressional (and presidential) acts invalid because they violate the Constitution.

K

Keynesian theory An economic theory stating that the government can stabilize the economy—that is, can smooth business cycles—by controlling the level of aggregate demand, and that the level of aggregate demand can be controlled by means of fiscal and monetary policies.

L

laissez faire An economic doctrine that opposes any form of government intervention in business.

legislative branch The lawmaking branch of government.

legislative liaison staff Those people who act as the communications link between the White House and Congress, advising the president or cabinet secretaries on the status of pending legislation.

liberalism The belief that states should leave individuals free to follow their individual pursuits.

liberals Those who are willing to use government to promote equality but not order.

libertarianism A political ideology that is opposed to all government action except as necessary to protect life and property.

libertarians Those who are opposed to using government to promote either order or equality.

lobby See *interest group*.

lobbyist A representative of an interest group.

M

majoritarian model of democracy The classical theory of democracy in which government by the people is interpreted as government by the majority of the people.

majority leader The head of the majority party in the Senate; the second-highest ranking member of the majority party in the House.

majority representation The system by which one office, contested by two or more candidates, is won by the single candidate who collects the most votes.

majority rule The principle—basic to procedural democratic theory—that the decision of a group must reflect the preference of more than half of those participating; a simple majority.

mandate A requirement that a state undertake an activity or provide a service, in keeping with minimum national standards.

mandatory spending In the Budget Enforcement Act of 1990, expenditures required by previous commitments.

mass media The means employed in mass communication; traditionally divided into print media and broadcast media.

means-tested benefits Conditional benefits provided by government to individuals whose income falls below a designated threshold.

media event A situation that is so "newsworthy" that the mass media are compelled to cover it. Candidates in elections often create such situations to garner media attention.

Medicaid A need-based comprehensive medical and hospitalization program.

Medicare A health insurance program serving primarily persons sixty-five and older.

minority rights The benefits of government that cannot be denied to any citizen by majority decisions.

Miranda warnings Statements concerning rights that police are required to make to a person before he or she is subjected to in-custody questioning.

modified closed primaries Primary elections that allow individual state parties to decide whether they permit independents to vote in their primaries and, if so, for which offices.

modified open primaries Primary elections that entitle independent voters to vote in a party's primary.

monetarists Those who argue that government can effectively control the performance of an economy mainly by controlling the supply of money.

monetary policies Economic policies that involve control of, and changes in, the supply of money.

municipal governments The government units that administer a city or town.

N

national committee A committee of a political party composed of party chairpersons and party officials from every state.

national convention A gathering of delegates of a single political party from across the country to choose candidates for president and vice president and to adopt a party platform.

national debt The accumulated sum of past government borrowing owed to lenders outside the government.

national sovereignty A political entity's externally recognized right to exercise final authority over its affairs.

necessary and proper clause The last clause in Section 8 of Article I of the Constitution, which gives Congress the means to execute its enumerated powers. This clause is the basis for Congress's implied powers. Also called the *elastic clause*.

New Deal The measures advocated by the Franklin D. Roosevelt administration to alleviate the Depression.

New Jersey Plan Submitted by the head of the New Jersey delegation to the Constitutional Convention, a set of nine resolutions that would have, in effect, preserved the Articles of Confederation by amending rather than replacing them.

newsworthiness The degree to which a news story is important enough to be covered in the mass media.

Nineteenth Amendment The amendment to the Constitution, adopted in 1920, that ensures women of the right to vote.

No Child Left Behind Act of 2001 (NCLB) A reauthorization of the Elementary and Secondary Education Act during the George W. Bush presidency.

nomination Designation as an official candidate of a political party.

non-means-tested benefits Benefits provided by government to all citizens, regardless of income; Medicare and Social Security are examples.

normal distribution A symmetrical bell-shaped distribution (of opinions) centered on a single mode, or most frequent response.

norms An organization's informal, unwritten rules that guide individual behavior.

O

Office of Management and Budget (OMB) The budgeting arm of the Executive Office; prepares the president's budget.

oligarchy A system of government in which power is concentrated in the hands of a few people.

open election An election that lacks an incumbent.

open primaries Primary elections in which voters need not declare their party affiliation and can choose one party's primary ballot to take into the voting booth.

order Established ways of social behavior. Maintaining order is the oldest purpose of government.

original jurisdiction The authority of a court to hear a case before any other court does.

oversight The process of reviewing the operations of an agency to determine whether it is carrying out policies as Congress intended.

P

parliamentary system A system of government in which the chief executive is the leader whose party holds the most seats in the legislature after an election or whose party forms a major part of the ruling coalition.

participatory democracy A system of government where rank-and-file citizens rule themselves rather than electing representatives to govern on their behalf.

party conferences A meeting to select party leaders and decide committee assignments, held at the beginning of a session of Congress by Republicans or Democrats in each chamber.

party identification A voter's sense of psychological attachment to a party.

party machine A centralized party organization that dominates local politics by controlling elections.

party platform The statement of policies of a national political party.

plea bargain A defendant's admission of guilt in exchange for a less severe punishment.

pluralist model of democracy An interpretation of democracy in which government by the people is taken to mean government by people operating through competing interest groups.

police power The authority of a government to maintain order and safeguard citizens' health, morals, safety, and welfare.

policy evaluation Analysis of a public policy so as to determine how well it is working.

policy formulation The stage of the policymaking process during which formal proposals are developed and adopted.

political action committee (PAC) An organization that collects campaign contributions from group members and donates them to candidates for political office.

political agenda A list of issues that need government attention.

political equality Equality in political decision making: one vote per person, with all votes counted equally.

political ideology A consistent set of values and beliefs about the proper purpose and scope of government.

political participation Actions of private citizens by which they seek to influence or support government and politics.

political party An organization that sponsors candidates for political office under the organization's name.

political socialization The complex process by which people acquire their political values.

political system A set of interrelated institutions that links people with government.

poll tax A tax of $1 or $2 on every citizen who wished to vote, first instituted in Georgia in 1877. Although it was no burden on most white citizens, it effectively disenfranchised blacks.

poverty level The minimum cash income that will provide for a family's basic needs; calculated using the Consumer Price Index.

precedent A judicial ruling that serves as the basis for the ruling in a subsequent case.

preemption The power of Congress to enact laws by which the national government assumes total or partial responsibility for a state government function.

presidential primary A special primary election used to select delegates to attend the party's national convention, which in turn nominates the presidential candidate.

primary election A preliminary election conducted within a political party to select candidates who will run for public office in a subsequent election.

prior restraint Censorship before publication.

procedural democratic theory A view of democracy as being embodied in a decision-making process that involves universal participation, political equality, majority rule, and responsiveness.

productive capacity The total value of goods and services that can be produced when the economy works at full capacity.

program monitoring Keeping track of government programs; usually done by interest groups.

progressive taxation A system of taxation whereby the rich pay proportionately higher taxes than the poor; used by governments to redistribute wealth and thus promote equality.

progressivism A philosophy of political reform based on the goodness and wisdom of the individual citizen as opposed to special interests and political institutions.

proportional representation The system by which legislative seats are awarded to a party in proportion to the vote that party wins in an election.

protectionism The notion that women must be protected from life's cruelties; until the 1970s, the basis for laws affecting women's civil rights.

public assistance Government aid to individuals who can demonstrate a need for that aid.

public figures People who assume roles of prominence in society or thrust themselves to the forefront of public controversy.

public goods Benefits and services, such as parks and sanitation, that benefit all citizens but are not likely to be produced voluntarily by individuals.

public opinion The collective attitudes of citizens concerning a given issue or question.

public policy A general plan of action adopted by the government to solve a social problem, counter a threat, or pursue an objective.

R

racial gerrymandering The drawing of a legislative district to maximize the chance that a minority candidate will win election.

reapportionment Redistribution of representatives among the states, based on population change. The House is reapportioned after each census.

recall The process for removing an elected official from office. Eighteen states allow recall.

receipts For a government, the amount expected or obtained in taxes and other revenues.

redistributional policies Policies that take government resources, such as tax funds, from one sector of society and transfer them to another.

redisricting The process of redrawing political boundaries to reflect changes in population.

referendum An election on a policy issue.

regulation Government intervention in the workings of a business market to promote some socially desired goal.

regulations Administrative rules that guide the operation of a government program.

regulatory commissions Agencies of the executive branch of government that control or direct some aspect of the economy.

representative democracy A system of government where citizens elect public officials to govern on their behalf.

republic A government without a monarch; a government rooted in the consent of the governed, whose power is exercised by elected representatives responsible to the governed.

republicanism A form of government in which power resides in the people and is exercised by their elected representatives.

responsible party government A set of principles formalizing the ideal role of parties in a majoritarian democracy.

responsiveness A decision-making principle, necessitated by representative government, that implies that elected representatives should do what the majority of people wants.

restraint A requirement prohibiting a state or local government from exercising a certain power.

rights The benefits of government to which every citizen is entitled.

rule making The administrative process that results in the issuance of regulations by government agencies.

rule of four An unwritten rule that requires at least four justices to agree that a case warrants consideration before it is reviewed by the U.S. Supreme Court.

S

school districts The government units that administer elementary and secondary schools and programs.

select committee A temporary congressional committee created for a specific purpose and disbanded after that purpose is fulfilled.

self-interest principle The implication that people choose what benefits them personally.

senatorial courtesy A norm under which a nomination must be acceptable to the home state senator from the president's party.

seniority Years of consecutive service on a particular congressional committee.

separate-but-equal doctrine The concept that providing separate but equivalent facilities for blacks and whites satisfies the equal protection clause of the Fourteenth Amendment.

separation of powers The assignment of lawmaking, law-enforcing, and law-interpreting functions to separate branches of government.

skewed distribution An asymmetrical but generally bell-shaped distribution (of opinions); its mode, or most frequent response, lies off to one side.

social contract theory The belief that the people agree to set up rulers for certain purposes and thus have the right to resist or remove rulers who act against those purposes.

social equality Equality in wealth, education, and status.

social insurance A government-backed guarantee against loss by individuals without regard to need.

Social Security Social insurance that provides economic assistance to persons faced with unemployment, disability, or old age. It is financed by taxes on employers and employees.

Social Security Act The law that provided for Social Security and is the basis of modern American social welfare.

social welfare programs Government programs that provide the minimum living standards necessary for all citizens.

socialism A form of rule in which the central government plays a strong role in regulating existing private industry and directing the economy, although it does allow some private ownership of productive capacity.

socioeconomic status Position in society, based on a combination of education, occupational status, and income.

sociotropic responses Opinions about how the country as a whole is doing affect political preferences more strongly than one's own personal circumstance.

soft news General entertainment programming that often includes discussions of political affairs.

solicitor general The third highest official of the U.S. Department of Justice, and the one who represents the national government before the Supreme Court.

sovereignty The quality of being supreme in power or authority.

Speaker of the House The presiding officer of the House of Representatives.

special districts Government units created to perform particular functions, especially when those functions are best performed across jurisdictional boundaries.

split ticket Voting for candidates from different parties for different offices.

stable distribution A distribution (of opinions) that shows little change over time.

stagflation The joint occurrence of slow growth, unemployment, and inflation.

standard socioeconomic model A relationship between socioeconomic status and conventional political involvement: people with higher status and more education are more likely to participate than those with lower status.

standing committee A permanent congressional committee that specializes in a particular policy area.

stare decisis Literally, "let the decision stand"; decision making according to precedent.

states' rights The idea that all rights not specifically conferred on the national government by the U.S. Constitution are reserved to the states.

straight ticket Voting for a single party's candidates for all the offices.

strict scrutiny A standard used by the Supreme Court in deciding whether a law or policy is to be adjudged constitutional. To pass strict scrutiny, the law or policy must be justified by a "compelling governmental interest," must be narrowly tailored, and must be the least restrictive means for achieving that interest.

substantive democratic theory The view that democracy is embodied in the substance of government policies rather than in the policymaking procedure.

suffrage The right to vote. Also called the *franchise*.

Supplemental Nutrition Assistance Program (SNAP) A federal program administered by the states that provides assistance for purchasing food to eligible beneficiaries.

supply-side economics Economic policies aimed at increasing the supply of goods (as opposed to decreasing demand); consists mainly of tax cuts for possible investors and less regulation of business.

supportive behavior Action that expresses allegiance to government and country.

supremacy clause The clause in Article VI of the Constitution that asserts that national laws take precedence over state and local laws when they conflict.

T

tax committees The two committees of Congress responsible for raising the revenue with which to run the government.

television hypothesis The belief that television is to blame for the low level of citizens' knowledge about public affairs.

Temporary Assistance for Needy Families (TANF) A 1996 national act that abolished the longtime welfare policy, Aid for Families with Dependent Children (AFDC). TANF gives the states much more control over welfare policy.

terrorism Premeditated, politically motivated violence perpetrated against noncombatant targets by subnational groups or clandestine agents.

totalitarianism A political philosophy that advocates unlimited power for the government to enable it to control all sectors of society.

trade association An organization that represents firms within a particular industry.

transfer payment A payment by government to an individual, mainly through Social Security or unemployment insurance.

treaty A legal agreement between two or more countries.

trustee A representative who is obligated to consider the views of constituents but is not obligated to vote according to those views if he or she believes they are misguided.

two-party system A political system in which two major political parties compete for control of the government. Candidates from a third party have little chance of winning office.

two-step flow of communication The process in which a few policy elites gather information and then inform their more numerous followers, mobilizing them to apply pressure to government.

U

unconventional participation Relatively uncommon political behavior that challenges or defies established institutions and dominant norms.

universal participation The concept that everyone in a democracy should participate in governmental decision making.

U.S. courts of appeals Courts within the second tier of the three-tiered federal court system, to which decisions of the district courts and federal agencies may be appealed for review.

U.S. district courts Courts within the lowest tier of the three-tiered federal court system; courts where litigation begins.

V

veto The president's disapproval of a bill that has been passed by both houses of Congress. Congress can override a veto with a two-thirds vote in each house.

Virginia Plan A set of proposals for a new government, submitted to the Constitutional Convention of 1787; it included separation of the government into three branches, division of the legislature into two houses, and proportional representation in the legislature.

voter turnout The percentage of eligible citizens who actually vote in a given election.

W

War on Poverty A part of President Lyndon Johnson's Great Society program, intended to eradicate poverty within ten years.

War Powers Resolution An act of Congress that forces that body to decide whether a commitment of troops into a war zone is permissible.

watchdog journalism Journalism that scrutinizes public and business institutions and publicizes perceived misconduct.

welfare state A nation in which the government assumes responsibility for the welfare of its citizens by providing a wide array of public services and redistributing income to reduce social inequality.

38. NBC News, San Bernadino Shooting: Timeline of How the Rampage Unfolded, 3 December 2015, http://www.nbcnews.com/storyline /san-bernardino-shooting/san-bernardino-shooting-timeline-how -rampage-unfolded-n473501.

39. John D. Donahue and Mark H. Moore (eds.), *Ports in a Storm: Public Management in a Turbulent World* (Washington, DC: Brookings, 2012).

40. 8 U.S.C. sections 1302 and 1304(e).

41. SB 1070, http://www.azleg.gov/legtext/49leg/2r/bills/sb1070s.pdf.

42. *Arizona* v. *United States*, 567 U.S. ___ (2012).

43. Elise Foley, "Obama Says He's Still Committed to Accepting Syrian Refugees," 16 November 2015, http://www.huffingtonpost.com /entry/obama-syrian-refugees_us_5649f552e4b045bf3defe6f6.

44. Polly Mosendz, "Map: Every State Accepting and Refusing Syrian Refugees," 16 November 2015, http://www.newsweek.com/where -every-state-stands-accepting-or-refusing-syrian-refugees-395050.

45. Dear Colleague letter from Robert Carey, Office of Refugee Resettlement, 25 November 2015, http://judiciary.house.gov/_cache/files /ad1921a5-383c-4053-8599-8c752ec484ea/orr-syrian-resettlement -letter.pdf.

46. *U.S. Term Limits, Inc.* v. *Thornton*, 514 U.S. 779 (1995).

47. David Brooks, "Divided They Stand," *New York Times*, 25 August 2005.

48. Zalmay Khalilzad and Kenneth M. Pollock, "How to Save Iraq," *The New Republic*, 22 July 2014, https://newrepublic.com/article/118794 /federalism-could-save-iraq-falling-apart-due-civil-war.

Chapter 5

1. Taryn Hillin, "More Than Half of Millennials Have Dated Outside Their Race," 4 February 2015, http://fusion.net/story/43228/more -than-half-of-millennials-have-dated-outside-their-race/.

2. Valerie Strauss, "For First Time, Minority Students Expected To Be Majority In U.S. Public Schools This Fall," *Washington Post*, 21 August 2014, https://www.washingtonpost.com/news/answer -sheet/wp/2014/08/21/for-first-time-minority-students-expected -to-be-majority-in-u-s-public-schools-this-fall/.

3. "Comparing Millennials to Other Generations," Pew Research Center, 19 March 2015, http://www.pewsocialtrends.org/2015/03 /19/comparing-millennials-to-other-generations/

4. "A Deep Dive Into Party Affiliation," Pew Research Center, 7 April 2015, http://www.people-press.org/2015/04/07/a-deep-dive-into -party-affiliation/; "Few Say Police Forces Do Well In Treating Races Equally," Pew Research Center, 25 August 2014, http://www.people -press.org/2014/08/25/few-say-police-forces-nationally-do-well-in -treating-races-equally/.

5. David Madland, and Ruy Teixeira, "The New Progressive America: The Millennial Generation" (Washington, DC: Center for American Progress, 2009).

6. Robert Jones, Daniel Cox, and Thomas Banchoff, "A Generation in Transition: Religion, Values, and Politics among College-Age Millennials" (Public Religion Research Institute, 2012); "Millennials in Adulthood," Pew Research Center, 7 March 2014, http://www .pewsocialtrends.org/2014/03/07/millennials-in-adulthood/.

7. "New Census Bureau Report Analyzes U.S. Population Projections," 3 March 2015, https://www.census.gov/newsroom/press-releases /2015/cb15-tps16.html.

8. "Race Relations," Gallup.com, http://www.gallup.com/poll/1687 /race-relations.aspx.

9. "America's New Drug Policy Landscape," Pew Research Center, 2 April 2014, http://www.people-press.org/2014/04/02/americas-new -drug-policy-landscape/.

10. Lindsay Cook, "Blacks and Whites See Race Issues Differently," USA Today, 15 December 2015, http://www.usnews.com/news/blogs/data -mine/2014/12/15/blacks-and-whites-see-race-issues-differently.

11. "What Americans Want to Do about Illegal Immigration," Pew Research Center, 24 August 2015, http://www.pewresearch.org/fact -tank/2015/08/24/what-americans-want-to-do-about-illegal -immigration/; Deborah Schildkraut, "Ambivalence in American Public Opinion about Immigration," in *New Directions in Public Opinion* 2nd ed., ed. Adam Berinsky (New York: Routledge, 2016), pp. 278–298.

12. E. Wayne Carp, "If Pollsters Had Been Around during the American Revolution" (letter to the editor), *New York Times*, 17 July 1993, p. 10.

13. See, for example, "Tea Party Image Turns More Negative," Pew Research Center for People and the Press, 16 October, 2013.

14. Sidney Verba, "The Citizen as Respondent: Sample Surveys and American Democracy," *American Political Science Review* 90 (March 1996): 3. For a historical discussion of the search for the "average" citizen, see Sarah E. Igo, *The Averaged American: Surveys, Citizens, and the Making of a Mass Public* (Cambridge, Mass.: Harvard University Press, 2007).

15. Robert Shapiro, "Public Opinion and American Democracy," *Public Opinion Quarterly* 75, no. 5 (2011): 982–1017.

16. Martin Gilens, *Affluence and Influence: Economic Inequality and Political Power in America* (Princeton, NJ: Princeton University Press, 2012).

17. "Kaiser Health Tracking Poll: January 2014," Kaiser Family Foundation, 30 January 2014, http://kff.org/health-reform/poll-finding/ kaiser -health-tracking-poll-january-2014/.

18. Nate Cohn, "Online Polls Are Rising. So Are Concerns about Their Results," *New York Times*, 28 February 2015, http://www.nytimes .com/2015/11/28/upshot/online-polls-are-rising-so-are-concerns -about-their-results.html. Emphasis added.

19. For a detailed discussion of the challenges of achieving a representative random sample, see D. Sunshine Hillygus, "The Practice of Survey Research: Changes and Challenges," in *New Directions in Public Opinion* ed. Adam J. Berinsky (New York: Routledge, 2012), pp. 32–51.

20. Peter Grier, "'Obamacare' vs. 'Affordable Care Act': Does the Name Matter?" *Christian Science Monitor*, 29 November 2013.

21. See, for example, Christopher Ellis and James Stimson, *Ideology in America* (New York: Cambridge University Press, 2012).

22. Steven A. Peterson, *Political Behavior: Patterns in Everyday Life* (Newbury Park, Calif: Sage, 1990), pp. 28–29. See also David O. Sears and Christia Brown, "Childhood and Adult Political Development," in *Oxford Handbook of Political Psychology*, 2nd ed., ed. David O Sears, Leonie Huddy, and Jack Levy (New York: Oxford University Press, 2013).

23. Stephen E. Frantzich, *Political Parties in the Technological Age* (New York: Longman, 1989); and M. Kent Jennings, Laura Stoker, and Jake Bowers, "Politics across Generations: Family Transmission Reexamined," *Journal of Politics* 71 (2009): 782–799.

24. Cliff Zukin et al., *A New Engagement: Political Participation, Civic Life, and the Changing American Citizen* (New York: Oxford University Press, 2006), pp. 142–144.

25. Janie S. Steckenrider and Neal E. Cutler, "Aging and Adult Political Socialization: The Importance of Roles and Transitions," in *Political Learning in Adulthood: A Sourcebook of Theory and Research*, ed. Roberta S. Sigel (Chicago: University of Chicago Press, 1989), pp. 56–88.

26. See, for example, Christopher Ellison, Heeju Shin, and David Leal, "The Contact Hypothesis and Attitudes Toward Latinos in the United States," *Social Science Quarterly* 92, no. 4 (2011): 938–958.

27. Diana Mutz and Jeffery Mondak. "The Workplace as a Context for Cross-Cutting Political Discourse." *Journal of Politics* 68, no. 1 (2006): 140–155; and David Jones, "The Polarizing Effect of a Partisan Workplace," *PS: Political Science & Politics* 46, no. 1 (2013): 67–73.

28. The American National Election Studies are jointly done by Stanford University and the University of Michigan, with funding by the National Science Foundation. Data reported here are from the ANES face-to-face interviews only. Responses are weighted using weights provided by the ANES. The 1 percent of respondents who did not answer this question was removed from subsequent discussions of this question.

29. Other scholars have analyzed opinion on abortion using six questions from the General Social Survey. See R. Michael Alvarez and

John Brehm, "American Ambivalence toward Abortion Policy," *American Journal of Political Science* 39 (1995): 1055–1082; and Elizabeth Adell Cook, Ted G. Jelen, and Clyde Wilcox, *Between Two Absolutes: Public Opinion and the Politics of Abortion* (Boulder, Colo.: Westview Press, 1992). Percentages reported here do not sum to 100 due to rounding.

30. Although some people view the politics of abortion as "single-issue" politics, the issue has broader political significance. In their book on the subject, Cook, Jelen, and Wilcox say, "Although embryonic life is one important value in the abortion debate, it is not the only value at stake." They contend that the politics is tied to alternative sexual relationships and traditional roles of women in the home, which are "social order" issues. See *Between Two Absolutes,* pp. 8–9.

31. Russell J. Dalton, *The Good Citizen* (Washington, DC: Congressional Quarterly Press, 2008), Chap. 5.

32. Ibid., p. 50.

33. See the exchange between Ronald Inglehart and Scott C. Flanagan, "Value Change in Industrial Societies," *American Political Science Review* 81 (December 1987): 1289–1319.

34. For analysis of regional trends over time, see Larry Bartels, "What's the Matter with *What's the Matter with Kansas?*" *Quarterly Journal of Political Science* 1 (2006): 201–226.

35. Nathan Glazer, "The Structure of Ethnicity," *Public Opinion* 1 (October–November 1984): 4.

36. According to CNN Exit Polls, 2016, available at: http://www.cnn .com/election/results/exit-polls.

37. "U.S. Census Bureau Projections Show a Slower-Growing, Older, More Diverse Nation Half a Century from Now," 12 December 2012, http://www.census.gov/newsroom/releases/archives/population /cb12-243.html.

38. Sandra L. Colby and Jennifer M. Ortman, "Projection of the Size and Composition of the U.S. Population: 2014–2060," U.S. Census Bureau, 2015, P25-1143. Note that the terms "Hispanic" and "Latino" are used interchangeably.

39. CNN Exit Polls.

40. CNN Exit Polls, 2016.

41. "The Asian Population: 2010," and "The American Indian and Alaska Native Population: 2010," U.S. Census Bureau.

42. Sandra L. Colby and Jennifer M. Ortman, "Projection of the Size and Composition of the U.S. Population: 2014–2060," U.S. Census Bureau, 2015, P25-1143.

43. CNN Exit Polls, 2016.

44. See, for example, "Obama Draws Nearly 90% of Native Vote," 31 October 2008, https://nativevotewa.wordpress.com/2008/10/31 /obama-draws-nearly-90-of-native-vote/.

45. Michael Dawson, Black Visions: *The Roots of Contemporary African American Political Ideologies* (Chicago: University of Chicago Press, 2001); John Garcia, *Latino Politics in America* (Lanham, Md.: Rowman & Littlefield, 2003); Thomas Kim, *The Racial Logic of Politics: Asian Americans and Party Competition* (Philadelphia: Temple University Press, 2007); Pei-te Lien, M. Margaret Conway, and Janelle Wong, *The Politics of Asian Americans* (New York: Routledge, 2004); and Katherine Tate, *Black Faces in the Mirror: African Americans and Their Representatives in the U.S. Congress* (Princeton, N.J.: Princeton University Press, 2003).

46. Glazer, "Structure of Ethnicity," p. 5; and Dennis Chong and Dukhong Kim, "The Experiences and Effects of Economic Status among Racial and Ethnic Minorities," *American Political Science Review* 100 (August 2006): 335–351.

47. "Nones on the Rise," Pew Research Religion and Public Life Project, 9 October 2012.

48. "Religious Landscape Study," Pew Research Center, http://www .pewforum.org/religious-landscape-study/.

49. "The Future of the Global Muslim Population," Pew Research Religion and Public Life Project, January 2011.

50. See David C Leege and Lyman A. Kellstedt (eds.), *Rediscovering the Religious Factor in American Politics* (Armonk, N.Y.: M. E. Sharpe, 1993); and "Many Americans Uneasy with Mix of Religion and Politics," Pew Forum on Religion and Public Life, 24 August 2006, http://pewforum.org/docs/DocID=153.

51. "A Portrait of Muslim Americans," Pew Research Center for People and the Press, 30 August 2011, http://www.people-press.org/2011 /08/ 30/a-portrait-of-muslim-americans/.

52. See, for example, "The Gender Gap: Three Decades Old, as Wide as Ever," Pew Research Center for People and the Press, 29 March 2012.

53. CNN Exit Polls, 2016.

54. Angus Campbell, Philip E. Converse, Warren E. Miller, and Donald E. Stokes, *The American Voter* (New York: Wiley, 1960); Michael Lewis-Beck, et al., *The American Voter Revisited* (Ann Arbor: University of Michigan Press, 2008); Marjorie Connelly, "A 'Conservative' Is (Fill in the Blank)," *New York Times,* 3 November 1996, sec. 4, p. 5; and Robert Erikson and Kent Tedin, *American Public Opinion,* 8th ed. (Boston: Pearson Longman, 2011).

55. American National Election Study, 2012.

56. However, citizens can have ideologically consistent attitudes toward candidates and perceptions about domestic issues without thinking about politics in explicitly liberal and conservative terms. See William Jacoby, "The Structure of Ideological Thinking in the American Electorate," *American Journal of Political Science* 39 no. 2 (1995): 314–335.

57. Ellis and Stimson, *Ideology in America.*

58. James L. Gibson, "Measuring Political Tolerance and General Support for Pro-Civil Liberties Policies: Notes and Cautions," *Public Opinion Quarterly* 77(S1) (2013): 45–68.

59. Herbert Asher, *Presidential Elections and American Politics,* 5th ed. (Upper Saddle River, N.J.: International Thomson Publishing Group, 1997).

60. Milton Rokeach also proposed a two-dimensional model of political ideology grounded in the terminal values of freedom and equality. See *The Nature of Human Values* (New York: Free Press, 1973), especially Chap. 6. Rokeach found that positive and negative references to the two values permeate the writings of socialists, communists, fascists, and conservatives and clearly differentiate the four bodies of writing from one another (pp. 173–174). However, Rokeach built his two dimensional model around only the values of freedom and equality; he did not deal with the question of freedom versus order.

61. In our framework, opposition to abortion is classified as a communitarian position. However, the communitarian movement led by Amitai Etzioni adopted no position on abortion (personal communication from Vanessa Hoffman by e-mail, in reply to a query of 5 February 1996).

62. William S. Maddox and Stuart A. Lilie, *Beyond Liberal and Conservative: Reassessing the Political Spectrum* (Washington, DC: Cato Institute, 1984), p. 68. From 1993 to 1996, the Gallup Organization, in conjunction with CNN and *USA Today,* asked national samples two questions: (1) whether individuals or government should solve our country's problems and (2) whether the government should promote traditional values. Gallup constructed a similar ideological typology from responses to these questions and found a similar distribution of the population into four groups. See Gallup's "Final Top Line" for 12–15 January 1996, pp. 30–31. For another typology that goes beyond liberal and conservative, see "Beyond Red vs. Blue: The Political Typology," Pew Research Center for People and the Press, 4 May 2011.

63. The same conclusion was reached in a major study of British voting behavior. See Hilde T. Himmelweit et al., *How Voters Decide* (New York: Academic Press, 1981), pp. 138–141. See also Aaron Wildavsky, "Choosing Preferences by Constructing Institutions: A Cultural Theory of Preference Formation," *American Political Science*

Review 81 (March 1987): 13; and Stanley Feldman and Christopher Johnston, "Understanding Political Ideology" (paper presented at the annual meeting of the American Political Science Association, Toronto, Canada, 2009).

64. Michael X. Delli Carpini and Scott Keeter, *What Americans Know about Politics and Why It Matters* (New Haven, Conn.: Yale University Press, 1996).

65. Ibid., p. 269. For more on this topic, see Scott L. Althaus, *Collective Preferences in Democratic Politics: Opinion Surveys and the Will of the People* (New York: Cambridge University Press, 2003).

66. "What the Public Knows—In Words, Pictures, Maps and Graphs," Pew Research Center for People and the Press, 5 September 2013.

67. Markus Prior and Arthur Lupia, "Money, Time, and Political Knowledge: Distinguishing Quick Recall and Political Learning Skills," *American Journal of Political Science* 52, no. 1 (2008): 169–183.

68. John Bullock et al., "Partisan Bias in Factual Beliefs about Politics," *Quarterly Journal of Political Science* 10, no. 4 (2015): 519–578; Markus Prior, Guarav Sood, and Kabir Khanna, "You Can't Be Serious: The Impact of Accuracy Incentives on Partisan Bias in Reports of Economic Incentives," *Quarterly Journal of Political Science* 10, no 4. (2015): 489–518.

69. "Modern Immigration Wave Brings 59 Million to U.S., Driving Population Growth and Change Through 2065," Pew Research Center, 28 September 2015, http://www.pewhispanic.org/2015/09/28/modern-immigration-wave-brings-59-million-to-u-s-driving-population-growth-and-change-through-2065/.

70. "The Impact of Media Stereotypes on Opinions and Attitudes Towards Latinos," National Hispanic Media Coalition and Latino Decisions, September 2012, http://www.latinodecisions.com/blog/2012/09/18/how-media-stereotypes-about-latinos-fuel-negative-attitudes-towards-latinos/; and Mark Koba, "$2 Trillion Underground Economy May Be Recovery's Savior," CNBC.com, 24 April 2013.

71. Benjamin I. Page and Robert Y. Shapiro, *The Rational Public* (Chicago: University of Chicago Press, 1992).

72. Brendan Nyhan and Jason Reifler, "When Corrections Fail: The Persistence of Political Misperceptions," *Political Behavior* 32, no. 2 (2010): 303–330. Also see Brendan Nyhan, Jason Reifler, and Peter A. Ubel, "The Hazards of Correcting Myths about Health Care Reform," *Medical Care* 51, no. 2 (2013): 127–132; and Brenan Nyhan, Jason Reifler, Sean Richey, and Gary Freed, "Effective Messages in Vaccine Promotion: A Randomized Trial," *Pediatrics,* forthcoming.

73. Self-interest is often posed as the major alternative to choice based on general orientations such as political ideology and moral values. A significant literature exists on the limitations of self-interest in explaining political life. See Jane J. Mansbridge (ed.), *Beyond Self-Interest* (Chicago: University of Chicago Press, 1990).

74. Richard D. Dixon et al., "Self-Interest and Public Opinion toward Smoking Policies," *Public Opinion Quarterly* 55 (1991): 241–254; David O. Sears and Jack Citrin, *Tax Revolt: Something for Nothing in California* (Cambridge, Mass.: Harvard University Press, 1985); and Robin Wolpert and James Gimpel, "Self-Interest, Symbiotic Politics, and Public Attitudes toward Gun Control," *Political Behavior* 20 (1998): 241–262.

75. "Public Opinion Runs Against Syrian Airstrikes," Pew Research Center for People and the Press, 3 September 2013.

76. For two classic investigations of self-interest and sociotropic responses, see Donald R. Kinder and D. Roderick Kiewiet, "Sociotropic Politics: The American Case," *British Journal of Political Science* 11, no. 2 (1981): 129–161; David O. Sears, et al. "Self-interest vs. Symbolic Politics in Policy Attitudes and Presidential Voting," *American Political Science Review* 74, no. 3 (1980): 670–684.

77. Henry Brady and Paul Sniderman, "Attitude Attribution: A Group Basis for Political Reasoning," *American Political Science Review* 79 (1985): 1061–1078; Samuel Popkin, *The Reasoning Voter*, 2nd ed. (Chicago: University of Chicago Press, 1994); and P. Sniderman, R. Brody, and P. Tetlock, *Reasoning and Choice* (Cambridge: Cambridge University Press, 1991). Psychologists have tended to emphasize the distorting effects of heuristics. See D. Kahneman, P. Slovic, and A. Tversky (eds.), *Judgment under Uncertainty: Heuristics and Biases* (Cambridge: Cambridge University Press, 1982); and R. Nisbett and L. Ross, *Human Inference: Strategies and Shortcomings of Social Judgment* (Englewood Cliffs, N.J.: Prentice-Hall, 1980).

78. Wendy M. Rahn, "The Role of Partisan Stereotypes in Information Processing about Political Candidates," *American Journal of Political Science* (1993): 472–496.

79. See, for example, LaFleur Stephens and Andrea Benjamin, "I Get So Emotional: Race, Gender, and Candidate Evaluations," paper presented at the Annual Meeting of the American Political Science Association, Chicago, Ill. 2013.

80. Stephen P. Nicholson, "Polarizing Cues," *American Journal of Political Science* 56, no. 1 (2012): 52–66.

81. On framing, see Dennis Chong and James N. Druckman, "Framing Public Opinion in Competitive Democracies," *American Political Science Review* 101 (November 2007): 637–655; James N. Druckman, "Political Preference Formation: Competition, Deliberation, and the (Ir)relevance of Framing Effects," *American Political Science Review* 98 (November 2004): 671–686; and Michael W. Wagner, "The Utility of Staying on Message: Competing Partisan Frames and Public Awareness of Elite Differences on Political Issues," *The Forum* 5, no. 3 (2007), http://www.be-press.com/forum/voll5/iss3/art8.

82. Benjamin I. Page, Robert Y. Shapiro, and Glenn R. Dempsey, "What Moves Public Opinion?" *American Political Science Review* 81 (March 1987): 23–43.

83. Lawrence R. Jacobs and Robert Y. Shapiro, *Politicians Don't Pander* (Chicago: University of Chicago Press, 2000).

84. "Beyond Distrust: How Americans View Their Government," Pew Research Center, 23 November 2015, http://www.people-press.org/2015/11/23/beyond-distrust-how-americans-view-their-government/.

Chapter 6

1. OxfordDictionaries.com, "New words added to OxfordDictionaries.com today include binge-watch, cray, and vape," August 2014, http://blog.oxforddictionaries.com/press-releases/new-words-added-oxforddictionaries-com-august-2014/; "live tweet" http://www.oxforddictionaries.com/us/definition/american_english/live-tweet; Tamara Keith, "Bernie Sanders Live Tweets GOP Debate, Gets Bored, Goes Home Early," NPR, 17 September 2015, http://www.npr.org/sections/itsallpolitics/2015/09/17/441004967/bernie-sanders-live-tweets-gop-debate-gets-bored-goes-home-early; John Wagner, "A Sarcastic Bernie Sanders Live-Tweets the GOP Debate," *Washington Post*, 17 September 2015, https://www.washingtonpost.com/news/post-politics/wp/2015/09/17/on-twitter-bernie-sanders-offers-a-running-often-sarcastic-commentary-on-the-gop-debate/.

2. Alex S. Jones, Losing the News, http://losingthenews.com/.

3. Richard Davis, *Typing Politics: The Role of Blogs in American Politics* (New York: Oxford University Press, 2009); Tom Price, "Future of Journalism," *CQ Researcher* 19, no. 12 (27 March 2009): 273–295; and Pew Project for Excellence in Journalism, http://www.stateofthemedia.org/2009/narrative_online_audience.php?media=58:cat=2.

4. Deena Zaru, "Beyoncé Gets Political at Super Bowl, Pays Tribute to 'Black Lives Matter,'" CNN.com, 9 February 2016, http://www.cnn.com/2016/02/08/politics/beyonce-super-bowl-black-lives-matter/.

5. "Michael Moore's Sicko: Broad Reach and Impact Even without the Popcorn?" Press release from Kaiser Family Foundation, 27 August 2007, http://www.kff.org/kaiserpolls/pomr082707nr.cfm.

6. See Markus Prior, *Post-Broadcast Democracy: How Media Choice Increases Inequality in Political Involvement and Polarizes Elections* (New York, NY: Cambridge University Press, 2007); and Bill Kovach and Tom Rosenstiel, *Blur: How to Know What's True in the Age of Information Overload* (New York: Bloomsbury, 2010).

7. S. N. D. North, *The Newspaper and Periodical Press* (Washington, DC: U.S. Government Printing Office, 1884), p. 27. This source provides much of the information reported here about newspapers and magazines before 1880. Also see Jonathan Ladd, *Why Americans Hate the Media and How It Matters* (Princeton, N.J.: Princeton University Press, 2011).

8. *Editor & Publisher, International Year Book, 2009* (New York: Editor & Publisher, 2009), p. xi.

9. Harold W. Stanley and Richard G. Niemi (eds.), *Vital Statistics on American Politics, 2015–2016* (Washington, DC: CQ Press, 2015). For a brief history of the newspaper business, see Paul E. Steiger, "Read All about It: How Newspapers Got into Such a Fix and Where They Go from Here," *Wall Street Journal*, 29–30 December 2007, p. 1.

10. See Ladd, *Why Americans Hate the Media and How It Matters*, pp. 48–52.

11. "Newspapers: Top 5 U.S. Daily Newspapers with Paywalls," http://www.journalism.org/media-indicators/top-5-u-s-newspapers-with-paywalls/.

12. "Yet Another Newspaper Paywall Goes Bust," http://www.techdirt.com, 14 August 2013.

13. On framing in the media, see Stephen D. Reese, Oscar H. Gandy, Jr., and August E. Grant (eds.), *Framing Public Life: Perspectives on Media and Our Understanding of the Social World* (Mahwah, N.J.: Erlbaum, 2001). More generally on how leaders mediate public deliberation on issues, see Doris A. Graber, *Media Power in Politics*, 7th ed. (Washington, DC: CQ Press, 2005).

14. "Broadcast Station Totals as of March 31, 2015," Federal Communications Commission, https://apps.fcc.gov/edocs_public/attachmatch/DOC-332923A1.pdf.

15. See radio statistics at *The State of the News Media 2015*, Pew Research Center, http://www.journalism.org/2015/04/29/audio-fact-sheet/.

16. Ibid.; and Jeffrey M. Berry and Sarah Sobieraj, *The Outrage Industry: Political Opinion Media and the New Incivility* (Oxford University Press, 2014).

17. Berry and Sobieraj, *The Outrage Industry*; David Barker and Kathleen Knight, "Political Talk Radio and Public Opinion," *Public Opinion Quarterly* 64 (Summer 2000): 149–170; and David C. Barker, *Rushed to Judgment: Talk Radio, Persuasion, and American Political Behavior* (New York: Columbia University Press, 2003).

18. Dana R. Ulloth, Peter L. Klinge, and Sandra Eells, *Mass Media: Past, Present, Future* (St. Paul, Minn.: West, 1983), p. 278.

19. "TV Basics," Television Bureau of Advertising, http://www.tvb.org/media/file/TV_Basics.pdf; and "Frequently Asked Questions," Corporation for Public Broadcasting, http://www.cpb.org/aboutpb/faq/stations.html.

20. Douglas Ahers, "News Consumption and the New Electronic Media," *Harvard International Journal of Press/Politics* 11 (Winter 2006): 29–52; Bill Carter, "CNN Last in TV News on Cable," *New York Times*, 27 October 2009, http://www.nytimes.com/2009/10/27/busi-ness/media/27rating.html?emc=etal; Prior, *Post-Broadcast Democracy*; Matthew Levendusky, *How Partisan Media Polarize America* (Chicago: University of Chicago Press, 2013); and Kevin Arcenaux and Martin Johnson, *Changing Minds or Changing Channels? Partisan News in an Age of Choice* (Chicago: University of Chicago Press, 2013).

21. "January 2016 Web Server Survey," Netcraft.com, http://news.netcraft.com/archives/category/web-server-survey/; International

Telecommunication Union, http://www.itu.int/en/ITU-D/Statistics/Pages/stat/default.aspx.

22. "The Demographics of Device Ownership," Pew Research Center, http://www.pewinternet.org/2015/10/29/the-demographics-of-device-ownership/, 10/29/15.

23. "Donald Trump's Twitter Insults: The Complete List (So Far)," *New York Times*, 5 February 2016, http://www.nytimes.com/interactive/2016/01/28/upshot/donald-trump-twitter-insults.html; and John Sides, "Why Does Trump Remain Atop the Polls? You Can Still Blame the Media," *Washington Post*, 28 August, 2015, https://www.washingtonpost.com/blogs/monkey-cage/wp/2015/08/28/why-does-trump-remain-atop-the-polls-you-can-still-blame-the-media/.

24. Katharine Q. Seelye, "Take That, Mr. Newsman!" *New York Times*, 1 January 2006, p. CI; and David Coursey, "You Be the Judge: Are Bloggers Journalists?" Forbes.com, 2 January 2012.

25. Matthew Hindman, *The Myth of Digital Democracy* (Princeton, N.J.: Princeton University Press, 2009); and Diana Mutz and Lori Young, "Communication and Public Opinion," *Public Opinion Quarterly* 75 (December 2011): 1018–1044.

26. Henry Farrell, "Why Glenn Greenwald's New Media Venture Is a Big Deal," *Washington Post*, 17 October 2013.

27. Eric Wemple, "BuzzFeed Expands Foreign Staff," *Washington Post*, 15 October 2015, https://www.washingtonpost.com/blogs/erik-wemple/wp/2015/10/15/buzzfeed-expands-foreign-staff/.

28. Jennifer Lai, "'Big Yellow Duck,' 'May 35th,' and Other Words You Can't Use On China's Twitter Today," Slate.com, 4 June 2013.

29. "American Public Television: Services," http://www.aptonline.org/aptweb.nsf/vServices/Index-Services ; "About CPB," Corporation for Public Broadcasting, http://www.cpb.org/aboutcpb/.

30. Doris A. Graber, *Mass Media and American Politics*, 8th ed. (Washington, DC: CQ Press, 2010), pp. 84–87. See also W. Lance Bennett, *News: The Politics of Illusion*, 3rd ed. (White Plains, NY.: Longman, 1996), Chap. 2.

31. John H. McManus, *Market-Driven Journalism: Let the Citizen Beware?* (Thousand Oaks, Calif: Sage, 1994), p. 85.

32. "Why Network News Still Matters," *New York Times*, 18 February 2015, http://www.nytimes.com/2015/02/19/upshot/why-network-news-still-matters.html.

33. "The Changing TV News Landscape," *The State of the News Media 2013*, stateofthemedia.org.

34. David D. Kurplus, "Bucking a Trend in Local Television News," *Journalism* 4 (2003): 77–94.

35. Bill Carter and Brian Stelter, "In NBC Universal Bid, Comcast Seeks an Empire," *New York Times*, 1 October 2009, http://www.nytimes.com/2009/10/02/business/media/02nbc.html.

36. "Network News Fact Sheet," *State of the News Media 2015*.

37. Thomas E. Patterson, *Doing Well and Doing Good: How Soft News and Critical Journalism Are Shrinking the News Audience and Weakening Democracy—and What News Outlets Can Do about It* (Cambridge, Mass.: Harvard University, Joan Shorenstein Center for Press, Politics, and Public Policy, 2000), pp. 2–5.

38. Johanna Dunaway, "Media Ownership and Story Tone in Campaign News," *American Politics Research* 41, no. 1 (2013): 24–53.

39. Price, "Future of Journalism"; and Amy Mitchell, et al., "Nonprofit Journalism: A Growing but Fragile Part of the U.S. News System," Pew Research Journalism Project, www.journalism.org, 10 June 2013.

40. Anita Balakrishnan, "What Does Rupert Murdoch Own? A Little Bit of Everything," *USA Today*, 11 June 2015, http://www.usatoday.com/story/money/business/2015/06/11/what-rupert-murdoch-owns/71089066/#.

41. Graber, *Mass Media and American Politics*, pp. 41–43.

42. Matthew Rose and Joe Flint, "Behind Media-Ownership Fight, an Old Power Struggle Is Raging," *Wall Street Journal*, 15 October 2003, p. 1. In 2003 the Federal Communications Commission (FCC) voted to increase the percentage share of the market to 45 percent. In 2007, the FCC ruled that no company can control more than 30 percent of the cable television market and relaxed newspaper-broadcast cross-ownership rules in the nation's twenty

largest media markets. See Stephen Labaton, "F.C.C. Reshapes Rules Limiting Media Industry," *New York Times*, 19 December 2007, p. Al.

43. Jennifer Lee, "On Minot, N.D., Radio, a Single Corporate Voice," *New York Times*, 31 March 2003, p. C7.

44. For a clear summary of very complex developments, see Robert B. Horowitz, "Communications Regulations in Protecting the Public Interest," in *The Institutions of American Democracy: The Press*, ed. Geneva Overholser and Kathleen Hall Jamieson (New York: Oxford University Press, 2005), pp. 284–302.

45. Graber, *Mass Media and American Politics*, p. 42.

46. Graber, *Mass Media and American Politics*, p. 342.

47. Jared Sandberg, "Federal Judges Block Censorship on the Internet," *Wall Street Journal*, 13 June 1996, p. Bl.

48. Robert Entman, *Democracy without Citizens: Media and the Decay of American Politics* (New York: Oxford University Press, 1989), pp. 103–108; and John Leland, "Why the Right Rules the Radio Waves," *New York Times*, 8 December 2003, sec. 4, p. 7.

49. Wes Allison, "Are Democrats Really Trying to Hush Rush?" *St. Petersburg Times*, 20 February 2009, p. 1A.

50. See Prior, *Post-Broadcast Democracy*; and Jason Gainous and Kevin Wagner, *Rebooting American Politics: The Internet Revolution* (Lanham, Md.: Rowman and Littlefield, 2011). For a discussion of the prevalence and possible consequence of incivility among fragmented media sources, see Berry and Sobieraj, *The Outrage Industry*.

51. For an alternative view of the functions of the media, see Graber, *Mass Media and American Politics*, pp. 5–11.

52. Harold W. Stanley and Richard G. Niemi (eds.), *Vital Statistics on American Politics, 2015–2016* (Washington, DC: CQ Press, 2015).

53. For a view from the point of view of a reporter who covered Washington for over sixty years, see Helen Thomas, *Watch-dogs of Democracy? The Waning Washington Press Corps and How It Has Failed the Public* (New York: Scribner, 2006).

54. For a discussion of the Bush years, see Scott McClellan, *What Happened: Inside the Bush White House and Washington's Culture of Deception* (New York: Public Affairs Books, 2008). For a discussion of Obama, see Adriel Bettelheim, "Meeting the Press Less Than Half Way," *CQ Weekly Online*, 20 July 2009, pp. 1700–1701, http://library .cqpress.com/cqweekly/weeklyreportl 11-000003170492.

55. Patrick Sellers, *Cycles of Spin: Strategic Communication in the U.S. Congress* (New York: Cambridge University Press: 2010), p. 198.

56. Dylan Byers, "ABC's 'World News' No Longer Has a Full-Time Congress Reporter," Politico.com, 2 June 2015, http://www.politico .com/blogs/media/2015/06/abcs-world-news-no-longer-has-a-full -time-congress-reporter-208097.

57. ActBlue, "Alan Grayson," http://www.actblue.com/entity /fundraisers/ 18665.

58. Dan Eggen and T.W. Farnam, "Michelle Bachmann, Others, Raise Millions for Political Campaigns with 'Money Blurts'," *Washington Post*, 19 June 2011.

59. Jon Garfunkel, "The New Gatekeepers Part 1: Changing the Guard," Civilites: Media Structures Research, 4 April 2005, http://civilites .net/TheNewGatekeepers-Changing.

60. Gainous and Wagner, *Rebooting American Politics*; and Lars Willnat and David Weaver, "The American Journalist in the Digital Age," Bloomington, IN: School of Journalism, Indiana University, 2014, http://news.indiana.edu/releases/iu/2014/05/2013-american -journalist-key-findings.pdf.

61. "Press Going Too Easy on Bush," *The State of the News Media 2007*, http://www.stateofthemedia.org.

62. Graber, *Mass Media and American Politics*, p. 259. For weekly content analysis of news topics, see the Project for Excellence in Journalism's "News Coverage Index," http://www.journalism.org.

63. Stephen J. Farnsworth and S. Robert Lichter, "The Nightly News Nightmare Revisited: Network Television's Coverage of the 2004 Presidential Election," (paper presented at the annual meeting of the Washington, DC. American Political Science Association,

2005); "Contest Lacks Content," *Media Tenor* 1 (2005): 12–15; Cristina Alsina, Philip John Davies, and Bruce Gronbeck, "Preference Poll Stories in the Last 2 Weeks of Campaign 2000," *American Behavioral Scientist* 44, no. 12 (2001): 2288–2305; C. Anthony Broh, "Horse Race Journalism: Reporting the Polls in the 1976 Presidential Election," *Public Opinion Quarterly* 44 (1980): 514–529; and David Paletz, Jonathan Short, Helen Baker, Barbara Cookman Campbell, Richard Cooper, and Rochelle Oeslander, "Polls in the Media: Content, Credibility, and Consequences," *Public Opinion Quarterly* 44 (1980): 495–513.

64. "Low Marks for the 2012 Election," Pew Research Center for People and the Press, 15 November 2012.

65. Amber Boydstun, *Making the News: Politics, the Media, and Agenda Setting* (Chicago: University of Chicago Press, 2013).

66. "The Evolving Role of News on Twitter and Facebook," Pew Research Center, 14 July 2015, http://www.journalism.org/2015/07/14/the -evolving-role-of-news-on-twitter-and-facebook/.

67. Maeve Duggan, "The Demographics of Social Media Users," Pew Research Center, 19 August 2015, http://www.pewinternet .org/2015/08/19/the-demographics-of-social-media-users/.

68. "What the Public Knows—In Pictures, Words, Maps and Graphs," Pew Research Center, 28 April 2015, http://www.people-press.org/2015 /04/28/what-the-public-knows-in-pictures-words-maps-and-graphs/.

69. W. Russell Neuman, Marion R. Just, and Ann N. Crigler, *Common Knowledge: News and the Construction of Political Meaning* (Chicago: University of Chicago Press, 1992), p. 10. See also Debra Gersh Hernandez, "Profile of the News Consumer," *Editor & Publisher*, 18 January 1997, pp. 6, 7. For a more optimistic assessment of television's instructional value, see Doris A. Graber, *Processing Politics: Learning from Television in the Internet Age* (Chicago: University of Chicago Press, 2001), esp. pp. 120–128. Another negative note is sounded by Alan B. Krueger, "Economic Scene," *New York Times*, 1 April 2004, p. C2.

70. James N. Druckman, "Media Matter: How Newspapers and Television News Cover Campaigns and Influence Voters," *Political Communication* 22 (October–December 2005): 463–481. For a complementary study finding that television news has little effect on campaign learning, see Stephen C. Craig, James G. Kane, and Jason Gainous, "Issue-Related Learning in a Gubernatorial Campaign: A Case Study," *Political Communication* 22 (October–December 2005): 483–503.

71. Diana Mutz, "Effects of 'In-Your-Face' Television Discourse on Perceptions of a Legitimate Opposition," *American Political Science Review* 101 (November 2007): 621–635.

72. James Avery, "Videoamalaise or Virtuous Circle? The Influence of the News Media on Political Trust," *International Journal of Press/ Politics* 14, no. 4 (2009): 410–433.

73. Jennifer Jerit, "Understanding the Knowledge Gap: The Role of Experts and Journalists," *The Journal of Politics* 71, no. 2 (2009): 444.

74. Jody Baumgartner and Jonathan Morris, "The Daily Show Effect: Candidate Evaluations, Efficacy, and American Youth," *American Politics Research* 34 (2006): 341–367; Michael Parkin, "Taking Late Night Comedy Seriously," *Political Research Quarterly* 63 (2010): 3–15; Xiaoxia Cao, "Hearing It from Jon Stewart," *International Journal of Public Opinion Research* 22 (2010): 26–46; Matthew A. Baum, "Sex, Lies, and War: How Soft News Brings Foreign Policy to the Inattentive Public," *American Political Science Review* 96 (2002): 91–110; and Matthew A. Baum and Angela S. Jamison, "The Oprah Effect: How Soft News Helps Inattentive Citizens Vote Consistently," *Journal of Politics* 68 (2006): 946–959.

75. Mutz and Young, "Communication and Public Opinion."

76. "Views of Government's Handling of Terrorism Fall to Post-9/11 Low," Pew Research Center, 15 December 2015, http://www.people -press.org/2015/12/15/views-of-governments-handling-of -terrorism-fall-to-post-911-low/.

77. Maxwell McCombs, "The Agenda-Setting Function of the Press," in Overholser and Jamieson, *Institutions of American Democracy*, pp. 156–168.

78. Danilo Yanich, "Kids, Crime, and Local TV News," report of the Local TV News Media Project, January (Newark: University of Delaware, 2005). See also Jeremy H. Lipschultz and Michael L. Hilt, *Crime and Local Television News: Dramatic, Breaking, and Live from the Scene* (Mahwah, N.J.: Erlbaum, 2002).

79. Lawrie Mifflin, "Crime Falls, but Not on TV," *New York Times*, 6 July 1997, sec. 4, p. 4.

80. John Tierney, "Talk Shows Prove Key to White House," *New York Times*, 21 October 2002, p. A13.

81. Doris Graber reviews some studies of socially undesirable effects on children and adults in *Processing Politics*, pp. 91–95, and in *Mass Media and American Politics*.

82. Jordan Shapiro, "Teenagers In The U.S. Spend About Nine Hours A Day In Front Of A Screen," Forbes.com, 3 November 2015, http://www.forbes.com/sites/jordanshapiro/2015/11/03/teenagers-in-the-u-s-spend-about-nine-hours-a-day-in-front-of-a-screen/#4afaf1867c34.

83. Douglas Kellner, *Television and the Crisis of Democracy* (Boulder, Colo.: Westview Press, 1990), p. 17.

84. James Fallows, *Breaking the News: How the Media Undermine American Democracy* (New York: Pantheon Books, 1996). Also see Paul Gronke and Timothy Cook, "Disdaining the Media," *Political Communication* 24 (July 2007): 259–281.

85. Ladd, *Why Americans Hate the Media and How It Matters*.

86. See Bernard Goldberg, *Bias: A CBS Insider Exposes How the Media Distort the News* (Washington, DC: Regnery Publishing, 2002); and Ann Coulter, *Slander: Liberal Lies about the American Right* (New York: Crown, 2002).

87. See Eric Alterman, *What Liberal Media? The Truth about Bias and the News* (New York: Basic Books, 2003); and Al Franken, *Lies and the Liars Who Tell Them . . . a Fair and Balanced Look at the Right* (New York: Penguin, 2003).

88. Lars Willnat and David Weaver, "The American Journalist in the Digital Age," Bloomington, IN: School of Journalism, Indiana University, 2014, http://news.indiana.edu/releases/iu/2014/05/2013-american-journalist-key-findings.pdf.

89. "Coverage of the Candidates by Media Sector and Cable Outlet," Pew Research Center, 1 November 2012, http://www.journalism.org/2012/11/01/coverage-candidates-media-sector-and-cable-outlet/.

90. Ibid.

91. *The People, the Press, and Their Leaders* (Washington, DC: Times-Mirror Center for the People and the Press, 1995). See also Pew Research Center, "Self Censorship: How Often and Why," a survey of nearly three hundred journalists and news executives in February–March 2000, released 30 April 2000.

92. Harold W. Stanley and Richard G. Niemi, *Vital Statistics on American Politics, 2013–2014* (Washington, DC: CQ Press, 2013).

93. Bob Kemper, "Bush: No Iraqi Link to Sept. 11," *Chicago Tribune*, 18 September 2003, pp. 1–6.

94. Steven Kull and others, "Misperceptions, the Media, and the Iraq War," Program on International Policy Attitudes (PIPA), 2 October 2003, http://www.pipa.org.

95. Valentino Larcinese, Ricardo Puglisi, and James Snyder, Jr, "Partisan Bias in Economic News: Evidence on the Agenda-Setting Behavior of U.S. Newspapers," *Journal of Public Economics* 95 (2011): 1178–1189.

96. See Bill Kovach and Tom Rosentstiel, *Blur: How to Know What's True in the Age of Information Overload*.

97. W. Lance Bennett and William Serrin, "The Watchdog Role," in Overholser and Jamieson, *Institutions of American Democracy*, pp. 169–188.

98. "Amid Criticism, Support for Media's Watchdog Role Stands Out," Pew Research Center for People and the Press, 8 August 2013.

99. For a historical account of efforts to determine voters' preferences before modern polling, see Tom W. Smith, "The First Straw? A Study of the Origin of Election Polls," *Public Opinion Polling* 54 (Spring 1990): 21–36. See also Susan Herbst, *Numbered Voices: How Opinion Polling Has Shaped American Politics* (Chicago: University of Chicago Press, 1993), Chap. 4.

100. See New York Times Polls at http://topics.nytimes.com/top/reference/ timestopics/subjects/n/newyorktimes-poll-watch/index.html.

101. Robert Shapiro, "Public Opinion and American Democracy," Public Opinion Quarterly 75 (2011): 982–1017. But for a critique of the class bias inherent in government responsiveness to polls, see Martin Gilens, *Affluence and Influence: Economic Inequality and Political Power in America* (Princeton, NJ: Princeton University Press, 2012).

102. William Schneider and I. A. Lewis, "Views on the News," *Public Opinion* 8 (August-September 1985): 6–11, 58–59. For similar findings from a 1994 study, see Times-Mirror Center for the People and the Press, "Mixed Message about Press Freedom on Both Sides of the Atlantic," press release, 16 March 1994, p. 65. See also Thomas E. Patterson, "News Decisions: Journalists as Partisan Actors" (paper presented at the annual meeting of the American Political Science Association, 1996), p. 21.

103. Pew Global Attitudes Project. Pew Global Attitudes Project Poll, Apr, 2015 [survey question]. USPSRA.111815G.R031C. Princeton Survey Research Associates International [producer]. Storrs, CT: Roper Center for Public Opinion Research, iPOLL [distributor], 26 February 2016.

104. Barton Gellman, Aaron Blake, and Greg Miller, "Edward Snowden Comes Forward as Source of NSA Leaks," *Washington Post*, 9 June 2013.

105. Aurelien Breeden, "Charlie Hebdo, Known for Its Satire, Commemorates Attack Accordingly," *New York Times*, 6 January 2016, http://www.nytimes.com/2016/01/07/world/europe/charlie-hebdo-attack-anniversary.html?_r=0.

Chapter 7

1. "Voting and Registration in the Election of November 2014," U.S. Census Bureau, Table 1, http://www.census.gov/data/tables/time-series/demo/voting-and-registration/p20-577.html.

2. M. Margaret Conway, *Political Participation in the United States*, 3rd ed. (Washington, DC: CQ Press, 2000), p. 3.

3. Michael Lapsky, "Protest as a Political Resource," *American Political Science Review* 62 (December 1968): 1145.

4. U.S. Department of State, "Patterns of Global Terrorism 2001" (Washington, DC: U.S. Department of State, May 2002), p. 17. The definition is contained in Title 22 of the U.S. Code, Section 2656f(d). On the problem of defining terrorism, see Walter Laquer, *No End to War: Terrorism in the 21st Century* (New York: Continuum International, 2003), esp. the appendix.

5. William E. Schmidt, "Selma Marchers Mark 1965 Clash," *New York Times*, 4 March 1985.

6. Frances Fox Piven, *Challenging Authority: How Ordinary People Change America* (Lanham, Md.: Rowman & Littlefield, 2006).

7. See Sidney Verba and Norman H. Nie, *Participation in America: Political Democracy and Social Equality* (New York: Harper & Row, 1972), p. 3.

8. 2005–2008 World Values Survey. The World Values Survey Association, based in Stockholm, conducts representative surveys in nations across the world. See http://www.worldvaluessurvey.org.

9. Jonathan D. Casper, *Politics of Civil Liberties* (New York: Harper & Row, 1972), p. 90.

10. U.S. Census Bureau, *2010 Statistical Abstract*, http://www.census. gov/compendia/statab/cats/elections/electedpublicofficialscharacteristics.html.

11. Steven Johnson, *Future Perfect: The Case for Progress in a Networked Age* (New York: Riverhead Books, 2012), p. 105.

12. Sean Captain, "The Demographics of Occupy Wall Street," 19 October 2011, http://www.fastcompany.com/1789018/demographics-occupy-wall-street.

13. Elaine B. Sharp, "Citizen Demand Making in the Urban Context," *American Journal of Political Science* 28 (November 1984): 654–670, esp. pp. 654, 665.

14. Verba and Nie, *Participation in America*, p. 67; and Sharp, "Citizen Demand Making," p. 660.

15. See Joel B. Grossman et al., "Dimensions of Institutional Participation: Who Uses the Courts and How?" *Journal of Politics* 44 (February 1982): 86–114; and Frances Kahn Zemans, "Legal Mobilization: The Neglected Role of the Law in the Political System," *American Political Science Review* 77 (September 1983): 690–703.

16. *Brown* v. *Board of Education,* 347 U.S. 483 (1954).

17. "Capital One Settles Litigation over Card Disputes," http://www.dailyherald.com/story/?id=345003.

18. USA.gov Reform Task Force, "State of the Federal Web Report," 16 December 2011, http://www.usa.gov/webreform/state-of-the-web.pdf.

19. The *Federal Register* is available via the Federal Digital System, http:// www.gpo.gov/fdsys/.

20. See http://www.opensecrets.org.

21. See http://www.followthemoney.org.

22. See http://www.foreffectivegov.org and http://truthinaccounting.org.

23. See Michael P. MacDonald and Samuel L. Popkin, "The Myth of the Vanishing Voter," *American Political Science Review* 95 (December 2001): 963–974. Traditionally, turnout had been computed by dividing the number of voters by the voting-age population (VAP), which included noncitizens and ineligible felons. Recent research excludes these groups, computing the *eligible* voting-age population, or VEP. Using VEP in estimating voter turnout has revised the U.S. turnout rates upward by three to five points in elections since 1980. See http://www.electproject.org/home/voter-turnout/voter-turnout-data. For a study of felon disenfranchisement, see Jeff Manza and Christopher Uggen, *Locked Out: Felon Disenfranchisement and American Democracy* (New York: Oxford University Press, 2006).

24. Max Kaase and Alan Marsh, "Political Action: A Theoretical Perspective," in *Political Action: Mass Participation in Five Western Democracies,* ed. Samuel H. Barnes and Max Kaase (Beverly Hills, Calif.: Sage, 1979), p. 168.

25. *Smith* v. *Allwright,* 321 U.S. 649 (1944).

26. *Harper* v. *Virginia State Board of Elections,* 383 U.S. 663 (1966).

27. Everett Carll Ladd, *The American Polity* (New York: Norton, 1985), p. 392.

28. Gorton Carruth et al. (eds.), *The Encyclopedia of American Facts and Dates* (New York: Crowell, 1979), p. 330. For an eye-opening account of women's contributions to politics before gaining the vote, see Robert J. Dinkin, *Before Equal Suffrage: Women in Partisan Politics from Colonial Times to 1920* (Westport, Conn.: Greenwood Press, 1995).

29. Jodie T. Allen, "Reluctant Suffragettes: When Women Questioned Their Right to Vote," Pew Research Center, 18 March 2009, http:// pewresearch.org/pubs/1156/women-reluctant-voters-after-suffrage-19th-amendment.

30. Ivor Crewe, "Electoral Participation," in *Democracy at the Polls: A Comparative Study of Competitive National Elections,* ed. David Butler, Howard R. Penniman, and Austin Ranney (Washington, DC: American Enterprise Institute, 1981), pp. 219–223.

31. International IDEA, "Frequently Asked Questions," http://www.idea.int/vt/faq.cfm#9.%20Which%20is%20the%20minimum%20 voting%20age?.

32. For an early history, see Thomas Goebel, *A Government by the People: Direct Democracy in America, 1890–1940* (Chapel Hill: University of North Carolina Press, 2007).

33. Politico, "2014 Ballot Measures Election Results," http://www.politico.com/2014-election/results/map/ballot-measures#.VpQ2Uza-_uU.

34. Initiative & Referendum Institute at http://www.iandrinstitute.org/BW%202015-2%20Results%20(v1).pdf.

35. David S. Broder, *Democracy Derailed: Initiative Campaigns and the Power of Money* (New York: Harcourt, 2000); and David S. Broder, "A Snake in the Grass Roots," *Washington Post,* 26 March 2000, pp. Bl, B2.

36. One could also select special bodies of citizens to decide policies. One scholar proposes creating large "citizens assemblies" consisting of randomly selected citizens statistically representative of the population to decide very critical issues. See James H. Snider, "Using Citizens Assemblies to Reform the Process of Democratic Reform," Joan Shorenstein Center on the Press, Politics and Public Policy, Spring 2008.

37. Caroline J. Tolbert, Ramona S. McNeal, and Daniel A. Smith, "Enhancing Civic Engagement: The Effect of Direct Democracy on Political Participation and Knowledge," *State Politics and Policy Quarterly* 3 (Spring 2003): 23–41. For a more critical look at initiatives as undermining representative government, see Bruce E. Cain and Kenneth P. Miller, "The Populist Legacy: Initiatives and the Undermining of Representative Government," in *Dangerous Democracy? The Battle over Ballot Initiatives in America,* ed. Larry J. Sabato, Howard R. Ernst, and Bruce A. Larson (Lanham, Md.: Rowman & Littlefield, 2001), pp. 33–62. For the role of interest groups in ballot issue campaigns, see Robert M. Alexander, *Rolling the Dice with State Initiatives* (Westport, Conn.: Praeger, 2002).

38. See http://www.isolon.org/ and http://www.brookings.edu/opinions/ 2011/0628_social_media_west.aspx.

39. Mark E. Warren and Hilary Pearse (eds.), *Designing Deliberative Democracy: The British Columbia Citizens' Assembly* (New York: Cambridge University Press, 2008).

40. Data on the elected state officials come from *The Book of the States 2013* (Lexington, Ky.: Council of State Governments, 2013). Estimates of the number of elected school board members come from *Chicago Tribune,* 10 March 1985.

41. Crewe, "Electoral Participation," p. 232. A rich literature has grown to explain turnout across nations. See Pippa Norris, *Democratic Phoenix: Reinventing Political Activism* (Cambridge: Cambridge University Press, 2002), Chap. 3; and Mark N. Franklin, "The Dynamics of Electoral Participation," in *Comparing Democracies* 2: *New Challenges in the Study of Elections and Voting,* ed. Lawrence LeDuc, Richard G. Niemi, and Pippa Norris (London: Sage, 2002), pp. 148–168.

42. Verba and Nie, *Participation in America,* p. 13.

43. Russell J. Dalton, *Citizen Policies,* 3rd ed. (New York: Seven Bridges, 2002), pp. 67–68. For the argument that greater economic inequality leads to greater political inequality, see Frederick Solt, "Economic Inequality and Democratic Political Engagement," *American Journal of Political Science* 52 (January 2008): 48–60.

44. Russell J. Dalton, The *Good Citizen: How a Younger Generation Is Reshaping American Politics* (Washington, DC: Congressional Quarterly Press, 2008).

45. Cliff Zukin et al., *A New Engagement?* (New York: Oxford University Press, 2006), pp. 188–191.

46. For a concise summary of the effect of age on voting turnout, see William H. Flanigan and Nancy H. Zingale, *Political Behavior of the American Electorate,* 11th ed. (Washington, DC: CQ Press, 2005).

47. Ibid., pp. 46–47.

48. M. Margaret Conway, Gertrude A. Steuernagel, and David W. Ahern, *Women and Political Participation: Cultural Change in the Political Arena* (Washington, DC: CQ Press, 1997), pp. 79–80.

49. Ronald B. Rapoport, "The Sex Gap in Political Persuading: Where the 'Structuring Principle' Works," *American Journal of Political Science* 25 (February 1981): 32–48. Perhaps surprisingly, research fails to show any relationship between a wife's role in her marriage and her political activity. See Nancy Burns, Kay Lehman Schlozman, and Sidney Verba, "The Public Consequences of Private Inequality: Family Life and Citizen Participation," *American Political Science Review* 91 (June 1997): 373–389.

50. Bruce C. Straits, "The Social Context of Voter Turnout," *Public Opinion Quarterly* 54 (Spring 1990): 64–73.

51. Sidney Verba, Kay Lehman Scholzman, and Henry E. Brady, *Voice and Equality: Civic Voluntarism in American Politics* (Cambridge, Mass.: Harvard University Press, 1995), p. 433.

52. Stephen J. Dubner and Steven D. Levitt, "Why Vote?" *New York Times Magazine,* 6 November 2005, pp. 30–31. The classic formulation of the rational choice theory of turnout is Anthony Downs, *An Economic Theory of Democracy* (New York: Harper and Row, 1957). For an empirical test of economic models, see David Levine and

Thomas Palfry, "The Paradox of Voter Participation? A Laboratory Study," *American Political Science Review* 101 (February 2007): 143–158.

53. Associated Press, "Voter Turnout Tops Since 1968," *St. Paul Pioneer Press*, 14 December 2008, p. A4

54. Stephen D. Shaffer, "A Multivariate Explanation of Decreasing Turnout in Presidential Elections, 1960–1976," *American Journal of Political Science* 25 (February 1981): 68–95; and Paul R. Abramson and John H. Aldrich, "The Decline of Electoral Participation in America," *American Political Science Review* 76 (September 1981): 603–620. However, one scholar argues that this research suffers because it looks only at voters and nonvoters in a single election. When the focus shifts to people who vote sometimes but not at other times, the models do not fit so well. See M. Margaret Conway and John E. Hughes, "Political Mobilization and Patterns of Voter Turnout" (paper presented at the annual meeting of the American Political Science Association, Washington, DC, September 1993).

55. See Jack Doppelt and Ellen Shearer, *America's No-Shows: Non-voters* (Washington, DC: Medill School of Journalism, 2001); Thomas E. Patterson, *The Vanishing Voter* (New York: Vintage Books, 2003); and Deborah J. Brooks and John Geer, "Beyond Negativity: The Effects of Incivility on the Electorate," *American Journal of Political Science* 51 (January 2007): 1–16.

56. Some scholars argue that Americans generally have become disengaged from social organizations (not just political parties), becoming more likely to act "alone" than to participate in group activities. See Robert D. Putnam, *Bowling Alone: The Collapse and Revival of American Community* (New York: Simon & Schuster, 2000).

57. See Eric Pultzer, "Becoming a Habitual Voter: Inertia, Resources, and Growth in Young Adulthood," *American Political Science Review* (March 2002): 41–56; Alan S. Gerber, Donald P. Green, and Ron Shachar, "Voting May Be Habit-Forming: Evidence from a Randomized Field Experiment," *American Journal of Political Science* (July 2003): 540–550; and David Dreyer Lassen, "The Effect of Information on Voter Turnout: Evidence from a Natural Experiment," *American Journal of Political Science* 49 (January 2005): 103–111. For the argument that turnout may be genetic, see Charles Q. Choi, "The Genetics of Politics," *Scientific American*, November 2007.

58. Center for Information and Research on Civil Learning and Engagement (CIRCLE) at the University of Maryland School of Public Policy, "The 2004 Youth Vote," http://www.civicyouth.org.

59. For the latest analysis of voting trends in the United States, see the research done by Michael McDonald, http://www.electproject.org/home/voter-turnout/voter-turnout-data.

60. Visit the Why Tuesday? website at http://www.whytuesday.org.

61. "High Turnout with Iowa's Election Day Registration Law," 5 February 2016, http://www.866ourvote.org/newsroom/news?id=0191.

62. Ruth Goldway, "The Election Is in the Mail," *New York Times*, 6 December 2006; and Randal C. Archibold, "Mail-in Voters Become the Latest Prize," *New York Times*, 14 January 2008.

63. "Hawaii's Internet Vote Is 1st in Nation," *St. Paul Pioneer Press*, 24 May 2009, p. 5A

64. Recent research finds that "party contact is clearly a statistically and substantively important factor in predicting and explaining political behavior." See Peter W. Wielhouwer and Brad Lockerbie, "Party Contacting and Political Participation, 1952–1990" (paper presented at the annual meeting of the American Political Science Association, Chicago, 1992), p. 14 Of course, parties strategically target the groups that they want to see vote in elections. See Peter W. Wielhouwer, "Strategic Canvassing by Political Parties, 1952–1990," *American Review of Politics* 16 (Fall 1995): 213–238.

65. Steven J. Rosenstone and John Mark Hansen, *Mobilization, Participation, and Democracy in America* (New York: Macmillan, 1993), p. 213.

66. For the differences between national and local elections, see J. Eric Oliver and Shang E. Ha, "Vote Choice in Suburban Elections," *American Political Science Review* 101 (August 2007): 393–408; and Brad T. Gomez, Thomas G. Hansford, and George A. Krause, "The

Republicans Should Pray for Rain: Weather, Turnout, and Voting in U.S. Presidential Elections," *Journal of Politics* 69 (August 2007): 649–663.

67. See Robert A. Jackson, "Voter Mobilization in the 1986 Midterm Election," *Journal of Politics* 55 (November 1993): 1081–1099; Kim Quaile Hill and Jan E. Leighley, "Political Parties and Class Mobilization in Contemporary United States Elections," *American Journal of Political Science* 40 (August 1996): 787–804; and Janine Parry et al., "Mobilizing the Seldom Voter: Campaign Contact and Effects in High Profile Elections," *Political Behavior* 30 (March 2008): 97–113.

68. Aaron Smith, "Civic Engagement Online: Politics as Usual," Pew Internet & American Life Project, 1 September 2009, http://pewresearch.org/pubs/1328/online-poltical-civic-engagement-activity.

69. Nonprofit Voter Engagement Network, "America Goes to the Polls: A Report on Voter Turnout in the 2006 Election," http://www.nonprofitvote.org.

70. Richard Niemi and Michael Hanmer, "Voter Registration and Turnout among College Students" (paper presented at the annual meeting of the American Political Science Association, 2006). Students at Northwestern University in 2008 were more likely to register and vote absentee if they came from a "swing" state. See Kim Castle, Janice Levy, and Michael Peshkin, "Local and Absentee Voter Registration Drives on a College Campus," CIRCLE Working Paper 66, October 2009.

71. Crewe, "Electoral Participation," p. 262.

72. For research showing that economic inequality depresses political engagement of the citizenry, see Frederick Solt, "Economic Inequality and Democratic Political Engagement," *American Journal of Political Science* 52 (2008): 48–60.

73. Barnes and Kaase, *Political Action*, p. 532.

74. Eric Lichtblau, "F.B.I. Watched Activist Groups, New Files Show," *New York Times*, 20 December 2005, p. 1

75. 1971 *Congressional Quarterly Almanac* (Washington, DC: CQ Press, 1972), p. 475.

76. Benjamin Ginsberg, *The Consequences of Consent: Elections, Citizen Control, and Popular Acquiescence* (Reading Mass.: Addison-Wesley, 1982), p. 13.

77. Ibid., pp. 13–14.

78. Ibid., pp. 6–7.

79. Some people have argued that the decline in voter turnout during the 1980s served to increase the class bias in the electorate because people of lower socioeconomic status stayed home. But later research has concluded that "class bias has not increased since 1964." Jan E. Leigh-ley and Jonathan Nagler, "Socioeconomic Class Bias in Turnout, 1964–1988: The Voters Remain the Same," *American Political Science Review* 86 (September 1992): 734. Nevertheless, Rosenstone and Hansen, in *Mobilization, Participation, and Democracy in America*, say, "The economic inequalities in political participation that prevail in the United States today are as large as the racial disparities in political participation that prevailed in the 1950s. America's leaders today face few incentives to attend to the needs of the disadvantaged" (p. 248).

Chapter 8

1. Jeffrey M. Jones, "Americans Continue to Say a Third Political Party is Needed," Gallup Politics, 24 September 2014, http://www.gallup.com/poll/177284/americans-continue-say-third-political-party-needed.aspx.

2. Steven Erlanger, "As Europe's Political Landscape Shifts, Two-Party Systems Fade," *New York Times*, 18 April 2015, p. A7.

3. The American National Election 2012 Time Series Study, http://www.electionstudies.org.

4. Gallup Poll 3–6, October 2013. N=1,028 adults nationwide.

5. See, for example, Peter Mair, "Comparing Party Systems," in *Comparing Democracies 2: New Challenges in the Study of Elections and*

Voting, ed. Lawrence LeDuc, Richard G. Niemi, and Pippa Norris (London: Sage, 2002), pp. 88–107.

6. E. E. Schattschneider, *Party Government* (New York: Holt, 1942).

7. See Lyn Carson and Brian Martin, *Random Selection in Politics* (Westport, Conn.: Praeger, 1999). They say: "The assumption behind random selection in politics is that just about anyone who wishes to be involved in decision making is capable of making a useful contribution, and that the fairest way to ensure that everyone has such an opportunity is to give them an equal chance to be involved" (p. 4).

8. See James M. Snyder, Jr., and Michael M. Ting, "An Informational Rationale for Political Parties," *American Journal of Political Science* 46 (January 2002): 90–110. They formalize the argument that political parties acquire "brand names" that help voters make sense of politics.

9. Edmund Burke, *Thoughts on the Cause of the Present Discontents* (1770).

10. Anthony Downs, *An Economic Theory of Democracy* (New York: HarperCollins, 1957), p. 25.

11. John H. Aldrich, *Why Parties? The Origin and Transformation of Political Parties in America* (Chicago: University of Chicago Press, 1995), p. 296.

12. See John Kenneth White and Daniel M. Shea (eds.), *New Party Politics: From Jefferson and Hamilton to the Information Age* (Boston: Bedford/St. Martin's, 2000), for essays on the place of political parties in American history.

13. See Jerome M. Clubb, William H. Flanigan, and Nancy H. Zingale, *Partisan Realignment: Voters, Parties, and Government in American History* (Beverly Hills, Calif.:: Sage, 1980), p. 163. Once central to the analysis of American politics, the concept of critical elections has been discounted by some scholars in recent years. See Larry M. Bartels, "Electoral Continuity and Change," *Electoral Studies* 17 (September 1998): 301–326; and David R. Mayhew, *Electoral Realignments: A Critique of an American Genre* (New Haven, Conn.: Yale University Press, 2002). However, the concept has been defended by other scholars. See Peter F. Nardulli, "The Concept of a Critical Realignment, Electoral Behavior, and Political Change," *American Political Science Review* 89 (March 1995): 10–22; and Norman Schofield, Gary Miller, and Andrew Martin, "Critical Elections and Political Realignments in the USA: 1860–2000," *Political Studies* 51 (2003): 217–240.

14. See Gerald M. Pomper, "Classification of Presidential Elections," *Journal of Politics* 29 (August 1967): 535–566. See also Walter Dean Burnham, *Critical Elections and the Mainsprings of American Politics* (New York: Norton, 1970). Decades later, an update of Gerald Pomper's analysis of presidential elections through 1996 determined that 1960, 1964, and 1968 all had realigning characteristics. See Jonathan Knuckley, "Classification of Presidential Elections: An Update," *Polity* 31 (Summer 1999): 639–653.

15. See Ronald Brownstein, "For GOP, a Southern Exposure," *National Journal Online,* http://www.nationaljournal.com/njonline/no_20090523_3656.php?.

16. In "Realignment in Presidential Politics: South and North?" (paper presented at the Citadel Symposium on Southern Politics, 4–5 March 2004), William Crotty argues that a political realignment definitely occurred in the South around 1968 that affected presidential politics and national voting behavior.

17. Earl Black and Merle Black, *The Rise of Southern Republicans* (Cambridge, Mass.: Harvard University Press, 2002), pp. 2–3.

18. Seth C. McKeen, "Rural Voters and the Polarization of American Presidential Elections," *PS: Political Science and Politics* 41 (January 2008): 101–108.

19. Jeffrey M. Stonecash, *Political Parties Matter: Realignment and the Return of Partisan Voting* (Boulder, Colo.: Lynne Rienner, 2006), pp. 129–130.

20. The discussion that follows draws heavily on Austin Ranney and Willmoore Kendall, *Democracy and the American Party System* (New York: Harcourt, Brace, 1956), Chapter 18, Chapter 19. For later

analyses of multiparty politics in America, see Steven J. Rosenstone, Roy L. Behr, and Edward H. Lazarus, *Third Parties in America: Citizen Response to Major Party Failure,* 2nd ed. (Princeton, N.J.: Princeton University Press, 1996); and John F. Bibby and L. Sandy Maisel, *Two Parties—or More?* (Boulder, Colo.: Westview Press, 1998).

21. J. David Gillespie, *Politics at the Periphery: Third Parties in a Two-Party America* (Columbia: University of South Carolina Press, 1993). Surveys of public attitudes toward minor parties are reported in Christian Coller, "Trends: Third Parties and the Two-Party System," *Public Opinion Quarterly* 60 (Fall 1996): 431–449. For a spirited defense of having a strong third party in American politics, see Theodore J. Lowi, "Toward a More Responsible Three-Party System: Deregulating American Democracy," in *The State of the Parties,* 4th ed., ed. John C. Green and Rick Farmer (Lanham, Md.: Rowman & Littlefield, 2003), pp. 354–377. For an analysis of third-party presidential campaigns in 2008, see Brian J. Brox, "Running Nowhere: Third Party Presidential Campaigns in 2008" (paper presented at the annual meeting of the Midwest Political Science Association, Chicago, 3–6 April 2008).

22. Ronald B. Rapoport and Walter J. Stone, *Three's a Crowd: The Dynamics of Third Parties, Ross Perot, and Republican Resurgence* (Ann Arbor: University of Michigan Press, 2005).

23. In a June 18–29, 2008, Pew Research Center Poll, 56 percent of the respondents agreed that "we should have a third major political party in this country in addition to the Democrats and Republicans."

24. Shigeo Hirano and James M. Snyder, Jr., "The Decline of Third-Party Voting in the United States," *Journal of Politics* 69 (February 2007): 1–6. See also Rapoport and Stone, *Three's a Crowd.*

25. In his study of party systems, Jean Blondel noticed that most three-party systems had two major parties and a much smaller third party, which he called two-and-a-half-party systems. (Britain, for example, has two major parties—Labour and Conservative—and a smaller Social Democratic Party. Germany has followed a similar pattern.) Blondel said, "While it would seem theoretically possible for three-party systems to exist in which all three significant parties were of about equal size, there are in fact no three-party systems of this kind among Western democracies." He concluded that "genuine three-party systems do not normally occur because they are essentially transitional, thus unstable, forms of party systems." See his "Types of Party System," in *The West European Party System,* ed. Peter Mair (New York: Oxford University Press, 1990), p. 305.

26. See Douglas J. Amy, *Real Choices, New Voices: The Case for Proportional Representation in the United States,* 2nd ed. (New York: Columbia University Press, 2002).

27. The most complete report of these legal barriers is contained in monthly issues of *Ballot Access News,* http://www.ballot-access.org. State laws and court decisions may systematically support the major parties, but the U.S. Supreme Court seems to hold a more neutral position toward major and minor parties. See Lee Epstein and Charles D. Hadley, "On the Treatment of Political Parties in the U.S. Supreme Court, 1900–1986," *Journal of Politics* 52 (May 1990): 413–432; and E. Joshua Rosenkranz, *Voter Choice 96: A 50-State Report Card on the Presidential Elections* (New York: New York University School of Law, Brennan Center for Justice, 1996), p. 24.

28. Samuel Issacharoff, Pamela S. Karlan, and Richard H. Pildes, *The Law of Democracy,* rev. 2nd ed. (New York: Foundation Press, 2002), pp. 417–436.

29. See James Gimpel, *National Elections and the Autonomy of American State Party Systems* (Pittsburgh, Pa.: University of Pittsburgh Press, 1996).

30. Measuring the concept of party identification has had its problems. For insights into the issues, see R. Michael Alvarez, "The Puzzle of Party Identification," *American Politics Quarterly* 18 (October 1990): 476–491; and Donald Philip Green and Bradley Palmquist, "Of Artifacts and Partisan Instability," *American Journal of Political Science* 34 (August 1990): 872–902.

31. Pew Research Center, "A Deep Dive into Party Affiliation," 7 April 2015, p. 2.

32. Susan Page, "Highly Educated Couples Often Split on Candidates," *USA Today*, 18 December 2002, pp. 1–2.

33. U.S. Census Bureau, "2014 National Population Projections: Summary Tables," http://www.census.gov/population/projections/data/national/2014/summarytables.html.

34. For recent research on the transmission of party identification, see Christopher Ojeda and Pater K. Hatemi, "Accounting for the Child in the Transmission of Party Identification," *American Sociological Review* 80 (December, 2015): 1150–1174.

35. The relationship between age and party identification is quite complicated, but research finds that it becomes more stable as people age. See Elias Dinas and Mark Franklin, "The Development of Partisanship during the Life-Course" (paper presented at the Midwest Political Science Association 67th Annual National Conference, Palmer House Hilton, Chicago, 2 April 2009), http://www.allacademic.com/meta/ p363000_index.html.

36. Two scholars on voting behavior describe partisanship as "the feeling of sympathy for and loyalty to a political party that an individual acquires—sometimes during childhood—and holds through life, often with increasing intensity." See William H. Flanigan and Nancy H. Zingale, *Political Behavior of the American Electorate*, 10th ed. (Washington, DC: CQ Press, 2002), p. 60.

37. See, for example, Gerald M. Pomper, *Elections in America* (New York: Dodd, Mead, 1968); Benjamin Ginsberg, "Election and Public Policy," *American Political Science Review* 70 (March 1976): 41–50; and Jeff Fishel, *Presidents and Promises* (Washington, D.C.: CQ Press, 1985).

38. Ian Budge and Richard I. Hofferbert, "Mandates and Policy Outputs: U.S. Party Platforms and Federal Expenditures," *American Political Science Review* 84 (March 1990): 111–131.

39. See Terri Susan Fine, "Economic Interests and the Framing of the 1988 and 1992 Democratic and Republican Party Platforms," *American Review of Politics* 16 (Spring 1995): 79–93.

40. Ian Budge et al., *Mapping Policy Preferences: Estimates for Parties, Electors, and Governments 1945–1998* (Oxford: Oxford University Press, 2001), p. 49.

41. See Ralph M. Goldman, *The National Party Chairmen and Committees: Factionalism at the Top* (Armonk, N.Y.: M. E. Sharpe, 1990). The subtitle is revealing.

42. Cornelius P. Cotter and Bernard C. Hennessy, *Politics without Power: The National Party Committees* (New York: Atherton Press, 1964).

43. Phillip A. Klinkner, "Party Culture and Party Behavior," in *The State of the Parties*, 3rd ed., ed. Daniel M. Shea and John C. Green (Lanham, Md.: Rowman & Littlefield, 1999), pp. 275–287; and Phillip A. Klinkner, *The Losing Parties: Out-Party National Committees, 1956–1993* (New Haven, Conn.: Yale University Press, 1994).

44. "Take the Lead: Political Parties and the Financing of the 2000 Presidential Election," in *The State of the Parties*, 4th ed., ed. John C Green and Rick Farmer (Lanham, Md.: Rowman & Littlefield, 2003), p. 97; and Klinkner, *The Losing Parties*.

45. Daniel J. Galvin, *Presidential Party Building: Dwight D. Eisenhower to George W. Bush* (Princeton, N.J.: Princeton University Press, 2010), pp. ix–x.

46. Dan Barry, "Republicans on Long Island Master Science of Politics," *New York Times*, 8 March 1996, p. AIS. Recent research suggests that when both major parties have strong organizations at the county level, the public has more favorable attitudes toward the parties. See John J. Coleman, "Party Organization Strength and Public Support for Parties," *American Journal of Political Science* 40 (August 1996): 805–824.

47. John Frendreis et al., "Local Political Parties and Legislative Races in 1992," in Shea and Green, *The State of the Parties*, p. 139.

48. Raymond J. La Raja, "State Parties and Soft Money: How Much Party Building?" in Green and Farmer, *The State of the Parties*, p. 146.

49. Robert Biersack, "Hard Facts and Soft Money: State Party Finance in the 1992 Federal Elections," in Shea and Green, *The State of the Parties*, p. 114.

50. Federal Election Commission, "2014 Individual Party Details," http://www.fec.gov/disclosure/committeeDetail.do.

51. See the evidence presented in Robert Harmel and Kenneth Janda, *Parties and Their Environments* (New York: Longman, 1982), Chapter 5; and the more recent assessment in Nicol C. Rae, "Be Careful What You Wish For: The Rise of Responsible Parties in American National Politics," *Annual Review of Political Science* 10 (2007): 169–191.

52. "The Factions in the House of Representatives," *New York Times*, 20 October 2013, p. 20.

53. Martin P. Wattenberg, *The Decline of American Political Parties, 1952–1994* (Cambridge, Mass.: Harvard University Press, 1996).

54. The model is articulated most clearly in a report by the American Political Science Association, "Toward a More Responsible Two-Party System," *American Political Science Review* 44 (September 1950): Part II. See also Gerald M. Pomper, "Toward a More Responsible Party System? What, Again?" *Journal of Politics* 33 (November 1971): 916–940. See also the seven essays in the symposium "Divided Government and the Politics of Constitutional Reform," *PS: Political Science and Politics* 24 (December 1991): 634–657.

55. Within the American states, parties also differ on policies, but to varying degrees. See John H. Aldrich and James S. Coleman Battista, "Conditional Party Government in the States," *American Journal of Political Science* 46 (January 2002): 164–172.

56. Jeffrey M. Jones, "Americans Lack Consensus on Desirability of Divided Gov't," *Gallup Poll Report*, 10 June 2010.

57. Recent research finds that voters do differentiate between policies backed by the president and by congressional candidates. See David R. Jones and Monika L. McDermott, "The Responsible Party Government Model in House and Senate Elections," *American Journal of Political Science* 48 (January 2004): 1–12.

Chapter 9

1. David Menefree-Libey, *The Triumph of Campaign-Centered Politics* (New York: Chatham House, 2000).

2. Stephen E. Frantzich, *Political Parties in the Technological Age* (New York: Longman, 1989), p. 105.

3. Reuven Y. Hazan and Gideon Rahat, *Democracy Within Parties: Candidate Selection Methods and Their Political Consequences* (Oxford: Oxford University Press, 2010). See also Krister Lundell, "Determinants of Candidate Selection: The Degree of Centralization in Comparative Perspective," *Party Politics* 10 (January 2004): 25–47.

4. Kenneth Janda, "Adopting Party Law," in *Political Parties and Democracy in Theoretical and Practical Perspectives* (Washington, DC: National Democratic Institute for International Affairs, 2005). This is a series of research papers.

5. *The Book of the States, 2013* (Lexington, Ky.: Council of State Governments, 2013), Table 6.3.

6. Pew Research Center, "2012 Republican Primary Voters: More Conservative Than GOP General Election Voters" (28 January 2016).

7. James A. McCann, "Presidential Nomination Activists and Political Representation: A View from the Active Minority Studies," in *Pursuit of the White House: How We Choose Our Presidential Nominees*, ed. William G. Mayer (Chatham, N.J.: Chatham House, 1996), p. 99.

8. "The Green Papers: 2014 General Election," http://www.thegreenpapers.com/G14/House.phtml/trackback/parties.phtml?v=l&p=DEM.

9. James M. Snyder, Jr., et al., "The Decline of Competition in U.S. Primary Elections, 1908–2004" (unpublished paper, MIT, Cambridge, Mass., June 2005), p. 22.

10. "Ninth Circuit Upholds Washington Top-Two System," *Ballot Access News* 27 (1 February 2012): 1–2; and "California Primary," *Ballot Access News* 28 (1 July 2012): 4.

11. "Turnout Change," *Ballot Access News* (1 March 2015): 2.

12. Richard Winger, "California Experience with Top-Two During 2013," *Ballot Access News* (1 January 2014): 3; Richard Winger, "Five New Papers Issued on Relationships between Primary Systems and Polarization," *Ballot Access News* (1 September 2013): 1–3.

13. E. McGhee, S. Masket, B. Shor, S. Rogers, and N. McCarty, "A Primary Cause of Partisanship? Nomination Systems and Legislator Ideology," *American Journal of Political Science* (2013), doi:10.1111/ajps.12070.

14. See "The Green Papers," http://www.thegreenpapers.com, for information on state methods of delegate selection in 2012.

15. "Election 2016," *Wall Street Journal* (27 January 2016), p. S4.

16. Alan Ware, *The American Direct Primary: Party Institutionalization and Transformation in the North* (Cambridge: Cambridge University Press, 2002). Ware argues that the primary system resulted less from the reform movement than the unwieldy nature of the caucus/convention system for nominating candidates.

17. These figures, calculated for voting-eligible population (VEP), come from elections, http://elections.gmu.edu/voter_turnout.htm. VEP is lower than voting-age population (VAP) because VEP excludes those ineligible to vote, usually noncitizens and felons.

18. Richard L. Berke, "Two States Retain Roles in Shaping Presidential Race," *New York Times*, 29 November 1999, p. 1; and Leslie Wayne, "Iowa Turns Its Presidential Caucuses into a Cash Cow, and Milks Furiously," *New York Times*, 5 January 2000, p. A16. See also Adam Nagourney, "Iowa Worries about Losing Its Franchise," *New York Times*, 18 January 2004, sec. 4, p. 3.

19. See James R. Beniger, "Winning the Presidential Nomination: National Polls and State Primary Elections, 1936–1972," *Public Opinion Quarterly* 40 (Spring 1976): 22–38.

20. Janet Hook, "Cleveland Set for a Trump Show," *Wall Street Journal*, 18 July 2016, pp. A1 and A6. Graphs in "A Preconvention Look at the Presidential Race," from a Wall Street Journal/NBC Poll of 1,000 registered voters taken on 9-13 July, 2016.

21. Thomas Kaplan and Maggie Haberman, "Trump Assails 'Rigged' System, Saying He Chooses Not to Exploit It," *New York Times* (28 April 2016), p. A13.

22. Bill Brock et al., "Let's Get This Straight about the Convention," *Wall Street Journal* (21 April 2016), p. A13.

23. "Unfavorable Views of the Front Runners," *Wall Street Journal* (4 May 2016), p. A5.

24. *The American Heritage Dictionary of the English Language,* 4th ed. (Boston: Houghton Mifflin, 2000), p. 362. Indeed, the entry on "Electoral College" in the 1989 Oxford English Dictionary does not note any usage in American politics up to 1875, when it cites a reference in connection with the Germanic Diet.

25. References to the electoral college in the U.S. Code can be found through the Legal Information Institute website, http://www4.law.cornell.edu/uscode/ch1.html.

26. Michael Nelson, *Congressional Quarterly's Guide to the Presidency* (Washington, DC: CQ Press, 1989), pp. 155–156. Colorado selected its presidential electors through the state legislature in 1876, but that was the year it entered the Union.

27. Who would have become president if the 538 electoral votes had been divided equally, at 269 each? According to the Constitution, the House of Representatives would have chosen the president, for no candidate had a majority. One way to avoid tied outcomes in the future is to create an odd number of electoral votes. To do this, one scholar proposes making the District of Columbia a state. That would give Washington three electoral votes—the same number as it has now without congressional representation. The Senate would increase to 102 members, while the House would remain fixed at 435. (Presumably, Washington's seat would come from one of the other states after decennial reapportionment.) This clever solution would produce an electoral college of 537, an odd number that could not produce a tie between two candidates. See David A. Crockett, "Dodging the Bullet: Election Mechanics and the Problem of the Twenty-third Amendment," *PS: Political Science and Politics* 36 (July 2003): 423–426.

28. Shlomo Slonim, "The Electoral College at Philadelphia: The Evolution of an Ad Hoc Congress for the Selection of a President," *Journal of American History* 73 (June 1986): 35. For a recent critique and proposal for reform, see David W. Abbott and James P. Levine, *Wrong Winner: The Coming Debacle in the Electoral College* (New York: Praeger, 1991). For a reasoned defense, see Walter Berns (ed.), *After the People Vote: A Guide to the Electoral College* (Washington, DC: American Enterprise Institute, 1992). For a detailed analysis of a congressional failure to enact proportional distribution of state electoral votes, see Gary Bugh, "Normal Politics and the Failure of the Most Intense Effort to Amend the Presidential Election System" (paper presented at the annual meeting of the Northeastern Political Science Association, Boston, 2006).

29. Lydia Saad, "Americans Would Swap Electoral College for Popular Vote," *Gallup Poll Report,* 24 October 2011.

30. For the most recent review, see Gary Bugh (ed.), *Electoral College Reform: Challenges and Possibilities* (Burlington, Vt.: Ashgate, 2010).

31. Walter Berns (ed.), *After the People Vote*, pp. 45–48. The framers had great difficulty deciding how to allow both the people and the states to participate in selecting the president. This matter was debated on twenty-one different days before they compromised on the electoral college, which, Slonim says, "in the eyes of its admirers . . . represented a brilliant scheme for successfully blending national and federal elements in the selection of the nation's chief executive" ("The Electoral College at Philadelphia," p. 58).

32. Observers suspect that the vote for Edwards instead of Kerry was cast by error. See http://news.minnesota.publicradio.org/features/2004/12/13_ap_electors.

33. See Alexis Simendinger, James A. Barnes, and Carl M. Cannon, "Pondering a Popular Vote," *National Journal*, 18 November 2000, pp. 3650–3656.

34. Harold W. Stanley and Richard G. Niemi, *Vital Statistics on American Politics, 2011–2012* (Washington, DC: CQ Press, 2011), Table 3.10.

35. Nate Silver and Andrew Gelman, "No Country for Close Calls," *New York Times*, 19 April 2009, p. WK11.

36. See Edward I. Sidlow, *Challenging the Incumbent: An Underdog's Undertaking* (Washington, DC: CQ Press, 2004), for the engaging account of the unsuccessful 2000 campaign by a young political scientist, Lance Pressl, against the most senior Republican in the House, Phil Crane, in Illinois' Sixth District. Sidlow's book invites readers to ponder what the high reelection rate of incumbents means for American politics.

37. Quoted in E. J. Dionne, Jr., "On the Trail of Corporation Donations," *New York Times*, 6 October 1980.

38. Federal Election Commission, *The First Ten Years: 1975–1985* (Washington, DC: Federal Election Commission, 14 April 1985), p. 1.

39. Michael J. Malbin, "Assessing the Bipartisan Campaign Reform Act," in *The Election After Reform: Money, Politics and the Bipartisan Campaign Reform Act*, ed. Michael J. Malbin (Lanham, Md.: Rowman & Littlefield, 2006).

40. Adam Liptak, "Justices, 5–4, Reject Corporate Campaign Spending Limit," *New York Times*, 22 January 2010, pp. A1, A16.

41. Editorial, "A Free Speech Landmark," *Wall Street Journal*, 22 January 2010, p. A18.

42. Editorial, "The Court's Blow to Democracy," *New York Times*, 22 January 2010, p. A20.

43. "Changing the Rules," *Wall Street Journal*, 22 January 2010, p. A6.

44. *SpeechNow.org* v. *FEC*, 599 F.3d 686 (DC. Circuit, 26 March 2010). See also http://www.fec.gov/press/press2011/FEC_Joint_Statement-Nov3.pdf.

45. "With New Political Committees, Possible Channels for Unlimited, Anonymous Donations," *New York Times*, 16 October 2011, p. 24.

46. "Super PACS," The Center for Responsive Politics, http://www.opensecrets.org/pacs/superpacs.php?cycle=2016.

47. James A. Barnes, "Matching Funds, R.I.P.," *National Journal*, 26 April 2008, p. 75.

48. Federal Election Commission, "2008 Presidential Campaign Financial Activity Summarized," News Release, 8 June 2009.

49. Dan Eggen, "The 2012 Election Brings a New Kind of Fundraiser: The Super Bundler," *Washington Post*, 16 August 2011.

50. "Candidate Summary, 2016 Cycle," OpenSecrets.org, 30 April 2016.

51. Colleen McCain Nelson, "Sanders Cash Keeps Flowing," *Wall Street Journal*, 4 April 2016, p. 1.

52. According to Brian F. Schaffner and Matthew J. Streb, less educated respondents are less likely to express a vote preference when party labels are not available. See "The Partisan Heuristic in Low-Information Elections," *Public Opinion Quarterly* 66 (Winter 2002): 559–581.

53. See Matt A. Barreto et al., "Bulls Eye or Ricochet? Ethnically Targeted Campaign Ads in the 2008 Election" (paper presented at the Chicago Area Behavioral Workshop, Evanston, Ill., 8 May 2009); and Michael G. Hagenand and Robin Kolodny, "Microtargeting Campaign Advertising on Cable Television" (paper presented at the annual meeting of the Midwest Political Science Association, Chicago, 3–6 April 2008).

54. See Eric W. Rademacher and Alfred J. Tuchfarber, "Preelection Polling and Political Campaigns," in Bruce I. Newman, *Handbook of Political Marketing* (Thousand Oaks, CA: Sage Publications. 1999), pp. 197–221.

55. Bruce I. Newman, "A Predictive Model of Voter Behavior," in Newman, *Handbook of Political Marketing*, pp. 259–282.

56. Timothy E. Cook, *Making Laws and Making News: Media Strategies in the U.S. House of Representatives* (Washington, DC: Brookings Institution, 1989).

57. Stephen J. Farnsworth and S. Robert Lichter, *The Nightly News Nightmare: Media Coverage of U.S. Presidential Elections, 1988–2008* (Lanham, Md.: Rowman & Littlefield, 2010), p. 52.

58. Julianne F. Flowers, Audrey A. Haynes, and Michael H. Crispin, "The Media, the Campaign, and the Message," *American Journal of Political Science* 47 (April 2003): 259–273.

59. Ann N. Crigler, Marion R. Just, and Timothy E. Cook, "Local News, Network News and the 1992 Presidential Campaign" (paper presented at the annual meeting of the American Political Science Association, Washington, DC, September 1993), p. 9.

60. Stephen Ansolabehere and Shanto Iyengar, *Going Negative: How Political Advertisements Shrink and Polarize the Electorate* (New York: Free Press, 1995), p. 145.

61. Darrell M. West, *Air Wars: Television Advertising in Election Campaigns, 1952–2004*, 4th ed. (Washington, D.C: CQ Press, 2010), p. 23.

62. Ted Brader, "Striking a Responsive Chord: How Political Ads Motivate and Persuade Voters by Appealing to Emotions," *American Journal of Political Science* 49 (April 2005): 388–405.

63. Darrell M. West, *Air Wars: Television Advertising in Election Campaigns, 1952–2009*, 5th ed. (Washington, D.C.: CQ Press, 2010), pp. 51–52.

64. Darrell M. West, *Air Wars: Television Advertising in Election Campaigns, 1952–2012*, 6th ed. (Washington, D.C.: CQ Press, 2014), p. 70.

65. This theme runs throughout Kathleen Hall Jamieson's *Dirty Politics: Deception, Distraction, and Democracy* (New York: Oxford University Press, 1992). See also John Boiney, "You Can Fool All of the People... Evidence on the Capacity of Political Advertising to Mislead" (paper presented at the annual meeting of the American Political Science Association, Washington, DC, September 1993).

66. West, *Air Wars*, 6th ed., p. 70.

67. Kathleen Hall Jamieson, Paul Waldman, and Susan Sheer, "Eliminate the Negative? Categories of Analysis for Political Advertisements," in *Crowded Airwaves: Campaign Advertising in Elections*, ed. James A. Thurber, Candice J. Nelson, and David A. Dulio (Washington, DC: Brookings Institution Press, 2000), p. 49.

68. David A. Dulio, Candice J. Nelson, and James A. Thurber, "Summary and Conclusions," in Thurber, Nelson, and Dulio, *Crowded Airwaves*, p. 172. Laboratory research found that even "uncivil" exchanges between candidates can be handled by the public. See Deborah Jordan Brooks and John G. Geer, "Beyond Negativity: The Effects of Incivility on the Electorate," *American Journal of Political Science* 51 (January 2007): 1–16.

69. Gregory A. Huber and Kevin Arceneaux, "Identifying the Persuasive Effects of Presidential Advertising," *American Journal of Political Science* 51 (2007): 957–977.

70. Ansolabehere and Iyengar, *Going Negative*, p. 112.

71. West, however, takes issue with the Ansolabehere and Iyengar analysis in *Going Negative*, saying that turnout is more dependent on mistrust than on negativity of ads. See West, *Air Wars*, 5th ed., pp. 71–72.

72. Richard R. Lau and Gerald M. Pomper, "Effectiveness of Negative Campaigning in U.S. Senate Elections," *American Journal of Political Science* 46 (January 2002): 47–66.

73. Richard R. Lau, Lee Sigelman, and Ivy Brown Rovner, "The Effects of Negative Political Campaigns: A Meta-Analytic Reassessment," *Journal of Politics* 69 (November 2007): 1176–1209.

74. Lee Sigelman and Mark Kugler, "Why Is Research on the Effects of Negative Campaigning So Inconclusive? Understanding Citizens' Perceptions of Negativity," *Journal of Politics* 65 (February 2003): 142–160; and Richard R. Lau, Lee Sigelman, and Ivy Brown Rovner, "The Effects of Negative Political Campaigns: A Meta-Analytic Reassessment," *The Journal of Politics* 69 (November 2007): 1176–1209.

75. The information on early campaign websites comes from Jill Zuckerman, "Candidates Spin Web of Support on Cybertrail," *Chicago Tribune*, 3 December 2003, p. 13.

76. Jeffrey Gottfied et al., "The 2016 Presidential Campaign—A News Event That's Hard to Miss," Pew Research Center, 4 February 2016.

77. Tanzina Vega, "Online Data Helping Campaigns Customize Ads," *New York Times*, 21 February 2012, pp. 1–13.

78. https://mobile.twitter.com/realDonaldTrump/tweets, 4 May 2016.

79. https://twitter.com/HillaryClinton?ref_src=twsrc%5Egoogle%7Ctwcamp%5Eserp%7Ctwgr%5Eauthor, 4 May 2016.

80. Michael Barbaro, "Pithy, Mean and Powerful: How Trump Mastered Twitter for the 2016 Race," *New York Times*, 6 October 2015, p. A22.

81. John Herrman, "Donald Trump Finds Support in the Web's Unruly Corners," *New York Times*, 11 April 2016, p. B1.

82. "Capitol Hill Takes the Social Stage," https://captiv8.io/presidential-race.

83. See the website for the American National Election Studies, http://www.electionstudies.org.

84. Michael M. Gant and Norman R. Luttbeg, *American Electoral Behavior* (Itasca, 111.: Peacock, 1991), pp. 63–64.

85. Janet Hook and Monica Langley, "Trump's Biggest Trophy Yet: The Republican Party," *Wall Street Journal*, 5 May 2016, pp. A1 and A6.

86. For a thorough review of studies on campaign effects, see Rian J. Brox and Daron R. Shaw, "Political Parties, American Campaigns, and Effects on Outcomes," in Katz and Crotty, *Handbook of Party Politics*, pp. 146–150.

87. Matthew A. Baum, "Talking the Vote: Why Presidential Candidates Hit the Talk Show Circuit," *American Journal of Political Science* 49 (April 2005): 213–234.

88. Electorates tend to be more engaged by campaigning in "battleground" states. See James G. Gimpel et al., "Battleground States versus Blackout States: The Behavioral Implications of Modern Presidential Campaigns," *Journal of Politics* 69 (August 2007): 786–797.

89. Neil King, Jr., "Map Looks Daunting for the GOP," *Wall Street Journal*, 5 May 2016, p. A4.

90. Chris Ariens, "2016 Debate Ranker So Far: GOP Averaging 15.8 Million Viewers," *TVNewser*, 22 February 2016, http://www.adweek.com/tvnewser/2016-debate-ranker-so-far-gop-debates-averaging-15-8-million-viewers/285264.

91. But for a contrary view, see Nicol C. Rae, "Be Careful What You Wish For: The Rise of Responsible Parties in American National Politics," *Annual Review of Political Science* 10 (2007): 169–191.

Chapter 10

1. Curtis Skinner and Valerie Vande Panne, "Students Across U.S. March over Debt, Free Public College," Reuters, 12 November 2015, http://www.reuters.com/article/us-usa-college-protests-idUSKCN0T116W20151113; Nancy Cook, "Confirmed: Millennials' Top Financial Concern is Student-Loan Debt," *The Atlantic*, 20 June 2015, http://www.theatlantic.com/business/archive/2015/06/millennials-student-loan-debt-money/396275/; and Susan Dynarski, "New Data Gives Clearer Picture of Student Debt," *New York Times*, 10 September, 2015, http://www.nytimes.com/2015/09/11/upshot/new-data-gives-clearer-picture-of-student-debt.html.

2. Kay Lehman Schlozman, Philip Edward Jones, Hye Young You, Traci Burch, Sidney Verba, and Henry E. Brady, "Organizations and the Democratic Representation of Interests," *Perspectives on Politics* 13 (December 2015): 1017–1029.

3. Alexis de Tocqueville, *Democracy in America, 1835–1839,* ed. Richard D. Heffner (New York: Mentor Books, 1956), p. 198.

4. *The Federalist Papers* (New York: Mentor Books, 1961), p. 79.

5. Ibid., p. 78.

6. See Robert A. Dahl, *A Preface to Democratic Theory* (Chicago: University of Chicago Press, 1956), pp. 4–33.

7. Art Swift, "Honesty and Ethics Rating of Clergy Slides to New Low," Gallup Poll, 16 December 2013, http://www.gallup.com/poll/103123/lobbyists-debut-bottom-honesty-ethics-list.aspx.

8. "Lobbying Database," Center for Responsive Politics, http://www.opensecrets.org/lobby/.

9. This discussion follows from Jeffrey M. Berry and Clyde Wilcox, *The Interest Group Society*, 5th ed. (New York: Longman, 2009), pp. 7–8.

10. Megan Wilson, "Poll: Congressional Staffers Find Lobbyist Chats Helpful," *The Hill*, 10 June 2013, http://fhehill.com/business-a-lobbying/304519-poll-congressional-staffers-find-lobbyist-chats-helpful.

11. "Union Members—2015," Bureau of Labor Statistics, 28 January 2016, http://www.bls.gov/news.release/union2.nr0.htm.

12. Juliet Eilperin and Tom Hamburger, "For Obama's Ex-Aides, It's Time to Cash in on Experience," *Washington Post*, 30 May 2013, http://www.washingtonpost.com/politics/for-obamas-ex-aides-its-time-to-cash-in-on-experience/2013/05/30/a649ccde-c867-lle2-9245-773c0123c027_story.html.

13. In political science this view was developed by David B. Truman in *The Governmental Process* (New York: Knopf, 1951).

14. Mitch Smith and Abby Goodnough, "Michigan Officials Defend Handling of Outbreak in Flint," *New York Times*, 9 February 2016; and Michael Wines and John Schwartz, "Holes in Safety Net Let Contaminants in Water," *New York Times*, 9 February 2016.

15. Adversity sometimes discourages the attraction of individuals to interest groups. See Adam Seth Levine, *American Insecurity* (Princeton, N.J.: Princeton University Press, 2015).

16. Robert H. Salisbury, "An Exchange Theory of Interest Groups," *Midwest Journal of Political Science* 13 (February 1969): 1–32.

17. See Mancur Olson, Jr., *The Logic of Collective Action* (New York: Schocken, 1968).

18. Marshall Ganz, *Why David Sometimes Wins* (New York: Oxford University Press, 2009).

19. "Education: Lobbying, 2015," Center for Responsive Politics, https://www.opensecrets.org/industries/lobbying.php?cycle=2016&ind=W04.

20. See David Karpf, *The Move On Effect* (New York: Oxford University Press, 2012).

21. See Olson, *The Logic of Collective Action.*

22. On the underlying motivation to contribute, see Hahrie Hahn, *Moved to Action* (Stanford, Calif.: Stanford University Press, 2009).

23. Beth L. Leech, *Lobbyists at Work* (New York: Apress, 2013), p. 19.

24. See Lee Drutman, *The Business of America is Lobbying* (New York: Oxford University Press, 2015).

25. Bob Herman, "AHIP CEO Karen Ignagni Leaving for EmblemHealth," *Modern Health Care*, 21 May 2015, http://www.modernhealthcare.com/article/20150521/NEWS/150529975.

26. Timothy LaPira and Herschel F. Thomas, "Revolving Door Lobbying and Interest Representation," *Interest Groups and Lobbying* 3 (March 2014): 4–29.

27. Eric Lipton, "Ex Lawmaker Still Working for Old Allies," *New York Times*, 6 August 2011; and Eric Lipton and Ben Protess, "Law Doesn't End Revolving Door on Capitol Hill," *New York Times*, 1 February 2014, http://dealbook.nytimes.com/2014/02/01/law-doesnt-end-revolving-door-on-capitol-hill/?_php=true&_type=blogs&_r=0.

28. Ted Johnson, "MPAA Chairman Chris Dodd's Compensation Was $3.3 Million in 2012," *Variety*, 19 November 2013, http://variety.com/2013/biz/news/chris-dodd-salary-2012-1200837496/.

29. Suzy Khimm, "Transformers," *New Republic*, 24 December 2008, p. 13.

30. Robert G. Kaiser, *Act of Congress* (New York: Knopf, 2013), p. 152.

31. "Statistical Summary of 24-Month Campaign Activity of the 2013–2014 Election Cycle," Federal Election Commission, 3 April 2015, http://www.fec.gov/press/press2015/news_releases/20150403release.shtml.

32. "PAC Contributions to Candidates January 1, 2013 through December 31, 2014," Federal Election Commission, 3 April 2015, http://www.fec.gov/press/summaries/2014/tables/pac/PAC2_2014_24m.pdf.

33. "Top 50 PACs by Contributions to Candidates and Other Committees January 1, 2013–December 31, 2014," Federal Election Commission, 3 April 2015, http://www.fec.gov/press/summaries/2014/tables/pac/PAC4c_2014_24m.pdf.Ibid.

34. Ibid.

35. Rogan Kersh, "To Donate or Not to Donate?" (paper delivered at the annual meeting of the American Political Science Association, Philadelphia, August 2003), p. 2.

36. Michael M. Franz, *Choices and Changes* (Philadelphia: Temple University Press, 2008).

37. One study concludes, "Scholars have struggled to document the impact of campaign contributions, but with inconsistent results." Frank R. Baumgartner, Jeffrey M. Berry, Marie Hojnacki, David C. Kimball, and Beth L. Leech, *Lobbying and Policy Change* (Chicago: University of Chicago Press, 2009), p. 193.

38. Marie Hojnacki and David Kimball, "PAC Contributions and Lobbying Access in Congressional Committees," *Political Research Quarterly* 54 (March 2001): 161–180; John R. Wright, "Contributions, Lobbying, and Committee Voting in the U.S. House of Representatives," *American Political Science Review* 84 (June 1990): 417–438; and Richard L. Hall and Frank W. Wayman, "Buying Time: Money Interests and the Mobilization of Bias in Congressional Committees," *American Political Science Review* 84 (September 1990): 797–820.

39. Baumgartner et al., *Lobbying and Policy Change*, pp. 166–189.

40. Eric Lipton and Liz Moyer, "Hospitality and Gambling Interests Delay Closing of Billion-Dollar Tax Loophole," *New York Times*, 20 December 2015, http://www.nytimes.com/2015/12/21/us/politics/hospitality-and-gambling-interests-delay-closing-of-dollar1-billion-tax-loophole.html.

41. S. Laurel Weldon, *When Protest Makes Policy* (Ann Arbor: University of Michigan Press, 2011), pp. 57–81.

42. Edward T. Walker, "The Uber-ization of Activism," *New York Times*, 6 August 2015, http://www.nytimes.com/2015/08/07/opinion/the-uber-ization-of-activism.html.

43. For a more optimistic assessment of protest politics, see Andrew S. McFarland, *Boycotts and Dixie Chicks* (Boulder, Colo.: Paradigm, 2011).

44. "States, School Districts Help Keep Junk Foods and Sugary Drinks Out of Elementary Schools" Robert Wood Johnson Foundation, 10 June 2013, http://www.rwjf.org/en/library/articles-and-news/2013/06/states--school-districts-help-keep-junk-foods-and-sugary-drinks-.html.

45. Anahad O'Connor, "Coca-Cola Funds Effort to Alter Obesity Battle," *New York Times*, 10 August 2015, http://well.blogs.nytimes.com/2015

/08/09/coca-cola-funds-scientists-who-shift-blame-for-obesity
-away-from-bad-diets/.

46. On competition and cooperation among Washington lobbies, see Thomas T. Holyoke, *Competitive Interests* (Washington, D.C.: Georgetown University Press, 2011).

47. Dara Z. Strolovitch, *Affirmative Advocacy* (Chicago: University of Chicago Press, 2007), p. 181.

48. Kay Lehman Schlozman, Sidney Verba, and Henry E. Brady, *The Unheavenly Chorus* (Princeton, N.J., Princeton University Press 2012). On what an ideal interest group system would look like, see David Lowery et al., "Images of an Unbiased Interest System," *Journal of European Public Policy* 22, no. 8 (2015).

49. Kay Lehman Schlozman, Traci Burch, and Samuel Lampert, "Still an Upper-Class Accent?" (paper presented at the annual meeting of the American Political Science Association, September 2004), pp. 16, 25.

50. See Jeffrey M. Berry with David F. Arons, *A Voice for Nonprofits* (Washington, DC: Brookings Institution, 2003).

51. See Jeffrey M. Berry and Kent E. Portney, "Sustainability and Interest Group Participation in City Politics," *Sustainability* 5 (2013): 2077–2097.

52. See Drutman, *The Business of America is Lobbying*.

53. Shalini Ramachandran et al., "Comcast's Lobbying Machine Faces Test in Washington," *Wall Street Journal*, 22 January 2015, http://www.wsj.com/articles/comcasts-lobbying-machine-faces-test-in-washington-1421983983; and "Comcast Reports 4th Quarter and Year End 2014 Results," http://www.cmcsa.com/releasedetail.cfm?ReleaseID=953074.

54. "Ranked Sectors," Center for Responsive Politics, https://www.opensecrets.org/lobby/top.php?indexType=c&showYear=2015.

55. Alexander Hertel-Fernandez and Theda Skocpol, "How the Right Trounced Liberals in the States," *Democracy* 39 (Winter 2016), http://democracyjournal.org/magazine/39/how-the-right-trounced-liberals-in-the-states/.

56. Anna Palmer and Tony Romm, "Spotify Turns Up Volume in DC," *Politico*, 15 April 2015, http://www.politico.com/story/2015/04/spotify-washington-lobbying-firms-117001.

57. Baumgartner et al., *Lobbying and Policy Change*, pp. 190–214. On the power of the status quo, see Amy McKay, "Negative Lobbying and Policy Outcomes," *American Politics Research* 40 (January 2012): 116–146.

58. Martin Gilens, *Affluence and Influence* (Princeton, N.J.: Princeton University Press, 2012).

Chapter 11

1. Levine, Marianne. "Paul Ryan Prizes Family Time, Opposes Family Leave," Politico.com, 21 October 2015, http://www.politico.com/story/2015/10/paul-ryan-family-leave-speaker-house-215034.

2. Ibid.

3. Amanda Terkel, "Paul Ryan Demands Family Time In His New Job. Many Americans Aren't So Lucky," *Huffington Post*, 21 October 2015.

4. Philip Bump, "The New Congress is 80 Percent White, 80 Percent Male, and 92 Percent Christian," *Washington Post*, 5 January 2015, https://www.washingtonpost.com/news/the-fix/wp/2015/01/05/the-new-congress-is-80-percent-white-80-percent-male-and-92-percent-christian/.

5. See, for example: Christian Grose, *Congress in Black and White: Race and Representation in Washington and at Home* (New York, NY: Cambridge University Press, 2011); Robert Preuhs, "Descriptive Representation as a Mechanism to Mitigate Policy Backlash: Latino Incorporation and Welfare Policy in the American States," *Political Research Quarterly* 60 no. 2 (2007): 277–292; and Katherine Tate, *Black Faces in the Mirror: African Americans and Their Representatives in the U.S. Congress* (Princeton: Princeton University Press, 2004).

6. Quoted in Susan Carroll, "Representing Women: Congresswomen's Perceptions of their Representational Roles," in *Women Transforming Congress*, ed. Cindy Simon Rosenthal (Norman, OK: University of Oklahoma Press, 2003), pp. 50–68.

7. Richard Fox and Jennifer Lawless, "Gendered Perceptions and Political Candidacies: A Central Barrier to Women's Equality in Electoral Politics," *American Journal of Political Science* 55, no. 1 (2011): 59–73.

8. Jennifer Lawless and Richard Fox, *Running From Office: Why Young Americans Are Turned Off to Politics* (New York: Oxford University Press, 2015).

9. Monika McDermott and David Jones, "Do Public Evaluations of Congress Matter? Retrospective Voting in Congressional Elections," *American Politics Research* 31, no. 2 (2003): 155–177.

10. Harold W. Stanley and Richard G. Niemi (eds.), *Vital Statistics on American Politics, 2011–2012* (Washington, DC: CQ Press, 2011), pp. 46–47.

11. For more on public opinion about Congress, see John Hibbing and Elizabeth Theiss-Morse, *Congress as Public Enemy: Public Attitudes toward American Political Institutions* (Cambridge: Cambridge University Press, 1995); John Hibbing and Elizabeth Theiss-Morse, *Stealth Democracy: Americans' Beliefs about How Government Should Work* (Cambridge: Cambridge University Press, 2002); and David Jones and Monika McDermott, *Americans, Congress, and Democratic Responsiveness* (Ann Arbor: University of Michigan Press, 2010).

12. Alan Abramowitz, Brad Alexander, and Matthew Gunning, "Incumbency, Redistricting, and the Decline of Competition in U.S. House Elections," *Journal of Politics* 68 (February 2006): 75–88.

13. Gary W. Cox and Jonathan N. Katz, *Elbridge Gerry's Salamander* (Cambridge: Cambridge University Press, 2002).

14. Micah Altman, Karin MacDonald, and Michael McDonald, "Pushbutton Gerrymanders? How Computing Has Changed Redistricting," in *Party Lines*, ed. Thomas E. Mann and Bruce E. Cain (Washington, D.C.: Brookings Institution, 2005), pp. 51–66; and Mark Monmonier, *Bushmanders and Bullwinkles* (Chicago: University of Chicago Press, 2001).

15. Steven Yaccino, "Illinois Redistricting Forces Republican Face-Off," *New York Times*, 21 September 2011, http://thecaucus.blogs.nytimes.com/2011/09/21/illinois-redistricting-forces-republican-face-off/.

16. Thomas E. Mann, "Polarizing the House of Representatives: How Much Does Gerrymandering Matter?" in *Red and Blue Nation*, ed. Pietro S. Nivola and David W. Brady (Washington, DC: Brookings Institution and Hoover Institution, 2006), pp. 263–283; and Sean Theriault, *Party Polarization in Congress* (New York: Cambridge University Press, 2011). For a contrasting view, see Nolan McCarty, Keith Poole, and Howard Rosenthal, "Does Gerrymandering Cause Polarization?" *American Journal of Political Science* 53, no. 3 (2009): 666–680.

17. Sean Theriault and David Rhode, "The Gingrich Senators and Party Polarization in the U.S. Senate," *Journal of Politics* 73, no. 4 (2011): 1011–1024. Note that this article claims that it is Senate *Republicans* who had served in the House who have been the main polarizing agent in the Senate.

18. Matthew E. Glassman, "Franking Privilege: Mass Mailings, and Mass Communication in the House, 1997–2014," CRS Report, 6 May 2015.

19. House Franking manual at: http://cha.house.gov/franking-commission/franking-information.

20. Jacob R. Straus and Matthew E. Glassman, "Social Media in the House of Representatives: Frequently Asked Questions," Congressional Research Service, 22 April 2015, https://www.fas.org/sgp/crs/misc/R43477.pdf.

21. Data on social media accounts in Congress are available at GovSM.com.

22. Sam Sanders, "Twitter Has A 136-Page Handbook for Politicians and It's Hilarious," 30 September 2015, http://www.npr.org/sections/itsallpolitics/2015/09/30/443128829/twitter-has-a-136-page-handbook-for-politicians-140-character-tweets.

23. Morris P. Fiorina, as cited in Roger H. Davidson and Walter J. Oleszek, *Congress and Its Members*, 11th ed. (Washington, D.C.: CQ Press, 2008), p. 144.

24. Center for Responsive Politics, "Incumbent Advantage: 2012 Election Cycle," http:// http://www.opensecrets.org/bigpicture/incumbs.php.

25. Gary Jacobson, *The Politics of Congressional Elections*, 8th ed. (Pearson, 2013).

26. Katie Long, "Most Members of Congress are Millionaires," slate.com, 9 January 2014.

27. Emily Heil, "Senate Women's Restroom Expanding to Accommodate Historic Numbers," *Washington Post*, 12 June 2013.

28. "Faith on the Hill," Pew Research Center, 5 January 2015, http:// www.pewforum.org/2015/01/05/faith-on-the-hill/.

29. See Beth Reingold, *Representing Women* (Chapel Hill, N.C.: University of North Carolina Press, 2000); and Michele L. Swers, *The Difference Women Make* (Chicago: University of Chicago Press, 2002).

30. Hanna Fenichel Ptikin, *The Concept of Representation* (Berkeley: University of California Press, 1967), pp. 60–91; and Jane Mansbridge, "Should Blacks Represent Blacks and Women Represent Women? A Contingent 'Yes,'" *Journal of Politics* 61 (1999): 628–657.

31. Hunter Schwartz, "Congress Decides to Get Serious about Tracking Police Shootings," *Washington Post*, 11 December 2014.

32. *Shaw v. Reno*, 509 U.S. 630 (1993).

33. *Bush v. Vera*, 116 S. Ct. 1941 (1996).

34. *Easley v.Cromartie*, 532 U.S. 234 (2001).

35. Ana Gonzalez-Barrera and Jeffery Passel, "An Awakened Giant: The Hispanic Electorate Is Likely to Double by 2013," *Pew Hispanic Center Report*, 14 November 2012.

36. Taeku Lee, "2014 Midterms: Patterns and Paradoxes in Voting Among Asian Americans," http://www.brookings.edu/blogs/fixgov/posts /2014/10/29-2014-midterms-asian-american-voting-patterns-lee.

37. See David Lublin, *The Paradox of Representation* (Princeton, N.J.: Princeton University Press, 1997). See, *contra*, Kenneth W. Shotts, "Does Racial Redistricting Cause Conservative Policy Outcomes?" *Journal of Politics* 65 (2003): 216–226.

38. See Frank R. Baumgartner et al., *Advocacy and Policy Change* (Chicago: University of Chicago Press, 2009).

39. Lisa Mascaro, "House Votes to Block Syrian Refugees Despite White House Veto Threat," *Los Angeles Times*, 19 November 2015, http://www.latimes.com/nation/politics/la-na-congress-refugees -20151119-story.html.

40. David Shribman, "Canada's Top Envoy to Washington Cuts Unusually Wide Swath," *Wall Street Journal*, 29 July 1985, p. 1.

41. Woodrow Wilson, *Congressional Government* (Boston: Houghton Mifflin, 1885), p. 79.

42. David Fahrenthold and Michelle Boorstein, "Rep. Peter King's Muslim Hearings: A Key Moment in an Angry Conversation," *Washington Post*, 9 March 2011, http://www.washingtonpost.com /wp-dyn/content/article/2011/03/09/AR2011030902061.html? sid=ST2011031002070.

43. Alessandra Stanely, "Terror Hearing Puts Lawmakers in Harsh Light," *New York Times*, 10 March, 2011, http://www.nytimes.com /2011/03/ 11/arts/television/at-muslim-hearing-finger-pointing -andtears. html?_r= 1 &ref=politics.

44. Greg Miller, Adam Goldman, and Julie Tate, "Senate Report on CIA Programs Details Brutality, Dishonesty," *Washington Post*, 9 December 2014, https://www.washingtonpost.com/world /national-security/senate-report-on-cia-program-details-brutality -dishonesty/2014/12/09/1075c726-7f0e-11e4-9f38-95a187e4c1f7 _story.html.

45. See Steven S. Smith, *Party Influence in Congress* (New York: Cambridge University Press, 2007).

46. Gary W. Cox and Mathew D. McCubbins, *Legislative Leviathan* (Berkeley: University of California Press, 1993); and Keith Krehbiel, *Information and Legislative Organization* (Ann Arbor: University of Michigan Press, 1992).

47. Matthew N. Green, *The Speaker of the House* (New Haven, Conn.: Yale University Press, 2010).

48. Jonathan Franzen, "The Listener," *New Yorker*, 6 October 2003, p. 85.

49. Robert Draper, "How Kevin McCarthy Wrangles the Tea Party in Washington," *New York Times*, 17 July 2011.

50. Charles O. Jones, *The United States Congress* (Homewood, 111.: Dorsey Press, 1982), p. 322.

51. Gregory Kroger, *Filibustering: A Political History of Obstruction in the House and Senate* (Chicago: Chicago University Press, 2010), p. 133.

52. Norman Ornstein, "Our Broken Senate," *The American*, May/April 2008, http://www.american.com/archive/2008/march-april-magazine -contents/our-broken-senate; and Barbara Sinclair, "The 60 Vote Senate," in *U.S. Senate Exceptionalism*, ed. Bruce Oppenheimer (Columbus: Ohio State University Press, 2002), pp. 241–261.

53. Barbara Sinclair, *Unorthodox Lawmaking: New Legislative Processes in the U.S. Congress* (Washington, D.C.: CQ Press, 2012); "Senate Action on Cloture Motions," http://www.senate.gov/pagelayout /reference/cloture_motions/clotureCounts.htm; and "Milestone: Most Closed Congress in History," http://democrats.rules.house .gov/press-release/milestone-most-closed-congress-us-history.

54. Sinclair, *Unorthodox Lawmaking*.

55. Gary W. Cox and Mathew D. McCubbins, *Setting the Agenda: Responsible Party Government in the U.S. House of Representatives* (New York: Cambridge University Press, 2005); and Smith, *Party Influence in Congress*.

56. These ideologies affect policy outcomes as well as the structure of the institution itself. See Nelson Polsby, *How Congress Evolves: Social Bases of Institutional Change* (New York: Oxford University Press, 2004).

57. See, for example, Sean Theriault, *Party Polarization in Congress* (New York: Cambridge University Press, 2008); Sean Theriault, *The Gingrich Senators* (New York: Oxford University Press, 2013); Thomas Mann and Norman Ornstein, *It's Even Worse than It Looks* (New York: Basic Books, 2013); Frances Lee, *Beyond Ideology: Politics, Principles, and Partisanship in the U.S. Senate* (Chicago: University of Chicago Press, 2009); and Hans Noel, *Political Ideologies and Political Parties in America* (New York: Cambridge University Press, 2014).

58. James Sterling Young, *The Washington Community* (New York: Harcourt, Brace, 1964).

59. Rebecca Kaplan, "Obama and Congress Look for Common Goals," CBSNews.com, 13 January 2015, http://www.cbsnews.com/news /obama-and-congress-look-for-common-goals/.

60. Sinclair, *Unorthodox Lawmaking*.

61. Joshua D. Clinton, "Representation in Congress: Constituents and Roll Calls in the 106th House," *Journal of Politics* 68 (May 2006): 397–409.

62. See John Cochran, "The Influence Implosion," *CQ Weekly*, 16 January 2006, p. 174; and Susan Ferrechio, "2005 Legislative Summary: House Ethics Investigations," *CQ Weekly*, 2 January 2006, p. 31.

63. Barry C. Burden, *The Personal Roots of Representation* (Princeton, N.J.: Princeton University Press, 2007).

64. "Life in Congress: The Member Perspective," Congressional Management Foundation Report, 11 March 2013, http://www .congressfoundation.org/projects/life-in-congress/the-member -perspective.

65. Louis I. Bredvold and Ralph G. Ross (eds.), *The Philosophy of Edmund Burke* (Ann Arbor: University of Michigan Press, 1960), p. 148.

66. "In Congress, Voting Your Own Way and Paying for It," *National Public Radio*, 18 July 2011, http://www.npr.org/2011/07/18/ 138473342 /in-congress-voting-your-own-way-and-paying-for-it.

67. Warren E. Miller and Donald E. Stokes, "Constituency Influence in Congress," *American Political Science Review* 57 (March 1963): 45–57.

68. Erin Kelly, "Some Want Earmarks Back to Help Congress Pass Bills," *USA Today*, 29 October 2013.

69. "Possible Negatives for Candidates: Vote for Bank Bailout, Palin Support," Pew Center for People and the Press, 6 October 2010, http://www.people-press.org/2010/10/06/possible-negatives -forcandi-dates-vote-for-bank-bailout-palin-support/.

70. Shanto Iyengar, Gaurav Sood, and Yphtach Lelkes, "Affect, Not Ideology: A Social Identity Perspective on Polarization," *Public Opinion Quarterly* 76, no. 3 (2012): 405–431.

/regwatch/labor/188427-under-perez-labor-department-produces
-a-blizzard-of-new-rules.

33. Joseph B. White, "Self-Driving Cars Spur New Guidelines," *Wall Street Journal*, 31 May 2013.

34. David Vogel, *The Politics of Precaution* (Princeton. N.J.: Princeton University Press, 2012).

35. Ron Nixon, "American Catfish Industry Could Suffer Under the Stricter Standards It Sought Out," *New York Times*, 21 March 2015, http://www.nytimes.com/2015/03/21/us/catfish-farmers-seeking
-regulation-to-fight-foreign-competition-face-higher-bills.html.

36. Maximus, "Child Support," http://www.maximus.com/services
/children-families/child-support.

37. Donald F. Kettl, "The Global Revolution in Public Management: Driving Themes, Missing Links," *Journal of Policy Analysis and Management* 16 (1997): 448.

38. Donald P. Moynihan and Stéphane Lavertu, "Does Involvement in Performance Management Routines Encourage Performance Information Use? Evaluating GPRA and PART," *Public Administration Review* 72 (July/August 2012): 592–602.

39. Ed Gerrish, "The Impact of Performance Management on Performance in Public Organizations: A Meta-Analysis," *Public Administration Review* 76 (January/February 2016): 48–66.

40. Ron Haskins and Greg Margolis, *Show Me the Evidence* (Washington, DC: Brookings Institution, 2015).

Chapter 14

1. Felix Frankfurter and James M. Landis, *The Business of the Supreme Court* (New York: Macmillan, 1928), pp. 5–14; and Julius Goebel, Jr., *The History of the Supreme Court of the United States, vol. 1, Antecedents and Beginnings to 1801* (New York: Macmillan, 1971).

2. Maeva Marcus (ed.), *The Documentary History of the Supreme Court of the United States, 1789–1800, vol. 3, The Justices on Circuit, 1795–1800* (New York: Columbia University Press, 1990).

3. Robert G. McCloskey, *The United States Supreme Court* (Chicago: University of Chicago Press, 1960), p. 31.

4. Cliff Sloan and David McKean, *The Great Decision: Jefferson, Adams, Marshall, and the Battle for the Supreme Court* (New York: Public Affairs, 2009).

5. *Marbury* v. *Madison*, 1 Cranch 137 at 177, 178 (1803).

6. Interestingly, the term judicial review dates only to 1910; it was apparently unknown to Marshall and his contemporaries. Robert Lowry Clinton, *Marbury* v. *Madison and Judicial Review* (Lawrence: University Press of Kansas, 1989), p. 7.

7. "Acts of Congress Held Unconstitutional in Whole or in Part by the Supreme Court of the United States," https://www.congress
.gov/content/conan/pdf/GPO-CONAN-REV-2014-11.pdf.

8. "Supreme Court Decisions Overruled by Subsequent Decision," https://www.congress.gov/content/conan/pdf/GPO-CONAN-REV
-2014-13.pdf.

9. *Martin* v. *Hunter's Lessee*, 1 Wheat. 304 (1819).

10. Epstein et al., *The Supreme Court Compendium*, 5th ed. (Washington, DC: CQ Press, 2011), Table 2-16.

11. Garry Wills, *Explaining America: The Federalist* (Garden City, N.Y.: Doubleday, 1981), pp. 127–136.

12. Robert LaFountain, et al., *Examining the Work of State Courts: An Overview of 2013 State Court Caseloads* (National Center for State Courts, 2015); John G. Roberts, Jr., "2015 Year-End Report on the Federal Judiciary," http://www.supremecourt.gov/publicinfo/year
-end/2015year-endreport.pdf (excludes bankruptcy cases).

13. William P. Marshall, "Federalization: A Critical Overview," *DePaul Law Review* 44 (1995): 722–723.

14. Chris Isidore, "Justice Scalia's Death Prompts Dow Chemical to Price-Fixing Case," CNN Money, 26 February 2016, http://money
.cnn.com/2016/02/26/news/companies/justice-scalia-death-dow
-chemical/.

15. Charles Alan Wright, *Handbook on the Law of Federal Courts*, 3rd ed. (St. Paul, Minn.: West, 1976), p. 7.

16. *Judicial Business of the United States Courts, 2015*, http://
www.uscourts.gov/statistics-reports/judicial-business-2015.

17. *Appointments of Magistrate Judges*, http://www.uscourts.gov/statistics
-reports/appointments-magistrate-judges-judicial-business-2014.

18. See note 16.

19. Linda Greenhouse, "Precedent for Lower Courts: Tyrant or Teacher?" *New York Times*, 29 January 1988, p. B7.

20. *Texas* v. *Johnson*, 491 U.S. 397 (1989); and *United States* v. *Eichmann*, 496 U.S. 310 (1990).

21. *Regents of the University of California* v. *Bakke*, 438 U.S. 265 (1978).

22. *Grutter* v. *Bollinger*, 539 U.S. 244 (2003); and *Gratz* v. *Bollinger*, 539 U.S. 306 (2003).

23. *Schuette* v. *Coalition to Defend Affirmative Action*, 572 U.S. __(2014).

24. "Reading Petitions Is for Clerks Only at High Court Now," *Wall Street Journal*, 11 October 1990, p. B7.

25. H. W. Perry, Jr., *Deciding to Decide: Agenda Setting in the United States Supreme Court* (Cambridge, Mass.: Harvard University Press, 1991); and Linda Greenhouse, "Justice Delayed: Agreeing Not to Agree," *New York Times*, 17 March 1996, sec. 4, p. 1.

26. Adam Liptak, "Friend of the Corporation," *New York Times*, 5 May 2013, p. BU1; and Jeffrey Rosen, "Supreme Court Inc.: How the Nation's Highest Court Has Come to Side with Business," *New York Times Magazine*, 16 March 2008, pp. 38 et seq.

27. Perry, *Deciding to Decide*; and Gregory A. Caldiera and John R. Wright, "The Discuss List: Agenda Building in the Supreme Court," *Law and Society Review* 24 (1990): 807.

28. Doris M. Provine, *Case Selection in the United States Supreme Court* (Chicago: University of Chicago Press, 1980), pp. 74–102.

29. Perry, *Deciding to Decide*, p. 286.

30. Justice Anthony M. Kennedy, quoted in Adam Liptak, "No Vote-Trading Here," *New York Times: Week in Review*, 16 May 2010, p. 4.

31. Kevin T. McGuire, "Repeat Players in the Supreme Court: The Role of Experienced Lawyers in Litigation Success," *Journal of Politics* 57 (1995): 187–196.

32. William H. Rehnquist, "Remarks of the Chief Justice: My Life in the Law Series," *Duke Law Journal* 52 (2003): 787–805.

33. "Rising Fixed Opinions," *New York Times*, 22 February 1988, p. 14. See also Linda Greenhouse, "At the Bar," *New York Times*, 28 July 1989, p. 21.

34. Jeffrey A. Segal and Harold J. Spaeth, *The Supreme Court and the Attitudinal Model* (Cambridge: Cambridge University Press, 1993).

35. Stefanie A. Lindquist and Frank B. Cross, *Measuring Judicial Activism* (New York: Oxford University Press, 2009), pp. 1–28.

36. Stuart Taylor, Jr., "Lifting of Secrecy Reveals Earthy Side of Justices," *New York Times*, 22 February 1988, p. A16.

37. Richard A. Posner, "The Courthouse Mice," *New Republic*, 12 June 2006, http://tnr.com/article/the-courthouse-mice.

38. Thomas G. Walker, Lee Epstein, and William J. Dixon, "On the Mysterious Demise of Consensual Norms in the United States Supreme Court," *Journal of Politics* 50 (1988): 361–389.

39. Linda Greenhouse, "Roberts Is at Court's Helm, but He Isn't Yet in Control," *New York Times*, 2 July 2006, sec. 1, p. 1. See also John P. Kelsh, "The Opinion Delivery Practices of the United States Supreme Court, 1790–1945," *Washington University Law Quarterly* 77 (1999): 137–181. For more on the Roberts Court, see Linda Greenhouse, "Oral Dissents Give Ginsberg New Voice," *New York Times*, 31 May 2007, p. A1; and Jeffrey Toobin, "Five to Four," *New Yorker*, 25 June 2007, pp. 35–37.

40. Stephen L. Wasby, *The Supreme Court in the Federal Judicial System*, 3rd ed. (Chicago: Nelson-Hall, 1988), p. 241.

41. Greenhouse, "At the Bar," p. 21.

42. "Survey of Judicial Salaries," *National Center for State Courts* 40, no. 2, (1 July 2015), http://www.ncsc.org/FlashMicrosites/
JudicialSalaryReview/2016/resources/CurrentJudicialSalaries.pdf.

43. M. P. McQueen, "The Big Boys Make $10 Million—How About You?" *The American Lawyer* 37, no. 1 (1 January 2015): 52; Elie Mystal, "Now That There Aren't As Many Law Students, Hiring Has Stabilized," *Above the Law*, 21 April 2016, http://abovethelaw.com

/2016/04/now-that-there-arent-as-many-law-students-hiring
-has-stabilized-nalp-2016/.

44. Supreme Court Justice Antonin Scalia, commenting on the state of the legal profession at the 2012 Midyear Meeting of the American Bar Association in New Orleans, http://abovethelaw.com/2012/02 /quotes-of-the-day-mo-superior-legal-minds-mo-problems/.

45. Lawrence Baum, *American Courts: Process and Policy*, 3rd ed. (Boston: Houghton Mifflin, 1994), pp. 114–129.

46. *Caperton* v. *A. T. Massey Coal Co.*, 556 U.S. 868 (2009).

47. Wikipedia, "List of Federal Judges Appointed by Barack Obama," http://en.wikipedia.org/wiki/List_of_federal_judges_appointed_by _Barack_Obama.

48. Tajuana D. Massie, Thomas G. Hansford, and David R. Songer, "The Timing of Presidential Nominations to Lower Federal Courts," *Political Research Quarterly* 57 (2004): 145–154.

49. Sheldon Goldman et al., "Picking Judges in a Time of Turmoil: W. Bush's Judiciary During the 109th Congress," *Judicature* 90 (May–June 2007): 252–283.

50. Eliot Slotnick, Sara Schiavoni, and Sheldon Goldman. "Writing the Book of Judges: Part 2," *Journal of Law and Courts* 4, no. 1, (Spring 2016): 187–242.

51. Paul Barrett, "More Minorities, Women Named to U.S. Courts," *Wall Street Journal*, 23 December 1993, p. B1; and Sheldon Goldman and Eliot Slotnick, "Clinton's Second Term Judiciary: Picking Judges under Fire," *Judicature* 92 (May-June 1999): 264–284.

52. Kenneth L. Manning and Robert A. Carp, "The Decision-Making Ideology of George W. Bush's Judicial Appointees: An Update" (paper presented at the annual meeting of the American Political Science Association, Chicago, 2–5 September 2004).

53. Charlie Savage and Raymond Hernandez, "Filibuster by Senate Republicans Blocks Confirmation of Judicial Nominee," *New York Times*, 7 December 2011, p. A16, http://www.nytimes.com/2011/12 /07/us/senate-gop-blocks-confirmation-of-caitlin-halligan-as-judg -e.html; and Joe Palazzolo, "With Rose Confirmation, Obama Sets a Record," The Wall Street Journal Law Blog, 11 September 2012, http://blogs.wsj.com/law/2012/09/11/with-rose-confirmation -obama-sets-record

54. Wasby, *Supreme Court*, pp. 107–110.

55. Jeffrey Toobin, *The Nine: Inside the Secret World of the Supreme Court* (New York: Doubleday, 2007), p. 269.

56. State News Service, "Statement of H. Thomas Wells Jr., President, American Bar Association re: American Bar Association Standing Committee on Federal Judiciary," 17 March 2009.

57. Sheldon Goldman. "Obama and the Federal Judiciary: Great Expectations but Will He Have a Dickens of a Time Living up to Them?" *The Forum* 7.1 (2010), http://works.bepress.com/ sheldon_goldman/l.

58. Peter G. Fish, "John J. Parker," in *Dictionary of American Biography*, supp. 6, 1956–1980 (New York: Scribner's, 1980), p. 494.

59. "Supreme Court Nominations, Present–1789," http://www.senate .gov/pagelayout/reference/nominations/Nominations.htm.

60. "CRS Report for Congress: Supreme Court Nominations Not Filled," p. 7, 9 January 2008, http://www.fas.org/sgp/crs/misc/RL31171.pdf.

61. "Supreme Court Nominee Sonia Sotomayor's Speech at Berkeley Law in 2001," *Berkeley La Raza Law Journal* (2002), http://law.berke -ley.edu/4982.htm.

62. Elena Kagan, "Confirmation Messes: Old and New," *The University of Chicago Law Review* 62, no. 2 (Spring 1995): 919–942, http:// www.scotusblog.com/wp-content/uploads/2010/03/Confirmation -Messes.pdf.

63. "Transcript: Kagan's Opening Statement," http://rn.npr.org/news /front/128171860?page=3.

64. *Brown* v. *Board of Education II*, 349 U.S.294 (1955).

65. Charles A. Johnson and Bradley C. Canon, *Judicial Policies: Imple- mentation and Impact* (Washington, DC: CQ Press, 1984).

66. *Whole Woman's Health* v. *Hellerstedt*, 579 U.S. ___ (2016).

67. Alexander M. Bickel, *The Least Dangerous Branch* (Indianapolis, Ind.: Bobbs-Merrill, 1962); and Robert A. Dahl, "Decision-Making

in a Democracy: The Supreme Court as a National Policy-Maker," *Journal of Public Law* 6 (1962): 279.

68. William Mishler and Reginald S. Sheehan, "The Supreme Court as a Countermajoritarian Institution? The Impact of Public Opinion on Supreme Court Decisions," *American Political Science Review* 87 (1993): 87–101.

69. Barry Friedman, *The Will of the People* (New York: Farrar, Straus and Giroux, 2009).

70. *Engel* v. *Vitale*, 367 U.S. 643 (1961).

71. James L. Gibson and Gregory A. Caldiera, "Knowing about Courts" (paper presented at the Second Annual Conference on Empirical Legal Studies, 20 June 2007), http://ssrn.com/abstract=956562.

72. Gallup Poll, "High Court to Start Term with Near Decade-High Approval, Supreme Court Trends," http://www.gallup.com/poll /4732/supreme-court.aspxhttp://gallup.com/poll/122858/High -Court-Start-Term-Near-Decade-High-Approval.aspx?CSTS=alert. Pew Research Center, "Negative Views of Supreme Court at Record High, Driven by Republican Dissatisfaction," 29 Jul 2015, http:// www.people-press.org/2015/07/29/negative-views-of-supreme -court-at-record-high-driven-by-republican-dissatisfaction/.

73. *Kelo* v. *City of New London*, 545 U.S. 469 (2005).

74. *Obergefell* v. *Hodges*, 576 U.S. ___ (2015).

75. G. Alan Tarr and M. C. Porter, *State Supreme Courts in State and Nation* (New Haven, Conn.: Yale University Press, 1988), pp. 206–209.

76. Kermit L. Hall, "The Canon of American Constitutional History in Comparative Perspective" (keynote address to the Supreme Court Historical Society, Washington, DC, 16 February 2001).

Chapter 15

1. "San Bernardino Shooting Updates," *Los Angeles Times*, 9 December 2015, http://www.latimes.com/local/lanow/la-me-ln-san-bernardino -shooting-live-updates-htmlstory.html.

2. Kevin Johnson, Jon Swartz, and Marco della Cava, "FBI Hacks into Terrorist's iPhone without Apple," *USA Today*, 29 March 2016, http://www.usatoday.com/story/news/nation/2016/03/28/apple -justice-department-farook/82354040/.

3. Ibid.

4. Emily Zackin, *Looking for Rights in All the Wrong Places: Why State Constitutions Contain America's Positive Rights* (Princeton, NJ: Princeton University Press, 2013).

5. Learned Hand, *The Bill of Rights* (Boston: Atheneum, 1958), p. 1.

6. Richard E. Berg-Andersson, "Of Liberties, Rights and Powers (Part One): Just How Far Is Too Far–Both Governments and Persons?" Green Papers Commentary, 27 April 2006, http://www.thegreenpapers .com/PCom/?20060427-0.

7. *Barron* v. *Baltimore*, 32 U.S. (7 Pet.) 243 (1833).

8. *Chicago B&Q Railroad* v. *Chicago*, 166 U.S. 226 (1897).

9. *Palko* v. *Connecticut*, 302 U.S. 319 (1937).

10. *Duncan* v. *Louisiana*, 391 U.S. 145 (1968).

11. Leonard W. Levy, *The Establishment Clause: Religion and the First Amendment* (New York: Macmillan, 1986); Leo Pfeffer, *Church, State, and Freedom* (Boston: Beacon Press, 1953); and Leonard W. Levy, "The Original Meaning of the Establishment Clause of the First Amendment," in *Religion and the State*, ed. James E. Wood, Jr. (Waco, Tex.: Baylor University Press, 1985), pp. 43–83.

12. Gallup, "Seven in 10 Americans are Very or Moderately Religious," 4 December 2012; Pew Research Global Attitudes Project, "The American-Western European Values Gap," 29 February 2012; and Pew Research Global Attitudes Project, "Worldwide, Many See Belief in God as Essential to Morality," 13 March 2014.

13. *Utah Highway Patrol Association* v. *American Atheists, Inc.*, 565 U.S. ___(2011) (Thomas, J. dissenting from a denial of certiorari).

14. *Reynolds* v. *United States*, 98 U.S. 145 (1879).

15. *Everson* v. *Board of Education*, 330 U.S. 1 (1947).

16. *Board of Education* v. *Allen*, 392 U.S. 236 (1968).

17. *Lemon* v. *Kurtzman*, 403 U.S. 602 (1971).
18. *Agostini* v. *Felton*, 96 U.S. 552 (1997).
19. *Zelman* v. *Simmons-Harris*, 536 U.S. 639 (2002).
20. *Lynch* v. *Donnelly*, 465 U.S. 668 (1984).
21. *Van Orden* v. *Perry*, 545 U.S. 677 (2005).
22. *McCreary County* v. *ACLU of Kentucky*, 545 U.S. 844 (2005).
23. *Solazar* v. *Buono*, 559 U.S. 700 (2010).
24. *Engle* v. *Vitale*, 370 U.S. 421 (1962).
25. *Lee* v. *Weisman*, 505 U.S. 577 (1992).
26. *Good News Club* v. *Milford Central School*, 533 U.S. 98 (2001).
27. *Town of Greece* v. *Galloway*, 572 U.S. ___ (2014).
28. Michael W. McConnell, "The Origins and Historical Understanding of the Free Exercise of Religion," *Harvard Law Review* 103 (1990): 1409.
29. *Sherbert* v. *Verner*, 374 U.S. 398 (1963).
30. Adam Winkler, "Fatal in Theory and Strict in Fact: An Empirical Analysis of Strict Scrutiny in the Federal Courts," *Vanderbilt Law Review* 59 (2006): 793.
31. McConnell, "Origins and Historical Understanding."
32. *Employment Division* v. *Smith*, 494 U.S. 872 (1990).
33. *Burwell* v. *Hobby Lobby Stores*, 573 U.S. ___ (2014).
34. Laurence Tribe, *Treatise on American Constitutional Law*, 2nd ed. (St. Paul, Minn.: West, 1988), p. 566.
35. Zechariah Chafee, *Free Speech in the United States* (Cambridge, Mass.: Harvard University Press, 1941).
36. Leonard W. Levy, *The Emergence of a Free Press* (New York: Oxford University Press, 1985).
37. *Brandenburg* v. *Ohio*, 395 U.S. 444 (1969).
38. *Schenck* v. *United States*, 249 U.S. 47 (1919).
39. *Gitlow* v. *New York*, 268 U.S. 652 (1925).
40. *Dennis* v. *United States*, 341 U.S. 494 (1951).
41. *Brandenburg* v. *Ohio*, 395 U.S. 444 (1969).
42. Anthony Lewis, *Freedom for the Thought That We Hate: A Biography of the First Amendment* (New York: Basic Books, 2008).
43. *Tinker* v. *Des Moines Independent County School District*, 393 U.S. 503 (1969).
44. Justin Jouvenal, "A Facebook Court Battle: Is 'Liking' Something Protected Free Speech?" *New York Times*, 8 August 2012; and Justin Jouvenal, "Facebook 'Liking' is Protected Free Speech, Federal Court Says," *Washington Post*, 18 September 2013.
45. Adam Bonica, Nolan McCarty, Keith T. Poole, and Howard Rosenthal, "Why Hasn't Democracy Slowed Rising Inequality?" *Journal of Economic Perspectives* 27, no. 3 (2013): 103–124.
46. *Citizens United* v. *Federal Election Commission*, 558 U.S. ___ (2010); and *McCutcheon* v. *Federal Election Commission*, 572 U.S. ___ (2014).
47. Adam Liptak, "Supreme Court Strikes Down Overall Political Donation Cap," *New York Times*, 2 April 2014.
48. *Chaplinsky* v. *New Hampshire*, 315 U.S. 568 (1942).
49. *Terminiello* v. *Chicago*, 337 U.S. 1 (1949).
50. *Cohen* v. *California*, 403 U.S. 15 (1971).
51. *Snyder* v. *Phelps*, 562 U.S. ___ (2011).
52. *Near* v. *Minnesota*, 283 U.S. 697 (1931). For a detailed account of *Near*, see Fred W. Friendly, *Minnesota Rag* (New York: Random House, 1981).
53. *New York Times* v. *United States*, 403 U.S. 713 (1971).
54. *Bartnicki* v. *Hopper*, 532 U.S. 514 (2001).
55. Chris Strohm and Del Quentin Wilber, "Pentagon Says Snowden Took Most U.S. Secrets Ever," *Bloomberg News*, 9 January 2014, http://www.bloomberg.com/news/articles/2014-01-10/pentagon-says-snowden-took-most-u-s-secrets-ever-rogers; and Ashby Jones, "Pentagon Papers II? On WikiLeaks and the First Amendment," 26 July 2010, http://blogs.wsj.com/law/2010/07/26/pentagon-papers-ii-on-wikileaks-and-the-first-amendment/.
56. *Branzburg* v. *Hayes*, 408 U.S. 665 (1972).
57. *Hazelwood School District* v. *Kuhlmeier*, 484 U.S. 260 (1988).
58. *Morse* v. *Frederick*, 551 U.S. 393 (2007).
59. *New York Times* v. *Sullivan*, 376 U.S. 254 (1964).
60. *Curtis Publishing Company* v. *Butts*, 388 U.S. 130 (1967); and *Associated Press* v. *Walker*, 398 U.S. 28 (1967).

61. *United States* v. *Cruikshank*, 92 U.S. 542 (1876); *De Jonge* v. *Oregon*, 299 U.S. 353 (1937); and *Constitution of the United States of America: Annotated and Interpreted* (Washington, DC: U.S. Government Printing Office, 1973), p. 1031.
62. Liane Hansen, "Voices in the News This Week," *NPR Weekend Edition*, 28 October 2001 (NEXIS transcript); and Dan Eggen, "Tough Anti-Terror Campaign Pledged: Ashcroft Tells Mayors He Will Use New Law to Fullest Extent," *Washington Post*, 26 October 2001, p. Al.
63. Matt Apuzzo and Joseph Goldstein, "New York Drops Unit That Spied on Muslims," *New York Times*, 15 April 2014, www.nytimes.com/2014/04/16/nyregion/police-unit-that-spied-on-muslims-is-disbanded.html.
64. American Civil Liberties Union, "Raza v. City of New York – Legal Challenge to NYPD Muslim Surveillance Program," 7 January 2016, https://www.aclu.org/cases/raza-v-city-new-york-legal-challenge-nypd-muslim-surveillance-program.
65. *United States* v. *Miller*, 307 U.S. 174 (1939).
66. *District of Columbia* v. *Heller*, 554 U.S. 290 (2008).
67. *McDonald* v. *Chicago*, 561 U.S.__(2010).
68. Robert Barnes, "Supreme Court Declines to Hear Gun Law Challenges," *Washington Post*, 24 February 2014.
69. *Caetano* v. *Massachusetts*, 577 U.S. ___ (2016); and Lyle Denniston, "The Second Amendment Expands, But Maybe Not By Much," *SCOTUSBlog*, 21 March, 2016, http://www.scotusblog.com/2016/03/the-second-amendment-expands-but-maybe-not-by-much/.
70. *McNabb* v. *United States*, 318 U.S. 332 (1943).
71. *Duncan* v. *Louisiana*, 391 U.S. 145 (1968); and *Baldwin* v. *New York*, 399 U.S. 66 (1970).
72. *Gideon* v. *Wainwright*, 372 U.S. 335 (1963). See also Anthony Lewis, *Gideon's Trumpet* (New York: Random House, 1964).
73. *Miranda* v. *Arizona*, 384 U.S. 436 (1966).
74. *Dickerson* v. *United States*, 530 U.S. 428 (2000).
75. *Wolf* v. *Colorado*, 338 U.S. 25 (1949).
76. *Mapp* v. *Ohio*, 367 U.S. 643 (1961).
77. *United States* v. *Leon*, 468 U.S. 897 (1984).
78. *Hudson* v. *Michigan*, 547 U.S. 586 (2006).
79. *Riley* v. *California*, 573 U.S. ___ (2014).
80. Paul Brest, *Processes of Constitutional Decision-Making* (Boston: Little, Brown, 1975), p. 708.
81. *Griswold* v. *Connecticut*, 381 U.S. 479 (1965).
82. *Roe* v. *Wade*, 410 U.S. 113 (1973).
83. *Webster* v. *Reproductive Health Services*, 492 U.S. 490 (1989).
84. *Hodgson* v. *Minnesota*, 497 U.S. 417 (1990); and *Ohio* v. *Akron Center for Reproductive Health*, 497 U.S. 502 (1990).
85. *Planned Parenthood of Southeastern Pennsylvania* v. *Casey*, 505 U.S. 833 (1992); *Stenberg* v. *Carhart*, 530 U.S. 914 (2000); and *Gonzales* v. *Carhart*, 550 U.S. 124 (2007).
86. Stuart Taylor, "Supreme Court Hears Case on Homosexual Rights," *New York Times*, 1 April 1986, p. A24.
87. *Bowers* v. *Hardwick*, 478 U.S. 186 (1986).
88. Dahlia Lithwick, "*Lawrence v. Texas*: How Laws Against Sodomy Became Unconstitutional," *The New Yorker*, 7 March 2012, http://www.newyorker.com/arts/critics/books/2012/03/12/120312crbo.booksJithwick; and Dale Carpenter, *Flagrant Conduct: The Story of Lawrence v. Texas* (New York: W. W. Norton & Company, 2012).
89. *Lawrence and Garner* v. *Texas*, 539 U.S. 558 (2003).

Chapter 16

1. *Fisher* v. *University of Texas*, 570 U.S. ___ (2013); *Fisher* v. *University of Texas*, Slip Opinion, No. 14-981. Argued December 9, 2015—Decided June 23, 2016, http://www.supremecourt.gov/opinions/15pdf/14-981_4g15.pdf; and Lyle Dennison, "Opinion Analysis: A Brief Respite for Affirmative Action?" 23 June 2016, http://www.scotusblog.com/2016/06/opinion-analysis-a-brief-respite-for-affirmative-action/.

2. "The Model Minority Is Losing Patience," *The Economist*, 3 October 2015, http://www.economist.com/news/briefing/21669595-asian -americans-are-united-states-most-successful-minority-they-are -complaining-ever.

3. David Palumbo-Liu, "A Willful Misreading of Racism Today: Fisher v. University of Texas is Part of a General Attack on Minority Rights," 18 December 2016, http://www.salon.com/2015/12/18/a _willful_misreading_of_racism_today_fisher_v_university_of _texas_is_part_of_a_general_attack_on_minority_rights/.

4. Pew Research Center, "Public Backs Affirmative Action, But Not Minority Preferences," 2 June 2009, http://www.pewresearch .org/2009/06/02/public-backs-affirmative-action-but-not-minority -preferences/; and Frank Newport, "Americans' Satisfaction with Ability to Get Ahead Edges Up," 21 January 2016, http://www.gallup .com/poll/188780/americans-satisfaction-ability-ahead-edges.aspx.

5. American National Election Studies, "Guide to Public Opinion and Electoral Behavior," Table 4A.4b Government Guaranteed Job /Standard of Living and Table 4B.4 Aid to Blacks/Minorities, http:// www.electionstudies.org/nesguide/gd-index.htm.

6. Rogers M. Smith, "Beyond Tocqueville, Myrdal, and Hartz: The Multiple Traditions in America," *American Political Science Review* 87, no. 3 (1993): 549–566.

7. *The Slaughterhouse Cases*, 83 U.S. 36 (1873).

8. *United States v. Cruikshank*, 92 U.S. 542 (1876).

9. *United States v. Reese*, 92 U.S. 214 (1876).

10. *Civil Rights Cases*, 109 U.S. 3 (1883).

11. Mary Beth Norton et al., *A People and a Nation: A History of the United States*, 3rd ed. (Boston: Houghton Mifflin, 1990), p. 490; and J. Morgan Kousser, *The Shaping of Southern Politics: Suffrage Restriction and the Establishment of the One-Party South, 1880–1910* (New Haven, CT: Yale University Press, 1974).

12. *Plessy v. Ferguson*, 163 U.S. 537 (1896).

13. *Cummings v. County Board of Education*, 17 5 U.S. 528 (1899).

14. *Missouri ex rel. Gaines v. Canada*, 305 U.S. 337 (1938).

15. *Sweatt v. Painter*, 339 U.S. 629 (1950).

16. *Brown v. Board of Education*, 347 U.S. 483 (1954).

17. *Boiling v. Sharpe*, 347 U.S. 497 (1954).

18. *Brown v. Board of Education* II, 349 U.S. 294 (1955).

19. Jack W. Peltason, *Fifty-Eight Lonely Men*, rev. ed. (Urbana: University of Illinois Press, 1971); and Matthew F. Delmont, *Why Busing Failed: Race, Media, and the National Resistance to School Desegregation* (Berkeley, CA: University of California Press, 2016).

20. *Alexander v. Holmes County Board of Education*, 396 U.S. 19 (1969).

21. *Swann v. Charlotte-Mecklenburg County Schools*, 402 U.S. 1 (1971).

22. *Milliken v. Bradley*, 418 U.S. 717 (1974); see also Delmont, *Why Busing Failed*.

23. Gerald N. Rosenberg, *The Hollow Hope: Can Courts Bring About Social Change*, 2nd ed. (Chicago: University of Chicago Press, 2008).

24. Robert Caro, *The Passage of Power: The Years of Lyndon Johnson* (New York: Knopf, 2012).

25. *Heart of Atlanta Motel v. United States*, 379 U.S. 241 (1964).

26. *Katzenbach v. McClung*, 379 U.S. 294 (1964).

27. J. Mitchell Pickerill, *Constitutional Deliberation in Congress: The Impact of Judicial Review in a Separated System* (Durham, NC: Duke University Press, 2004).

28. *Grove City College v. Bell*, 465 U.S. 555 (1984).

29. *Martin v. Wilks*, 490 U.S. 755 (1989); *Wards Cove Packing Co. v. Atonio*, 490 U.S. 642 (1989); *Patterson v. McLean Credit Union*, 491 U.S. 164 (1989); *Price Waterhouse v. Hopkins*, 490 U.S. 228 (1989); *Lorance v. AT&T Technologies*, 490 U.S. 900 (1989); and *EEOC v. Arabian American Oil Co.*, 499 U.S. 244 (1991).

30. "What Happened in Ferguson?" *New York Times*, 10 August 2015, www.nytimes.com/interactive/2014/08/13/us/ferguson-missouri -town-under-siege-after-police-shooting.html.

31. U.S. Department of Justice, "Justice Department Announces Findings of Two Civil Rights Investigations in Ferguson, Missouri," 4 March 2015, https://www.justice.gov/opa/pr/justice-department-announces -findings-two-civil-rights-investigations-ferguson-missouri; and

U.S. District Court for the Eastern District of Missouri, *United States of America* v. *The City of Ferguson*, Consent Decree, 17 March 2016, https://www.justice.gov/opa/file/833431/download.

32. Cited in Martin Gruberg, *Women in American Politics* (Oshkosh, Wise: Academic Press, 1968), p. 4.

33. *Bradwell v. Illinois*, 83 U.S. 130 (1873).

34. *Muller v. Oregon*, 208 U.S. 412 (1908).

35. *International Union, United Automobile, Aerospace and Agricultural Implement Workers of America v. Johnson Controls, Inc.*, 499 U.S. 187 (1991).

36. Kaiser Family Foundation, "Women's Health Indicators: Abortion Statistics and Policies," http://kff.org/state-category/womens-health /abortion-statistics-and-policies/.

37. *Minor v. Happersett*, 88 U.S. 162 (1875).

38. The Library of Congress, "Today in History: August 28, Picketing for Suffrage," https://memory.loc.gov/ammem/today/aug28.html.

39. Jane J. Mansbridge, *Why We Lost the ERA* (Chicago: University of Chicago Press, 1986).

40. Melvin I. Urofsky, *A March of Liberty* (New York: Knopf, 1988).

41. The Equal Rights Amendment, Unfinished Business for the Constitution, http://www.equalrightsamendment.org/.

42. United States House of Representatives, "History, Art, and Archives: Griffiths, Martha Wright," http://history.house.gov/People/Listing /G/GRIFFITHS,-Martha-Wright-%28G000471%29/.

43. *Ledbetter v. Goodyear Tire and Rubber Company*, 550 U.S. 618 (2007).

44. Sheryl Gay Stolberg, "Obama Signs Equal-Pay Legislation," *New York Times*, 30 January 2009.

45. *Reed v. Reed*, 404 U.S. 71 (1971).

46. *Frontiero v. Richardson*, 411 U.S. 677 (1973).

47. *Craig v. Boren*, 429 U.S. 190 (1976).

48. *J.E.B. v. Alabama ex rel. T.B.*, 511 U.S. 127 (1994).

49. U.S. Department of Education, Office for Civil Rights, "Title IX and Sex Discrimination," http://www2.ed.gov/about/offices/list/ocr/docs /tix_dis.html.

50. *United States v. Virginia*, 518 U.S. 515 (1996).

51. Mike Allen, "Defiant V.M.I, to Admit Women but Will Not Ease Rules for Them," *New York Times*, 22 September 1996.

52. U.S. Department of Education, "Table 104.20. Percentage of persons 25 to 29 years old with selected levels of educational attainment, by race/ethnicity and sex: Selected years, 1920 through 2015," *Digest of Education Statistics*, https://nces.ed.gov/programs/digest/d15/tables /dt15_104.20.asp.

53. "Stonewall and Beyond: Lesbian and Gay Culture," Columbia University Libraries exhibition, 25 May–17 September 1994, http:// www.columbia.edu/cu/libraries/events/sw25/.

54. John D'Emilio, William B. Turner, and Urvashi Vaid, eds., *Creating Change: Sexuality, Public Policy, and Civil Rights* (New York: St. Martin's Press, 2000).

55. The Human Rights Campaign, http://www.hrc.org/.

56. Rachel Maddow interview, 10 May 2012, Today on NBC, http:// video.today.msnbc.msn.com/today/47368691; and Jesse McKinley, "Closing Arguments in Marriage Trial," *New York Times*, 16 June 2010, http://www.nytimes.com/2010/06/17/us/17prop.html.

57. *Hollingsworth v. Perry*, 570 U.S.___(2013).

58. Jackie Calmes and Peter Baker, "Obama Says Same-Sex Marriage Should Be Legal," *New York Times*, 9 May 2012.

59. *United States v. Windsor*, 570 U.S.12 (2013).

60. *Obergefell v. Hodges*, 576 U.S. __ (2015).

61. *Boy Scouts of America v. Dale*, 530 U.S. 610 (2000).

62. Elizabeth Bumiller, "Obama Ends 'Don't Ask, Don't Tell' Policy," *New York Times*, 22 July 2011, http://www.nytimes.com/2011/07/23 /us/23military.html.

63. *V.L. v. E.L., et al.*, 577 U.S. ___ (2016).

64. Francis Paul Prucha, *The Great Father: The United States Government and the American Indian*, vol. 2 (Lincoln: University of Nebraska Press, 1984); James S. Olson and Raymond Wilson, *Native Americans in the Twentieth Century* (Urbana, IL: University of Illinois Press, 1984); and U.S. Census Bureau, "Overview of Race

and Hispanic Origin, 2010 Census Briefs," March 2011, http://www.census.gov/prod/cen2010/briefs/c2010br-02.pdf.

65. Dee Brown, *Bury My Heart at Wounded Knee: An Indian History of the American West* (New York: Holt, Rinehart & Winston, 1971).

66. Prucha, *The Great Father*; and Olson and Wilson, *Native Americans in the Twentieth Century*.

67. Fergus M. Bordewich, *Killing the White Man's Indian: Reinventing Native Americans at the End of the Twentieth Century* (New York: Anchor Books, 1996).

68. Jennifer Ludden, "1965 Immigration Law Changed the Face of America," NPR All Things Considered, 9 May 2006, http://www.npr.org/templates/story/story.php?storyId=5391395.

69. *Yick Wo v. Hopkins*, 118 U.S. 356 (1886).

70. *Lau v. Nichols*, 414 U.S. 563 (1974).

71. U.S. Department of Education, "English Language Learners in Public Schools," *The Condition of Education*, May 2016, http://nces.ed.gov/programs/coe/indicator_cgf.asp.

72. Department of Commerce, Bureau of the Census, "Voting Rights Act Amendments of 2006, Determinations Under Section 203," *Federal Register*, 13 October 2011, https://www.justice.gov/sites/default/files/crt/legacy/2011/10/13/2011_notice.pdf.

73. *Arizona v. United States*, 567 U.S. ___ (2012); and Carli Brosseau, "ACLU Files Lawsuit Precursor in SB 1070 Challenge Case," *Arizona Daily Star*, 13 November 2013, tucson.com/news/local/border/aclu-files-lawsuit-precursor-in-sb-challenge-case/article_24900305-4cd5-5edb-a408-81a7aa70ea9f.html.

74. Stephen Ceasar, "Hispanic Population Tops 50 Million in U.S.," http://articles.latimes.com/2011/mar/24/nation/la-na-census-hispanic-20110325.

75. U.S. Department of Justice, Civil Rights Division, https://www.ada.gov/; and U.S. Department of Education, http://idea.ed.gov/.

76. Lennard J. Davis, *Enabling Acts: The Hidden Story of How the Americans with Disabilities Act Gave the Largest US Minority Its Rights* (Boston: Beacon Press, 2015).

77. U.S. Equal Employment Opportunity Commission, "Americans with Disabilities Act of 1990 (ADA) FY 1997–FY 2013," http://www.eeoc.gov/eeoc/statistics/enforcement/adacharges.cfm.

78. Lisa J. Stansky, "Opening Doors," *ABA Journal* 82 (1996): 66–69; and *Parents Involved in Community Schools v. Seattle School District No. 1*, 551 U.S. (2007).

79. U.S. Department of Labor, Bureau of Labor Statistics, "Table A-6. Employment Status of the Civilian Population by Sex, Age, and Disability Status, Not Seasonally Adjusted," 3 June 2016, http://www.bls.gov/news.release/empsit.t06.htm; and U.S. Department of Labor, "National Disability Employment Awareness Month 2016," https://www.dol.gov/odep/topics/ndeam/.

80. *Foster v. Chapman, Warden*, slip opinion at http://www.supremecourt.gov/opinions/15pdf/14-8349_6k47.pdf; and Ariane de Vogue, "Supreme Court Sides with Death Row Inmate in Racial Discrimination Case," 23 May 2016, http://www.cnn.com/2016/05/23/politics/supreme-court-racial-discrimination/.

81. Dana Ford, "Jonathan Butler: Meet the Man Whose Hunger Strike Flipped the Script at Mizzou," CNN.com, 10 November 2015, http://www.cnn.com/2015/11/09/us/jonathan-butler-hunger-strike-missouri-profile/.

82. Kasia Kovacs, "UPDATE: MU Student Embarks on Hunger Strike, Demands Wolfe's Removal from Office," *Columbia Missourian*, 2 November 2015, http://www.columbiamissourian.com/news/higher_education/update-mu-student-embarks-on-hunger-strike-demands-wolfe-s/article_35ab864a-8186-11e5-902b-6f136a45260b.html.

83. Michael Pearson, "A Timeline of the University of Missouri Protests," CNN.com, 10 November 2015, http://www.cnn.com/2015/11/09/us/missouri-protest-timeline/.

84. Kenneth Jost, "Voting Controversies: Are U.S. Elections Being Conducted Fairly?" *CQ Researcher*, 21 February 2014, http://library.cqpress.com/cqresearcher/document.php?id=cqresrre2014022100.

85. Pew Center on the States, *Inaccurate, Costly, and Inefficient: Evidence that America's Voter Registration System Needs an Upgrade*, February 2012, http://www.pewtrusts.org/en/research-and-analysis/reports/2012/02/14/inaccurate-costly-and-inefficient-evidence-that-americas-voter-registration-system-needs-an-upgrade.

86. David Goldman, "North Carolina Loses 400 Jobs as PayPal Pulls Facility," 5 April 2016, http://money.cnn.com/2016/04/05/technology/paypal-north-carolina-lgbt/; and Laura Wagner, "Bruce Springsteen Cancels Show in North Carolina to Protest 'Bathroom Bill,'" NPR.org, 8 April 2016, http://www.npr.org/sections/thetwo-way/2016/04/08/473566753/bruce-springsteen-cancels-show-in-north-carolina-to-protest-bathroom-bill.

87. U.S. Department of Labor, OFCCP 50th Anniversary Celebration," https://www.dol.gov/ofccp/about/50thAnniversary.html.

88. Peter Katel, "Affirmative Action: Is It Time to End Racial Preferences?" *CQ Researcher*, 17 October 2008, http://library.cqpress.com/cqresearcher/document.php?id=cqresrre2008101700.

89. *Regents of the University of California v. Bakke*, 438 U.S. 265 (1978).

90. *Gratz v. Bollinger*, 539 U.S. 244 (2003).

91. *Grutter v. Bollinger*, 539 U.S. 306 (2003).

92. *Parents Involved in Community Schools v. Seattle School District No. 1, 551* U.S. 701 (2007).

Chapter 17

1. Address to the Nebraska Republican Conference, in Lincoln, Nebraska, on 16 January 1936. Herbert Hoover, *Addresses upon the American Road, 1933–1938* (New York: Scribner's Sons, 1938), p. 105.

2. Estimates vary concerning the debt in 1936. A 1936 citation said $34.5 billion. See R. M. Boeckel, "The Deficit and the Public Debt," *Editorial Research Reports 1936*, Vol. I (Washington, DC: CQ Press, 1936). Data compiled recently by Christopher Chantrill put the debt higher. See http://www.usgovernmentspending.com/spending_chart_1930_2017USp_15sllilllmcn_H0f#tabbed.

3. Chantrill at http://www.usgovernmentspending.com/spending_chart_1930_2017USp_15sllilllmcn_H0f#tabbed.

4. Office of Management and Budget, *Budget of the U.S. Government, Fiscal Year 2015* (Washington, DC: U.S. Government Printing Office, 2014), Table S-13.

5. You won't learn basic economics in this chapter. For a quick summary of "ten principles of economics," see N. Gregory Mankiw, *Principles of Economics*, 7th ed. (Boston: Cengage Learning 2014), p. 3.

6. Dan Usher, in *Political Economy* (Maiden, Mass.: Blackwell Publishing, 2003), offers this interpretation of Adam Smith's "invisible hand" metaphor: "Self-interested people are guided by market-determined prices to deploy the resources of the world to produce what people want to consume. This assertion, made commonplace by repetition, is so extraordinary and so completely counter-intuitive that it cannot be strictly and unreservedly true. A central task of economics is to show when the assertion is true, when public intervention in the economy might be helpful, and when markets are best left alone because public intervention is likely to do more harm than good" (p. xiv).

7. Two of the ten principles of economics that Mankiw cites in *Principles of Economics* are "#6: Markets are usually a good way to organize economic activity" but "#7: Governments can sometimes improve market outcomes."

8. Justin Fox, *The Myth of the Rational Market* (New York: Harper Collins, 2009), pp. xii–xiii.

9. National Bureau of Economic Research, "Business Cycle Expansions and Contractions," 1 December 2008, http://www.nber.org/cycles.html.

10. Shaun P. Hargraves Heap, "Keynesian Economics," in *Routledge Encyclopedia of International Political Economy*, vol. 2, ed. R. J. Barry Jones (London: Routledge, 2001), pp. 877–878.

11. "We're All Keynesians Now," *Wall Street Journal*, 18 January 2008, p. A12.

12. Kathleen R. McNamara, "Monetarism," in Jones, *Routledge Encyclopedia of International Political Economy*, pp. 1035–1037.

13. The Federal Reserve Act (as amended over the years) cites "maximum employment, stable prices, and moderate long-term interest rates"; see http://www.federalreserve.gov/aboutthefed/section2a.htm.

14. See Allan H. Meltzer, *A History of the Federal Reserve, vol. 1, 1913–1951* (Chicago: University of Chicago Press, 2003). Meltzer writes that the leading banks in 1913 were privately owned institutions with public responsibilities. Fears were that they would place their interests above the public interest, but there was also concern about empowering government to control money. "President Wood-row Wilson offered a solution that appeared to reconcile competing public and private interests. He proposed a public-private partnership with semiautonomous, privately funded reserve banks supervised by a public board" (p. 3).

15. Luca LiLeo, "Fed Gets More Power, Responsibility," *Wall Street Journal*, 16 July 2010, p. A5.

16. The quote, attributed to William McChesney Martin, Jr., is in Martin Mayer, *The Fed* (New York: Free Press, 2001), p. 165.

17. Federal Reserve Bank of San Francisco, *Weekly Letter 96-08*, 23 February 1996.

18. Pew Research Center, "Economic Discontent Deepens as Inflation Concerns Rise," news release, 14 February 2008.

19. Fox, *The Myth of the Rational Market*, pp. xi–xii.

20. Jeff Cox, "Fed Raises Rates by 25 Basis Points, First Since 2006," http://www.cnbc.com/2015/12/16/fed-raises-rates-for-first-time-since-2006.html.

21. Mankiw, *Principles of Economics*, pp. 170–171.

22. See the editorial "How to Raise Revenue," *Wall Street Journal*, 24 August 2007, p. A14; and Austan Goolsbee, "Is the New Supply Side Better Than the Old?" *New York Times*, 20 January 2008, p. BU6.

23. One such "national debt clock" is at http://www.usdebtclock.org.

24. U.S. Treasury, "The Debt to the Penny and Who Holds It," http://www.treasurydirect.gov/NP/debt/current.

25. For the federal budget of the current fiscal year, go to http://www.whitehouse.gov/omb/budget.

26. Concord Coalition, "Budget Process Reform: An Important Tool for Fiscal Discipline, but Not a Magic Bullet," *Issue Brief*, 5 February 2004.

27. Concord Coalition, "Budget Process Reform," p. 3.

28. James V. Saturno, *A Balanced Budget Constitutional Amendment: Procedural Issues and Legislative History*, Congressional Research Service Report 98-671 (5 August 1998), p. 14.

29. Peter H. Schuck, "The Balanced Budget Amendment's Fatal Flaw," *Wall Street Journal*, 22 July 2011, p. A15.

30. D. Andrew Austin, *The Debt Limit: History and Recent Increases*, CRS Report for Congress, RL31967 (29 April 2008), p. 3.

31. "The Budget for Fiscal Year 2015, Historical Tables," Table 7.3, http://www.whitehouse.gov/sites/default/files/omb/budget/fy2015/assets/hist.pdf.

32. Amy Bingham, "Only One Democratic Country, Besides America, Has a Debt Ceiling," *ABC News*, 19 July 2011.

33. Richard A. Musgrave and Peggy B. Musgrave, *Public Finance in Theory and Practice*, 2nd ed. (New York: McGraw-Hill, 1976), p. 42.

34. If you can spare twenty-four megabytes of storage, you can download the complete text of the U.S. Internal Revenue Code, Title 26 of the U.S. Code, http://www.fourmilab.ch/uscode/26usc. If you print the tax code, expect more than 7,500 pages.

35. Office of Management and Budget, "Historical Tables, FY 2017 Budget," Table 2.2, http://www.whitehouse.gov/omb/budget/Historicals.

36. David Cay Johnston, "Talking Simplicity, Building a Maze," *New York Times*, 15 February 2004, Money and Business section, pp. 11, 14.

37. Over a dozen surveys from 1992 to 2013 found that 60 percent or more of respondents felt that "upper-income people" were paying too little in taxes. See http://www.pollingreport.com/budget2.htm.

38. Jill Barshay, "'Case of the Missing Revenue' Is Nation's Troubling Mystery," *CQ Weekly*, 17 January 2004, p. 144.

39. Tax Policy Center, "Historical Income Tax Rates for a Family of Four," 1 July 2015, http://www.taxpolicycenter.org/taxfacts/displayafact.cfm?Docid=226.

40. Pew Research Center for the People and the Press, "Economic Inequality Seen as Rising, Boom Bypasses Poor," *Survey Report*, 21 June 2001.

41. Spending as percentage of GDP is a common way of measuring social welfare benefits, but it is not the only way. If spending is measured by dollars per capita, the United States, with a very high GDP, rates much more favorably. See Christopher Howard, "Is the American Welfare State Unusually Small?" *PS: Political Science and Politics* 36 (July 2003): 411–416.

42. Thorn Shanker, "Proposed Military Spending Is Highest Since WWII," *New York Times*, 4 February 2008, p. A10.

43. National Priorities Project, "The Cost of War," http://costofwar.com/en/.

44. Executive Office of the President, *Budget of the United States Government, Fiscal Year 2017: Historical Tables* (Washington, DC: U.S. Government Printing Office, 2016), Table 8.3.

45. Pew Survey of 10 February 2011 at http://www.people-press.org/2011/02/10/section-3-the-deficit-and-government-spending/.

46. Fay Lomax Cook et al., *Convergent Perspectives on Social Welfare Policy: The Views from the General Public, Members of Congress, and AFDC Recipients* (Evanston, III: Center for Urban Affairs and Policy Research, Northwestern University, 1988), Table 4-1.

47. Pew Research Center, "Budget Deficit Slips as Public Priority," 22 January 2016, p. 1.

48. Cynthia Crossen, "Not Too Long Ago, Some People Begged for an Income Tax," *Wall Street Journal*, 4 June 2003, p. B1.

49. Ron Nixon, "Billionaires Received U.S. Farm Subsidies, Report Finds," *New York Times*, 7 November 2013), online.

50. Arthur C Brooks, "The Left's 'Inequality' Obsession," *Wall Street Journal*, 19 July 2007, p. A15. Federal income taxes do make income distribution slightly more equal. See David Wessel, "Fishing Out the Facts on the Wealth Gap," *Wall Street Journal*, 15 February 2007, p. A10.

51. Scott Greenberg, "Summary of Latest Federal Individual Income Tax Data, 2015 Update," *Fiscal Facts* (Washington, DC: Tax Foundation), 19 November 2015.

52. Ibid.

53. Warren E, Buffett, "Stop Coddling the Super-Rich," *New York Times*, 16 August 2011, p. A19.

54. Tax Policy Center, "Distribution of Federal Payroll and Income Taxes by Expanded Cash Income Percentile, 2017," 25 June 2015, http://www.taxpolicycenter.org/numbers/displayatab.cfm?Docid=4268&DocTypeID=2.

55. Joseph A. Pechman, *Who Paid the Taxes, 1966–1985?* (Washington, DC: Brookings Institution, 1985), p. 80. See also Lawrence Mishel, Jared Bernstein, and Heather Boushey, *The State of Working America, 2002–2003* (Ithaca, NY.: Cornell University Press, 2003), p. 66.

56. OECD, *In It Together: Why Less Inequality Benefits All* (Paris: OECD Publishing, 2015), http://dx.doi.org/10.1781/9789264235120-en, Table 1.A1.1.

57. Sylvia A. Allegretto, "The State of Working America's Wealth, 2011," Economic Policy Institute, Briefing Paper #292 (23 March 2011), p. 5.

58. U.S. Bureau of the Census, *Statistical Abstract of the United States 2012* (Washington, DC: U.S. Government Printing Office, 2012), Table 697.

59. Benjamin I. Page, *Who Gets What from Government?* (Berkeley: University of California Press, 1983), p. 213.

60. Frank Newport, "Americans Continue to Say U.S Wealth Distribution Is Unfair," Gallup Poll Report, 4 May 2015 http://www.gallup.com/poll/182987/americans-continue-say-wealth-distribution-unfair.aspx?g_source=wealth&g_medium=search&g_campaign=tiles.

61. Karlyn Bowman and Andrew Rugg, *Public Opinion on Taxes: 1937 to Today* (Washington, DC: American Enterprise Institute, 2012).

62. James Sterngold, "Muting the Lotteries' Perfect Pitch," *New York Times*, 14 July 1996, sec. 4, p. 1.

63. "Taxes: What's Fair?" *Public Perspective* 7 (April–May 1996): 40–41.

64. Robert J. Blendon et al., "Tax Uncertainty: A Divided America's Uninformed View of the Federal Tax System," *Brookings Review* 21 (Summer 2003): 28–31.

65. Jason White, "Taxes and Budget," *State of the States: 2004* (Washington, DC: Pew Center on the States, 2004), p. 30.

66. Shailagh Murray, "Seminary Article in Alabama Sparks Tax-Code Revolt," *Wall Street Journal*, 12 February 2003, pp. A1, A8.

Chapter 18

1. Carmen DeNavas-Walt and Bernadette D. Proctor, "Income and Poverty in the United States: 2014," (Washington, DC: U.S. Census Bureau, 2015.)

2. Kathleen Romig, "Social Security Lifts 21 Million Americans Out of Poverty," Center on Budget and Policy Priorities, 2015, http://www.cbpp.org/blog/social-security-lifts-21-million-americans-out-of-poverty-0.

3. "Chart Book: Accomplishments of the Safety Net," Center on Budget and Policy Priorities, 2015, http://www.cbpp.org/research/poverty-and-inequality/chart-book-accomplishments-of-the-safety-net#part1_6.

4. "Chart Book: SNAP Helps Struggling Families Put Food on the Table," Center on Budget and Policy Priorities, 2015, http://www.cbpp.org/research/food-assistance/chart-book-snap-helps-struggling-families-put-food-on-the-table.

5. Adam Nagourney, "For Cowboy Poets, Unwelcome Spotlight in Battle Over Spending," *New York Times*, 10 April 2011; and Danielle Switalski, "Cowboy Poetry Gathering Drawn into Budget Battle," *Elko Daily Free Press*, 10 March 2011.

6. "State Tax Codes as Poverty Fighting Tools," Institute on Taxation and Economic Policy, September 2011, http://www.itepnet.org/pdf/poverty2011report.pdf; and Josh Goodman, "Kansas and Oklahoma Income Tax Won't Reach Zero," *Stateline: The Daily News Service of the Pew Charitable Trusts*, 18 May 2012.

7. Peter Katel, "Food Safety," *CQ Researcher*, 17 December 2010, www.cqresearcher.com; and U.S. Food and Drug Administration, "The New FDA Food Safety Modernization Act," http://www.fda.gov/Food/FoodSafety/FSMA/default.htm.

8. According to the FDA, it is four or fewer rodent hairs per twenty-five grams. See the FDA's "Defect Levels Handbook," http://www.fda.gov/food/guidancecomplianceregulatoryinformation/guidancedocuments/sanitation/ucm056174.htm#intro.

9. Gardiner Harris and William Neuman, "Senate Passes Sweeping Law on Food Safety," *New York Times*, 20 November 2010.

10. This typology is adapted from Theodore Lowi's classic article, "American Business, Public Policy Case Studies, and Political Theory," *World Politics* 16 (July 1964): 677–715.

11. "What America Thinks: Americans Are in a Giving Mood This Christmas," 16 December 2014, http://www.rasmussenreports.com/public_content/what_america_thinks/2014_12/what_america_thinks_americans_are_in_a_giving_mood_this_christmas; and "Charitable Giving Statistics," National Philanthropic Trust, http://www.nptrust.org/philanthropic-resources/charitable-giving-statistics/.

12. Diane Stafford, "FDA Intends to Clear the Air on E-Cigarettes," *Kansas City Star*, 8 January 2014; and Michael Erikson, "Could FDA E-Cigarette Regulations Help More People Quit Smoking?" *US News & World Report*, 16 February 2016, http://www.usnews.com/news/articles/2016-02-16/could-fda-e-cigarette-regulations-help-more-people-quit-smoking.

13. Roger W. Cobb and Charles D. Elder, *Participation in American Politics*, 2nd ed. (Baltimore, Md.: Johns Hopkins University Press, 1983), p. 14.

14. Lawrence D. Brown and Lawrence R. Jacobs, *The Private Abuse of the Public Interest* (Chicago: University of Chicago Press, 2008).

15. Dana Lee Baker and Shannon Stokes, "Brain Politics: Aspects of Administration in the Comparative Issue Definition of Autism-Related Policy," *Public Administration Review* 67 (July–August 2007): 757–767.

16. Frank R. Baumgartner, Suzanna L. De Boef, and Amber E. Boydstun, *The Decline of the Death Penalty and the Discovery of Innocence* (New York: Cambridge University Press, 2008).

17. Julian Hattam, "Obama Signs Drug Compounding Bill," *The Hill*, 27 November 2013.

18. U.S. Department of Transportation, "2004 Automotive Fuel Economy Program," http://www.nhtsa.gov/Laws+&-|-Regulations/CAFE+-+Fuel+Economy/2004+Automotive+Fuel-|-Economy-|-Program; and Juliet Eilperin, "EPA Issues New Fuel-Efficiency Standard: Autos Must Average 54.5 mpg by 2025," *Washington Post*, 29 August 2012.

19. "Claims Information," BP.com; Clifford Krauss, "In BP Trial, the Amount of Oil Lost Is at Issue," *New York Times*, 29 September 2013; and Campbell Robertson, John Schwartz, and Richard Pérez-Peña, "BP to Pay $18.7 Billion for Deepwater Horizon Oil Spill," *New York Times*, 6 July 2015, http://www.nytimes.com/2015/07/03/us/bp-to-pay-gulf-coast-states-18-7-billion-for-deepwater-horizon-oil-spill.html?smid=nytcore-iphone-share&smprod=nytcore-iphone&_r=0.

20. Eric Lipton and Gardiner Harris, "In Turnaround, Industries Seek U.S. Regulations," *New York Times*, 16 September 2007.

21. "H.R. 2154: Distracted Driving Prevention Act of 2015," https://www.govtrack.us/congress/bills/114/hr2154; data on deaths and injuries from Distraction.gov, http://www.distraction.gov/stats-research-laws/facts-and-statistics.html.

22. Lipton and Harris, "In Turnaround."

23. Jeffrey M. Berry and Clyde Wilcox, *The Interest Group Society*, 5th ed. (New York: Pearson Longman, 2009), pp. 155–176.

24. Michael T. Heaney, "Coalitions and Interest Group Influence over Health Care Policy" (paper presented at the annual meeting of the American Political Science Association, Philadelphia, August 2003), p. 16.

25. Robert Shapiro, "Public Opinion and American Democracy," *Public Opinion Quarterly* 75 (2011): 982–1017.

26. See, for example, Kim Parker, "Where the Public Stands on Government Assistance, Taxes, and the Presidential Candidates," Pew Research Social and Demographic Trends, 20 September 2012.

27. Data available from U.S. Department of Labor, Bureau of Labor Statistics, http://www.bls.gov/cps/prev_yrs.htm.

28. Charles Kenny, "50 Years After the War on Poverty, Poor People are Not Better Off," *Bloomberg Businessweek*, 13 January 2014; and Jared Bernstein, "The War on Poverty at 50," *New York Times*, 6 January 2014.

29. "OASDI and SSI Program Rates & Limits, 2016," https://ssa.gov/policy/docs/quickfacts/prog_highlights/index.html.

30. Harold W. Stanley and Richard G. Niemi (eds.), *Vital Statistics on American Politics, 2015–2016* (Washington, DC: CQ Press, 2015).

31. "CBO's 2015 Long-Term Projections for Social Security: Additional Information," https://www.cbo.gov/publication/51047.

32. Clea Benson, "How Long Can Americans Work?" *CQ Weekly*, 5 July 2010, pp. 1616–1617.

33. Social Security Administration, "2016 Social Security Changes," https://www.ssa.gov/news/press/factsheets/colafacts2016.html.

34. Pew Research Center, "Millennials in Adulthood," 7 March 2014, http://www.pewsocialtrends.org/2014/03/07/millennials-in-adulthood/.

35. *Retirement Security and Quality Health Care: Our Pledge to America*, n.d., GOP Platform, http://abcnews.go.com/Politics/story?-id=123296ftpage=l.

36. Matt Berman, "What Is Chained CPI?" *National Journal*, 31 December 2012; and Pete Kasperowicz, "Dems Reject Obama's Chained CPI Formula for Social Security," *The Hill*, 22 April 2013.

37. Diana DiNitto and David Johnson, *Social Welfare: Politics and Public Policy*, 8th ed. (Boston: Pearson, 2016); and "Hard Choices on Social Security: Survey Finds Most Americans Would Pay More to Fix Its Finances and Improve Benefits," National Academy of Social

Insurance, 23 October 2014, https://www.nasi.org/press/releases /2014/10/press-release-hard-choices-social-security-survey-finds-m.

38. Although it has been the source of endless debate, today's definition of poverty retains remarkable similarity to its precursors. As early as 1795, a group of English magistrates "decided that a minimum income should be the cost of a gallon loaf of bread, multiplied by three, plus an allowance for each dependent." See Alvin L. Schorr, "Redefining Poverty Levels," *New York Times*, 9 May 1984, p. 27; and Louis Uchitelle, "How to Define Poverty? Let Us Count the Ways," *New York Times*, 26 May 2001, http://www.nytimes.com/2001/05 /26/ arts/how-to-define-poverty-let-us-count-the-ways.html ?pagewanted=l.

39. U.S. Census Bureau, "Poverty Data," http://www.census.gov/hhes /www/poverty/data/threshold/. The poverty guideline for 2016 was $24,300 (see the 2012 HHS Poverty Guidelines, http://aspe.hhs.gov /poverty-guidelines).

40. Nicholas Eberstadt, "The Mismeasure of Poverty," *Policy Review* 138 (August–September 2006): 1–21.

41. U.S. Census Bureau, *Income and Poverty in the United States: 2014* (Washington, DC: U.S. Government Printing Office, 2015).

42. Ibid.

43. U.S. Census Bureau, "The Supplemental Poverty Rate: 2014," September 2015, https://www.census.gov/content/dam/Census /library/publications/2015/demo/p60-254.pdf.

44. Juan Williams, "Reagan, the South, and Civil Rights," National Public Radio, 10 June 2004, http://www.npr.org/templates/story /story.-php?storyld=1953700.

45. Peter T. Kilborn, "With Welfare Overhaul Now Law, States Grapple with the Consequences," *New York Times*, 23 August 1996, p. A10.

46. DiNitto and Johnson, *Social Welfare*.

47. DiNitto and Johnson, *Social Welfare*; and "TANF Caseload Data: 2015," http://www.acf.hhs.gov/programs/ofa/programs/tanf /data-reports.

48. Alan Weil and Kenneth Feingold (eds.), *Welfare Reform: The Next Act* (Washington, DC: Urban Institute, 2002).

49. Andrea Hetling et al., "Symbolism vs. Policy Learning," *American Politics Research* 36, no. 3 (May 2008): 335–357; and Joshua Dyck and Laura Hussey, "The End of Welfare As We Know It? Durable Attitudes in a Changing in Formation Environment," *Public Opinion Quarterly* 72, no. 4 (2008): 589–618.

50. Eugenie Hildebrandt and Patricia Stevens, "Impoverished Women with Children and No Welfare Benefits: The Urgency of Researching Failures of the Temporary Assistance for Needy Families Program," *American Journal of Public Health* 99, no. 5 (2009): 793–801; and Robert Wood, Quinn Moore, and Anu Rangarajan, "Two Steps Forward, One Step Back: The Uneven Economic Progress of TANF Recipients," *Social Service Review* 82, no. 1 (2008): 3–28.

51. LaDonna Pavetti and Liz Schott, "TANF's Inadequate Response to Recession Highlights Weakness of Block Grant Structure," Center for Budget and Policy Priorities, July 2011, http://www.cbpp.org/cms /index.cfm?fa=view&id=3534.

52. "Policy Basics: Introduction to the Supplemental Nutrition Assistance Program," Center on Budget and Policy Priorities, 8 January 2015, http://www.cbpp.org/research/policy-basics-introduction-to-the -supplemental-nutrition-assistance-program-snap; and Michael Shear, "In Signing Farm Bill, Obama Extols Rural Growth," *New York Times*, 7 February 2014.

53. Jessica C. Smith and Carla Medalia, *Health Insurance Coverage in the United States: 2014* (Washington, DC: U.S. Government Printing Office, 2015).

54. Association of American Medical Colleges, "Physician Supply and Demand Through 2025: Key Findings," https://www.aamc.org /download/426260/data/physiciansupplyanddemandthrough2025 keyfindings.pdf.

55. "National Health Expenditures 2014 Highlights," https://www.cms .gov/research-statistics-and-systems/statistics-trends-and -reports/nationalhealthexpenddata/downloads/highlights.pdf; and "National Health Expenditure Projections 2014–2024," https://www

.cms.gov/Research-Statistics-Data-and-Systems/Statistics-Trends -and-Reports/NationalHealthExpendData/downloads/proj2014 .pdf.

56. OECD Health Statistics 2013 - Frequently Requested Data, http:// www.oecd.org/els/health-systems/oecdhealthdata2013 -frequentlyrequesteddata.htm.

57. Paul Starr, *The Social Transformation of American Medicine* (New York: Basic Books, 1982), pp. 279–280.

58. Theodore Marmor, *The Politics of Medicare* (Chicago: Aldine, 1973).

59. Martha Derthick, *Policymaking for Social Security* (Washington, DC: Brookings, 1979), p. 335.

60. "A Primer on Medicare: Key Facts About the Medicare Program and the People It Covers," Kaiser Family Foundation, 20 March 2015, http://kff.org/medicare/report/a-primer-on-medicare-key-facts -about-the-medicare-program-and-the-people-it-covers/.

61. "The Medicare Part D Prescription Drug Benefit," Kaiser Family Foundation, 13 October 2015, http://kff.org/medicare/fact-sheet /the-medicare-prescription-drug-benefit-fact-sheet/.

62. "Medicaid Enrollment Data Collected through MBES," Medicaid .gov, https://www.medicaid.gov/medicaid-chip-program-information /program-information/medicaid-and-chip-enrollment-data/medicaid -enrollment-data-collected-through-mbes.html.

63. "By Population," Medicaid.gov, https://www.medicaid.gov/medicaid -chip-program-information/by-population/by-population.html.

64. Julia Paradise, "Medicaid Moving Forward," The Kaiser Family Foundation, 9 March 2015, http://kff.org/health-reform/issue-brief /medicaid-moving-forward/.

65. "Current Status of State Medicaid Expansion Decisions," Kaiser Family Foundation, 14 March 2016, http://kff.org/health-reform /slide/current-status-of-the-medicaid-expansion-decision/.

66. Robin Rudowitz, Laura Snyder, and Vernon K. Smith, "Medicaid Enrollment & Spending Growth: FY 2015 & 2016," Kaiser Family Foundation, 15 October 2015, http://kff.org/medicaid/issue-brief /medicaid-enrollment-spending-growth-fy-2015-2016/.

67. "Health Timeline 2010–2015," *CQ Weekly*, 5 April 2010, p. 818; Robert Pear and David M. Herszenhorn, "Obama Hails Vote on Health Care as Answering 'the Call of History,'" *New York Times*, 21 March 2010, http://www.nytimes.com/2010/03/22/health/policy/22health .html?scp=lasq=obamao/o20hailso/o20voteo/o20ono/o20helatho /o20careast=cse; and "Health Care Reform, at Last," *New York Times*, 22 March 2010, http://www.nytimes.com/2010/03/22/opinion/22 -mon5.html?scp=msq=healtho/o20careo/o20reform,o/o20ato /o20 lastast=cse.

68. MaryBeth Musumeci, "Are Premium Subsidies Available in States with a Federally-run Marketplace? A Guide to the Supreme Court Argument in King v. Burwell," Kaiser Family Foundation, 25 February 2015, http://kff.org/health-reform/issue-brief/are-premium-subsidies -available-in-states-with-a-federally-run-marketplace-a-guide-to -the-supreme-court-argument-in-king-v-burwell/.

69. Kerry Young, "Controlling Medicare Costs," *CQ Weekly*, 5 April 2010, p. 826; "How Health Care Reform Reduces the Deficit in 5 Not-So-Easy Steps," *Newsweek*, 20 March 2010, http://www.newsweek .com/2010/03/20/how-health-care-reform-reduces-thedeficit-in -5-not-so-easy-steps.html; and Peter Grier, "Health Care Reform Bill 101: Who Will Pay for Reform?" *Christian Science Monitor*, 21 March 2010, http://www.csmonitor.com/USA/Politics/2010/0321 /Health-care-reform-bill-lOl-Who-will-pay-for-reform.

70. U.S. Department of Education, "Federal Role in Education," http:// www2.ed.gov/about/overview/fed/role.html?src=ln.

71. National Center for Education Statistics, *The Nations Report Card* (Washington, DC: U.S. Department of Education, 2011), http:// nces.ed.gov/nationsreportcard/pdf/main2011/2012459.pdf

72. See relationship between educational attainment and earnings at "Employment Projections," Bureau of Labor Statistics, http://www .bls.gov/emp/ep_chart_001.htm.

73. Paul Manna, "Federalism, Agenda Setting, and the Development of Federal Education Policy, 1965–2001" (Ph.D. diss., University of Wisconsin-Madison, 2003).

74. Kenneth Jost, "Revising No Child Left Behind," *CQ Researcher*, 16 April 2010, http://www.cqresearcher.com.

75. Alyson Klein, "Obama Administration Aloof as Lawmakers Tangle over ESEA," *Education Week*, 8 August 2013.

76. Lyndsey Layton, "Some States Rebrand Controversial Common Core Education Standards," *Washington Post*, 31 January 2014.

77. Vote totals reported at Congress.gov: https://www.congress.gov/bill/114th-congress/senate-bill/1177/summary/00.

78. Julie Hirschfeld Davis, "President Obama Signs Into Law a Rewrite of No Child Left Behind," *New York Times*, 10 December 2015, http://www.nytimes.com/2015/12/11/us/politics/president-obama-signs-into-law-a-rewrite-of-no-child-left-behind.html?rref=collection%2Ftimestopic%2FNo%20Child%20Left%20Behind%20Act.; and Alan Singer, "Will Every Student Succeed? Not With This New Law," *The Huffington Post*, 6 December 2015, http://www.huffingtonpost.com/alan-singer/will-every-student-succee_b_8730956.html.

79. Lyndsey Layton, "Obama signs new K-12 education law that ends No Child Left Behind," *Washington Post*, 10 December 2015, https://www.washingtonpost.com/local/education/obama-signs-new-k-12-education-law-that-ends-no-child-left-behind/2015/12/10/c9e58d7c-9f51-11e5-a3c5-c77f2cc5a43c_story.html.

80. Jie Zong and Jeanne Batalova, "Frequently Requested Statistics on Immigrants and Immigration in the United States," Migration Policy Institute, 26 February 2016, http://www.migrationpolicy.org/article/frequently-requested-statistics-immigrants-and-immigration-united-states#Unauthorized%20Immigration.

81. U.S. Census Bureau, *Income and Poverty in the United States: 2014* (Washington, DC: U.S. Government Printing Office, 2015), and

U.S. Census Bureau, *Health Insurance Coverage in the United States: 2014* (Washington, DC: U.S. Government Printing Office, 2015).

82. U.S. Department of Homeland Security, "2013 Yearbook of Immigration Statistics," https://www.dhs.gov/publication/yearbook-2013.

83. Congressional Budget Office, *Immigration Policy in the United States: An Update*, December 2010.

84. Migration Policy Institute, "Public Benefits Use," http://www.migrationinformation.org/integration/publicbenefits.cfm.

85. U.S. Immigration and Customs Enforcement, "FY 2015 ICE Immigration Removals," https://www.ice.gov/removal-statistics.

86. Deborah J. Schildkraut, "Ambivalence in American Public Opinion about Immigration," in *New Directions in Public Opinion*, 2nd ed., ed. Adam J. Berinsky (New York: Routledge, 2016), pp. 278–298

87. "Data on Individual Applications and Petitions," U.S. Citizenship and Immigration Services, http://www.uscis.gov/tools/reports-studies/ immigration-forms-data/individual-applications-and-petitions/ data-individual-applications-and-petitions.

88. Nina Totenberg, "Supreme Court To Review If Obama Immigration Actions Were 'Faithfully Executed,'" NPR.org, 19 January 2016, http://www.npr.org/2016/01/19/463622789/supreme-court-agrees-to-review-obama-executive-actions-on-immigration; and Jens Manuel Krogstad, "Key facts about immigrants eligible for deportation relief under Obama's expanded executive actions," Pew Research Center, 19 January 2016, http://www.pewresearch.org/fact-tank/2016/01/19/key-facts-immigrants-obama-action/.

89. David Harrison, "Of Boundaries and Borders: Court Case Seeks the Line," *CQ Weekly*, 22 December 2011, pp. 2646–2647.

Index